Rock Island

An American History

A Brief — But Tantalizing — History of Rock Island
From 25,000 BC to 1962

Steve Urie

ROCK ISLAND: AN AMERICAN HISTORY. Copyright © 2012 by Steve Urie. All rights reserved. No part of this book may be reproduced or transmitted in any form or by any means, electronic of mechanical, including photocopying, recording, or by any information storage and retrieval system (except for flattering review), without permission from Small Pond Publishing, Inc., and Steve Urie: steveurie.org.

PRINTED IN THE UNITED STATES OF AMERICA

First trade edition published 2012

Design by Small Pond Publishing, Inc.; Cover photo: Anonymous 1887 drawing of Rock Island; Cover photo assistance from Jill Doak, Rock Island City Planner and Unofficial City Historian.

ISBN: 978 06 1566 1827

For Huck, so you understand why the sun always shines on Truckee; in memory of my father, Hod, who showed how to enjoy the journey and the people along the way; and for Kevin Miller, so you will know that Gersick isn't making all that stuff up.

The inhabitants of the town [Rock Island] *and its environs could not be surpassed, if equaled, by any city in the west, for men of intelligence — courteous and kind in everything.* ~ Henry C. McGrew, Newspaperman, 1840

Table of Contents

Introductory Notes	1
The Early Years	9
The Frontier	26
With Liberty and Justice for All	46
A New Nation Finds its Way	64
Black Hawk Reigns	81
Culture Clashes	91
Crossroads of the Nation	112
Engineers and Businessmen	122
First Amendment Rights	134
Prosperity	147
A Divided Nation	161
The War at Home	174
A Nation Rebuilds	186
Taming the West	205
Play Ball!	224
The Gilded Age	237
The Progressive Era	265
Trouble Comes to River City	278
Great Migrations	295
The Looney Years	310
A Conservative Time	339
Serious Depression	364
Happy Days are Here Again	377
Government Waste	390
Another Great War	407
Subversives	420
New Rules	439
After Notes	458
Bibliography	462
Index	464

Introductory Notes

The day after Labor Day in 1949, my classmates at Longfellow Grade School and I began a 13-year romp through the public school system in Rock Island, Illinois. Then, and for the next dozen years, I was blissfully unaware of what happened in the world beyond the towns that had high schools in the Mississippi Valley Conference, much less what had transpired before 1950. Part of my social ignorance and lack of global awareness was because, unlike most of my friends, I grew up without a TV.

One memorable evening during the summer before second grade, my father came home with a huge wooden-encased, 21" black and white Magnavox television from Frank's Furniture in Davenport, where he worked. In his best authoritarian voice, which came very naturally to him, he said, "If you sit in front of the TV all day, it's going back." We did, and two weeks later it did. That began a decade of family media deprivation that I'm sure would have continued to my father's grave, if the Chicago Bears didn't start televising their Sunday afternoon games.

I would like to say that the countless hours spent reading when I was young were the result of my parents' good example and the treasures I found at the Rock Island Public Library — this is where my mother would later work and where she dragged me every Saturday morning after buying our groceries at DeVaught's IGA on 14th Avenue — but they weren't. Reading was just less boring than listening to the big-band swing music on WHBF radio that came on every evening after the Lone Ranger signed off with a hearty "Hi-yo, Silver! Away!" and rode into the sunset with his faithful sidekick Tonto to the stirring accompaniment of the William Tell Overture.

For many years after leaving Rock Island, whenever I was asked where I was from, I would answer, "Rock Island, Illinois, the only place the Mississippi River runs east to west and where the sun always shines." And during the 1950s, both were absolutely true for me — a white, middle-class boy. The only attribute that set me apart from my peers was that I was born with an extra thumb on my right hand. (Unbelievably, for cosmetic purposes I've always resented, my parents removed the sixth digit from my pitching hand before I made my first throw — never considering that they might be ruining a Major League career.)

Except for the occasional grimy soot from the IH Farmall foundry that I had to wash from the windshield of my Dad's pea-green 1950 Ford, there were few issues at 4320 7th Avenue. Mowing the summer grass, shoveling winter's perpetually ice-covered sidewalks, drying the dishes, and random household chores took about an hour a day. The rest of the time was mine, except for the 36 school weeks, which I shared with the teachers at Longfellow. Born midway between sisters, Lynne and Gail, who were separated by nine years, and 12 years senior to my little brother, Mike, there were no sibling rivalries and no family playmates. And that was okay, because in the 1950s everyone living within a quarter-mile radius was family, and the gravelly, weed-coved Longfellow playground was the best sandlot ball field a kid could ask for.

After-school hours were filled with pickup spring softball games and fall touch football and year-round basketball with a 9'8" hoop that tilted to the right and ruined the shot of a generation of Longfellow boys. During the bitter cold, gray winters, skating and sledding were endured by the hardy at Lincoln Park. We knew kids our age were doing the same things only two miles to the west at Longview Park, but from our infrequent contact with them they could just as easily have been living in Des Moines as on the other side of the 7th Avenue Hill. Lying between them and us was the vast Augustana College campus, a school that seemingly admitted only robust, blue-eyed, blond-haired Scandinavians. "Augie" was in our domain. There we learned to swim, listened to the *Messiah* at Christmas, watched countless football, basketball, and baseball games, and wondered if we would ever be big enough and blonde enough to be an Augustana Viking.

Summers were a total escape from all things scholarly. There was little time for reading from Memorial Day until Labor Day. During the endless hot and humid, pre-air conditioned summers, the neighborhood rule was that kids were free from when they were shooed out of the house after morning chores until the street lights came on. We could ride our bikes on the pot-holed, concrete alley connecting our houses to the back door of Longfellow and make any stop along the way to visit kids and/or their moms in the two blocks in between. On the fly we could join the endless games of tag, kick-the-can, and capture-the-flag. We would round up some pals and take an excursion into Lincoln Park where a new adventure always awaited us, and we would giggle at the Holy Rollers' Wednesday night's incantations and hallelujahs that emanated from the open windows at the Bethel Assembly of God.

In the 1950s the Longfellow School District was a working-class neighborhood of older homes separated from the rest of Rock Island by Augustana to the west, (a pleasant stroll up 7th Avenue, then a two-way street that traversed the campus and whose single lanes were separated by a flower-bedded boulevard); the Farmall factory and the Mississippi River to the north; the great abyss of Moline to the east; and Lincoln Park, the world's most kid-friendly park to the south. Lincoln Park was a pre-adolescent paradise with all the standard municipal park paraphernalia: playground, ball diamond, basketball and tennis courts, but the extras made it world class.

The over-the-top bonuses began with the ribbons of medieval woods that flanked the park, which during the 1950s only boys under ten and a few privileged sisters were allowed to enter. The woods snaked up the hill and were dotted with kid-dug caves and bough-covered traps along a path that followed a trickle of a creek that was home to frogs and toads. Several huge oaks sported knotted-rope Tarzan swings looped over elbowed limbs, and beds of poison ivy abounded where we initiated new neighborhood kids. At the top of the hill was the best extra ever: two World War I howitzers stood at the highest point in the park and were constantly manned by a brigade of children who volunteered to guard the softball field against enemy soldiers that might be hiding out on the Augustana campus. As if that weren't enough to assure a happy childhood, Lincoln Park had a perfectly sculpted sledding hill that rose steeply above a flat run-out area where in the spring city workers transplanted beds of flowers just in time to gather Mother's Day bouquets.

But summertime was when Lincoln Park came alive and ascended to world-class status. Then the broad sidewalk that encircled the wading pool surrounded by Greek columns and arches became a promenade for the annual bicycle parade and a stage for the dress rehearsal for the citywide lantern parade around the track in the Rocky football stadium. Friday evenings the band shell featured an eclectic musical mix, showcasing the Quad City Symphony Orchestra, the Rock Island Band, barbershop quartets, an occasional boring opera singer, and recitals by students from the Augustana Music Department. Where else could kids chase lightening bugs with their buddies to the accompaniment of a live symphony playing *Flight of the Bumblebee*?

The most memorable adult during Lincoln Park's golden era was a kindly old man who lived in a rooming house by the bus station on 5th Avenue, and who came to the park every morning at about 11:00 when the crafts classes ended. He was tall, weather-beaten, and grandfatherly. He called himself Mr. Love. Kids lined up next to his park bench that overlooked the softball field and then sat next to him while, with his huge hands, he delicately carved whistles, tops, and spinning propellers to the endless delight of his tiny admirers. In the winter when the upper tennis courts were transformed to an ice rink, the same line of kids patiently waited their turn for Mr. Love to tightly lace their skates. Life was sweet on our island in Rock Island.

In the 3rd grade, we studied the Sauk and Fox Indians and took a field trip to the Hauberg Indian Museum in the park named after the heroic Sauk warrior, Black Hawk.

We all knew who he was. A statue of the proud man stood in Spencer Square, Rock Island's charming downtown park for old men, kids, and pigeons. And Carse & Ohlweiler, the local soft drink company, named the world's best wild cherry pop after him. But things often didn't jibe in the adult world, and Indians were one of them.

There wasn't a kid in Mrs. Armstrong's third grade class that didn't know from the Saturday matinees at the Rocket Cinema that Indians were vicious savages — crazy, wild people who burned intrepid settlers' cabins, scalped the men, and kidnapped the women and children. Miraculously, the pioneer kids were always rescued in the nick of time by the U.S. Cavalry that swooped into the Indian village led by a soldier blowing *Charge* on his bugle while carrying a huge American flag and picking off Indian braves with his six-shooter. But those were Indians from out West, not the gentle souls who lived on the bluffs of the Rock River and peacefully slipped into the night to graciously make way for America's progress.

My first awareness that things weren't always what adults wanted kids to believe was when the *Rock Island Argus* celebrated their centennial the summer after 3rd grade. Roy Rogers was the parade marshal, and on our way home a group of neighborhood kids swung by the train station to see if we might catch an up-close look at the "King of the Cowboys" before he left town. We did — he was smaller than he looked in the movies. He was wearing a white cowboy hat and a plain white, short-sleeved shirt that revealed thin, pealing sunburned arms. He stood inside the white line where only passengers could go and casually smoked a cigarette while chatting up two adoring young women. He was oblivious to the throng of boys who were trying to catch his eye and maybe an autograph. It was a quiet walk home.

Unlike everything that happened on Longfellow's playground, I remember little that happened inside its classrooms. But I somehow learned how to read and write, albeit with terrible penmanship, and how to do arithmetic. By the time I started making the two-mile trip over the 7th Avenue Hill to Central Junior High School, I could name all the states, their capitals, and their nicknames, and could recite, in order, the presidents from George "the Father of Our Country" Washington to Dwight "I Like Ike" Eisenhower, who was serving his first term at the time — academic achievements that, even as an 11-year-old, I knew would be of limited future use.

At Central I was taught the difference between "book smart" and "street smart." While I was waiting outside the back entrance for the first bell the first day, Jimmy Davis, a black kid from Hawthorne Grade School, began my street education. He asked if he could "see" my lunch money. I showed him a quarter my mom had given me. He said thank you and slipped it into his pocket. For the next three years, I took a brown-bagged lunch of sandwiches, fruit, and things like celery and carrot sticks that Jimmy didn't care for. Jimmy also taught me to throw the first punch, what was politically correct between the races (which was simply, black boys go first), and what "elbow grease" is.

In what had to be one of the first academic, gender crossover experiments in the nation, in ninth grade at Central the girls took Shop and the boys took Home Ec for six weeks. As good fortune would have it, Jimmy was one of my five kitchen mates. The first time it was my turn to clean up, after baking beans or wheat flour muffins or some equally tasty dish, I asked where the cleanser was. Jimmy said, "Just use some elbow grease." I respectfully asked, "Where is it?" After peering under the sink, he shook his head, appeared bewildered, and said that it looked as if we were plumb out of elbow grease, and that before the bell rang I had better hustle over to the administration building and ask the secretary for a new bottle. The "tardy" bell rang just after the school secretary gathered her co-workers around, smiled sweetly, and earnestly said, "Tell me again what you need." (Jimmy Davis is not to be confused with the very admirable and Honorable Jim Davis who was a year older and already at Rocky at the time of my humiliation and would later become principal at Hawthorne and Rock Island mayor.)

After Central, Rock Island Senior High School was a breeze, although a lot of Mr. Sias' sophomore American History class confused me. There was an improbable gap of almost 300 years between when America presented a formidable barrier to Columbus on his westward voyage to India and the American Revolution. It appeared that the only significant things that happened were that some very righteous religious dissenters settled in Massachusetts and some enterprising farmers built beautiful plantation homes in Virginia. Years later I discovered not much did happen — except for the extermination of at least 50 million American Indians and the importation of more than 600,000 African slaves to farm cotton and tobacco for export to England.

During the spring of our junior year at Rocky, a group of Northern black and white "Freedom Riders," led by Eastern college professors, made what seemed to be an apparently unwise decision to get on a Greyhound bus and ride into Montgomery, Alabama with each other just because the law said they could. Predictably, they got thrown into jail after the local sheriff gave a mob of angry white citizens 15 minutes to beat the bejeezus out of them — equally and without regard to skin color. At Central we had had some minor racial tensions, but the white kids put schoolyard racial issues behind us when at Rocky a pair of superlative black guards led us into the state basketball finals. Some of us occasionally wondered what happened to all the black kids that were in our 9th grade class at Central. In the RIHS '62 class of 472, there were only 12 black graduates other than our magnificent guards. Whereas at Central we had a couple dozen black 9th grade graduates and Franklin Junior High had more black students than Central. (Washington Junior High, where the kids who lived on "The Hill" went to school, had no black students during the 18 years I lived in Rock Island.) And I really didn't understand what went haywire when my brother got out of school for a week in 1972 as the National Guard was called in to "quell racial violence" at Rocky.

My father's whale-shaped '55 Buick didn't fit the prototype of cars that cruised "The One Ways." But there were many fond memories generated from the Buick's vinyl covered interior, where seven or more of us crammed onto the Buick's bench seats for visits to the Black Angel statue in Moline's Riverside Cemetery, the haunted house in Davenport, and the asylum in East Moline — all spots that had genuine historical significance that none of us knew, or would have cared about if we did. One place we knew was rich in history and folklore and always drew a twitter was the "red light district" on 4th Avenue between 22nd and 24th Streets. The famous madam, Jenny Mills, had continuously run brothels in "The District" from 1918 until her death in 1958.

The vague realization that my male pals and I had cruised through school with advantages and extra assistance not afforded our female friends didn't set in until several years after we graduated from Rocky. Then some of our female classmates started "burning" their bras. The decision of feminists to go braless was greeted with great enthusiasm by young males until we found out that it wasn't for our convenience or viewing pleasure but was a symbolic defiance against the unfair gender role expectations and social structures our female classmates inherited. After many millennia of male rule, the sexual equality thing was a big bite for boys from the '40s and '50s to swallow, and decades later when the glass ceiling cracked and then shattered, most of us were dumbstruck as our daughters raced past our sons.

In the early '70s few men paid much attention to militant women demanding equal footing — there were bigger issues to deal with, like one's personal safety. African American men had spent more than a decade being beaten and killed for their insistence on equal rights and opportunity while President Kennedy and his Attorney General brother, Bobby, were taking their time enforcing the laws of the land. And black, brown, yellow, and white draft-age men alike were angry about how the old, white men who ran the government were insisting that it was their turn to defend the nation — only this time the enemy wasn't a run-amok Germanic nation but a bunch of brown-skinned Communist peasants living in Southeast Asia who posed little threat to America or its way of life.

To the dismay of most white Christian men, Olympic gold medalist and the "world's most recognizable man," Cassius Clay, changed his name to Mohammed Ali while holding the title of World Heavyweight Boxing Champion. When he got his

"Greetings from the President of the United States" to take his draft physical, Ali declined and turned up the rhetoric when he stated the attitude of most black men under age 30 by saying, "I ain't got no quarrel with the Vietcong. No Vietcong ever called me nigger." In a nation that 190 years earlier had declared their independence, stating that "all men are created equal," and whose Constitution guaranteed freedom of religion, Ali was stripped of his boxing title and was ineligible to fight while the U.S. Courts decided if his Islamic deistic belief qualified him for status as a religious conscientious objector. After four years, the U.S. Supreme Court decided it did.

My understanding of natural history and anthropology was also a bit distorted. During the summer before my junior year at Rocky, a carload of friends and I watched a sneak preview of *Inherit the Wind*, the controversial movie about the Scopes Monkey Trial. Until then I had pretty much taken Sister Theresa's word that the earth was 6,000 years old and had been created in six days. Our Saturday morning catechism class at Sacred Heart School later proved to be a veritable trove of misinformation spanning many subjects, but in retrospect that's forgivable since even today some state school systems still don't accept evolution as scientific fact.

My knowledge of when and how my hometown was settled and how its history fit into what had happened in the adjacent cities, much less Chicago or San Francisco or Paris, was woefully limited. It was not until the Internet reunited a group of Rocky '62 classmates spread across the country who shared memories, pictures, stories, and Rock Island history that I put aside my blasé acceptance that Rock Islanders are just naturally exceptional and investigated why. Turns out we aren't — we were lucky and were born in a prosperous community at the beginning of a dynamic generation. After critically reading our nation's history for the first time, I realized that it was not where in the United States Baby Boomers were born — we all shared the same fortuitous accident of birth.

When I lived in Rock Island, it seemed that no place could be better. Then I lived in Milwaukee, and I believed it to be the perfect place. Now that I live in Truckee, California, I'm convinced that it makes little difference where anyone chooses to live in the United States; we all have the opportunity to live where we want and to pursue whatever makes us happy, as long as it's not at the expense of others. *Rock Island* is not only about the city where I grew up, but is a history of the country where I was born. I believe a similar history could be written about every community in the United States — even Moline and Davenport. Throughout the book I'm critical of those who abused power or were unjust to minorities. There are no do-overs, but future mistakes can be avoided, and we can be more accepting of those we disagree with and more tolerant of those who are different from us — even those from Moline and Davenport.

Two books published by Quad City newspapers were the most helpful. The first, *The Town Crier,* a collection of articles by George Wickstom in the *Rock Island Argus* on the interesting people and events that built and shaped Rock Island, was published in 1948 and was invaluable in sorting out the who, what, when, and where of Rock Island. The second, the *Quad-City Times', A Time We Remember,* is a picture-filled collection of *Times* articles and readers' remembrances assembled by Bill Wundram for the paper's centennial. It is an impressive nostalgia-inducing book for anyone born before 1985. My sister, Gail, retrieved *A Time We Remember* from my mother's belongings after her death in 2010. He had signed his book for my mother when it was published in 1999 and wrote a nice note about his memory of my father. As I wrote *Rock Island,* I felt Wundram, a *Times'* writer for more than 65 years, looking over my shoulder tsk-tsking whenever I filled in the blanks without being as sure of the facts as possible. I have never met him, but this book is immeasurably more accurate because of him.

Reading about the politics and events that shaped Rock Island's history made me realize that I should have paid closer attention during history classes instead of replaying the previous day's ballgame in my mind or musing about what it was that made Nancy Van Dine so distracting. My mind was full then, and remained so, of a collection of fragmented historical facts and out-of-context quotes that I had learned for tests or that a teacher had promised I would appreciate knowing at some vague future time. And all of history's patriots, villains, and great thinkers were bunched together, as if in a large school photo where there were so many faces and the picture was so large that everyone was indistinguishable from one another. Attila the Hun was standing next to Alexander the Great, and I didn't know who was who or if he lived before the fall of Rome or after the signing of the Magna Carta — and, again, exactly why was the Magna Carta important?

Reading about my hometown was fun. And it nudged me into finding out what was happening outside of Rock Island's city limits while history was being made in one of the world's greatest little cities and its best hometown, who did what when, finding amusing anecdotes and fun facts about those who shaped our world, and learning if my prejudices were reasonable, and if my instincts were correct. Of course, Rock Islanders' roots go back to the beginning of mankind, and to understand why the best and the brightest were drawn to the nation's crossroads, it's necessary to trace how Rock Island's superior gene pool was formed and why immigrants of strong character, good looks, and superior intelligence, settled there. So before getting to the fascinating history of Rock Island, a brief history of the evolution of man and his development in America will give context to the city's magnificent saga. ~ Steve Urie, RIHS 1962

Chapter 1

The Early Years

And God said, Let us make man in our image, after our likeness: and let them have dominion over the fish of the sea, and over the fowl of the air, and over the cattle, and over all the earth, and over every creeping thing that creepeth upon the earth.
~ Genesis 1:26 (King James Version)

THE FIRST IMMIGRANTS TO SETTLE at the mouth of a 14-mile stretch of Mississippi River rapids where Rock Island, Illinois, now stands were descendants of an adventuresome band of Asian nomads. After taking four and a half million years to evolve into humans, a small, black-skinned people had lived comfortably in central Africa for more than 50,000 years while developing their physiques and behavioral skills. Then, the females of the clans acquired rudimentary verbal skills and the ability to instruct their mates through grunts and hand signals to ask other equally uninformed males for directions. Soon, Rock Island's future native ancestors left the comforts of central Africa and immigrated into southern Asia in search of better food.

Thus, an 110,000-year odyssey began before the first humans made their way to Rock Island 25,000 years ago. After a couple of false starts, 90,000 years ago the natives raced across the Arabian Peninsula, where they then slowed down and lived comfortably as beachcombers and fishermen on the shores of the Indian Ocean. Indonesia was then part of the mainland, and although colder than today, living on the shores of the Bay of Bengal and the South China Sea was about as easy as life got 75,000 years ago. But then things took a turn for the worse. Spectacularly, Mt. Toba erupted, covering parts of India and Pakistan with 15 feet of volcanic ash and plunging the world into a 6-year nuclear winter and a 1,000-year ice age. African hunter-gatherers and Asian beachcombers were unprepared for year-round winter, and it's estimated that the world's population may have shriveled to fewer than 10,000 adults. Recovering slowly over the next 10,000 years, the few survivors in the South China Sea region were joined by new African immigrants. Never venturing far inland, the natives crept northward up the China coast.

After waiting 20,000 years for the glaciers to recede, 45,000 years ago inland travel through Asia became possible. Over a few millennia, South Central Asia and Europe were colonized — "modern man" had arrived, and he started exploring. It took humans, anatomically very similar to what we are today, only 5,000 years to colonize lower Siberia, Japan, and Korea. Then taking advantage of a span of 15,000 years of decent weather, the ancestors of the first North Americans left behind more hospitable climates and split from their neighbors; some of them went south to Fiji, New Guinea, and other warm islands, and others inexplicably moved to the edge of the Asian Artic Circle. This later proved to be a good move — for their descendants.

Tracking animal herds that had begun migrating east across the Bering Land Bridge 30,000 years earlier, the first Americans were not to meet up with their Siberian friends and neighbors, who took the west fork in the road to Europe, for another 25,000 years. In a veritable 3,000-year dash, Asians plunged across the land bridge into Alaska and migrated south along two temporarily ice-free corridors. The first route hugged the coast of the Gulf of Alaska and traversed south through the Yukon Territory and into British Columbia, while the other route skirted the eastern edge of the Canadian Rockies and dipped south into the valleys and Midwest plains. It was the adventuresome Asian pioneers who forged into the Great Plains east of the Rocky Mountains that first settled the scenic river bluffs that Rock Islanders now call home.

Forty thousand years before the first person left Africa and 105,000 years before the first person lived on the site of Rock Island, Mother Nature had carved a magnificent drainage system that flowed into the mightiest river of them all. The middle prong of the Missouri-Mississippi-Ohio Rivers that flow into the Lower Mississippi River followed the basin that the Illinois River now follows. Twenty thousand years ago when the first Asians were working their way down the Pacific coast and the eastern slope of the Rockies, glacial ice blocked the Mississippi River just north of Rock Island. As the ice receded, the river slowly shifted west to roughly its present course. Finishing touches to the river and its tributaries were added at the end of the last glacial period 10,000 years ago.

Peak glaciations during the last period of the Ice Age occurred 18,000 years ago, and by its end, few of the first wave of Asian immigrants had survived the cold spell, but those who did were tough, smart, and adaptable. In 2012 carbon dating of projectile points and DNA extracted from dried-up feces that were found in Oregon's Paisley Caves date the earliest humans in North America to 14,500 years ago. North America was especially hard hit during the last glacial period, and only a few small, isolated pockets of Native Americans endured. As the Ice Age begrudgingly gave way, the dogged survivors prospered, and Siberians seeking a more luxurious lifestyle again traversed the Bering Land Bridge. Later dubbed the Clovis culture, the second wave of Asian immigrants was greeted by the old-timers who had ridden out the cold years in Florida and Mexico.

Life was good in America. Wooly mammoths were plentiful and the weather progressively improved. But just when it looked as if it were time to branch out, expand families, and start new enterprises, the cosmos intervened. About 12,800 years ago, a comet exploded over North America, bringing on a 1,300-year cold snap scientists call the "Big Freeze." Year-round winter in North America killed off the mastodons, camels, tapir, sloths, and saber-tooth tigers along with most of the Native Americans that had survived the comet's blast and the resulting coast-to-coast forest and range fires — squirrels, rodents, and other small, furry animals fared somewhat better.

Finally, the Big Freeze thawed and the Ice Age collapsed, and with it the Asian land bridge disappeared, cutting off the migration of large Eurasian mammals and people to America. The recent discovery of 11,500-year-old remains of a small Alaskan child, who was cremated and buried on the cooking hearth of his home, gives solid evidence that the Asian-North American hunter-gathers were highly evolved and began to establish permanent communities shortly after the ice melted. It is believed that the child's family was living in the simple house when the child died. Archeologists surmise the child was laid on the surface of the hearth "because all of the food elements were below the human remains. The site was immediately backfilled and probably abandoned at that point," using their former home as a crypt for the child.

Although not always historically accurate, Native American oral tradition also dates many clans to the time of the "great ice." After the Big Freeze, large animal populations started to reemerge in North America, and 2,000 years later the weather stabilized to conditions that remained somewhat constant and were similar to current weather patterns. Asian mountain sheep, bear, fox, wolves, beavers, badgers, squirrels, rabbits, antelope, elk, deer, and horses and hundreds of species of songbirds, waterfowl, and fish were particularly well adapted to the temperate, mixed deciduous-coniferous forests and plains carved by rivers and streams and spotted with thousands of lakes. On the vast open plains east of the Rockies, prairie dogs and buffalo thrived. More than 50 million bison ranged on the Great Plains. With as many buffalo as Native Americans, and even greater numbers of deer and antelope, pre-Columbian Midwest living was easy. The abundance of fish and animals along with grains, squash, roots, berries, and nuts provided a sustainable, well-rounded organic diet that was much superior to today's average American's diet. There was no alcohol in the Americas until Europeans arrived, and there were no obese Native Americans, but tobacco was one of the first crops the aboriginals farmed.

About 1,000 years before the birth of Jesus, natives living at the confluence of the Mississippi and Rock Rivers settled with other similar speaking Algonquin-language tribes, who had nestled in the valleys of the Missouri, Mississippi, and Ohio Rivers. The tribes began to build permanent villages where they summered and farmed and where often old men and women and young children lived year-round tending the maintenance of the village. During the autumn and winter, the able-bodied men, accompanied by their wives and older children, followed animal herds south, using the women and children to pack meat, pelts, and goods traded from other tribes back to the villages.

Derivations of the Algonquin language were spoken throughout the Ohio Valley and as far west as Arkansas, Missouri, and Iowa. The indigenous folk that settled along the Mississippi River north and west of the Ohio and Wabash Rivers called themselves Illiniwek, meaning "people." Similar to their tribal neighbors to the east, they built elaborate burial mounds that after dozens of generations rose to heights of 50 feet and spread to 200 feet in diameter. The mounds stood apart from the villages, which were protected by the spirits of the departed buried in the mounds. After white men took control of Illinois, in the 1870s amateur archeologists and scavengers excavated most of the burial mounds. One of the archeologists, Clarence Lindley, collected artifacts from a series of mounds between Black Hawk State Historic Site and present day 30th Street. Lindley described one of the mounds west of 9th Street within 10 yards of the Rock River:

> This mound, as well as the others, was about 6 feet high and 35 feet across the base. When we reached the floor of the mound, we found five skeletons, all stretched out east and west. The middle one was slightly larger of frame than the others and the arms were stretched out nearly to full length. Near the fingers of the right hand was a flint spearhead five inches long, and 21 arrowheads. At the feet was an earthen vase. Near the shoulders and breastbone were two polished stones, about six inches long. By the side of one jawbone was a piece of worked deer bone resembling a knife handle; near this knife handle were several bones of some animal, and the jawbone of a deer.

The Illiniwek practiced the common Indian tradition of dividing labor along gender and age lines. The young men and boys performed tribal security, hunted, fished, built wigwams and long houses, and made weapons and tools. The women planted and harvested maize, squash, and tobacco; they made clothing, baskets, and pottery and cared for the small children. The old men smoked the tobacco and passed their wisdom on to the young men. Illiniwek shamans were female, and these wise women were granted organizational and governance responsibilities. However, female authority ended in matters of adultery, which, of course, was acceptable for men but punishable by mutilation or death for women.

Contrary to the nickname of University of Illinois athletic teams, the Fighting Illini, the Illiniwek were a confederation of moderately peaceful tribes. But likely because they had staked out such prime territory, they had many enemies. In particular, the Iroquois were a confrontational confederation of tribes from the East with the most aggressive of the six confederate nations being from the future state of New York. The Iroquois were larger in number and more powerful than the Illiniwek, harassed them for centuries, and with the Shawnee, Dakota, Osage, and Winnebago to the north and west, boxed the Illiniwek into an area that roughly included what is now Illinois.

While Rock Island's plucky native ancestors had slowly moved north along the coast of China after the Mt. Toba fireworks and resultant ice age, equally resolute bands had retraced the routes of their ancestors along the coast of India and moved north through the Biblical Lands into Syria, Egypt, and Turkey. There they mixed in with established clans that had wandered out of Africa starting about 50,000 years before Jesus was born. From Turkey it was a short hop into Greece and Southern Europe. Early Asian immigrants to Europe arrived just as the Neanderthals were leaving. The Neanderthals were not related to the Asians, and even though they could produce fertile offspring with them, they were a different species and have been extinct now for at least 25,000 years. Since almost 2 percent of the Eurasian genome is Neanderthal, the hairy, short, stocky men were around long enough to seduce more than a few Homo sapiens women. It appears that two mega-volcanoes near Naples, Italy, 40,000 years ago dramatically changed the weather and weakened the Neanderthals, and that they were absorbed by the more advanced Homo sapiens.

The new Europeans were an industrious lot, and they immediately began to improve the crude stone tools that had been the standard for 100,000 years. Fighting the bitterly cold winters for 15,000 years that helped do in the Neanderthals, progress was slow. But early Europeans were tenacious, and 30,000 years ago the French were starting to decorate their caves with exquisite drawings that were much more artistic than the simple drawings the Neanderthals used to deck out their Spanish caves. Then, as in North America, the last glacial period of the Ice Age wiped out all but the hardiest Europeans. And as in North America, when the weather started to improve about 12,000 years ago, Asians repopulated Europe and mixed with those who had survived the Big Freeze. In the period between 9,000 and 5,000 years ago (the New Stone Age), life in Europe closely paralleled that in Asia and North America. Small clans lived as hunter-gatherers in communities, often clashing with other clans over more favorable territory and hunting grounds.

With the invention of the wheel, the Stone Age, which had begun 3.4 million years earlier, was pushed out and the Bronze Age rolled in. In the middle of the 4th millennium BC, simultaneously in Mesopotamia, the Northern Caucasus, and Central Europe wheeled vehicles became the rage, but left the question of who invented the wheel forever unanswered. However, contrary to cartoonists' depictions, the wheel's inventor was not a troglodyte (caveperson). The earliest drawing of a wheeled vehicle — a four-wheeled wagon with two axles — is on a clay pot found in southern Poland. The pot was thrown between 3500 and 3350 BC.

A little over 5,000 years ago, the people in the Ancient Near East, an area that roughly corresponds to the modern Middle East, began to improve living standards by smelting ores, especially copper and tin to make durable bronze tools and weapons. Early in the period and trailing Asians by little more than a century, Greeks adopted grain farming and animal domestication from the Ancient Near East. Over the next millennium agrarian practices and cultivation techniques were refined and spread north and west throughout Europe. Bronze axes, scythes, hoes, and spades made farming and gardening easier, and harvested grains provided a year-round source for breads. Hunter-gatherers and fishermen around the Mediterranean Sea settled into larger communities that had divisions of labor and specialization. Copper-based metal pots, cups, plates, spoons, knives, and forks improved table manners, and swords, maces, and metal-tipped spears made soldiers more deadly effective. For more than 2,000 years, southern Europeans and those in the Ancient Near East slowly advanced their societies, built stable tribal communities, and began to use symbols and characters to represent ideas and words. Blessed with good soil and a benign climate, they cultivated rudimentary crops — including grapes for wine and barley and hops for beer.

During this period, in the area that became known as the Fertile Crescent, civilized communities became rooted in the valleys along the Tigris and Euphrates Rivers, which flow to the Persian Gulf, and spread along the eastern Mediterranean seaboard from Turkey to Egypt. In the moist, fertile plains that became known as Mesopotamia, reliably good weather allowed for growing a range of crops and led to improved farming techniques. And the tribal city-states that evolved in the valleys began making glass, used the wheel for transport, and began written languages. At the center of Mesopotamia was Babylonia, a region with the largest city, Babylon, as its capital. During a 17th century consolidation of tribes under Hammurabi, the sixth king of Babylonia, Mesopotamia and Babylonia were briefly the same. For religious purposes, the united region retained the Sumerian language, which was no longer spoken, and for speaking, the written Semitic Akkadian language — it was the basis of Hebrew.

Phoenicia, a land of independent Mediterranean seaports ruled by monarchs, stretched southwest from Mesopotamia along the Mediterranean to Egypt. The Tigris and Euphrates River valleys provided the easiest routes from Asia to Europe and were traveled for millennia by traders, emigrants, and conquering armies. The trade of goods between East and West and the mixing of cultures — often by force — stimulated progress and stirred the gene pools. The lands at the eastern end of the Mediterranean Sea were the crossroads of western Asia and northeast Africa and were the "cradle of civilization." The fall of Babylon — which historians place between 1651 and 1499 BC — began a four-century period of self-destructive imperialism that destroyed many of the major cities and caused widespread cultural regression around the Mediterranean Sea from Troy to Gaza and ended the Bronze Age. War-savaged societies experienced famine and depopulation and palace economies devolved back into village cultures. The period from 1200 to 800 BC is known as the Ancient Dark Age; it was during this period that Judaism, the West's oldest living religion, began to evolve.

Those living in the Fertile Crescent led Europeans out of the Ancient Dark Age and into the Iron Age. Although biased with primitive religious beliefs and scientific misconceptions, around 900 BC written records became more numerous, and historical events and dates become more precise. The rise of the Neo-Assyrian Empire in Babylonia produced classical historical sources such as Ptolemy's *Canon of Kings* and the *Hebrew Bible.* In 626 BC a renaissance began in Babylonia, and the Neo-Babylonia Empire, which encompassed all of the Fertile Crescent and spread south along the Red Sea, rose to world dominance. Ambitious architectural projects were built, the arts and sciences flourished, and imperial states were formed. The kings granted large rural estates to government officials who had autocratic control and answered only to their king. The cities were also governed autonomously by religious hierarchies. In Babylonia, south of Phoenicia along the Mediterranean Sea, lay the Kingdom of Israel, and south of Israel, separated from the Mediterranean by the Philistine States, was the Kingdom of Judah. For almost a century, harmony reigned in the earth's most advantaged region. But in 587 BC the Kingdom of Judah fell to the Babylonian Army, and then crumbled when Cyrus the Great of Persia conquered Babylon in 539 BC. (Cyrus is one of the earliest recorded egotists to append his name with "the Great" — the affectation was usually self-granted.) It was during the period between 600 and 400 BC that the *Torah* (the first five books of the *Hebrew Bible*) was written.

Then it became the Persians turn at the top of the social scale. By 500 BC Persia had swallowed Babylonia and conquered Turkey, Ancient Egypt, Asia Minor, Central

Asia, and Pakistan. By 480 BC, almost half of the world's population lived in the Persian Empire, making it the largest empire by percentage of world population in history. For two centuries, Persian kings connected their empire with a vast network of roads and controlled it with a well-organized and trained army. The only land that Persia was unable to conquer was Greece, and the world is a better place because of their failure. It's not that the Persians didn't give an all-out effort, or that they hadn't ratcheted up civilization a notch or two, it's only that the Greeks arguably contributed more to mankind's cultural advancement than any other nationality.

In 490 BC after capturing Eretria, Persian King Darius the Great attacked Marathon with 25,000 soldiers. Outnumbered more than two to one, the Greeks turned back Darius' Army. In the first recorded ultra-marathon, before the battle at Marathon a Greek runner, Pheidippides, was dispatched from Athens to Sparta to seek assistance in the impending showdown against the Persians. He covered the distance of 140 miles in less than two days. Then, following the victorious battle, 10,000 Athenian troops marched about 26 miles 365 yards back to Athens to head off Persian ships that were planning a second attack on the unguarded city. The Athenian Army arrived in time to force the Persians to turn away from Athens. Fortunately for weekend runners, when the modern Olympics were first held in 1896, Pierre de Coubertin confused the two distances and set the length for the games longest race at the distance that 10,000 soldiers in heavy armor covered in a day's time, instead of the 140 miles Pheidippides had run.

Ten years later, the Persians were back for another go at the Greeks. This time they came prepared to stay and with a much larger army. Over the course of a year and a half, the Persians gained control of a large swath of territory in northern Greece and again threatened Athens. In the summer of 479 BC, the Greeks began a year-long counterattack that ended by pushing the Persians to the Asian side of the treacherous two-mile wide strait at Byzantium, one of the world's most strategically located cities. Called the Bosporus, the strait separates the Black Sea from the Mediterranean Sea and is a geographical division between Asia and Europe. In AD 330 Byzantium was renamed Constantinople in honor of Roman Emperor Constantine the Great, and in 1453 it became the capital of the Ottoman Empire and for the first time was called Istanbul (from the Greek phrase "eis ten polin," meaning "in the city"). In 1930 the city's name officially became Istanbul.

With control of the west side of the Bosporus, Greece remained secure for the next three centuries, and until conquered from the northwest by the Romans in 146 BC, the Greeks influenced virtually all European life and culture, except that of the Scandinavians who were too consumed with winters to deal with much else. The

Greeks lay the foundation for all European literature and art, architecture and science, and Western philosophy and law. And the Greeks achieved new levels of economic prosperity and social evolution. Greek religious practices centered on the stories and mythology of how their ancient gods controlled the earth's movements and its nature. We know most of the history of Greece and Persia during this period because of Herodotus, the "Father of History," who was the first person to systematically collect historical materials, test their accuracy, and arrange them in a well-constructed narrative. He produced one work, *Historía,* a Greek word meaning "inquiries" that passed into Latin and means "histories."

During the 4th century BC, the Greeks were free from holding off invaders and turned inward. Athens became the most advanced city and the intellectual center of the Western World. Socrates was one of its young intellectuals. A rabble-rousing heretic, he was constantly in trouble with the city-state's rulers for mocking their lifestyles and challenging their ethics. One of the founders of Western philosophy, he was tried and found guilty of "corrupting the minds of the youth of Athens" and of "not believing in the gods of the state." One of the minds Socrates corrupted was that of his student, Plato, who considered pure mathematics to be the highest attainable level of human thought. Over the entrance to the Academy of Athens, which he founded, Plato posted, "Let no one ignorant of mathematics enter here." When a student asked Plato, "What practical end do these theorems serve? What is to be gained by them?" Plato turned to a slave and said, "Give this man an obol [a coin] that he may feel that he has gained something from my teachings, and then expel him." Reputedly, another observation Plato made, and one that students and scholars throughout the ages have seldom challenged, is: "He was a wise man who invented beer."

A student of Plato's that understood the value of mathematics, and everything else worth knowing, was Aristotle. Unlike Socrates, who was too busy asking questions to write anything down, Aristotle liked to write — Cicero described his treatises as "a river of gold" — and although it is estimated that only about a third of Aristotle's works have survived, those that made it through the 2,300 years since his death form the foundation of Western philosophy and encompass logic, morality, aesthetics, and metaphysics. There has never been much money in philosophy, so most of history's great minds supported themselves by teaching. Aristotle got lucky and was selected by Philip II, the king of Macedon, to tutor his son Alexander III. However, Aristotle was a tough negotiator, and he didn't accept Alexander as a student until Philip agreed to rebuild Stageira, Aristotle's hometown, which Philip had sacked, and free its citizens, who he had enslaved. Demonstrating that responsible parents put their children's education first, Philip did as he promised and moved Aristotle into the Temple of Nymphs at Mieza for Alexander's instruction.

For three years, Aristotle taught Alexander along with the children of other Macedonian nobles. Alexander was a passionate student who was particularly fond of Homer and his great work, the *Iliad*. Aristotle gave his bright pupil an annotated copy, which he carried with him throughout his life. At age 16, Alexander began his life's work of conquering the world all the way to the "Great Outer Sea" (the Indian Ocean) and ended Greece's period of external strife. He was very good at what he did, and by the time he was 30, his empire stretched from Greece to the Himalayas, and he was known as "Alexander the Great." Alexander died at age 61 without conquering India or Arabia, and after his death his empire was torn apart by civil war and Greece began a slow decline. Alexander's legacy includes spreading Greek culture and civilization and developing military tactics that are still taught.

Around 900 BC, while the tribes in the Fertile Crescent were crawling out of the Ancient Dark Age, the Iron Age in Italy was still more than a century off. Italian tribes were culturally and linguistically divided into Oscans, Umbrians, and Latins. The Latin culture became dominant and absorbed the other Italian tribes. Rome emerged as a powerful city-state, and in 509 BC, Italy, which was geographically protected on its boot-shaped peninsula, formed a stable, democratic republic that would endure for five centuries. In 146 BC the Romans defeated the Greeks at the Battle of Corinth, and Europe's power center transferred to Rome, where it would remain for the next six centuries. Julius Caesar's appointment as "perpetual dictator" in 44 BC marks the end of the Roman republic and the beginning of the autocratic Roman Empire. The Romans were as militaristic as their Persian and Greek predecessors, and during the 1st century, they conquered the lands surrounding the Mediterranean Sea and England and controlled almost as much area and population as the Persians had. For the next two centuries, the Romans, who had absorbed the Greek culture, spread their language, architecture, philosophy, law, and governmental forms throughout Europe.

Like the Greeks, the Romans believed gods controlled natural phenomena, and Caesar introduced the new twist that Roman emperors became gods after their death — although some emperors like Caligula claimed to be gods while they were alive. Now known as the Imperial Cult, Roman religion was at odds with those who started preaching the word of a Jew from Nazareth. Called māshīaḥ (messiah; Greek, chrīstos) by some Jews, the birth of Jesus Christ changed the religious practices of most of Europe and later reset the Western world's calendar to year AD 1. The Roman rulers were threatened by those who worshipped the Messiah and believed there was but one

God who existed as three distinct, divine entities — the Father, the Son (Jesus Christ), and the Holy Spirit — and coexisted in unity and equality. After crucifying Jesus for his dissident ways, the Roman Army started rounding up the heretics and crucifying them as a lesson to others.

One martyr, Simon Peter, was one of the twelve Apostles and the first pope. Peter had gone to Rome to preach Christianity, and when he was sentenced to death by the Roman Emperor Nero, he requested to be crucified on an upside down cross because he felt he was unworthy to die as Jesus had. He was buried within 500 feet of his crucifixion, and a simple shrine was built on the spot of his grave. Three centuries later, Old St. Peter's Basilica replaced the shrine when Constantine became the first Christian Roman emperor in 324. Fifty-five years after Old St. Peters was consecrated, Theodosius I made Christianity Rome's official religion.

Roman religious life had become less important to its citizens as the plunder from its conquests raised the lifestyles of the emperors and their courts to new levels of decadence. However, it is untrue that debauchery and orgies were responsible for Rome's fall, which happened 200 years after the wildest parties were only faded memories. A 50-year stretch of invasion, plague, economic depression, and civil war that began with the 235 assassination of Emperor Alexander Severus by his own generals weakened the Roman Empire and set it up for its fall. Romans were not prepared for the Huns who swept into Eastern Europe like a cold wind from the Northeast during the 3rd century and softened the Romans for their defeat in 476 to the Germanic warlord, Odoacer. During the 1,400 year stretch that the Greeks and Romans led the development of Western civilization, they introduced virtually every philosophical, scientific, and socially important idea of modern times. The one exception was the precepts of Christianity — those they borrowed from the Jews in the Fertile Crescent.

While Romans were occupying the Ancient Middle East, they noticed the dignity of Jewish worship and the simplicity of worshiping a single god instead of multitude gods, and that Jesus' humanistic message was more relevant and comforting to the soldiers than believing their emperor was a god. Early Christians also found the earth's creationist explanation more plausible than their natural phenomena explanations such as Helios driving the chariot of the sun across the sky each day and Diana tossing the moon into the sky at night. When they returned to Rome, they took the stories of the ancient Jews and the parables of the modern-day Christ with them. Romans also took Jesus' moral stories to Byzantium, where they were interpreted somewhat differently, and the Eastern Orthodox Church evolved in a parallel fashion to the Roman

Catholic Church with one notable difference — the Eastern Orthodox Catholic Church does not believe in the Pope's infallibility in matters of faith and morals.

Finally, more than a thousand years after Judaism was solidly established and after taking generations to migrate to the North Mediterranean regions, early Christians took the best from Jewish customs and theology, blended in the oral history of the Apostles that Jesus Christ was God — even though He never made any such direct claim — and started to write down the Apostles' accounts of Christ's life and teachings in Hellenistic Greek, Hebrew, and Aramaic. Christian interpretations of the New Testament have been refined and redefined by a dozen major Christian religions divided into as many as 20,000 worldwide sects — albeit, some as small as three people.

Apparently, the Devil wasn't too keen on the new religious views, and he started to send demons to randomly possess the bodies of early Christians. Early demonic possession was usually associated with bizarre behavior that in recent decades is more commonly diagnosed as hysteria, schizophrenia, Tourette's syndrome, or dissociative identity disorder. However before the discovery of psychological diseases and the rise of modern pharmacology, exorcism was the only sure way to cast out demons. The Catholic Church states that the religious rite of exorcism does not depend "on the rigid use of an unchanging formula or on the ordered sequence of prescribed actions. Its efficacy depends on two elements: authorization from valid and licit Church authorities, and the faith of the exorcist." In 1999 the Vatican issued the guideline that a person "who claims to be possessed must be evaluated by doctors to rule out a mental or physical illness" before they could send a Jesuit priest trained in exorcisms to get rid of the demon.

The Roman Catholic Church became Western Europe's oldest institution and largest religion, and by translating the Greek and Roman classics into Latin, Catholic monks, Italian priests, and Catholic monarchs and patrons are credited with preserving them. While the monks were painstakingly hand-copying the classics and recording God's Word in the first Bibles during the 4th century, they also did a little creative writing. One of the religious legends that emerged was that of a Roman soldier whose full name has been lost but is known throughout the West simply as Saint George (c. 275/281 – April 23, 303). Three hundred years after his heroics, during the 7th century, some pictures of Saint George's feat were drawn, but the first written description of his awe-inspiring gallantry didn't appear until 400 years after the early pictorial accounts. The written versions of Saint George's courageous feat describe how he came to the rescue of the citizens of Silene (modern day Cyrene, Libya) who were inconvenienced by a fire-breathing dragon that made its nest in the spring-fed pond that supplied the village's water. The only way the villagers could lure the dragon away from the spring was to tie a lamb to a stake far enough from the spring so that when the dragon lumbered out to devour the lamb, the inventive villagers could rush in and fill their water vessels.

Accounts are fuzzy whether the villagers ran out of sheep or if the dragon got tired of lamb, but soon young maidens were being tied to the stake instead of lambs. The locals were a democratic group, so to be fair, they drew lots to see who among the young women would be the next dragon bait. One day the village princess' number came up, and although her father, the king, begged for her life, the townspeople wouldn't change the lottery rules. As fate would have it, George was riding through town as the princess was being tied to the stake. Protecting himself with the sign of the cross, George slayed the dragon. The citizens were so amazed and grateful that they abandoned paganism and converted to Christianity, and there was never another dragon spotting in Silene. George not only got his reward in heaven, but his feat came to the attention of the Vatican, and he was made a saint. He is one of the most venerated of the more than 10,000 named Catholic saints, and he has been given a feast day of April 23. Saint George is the patron saint of boy scouts and horses and a multitude of professions including agricultural workers, archers, butchers, cavalry, farmers, knights, saddlers, shepherds, and soldiers. And if afflicted with a skin disease, herpes, leprosy, plague, or syphilis, he's the saint to pray to.

After Attila took power in Europe in 434, the Huns, a mean-spirited and uncouth group from the Volga River region, precipitated a westward European migration that caused European cultural development to flounder for the next 400 years. The Western Iron Age introduced by the Greeks and Romans ground to a halt, and the Middle Ages began their dreary 1,000-year-long run. The barbarians not only ruthlessly destroyed social structures everywhere in Europe except southern Italy and Scandinavia, but also depopulated the continent. Unaware they were only half way through medieval times, at the end of the first millennium Europe began to pull itself together. Barbarian invasions and occupation petered out in western and central Europe, and apparently tired of salted fish and dark, cold winters, the Vikings moved south and settled in with the natives in the British Isles and Northern France.

In 1066, William the Conqueror (Guillaume le Conquérant as he was later known to his friends in Normandy) overran England and made himself King. Before his conquest and because of his illegitimate birth and possibly because of a reputed mean streak, the French called him "Guillaume le Bâtard" (William the Bastard). Historians can find no evidence that the English called him anything other than "Your Majesty." After William the Conqueror's death, his third son, the tyrannical William Rufus inherited the throne. When the despised king was mysteriously killed in a hunting accident, William Rufus' younger brother, Henry, ascended to the throne. King Henry I was much kinder and gentler and more popular than his older brother had been. Yielding to the powerful Anglican/Catholic clergy, Henry signed the Charter of Liberties, which bound the King to certain laws regarding the treatment of church officials and nobles and paved the way for the Magna Carta a century later. First signed in 1215, the Magna Carta (Latin for Great Charter) was a series of laws that limited the monarchy's power. Often revised during the 13th century, the charter has been described as "the greatest constitutional document of all times — the foundation of the freedom of the individual against the arbitrary authority of the despot."

While England and France were struggling over who controlled the British Isles, Vatican-based Catholics began two centuries of Crusades to gain control of the Holy Land. Charitably giving heretics and pagans the choice to convert or be killed, the Holy See helped Italy regain its lost power. Before they were over, the Crusades attempted to conquer and convert Jews, Mongols, Slavs, Balts, Greek Orthodox Christians, Muslims, and everyone else who might be suspected of being a non-Catholic heretic. Using "the remission of sin" ploy as a recruiting tool to join the Crusades, the papacy promised all sinners that they would avoid eternal damnation in hell by joining the cause to retake Jerusalem from the Jews and Muslims — few sinners could pass up a ticket to heaven. Five hundred years earlier, a 40-year-old Jewish merchant, Muhammad bin `Abd Allāh had become discontented with life in Mecca and retreated to a mountain cave. There he received a revelation from God. Three years later, Muhammad started preaching his revelation and proclaimed that "God is one" and that complete "surrender" to Him is necessary — and that he, Mohammad, was a prophet and the creator of Islam.

In 1184 starting under Pope Lucius III's direction, Catholic bishops were charged to "do away with" heretics, and many bishops took this command literally. The papal order was specifically aimed at the Cathar, or Good Christians, Catholic heretics in southern France. The Catharist inquisition failed, and 20 years later in 1204 Pope Innocent III organized a Crusade that deviated from their assigned objective of retaking Jerusalem and instead sacked Constantinople, the home of the Christian Eastern Orthodox Church and Europe's largest and wealthiest city throughout the Middle Ages. In defiance of Innocent III's directive, the Roman clergy convinced 20,000 Crusaders that an attack on Constantinople was spiritual and that the Eastern Orthodox Greeks were heretics and traitors and "were worse than the Jews." When many balked, the bishops threatened them with excommunication, which was a direct trip to Hell with no stop in Purgatory — inspired, the Catholics heroically conquered Constantinople.

Never conquering the Holy Land, the Vatican then turned its attention to Western Europe, where there were more than enough heretics to keep the Crusaders occupied. In 1242 the Inquisition condemned the *Talmud*, Jewish cultural history, philosophy, customs, and laws. Not content with burning thousands of copies of the ancient writings, the Inquisition got to the heart of the issue and started burning Jews. In 1288 in Troyes, France, 13 wealthy Jews were randomly selected from the community and burned at the stake for the supposed murder of a Christian child. Thus began Christian persecution of Jews that has since ebbed and flowed but never ceased.

While Europe was haphazardly ridding themselves of infidels, Genghis Kahn was uniting the tribes of northeast Asia. Moving savagely westward, the Mongols conquered Central and Western Asia and invaded Eastern Europe during the first half of the 12th century — establishing a Mongol empire that lasted into the 15th century in Persia and the 19th century in India. By the late 12th century, Europeans had staved off and driven back the Mongols. Just when it appeared that European culture might reestablish itself, the continent suffered a succession of calamities. The first was the Great Famine, which began in 1315, and in less than three years reduced the population by ten percent through starvation and malnutrition. Then in 1337 the French and English launched their Hundred Years' War, which killed off three-fourths of the people in Normandy. And to cap off the 14th century, the first wave of the Bubonic Plague swept through Europe. By the mid-15th century, France's population was halved and Paris numbered only a third of the people it had a century earlier. Devastated by the Black Death, the world lost at least 100 million people from a pre-plague high of 450 million. It took the continent 150 years to recover. While Paris was being devastated by the plague, Robin Hood and his band of merry men were redistributing the wealth in Nottinghamshire, England.

In the mid-13th century, the Mongols also invaded the Kievan Rus', the vast territory of Finnic and Slavic tribes that lived northeast of the Baltic Sea. In 976 Vladimir, the prince of Novgorod, fled to Scandinavia after his half-brother Yaropolk murdered his other brother Oleg and took control of Rus'. With help from Earl Håkon Sigurdsson, ruler of Norway, Vladimir assembled a Viking Army and reconquered Novgorod and Kiev from Yaropolk. While in power, Vladimir's most notable achievement was the Christianization of Kievan Rus', a quick process that began in 988. Rejecting the nonsense of traditional idol-worship, Vladimir sought a new faith. He sent his most trusted advisors as emissaries to different parts of Europe to visit and scrutinize Jews, Muslims, and Christians of the Latin Rite and the Eastern Orthodox Rite. The advisors rejected Judaism because the God of the Jews had permitted his chosen people to be left without a country, Islam because it prohibited the consumption of alcohol, and Roman Catholicism because it was oppressively restrictive. (It was during this period that the Church started strongly suggesting that popes and priests should practice celibacy. Before then Catholic clergy were sexually active and married, and it wasn't until the mid-16th century that celibacy vows became canon law.) But proving that it pays to be the last to present, at Constantinople Vladimir's emissaries were astounded by the beauty of the cathedral of Hagia Sophia and the services held there, and they selected the Eastern Orthodox religion and sold the faith to Vladimir. Demonstrating Russians' tendency towards compulsive behavior, Vladimir immediately journeyed to Constantinople and arranged to marry Princess Anna, the sister of the emperor.

Over the next five centuries, Russia changed little. The land remained Christian and isolated, and the feudal society remained as primitive as Western Europe. But as the Medieval Period faded away, that changed when Ivan Vasilyevic inherited the throne in 1547 at age 17 and proclaimed himself "Tsar" (Caesar). The same year, after being presented with about 1,000 suitable women from noble families to wed, he selected Anastasia Romanovna Zakharyina-Yurieva. He loved her, and Anastasia had a moderating and stabilizing effect on her volatile husband who suffered from "periodic bouts of madness." Unfortunately, she died the month Ivan turned 30, and without her calming influence, he took off on a 20-year reign of conquest and terror. Expanding his control of Asia from Moscow to the east, he first seized Kazan and the Caspian Sea port of Astrakhan from the Tartars and then moved south against Livonia and west to Siberia. The tyrannical Ivan wisely massacred nobles and their heirs as he conquered their regions, leaving the peasants without leadership and dependent on their conquerors.

At a time when all of Europe believed that nobility was God-given, Ivan IV cleverly announced he would abdicate his throne because of lack of loyalty — but consented to stay on if he were allowed to deal with the disloyal at his own discretion. The pronouncement was the same as if God had spoken, and the people insisted he stay. Ivan formed a large personal army to enforce his discretionary whims. It was the arbitrary enforcement of the loyalty clause of his pact with the people by his soldiers that earned him the moniker: Ivan the Terrible. He married six more times, disposing of wives quickly when they didn't meet the standard set by Anastasia. Ivan and Anastasia's oldest son was heir to the throne. While he was beating his son's pregnant wife for dressing immodestly, his son came to her aid. Enraged by his son's impudence, Ivan whapped his son with his staff and killed the heir to the Russian throne. Ivan the Terrible's death in 1584 began an era of Russian intrigue that some say is ongoing.

The Inquisition was the most enduring enterprise during the Middle Ages. Carrying out Papal orders, in March 1492 Spain's King Ferdinand and Queen Isabella gave Jews 90 days' notice to get out of Spain but to leave their gold, silver, money, arms, and horses behind. After splitting up the bounty with a Dominican Friar, Tomás de Torquemada, the Catholic monarchs found themselves sitting on a pile of extra cash. Demonstrating extraordinary vision, the Spanish couple commissioned Christopher Columbus to initiate the Golden Age of Exploration and Colonization that put an end to the fun-starved Medieval Period.

Chapter 2

The Frontier

It would be difficult to conceive of any more dogmatic and less tolerant people than the first settlers on New England shores. ~ Paul Harris, Rotary Club founder

AFTER GROSSLY UNDERESTIMATING THE EARTH'S circumference, Christopher Columbus got credit for discovering the "New World" when he became the first European to step foot on lands east of the Atlantic Ocean since Leif Eriksson visited Nova Scotia and the Northeast seaboard 500 years earlier. In 1002 or 1003, after hearing a report from a sea captain who was blown off course and spotted "thick forests on a land to the west," Eriksson, who was a son of Erik the Red, left treeless Greenland in search of the timber. There is some dispute exactly where in North America Eriksson landed and wintered; however, written descriptions indicate it was near Massachusetts' Nantucket Island. After Leif's brother, Thorwald, was killed by a Native American's arrow on a later voyage, there is no dispute that Eriksson's was the first rendezvous in 25,000 years between the Asians that took the eastern shortcut to North America and the Asians that took the longer western route through Europe.

Over the millennia, their diet and environment had changed the physical characteristics of the distant relatives as they adapted to their climates. Both family lines had started as black Africans less than 100,000 years earlier, but having spent the prior 10,000 years in Scandinavia, where year-round warm clothing and beards covered all but their noses, the Vikings had lost their protective skin pigmentation and their eyes had turned from brown to blue and their hair from black to blond. Living in more moderate climes, the Native Americans, who were not called Indians for another five centuries, had retained many of their Asian features and the dark Asian skin coloring. The most prominent physiological difference, however, was that Europeans had endured a large spectrum of diseases since they separated and had developed immunities that the less exposed and clean-living American aborigines had not.

Culturally, Europeans had benefited from the necessity to domesticate animals for food and work, improve tools and weapons, and transport goods. Competition and specialization led to metalworking, the development of written language, and the design of wheeled carts, wagons, and ships. Native Americans' environment was more benign; they were not as hostile as their European brothers, and food was more varied and naturally plentiful. Even though it was 1,000 years after the birth of Jesus, during Leif Eriksson's time, the spiritual and religious practices of Vikings and Native Americans were very similar. Both believed in gods and goddesses that controlled and directed life's natural phenomena: the sun, moon, stars, and seasons. There was one notable difference — the Vikings had Aegir, the god of beer.

When Columbus bumped into what was to become San Salvador, he remained politically correct and faithful to his Spanish Roman Catholic patrons and named the island after the "Holy Savior." He thought he had discovered an oceanic trade route to India, so he named the region the Indies, and the inhabitants, Indians. To verify his discovery of a shortcut to India, Columbus packed up some local Taino Indians and headed back to a hero's welcome in Spain. During his first voyage, Columbus kept two logs. He fudged the open ship's log in an effort to reassure his men that they were not that far from home. The secret log was a record of what he actually reckoned. Ironically, the falsified log proved to be more accurate than his "actual" calculations.

Returning the following year with 17 ships and 1,500 men to search for gold and to capture Indians to be sold as slaves, Columbus and his fleet discovered two more large Islands, which they named Cuba and Dominica. They found no gold, but captured many slaves. Columbus returned to the Americas two more times to explore, search for gold, and enslave Indians. On his second voyage, as he was preparing to return to Spain, Columbus found himself in Jamaica in dire need of provisions for his return voyage. The Jamaican Indians were not cooperative and refused to trade food for trinkets. Desperate, Columbus fortuitously saw in his almanac that a lunar eclipse was due in a few days. Through drawings and sign language, he conveyed that if the Indians didn't give him what he wanted, he would black out the moon. The Indians were amused and left the meeting, only to hurry back in terror as the moon slowly disappeared. After receiving promises for the supplies he needed, Columbus restored the moon.

At the beginning of the 15th century, when there were more than 50 million Native Americans living in relative harmony in North America, the Catholic Church's efforts to rid Europe of infidels was fizzling out, and a movement to reintroduce Greek literary, historical, and theological texts into Western European education created a renaissance in scholarly thought. The Black Death had decimated Europe, and those that survived became more focused on daily life than on the prospect of an afterlife. A method of learning, called "Humanism," evolved, which sharply deviated from the didactic, medieval educational approach of memorizing and trying to live the Church's ecclesiastical law. Instead Humanism focused on studying and appraising ancient texts by using reasoning and empirical evidence. Italy had been particularly hard hit by the plague, and the Medici, a Florentine banking family, promoted and underwrote a cultural and artistic revival that produced three of history's most talented artists: Leonardo da Vinci, Sandro Botticelli, and Michelangelo Buonarroti. The cultural movement spread from Florence, and in 1564, the year Michelangelo died, Galileo Galilei was born. Some, who study such things, have estimated his IQ was as high as 200, but it was not his genius that distinguished Galileo as the most famous "renaissance man," it was his defiance of the system. Known as the "Father of Science," he made lasting break-through contributions in the fields of mathematics, physics, astronomy, and philosophy. However, when he postulated that the earth revolved around the sun and that it was not the center of the universe, he got crosswise with Pope Urban III and the Jesuits, and the Inquisition found him "vehemently suspect of heresy." He was forced to recant (but defiantly muttered, "But yet it [the earth] moves"), and he spent the last nine years of his life under house arrest.

While the Italians da Vinci and Michelangelo were creating artistic masterpieces and Galileo was reintroducing science and logic to Europeans, an English actor, poet, and playwright, William Shakespeare, was setting a worldwide writing standard that has yet to be matched. With European life becoming fun again, there were few compelling reasons to leave home, and colonization of North America was slow to gain momentum. Passage to the New World was treacherous and expensive, there wasn't any gold, there were no jobs, and farming in the Northeast, where the winds and currents landed most English ships, was more difficult than in Western Europe. Tobacco, sugar, and cotton farming in the South required slave labor to be bearable and profitable, and slaves required a large initial investment and were expensive to maintain. Indians didn't take to slavery well and could only be sold to island plantations, or they ran back to their tribes at the first opportunity. And due to their mortal susceptibility to European diseases, Indians quickly became much less valuable than African slaves.

Twenty-five years after Columbus rediscovered America, Martin Luther, a German monk, wrote a protest against Catholic bishops and priests selling indulgences as a method for sinners to receive pardon for their sins. While he was at it, he wrote down 94 other practices he found to be outside what he thought Jesus would do that had crept into Catholic Church liturgy over the preceding 1,500 years. As it turned out, Luther was just one of many who were displeased with Church dogma and policy. As a result of schisms caused by ethical conflict, disorganization, and failures during the Inquisition, Catholic Bishops had pointed fingers, and major disputes had arisen within the Church's hierarchy — at one point, three men simultaneously claimed to be pope. A disgruntled French theologian, John Calvin, sought to reform the Church along strict

Biblical lines, and gave the written Word of God a literal interpretation when he defined the basis for the Presbyterian Church. And England's King Henry VIII found the Catholic Church's rules on marriage to be inconvenient after he was smitten by his wife's consort, Anne Boleyn. When Boleyn refused to be his mistress and Pope Clement VII wouldn't annul his marriage, he broke from the Church of Rome, established the Church of England, had his first marriage annulled, and married Boleyn.

Henry was desperate for a male child to succeed him, and when the second queen failed to deliver one, he declared that his marriage was the product of witchcraft. Queen Anne was arrested and taken to the Tower of London. She was accused of adultery, incest, and high treason; found guilty and executed. The third queen proved to be the charm. The day after Queen Anne's execution, Henry married his mistress — after defining the rules for Christian divorce, he would marry three more times — and Queen Jane delivered Prince Edward. The movement started by Martin Luther to reform the Church of its excesses and to realign Christianity to European cultures is appropriately called the "Reformation."

While most of Europe was synchronizing religion with culture, Spanish and Portuguese conquistadors were conquering Indian tribes in South America, Mexico, and the extreme southeast of North America. In South America, the Aztec and Inca cultures were sophisticated and had built technically advanced civilizations. They also had refined gold and silver for adornments and jewelry. The conquistadors wiped out the natives and their culture and plundered their riches. One of the things the conquistadors stole from the South Americans was potatoes. In 1537 Jimenez de Quesada and his forces encountered a village in Columbia where the natives had fled. Among the food stuffs the Spanish troops plundered were potatoes, which the Spanish called "truffles." It would be another 200 years before Belgians first learned to cut them into long strips and fry them in lard, and then another century before the French introduced fried potato strips to the United States.

By the late 1500's, South American silver accounted for 20 percent of Spain's gross economy. In return for Indian gold and silver, the conquistadors introduced small pox, cholera, mumps, measles, and syphilis to the natives. It is estimated that although hundreds of thousands of Indians were killed by the Spanish Conquistadors and their Indian allies, many times more were killed by European diseases, and that as much as 95 percent of the total native population of the Americas was wiped out by disease between 1500 and 1620, when the Pilgrims in Massachusetts were first meeting Indians. The word "genocide" is rarely found in student textbooks or histories when referencing the colonization of the Americas. The only positive Spanish contribution to Indian culture was the reintroduction of horses, which Indians had hunted to extinction

9,000 years earlier. Anthropologists estimate that in Mexico the Indian population fell by more than 97 percent from 25 million in 1518 to less than one million a century later.

While the Spanish and Portuguese were pillaging everything south of Alabama, the Dutch, French, and English set their sights on the colder stretches of the Atlantic coast. Whereas early English colonists were mostly ostracized separatists from the Church of England, the French and Dutch were drawn to the New World for commercial opportunities. In 1609 English Captain Henry Hudson conducted the first exploration of the area now called New York Bay. Surreptitiously, the Englishman was seeking a navigable northwest passage to the Pacific Ocean for the Dutch East India Company. Unsuccessful, Hudson returned with glowing reports of beautiful streams and rivers bountifully populated with beavers. This was very good news. Beavers were highly prized in Europe because the fur from their pelts could be "felted" to make waterproof hats, and a valuable secretion of their anal glands was used for medicinal purposes.

Strangely, the first non-Native American to settle on what is now Manhattan Island was a black man from Santo Domingo. Jan Rodriguez, the son of a Portuguese sailor and an African woman, was also the island's first merchant. Set up on a Dutch fur trading post in late 1613 and reassured that Dutch traders would return the next year, Rodriguez was left for the winter with hatchets and knives to trade to the Indians for provisions and to reconnoiter the island. Early the next fall, three Dutch ships arrived at the trading post. Hendrick Christiaensen, the official founder of New York City, captained one of the ships. Christiaensen's log states that Rodriguez came aboard his ship and presented himself as a freeman and offered to work for Christiaensen trading for furs and anal glands with the Indians he had befriended.

Unlike the English who soon followed, Dutch traders were kind and fair with the local Indians who supplied them with pelts and glands in exchange for goods and tools. In 1621 the Dutch West India Company was founded, and over the next two years the government-backed company drove out the non-Dutch and the private traders, which opened the territory to Dutch settlers and company traders. It also allowed the laws of Holland to apply, whereas before the "law of the ship" — which gave the ship's captain absolute power — applied. The Dutch named the region "Nieuw-Nederland" (New Netherland). Because it provided ice-free access to the beaver-rich country to the north and easy access to the ocean, the mouth of the Hudson River was selected as the location for the new settlement. And In 1626 Peter Minuit made a particularly good real estate purchase for the Dutch West India Company when he bought present day Manhattan Island from the Canarsee Indians for 60 Dutch guilders ($900 in 2012 dollars).[1] Initially, the Canarsee may have received the better end of deal — they lived on Long Island, not in Manhattan.

The year before the purchase of Manhattan Island from the Canarsee, the Dutch West Indies Company had set up operations at the approximate site where Wall Street is now located. Using eleven African slaves, the Dutch built a wall around their tiny colony to protect themselves from the Indians and English. They called their enclave Fort Amsterdam. In August of 1654, a group of Ashkenazic Jews arrived from Amsterdam. The next month a group of Sephardic Jews, fleeing from the Portuguese conquest, joined them. Always a socially liberal people, the Dutch welcomed the Jews, who settled in an area of New Netherland called Nieuw Haarlem (now known only as Harlem), which became part of Nieuw-Amsterdam's (New Amsterdam) cultural core.

The Dutch owned and controlled New Amsterdam until 1664, when — even though the Dutch and English were at peace — four English frigates sailed into New Amsterdam's harbor, and their commander demanded that New Netherland surrender. The Dutch Director-General Peter Stuyvesant did, but the aggression led to the Second Anglo-Dutch war, which the Dutch lost. New Amsterdam was reincorporated under English law as New York City, named after the Duke of York, the arrogant brother of King Charles II who had been granted the lands. A story is told that one morning on his walk in Hyde Park, King Charles II dismissed his guards and strode into the park with two lords. As he crossed the road, his brother, James, the Duke of York, drove up in his carriage. The duke stopped his coach and expressed surprise at seeing his brother unattended and said that he thought it unwise for the king to expose himself to such danger. "No danger," said King Charles, "for no man in England would take away my life to make you king."

The Dutch treated their slaves much better than the English treated theirs. Dutch slaves were permitted to join the Dutch Reform church, they had most of the same legal rights as whites, families were kept intact, and they had better workers' rights — including wages for overtime. Two centuries later, slavery was abolished in New York, and on July 4, 1827, 10,000 New York slaves were freed without compensation to their owners, establishing a nucleus of free African-Americans in

---

[1] A note about the parenthetical inflation-adjusted 2012 dollar comparisons that are appended to dollar values throughout the text: From when the Continental Congress first issued Continentals until the modern economy began at the beginning of the 20th century, the value of the dollar was very stable. In fact, the value of the 1776 Continental bought exactly the same as the dollar did 130 years later in 1906, as did the dollar during the Black Hawk War, at the start of the Civil War, and during the Spanish-American War. During the U.S. currency's first 130 years, the dollar's value fluctuated within a range of two. In the last century, the dollar has inflated by a factor of 25. It is this incredible inflationary increase that distorts the value of everything after the First World War and why the parenthetical values to 2012 dollars comparisons are given.

North America and inflaming resentments over slave ownership between Northerners and Southerners. At first Northerners' criticism of Southern slave owners was that they treated their slaves poorly, granted them few freedoms, and considered them chattel. A generation later, their children took a higher moral ground and expanded Northern judgment to include cultural and ethical issues.

In 1607 the English Territory of Virginia was established. It included virtually all of the land east of the Mississippi River, south of New York, and north of South Carolina. Twelve years later about 20 African slaves were brought to Virginia, and a slave system was established in the English colonies, similar to the one that was thriving in the Spanish colonies. One hundred years earlier, under abominably inhumane conditions, the Spanish had captured and imported African slaves to work on their Caribbean sugar plantations. By the start of the Civil War, 240 years after the first slaves were brought to Virginia, the North American slave population grew from 20 to 4 million and further divided the North, where slavery was no longer of economic importance, from the South, where plantation farming was dependent upon slave labor.

The earliest permanent New England settlers arrived aboard two ships, the *Mayflower* and *Speedwell*, in early November 1620. The passengers that left England were a ragtag collection of 102 Protestants, separatists, servants, and child laborers, who were orphans, or poor or illegitimate children who had been taken from their parents and given to church members. One crewmember and one passenger died on the stormy 65-day voyage, one child was born, and most were sick when the ships dropped anchor at Cape Cod. The first ashore found vacant Indian buildings and fresh burial mounds. In a journal written before 1647, William Bradford, the leader of the Plymouth Colony wrote of the Pilgrims' landing:

> They also found two of the Indians houses covered with mats, and some of their implements in them; but the people had run away and could not be seen. They also found more corn, and beans of various colours. These they brought away, intending to give them full satisfaction [repayment] when they should meet with any of them — as about six months afterwards they did. And it is to be noted as a special providence of God, and a great mercy to this poor people, that they thus got seed to plant corn the next year, or they might have starved; for they had none, nor any likelihood of getting any, till too late for the planting season.

Over the next three weeks, several expeditions ashore didn't produce a suitable settlement site, but did result in the first encounter with Native Americans — the Pilgrims shot at them. Wisely fearing the local Indians may be angry with them for stealing corn meant for the dead and trying to kill them, the Pilgrims decided to move on and try somewhere else. They dropped anchor in Plymouth Harbor on December 17 and four days later a flat hilltop was selected for the site; Plymouth Colony was established. Twenty men permanently remained ashore while the others were protected in the relative comfort of the ship. Over the next two months, the shore crew and daily work crews, formed from those on the ship who were well enough to work, constructed a fort with five cannons, four common houses, and seven of the 19 planned residences. Conditions were brutal, and 45 of the 102 who landed at "New Plimouth" died before spring. The housing shortage was not as problematic as were the lack of provisions and absence of sanitary facilities.

The Pilgrims were not the first to land in the area. Europeans had fished the waters for almost a century, and Captain John Smith had explored the area in 1614. Seven years before that, Smith had founded James Fort, which in 1619 became Jamestown, the first permanent English settlement. Smith is credited with naming the region New England, and he named the future site of the Pilgrim's settlement "Accomack." The year after Smith's exploration and 15 years before the Pilgrims landed, a Frenchman, Samuel de Champlain, had extensively explored and mapped Plymouth Harbor. Champlain called the area "Port St. Louis" and wrote of a thriving Patuxet Indian village. The Patuxet were a tribe of the Wampanoag nation, and their sprawling former village carried the same name. In the three years before Plymouth Colony was established, the tribe had been reduced to a tenth of the number Champlain saw. Smallpox had decimated the Indian population along the New England coast, and very likely had the disease not reduced the Native American population to the lowest levels since the Ice Age, English colonization of New England would have been more aggressively opposed by the natives.

On March 16, 1621, an Indian named Samoset boldly walked into the Pilgrim settlement and said, "Welcome, Englishmen!" — he had learned broken English from English fishermen. No record is found of the normally imperturbable Puritans' reaction to their first close encounter with a Native American. After spending the night with the Pilgrims, Samoset came back two days later with Squanto (who preferred to be called Tisquantum), and who spoke even better English than Samoset. Tisquantum had been kidnapped along with other Indians in 1614 by one of John Smith's lieutenants who intended to sell him in Spain as a slave. Instead, some English friars took him and instructed him in Christianity. After a couple years, Tisquantum became homesick and asked to return to America. The Friars gave him to an English shipbuilder who taught him carpentry and more English and arranged passage for him to Newfoundland, where plans fell through for a connection to New England, so Tisquantum returned to England. Finally in 1619, after five years of living in England and at sea, he came home to Patuxet, only to find his tribe had been decimated by smallpox.

Tisquantum settled with the Pilgrims at the site of his former village. He taught them how to grow maize, catch eels and fish, and he helped them recover from their tragic first winter and establish their colony. The Pilgrims were grateful for his assistance and treated him with respect. Contrary to current practice, the Pilgrims thought of "Thanksgiving" as a solemn ceremony of prayer and thanks to God, and the first Pilgrim Thanksgiving wasn't held until July 1623. The holiday that Americans now celebrate on the 4th Thursday of November was a Pilgrim "harvest festival" and was first held in October 1621. The 53 surviving Pilgrims and Massasoit, the Wampanoag chief, and 90 of his men attended the three-day festival. The first Thanksgiving Day football game was still two and a half centuries off, so the celebration was all about eating. The colonists brought waterfowl, wild turkeys, and fish, and the Indians brought five deer.

There are many recorded instances where Indians provided food and assisted newly-arrived, smallpox-infested Europeans, and the Plymouth Pilgrims were one of the many boatloads of immigrants aided by the Wampanoag. Without Tisquantum's lessons and the acceptance and aid of his tribe, Plymouth's Pilgrims, who numbered half as many as when they left England, may have gone the way of the Lost Colony on Roanoke Island — a settlement that simply disappeared between late 1587 and August 1590. A half a century earlier, the Spanish had celebrated the first recorded North American Thanksgiving in September 1565 in what is now Saint Augustine, Florida. If any of *la Florida's* Native Americans were invited to Thanksgiving dinner, they probably sent their regrets. For two generations, the Spanish had been raiding the peninsula for Indian slaves. Nor were Indians asked to dinner when Sir Martin Frobisher, observed the first Canadian Thanksgiving in 1578. He threw a joyful late-autumn party for his crew to celebrate their safe return to Newfoundland after failing to find a Northwest Passage.

Although Frobisher was more fortunate than English explorer Henry Hudson, who was cast adrift by his mutinous crew when he refused to give up looking for the Northwest Passage, and Rear-Admiral Sir John Franklin and his icebound crew, who perished from starvation and hypothermia while mapping the Canadian coastline, the intrepid Frobisher stopped exploring and started mining when he found what he thought was gold ore on Canada's Baffin Island. His Initial assays determined the ore to be worth £5.1 per ton. After mining and carting 1,550 tons of ore back to England (an anticipated value of approximately $38,000), it was determined that the ore was worthless iron pyrite, a metal the English were unfamiliar with — Frobisher then gave up on legitimate enterprises and turned to pirating and privateering.

There are many early examples of pre-Pilgrim exploitation of Native Americans and their resources, but English emigrants seeking religious freedom were the first to declare war on the natives. American settlers backed by local posses, state militias, and later the U.S. Army waged a continuous war against North American Indians for 284 years, finally ending in January 1918 when the U.S. Army's 10th Calvary Company captured the last unruly band of Indians in Bear Valley, Arizona. History tends to justify, minimize, and obscure the brutality of the more than two and a half centuries of Indian battles east of the Mississippi River. The Indian Wars during the Colonial Period, which is considered to have extended from Columbus' landing to the American Revoultion, involved millions more Indians and resulted in a far greater loss of life and culture than the conflicts west of the Mississippi that provided background material and spectacular scenery for decades of Hollywood scripts. With few exceptions, Indians were grossly exploited and treated inhumanely. The fighting was relentless, and the last battle east of the Rockies was not until October 1898, only 20 years before the last Indian battle in Bear Valley. Because of his bravery in the battle of Sugar Point at Leech Lake, Minnesota, Pvt. Oscar Burkhard received the last Medal of Honor awarded for killing Native Americans.

Although skirmishes between Europeans and Indians are recorded from the time when natives first resisted Christopher Columbus' attempts to capture and enslave them, the brutal, non-stop conflict between the cultures began in 1634 when Massachusetts Bay colonists clashed with local Pequot tribes who resisted leaving their traditional lands to make way for the British immigrants. The Pequot Nation was a powerful New England clan of about 8,000 whose territory the white men coveted — mostly because it's where they had randomly dragged themselves ashore. The Pequot split between those who wished to coexist with the British, the Mohegan, and those who chose not to quietly pack up and leave. In retaliation for killing an Englishman, in 1636 a Pequot village was burned. The following summer militia from the Massachusetts and Connecticut colonies organized with warriors from the Narragansett and the Mohegan tribes to further the punishment.

Surrounding a Pequot fort at Mystic, Connecticut, where the Pequot were making a last stand, the fort was set afire, and in less than an hour more than 600 Pequot were killed by the flames or gunned-down while trying to escape. Most of the Indian men who were allowed to surrender were sold into slavery in the West Indies and Bermuda, and most of the Pequot women and children were divided among the Narragansett and the Mohegan. The scattering of the Mystic survivors effectively eliminated the Pequot Nation, and in 1935 the tribal census was 42, all of whom were destitute and living on a 213-acre reservation. Forty years after the 1935 census, all but two tribal members had dispersed and left the reservation. One of the remaining, Elizabeth George, appealed to other tribal members to reunite and to revitalize the tribe. They did and in 1992 the Mashantucket Pequot Nation opened the Foxwoods Casino on their reservation — one of the world's largest casinos with over seven acres of casino gaming space. The Pequot have been methodically gaining their economic revenge on the white man ever since, as have their 480 Shakopee brothers at Mystic Lake, Minnesota, each of whom receives more than a million dollars a year for being part owners of the Mystic Lake Casino.

At the same time the Massachusetts Bay colonists were setting the Pequot on fire, they were also killing their own women. Although Pope John XII had authorized the Inquisition to prosecute sorcerers in 1320, "witch hunting" didn't become a widespread sport until a Franciscan priest, Bernardine of Siena, gained immense popularity when he held "bonfires of vanities" where those at his sermons burned objects of temptation. (Since women are the greatest temptation for straight men, it was a short leap.) Father Bernardine was a convincing speaker who preached fiery sermons that called for Jews and sodomites to be isolated or eliminated from the community, and he demonized many women as "witches." He praised the burning of homosexuals, and was equally zealous about torching witches — ironically, women comprised the majority of his audience. Six years after his death in 1444, he was canonized as a saint.

Saint Bernardine is the patron saint of compulsive gambling, respiratory issues, and advertising. Being the designated saint for advertising is understandable. It was his fiery sermons against witches that sold the concept of witchcraft and spread the fear that witches were an organized band of devil-worshippers that needed to be eliminated. Within a century, the popularity of witch hunting spread throughout Central Europe, and although sometimes trials were held, by church edict or popular vote of the faithful, most accused witches ended up being burned at the stake. By the mid-16th century, witch hunts made their way to Great Britain, and women were blamed for just about everything that went wrong — in Berwick, Scotland, more than 100 women were accused of witchcraft, and one was burned at the stake because of bad weather.

Puritans, who immigrated to the New World, were mostly Anglicans who were annoyed that they were marginalized by the Church of England and were controlled by the king's laws in their practice of religion. Their church was only 100-years-old, and already a religion born during the Reformation needed reforming. The Puritans were particularly distressed over the flamboyant dress of Episcopal clerics and preferred the understated style seen today in children's illustrated books of Pilgrims enjoying a

Thanksgiving feast. Also, they believed that the Reformation had not gone far enough and resented that the Church of England had not further distanced itself from Roman Catholicism. One of the Catholic canons they did embrace was that witches were a constant threat. The Plymouth Pilgrims were too preoccupied with survival, and women were in too short of supply to carelessly waste them, but after two generations, things normalized, and witch-hunting became popular in the colonies.

An English philosopher and clergyman, Joseph Glanvill, taught that smart men should believe in witches and demons, and that if they doubted the reality of spirits, they not only denied devils, but also the almighty God. Glanvill built a career on that bit of circular logic, and as more Puritans made their way to America and brought the latest theological revelations with them, Massachusetts's colonists started actively rooting out the causes of their misfortunes. Men and some righteous women believed that such things as infant death, crop failures, illness, or conflicts among the congregation were the work of the devils that possessed wanton women and the men who hunkered up to them.

During the early 1690s, the Salem area of Massachusetts was a contentious place to live. Salem Village was at constant odds with Salem Town over property lines, grazing rights, and church privileges. Both villages were seen as "quarrelsome," and in 1672 Salem Village hired its own minister. This brazen and needlessly expensive act escalated the tension between the two burgs and nearby hamlets that worshipped with the Salem Town minister. Most of the area's inhabitants were ultra-strict Calvinists, whose lives were governed by the Church. Music, singing, dancing, holiday celebrations, children's games, and toys were forbidden, and there were no taverns. The only schooling children received was religious doctrine, and the only book read was the Bible.

Inexplicably, a 9-year-old girl and her 11-year-old cousin started behaving strangely. The girls would scream, growl, and throw things about the room. Soon, other girls in Salem Village started doing the same bizarre things. When the young women started screaming during the twice-a-week three-hour church services, something had to be done. Three women from neighboring villages were identified as witches and accused of afflicting the girls. One of the usual suspects was a homeless beggar, another was a widower who married an indentured servant, and the third was a slave. People from other villages started pointing fingers and making accusations about Salem Village women, and soon every available witch suspect within miles had been hunted down and arrested.

Although they didn't wear black pointy hats, witches were easy to identify because of their conduct and absence from church services. However, it was America, and an early belief emerged that everyone was innocent until proven guilty. It was commonly held that an effective method of positive identification of an accused witch was to bake a witch cake. The important ingredients in a witch cake are rye meal and the urine of the bewitched. The cake is then fed to a dog — any dog will do. Invisible particles that the witch used to afflict her target passes in the urine of the inflicted, and after the dog eats the cake, if acts a little crazy, there is solid circumstantial evidence of witchcraft.

Not all the witches were women. Often men were accused of witchcraft or of making a pact with the devil. One Salem man who was convicted was John Willard, a constable in Salem Village. After he began to doubt the truth of the allegations against the people he was arresting, he quit his job. In retaliation for his insubordination, he was accused of witchcraft and of murdering 13 people — he was hung. The total number of Salem witches arrested was 172, and after passing through several courts to sort out the true witches — 28 were convicted. Of those convicted, 21 were executed, six were pardoned, and one escaped. Of those who were pardoned, two were spared because they were pregnant and four because the bewitched girls stopped misbehaving, so apparently all of the Salem witches had already been eliminated. One 80-year-old farmer who had been arrested refused to enter a plea when he was brought before the court, so the judges sentenced him to have stones piled on his chest until he offered a plea — after two days he died.

Driven from their lands by whites, virtually all of the Northeastern Indian tribes relocated during the Colonial Period. The Sau-Kee (a name meaning "people of the yellow or parched earth," which later became an appropriate name for a Rock Island public golf course) and the Mus-qua-Kee (meaning "red or flaming earth people") were aggressively driven west from their native lands along the St. Lawrence River near present day Montreal and Quebec by the Iroquois. The Iroquois had originally lived in the Finger Lakes region west of the Hudson River until the colonists drove them from their native lands. About the same time the Pilgrims were building their first cabins at Plymouth, the Sau-Kee had settled near present day Saginaw, Michigan, and the Mus-qua-Kee near Detroit.

During the mid-17th century, the two tribes were pushed even farther west by the Iroquois and Wyandotte. They relocated to Wisconsin's Fox River region and became allies, fighting against the area's native Indian tribes, principally the Winnebago. Later, the French, who were beginning to trade with the Winnebago for animal pelts, also became an enemy. In 1634 Jean Nicolet, the first white man to traverse Wisconsin, befriended the Winnebago at Red Banks, just north of the present-day University of Wisconsin-Green Bay campus. However it would be another 20 years before the first fur traders and the first Jesuit missionary, Father René Menard, established a continuing relationship with the tribes. Fr. Menard spoke six Indian languages, and he may have been the first to call the Sau-Kee "Sauk" and rename the Mus-qua-Kee (Meskwaki) "Renards," which is French for "fox."

As an increasing number of French traders arrived in Green Bay, the Sauk and Meskwaki, who then did only minimal fur trading, demanded tributes from them, which of course the traders resisted. In 1722 after more than two decades of minor skirmishes and isolated attacks, as the fur trade prospered, the traders had had enough, and the French commander at the Green Bay fort ambushed the Meskwaki's main village from boats. Local Menominee warriors, who were allied with the French, created diversionary attacks from land that drove the Meskwaki into the soldiers' trap. The resulting slaughter greatly weakened the Meskwaki, and as the French grew stronger, the Meskwaki further allied themselves with the Sauk. In 1735 the two closely affiliated tribes fled Packerland and migrated west to the Mississippi River.

Fighting their way south along the river against long-established tribes, the Sauk and Meskwaki made their way to the confluence of the Mississippi and Rock rivers where they drove the Illiniwek south of the Rock River. The Meskwaki, who numbered about 1,600, settled on the west side of the Mississippi River and the Sauk on the east side. Most of the Sauk, including the Thunder and Fox clans, settled on the south banks of a 14-mile stretch of the Mississippi that is the only place where the river runs east to west. Picking a scenic and strategically well-situated site on the bluffs overlooking the Rock River near the confluence with the Mississippi, the Sauk built their primary village, which they called Saukenuk. The orderly village consisted of about 100 long houses on the north bank of the Rock River and was laid out in a neat grid, not unlike present day Rock Island. The Sauk nation numbered about 5,000.

The westward-flowing stretch of the Mississippi River was a rocky chain of rapids that extended the length of the northern shore of a narrow strip of land bordered to the south by the Rock River. The rapids provided several crossing points and excellent fishing, and before the Sauk arrived in the early 18th century, the ribbon of land between the two rivers had served as a hub of Native American settlement and trade. The fast-running stretch of clear river water would later be named the Rock Island Rapids. In 1673 white men first saw the ancient river's three-quarter-mile wide racing waters, dotted with small islands and sandbars that allowed the river to be easily canoed across in the summertime, and its frozen ponds that allowed it to be walked across in the wintertime. French explorers Louis Jolliet and Jacques Marquette canoed down the Wisconsin River and then down the Upper Mississippi to the mouth of the Arkansas River. When Marquette and Jolliet passed through the Rock Island Rapids, the Illiniwek occupied the land along the riverbanks.

Born in Laon, France, Marquette joined the Society of Jesus at age 17. Twelve years later the Jesuits sent him as a missionary to Quebec City and assigned him to convert the "indigenous peoples of the Americas." Apparently assisted by learning Latin at an early age, Marquette became proficient in several Indian languages. Marquette requested to extend his mission and to search for the "great river" described to him by Illiniwek he met while establishing a mission near Ashland, Wisconsin. He recruited a local frontiersman, Louis Jolliet, to guide and assist him. Jolliet was born near Quebec City and was the stepson of a prominent merchant. Educated at a Jesuit school, he learned English, Spanish, Latin, and several Indian dialects at an early age. He had taken his first vows to become a Jesuit, but before taking final vows, he dropped out of the seminary and became an adventurer and local bon vivant.

The Frenchman and the Canadian left St. Ignace in two canoes in May with five Métis, men of French and Indian ancestry. Both men kept journals and mapped their expedition, but Jolliet lost his when his canoe tipped over on the return trip, so the recorded history of the journey is totally from Marquette's viewpoint. Although the priest was less experienced as an explorer and a less detailed chronologist than Jolliet, historians use his description of landing on the west bank of the Mississippi as solid evidence that a French Catholic missionary discovered Iowa. Taking the advice of local Indians, Jolliet led the expedition's return to St. Ignace up the Illinois River and across the "Chicago Portage" into Lake Michigan. Jolliet noted that the portage was "only half a league" (less than 2 miles) and saved weeks of travel up the Mississippi and Wisconsin Rivers. It would be another 175 years before engineers took advantage of Jolliet's observation and connected the Great Lakes to the Mississippi River via the Illinois and Michigan canal.

Marquette called the great river the *River of the Immaculate Conception*, which wasn't much catchier than Spanish explorer, Hernando de Soto's, name for the Mississippi when he boated up the river to the site of present day Memphis two centuries earlier and dubbed it the *River of the Holy Spirit*. (Spanish maps before the first Treaty of Paris in 1763 show the land comprising all of Illinois south of the Illinois River as part of Florida.) De Soto's and Marquette's names didn't stick, and fortunately for secularists, the French translated, Anishinaabe, the Algonquin name for the river, which means "Father of Waters" to Messipi, and the English Anglicized the name. In 1543 when de Soto canoed up the Lower Mississippi, he noted in his journal the first recorded Mississippi flood. Fields near an Indian village at the confluence of the Mississippi and Arkansas Rivers were under water.

Historians' believe that 670 years after Leif Eriksson discovered the Americas and 180 years after Columbus rediscovered them that Marquette and Jolliet were the first white men to walk Rock Island's riverbanks. They believe this because the rapids required portaging; the site was home to a large band of Indians, an observation made in Marquette's journal; Rock Island's topography matches descriptions in his journal; the rapids emptied into a vast marshland below where the Rock River flows into the Mississippi, making the Illinois side of the river easier to traverse than the Iowa side; and of course, the French explorers would have preferred the esthetics of the Illinois side of the river.

Marquette and Jolliet's glowing descriptions of expansive lands lush with rich vegetation and teeming with valuable animal pelts opened the Upper Mississippi River to the fur trade. The present day Upper Mississippi begins as a stream near Lake Itasca in north-central Minnesota. From there, the river meanders through wooded valleys for over 500 miles until it reaches the Minneapolis/St. Paul area where it becomes navigable by large craft. As the river flows 665 miles south from St. Paul to the confluence with the Missouri River just above St. Louis, the Minnesota, St. Croix, Chippewa, Wisconsin, Rock, Des Moines, and Illinois Rivers and hundreds of streams and creeks feed into it. Finally, 170 miles south of St. Louis at Cairo, Illinois, the Ohio River joins the Upper Mississippi to form the magnificent river that Mark Twain described as a "mile-wide tide, shining in the sun."

Nine years after Marquette and Jolliet journeyed down the Mississippi, French explorer, Robert de La Salle, led an expedition south from the Illinois River to the mouth of the Mississippi and claimed the entire river valley for France. Soon French traders were using a centrally located Mississippi River island in the marsh on the north side of the river at the mouth of the Rock River as a base for trading operations. The flat, low-lying island was easily defended and afforded easy access to the river channel. The Mississippi River's largest island, which lies across a narrow slough from the south side of the river, is located only two miles upstream but was considered sacred to the Indians and was off-limits to white men. On the downstream island, traders advanced credit to Indians for traps, guns, and provisions, and promised more goods, whiskey, and cancellation of the IOU's with the delivery of a certain number of pelts. The island became known as Credit Island, a name it retains today.

In the early 18th century, France claimed and controlled the vast American territory that extended west from Newfoundland to the Rocky Mountains and south from the Hudson Bay to the Gulf of Mexico. Nouveau France included everything in the New World except the original thirteen colonies, Florida, whose white sand beaches had been staked out by the Spanish several centuries earlier, and the Appalachian

Mountains, which weren't in high demand by anyone except some Scots-Irish who found them a suitable place to build gin mills and play banjos free of complaining neighbors. The French and English were not good neighbors either in the New or Old World. After William the Conqueror's invasion of England in 1066, they had become relentlessly hostile adversaries.

In 1756 matters between the two nations had once again become hotly contentious, and they fought until early 1763, a period creatively called the Seven Years War. England had the stronger navy, and they initiated attacks on the European mainland, where most of the war's land battles were fought. Two years before war broke out in Europe, in the American colonies the uneasy truce between French and English immigrants and the French and English armies that protected them was broken by a dispute over who owned the land where Pittsburgh now stands. Fighting on what was then the western frontier, for the next few years the French had the upper hand on the continent they called the Nouveau Monde.

Unlike the English, the French weren't interested in acquiring land and farming it. They were more driven by the commerce of trading trinkets, tools, guns, and whiskey with young male Indians for animal skins and sending the pelts back to France where they were made into fashionable hats and overcoats. And being solid Catholics from a Catholic country, they weren't looking for a place to avoid religious persecution. French commercial interests were more compatible to Indian pursuits, and by trading woven clothes and guns and goods and liquor and glass beads and promises to stay off their land to the Indians, the French captured Indian loyalty and then craftily turned them against the English, who were mostly interested in finding a fertile tract with a nice creek running through it.

During the early years of the Seven Years War, the warring parties in Europe, knowing that whoever won at home would get the worldwide spoils, were not particularly invested in who was winning in the colonies. However in the colonies, the French, with considerable help from the Indians, were clearly getting the best of the English. That changed when the English put William Pitt, the Elder, in charge of the war effort and English forces were increased in America. The French didn't match the British commitment and the tide turned against them.

On the Continent after seven years of the English taking on all comers, which included almost every country in Central Europe, and after killing more than a million, the antagonists fought to a bloody draw. North American boundary and governance compromises, made in the 1763 Treaty of Paris, assured that English would be the common language in the future United States. Spain ceded Florida to Great Britain and France ceded all the land in North America east of the Mississippi River and south of what is now Canada to the English — Illinois was now British territory. The land west of the Mississippi was given to the Spanish, and the French got nothing. Because the English won the war, they got to write the history, and they named the nine years of strife in North America, the French and Indian War, which it was from their point of view.

The English were particularly pleased in gaining control of French Canada and Acadia, the land between Maine and Quebec, which they had fought over with the French for more than two hundred years, and they began seizing property and deporting the region's widely scattered 80,000 French-speaking Roman Catholics. Most of the Acadians dispersed throughout the British provinces, but many returned to France, and a large group went to New Orleans on the western banks of the Mississippi, which was technically owned by the Spanish but still occupied by the French. The Acadian Frenchmen who relocated to Louisiana were called "Cadiens," which, in that lazy Southern way, evolved into "Cajuns."

Because the Treaty of Paris gave the disputed and ethnically-mixed frontier territory west of the established East Coast colonies to the English, anti-British alliances were solidified and most Indian loyalties drifted to the French. Oppressive, post-war Indian policies and the Indian's reluctance to leave their traditional lands hardened English/Indian relationships, and led to Pontiac's Rebellion, a conflict that was fought in the eastern Great Lakes region. The Indians continued to fiercely battle the English for two years after the Europeans had settled their differences.

Fighting in the colonial frontier period was brutal. The pillaging and burning of immigrant settlements and Indian villages were common, and the murder of prisoners and civilians and atrocities against women and children by both whites and Indians were widespread. Even though the Treaty of Paris brought Great Britain, France, Spain, and Portugal into agreement over the European distribution of territory in the New World, the natives weren't included in the negotiations and they became increasingly restless.

West of the Great Lakes, the French and Indians had coexisted comparatively peacefully for more than a hundred years, and many tribes were dismayed to learn that French agreements and relationships no longer mattered and that now they were subject to the British — in many cases their adversaries for generations. Others were indifferent to the ethnicity of their white adversaries; they didn't like any whites. The English did little to improve their image with the Indians. Although having a strict code of military honor and justice, they chose not to extend the courtesies and rules of military conduct to non-whites. In one of the first recorded cases of American biological warfare, at the beginning of Pontiac's Rebellion, the Delaware laid siege to Fort Pitt.

Surrounded and greatly outnumbered, the fort's commander, "out of our regard to them" gave each of the Delaware two blankets and a handkerchief courtesy of the Pittsburgh smallpox hospital. The ensuing epidemic among the Delaware weakened their resolve and greatly diminished their number of warriors.

Hostilities were abated when King George III, who was unclear on what he was giving away, made the Royal Proclamation of 1763, which created an "Indian Reserve," that gave ownership of land west of the crest of the Appalachians to the Indians. The land concession appeased the Indians, gave sanctuary to the French, and enraged British colonists who had settled west of the Appalachians or who had been previously granted land in the territory King George so blithely gave back to the Indians. King George's magnanimous compromise and recognition of Indian land rights was one of the major causes leading to the American Revolution. The Indian Reserve encompassed virtually all of the land the English had received eight months earlier in the Treaty of Paris, except what was in Canada.

With King George's proclamation, overnight American politics became as muddled and contentious as anytime in American history. Those living the colonies were least affected, unless they weren't English, but those residing in the massive territory, which was three times as large as the colonies were turned upside down. Many Indian tribes had been long-time allies of the French and some had made peace with the British for concessions on their traditional lands, but were now being asked to move west into the Indian Reserve. The French, who were mostly concentrated in the Upper Mississippi Valley portion of the Indian Reserve and were not tied to the land, were better liked and more compatible with the Indians than the English who owned the land. Wisely seizing the opportunity to establish domain over the land ceded to them by King George III, many of the Sauk living at Saukenuk, became loyal to the British — the Americans, Spanish, and French, who greatly outnumbered British Loyalists in the region, commonly referred to them and other Sauk and Meskwaki that were loyal to the English as the "British Band."

The Sauk and Meskwaki were among the most respected of the Indian tribes. They were given faint praise when an early historian wrote of them, "The Sacs and Foxes are a truly courageous people, shrewd, politic and enterprising, with not more of ferocity and treachery of character than is common among the tribes by whom they were surrounded." To foster competitiveness, at birth each Sauk child was given a black or white designation — proudly displaying for life a black charcoal mark or white clay mark. With each new birth, the colors were alternated so that the nation was evenly divided between blacks and whites, perpetually creating two competing teams. Besides saving time when choosing sides for Indian games, the marking created a sense of teamwork and accountability in all things from providing meat and pelts to the taking of scalps.

Marriage ties were not strong among the Sauk, but family ties were. Heredity rights were traced through the male line and were designated for each Sauk clan by a totem, such as a bear or eagle or hawk. The name of the clan's totem was part of the family surname, and Sauk and Meskwaki men and women took great pride and showed lasting loyalty to their clan (a loyalty similar to that of those who graduate from Rocky and Alleman). And the prohibition of men marrying women of the same clan protected against inbreeding.

Although not without conflicts, the twenty-year period from King George's creation of the Indian Reserve until the 1783 Treaty of Paris (the second Treaty of Paris) that formally ended the American Revolution was the least contentious for the Indians west of the colonies. Indisputably, if other Indian nations had joined the British Band and supported the English during the war, and if England had won the war, the Indians would have fared better — they could not have been treated worse — and very probably today they would live as their Canadian brothers do. Native Canadians have always been treated more fairly and with greater respect and been given greater land concessions and sovereignty than Native Americans.

After King George's proclamation, circumstances fell against the English. Some historians write that Indian warfare taught American colonists how to fight the British and hardened them for the American Revolution. Also, the French, who were always looking for others to fight their battles and who wanted another bite of the North American colonization apple, fostered strong relationships with the Indians through trade and weapons support and encouraged the Indians to oppose the British. The Spanish were most happy to stay out of the revolutionary fracas and tend to business in the warmer climes of the Caribbean Islands, Florida, Mexico, and South America, but they too opposed the British during the Revolution.

However, in the final analysis England's rigid imperialistic policies and laws were their undoing, and English, Spanish, and French colonists, who had been enemies for generations became allies against King George. And except for those tribes that had received major land concessions from the British, most Indian clans opposed them or sought passive neutrality during the Revolution. With little to gain, the tribes that were actively engaged in the war were fragmented in their allegiances and were quick to give up their positions. Native Americans can only wonder what their destiny would have been had they banded together and helped the British defeat the colonists.

Chapter 3

With Liberty and Justice for All

Democracy is two wolves and a lamb voting on what to have for lunch. Liberty is a well-armed lamb contesting the vote. ~ Benjamin Franklin

IN THE MID-18TH CENTURY, the lands and culture surrounding Saukenuk were virtually unchanged from antiquity, and Indians outnumbered white men by more than 1,000 to one. In the decades before the American Revolution, whites had settled along the East Coast from Massachusetts to Florida, and Indian tribes had been pushed to the interior from shorelines and white settlements by only about ten miles. The white population of the colonies was 1.5 million with most living in the urban areas of Boston, New York, Philadelphia, and Charleston and in the coastal agricultural regions of New Jersey, Maryland, and Virginia.

The colonies spawned a strongly independent, self-reliant group of men, who were schooled in English culture, law, and social order. However, separated from London by a treacherous month at sea, as succeeding generations were born on American soil, European ties diminished and regional and colony loyalties strengthened. In a classless society where community contributions were valued, old social concepts and limitations vanished and unregulated opportunity was available to all white men. Given a blank slate upon which to write the future of a country, a generation of intellectuals, entrepreneurs, social reformers, and patriots emerged to form a democratic nation unmatched in history.

No man contributed more to the evolving American culture than Benjamin Franklin. The 15th of 17 children fathered by Josiah Franklin, Benjamin was born on Boston's Milk Street. An avid reader, he received two years of formal education at Boston's Latin School and then became self-taught. At age twelve, he was forced to become an apprentice printer to his brother, James. Three years later, James began publishing *The New-England Courant*, the first independent newspaper in America. Denied permission by his brother to write for the paper, Franklin assumed the pseudonym of "Mrs. Silence Dogood," and soon his letters to the paper were the talk of Boston. His brother was outraged when he found out that Franklin was Mrs. Dogood, and the 15-year-old Franklin was forced to run away and become a legal fugitive.

Seeking a new start, Franklin fled to Philadelphia where he found work as a typesetter. Joining with like-minded young men, he formed a reading club. But books were scarce and expensive, so Franklin expanded his club to the general public so that anyone could borrow a book after paying a subscription fee, which was used to purchase more books. Named the Philadelphia Library Company, it was the first public library. Eight years after opening, the books were moved from the home of the librarian to the building now called Independence Hall. In 1791, a new building was constructed for the Library Company, and today it houses one of the world's foremost historical research libraries with a collection of over 500,000 rare books and pamphlets.

At age 17, Franklin proposed to 15-year-old Deborah Read, the daughter of his landlord. Her mother opposed the marriage, and while Franklin was in London on official business for the Pennsylvania governor, Deborah married another man, who then fled to Barbados with her dowry. Because of bigamy laws, Franklin was not allowed to marry her, but six years later they formed a common law marriage. In addition to Franklin's illegitimate son, William, who lived with them, the couple had Francis Folger, who died of smallpox at age four, and Sarah, who in addition to mothering seven children, cared for her father in his last years. The Franklin marriage was not a close one, and afraid of the sea, Deborah refused to accompany him on his frequent trips abroad. She died of a stroke at age 66 while he was on an extended trip to England.

At age 27, Franklin began a 26-year stint publishing *Poor Richard's Almanack*. At the height of its popularity, 10,000 copies were sold annually (relative to the country's population, today the *Almanack's* sales would equal 2 million annually). During the same period, Franklin voraciously read about science and formed an extensive foundation of scientific and engineering knowledge that led to an array of inventions, which included the lightening rod, Franklin stove, bifocals, and very probably his most humanitarian invention, the flexible urinary catheter. After he left printing, Franklin primarily occupied himself with scientific inquiry, but he never patented any of his inventions. He explained, "As we enjoy great advantages from the inventions of others, we should be glad of an opportunity to serve others by any invention of ours; and this we should do freely and generously."

However, he did enjoy the good life, and he was not above making money from his writings and inventions — he wrote in the *Almanack*, "The only thing sweeter than honey is money." In addition to human biology, his physical science interests spanned the fields of physics, meteorology, oceanography, and astronomy, and his research greatly contributed to the wave theory of light and the thermodynamics of temperature on electrical conductivity. His recreations were as varied as his professional interests and included chess (he wrote *The Morals of Chess*) and music (he played the violin, harp, and guitar, and he invented the glass armonica). He did not paint or play lacrosse.

Franklin greatly enjoyed good food and fine wine. And he apparently believed in divine intervention, saying, "Behold the rain which descends from heaven upon our vineyards, there it enters the roots of the vines, to be changed into wine, a constant proof that God loves us, and loves to see us happy." (This quote has been crassly shortened and distorted by tee-shirt manufacturers to widen its appeal to the masses by saying, "Beer is proof that God loves us and wants us to be happy." Although Franklin would probably agree, he didn't say it.)

After founding the first public library, Franklin's societal contributions expanded into virtually all areas of public service. At age 30 he created the Union Fire Company, one of the nation's first volunteer fire departments, and the same year he invented a currency that was difficult to counterfeit. Seven years later, he devised a graduate and post-graduate curriculum for the Academy and College of Philadelphia (later merged with the University of the State of Pennsylvania to become the University of Pennsylvania), and the man who with two years of elementary education was made president of the college — Franklin later became the first person to receive honorary degrees from both Harvard and Yale.

Franklin didn't hold his first political office until age 42, when he was elected councilman. The following year, he was elected justice of the peace, and in 1751 at the age of 45, he was elected to the Pennsylvania Assembly. The same year, Franklin and Thomas Bond received a charter from the State of Pennsylvania to form a hospital — it was the first in North America. Two years later he was appointed to be deputy postmaster-general where he reformed a shoddy operation and assured that mail to Europe would be shipped every week.

In 1754 Franklin headed the Pennsylvania delegation to the Albany Congress, a convention assembled by the Board of Trade in England to improve relations with the Indians and to plan defenses against France. Language from the adopted plan found its way into the Articles of Confederation and the Constitution. Two years later, Franklin organized the Pennsylvania militia. Successfully enlisting recruits at Philadelphia's Tun Tavern (a popular meeting place that was also the "birthplace of Masonic teachings in America") to fight Indians in the colony's western regions. Franklin was elected colonel of the militia but declined the position, most probably because he was a pacifist who strongly believed in negotiated settlements and that war was the last resort.

Franklin was deeply humane and had an insightful understanding of the human condition that he extended to men of all races, and because of his pacifist and egalitarian views, it is unlikely that he would have harmed an Indian or any other man. The *Quebec History Encyclopedia* says of Franklin and his views on Indian culture:

> In one of his *Essays* Benjamin Franklin offered some considerations regarding the Indians which are well worthy of remembrance, and of special application to those of Canada [and the rest of the Americas]. He points out that the Indian men, when young, were hunters and warriors; when old, counselors; that all their government was by the counsel or advice of the sages; that there was no force, there were no prisons, and no officers to compel obedience, or inflict punishment. Hence they generally studied oratory, the best speaker having the most influence. The Indian women tilled the ground, dressed the food, nursed and brought up the children, and preserved and handed down to posterity the memory of public transactions. These employments of men and women were accounted natural and honourable. Having few artificial wants they had abundance of leisure for improvement in conversation. Our labourious manner of life, compared with theirs, they esteemed slavish and base, and the learning on which we value ourselves they regarded as frivolous and useless.

Before the American Revolution, few colonists had this deep understanding of the Indian culture or shared Franklin's views. He was equally outspoken on slavery, and these views were only slightly less popular than those on Indian rights. During the last five years of his life, he became a strident abolitionist and was president of the Pennsylvania Abolition Society. He wrote extensively of the evils of slavery and the necessity of assimilating blacks into mainstream society. He was not a religious man, and he observed, "Lighthouses are more helpful than churches."

Franklin was a Freemason, which speaks well of the enigmatic fraternal organization whose members today argue that they are an "esoteric" society not a "secret" society. The semantics of the description are irrelevant, because other than dozens of conspiracy theories that range from being a Jewish front for world domination to being behind the assassination of John Kennedy, nothing dastardly that has happened in the 500 years since the fraternity was founded can be attributed to Freemasons. Also there are an extraordinary number of remarkable good works associated with their lodges, and if an organization can be judged by its membership, the 14 U.S. Presidents and thousands of well-respected elected officials, military leaders, and business and community leaders that have been members commend the organization and reflect well on the almost 2 million current U.S. Freemasons.

In 1757 the Pennsylvania Assembly dispatched Franklin to England to protest the political control of the Penn family, the proprietors of the colony. Suffering one of the few defeats of his life, he spent five years lobbying the British Parliament to end the Penn's tax exclusion and their ability to overturn legislation from the elected Assembly. As much as any other British act of arrogance and indifference, rebuffing Franklin pushed him and the colonies toward revolution and aligned the colonists with the

French. While in London, Franklin's politics moved from conciliatory to revolutionary, and he became involved with the Club of Honest Whigs and with his landlady's daughter, Mary "Polly" Stevenson. Before returning to Pennsylvania, in 1762 Oxford University bestowed an honorary doctorate on him for his scientific achievements, and from then on he went by "Doctor Franklin" — his only concession to his extraordinary accomplishments.

In 1763 when Franklin returned to Pennsylvania, the western frontier, which was then the Great Lakes Region, was engulfed in Pontiac's Rebellion. After murdering 20 peaceful Susquehannock Indians in central Pennsylvania, the Paxton Boys, a group of vigilante settlers, marched on Philadelphia in an attempt to convince the Pennsylvania government that not enough was being done to protect settlers from Indian raids. Franklin helped organize a local militia to defend the capital against the mob, and then met with the Paxton leaders and persuaded them to disperse. Franklin wrote a scathing attack against the racial prejudice of the Paxton Boys. "If an Indian injures me," he asked, "does it follow that I may revenge that Injury on all Indians?"

Also upon his return to Philadelphia, he resumed his feud with the Penns, and as the leader of Pennsylvania's Anti-proprietary Party was elected Speaker of the Pennsylvania House. Fears initiated by the Penn family that Pennsylvanians could lose their religious and political freedoms turned the electorate against Franklin and he lost his Assembly seat in 1764. Being dispatched back to England to continue the political struggle with the Penn family proved fortuitous for America — it placed the right person in the right spot at the right time.

Shortly after Franklin arrived in London, the 1765 Stamp Act was passed. The act imposed a tax on printed materials, and the tax revenue was used to support British troops in the American colonies after the Seven Years War. The furor over taxing citizens to pay for British troops to police them unleashed the highly respected Franklin to successfully champion the repeal of the act before the House of Commons. Suddenly Franklin became the most influential American in England. He published persuasive essays on behalf of the colonies, and Massachusetts, Georgia, and New Jersey also appointed him as their agent to the Crown. At the time the Stamp Act was repealed, Parliament stated that their authority was the same in America as in Britain and asserted their right to make binding laws on the American colonies. This was the tipping point for the American Revolution.

For the next decade, Franklin spent most of his time in Great Britain with frequent trips to France. He was alternately a representative of the colonies, a goodwill ambassador to England and France, and a spy for the colonists. In the latter role, he obtained private letters written by Massachusetts' governor Thomas Hutchinson that encouraged London to crack down on the rights of Bostonians. Franklin sent the letters to America where they further escalated tensions. His former British patrons ostracized and shunned Franklin, and all hope for a peaceful resolution between the Americans and British ended with he left London in March 1775.

While Franklin was at sea, fighting between the New England militia and the British Army flared up at Lexington and Concord, and the militia trapped the main army in Boston. The Pennsylvania Assembly unanimously chose Franklin as their representative to the Second Continental Congress. A month later, Congress established the United States Post Office and named him Postmaster General. In June 1776 Congress appointed him a member of the Committee of Five, which drafted the Declaration of Independence. Disabled by gout, which affected him most of his life, he was unable to actively participate in the drafting meetings, but made suggestions and minor changes to the drafts sent to him by Thomas Jefferson.

When Jefferson complained to Franklin about the edits that the Committee of Five made to his cherished draft, Franklin took him aside and told him a story about when he was a young man and a friend, who was a hatter, opened a shop. His friend was anxious to have a fine signboard and composed one that said, "John Thompson, hatter, makes and sells hats for ready money." Underneath the script was a picture of a hat. When he asked his friends what they thought, one said, "hatter" was superfluous, as "makes and sells hats" showed the nature of the business. A second friend said that "makes" could be left out since prospective customers were unlikely interested in who made the hat. A third friend said that since few merchants extended credit, the words "for ready money" were also superfluous, and they too were struck. "No one would expect you to give them away," said a fourth friend, "so what is the point of 'sells'?" Finally someone said that it seemed unnecessary to have the word "hats" on the sign since there was a painted picture of one. So the finished sign read "John Thompson" with a picture of a hat underneath the name. Jefferson was mollified and agreed that the changes improved the Declaration of Independence.

Experiencing quite different circumstances than the self-made Franklin, George Washington was born of landed gentry in Colonial Virginia, and his father and two older half-brothers home schooled him. His father died when he was 11, which prevented him from going to school in England as his brothers had, and at 17, when most young men of his age and station were enrolled in college or serving in the Royal Navy or British Army, Washington was appointed to the prestigious and responsible position of official surveyor of the Shenandoah Valley.

When he was 19, Washington went to Barbados with his oldest brother in the hopes of improving and easing his brother's tuberculosis. While there, he contracted the dreaded smallpox, which permanently scarred his fair-skinned face. His brother's health deteriorated, so they returned to their Mount Vernon plantation, where his brother soon died. Joining the Virginia militia, Washington was given the rank of major. A man of commanding presence, a fellow officer described him when he was 26:

> Straight as an Indian, measuring six feet two inches in his stockings, and weighing 175 pounds ... his frame is padded with well-developed muscles, indicating great strength. His bones and joints are large, as are his hands and feet. He is wide shouldered but has not a deep or round chest; is neat waisted, but is broad across the hips and has rather long legs and arms. His head is well shaped, though not large, but is gracefully poised on a superb neck. [He has] a large and straight rather than a prominent nose and blue gray penetrating eyes, which are widely separated and overhung by a heavy brow. His face is long rather than broad, with high round cheekbones, and terminates in a good firm chin. He has a clear though rather a colorless pale skin which burns with the sun -- a pleasing and benevolent though a commanding countenance, dark brown hair, which he wears in a cue.
>
> His mouth is large and generally firmly closed, but which from time to time discloses some defective teeth. His features are regular and placid with all the muscles of his face under perfect control, though flexible and expressive of deep feeling when moved by emotions. In conversation, he looks you full in the face, is deliberate, deferential, and engaging. His voice is agreeable rather than strong. His demeanor at all times composed and dignified. His movements and gestures are graceful, his walk majestic, and he is a splendid horseman.

In the early years of the French and Indian War, Washington was commissioned as "Colonel of the Virginia Regiment and Commander in Chief of all forces now raised in the defense of His Majesty's Colony" and given the task of defending Virginia's frontier. The Virginia Regiment was the first fulltime American military unit. Washington was a strict disciplinarian who emphasized training, and he led his men in brutal campaigns against the Indians. In ten months, his regiment fought 20 battles, losing a third of its men — the number of Indian deaths is unknown. Washington — and all future citizens of the United States — benefited immensely from the three years he served during the French and Indian War, where he learned to organize, train, drill, and discipline raw recruits and volunteers. And by observing his British superiors, he learned the basics of battlefield tactics and gained a strong understanding of organization, logistics, and overall strategy. Most importantly, he learned the effectiveness of "Indian warfare" and British vulnerability to surprise strike-and-run tactics.

After leaving the Virginia Regiment, Washington married Martha Dandridge Custis, a wealthy widow with two children. Although he would universally become regarded as the "father of his country," he was apparently sterile from his bout of smallpox, and he never fathered any children, which deeply grieved him. For the fifteen years between his service in the French and Indian War and the Revolutionary War, Washington lived the life of an aristocratic Virginia planter — fox hunting was his favorite leisure activity. He enjoyed parties and dances, the theater, horse races, and cockfights. Washington also was known to profitably gamble at cards, backgammon, and billiards, and to raise a glass of the bourbon made at his still.

In 1774 a meeting of delegates from the Thirteen Colonies was called together to discuss the colonies' common complaint of increasing taxation without Parliamentary representation. The convention of representatives named themselves the Continental Congress. Initially, there was opposition to breaking from the Crown, but as the British hardened their position against the colonies, on July 4, 1776 the new Congress issued a Declaration of Independence, proclaimed the "United States of America" the name of the new nation, and established the Continental Army. A year later a constitution called the "Articles of Confederation" was sent to the colonies for ratification. The Continental Congress was the United States' governing body during the American Revolution.

Two months before the Declaration of Independence was signed, the Revolution's first battles were fought at Lexington and Concord. Signaling that he was ready to serve, Washington arrived at a session of the Second Continental Congress wearing his old military uniform — sans the British insignia. Understanding the implications and seizing the opportunity, John Adams nominated him as Major General and Commander-in-chief of the Continental Army. Although his primary responsibilities were to organize and train an army and to plot the war's strategies, Washington played a greater intangible role.

Because he had served as an officer for the British Army and because he was a wealthy and privileged man who had everything to lose by not remaining a British loyalist — including his life because he would surely be hung for treason if the Americans were to lose the war — his stature and dedication kept Congress, the Army, the French, the militias, the states, and even some Indian tribes united. Early in the Revolutionary War, Washington sent an officer to requisition horses from local landowners. Stopping at a country mansion, the officer was received by an elderly women, "Madam, I have come to claim your horses in the name of the government," he began.

"On whose orders?" the woman sternly demanded.

"On the orders of General George Washington, Commander in Chief of the American Army," replied the officer.

The lady smiled and said, "You go back and tell General George Washington that his mother says he cannot have her horses."

After driving the British from Boston, Washington's Army endured a string of losses including New York City. Then using a strategy of quick raids, he won back

Trenton and Princeton, New Jersey, a quaint college town that was the site of the fourth oldest college in the colonies. Changing tactics to large-scale assaults, he had some moderate successes and some failures and then hunkered down for the bitterly cold winter at Valley Forge in Pennsylvania.

One day while reviewing the restive troops, he came upon a private who was drinking stolen wine with his companions. Already buzzed, the private invited the Commander of the Continental Army to "drink some wine with a soldier."

Washington replied, "We have no time for drinking wine," and turned away.

The private exclaimed, "Damn your proud soul! You're above drinking with soldiers?"

Turning back, Washington said, "Come, I will drink with you," and took a long pull on the jug before handing it back.

"Give it to your servants," said the soldier, gesturing towards Washington's aides, and the jug was passed around.

After receiving the jug back, the private said, "Now, I'll be damned if I don't spend the last drop of my heart's blood for you."

The next summer, Washington drove the British from Philadelphia and fought them to a draw at Monmouth, New Jersey. In the summer of 1779, he ordered a "scorched earth" policy against the Iroquois, who supported the British. Forty villages in Upstate New York were burned. The following summer as a result of extensive negotiations by two Pennsylvanians — Robert Morris, the Superintendent of Finance, and Benjamin Franklin, the Minister to France — France sent 5,500 troops and extended more credit and gave more money to aid the Americans. The strong alliance with France was a major factor in lessening British resolve. And by enlisting and maintaining France's military and financial support, arguably Morris and Franklin did as much to assure America's independence as Washington and his armies did. The combination of strong French support and Washington's victories in the field eroded British commitment and moved the war towards it inevitable conclusion.

Virtually all of the Revolution's battles were fought in the colonies. And the farther west settlers lived from the Atlantic Coast, the less passionate they were about the cause for political freedom — they were already free of social conventions, taxes, and imperialistic laws. The Indian Reserve territory northwest of the Ohio River was virtually unsettled by whites, and along the Mississippi River, the Spanish, who had initially explored the Lower Mississippi Valley and claimed the area for Spain, were greatly outnumbered by the French and Métis who didn't care who claimed the land as long as the Indians traded with them.

More than 50 years before the Revolutionary War, the French had established a community of "wretched hovels in a malarious wet thicket of willows and dwarf palmettos, infested by serpents and alligators" where the City of New Orleans now stands. (For six months after December 1734, New Orleans was flooded. Because the French-Americans were too stupid or too lazy to build on high ground, for the next 200 years engineers would attempt to hold back the Mississippi from swamping their hovels. In 2005 the engineers' efforts colossally failed, and it is doubtful that New Orleans will ever regain its former charm.) In 1764 after the Treaty of Paris, the French had built a trading post and fort in the Spanish Territory on the west bank of the Mississippi near the confluence of the Missouri and Mississippi rivers. Initially, the settlement of St. Louis consisted of about 30 French trappers and traders who were soon joined by some fearless farmers. During the Revolution, communities in Louisiana and around St. Louis were the only significant villages on the Mississippi.

In the wilderness north of St. Louis along the Upper Mississippi, the Sauk and Meskwaki were also relative newcomers, and their primary battles were against other tribes to retain the land they had recently called their own. They had few Indian allies outside of the Potawatomi, Menominee, and Winnebago who sided with them when the Sauk and Meskwaki's purposes aligned with theirs. And their Indian enemies sided with the colonists, the French, and the Spanish. Although divided in loyalties, many of the Sauk picked the losing side and fought with the British during the American Revolution.

In 1779 a planned British attack on New Orleans was broken up when a communiqué from King George III was intercepted that exposed the plan. The Louisiana governor quickly organized troops that defeated the British colonial forces at Manchac, Baton Rouge, and Natchez before an attack on New Orleans could be mounted. The next year a force of about 1,000 Sauk, Meskwaki, Sioux, Winnebago, and a few British fur traders were led by a British militia commander in an attack on St. Louis. The Spanish-governed town repulsed the attack. Simultaneously five miles east of St. Louis and across the river in Cahokia, Illinois, British-led Indians attacked an American village of 105 households. The Americans had settled in a lush valley that had been the site of one of North America's largest Indian settlements. When the settlers moved onto the Indians' sacred grounds, they found 120 burial mounds spread over a six-square-mile area. The settlers also withstood the Indian raid, which was primarily motivated by the Indian's desire to reclaim their land; they failed because they brought bows and arrows to a gun fight. With no major successes, the British failures at New Orleans and St. Louis effectively ended British attempts to gain control of the Mississippi River. However, it didn't end the American's war efforts along the river.

In June of 1780 the month after the attack on St. Louis and in retribution for the Sauk's British alliance, a force of 350 Americans, Spanish, and French under the command of John Montgomery moved up the Illinois River in flatboats to Peoria and then marched along a half-mile-wide buffalo trail to Saukenuk where they burned the village. Although there were no permanent white settlements in the area, the future city of Rock Island became the westernmost battleground of the American Revolution. The buffalo trail that Montgomery followed had been used for centuries by herds of migrating animals and Native Americans, and later it became the easiest western route between the Illinois and Mississippi rivers for trappers and settlers and stagecoaches. The trail that buffalo stamped out became known as the Knoxville Road and is now Interstate 74 north of Peoria, which then joins U.S. Hwy 6 north of Orion.

After a year of scattered minor land battles, in September 1781 a French naval victory allowed American and French forces to trap a British Army commanded by Lord Cornwallis at Yorktown, Virginia. Even though the British had 26,000 troops occupying several major American cities and a powerful naval fleet, Cornwallis' surrender was the final straw that broke the will of the British Army and no more land battles were fought. The colonies were free of British rule — it was several years before the concept sank in.

Compared to European wars at the time and the Civil War nearly a century later, the Revolution was relatively bloodless, and although the war dragged on for eight years, there were fewer than 8,000 combat deaths. As with most wars when viewed in hindsight, there was inevitability in America's victory. Benjamin Franklin's admonishment at the signing of the Declaration of Independence that "We must all hang together, or assuredly we shall all hang separately" was fully appreciated by all the signers — King George was not nearly as invested in the outcome.

After the signing of the second Treaty of Paris in September 1783 ended the Revolutionary War, the nation was left with the classic dilemma of "What do we do now?" Although democracy first appeared in Athens in 508 BC, there were no contemporary examples of how 13 distinct regions with different ethnicities, cultural and religious heritages, and economic interests could structure a lasting democratic nation where every free man had his interests equally protected and was given equal voice in selecting his political representatives. With a weak federal government, the states became more autonomous, and state politicians, slave owners, landowners, and powerful businessmen viewed the increasingly weakened Congress operating under the Articles of Confederation as a good thing. The root of the growing problem was in the immortal words of George Washington — "no money."

By 1786 the 625-man U.S. Army was not being paid and desertions were rampant; in violation of the treaty with Great Britain, New York and South Carolina were prosecuting Loyalists; Congress was paralyzed; and the Federal Government was about to default on its wartime debts. In addition to having no money and no respect for the federal government in Philadelphia, the Articles of Confederation did not adequately define and structure a centralized government. The vision of a "respectable nation among nations" with power derived from the people in frequent elections was rapidly fading. To the new nation's rescue came many of the same patriots who had guided it through the Revolution: Virginia's George Washington, Thomas Jefferson, and James Madison, New York's John Jay and Alexander Hamilton, Massachusetts' Samuel Adams and Henry Knox, Pennsylvania's Benjamin Franklin and Robert Morris, and 47 others from all of the states but Rhode Island, which decided they liked things as they were. The representatives gathered to write a constitution, and over four months during the summer of 1787 the U.S. Constitution was forged.

Three issues pushed aside all others: state's rights, state representation in the proposed government, and slavery. Creating the House of Representatives and the Senate and counting each slave as three fifths of a person for enumeration for taxes and representation mollified the strong states' rights and equal representation advocates. And the ethical issue of slavery was put aside for another day. It was decided that Congress would have the power to ban the importation of slaves — but not for 20 years. That compromise created a nation doomed to a civil war that would take nearly as many American military lives as the all of the combined American wars before and since.

One of the common misconceptions about the U.S. Constitution is that its framers considered black people to be three-fifths of a human being. (At the time of the War of Independence there were approximately 450,000 enslaved African Americans, which comprised 20 percent of the population of the colonies.) As perverse as the three-fifths compromise was, the 40 percent devaluation was not meant to indicate a relative social value of slaves but the extent to which the whites who owned them would be rewarded with additional political power. Ironically, it was those who enslaved blacks and treated them as less than human who wanted slaves to count as a whole person for voting allocation purposes, and those who would eventually free them who wanted them to count as nothing when allocating House representatives.

By summer's end, after a speech by Benjamin Franklin, Congress unanimously resolved to send the Constitution to state legislatures for ratification. A year later after state-by-state battles, 11 states voted favorably and Congress certified that the Constitution was ratified. George Washington was unanimously elected by the Electoral

College as President. To help alleviate the fears of some states that Congress could become oppressive of personal rights, under the leadership of James Madison, the first ten amendments to the Constitution — which immediately became known as the Bill of Rights — were added in Congress' first session. A year later, North Carolina begrudgingly ratified the Constitution. And 20 months after George Washington began his first term, by a vote of 34 to 32, laggard Rhode Island slithered onto the bandwagon.

After its approval and long before the Age of Entitlement began, Benjamin Franklin said of the document, "The Constitution only gives people the right to pursue happiness. You have to catch it yourself." When Franklin returned to the United States in 1785, he was second only to George Washington as a champion of American independence. Franklin died on April 17, 1790 at the age of 84. More than 20,000 people attended his funeral.

The document produced by the Constitutional Convention that George Washington presided over and Benjamin Franklin actively backed is generally regarded as history's finest example of a dynamic framework for government and its societal relationships. It was not initially recognized as such. As with most negotiations and compromises, everyone left the Philadelphia Convention with less than they hoped for. A series of 85 essays, now called the *Federalist Papers*, rebutted opponents of the proposed Constitution and promoted its adoption. Published in the year following the Constitution's submission to the states for their approval, the collection of essays is equally regarded, along with the Constitution, as one of the best political philosophy treatises written. Historian Richard Morris said they are an "incomparable exposition of the Constitution, a classic in political science unsurpassed in both breadth and depth by the product of any later American writer." Although anonymously published, 20th century historians believe and computer analysis verifies that 51 of the articles were written by Alexander Hamilton, 26 by James Madison, five by John Jay, and three were a corroboration between Hamilton and Madison. James Madison is generally credited with being "The Father of the Constitution," but its wording and construction evolved over more than a decade, and the unprecedented expression of freedoms and personal rights for all white men, that it exquisitely defined, had been evolving for more than a century.

Considering that Americans had waged war on Indian nations for 150 years and dismissed Indians as sub-human primitives, it is ironic that Indians were a significant influence on the U.S. Constitution. The people of the Six Nations, also known by the French term, Iroquois, lived in the regions north of Hudson Bay. Originally, the Six Nations numbered five and included the Mohawk, Oneida, Onondaga, Cayuga, and Seneca. The sixth nation, the Tuscarora, migrated into Iroquois country in the early 18th century. Together, these tribes comprise the oldest living participatory democracy on earth. Their governance, based on the consent of the governed, provided insights for some of the founding fathers. Benjamin Franklin and Thomas Jefferson, in particular, drew inspiration from the Six Nation confederacy in which a council of chiefs determined the societal rules and separate chosen elders determined punishments for disobedience.

After the important details of federal governance were taken care of, the only remaining task was the design and adoption of a national flag. During the war, the Revolutionary Army carried the "Grand Union," a thirteen red-and-white-striped flag with the Union Jack where the field of stars is now placed. Francis Hopkinson, a signer of the Declaration of Independence, designed the Grand Union flag., and no one can say for certain, but many historians believe he also designed the first official American flag. This is not to say that Betsy Ross and others may not have contributed.

One version of the flag's origins says that George Washington, Robert Morris, and George Ross (no relation) approached Betsy Ross to see if she could make a large number of flags in her upholstery shop. Ross was a member of the same church as Washington, and besides agreeing to make these flags, her major contribution may have been to demonstrate that it would be easier to cut five-pointed stars instead of the more difficult six-pointed stars that Hopkinson proposed. And, of course, the six-pointed star was the generally recognized symbol of Judaism, the Star of David. Ross led a full life, married three times, mothered seven daughters, and died at age 84. What she almost certainly didn't do was sew the first American flag, a story that appeared when, during the buildup to the 1876 Centennial, Ross' grandson presented a paper to the Pennsylvania Historical Society in which he claimed that his grandmother "made with her hands the first flag" of the United States.

Before the Revolution, Washington had no moral reservations about slavery. As an 11-year-old, he was bequeathed ten slaves from his father, and during his lifetime he owned hundreds. But during the war, his views did an about face, and in 1779 he told his manager at Mount Vernon that if the war ended in an American victory, he wished to sell his slaves. This change in attitude was probably caused by the bravery of the Freemen who fought with him — several hundred of whom suffered through the winter at Valley Forge. In 1786, he wrote to the wealthy Pennsylvania merchant, Robert Morris, saying, "There is not a man living who wishes more sincerely than I do, to see a plan adopted for the abolition of slavery." In his will, he freed his slaves upon Martha's death.

While president, Washington also put forth a 6-point plan to "civilize the Indians:"

1. Impartial justice toward Native Americans
2. Regulated buying of Native American lands
3. Promotion of commerce
4. Promotion of social experiments to improve Native American society
5. Presidential authority to give presents
6. Punishing those who violated Native American rights

Washington's Indian program was one of the few plans he presented as president that was not implemented.

Another framer of the Constitution, John Adams joined Franklin, Washington, and Jefferson, as avid readers of the European authors of The Enlightenment, which included Descartes, Rousseau, Locke, and Voltaire. All were also compatriots of Thomas Paine, the English-born author of *The Age of Reason*, which promoted the radical idea that a person could believe in God based on reason and nature, and not religious dogma. (Voltaire may have made one of the most reasonable medical observations in the history of mankind when he said, "The art of medicine consists in amusing the patient while nature cures the disease.") In addition, Paine's pro-revolutionary pamphlet series, *Common Sense,* was so influential that Adams said, "Without the pen of the author of *Common Sense*, the sword of Washington would have been raised in vain." Although Paine's religious convictions were very similar to Benjamin Franklin's, his mentor, his written ridicule of Christianity earned him the scorn of a nation. Six people attended the American patriot's funeral — fewer than one in a million of the 7,239,881 U.S. citizens in 1810.

John Adams, an erudite Boston lawyer and patriot, assisted Jefferson in drafting the Declaration of Independence, and during the latter years of the Revolution, he served as Ambassador to Great Britain — a tough job considering the warring parties. After the Revolution, the flamboyant Adams was rewarded for his work in forming the new nation by being elected George Washington's vice-president. He hated the job. He wrote of the position: "My country has in its wisdom contrived for me the most insignificant office that ever the invention of man contrived or his imagination conceived."

Smitten with his petite 17-year-old third cousin, who was keenly knowledgeable about philosophy, poetry, and politics, 26-year-old Adams asked Abigail Smith to become the woman, who would be the first second lady and the second first lady, to marry him. As intelligent and outspoken as her husband and a political activist at a time when "respectable women" were only seen outside their homes in the company of their husbands, Abigail Adams would help shape the man who helped shape the nation. Born into a political family at a time when few women knew how to read and write, she was home-schooled and learned French and studied English and French literature from her family's extensive library.

Abigail's ideas on slavery, women's rights, religious freedoms, and government greatly influenced her husband's political views. Her letters to him chronicle many of the radical ideas that found their way into the new nation's founding documents. Notably, John Adams was the primary author of the Massachusetts State Constitution, which became the model for the U.S. Constitution, and which, from its language, led to the end of slavery in the Bay State. The cultured woman never owned a slave and declined on principle to employ slave labor; instead she employed free blacks. In 1791 a free black boy came to the Adams' house and asked to be taught to read and write. Over her neighbors' objections, Abigail placed him in a local evening school. When challenged, she said that he was "a Freeman as much as any of the young Men and merely because his Face is Black, is he to be denied instruction? How is he to be qualified to procure a livelihood? ... I have not thought it any disgrace to myself to take him into my parlor and teach him both to read and write."

While the couple was living in London at the end of the Revolution, Abigail and Mary Wollstonecraft, author of *A Vindication of the Rights of Woman* and mother of Mary Shelly of *Frankenstein* fame, became friends, and Abigail's idealism became radicalized. One of the first American women's rights activists, Adams believed that women should not summit to laws that were not in their interest, should be more than homemakers and companions of their husbands, should educate themselves so that they would be recognized for their intellects, and asked, "When will Mankind be convinced that true Religion is from the Heart, between Man and his Creator, and not the imposition of Man or creeds and tests?" — all of which was heretical during the 18th century, and a century earlier might have caused her to be burned at the stake.

During the First Continental Congress as the initial laws were being drafted, Abigail wrote to John, "Remember the ladies, and be more generous and favorable to them than your ancestors. Do not put such unlimited power into the hands of the Husbands. Remember all Men would be tyrants if they could. If particular care and attention is not paid to the Ladies we are determined to foment a Rebellion, and will not hold ourselves bound by any Laws in which we have no voice or Representation." John wrote back, "We have only the name of masters, and rather than give up this, which would completely subject us to the despotism of the petticoat, I hope General Washington and all our brave heroes would fight." During her term as first lady, the White House servants called the 5'1" dynamo "Mrs. President." Abigail had five children, and her oldest boy, John Quincy, became the sixth president.

After George Washington retired to his farm and distillery at Mount Vernon, John Adams (whose descriptive nickname, "The Colossus of Independence," was given to him by his friend and political foe, Thomas Jefferson) was elected the second U.S. President. Unfortunately Washington had set the bar incredibly high, and even though no one was more qualified to be president, Adams was criticized for everything he did, including his grand lifestyle. A scandalous story made the rounds that Adams had sent General Charles C. Pinckney to England to select four pretty girls as mistresses — two for Pinckney and two for himself. When Adams heard the slander, he wrote to a friend, "I do declare, if this be true, General Pinckney has kept them all for himself and cheated me out of my two."

During the Second Continental Congress, when Thomas Jefferson proposed that Adams draft the Declaration of Independence. The following exchange was delivered before Congress:

> Adams: I will not.
> Jefferson: You should do it.
> Adams: Oh! No.
> Jefferson: Why will you not? You ought to do it.
> Adams: I will not.
> Jefferson: Why?
> Adams: Reasons enough.
> Jefferson: What can be your reasons?
> Adams: Reason first, you are a Virginian, and a Virginian ought to appear at the head of this business. Reason second, I am obnoxious, suspected, and unpopular. You are very much otherwise. Reason third, you can write ten times better than I can.
> Jefferson: Well, if you are decided, I will do as well as I can.
> Adams: Very well. When you have drawn it up, we will have a meeting.

One of the most brilliant of all American political philosophers, Jefferson did as Adams suggested and became the primary author of the Declaration of Independence. He was aggressively expansionist, totally distrusted the British, favored states' rights, espoused the wide separation of church and state, promoted education above all other public services, and was a champion of the small, land-owning farmer. Without his founding guidance, the United States might well be governed in a different manner today. Jefferson is always rated near the top of any list that ranks U.S. Presidents by their contributions.

The third of ten children, Jefferson was born into a prominent Virginia family. He had an inquiring mind and received a fine education. At age 16 he enrolled in the College of William & Mary where he studied mathematics, metaphysics, and philosophy and read the historically great authors and thinkers, graduating with highest honors. He spoke five languages and read three; he was a voracious reader and accumulated one of the largest private libraries in the world. At age 29 Jefferson married 23-year-old

Martha Wayles Skelton. They had seven children during their 11 years of marriage, but only one, Martha Washington Jefferson survived beyond age 25. Her mother died of diabetes at age 33, and Jefferson deeply mourned her loss and never remarried. Through DNA testing it is now well established that after Martha's death, Jefferson had six children with Martha's slave half-sister, Sally Hemings — Martha and Sally's father was John Wayles. Although Jefferson held the racial beliefs of most whites of his time, he was truly egalitarian with Caucasians. One morning he started his day from a modest Washington rooming house. He dressed and went to his inauguration as the third U.S President. After being sworn in, he returned to the rooming house for dinner and to stay the night before returning to Monticello, his Virginia estate. At the rooming house, he found no space at the dinner table. So quietly accepting the democratic principle of first come, first served, on his first night as U.S. President, he went to bed without dinner.

Although Jefferson and John Adam's political views differed dramatically and Jefferson ran against and defeated Adams in his bid for a second term, the second and third presidents admired each other's intelligence, selfless patriotism, and dedication to the new republic. After Jefferson's presidency, over a 14-year period the two men wrote a series of 158 letters and became tight friends. Fittingly, Adams and Jefferson died on the same day — July 4, 1826, the 50th anniversary of the signing of the Declaration of Independence. With his life ebbing rapidly, on the evening before his death, Jefferson asked an attending friend if it was the 4th. His friend couldn't bring himself to tell him it wasn't — Jefferson lived until the following day.

With his health rapidly deteriorating for more than a month, the 90-year-old Adams, who was seven years older than Jefferson, was equally determined to survive until the 50th anniversary. Upon awakening on the morning of the holiday, a servant told him it was the 4th day of July. Adams said, "Oh yes, it is the glorious 4th of July, God bless it. God bless you all." He then fell into a coma. Later, he rallied briefly and murmured, "Thomas Jefferson survives." Those were his last words.

Chapter 4

A New Nation Finds its Way

Children should be educated and instructed in the principles of freedom. ~ John Adams, in defense of the Constitution

ANDREW JACKSON, an American success story of Horatio Alger proportions, was born in March of 1767 of parents who, two years before his birth, had emigrated from County Antrim, Ireland, to the frontier region of South Carolina. Jackson's father died in an accident three weeks before he was born. The youngest of three boys, at age thirteen Andrew and his brother Robert served as couriers in the Revolutionary War. His older brother Hugh died during the Battle of Stono Ferry, and the British captured the younger brothers. Shortly after being captured, Jackson was slashed across the head and left hand while deflecting a blow from a British officer's sword — delivered when he refused to polish the major's boots.

Nursed by Robert, Jackson recovered from his wounds, but while imprisoned, the brothers caught smallpox and Robert died. After securing his release and assured that Andrew would survive, his mother volunteered to nurse prisoners of war with cholera who were held on two ships in Charleston Harbor — she soon contracted the disease and died. Orphaned, and with the loss of his brothers to the war, a 15-year-old Jackson, nurturing a deep hatred for the British, set out to make his way through life.

Distancing himself from the war by moving to the frontier town of Jonesborough, now the oldest town in Tennessee, Jackson studied law and supported himself by teaching. He prospered in the rough-and-tumble world of frontier law. As a handsome, mostly self-taught, and life-hardened 19-year-old, Jackson was appointed Solicitor of the Western District and moved to Nashville in 1788. Two years later, he married Rachel Donelson Robards, and the couple joined the social elite in the genteel frontier town. In 1796 he was a delegate to the Tennessee Constitutional Convention, and when Tennessee was granted statehood later that year, Jackson was elected its U.S. Representative. Upon concluding his first term, he ran for the U.S. Senate and won, only to resign after the first year and accept an appointment to the Tennessee Supreme Court. He served on the court for six years until 1804. In 1801 while a still a justice, Jackson was appointed commander of the Tennessee militia. Then after retiring from the Court, Jackson bought a 640-acre cotton plantation near Nashville. Starting with nine slaves, within 15 years he doubled the size of the plantation and owned 44 slaves; at age 38 he was a wealthy man.

A year after Jackson was appointed Solicitor and the U.S. Constitution was ratified, Congress affirmed the incorporation of the Northwest Territory (not to be confused with the Pacific Northwest or the Canadian territory of the same name), a sizeable chunk of land that included the future states of Ohio, Indiana, Michigan, Wisconsin, and Illinois — a major portion of the same land that 25 years before King George III had given perpetual rights to the Indians. About 4,000 British and French immigrants and a smattering of other Western Europeans had settled among more than ten times that number of Indians in the five-state territory with most of the white settlers clustered north of the Ohio River and south of Lake Erie in the Ohio River Valley.

On July 4th 1803, sticking to the sound business principle of not overpaying for undeveloped property, the U.S. paid $15 million ($300 million) to France to settle their war debts and to buy all of the French-claimed land west of the Mississippi that extended from Louisiana to Montana. Although no one had a firm idea of how much land was involved, the purchase price later worked out to be 3¢ (60¢ in 2012 pennies) an acre, and the territory more than doubled the size of the United States. Today, the "Louisiana Purchase" represents about a quarter of the current U.S. land area. Along with the land, the United States acquired 93,000 people of mixed-European descent and a far larger number of Native Americans. The white men's sense of entitlement to land that Indians had lived on for more than 10,000 years did not sit well with the Native Americans.

Readily acknowledging that the U.S. Constitution contained no provision for the acquisition of property, Thomas Jefferson went ahead with the Louisiana Purchase because he was concerned that the French and/or Spanish could block access to the Port of New Orleans — even though they had shown no intent to do so and had been compliant with the terms of the Treaty of Paris since its signing. Jefferson never explained why he was concerned about a potential event that, in light of superior logistics and military forces, seemed improbable. As always, Native Americans were not consulted about the sale of the land that was literally sold out from under them.

Except in the Gulf Area, at the time of the Louisiana Purchase, few whites had ventured west of the Mississippi. Those who had were mostly French and English explorers, whose accounts of plentiful wild animals and cheap Indian labor to hunt and skin the animals had attracted rugged trappers and traders. No one was too sure what lay to the west in the territory purchased from the French, and it was generally believed that only the poorly mapped territories of Texas, California, and Oregon were left to be acquired to create a land stretching from sea to shining sea.

The signing of the 1783 Treaty of Paris (the second Treaty of Paris) settled many North American boundary disputes between the United States, Great Britain, France, Spain, and the Netherlands — but there was no more Indian Reserve, as had been guaranteed earlier by King George. Although some tribes had allied with the British, many of the northeastern tribes that had been pushed out of their traditional lands and that remained neutral or supported and fought alongside the American colonists during the war hoped to reclaim their lost territory. During the war, the tribes were led to believe that, if victorious, their American allies would reward their loyalty and sacrifice. But when it came time to divide the war spoils, Indians were left out of the discussion and no mention was made of Native Americans in the second Treaty of Paris. Joseph Brant, a Mohawk chief and one of the leaders of the Western Confederacy of Indians, summed it up when he said, "The Indians were sold to Congress."

The end of fighting between the colonists and the English over who had sovereignty to the Indians' land kindled conflicts that had been dormant for 18 years. In the massive former Indian Reserve, British Loyalists, who before the war were the Indians' primary nemesis, now became their allies by supplying them with munitions and provisions to hold back the victorious colonists who, feeling no obligation to uphold English treaties, in a massive land grab overran the area that would become the five Midwestern states east of the Mississippi River and then comprised the Northwest Territory.

Not only did newly independent Americans put aside inconvenient Indian treaties, but they also rebelled against impractical social conventions. One of the most significant breaks from British customs after America gained its independence was that colonial teamsters drove their wagons on the right side of the road instead of the left as had been the worldwide standard to that time. In 1300 Pope Boniface VIII made the custom official when he handed down the edict that pilgrims headed to Rome should keep left. The "always stay left" practice had started during the Dark Ages when it was never known who would be met on the road, and it was desirable to have the sword hand at the ready. The Pope's imprimatur prevailed until American teamsters started pulling large wagons with as many as six pairs of horses. The driver sat on the left rear horse so that his whipping hand was free and allowed him to make sure he cleared the wheels of oncoming wagons. This practical method was embraced by all except the British, many of whom still don't acknowledge that the sun has set on their Empire.

William Henry Harrison was an ambitious man, who along with Andrew Jackson oversaw the systematic plundering of Indian lands after the Revolution. The son of a wealthy career politician who was a signer of the Declaration of Independence, Harrison entered medical school as a 17-year-old, but with little interest in becoming a doctor. Before his second year of med school, Harrison's father died, and for lack of funds he was forced to drop out. A year later he found his calling as an Indian fighter.

Commissioned an ensign, Harrison rose to aide-de-camp to General Anthony Wayne during the Northwest Indian War — a ragged conflict that began in 1785 between the U.S. Government and the Western Confederacy of tribes, a loose alliance formed by almost two-dozen displaced Northeastern clans. The new nation was haphazardly finding its way, and with the ratification of the Constitution still three years away, territory outside of the 13 states was a deadly free-for-all. Joining halfway through the ten-year war, Harrison was at the concluding Battle of Fallen Timbers near present day Toledo, Ohio. Although fewer than 100 died on both sides at the battle, 3,000 U.S. Army regulars decisively defeated half that number of Indian warriors. Eastern Indian hostilities would smolder for a generation and become violent again in 1811 in Tecumseh's War. Tecumseh, who was a young Shawnee warrior at Fallen Timbers, was destined to again cross paths with Harrison.

Harrison's mother had died in 1793, leaving him 3,000 acres of land and several slaves, all of which he sold to his brother. While still in the Army, two years later he met and fell in love with Anna Symmes, the daughter of a prominent Ohio judge. When the judge flatly turned down his request to marry Anna, Harrison waited until Judge Symmes left town on business and eloped with her. A 1915 issue of the *Indiana Magazine of History*, which was published 75 years after Harrison's death, describes him as "commanding with prepossessing manners … about six feet high, of rather slender form, straight, and of a firm elastic gate. … He had a keen penetrating eye, denoting quickness of apprehension, promptness and energy." But Harrison was, in fact, 5'8" tall, frail, and had a disconcerting beak-like nose. There is no dispute that he was smart and convincing. Having gone through his inheritance and unable to support Anna on peacetime Army pay, Judge Symmes gave Harrison 160 acres to farm.

He did not adapt well to the life of a farmer, and through friends Harrison received a civil service appointment as Secretary to the Governor of the Northwest Territory. He renewed social contacts in the East, where he promoted his reputation as an Indian fighter and frontiersman. At age 26, running for Congressional Delegate from the Northwest Territory and campaigning on the single issue of lower government land prices, Harrison defeated his boss's son for the position. With the passage of the 1800 Harrison Land Act, settlers received the right to purchase land in the Northwest Territory for a minimum of $2 ($35) an acre. Harrison became a very popular politician — so popular that when President John "His Rotundity" Adams split the Northwest

Territory into the Ohio and Indiana Territories, Harrison was appointed Governor of the Indiana Territory.

Harrison's first task as governor was to build a plantation style mansion for Anna in Vincennes. He then built a "second capital" in Corydon. Suitably housed, he set about performing the duties given to him by his new president, Thomas Jefferson, which were primarily to negotiate Indian treaties. Using questionable methods and tactics and unquestionable aggressiveness, in little over a decade Governor Harrison acquired 60 million acres of land for the United States from the Indians — more land than the combined states of Illinois and Indiana. The Indians received far less per acre for their land than the Canarsee did for Manhattan Island, and at the price he had created under his land act, Harrison acquired Indian Territory that had a sale value of $120 million ($2 billion) for the U.S. government. At the time the annual federal budget ran about $10 million a year.

The Indian treaties always included small monetary payments that meant nothing to the Indians but satisfied the American concept, taken from English common law, of giving monetary compensation to make a contract legally binding — even if the government agents knew that they weren't giving true value and that the agreements were so full of loosely worded loopholes that they would never be fulfilled. Harrison's primary negotiating chips when writing treaties were promises not to use further military force and that the Indians could always live and hunt on the land, as long as they behaved as the white men told them. For example, five years after Congress ratified the second Treaty of Paris, the Sauk and Meskwaki entered into their first treaty with the United States. Signed at Fort Harmar in southeastern Ohio, the treaty stated: "The individuals of said nations shall be at liberty to hunt within the territory ceded to the United States, without hindrance or molestation, so long as they demean themselves peaceably and offer no injury or annoyance to any of the subjects or citizens of the said United States."

The clause in the Harmar Treaty appeared in similar form in all of Harrison's Indian treaties. Although it gave the Indians what they wanted and readily agreed to, as soon as a treaty became inconvenient for American squatters, it was totally ignored. However, since squatters had no legal rights to the land the U.S. Government took from the Indians, when another white man purchased the land, squatters were forcibly evicted from the property. Most displaced squatters simply picked up and moved farther into the frontier.

Because Americans were still adjusting to not being under English rule, and because the "manifest destiny" concept that stated white men were destined to rule the New World had not yet taken complete hold, Harrison's boss, President Jefferson was conflicted about the "Indian situation." In January 1803, Jefferson secretly took a proposed Indian Policy to Congress:

> [1] *Gentlemen of the Senate and of the House of Representatives:* As the continuance of the act for establishing trading houses with the Indian tribes will be under the consideration of the Legislature at its present session, I think it my duty to communicate the views which have guided me in the execution of that act, in order that you may decide on the policy of continuing it in the present or any other form, or discontinue it altogether if that shall, on the whole, seem most for the public good.
>
> [2] The Indian tribes residing within the limits of the United States have for a considerable time been growing more and more uneasy at the constant diminution of the territory they occupy, although effected by their own voluntary sales, and the policy has long been gaining strength with them of refusing absolutely all further sale on any conditions. ... A very few tribes only are not yet obstinately in these dispositions.
>
> [3] In order peaceably to counteract this policy of theirs and to provide an extension of territory, which the rapid increase of our numbers will call for, two measures are deemed expedient. First: To encourage them to abandon hunting, to apply to the raising [of live]stock, to agriculture, and domestic manufacture, and thereby prove to themselves that less land and labor will maintain them in this better than in their former mode of living. The extensive forests necessary in the hunting life will then become useless, and they will see advantage in exchanging them for the means of improving their farms and of increasing their domestic comforts.
>
> [4] Secondly: To multiply trading houses among them, and place within their reach those things which will contribute more to their domestic comfort than the possession of extensive but uncultivated wilds. Experience and reflection will develop to them the wisdom of exchanging what they can spare and we want for what we can spare and they want. In leading them thus to agriculture, to manufactures, and civilization, in bringing together their and our sentiments, and in preparing them ultimately to participate in the benefits of our Government, I trust and believe we are acting for their greatest good.

Although patronizing, unrealistic, and demonstrating the American attitude of cultural superiority, Jefferson's official position was well meant. But it was unpopular with Congress and was rejected. As a result, the 31-year-old Harrison quietly went about doing the dirty work needed to pave the way for civilizing the wild frontier.

In 1804 at Fort St. Louis, Governor Harrison struck a typically advantageous deal with five Sauk men when he bought all of the Sauk lands east of the Mississippi running north from the Missouri River to the Wisconsin River. The Indians received an upfront payment of $2,200 in goods and services and annual payments of $1,000 ($18,500) to be given in goods and services. The Sauk lands were some of the most fertile that Harrison purchased, and they comprised about a third of the acreage he negotiated treaties for during his governorship. The 1804 value of the Sauk land was approximately $40 million ($670 million).

The five Sauk who placed their marks on the Treaty of St. Louis were not tribal chiefs or leaders and had no tribal authority — it is unclear why they were even there. However, while they were at Fort St. Louis, they were apparently treated well and wined and dined by Harrison and his agents and then given their bounty of gifts for their "X"s on a treaty written in English that they could not understand much less read. The five men signed away lands that extended far beyond what they had even seen. Since Indians were virtually the only residents of the area at the time, the drunken escapade of the Sauk men was then of little consequence. Twenty-five years later all of that would change. A Saukenuk village leader, *Ma-Ka-Tai-Me-She-Kia-Kiak*, (literally, Black Sparrow Hawk) who for obvious reasons was called Black Hawk by non-Algonquin speakers, later wrote of the transaction in his autobiography:

> It subsequently appeared that they had been drunk the greater part of the time while at St. Louis. This was all myself and the nation knew of the treaty of 1804. It has since been explained to me. I found by that treaty, that all of the country east of the Mississippi, and south of Jefferson was ceded to the United States for one thousand dollars a year. I will leave it to the people of the United States to say whether our nation was properly represented in this treaty? Or whether we received a fair compensation for the extent of country ceded by these four individuals? I could say much more respecting this treaty, but I will not at this time. It has been the origin of all our serious difficulties with the whites.

Until his death, Black Hawk maintained that the treaty was invalid because the five who placed their marks on it were not authorized to represent the tribe. In any case, as with the Fort Harmar agreement, the treaty wasn't followed anyway. Article 7 says: "As long as the lands which are now ceded to the United States remain their property, the Indians belonging to the said tribes shall enjoy the privilege of living and hunting upon them." Harrison understood that the language of the treaty with the Sauk wasn't followed by settlers or the government — over the next 12 years, two more restrictive treaties were initiated with the Sauk for most of the same land covered under the 1788 and the 1804 treaties.

Harrison and virtually every other government agent greatly underestimated the intelligence and sophistication of Indian leaders and believed that the Indians were so unsophisticated that they would neither remember nor care what they had been told years before. In fact, the oral tradition that Indians used to anchor and perpetuate their cultures for thousands of years uniquely conditioned them to precisely recall what they were told and what they agreed to. Unlike white politicians and government officials, the Indian leaders did as they agreed until their trust was violated. All of Harrison's treaties were one-sided, hypocritical justifications to take Indian lands and to legally slaughter the Indians if they fought to hold onto their territory or culture. And it must have been a very good future political consultant that came up with the schoolyard taunt of "Indian giver," because it was always white men who took back what they gave or who reneged on their promises.

In 1812 Harrison retired as Governor of the Indiana Territory, and four years later Black Hawk attached his mark to the fourth and final Sauk treaty. As with all of the Sauk who preceded him in treaty negotiations, Black Hawk could not speak English, much less read it, and he relied on government interpreters to truthfully explain the treaty. For little consideration other than not being aggressively and immediately driven from their hereditary lands, each treaty successively reduced Indian lands and rights. Black Hawk later said of the treaty he signed:

> Here, for the first time, I touched the goose quill to the treaty not knowing, however, that by the act I consented to give away my village. Had they explained to me I should have opposed it and never would have signed their treaty.

The same year, and in conjunction with the treaty Black Hawk signed, the United Tribes of the Ottawa, Chippewa, and Potawatomi in eastern Illinois and Wisconsin signed another treaty, and the two treaties permitted the Indian Boundary Line to be drawn. The treaties required that Indians forfeit their claims to land south of a latitudinal line that extended from the southern tip of Lake Michigan west to the Mississippi River. And in 1817, the year after the treaty was signed, the boundary was surveyed. Monuments on the western edge of Lincoln Park and on the Augustana campus mark the Indian Boundary line as it passed through Rock Island near present day 9th Avenue. It now appears that erroneous maps caused government surveyors to miscalculate where the latitudinal line would reach the Mississippi River.

It was the government's intent to create a border so that all land south of the Mississippi River as it ran west through the rapids would be reserved exclusively for white people and to assure that a recently constructed fort on a three-mile-long island on the south side of the river would not be in Indian Territory. The Indians would have the land in the cold, rocky-soiled wilderness of the Michigan Territory that ran all the way to the Canadian border and wrapped around the north side and down the east side of Lake Michigan. But when the latitudinal line was surveyed, it unfortunately missed the anticipated mark by more than a mile. The Indian Boundary Line was also intended to be the northern border of Illinois, and if the government had honored its two-year-old agreement with the Sauk and not redrawn the line 60 miles farther north, all of Chicago and downtown Rock Island would now be in Wisconsin.

The year following the survey, Illinois entered the Union as the 21st state, and leaving nothing to chance, Illinois' northern border was established where it is currently drawn — even though much of the land north of the Indian Boundary Line was not covered by treaty and was still sovereign to the Indians. This disregarded fact is one of many examples of the complete contempt with which elected politicians and their government agents held the Sauk, Meskwaki, and all other tribes, and how they didn't let their agreements stand in the way of their plans.

While William Henry Harrison was pushing the Indians out of Illinois, in the eastern region of the Northwest Territory during the two decades after the battle of Fallen Timbers, Tecumseh rose to become a Shawnee war chief. He had fostered close relationships with the British and had become friends with James Galloway and his family in Greene County, Ohio. He was taught to read and write by Rebecca Galloway, and he read books ranging from the Bible to Shakespeare. Some accounts say that he fell in love with Rebecca, and that he asked her father to marry her. James gave his permission, but Rebecca said she would marry Tecumseh only if he would give up his Indian traditions and live with her as a white man. For a month, Tecumseh pondered the decision and finally told Rebecca that he could never abandon his people — he never took a wife, either Indian or white.

With the 1809 Treaty of Fort Wayne, William Henry Harrison snatched up 3 million acres of Illinois and Indiana from the Delaware, Miami, Lenape, Eel River, and Potawatomi tribes. In the negotiations, Harrison convinced tribal leaders that, instead of a lump sum payment, it was better to receive annual payments in perpetuity, thereby assuring land and financial security to future generations. After obtaining signatures to the treaties, Harrison left it to the Indians to determine who was entitled to what land, and when negotiations got contentious, he gave his support and protection to those tribes most loyal to him. Hostilities arose when the Indian clans realized that Harrison had made individual payments and off-the-record promises of the same territory to different tribes. Tecumseh came to the aid of the disenfranchised tribes and formed a cooperative confederacy, and the following August, he led 400 warriors, representing the Indian Confederation, to Vincennes to confront Harrison at the governor's mansion about the inequities and false promises. Harrison rejected Tecumseh's demand to discuss the treaties, saying that only individual tribes could negotiate with the United States government, and that Tecumseh's interference was unwelcome by the Potawatomi and Winnemac. The two tribes had capitulated to Harrison's strong-arm policies and were allowed to stay on their lands and temporarily granted favored status. Apparently not understanding Harrison's agenda and the general racial attitudes of the white settlers Harrison represented, the articulate Tecumseh responded in English:

> (Governor Harrison), you have the liberty to return to your own country ... you wish to prevent the Indians from doing as we wish them, to unite and let them consider their lands as common property of the whole ... You never see an Indian endeavor to make the white people do this ... Sell a

country! Why not sell the air, the great sea, as well as the earth? Did not the Great Spirit make them all for the use of his children? How can we have confidence in the white people?

Defensively, Harrison, who was backed up by the armed militia that defended the capital, drew his sword and told the warriors to leave in peace. After calmly informing Harrison that unless he rescinded the treaty, he would seek an alliance with the British, Tecumseh withdrew. The following summer Tecumseh returned again to Vincennes to try to persuade Harrison to rescind the treaty. Always the condescending gentleman, Harrison met Tecumseh in the courtyard of the governor's mansion. A soldier brought Tecumseh a chair and said, "Your father, General Harrison, offers you a seat." "My father!" Tecumseh exclaimed, "The sun is my father and the earth is my mother, and on her breast I will lie." He stretched out on the ground next to the chair; of course, the Indian leader obtained the same results as he had before — war was inevitable. That November with 1,200 regulars, cavalry, militia, and Indian mercenaries, Harrison battled Tecumseh and 600 warriors of the Tribal Confederation about 100 miles north of Vincennes at the confluence of the Wabash and Tippecanoe Rivers. Harrison's troops initially suffered heavy losses before turning the Indians back; however, never one to look bad, Harrison reported to Washington that the battle was won and Indian scalps were taken — in fact, many Indian scalps were taken after digging up fresh Indian graves. It is unclear who gave Harrison the nickname, "Old Tippecanoe."

Harrison's exaggerated claims of defeating Tecumseh's warriors and the Tribal Confederation were ambivalently received by James "His Little Majesty" Madison, a pacifist who deferred military actions to the Congressional "War Hawks." A brilliant governmental theorist and one of the preeminent founding fathers, Madison was a Princeton-educated political philosopher — the primary author of the Constitution and 26 of the 85 Federalist Papers. He was a staunch defender of the new nation's sovereignty; however, his political philosophies of national sovereignty did not extend to Native Americans. Nevertheless, Madison's greatest contributions were before his presidency. As a young lawyer, he persuaded Virginia to give up its claims to the land that comprised the Northwest Territory, he was the chief architect of the Constitution, and he became George Washington's primary political adviser. Of Madison, George Will wrote, "That If we truly believed that the pen is mightier than the sword, our nation's capital would have been called "Madison D.C.," instead of Washington D.C." — instead Wisconsin's state capital was named after him.

Elected the fourth U.S. President in 1808 — and shortest ever at 5'4" — Madison set out to consolidate the interests of the United States. He appointed a young political opponent, James Monroe Secretary of State and allowed him to double dip in the unpopular position of Secretary of War. Monroe was directed to lead a poorly-trained and ill-equipped U.S. Army into their first declared war. In 1812 the United States opportunistically took on the British Empire, which was again fighting with the French and was deeply engaged in dealing with Napoleon Bonaparte's imperialistic designs. (The famously diminutive Napoleon was taller than Madison, as was Madison's wife, Dolley, who towered over him by three inches.)

The two decades between the ratification of the U.S. Constitution and the start of Madison's presidency had been a politically chaotic time. In 1803 Napoleon Bonaparte began his conquest of Europe, and Great Britain was preoccupied with saving their empire. When Napoleon completed the Louisiana Purchase that year, he planted the seeds of U.S. imperialism when he said, "This accession of territory affirms forever the power of the United States, and I have given England a maritime rival who sooner or later will humble her pride." By 1812 England was stretched thin after a decade of land and naval battles and Napoleon's defeat at the Battle of Waterloo was still three years off. Seizing the moment to expand into the Northwest Territory beyond the boundaries established during the Revolution — Vermont (1791), Kentucky (1792), Tennessee (1796), and Ohio (1803) had been carved out of land included in former colonies. Citing among other offenses, British support of Indians who resisted U.S. expansion into Indian territory, the United States flexed its newly found military muscle and U.S. troops engaged the British from New Orleans to Toronto.

In August of 1812, Tecumseh and warriors from the depleted tribes of the Indian Confederation supported the British and defeated the Americans at the well-fortified Fort Detroit. Located on the present site of the Detroit Civic Center, Fort Detroit had been established more than a century earlier by the French officer Antoine de la Mothe Cadillac and had been a French stronghold on the western frontier until 1760 when it surrendered to the English at the end of the French and Indian War. After holding the fort for more than three decades, in 1796, the British surrendered it to the Americans who held it until they were fooled into giving it back to the British in August of 1812. The British regained the fort in a plan some historians credit to Tecumseh — British commander, Isaac Brock, said of the Indian leader "a more sagacious and a more gallant warrior does not I believe exist." To appear to the Americans that they had a much greater force, British Loyalist militia dressed in cast-off regular army uniforms and at mealtime formed lines in view of the American fort. After taking their rations, the militiamen dumped their meals in hidden pots and returned to the line. At night, instead of lighting one campfire per unit, they lit many. And during the day, units marched to field positions against the fort, then ducked out of view and repeated the maneuver.

After performing this ruse for two days, the British began to bombard the fort. Meanwhile, "Tecumseh extended his men, and marched them three times through an opening in the woods at the rear of the fort in full view of the garrison, which induced them to believe there were at least two or three thousand Indians." The British sent a surrender demand to the Americans stating, "The force at my disposal authorizes me to require of you the immediate surrender of Fort Detroit. It is far from my intention to join in a war of extermination, but you must be aware, that the numerous body of Indians who have attached themselves to my troops, will be beyond control the moment the contest commences." Commanded by William Hull, the Americans hoisted a white flag over the garrison.

Hull asked for three days to agree on terms of surrender — Brock allowed him three hours. Hull, who supposedly was drinking heavily before he surrendered, said the Indians were "numerous beyond example" and "more greedy of violence than the Vikings or Huns." After Hull surrendered, 1,600 Ohio militiamen at the fort were paroled and safely escorted south away from the bloodthirsty Indians — a large force of Michigan militia had already deserted. The English seized 30 cannons, 300 rifles, and 2,500 muskets, and the fort's 582 American Army regulars were sent as prisoners to Quebec City.

A year later, Creek Indians massacred 517 at Fort Mims, about 40 miles north of present day Mobile, Alabama. The Creek Nation was divided between those who supported the Americans in the War of 1812 and the majority who did not. Fort Mims was a shoddily-run outpost, and although two black slaves, who were tending the fort's cattle, reported seeing Indians in war paint, the garrison commander had the black messengers flogged for raising a "false alarm." The next day, after patiently waiting for the soldiers to go inside for lunch, 800 Creek warriors rushed through an open and unguarded gate and slaughtered all but 36. All the African slaves were spared, and the Creek kept them as their own.

With their primary focus on battling the French in Europe, the British started the war with a defensive strategy and were able to turn back several American invasions of the Canadian provinces. The conflict tipped towards the Americans when late in the summer of 1813 Commander Oliver Perry defeated the British in a series of naval battles on Lake Erie. While Perry was taking control of Lake Erie, William Henry Harrison, who had been promoted to general, established a fort on the Maumee River, which was to serve as temporary supply depot and staging area for an invasion of

Canada. Named for the Ohio Governor, Return J. Meigs, the garrison was home quarters for more than 2,000 regular army and state militia.

Knowing the importance of disrupting the supply lines and staging areas, the British and Tecumseh-led Indians laid siege to Fort Meigs in early May of 1813. After being repulsed after more than a week of battle, the British lifted the siege and returned to Canada. To appease the aggressive Tecumseh, the British returned in July and again attacked the fort. Failing a second time, the British moved on to Fort Stephenson, which was located where Fremont, Ohio now stands. That attack also failed, and the British and Tecumseh's Indian Confederation suffered heavy losses. Harrison pushed his advantage and cut the British supply lines to Fort Detroit. Then after first burning all of the public buildings and the fort, the British retreated into Canada along the Thames Valley.

During the early spring, Black Hawk, who remained loyal to the British, and his British Band of warriors had joined Tecumseh and the Indian Confederation. The British Band fought in the battles at Fort Meigs and Fort Stephenson. Despairing over the defeats and the carnage caused by British attack methods, Black Hawk quit the Indian Confederacy, and with his warriors returned to Saukenuk, where he found that Keokuk, his life-long adversary, had become the tribe's war chief.

With 3,500 American infantry and cavalry, Harrison pursued the British into Canada. Tecumseh and 500 of his warriors followed the Americans, fighting rearguard actions to slow their advance. Major-General Henry Proctor, who led the British retreat, was an undistinguished timid sort, who was disliked by his men and the Indians alike. In early October with winter approaching, Proctor retreated farther into Canada, causing the Americans to rethink their pursuit of the British. Knowing the Americans were not eager to enter into a major campaign before the winter, Tecumseh implored Proctor to give his heavy guns and ammunition to the Tribal Confederation so that they could strike the hesitant Americans.

In an impassioned speech to Proctor and his officers, he concluded:

> Father, listen! We wish to remain here and fight our enemy, should they make their appearance. ... Father, you have the arms and the ammunition, which our Great Father sent for his red children. If you have an idea of going away, give them to us. Our lives are in the hands of the Great Spirit. We are determined to defend our lands, and if it be his will, we wish to leave our bones upon them.

Unmoved and not wanting to lose heavy guns to the Americans, Proctor gave minimal munitions and personnel support to Tecumseh who engaged Harrison 30 miles west of Fort Detroit near Chatham, Ontario. Harrison's vastly greater number of troops overwhelmed the Indians, and the U.S. won a decisive victory — and Tecumseh was killed. The actual circumstances of Tecumseh's death are unknown; however, his death was a celebratory event for the Americans. A historian at the time wrote:

> Several of Harrison's Army claimed to have killed Tecumseh. "I killed Tecumseh; I have some of his beard" one would say; "I killed Tecumseh," another would clamour; "I have a piece of his skin to make me a razor strop!" None of these braggadocios were in the last battle, in which the brave Chief received his mortal wound.

With Harrison's victory, the war in the Northwest Territory was all but over, and the Tribal Confederation was permanently destroyed. Significantly, Napoleon's abdication in April 1814 dissolved French support of the Indians and allowed the Americans to take an even more aggressive posture towards the tribes. Indian fortunes rapidly deteriorated. Because the U.S. Army was engaged in the North pursuing Proctor, a retaliatory response to the Fort Mims massacre had been delayed, but after Harrison secured the North, the Americans were able to move forces to the Deep South.

Commander-In-Chief James Madison dispatched General Andrew Jackson and his Tennessee Volunteers to win back and defend the South. Among the 2,000 well-trained Volunteers serving under Jackson were an affable, 38-year-old illiterate farmer named Davy Crockett and a 21-year-old Third Lieutenant named Sam Houston. Five years earlier, Houston had run away from home because he hated working as a clerk in his older brother's store. He then lived for a few years with the Cherokee, who called him *Colonneh* (the Raven).

In March of 1814, reinforced with an additional 700 U.S Army troops and 600 Cherokee and Choctaw, Jackson engaged the Creek at Horseshoe Bend near present day Dadeville, Alabama. The battle was a complete reversal of the Fort Mims Massacre — Jackson's forces caught the Creek in a crossfire, killing 857 while suffering only 47 fatalities. One of the first over the Creek's barricade was Sam Houston, who caught an arrow in the groin. The wound bothered him for the rest of his life — but apparently it was not debilitating, since he would later father seven children. After Horseshoe Bend, Andrew Jackson was promoted to Major General, and Jackson's men started calling him "Old Hickory" because he was as "tough as old hickory." The Creek called him "Sharp Knife."

Although the Great Lakes region had been conquered and the war's fortunes had turned to the Americans, their most humiliating defeat was still to come. The British Royal Navy controlled Chesapeake Bay, and with 16,000 additional Red Coats freed from fighting the French, on August 23, 1814, only five months after Horseshoe Bend, the British rallied at the Battle of Bladensburg, a village on the Potomac River northeast of Washington D.C. Five days earlier, the British had created a diversionary landing near Baltimore, while their main fleet proceeded up the Potomac with 4,370 marines. The marines included a company (160 troops) of black slavery refugees recruited by the British. After creating several diversions, they surprised the American militia at Bladensburg, less than ten miles from Washington D.C. The American militia retreated and scattered. Their disorganized evacuation is often referred to as "the Bladensburg Races," taken from a satirical poem of the time.

Marching virtually unopposed on Washington — fewer than two-dozen Americans died in defense of their Capital that was still under construction — and in retaliation for the U.S. Army's ransacking, looting, and burning of York (present day Toronto) 16 months earlier, the British Army was ordered to conquer and burn Washington's new public buildings. With little looting or damage to private property, they efficiently carried out orders. President Madison and other government officials, along with the few remaining militia that hadn't already left town, fled to Virginia. Abandoning Washington D.C. and the rising of the British Jack over the nation's Capital is called the "the most humiliating episode in American history."

History books proclaim that the buxomly, strikingly attractive and vivacious first lady, Dolley Madison, heroically remained behind to save valuables from the White House, including Gilbert Stuart's famous full-length portrait of George Washington, which still hangs in the White House's West Wing. The valorous act is refuted by one of the Madison's slaves, Paul Jennings, who wrote:

> It has often been stated in print, that when Mrs. Madison escaped from the White House, she cut out from the frame the large portrait of Washington ... and carried it off. This is totally false. She had no time for doing it. It would have required a ladder to get it down. All she carried off was the silver in her reticule, as the British were thought to be but a few squares off, and were expected every moment.
> John Susé (a French door-keeper) and McGraw, the President's gardener, took it down and sent it off on a wagon, with some large silver urns and such other valuables as could be hastily got hold of. After this he said, 'when the British did arrive, they ate up the very dinner, and drank the wines that I had prepared for the President's party.'

And after dining at the White House, the British set it on fire.

Having accomplished the first leg of a dual assault on Washington D. C. and New York State, the British marines returned to their ships. The second leg of the assault was 18 days later at Plattsburg, New York, on the banks of Lake Champlain, and was not as successful. For the engagement, U.S. and British naval strength was about equal, but with 10,000 marines, the British had three times the number of foot soldiers. After killing the British naval commander, the U.S. won a hard-fought battle on the lake, and the British foot soldiers retreated into Canada. With the British in retreat and hiding in Canada for the winter, continuing the war seemed irrelevant, and three months later on Christmas Eve at Ghent, Belgium, a treaty was signed.

Although the war took more than 20,000 lives, the Treaty of Ghent, which ended the nearly three-year War of 1812, made no major changes to the pre-war borders; however, the British made several promises. One was to return all the black slaves that had defected to their side. But a few years later, the English decided to keep the slaves and paid the United States $350,000 ($5.8 million) to purchase them. Because the laying of the transatlantic telegraph cable was still five decades away, it was more than a month before word that Great Britain and the United States were at peace reached the States.

The day before the Treaty of Ghent was signed, the British landed a force nine miles south of New Orleans in preparation for an assault on the city. Fortunately for the Cajun community, Old Hickory and the Tennessee Volunteers had already arrived. After decimating the Creek at Horseshoe Bend, General Andrew Jackson advanced to safeguard New Orleans. Learning of the British encampment, Jackson said, "By the Eternal, they shall not sleep on our soil" — and he meant it literally. That same evening Jackson surprised the British with a three-pronged attack. The British retreated and although the battle would sporadically rage for more than two weeks, the British were freed of thoughts of an easy victory, and the momentum swung to the defenders. At the battle's conclusion, the final toll was 2,459 British killed, wounded, or missing versus 333 Americans. At age 46, Andrew "Old Hickory" Jackson was the most revered man in America.

British and U.S. warships that were not notified of the peace continued to fight for several months after the truce. On the frontier, a year after the Battle of Fort Meigs some of the British Band of Sauk attacked a small force of U.S. troops near Fort St. Louis. The British Band continued to attack American settlements for another two years, but it is unclear whether they were fighting for the British or against the Americans. The United States was successful in its first international war, but an unfortunate consequence was the composition of *The Stars-Spangled Banner*. The difficultly-worded song has a range of an octave and a half and has thrown off celebrity singers from Ozzy Osbourne to Christina Aguilera. The song's lyricist, Francis Scott Key, had been detained on a British warship where he had gone to negotiate an exchange of prisoners. Kept awake by "bombs bursting in air" over Baltimore, at dawn after blearily watching the stars and stripes raised over Fort McHenry, the sleep-deprived, 35-year-old lawyer was inspired to write a poem about his experience. Later sung to the tune of a popular British drinking song, the poem turned song took 120 years to push aside other deserving candidates as the national anthem. Melodious and inspiring tunes such as *God Bless America; Hail, Columbia; and My Country, 'Tis of Thee* and rousing marches like *Stars and Stripes Forever* were rejected. In 1931 in one of Congress' most disputed acts *The Star-Spangled Banner* was selected as the National Anthem.

Although nothing was won or lost in the War of 1812, the U.S. Government let the British know that the territory south of Canada and north of Mexico was under their control and would remain so, and it effectively forever suppressed armed Indian rebellion within the original 13 colonies. A clear message was sent to the tribes that all prior promises of Indian sovereignty were worthless and would not be honored. The war demonstrated the necessities and advantages of a strong federal government with an organized, professional army and unified the states. The year the war ended, the "Year Without a Summer" began — 1815 was a bitter cold year in northern Europe and in the Northeastern United States. Napoleon met his Waterloo in June 1815 and retired to St. Helena, a barren wind-swept rock in the South Atlantic. And weary of war, England decided to expand its Empire in places other than North America.

In 1816 James Monroe was elected president. He became the last of the U.S. Founding Fathers and the last from the "Virginia Dynasty" — four of the first five presidents were from Virginia — to be elected president. In 1774 at the age of 16, Monroe had inherited his father's fortune, and joined the elite class of wealthy, slave-owning Virginia planters. That same year, Monroe enrolled in the College of William and Mary, but like most students, he was distracted by the prospect of rebellion against King George, and the following spring, he dropped out of college and joined the Continental Army. After the Revolution, he served in the Continental Congress, and later as a political ally of Jefferson and Madison in the U.S. Senate. Before being elected president, Monroe was elected to two terms as Governor of Virginia and served as Minister to France and Ambassador to England. He was well qualified to be the fifth U.S. President, but his keen intellect and deep experience were unneeded and went mostly unused. The "Era of Good Feelings," which spanned James Monroe's presidency from 1817 to 1825, began a period of economic prosperity and community growth, and Americans discovered their unprecedented freedoms and began to exploit their vast resources. Monroe may have presided over the least contentious decade in U.S. history.

Chapter 5

Black Hawk Reigns

How smooth must be the language of the whites, when they can make right look like wrong, and wrong like right. ~ Black Hawk

DURING THE WAR OF 1812, Black Hawk was still smarting from William Henry Harrison's trickery and the encroachment of white squatters, so he had again aligned much of the Sauk Nation with the British and re-formed the British Band of Sauk warriors. French trappers and fur traders operating from Credit Island were the only whites that many Saukenuk residents had seen in their region during their lifetimes. The traders had introduced alcohol, to which Indians had no addictive resistance, and deadly diseases including smallpox, measles, chickenpox, and syphilis, to which the Indians had no immunity. Black Hawk, who was a moral and ethical man, deeply resented the devastating destructiveness the French had introduced into the Sauk culture. Although the traders had ostensibly upgraded the region's material welfare by introducing wool and cotton clothing, traps, guns, and steel tools, Black Hawk understood that whites were a long-term threat to the Sauk way of life. Many of the Sauk viewed British Loyalists defeated in the Revolution as the oppressed and less of a threat than the French, government bureaucrats, and the American Army. Out of desperate self-interest, they sided with the British in an effort to restrain whites from moving onto their lands. Other Sauk leaders, such as Keokuk, were drawn to the materialistic lifestyle the white men brought with them.

Because the second Treaty of Paris granted the territory east of the Mississippi River to the United States, British Loyalists were left with either Iowa or Canada as their only choice of destinations. But because territorial sovereignty had been in continuing flux for more than two centuries and little federal government or military control existed on the frontier, many Loyalists were slow to vacate the wilderness regions of northern Illinois and southern Wisconsin. In the early 19th century, the westernmost U.S Government outpost was Fort St. Louis, and there agents were busy rewriting Harrison's treaties to assure that moving Indians out of the way of progress was legal under U.S. law — even if it was not moral.

In one of the westernmost battles of the War of 1812, three American riverboats led by John Campbell and carrying 106 U.S. soldiers and rangers on their way to Fort Shelby at Prairie du Chien were met by Black Hawk and 500 British Band warriors on a Mississippi River island at the head of the Rock Island Rapids. After one of the riverboats was grounded, the Indians attacked the boats from canoes, killing 16 and wounding 21 and forcing the Americans to retreat back to Fort St. Louis. From then on, the Island where the Sauk launched their attack was called Campbell's Island. After plundering the grounded boat and disposing of the dead, Black Hawk and his warriors returned to a Meskwaki village on the Illinois side of the Mississippi across the channel from Rock Island. There, Black Hawk wrote, "We put up our new lodges and hoisted the British flag; we placed our sentinels and commenced dancing over the scalps we had taken." Rock Island was to remain British territory until the end of the war.

Two months later, the Americans were back for more. This time the Army sent 350 troops up the river under the command of Major Zachary Taylor. When Taylor's troops reached the Rock River, they camped before crossing. During the night, Black Hawk's braves attacked Taylor's guards and killed two of his men. The next day, Indian warriors attacked Taylor's boats at the foot of the rapids. Black Hawk wrote of the battle in his autobiography:

> I discovered that one boat was badly managed, and was suffered to be drawn ashore by the wind. They landed by running hard aground and lowered their sail. The others passed on. This boat the Great Spirit gave to us. All that could, hurried aboard, but they were unable to push off, being fast aground. We advanced to the river's bank undercover, and commenced firing on the boat. I encouraged my braves to continue firing. Several guns were fired from the boat, but without effect. I prepared my bow and arrows to throw fire to the sail, which was lying on the boat. After two or three attempts, I succeeded in setting it on fire. The boat was soon in flames.
>
> About this time, one of the boats that had passed returned, dropped anchor and swung in close to one, which was on fire, taking off all the people except those who were killed or badly wounded. We could distinctly see them passing from one boat to the other, and fired on them with good effect. We wounded the war chief in this way. Another boat now came down, dropped her anchor, which did not take hold, and drifted whore. The other boat cut her cable and drifted down the river, leaving their comrades without attempting to assist them. We then commenced an attack upon this boat, firing several rounds, which were not returned. We thought they were afraid or only had a few aboard. I therefore ordered a rush toward the boat, but when we got near enough they fired, killing two of our braves — these being all we lost in the engagement.
>
> Some of their men jumped out and shoved the boat off, and thus got away without losing a man. I had a good opinion of this war chief, as he managed so much better than the others. It would give me pleasure to shake him by the hand. We now put out the fire on the captured boat to save the cargo, when a skiff was seen coming down the river. Some of our people cried out, "Here comes an express from Prairie du Chien" We hoisted the British flag, but they would not land. They turned their little boat around, and rowed up the river. We directed a few shots at them, but they were so far off that we could not hurt them.

I found several barrels of whisky on the captured boat, knocked in the heads and emptied the bad medicine late the river. I next found a box full of small bottles and packages, which appeared to be bad medicine also, such as the medicine men kill the white people with when they are sick. This I threw into the river. Continuing my search for plunder, I found several guns, some large barrels filled with clothing, and a number of cloth lodges, all of which I distributed among my warriors.

We now disposed of the dead, and returned to the Fox village opposite the lower end of Rock Island, where we put up our new lodges, and hoisted the British flag. A great many of our braves were dressed in the uniform clothing which we had taken from the Americans, which gave our encampment the appearance of a regular camp of soldiers. We placed out sentinels and commenced dancing over the scalps we had taken. Soon after several boats passed down, among them a very large one carrying big guns. Our young men followed them some distance, but could do them no damage more than scare them.

We were now certain that the fort at Prairie du Chien had been taken, as this large boat went up with the first party who built the fort. In the course of the day some of the British came down in a small boat. They had followed the large one, thinking it would get fast in the rapids, in which case they were sure of taking her. They had summoned her on her way down to surrender, but she refused to do so, and now, that she had passed the rapids in safety, all hope of taking her had vanished.

The British landed a big gun and gave us three soldiers to manage it. They complimented us for our bravery in taking the boat, and told us what they had done at Prairie do Chien. They gave us a keg of rum, and joined with us in our dancing and feasting. We gave them some things, which we had taken from the boat, particularly books and papers. They started the next morning, promising to return in a few days with a large body of soldiers. We went to work under the direction of the men left with us, and dug up the ground in two places to put the big gun in, that the men might remain in with it and be safe. We then sent spies down the river to reconnoiter, who sent word by a runner that several boats were coming up filled with men.

I marshaled my forces and was soon ready for their arrival. I resolved to fight, as we had not yet had a fair fight with the Americans during the war. The boats arrived in the evening, stopping at a small willow island, nearly opposite to us. During the night we removed our big gun further down, and at daylight next morning commenced firing. We were pleased to see that almost every shot took effect. The British, being good gunners, rarely missed. [The British had a single 3-pounder under the direction of Sgt. James Keating. The Americans had 20 cannons on their gunboat.]

They pushed off as quickly as possible, although I had expected they would land and give us battle. I was fully prepared to meet them but was sadly disappointed by the boats all sailing down the river. A party of braves followed to watch where they landed, but they did not stop until they got below the Des Moines Rapids, where they came ashore and commenced building a fort. ~ As told to Antoine LeClaire in 1833.

Black Hawk's life story is the first Native American autobiography. After translating Black Hawk's descriptions, LeClaire had a newspaper editor, John Patterson, write the prose. LeClaire read and explained the book to Black Hawk who made no material changes. Although Black Hawk would not have spoken as the text is written, historians have found no major factual errors in it. As a result of winning the battles of the Rock Island Rapids, the Sauk maintained control of their homeland for another two decades.

The only other chain of rapids on the Mississippi River was an 11-mile stretch located between Montrose, Iowa, and Nauvoo, Illinois. Called the Des Moines Rapids, the rocky chute of whitewater was the only other barrier on the river for large gunboats going north. British Band victories during the War of 1812 demonstrated that not having the big guns provided by gunboats made maneuverable Indian canoes the most effective river craft. Because of this disadvantage on the river, the U.S. Secretary of Defense thought it prudent to construct a string of forts on the Upper Mississippi to protect the land they had won from the British and bought from the Indians.

Seven years before the War of 1812 when President Thomas Jefferson sent Lewis and Clark up the Missouri River, he also sent Lieutenant Zebulon Pike and Major Stephan H. Long to the Upper Mississippi River to locate strategic sites to build forts. A three-mile-long island at the end of the rapids near the Rock River confluence was their first choice. Initially called "Big Island" by Pike, in 1809 Congress appropriated the island for military use and renamed it "Rock Island." The fort built on the western tip of Rock Island was named after John Armstrong who was briefly the Secretary of War during the War of 1812. Why the fort was named after Armstrong was questioned from the beginning. Armstrong, a New England dilettante, was hastily named Secretary of War by President Madison and was narrowly confirmed by the Senate. He was forced to resign the position when, on his watch, the British burned Washington. Historian Henry Adams wrote of him: "In spite of Armstrong's services, abilities, and experience, something in his character always created distrust. He had every advantage of education, social and political connection, ability and self-confidence ... he suffered from the reputation of indolence and intrigue."

In 1815, 800 soldiers commanded by Colonel William Lawrence unwisely waited until September to leave St. Louis and make the 200-mile trip up the Mississippi to construct Fort Armstrong. They only got only as far as the mouth of the Des Moines River before they were stopped by ice in mid-November. Keelboats carried the construction equipment and supplies, and the boats, which usually averaged five miles a day, normally would have reached Rock Island by late November. However, the combination of weather-caused delays and earlier than normal ice forced the party to stop only half way to their destination and winter at the present-day site of Warsaw, Illinois.

Keelboats were a laborious form of transport, and a crew of 20 manned each of the boats. They were propelled by six of ten men on each side who leaned on 20-foot poles as they walked toward the stern. As each man reached the stern, he jumped to the cabin roof and walked to the bow to take his place in line again. When the river was too deep for the poles, sails were hoisted, and if there was inadequate wind, the men pulled the boats with ropes from shore. Each day, the soldiers walked the shoreline, carrying their personal equipment and supplies, and bivouacked upstream to set up camp for the 160 men who manned the eight supply keelboats. A retired Army officer and civilian supplier, George Davenport, commanded the keelboats. He was accompanied by his family and was planning to stay at Rock Island and build a private trading post.

As an 18-year-old, Davenport, who was then called George King, had left his home in England and gone to sea on his uncle's merchant ship. He was left behind in New York City when he shattered his leg in a dockside accident while unloading freight. After recovering and needing a job, King joined the U.S. Army. The officer who recruited him encouraged King to change his name because it was so similar to King George, the reviled monarch who America had so recently won her independence from. Why George King selected "Davenport" for his new surname is unknown, but speculation says it was because he was born near Davenport Cheshire, England.

After ten years of Army service, Davenport was honorably discharged the year before he contracted to supply the construction of Fort Armstrong. Following his discharge he visited Cincinnati, where he met Margret Lewis. Davenport married Lewis, a widow with two children, William and Susan. Davenport's new family accompanied him on the extended journey up the river. Although records are unclear when William, Davenport's stepson, died, he did not survive the trip to Rock Island. After spending the winter encamped on the riverbank and shortly after arriving at Rock Island, Davenport's 16-year-old stepdaughter, Susan, bore him a son, George L'oste Davenport. Called L'oste, the boy is presumed to be the first white baby born in the region. Six years later Susan would bear him a second son, Bailey. Davenport's wife, Margret, bore him no children, and L'oste and Bailey were his only sons. However when he was 52, he had a daughter, Elizabeth, with Cathrine Fourt, one of the family's servants.

When the Davenports, boat crews, and soldiers reached Rock Island on May 10, 1816, they found approximately 10,000 Indians living in the current Quad City Area. There were three main Indian villages: the Oshkosh lived in what is now Davenport, the Meskwaki led by Chief Wapello were located in present-day downtown Rock Island, and the Sauk lived on the north banks of the Rock River near its confluence — even then the land where Moline and Milan now stand was less desirable. Some Indians welcomed the first large group of whites to descend on their villages. They brought gifts of sweet corn, beans, pumpkins, and tobacco to the soldiers; in return they were given iron tools and whiskey.

The Army construction regiment was ordered to build a 300-foot by 300-foot square stone and timber fortress on the western end of the island site identified by Zebulon Pike. One of the first buildings constructed was a lookout tower that supported a flagstaff that reached 130-feet and flew an American flag with 18 stars. Blockhouses were erected at three of the fort's corners. (In 1916 for Fort Armstrong's centennial celebration, the blockhouse on the causeway near the entrance to the Government Bridge was erected. It is a replica of the fort's original blockhouses.)

Soon after establishing a supply base for the construction crew and building a large log cabin on the island for his family that also doubled as a trading post, Davenport continued up the Mississippi to Galena, which was the largest American settlement west of Chicago. In the 1790s French trappers had discovered lead in the Galena river bluffs. On the frontier, the malleable metal was called "black gold" and was used for pipe, solder, pewter, weights, and musket and cannon balls. George Davenport shipped the first boatload of lead ore downriver from Galena to Rock Island, changing how and where lead was smelted and transported. Within months of establishing the army fortress, Rock Island became a principal transportation center.

In the decade after arriving at Rock Island, Davenport became a successful trader who was trusted by all. In his first summer, he acquired an Indian name: Saganosh. Some of his cattle had strayed from the island and he went looking for them. Mistaken for a squatter, he was attacked and beaten by a party of Sauk braves when an Indian, who knew Davenport and his English accent, rushed up, crying "Saganosh, Saganosh" — Englishman, Englishman. The Sauk braves, who had been allies of the British during the War of 1812, apologized and from then on all of the tribes called Davenport, "Saganosh."

Becoming the 21st state in December 1818, Illinois had grown to a population of 34,000, most who either lived in Galena, along the shores of Lake Michigan, or in the less weather-challenged southern portion of the state. War of 1812 veterans received 160-acre land warrants in the south central portion of Illinois, and in 1819 when the Kickapoo tribes were moved west of the Mississippi into the Missouri Territory, farms began to sprout up south of the Illinois River. North of the Illinois River was prairie and wilderness that was controlled for the first half of the 19th century by Métis. A tough, cliquish culture of second-generation traders and trappers, the Métis were bilingual and savvy and were accepted and respected by both whites and Indians.

In 1823 the first steamboat, the *Virginia*, arrived at the foot of the Rock Island Rapids. Because of his knowledge of the river, Davenport was called upon to pilot the small steamer through the fast-flowing rapids to Port Byron. It took him three days to negotiate the 14-mile journey. Two years later, Davenport received a letter from

Washington appointing him postmaster at "Rock Island, Missouri." Although Illinois had been a state for seven years, the mail to the frontier had been sent through the post office at Clarksville, Missouri. For the next three years because there was no one to administer the oath of office and to correct the error, Davenport served as postmaster of Rock Island, Missouri.

As the U.S. Army and state militias pushed the Algonquin tribes of the Great Lakes region — including those of the Sauk, Meskwaki, Winnebago, Menominee, and Chippewa — across the Mississippi into the Iowa Territory, the indigenous Ioway and Potawatomi tribes futilely fought their Indian brothers to retain their ancestral land. To settle the Indians' issues to the U.S. Government's satisfaction, in 1825 a "neutral line," creating "open" Indian Territory was drawn. The boundaries ran from the mouth of the Upper Iowa River at the Mississippi, northwest to the present Iowa and Minnesota border, and then southwest to the Des Moines and Missouri Rivers. Then the government told the tribes to work it out.

The huge trapezoid of land, which encompassed much of the known "uninhabitable frontier," created an untenable mixing of the tribes, who because of their competition for the best hunting grounds were anything but friendly or "neutral" towards each other, and the government's edicts and boundaries were ignored. It is often claimed that Indians were as hostile to each other as they were to whites, and this may have been the case in the later years of the Colonial Period and during the settling of the West. However, before white men took Indian lands in the East and started a dominoes effect of shoving ever greater numbers of Native Americans into less desirable hunting grounds, it appears that with few exceptions a social equilibrium existed among the North American tribes that was dependent on intertribal trade and was upset only when territories were breached.

Fort Armstrong remained an active garrison for only 20 years. Before the U.S. Government had taken possession of the island, Black Hawk's biography notes it was considered sacred by the Sauk:

> This [island] was the best one on the Mississippi, and had long been the resort of our young people during the summer. It was our garden, like the white people have near their big villages, which supplied us with strawberries, blackberries, gooseberries, plums, apples and nuts of different kinds. Being situated at the foot of the rapids its waters supplied us with the finest fish. In my early life I spent many happy days on this island. A good spirit had charge of it, which lived in a cave in the rocks immediately under the place where the fort now stands. This guardian spirit has often been seen by our people. It was white, with large wings like a swan's, but ten times larger. We were particular not to make much noise in that part of the island, which it inhabited, for fear of disturbing it. But the noise at the fort has since driven it away, and no doubt a bad spirit has taken its place.

As quaint as Black Hawk's spiritual beliefs may now seem, those of the white men who had squatted on his tribe's lands were no less curious. At that time in the Illinois Territory, laws forbade travel on the Sabbath "except in a pious going to and from the Church of God." Likewise "whistling or other boisterous conduct on that sacred day" was forbidden, and woe to "ye good man ye kissing of his wife on ye Sabbath day."

It was during this period that Illinois became known as the "Sucker State." Credit for the less than flattering nickname is attributed to the miners who walked north to Galena when the winter's ice melted and worked the lead and coal mines until the ground froze and they were forced south for the winter. Most of the miners came from Missouri and Kentucky and their home state pals called them "suckers" in reference to the ugly, dead-eyed fish that swam up the Mississippi in the spring and returned south in the fall. In fact, in the spring of 1827 so many Missourians showed up in Galena to work the mines, locals said that it appeared that "the State of Missouri took a puke." Then, among many other derogatory names, Missouri was known as the "Puke State," and was called that descriptive name until the late 1890s, when some original PR man came up with the ambiguous tag of the "Show Me State."

Setting out for this spiritually unenlightened and racially intolerant region, in the spring of 1827, 26-year-old John Spencer left his farm in Morgan County, Illinois, and ascended the Mississippi to become one of the Suckers in the Galena lead mines. Passing by the Rock Island Rapids, Spencer was "attracted by the area's natural beauty and of the adjacent country." Late the same year, Louden Case, whose daughter Spencer married the following year, and a couple of others accompanied him to Rock Island to explore the area and to stake out a farm. Arriving at Rock Island in early December, the party of men moved into an empty barn-sized Saukenuk lodge, known as a longhouse, which was large enough to house four Indian families.

The Sauk had temporarily vacated the longhouse to go south for the winter hunt. Spencer would later write of the Sauk winter hunt:

> It was the practice of our Indians to leave here for their fall and winter hunting grounds about the middle of September, and return about the middle of April... Our Indians consisted of the Sauk and Fox, these two tribes owning their lands jointly... Before starting [for their winter hunt,] it was understood by the two tribes where each should go, so as to avoid confusion. In hunting, the Sauk occupied southern and middle Iowa, the Fox northern Iowa. Our Indians ascended the Iowa, Skunk, Des Moines [Rivers], and all smaller streams that would admit of a canoe. After the fall hunt they had a rendezvous appointed where they assembled for winter quarters ... after making their maple sugar in the spring, they were now ready to start for the old village [Saukenuk]. As soon as possible, they would gather on the Mississippi, those that went to the more northern streams would wait for those who went

farther south. They would all gather together about the Iowa River and move up the river ... making at best not more than eight or ten miles a day.

They brought home little besides the sugar just made and dried meat, their skins and furs having been disposed of to the Indian traders where they had been. Now they commenced looking for their corn, beans, and dried squashes they had cached in the fall. It depended on the hiding whether there would be any corn in the spring, for as soon as they were gone the Winnebago and other Indians came here hunting for their treasure. These Indians, by the aid of their muskrat spears, feeling in the ground, often succeeded in finding, and would take the supplies of several families.

Four months later, Spencer and Case and his three sons returned to the Rock Island Rapids. Again instead of building a cabin, they moved into another vacant Saukenuk longhouse on the bluffs overlooking the Rock River. At the time, there were fewer than a dozen white settlers squatting land within a 50-mile radius of Rock Island. Hearing that white men were occupying his village, Black Hawk hurried north with a companion. Spencer later wrote of his first meeting with the 60-year-old Black Hawk:

We were here but a few days when two Indians came. One of them commenced talking in a loud voice in the Indian language, of which we could not understand a word. We understood he claimed the land and the wigwam belonged to the Indians. This man proved to be Black Hawk. ... He had heard, way out at his winter hunting grounds that the white man had taken possession of their lands and their wigwams; and he, with the Indian who accompanied him, had walked in all the way, to find the report too true. ... About six weeks after Black Hawk's visit here, he, with the rest of the Indians, returned, and by this time [I] was living in [my] own cabin, in their village. They were very much displeased to find white settlers so near ... [However,] they soon became quiet, and we got along pretty well during the season.

In December of Spencer's first year on the mainland south of Rock Island, Davenport promised him a payment of $5.00 ($115) if he would take the mail to the post office and find out who had won the presidential election the previous month. The post office was in Galena. Ice skating up the frozen Mississippi River with the mailbag, fur pelt sleeping bag, and provisions, Spencer completed the 200-mile roundtrip in one week — setting a Rock Island to Galena to Rock Island ice skating record that still stands — and arrived on Christmas Day to tell Rock Island residents that Andrew Jackson was the seventh U.S. President.

The same year John Spencer built his cabin, Rinnah Wells came to the area and settled among a band of Kickapoo who lived south of the Rock River across from Saukenuk. The next year, Joshua Vandruff became the second settler in the area where Milan now is. These are the only two white men who are recorded to have lived among the Kickapoo until the Indians were forced from their land into the Iowa Territory in 1831. On December 27, 1828, twelve years after becoming the first permanent resident of Rock Island and two days after John Spencer returned to Rock Island to spread the news of Jackson's victory, George Davenport wrote in his journal, "Geo. Wells came down for provisions, he having settled on the Rapids. He makes the tenth settler in our neighborhood, and one preacher, Rev. John Kinney, who preached for the first time on the Island 29th January."

It was also during this early stage of settlement that the first blacks came to the region. Most officers at Fort Armstrong had black slaves, and according to *Historic Rock Island County*, a "man, whose name is unknown," brought "about 75 negroes" from Louisiana to an area above Moline with the intention of establishing a plantation with freedmen. After enduring a Midwest winter and living a year in Moline, the freed slaves chose to return to Louisiana. Never missing a new source of public revenue, in 1829 the Rock Island County commissioners passed a tax of one-half per cent "to be levied on slaves or indentured negro or mulatto indentured servants, pleasure carriages, distilleries, horses, mules, cattle, watches and their appendages, and on household furniture, clocks, wagons, carts, sheep and town lots."

Chapter 6

Culture Clashes

A culture is made — or destroyed — by its articulate voices. ~ Ayn Rand, author and political philosopher

    THE 1828 ELECTION pitted the socially liberal politics of the sophisticated Northeastern establishment against those of the rugged libertarian frontiersmen. Incumbent John Quincy "The Abolitionist" Adams (who had inherited his mother's social values), was an anti-slavery New Englander, who opposed Andrew "Old Hickory" Jackson, a slave owner from Western Tennessee. Adams' Vice President, John C. Calhoun, a pro-slavery South Carolinian, effectively threw the election to the challenger Jackson because he opposed his president's views on slavery. In 1804 the Twelfth Amendment had changed the method of electing the vice president. The amendment provided that the president and vice president run on the same ticket but be elected on different ballots of the Electoral College. As politically bizarre as the 1828 election was, the previous election had been stranger.

    Because it was no longer relevant, the Federalist Party had dissolved a few years before the election, and John Quincy Adams, then known as "Old Man Eloquent," had run against Jackson; William H. Crawford, a Georgian; and Henry Clay, a Kentuckian — all four candidates were Democratic-Republicans, the party founded by Thomas Jefferson and James Madison. Crawford and Clay were also-rans in the election; however, they drew off Southern voters from Jackson who received more popular and more electoral votes but didn't receive a majority of the electoral vote. The House of Representatives decided the election in Adams' favor.

    Of the four candidates, Henry Clay may have been the most qualified. He was a Southerner and slave owner who understood the inevitability of freeing all slaves. He strongly opposed the popular Jackson because of his autocratic ways, his opposition to a national bank, and his tacit support of Manifest Destiny. Clay was a Unionist and a statesman who served as Secretary of State to John Quincy Adams — the man who first defeated him. Clay also served six terms as a member of the House of Representatives and was House Speaker for three. After being defeated again for president in a close 1844 election, he ended his career serving as a U.S. Senator. In 1957 a Senate

Committee voted him one of the five "greatest U.S. Senators." One of his Senatorial colleagues said of him, "Had there been one such man in the Congress of the United States as Henry Clay in 1860-61 there would, I feel sure, have been no Civil War." Abraham Lincoln was a great admirer of the levelheaded Southerner, saying he was "my ideal of a great man."

Although a career politician and deservedly known as the "Great Compromiser," Clay was not one to back down from confrontation. As the 32-year-old Speaker of the Kentucky House of Representatives, to help support U.S. industry, he introduced a bill before the General Assembly to require its members to wear homespun suits instead of British broadcloth. One of the two who opposed the bill was Humphrey Marshall, an "aristocratic lawyer." After nearly coming to blows on the Assembly floor, Clay challenged Marshall to a duel. Marshall fired first and missed; Clay fired and missed; in turn, each man fired again and missed. On his third shot, Marshall shot Clay in the thigh. Staggered, Clay grazed Marshall below the ribs — the representatives retired to lick their wounds.

Clay was a much better orator than a marksman. Exceptionally quick-witted and always ready with the humorous jibe, once when he encountered a legislative rival on a narrow pathway, the two men came nose to nose with neither giving way. Clay's adversary growled, "I never give way to scoundrels." Clay smiled and stepped off the path saying, "I always do." Another time, while sitting outside of Washington's National Hotel with Massachusetts' Senator Daniel Webster, when a man walked by leading a pack of mules, Webster poked fun at him saying, "There goes a number of your Kentucky constituents." "Indeed, they must be going to Massachusetts to teach school," Clay retorted.

The 1828 election again pitted John Quincy Adams against Andrew Jackson. Thinking that it was unseemly to promote oneself by campaigning, neither candidate did. That left their supporters and the press to wage what is generally thought to be the meanest of all presidential elections. To prevent a reenactment of the 1824 split ticket debacle and to separate himself from the other pro-slavery candidates, with savvy political support from New Yorker, Martin Van Buren, Jackson created his own party by reviving the dormant Republican Party and renamed it the Democratic Party, as it remains today.

During the campaign, Jackson's detractors referred to him as "Jackass" Jackson. Jackson turned the slur to his advantage by adopting a cartoon caricature of a jackass as his party's symbol. Not to be outflanked, Adams also abandoned the Democratic-Republican Party and with Henry Clay formed the National Republican Party, which in 1833 became the Whig Party and in 1854 morphed into the modern Republican Party.

Out-politicked and not nearly as good-looking as the 6'1" and ruggedly handsome Jackson, the pudgy and balding Adams lost. Also during the campaign, Clay's supporters publicized the fact that Jackson's wife, Rachel, was a bigamist when she married Jackson. Although late-life portraits of Rachel tend to obscure it, she is said to have been an extremely beautiful young woman. And until John and Jacqueline Kennedy moved into the White House 130 years later, historians of such matters agree that the Jacksons were the most attractive First Couple.

In 1790 Rachel Donelson Robards had separated from her husband Captain Lewis Robards, a man reputed to be mean-spirited and subject to fits of jealous rage. Two years earlier, 19-year-old Andrew Jackson **was** appointed District Solicitor and became a boarder in Rachel's mother's Nashville house. Unaware that she was married, Jackson courted and married Rachel in 1791. Upset, Captain Robards sued for a divorce from Rachel, which was granted in 1793 — it was the new state of Kentucky's first divorce. Apparently confident about the outcome of his lawsuit, while still married to Rachel, in 1792 Captain Robards married Hannah Withers. At the time the divorce was granted, Jackson appears to have been the love triangle's only non-bigamist. The year after the Robards' divorced, Andrew and Rachel married again.

Twelve years later, a wealthy Tennessee attorney and horse breeder Charles Dickinson picked a fight with Jackson. Dickinson was an accomplished gunfighter and had killed 26 men in duels. Jackson was also a well-known tough guy. Several years earlier when Jackson was a presiding judge at a small town in Tennessee, a local bad man, Russell Bean, created a ruckus outside the courthouse. Swearing to shoot anyone who came within ten feet of him, he caused the sheriff to back off. Finally Jackson, who was on the bench, coolly made his way through the crowd and commanded, "Surrender this instant or I'll blow you through." Bean eyed Jackson and allowed himself to be led away. When asked why he let Jackson cow him, Bean answered, "When he came up I looked him in the eye, and I saw shoot, and there wasn't any shoot in nary an eye in the crowd; and so I says to myself, says I, hoss, it's about time to sing small, and so I did."

Two years before Jackson challenged Dickinson, he had been mocked by Dickinson in front of his men at a Tennessee militia muster when Dickinson asked Jackson, who was wearing an elaborate uniform, why he was sporting "such gorgeous trappings." A year after the public dig, angered over how a horserace bet was handled by a friend of Jackson's, Dickinson pulled Jackson into the argument by calling Jackson "a coward and an equivocator." A half-year later Dickinson published an article in the *Nashville Review saying* that Jackson was a "worthless scoundrel ... a poltroon and a coward." Jackson shrugged off the escalating insults, until Dickinson brought Rachel into it. Dickinson commented at a Nashville social event, "Why, gentlemen, General

Jackson has done a most daring exploit. He has captured another man's wife." Dickinson knew that if he kept up the insults, Jackson would have to challenge him to preserve his honor, and there was no clearer way to make a name for oneself on the frontier than to kill a famous man in a duel. He also knew that as the challenged, he would have first shot. Everyone knew that this had been a death sentence for all who had challenged Dickinson before.

Firing first, Dickinson wounded Jackson in the chest. With blood dripping onto his boots, Jackson stood straight and took aim, but half-cocked, his gun didn't fire. Cocking again, Old Hickory slowly aimed and shot Dickinson dead. Dickinson had aimed true — the bullet broke Jackson's ribs and lodged inches from his heart. Most men would have fallen. Jackson later said, "I intended to kill him. I would have stood up long enough to kill him if he had put the bullet in my brain."

As troubled as their marriage had begun, Jackson and the vivacious Rachel were devoted to each other. However, she didn't share Jackson's taste for public life, and throughout their marriage she stayed close to home where she greatly enjoyed smoking her pipe and reading the Bible. Tragically, immediately before the electoral ball, Rachel died suddenly of undetermined causes — Jackson was disconsolate. He refused to believe she was dead and instructed that blankets be placed over her so when she awoke she would be warm. Rachel was buried in a tomb built in her garden, and every night he was home, Jackson visited her grave at sunset. He said, "Heaven will be no heaven for me if she is not there." Jackson and Rachel had no natural children but adopted ten during their 37-year marriage.

Prior to his election, Jackson was supportive of Indian Removal; however, in his first Annual Message to Congress Jackson became presidential and said:

> This emigration should be voluntary, for it would be as cruel as unjust to compel the aborigines to abandon the graves of their fathers and seek a home in a distant land. But they should be distinctly informed that if they remain within the limits of the States they must be subject to their laws. In return for their obedience as individuals they will without doubt be protected in the enjoyment of those possessions, which they have improved, by their industry.

His proposed humane and just position was met with passionate Congressional objection, especially by those Congressmen who represented districts that had large Indian populations — which was just about everyone. So bowing to political pressure, Jackson returned to his original position and took the popular course of action, flip-flopping on his "stated" position. A year after saying that it would be "cruel ... to compel [Indians to] ... seek a home in a distant land," he signed the Indian Removal Act.

Although the May 1830 act provided for the "voluntary" migration of the tribes to designated lands west of the Mississippi, the military and state militias of all the states and territories, especially those in the South, viewed it as an open permit to drive the tribes from any land found desirable by white squatters. Within seven years, the government relocated 46,000 Indians and acquired 25 million acres of choice land. The act was strongly supported in the South, where plantation owners were eager to acquire the lands of the Five Civilized Tribes: the Cherokee, Chickasaw, Choctaw, Creek, and Seminole. And although most white Americans favored the Removal Act, there was significant opposition from some powerful Congressmen, such as Davy Crockett and Abraham Lincoln.

The five tribes were called "civilized" because they had acquired diverse cultural, agricultural, and lifestyle practices from Southeastern settlers and were assimilating into the plantation culture of that time; some even owned large numbers of slaves. George Washington and Henry Knox had proposed the process of "civilizing" the tribes, and Thomas Jefferson had tried futilely to refine and popularize the process. In a letter to Washington, Knox wrote:

> How different would be the sensation of a philosophic mind to reflect that instead of exterminating a part of the human race by our modes of population that we had persevered through all difficulties and at last had imparted our Knowledge of cultivating and the arts, to the Aboriginals of the Country by which the source of future life and happiness had been preserved and extended. But it has been conceived to be impracticable to civilize the Indians of North America — this opinion is probably more convenient than just.

Reluctantly but peacefully, for two generations the five tribes went along with the assimilation plan. They began restructuring their societies to emulate whites in many ways, including the building of schools and in some instances converting to Christianity. Because of their peaceful and accommodating ways and because they outnumbered whites in the regions away from the Atlantic coast, the Civilized Tribes were allowed to coexist; however, increasingly the demand for their lands created pressure on federal politicians. Then the 1830 Indian Relocation Act reversed the Jeffersonian policy. All of the five nations were victimized, but the Cherokee the most.

In late 1829, the discovery of gold in Georgia had stoked whites' determination to see the Cherokee removed from their ancestral lands. Cherokee were forbidden to dig for gold, and the state surveyed their lands in anticipation of a lottery to distribute it to white Georgians. Also, the Georgia legislature stripped the Cherokee of all land except their residences. The aggressive laws caused the Cherokee to fight back in the federal courts. In 1832 arguing that the United States inherited common law rights of Great Britain dating back to the Magna Carta, the U.S. Supreme Court, headed by Chief Justice John Marshall, ruled in *Worcester v. Georgia* that that the Cherokee Nation was a "distinct community" with self-government "in which the laws of Georgia can have no force," establishing the doctrine that the federal government, and not individual states, had authority in Indian affairs and that Indian lands were sovereign.

Shortly after the Supreme Court's ruling, President Jackson met with a delegation from the Cherokee National Council. When asked by the Indian leaders, who lived principally in Georgia but also in parts of North Carolina, Alabama, and Tennessee, whether he would use federal force against Georgia to enforce the Supreme Court's decision, Jackson bluntly said he would not and urged the Cherokee to accept removal. After his meeting with the Cherokee, Jackson, who apparently was unclear on the oath he had taken and the duties of his office, defiantly and famously said, "John Marshall has made his decision; now let him enforce it! ... Build a fire under them. When it gets hot enough, they'll go."

Georgia, then the largest state in size, built a bonfire. Following Jackson's lead, the state courts ignored the Supreme Court decision. Tensions heightened, and in October of 1835 an envoy from President Jackson agreed that the United States would pay the Cherokee people $5 million ($125 million) to be disbursed on a per capita basis, amounting to about $350 ($8,500) per person. The proposed treaty also provided an additional $500,000 dollars for education and title in perpetuity to an equal amount of land in Indian Territory. Most significantly, the proposed treaty allowed all Cherokee men, who desired to remain and become citizens of the states where they resided, to receive 160 acres of land.

The majority of Cherokee favored the plan until Jackson arbitrarily reneged on the citizenship and land offers and struck them from the treaty. (Arguably, Jackson's reversal was the government's single most devastating Indian policy.) Then, the Cherokee became divided in their support of it, and even though a faction of the tribal membership signed it, most opposed the treaty and petitioned Congress not to pass it. The disputed treaty passed by a single vote — this marked the 34th of 41 treaties the Cherokee entered into with white men. Enforcement of the act was left to Jackson's successor, Martin Van Buren, who in 1838, mobilized an armed force of 7,000 militia and regular army to round up 13,000 Cherokee and move them to camps near Red Clay, Tennessee, the Eastern Cherokee capital, before they were herded to Oklahoma. The militia then burned the Cherokees' homes, and the State of Georgia distributed their land to white settlers in a lottery.

The U.S. Army oversaw the thousand-mile winter march. The Cherokee were accustomed to the warm Georgia climate and had insufficient clothing and provisions for Midwest winters. Most walked barefoot or in moccasins over the frozen trails to Oklahoma, and more than 4,000 died of exposure, starvation, or smallpox from infected hospital blankets that the Army gave them. U.S. Army private, John Burnett, later wrote,

"Future generations will read and condemn the act, and I do hope posterity will remember that private soldiers like myself, and like the four Cherokee who were forced by General [Winfield] Scott [the commander of the march] to shoot an Indian Chief and his children, had to execute the orders of our superiors. We had no choice in the matter." Another soldier who participated in the removal later wrote, "I fought through the War Between the States and have seen many men shot, but the Cherokee Removal was the cruelest work I ever knew." The Cherokee called the march from their homelands to Oklahoma *Nunna daul Isunyi* — "the Trail Where They Cried." Everyone now calls it the "Trail of Tears."

Many frontiersman who had grown up among Indians, opposed their removal — one was Davy Crockett. Although Crockett was illiterate, he was smart in the ways of the frontier, understood men, and was politically astute — and was uncompromising in his ethics. In 1826 he was elected to the U.S. House of Representatives as a Jacksonian. After Jackson signed the Indian Removal Act, Crockett turned on him and said, "I bark at no man's bid. I will never come and go, and fetch and carry, at the whistle of the great man in the White House no matter who he is." His position on Indian removal cost him reelection to a third term, but he was again elected to the House two years later. While in office, Crockett was an outspoken proponent of squatters' land rights, even though it was generally thought to be contradictory to his position on Indian relocation. A man who grew up among Indians had the quaint concept that whites and Indians could live side-by-side in harmony, and he did not believe the Sauk and other tribes should be forced to move west of the Mississippi into the rolling plains of Iowa. However at the time, most people thought Iowa would be marvelous Indian Territory, and virtually all who had visited the Territory of Iowa, did not think that the United States would extend west of the Mississippi — nor did they see any reason for it to do so.

Another who understood the inflammatory dynamics of Indian removal was George Davenport, and he traveled to Washington to express his concerns to Jackson. Davenport suggested that the Indians could be persuaded to move to the Iowa side of the Mississippi River for a few thousand dollars. Jackson said that it was unnecessary to pay the Indians, that they would be driven across the river at no cost to the government. Jackson's humanity appears to have died with Rachel. Historians rank Jackson in the top quartile of presidents, but with Indians and blacks, his ranking is considerably lower. During his two terms from 1829 to 1837, he was revered by the conservative Democratic Party and his frontier constituency but was held in contempt by the liberal National Republican Party. Jackson's combative personality always evoked strong opposing emotions, and on the last day of his presidency, a time most presidents thank their staffs and praise their supporters, Jackson said that he had but two regrets, that he "had been unable to shoot Henry Clay or to hang John C. Calhoun."

Uninvolved in and uninformed of the politics, Black Hawk and his band returned to Saukenuk in April of 1830. The next month, the Indian Removal Act passed, and emboldened by the security provided by the soldiers at Fort Armstrong, squatters began to settle on the fertile plain between the Mississippi and Rock Rivers. Their brazen encroachment on the Sauk and Meskwaki lands inevitably led to greater resentments and tensions. After the 1831 winter hunt, Black Hawk returned with 1,500 tribesmen, including many Potawatomi he had recruited who were equally dedicated to maintain control of their lands. He demanded that the squatters leave Saukenuk and the surrounding area. The white men appealed to Illinois Governor John Reynolds who contacted General Edmund Gaines at Jefferson Barracks, Missouri. General Gains arranged a meeting at the garrison with Black Hawk, who again pled that the Sauk had not knowingly sold their land and contended that the five tribesmen, who had signed the treaty in 1804, had no authority to do so, and that he had not been told that he was signing away Saukenuk when he put his mark on the 1816 Treaty.

Black Hawk's arguments fell on uncaring ears, and during the conferences, a state militia, the Rock River Rangers, were surreptitiously formed by Reynolds, who had been a private and served as an Indian scout during the War of 1812. He bestowed the name of "Old Ranger" on himself and was made field commander and given the rank of Major General by President Jackson. The governor took his military assignment seriously and spent much of the summer supervising the Rock River Rangers. John Spencer was made a first lieutenant of the militia; his brother-in-law, Charles Case, was made a sergeant; and Jonah Case became one of a force that would grow to 1,600. Fifty-eight of the Rangers were from Rock Island County — 11 of those had "Wells" as their surname. Another who joined the militia was 30-year-old Thomas Ford, who a decade later would become the eighth governor of Illinois. In his 1854 *A History of Illinois*, Ford wrote of the area he helped protect from the Indians:

> The volunteers marched to Rock Island next morning and here they encamped for several days, precisely where the town of Rock Island is situated. It was then in a complete state of nature, a romantic wilderness. Fort Armstrong was built upon a rocky cliff on the lower point of an island, near the centre of the river a little way above; the shores on each side, formed of gentle slopes of prairie extending back to bluffs of considerable height, made it one of the most picturesque scenes in the western country. The river here is a beautiful sheet of clear, swift-running water, about three-quarters of a mile wide; its banks on both sides were inhabited only by Indians, from the Lower Rapids to the fort; and the voyage up stream, after several days progress through a wilderness country, brought the traveler suddenly in sight of the fort, perched upon a rock, surrounded by the grandeur and beauty of Nature, which at a distance gave it the appearance of one of those enchanted castles in

an uninhabited desert, so well described in the *Arabian Night's Entertainments.*

Governor Reynolds' Rock River Rangers joined with regular forces under General Gaines, and in May they attacked Saukenuk, only to find the village deserted. Out of frustration and not wanting to waste a three-mile ride through the rain and mud by 1,800 bumbling militia, the commanding officer ordered Saukenuk to be burned. The village was looted and totally destroyed. After a number of light retaliatory skirmishes and to prevent further reprisals and with no permanent shelters or land to cultivate, six weeks later Black Hawk signed Articles of Agreement and Capitulation.

Black Hawk and his tribe were forced to summer in Iowa on land that was controlled by Keokuk, a smoothly political Sauk leader who did not resist the white men and who followed their edicts. Black Hawk opposed Keokuk — who was 13 years younger than he, and who had also been born in Saukenuk but carried the white mark. Black Hawk had been given the black mark at birth. A member of the Fox clan, Keokuk, whose mother was said to be half French, was a brilliant leader and an unscrupulous politician. He was quick to be inoffensive, but was continuously involved in diplomatic intrigue and often skillfully played one side against the other. He was also narcissistic and given to worldly pleasures; he had seven wives and a fondness for whiskey, gambling, and money. He rode a white Arabian pony, wore elaborate robes made by his wives, and was often guarded by as many as fifty warriors who also rode the finest horses. In stark contrast, Black Hawk lived equally with his warriors, usually walked alone or with one or two braves, and had but one wife, of whom he said, "She was the best, and only, wife I ever had, or ever wanted."

Resentful of being told to live in Keokuk's territory but with nowhere else to go, in the spring of 1832 with 600 non-combatants and a band of 500 warriors Black Hawk crossed the Mississippi River north of the Yellow Banks, which is halfway between the Des Moines Rapids and the Rock Island Rapids. The drifting band of Indians headed north along the Rock River to a village (now the site of Prophetstown, Illinois) about 35 miles from the Saukenuk ruins on the Rock River. A friend and advisor of Black Hawk was the village's medicine man and tribal leader, Wabokieshiek (White Cloud) who was half Winnebago and half Sauk and was known by all as "The Prophet." White Cloud also was known for his hostility toward American squatters, and he was always ready for a fight with them. When Black Hawk arrived at The Prophet's village, The Prophet told him that he had a vision that the Great Spirit and a large army would enable him to drive away the whites and regain possession of his old village. The Prophet's prediction and a false report that British in Canada would join their old allies to fight the

Americans induced Black Hawk to wage the war that now bears his name. Keokuk later blamed The Prophet for all the frontier trouble in 1832.

Four hundred Winnebago under The Prophet's leadership joined Black Hawk's warriors, and the combined bands of Indians defiantly took a position near The Prophet's village. Alarmed by the large number of Indians, squatters fled the region and again appealed to Reynolds for protection. To back up the 100 Army Regulars at Fort Armstrong, a brigade of soldiers under Brigadier General Henry Atkinson was dispatched to the fort. The Indians had committed no acts of aggression and had attempted to avoid white settlements, but by entering Illinois instead of staying in Iowa, Black Hawk violated the terms of the prior summer's capitulation agreement. Atkinson reached Fort Armstrong before Black Hawk passed through the region as the Indians traveled northeast along the Rock River, but chose not to engage him. Instead, Atkinson asked Reynolds again to call out the Illinois militia, ironically, exhorting that "no one should remain at home while the country was being invaded."

In the spring of 1832, 90 white men and boys were identified as "settlers" in the 450-square mile Rock Island County peninsula that was bounded by the Mississippi River to the north and the Rock River to the south. In a letter, Henry C. McGrew, the publisher of Rock Island's first newspaper, describes the town in the first summer that Black Hawk was forbidden to live in his birthplace:

> Although thirty-eight years have passed since I first landed at Rock Island, I shall never forget my first impressions of the place. It was a beautiful moonlight night in June, and as I stood upon the deck of the steamer, as we rounded the bend below the village, and beheld old Fort Armstrong on the island in the river, with its whitewashed walls, pretty gardens and officers' houses, the scene was charming, presenting the appearance of some ancient castle. ... The panorama inspired me with a feeling of happiness I shall never forget; and coupled with the idea that I was on the outskirts of civilization, gave the whole scene an air of romance.

The call to help the army regulars defend the settlers and drive the Sauk west of the Mississippi River was answered by 3,000 volunteers, including 30 settlers from Rock Island County and 23-year-old Abraham Lincoln from Sangamon County. Lincoln was elected captain of his militia unit, and his entire military career consisted of the three months he served in the Black Hawk War. The closest Lincoln came to battle action was after the Battle of Stillman's Run where he helped to bury the dead at Kellogg's Grove. Years later he said of the scene, "I remember just how those men looked as we rode up the hill where their camp had been. The red light of the morning sun was streaming upon them as they lay, heads toward us, on the ground. Every man had a round red spot on the top of his head about as big as a dollar, where the redskins had taken off his scalp. It was frightful, but grotesque."

Having no previous military training or formal instruction in command procedures, Lincoln relied on his intelligence to lead his troops through the summer-long war. One morning while drilling a squad of 20 men in a field, he said that he "could not for the life of me remember the proper word of command for getting my company endwise. So as we came near the gate I shouted, 'this company is dismissed for two minutes, when it will fall in again on the other side of the gate."

All physical descriptions and later portraits of Abraham Lincoln depict him as a stern, tall, strong, and homely man. There may be some question as to how homely he was (a sketch during this period of a beardless Lincoln with a good haircut shows him to be rather handsome), but there is little question of his physical strength. At 6'4" and 190 pounds — at the time the average American man was 5'8" and weighed 143 pounds — Lincoln was "strong enough to intimidate any rival." Before bare-knuckled boxing became the rage after the Civil War, wrestling was America's sport, and Lincoln was to wrestling what Lou Gehrig would become to baseball. He was smart, big, tough, and athletic, and he had won many wagers for his men, the Sangamon County Boys, and himself by his wrestling exploits. A wrestling match was arranged in what is now South Rock Island between Lincoln and a brute of a man named Dow Thompson, who fought with the Union County Division. Backing their men with all of their "slick and well-worn quarters," the first fall went to Thompson. Lincoln had never before been thrown, and his backers claimed that it was a "dog fall." Lincoln was thrown a second time, and his supporters cried "foul." Lincoln calmly said, "Boys, give up your bets. This is the strongest man I ever met. If he has not thrown me fairly, he could."

The base pay for a private in the Illinois militia during the Black Hawk War was $6.66 a month, but rose to more than $20 if the militiaman brought his own horse and gun. As an officer, Lincoln was paid a veritable windfall. He received $125 ($3,200) plus room, board, and supplies for less than 100 days of service — and later he was given 160 acres of land in Iowa, which had been purchased from the French in the Louisiana Purchase for 3¢ an acre — and taken from the Sauk as a peace condition at the conclusion of the Black Hawk War.

Although hardly deserving to be called a "war," the fifteen-week conflict consisted mostly of spotty skirmishes as the soldiers relentlessly pursued the Indians northwest from the Rock River into the southwestern corner of the Michigan Territory (now Wisconsin). Overwhelmingly outnumbered, the Sauk were abandoned by their few allies — the promise of British aid and munitions was a complete sham — and actively opposed by their Indian enemies. Although they were triumphant in their first engagement with the Illinois militia at Stillman's Run, which is 100 miles up the Rock River from Rock Island, it was the Sauk's only noteworthy victory. Outnumbered four to one and using hit and run tactics, Black Hawk's warriors routed a militia force of 275 and killed 12 militiamen. The loss enraged the volunteer militia and assured the Indians' destruction.

Black Hawk soon realized that he was overwhelmingly outnumbered and that there would be no return to Saukenuk. With the safety of the Indian Territory west of the Mississippi River as his destination, he retreated from the area near present day Rockford, north into the Michigan Territory and then west towards the river. Moving as fast as the slowest of his old people and small children allowed, diversionary skirmishes were fought to allow the non-combatants to scavenge for food as they retreated into what only a few years earlier had been wilderness inhabited only by Indian tribes. Not understanding the inexorable forces of white colonialism, Black Hawk had entered Illinois under the delusion that the British, other tribes, and other Sauk and Meskwaki clans would support his efforts to reclaim his homeland.

The war ended abruptly. Knowing he could not prevail, Black Hawk moved his tribe west as fast as they could travel with the hope of reaching the Mississippi and crossing into Iowa. Relentlessly pursued by the militia, who were bent on revenge, and eating roots and bark to survive, many of the elderly and young children died on the hasty retreat. Finally reaching the Mississippi, a mile from the river on a ridge north of Prairie du Chien, Black Hawk and 50 warriors confronted the militia, hoping to gain time for the women and children to cross the river into Iowa. For a day the warriors successfully held off the militia, allowing some of the women, children, and elderly to raft across the river into the sanctuary of Indian Territory — many more drowned or were stranded, unable to cross the river before the bloodthirsty militia closed in the next day. With the Illinois volunteers encircling the remaining Indian band, Black Hawk knew that the situation was hopeless. He tried to surrender at river's edge to a gunboat (the *Warrior*) that had positioned itself to cut off the river retreat. In his autobiography, Black Hawk describes how the war ended:

> We had been here but a little while, before we saw a steamboat coming. I told my braves not to shoot, as I intended going on board, so that we might save our women and children. I knew the captain [Throckmorton] and was determined to give myself up to him. I then sent for my white flag. While the messenger was gone, I took a small piece of white cotton, and put it on a pole, and called to the captain of the boat, and told him to send his little canoe ashore, and let me come on board.
>
> The people on the boat asked whether we were Sacs or Winnebago. I told a Winnebago to tell them we were Sacs, and wanted to give ourselves up! A Winnebago on the boat called to us "to run and hide, that the whites were going to shoot!" About this time one of my braves had jumped into the river, bearing a white flag to the boat — when another sprang in after him, and brought him to shore. The firing then commenced from the boat, which was returned by my braves, and continued for some time. Very few of my people

were hurt after the first fire, having succeeded in getting behind old logs and trees, which shielded them from the enemy's fire.

The Winnebago, on the steamboat, must either have misunderstood what was told, or did not tell it to the captain correctly; because I am confident that he would not have fired upon us if he had known my wishes. I have always considered him a good man, and too great a brave to fire upon an enemy when suing for quarters. [Throckmorton later claimed that he thought the white flag was a hoax. He said he killed 23 of Black Hawk's band.]

After the boat left us, I told my people to cross, if they could and wished; that I intended going into the Chippewa country. Some commenced crossing, and such as had determined to follow them, remained — only three lodges going with me. Next morning, at daybreak, a young man overtook me, and said that all my party had determined to cross the Mississippi — that a number had already got over safe, and that he had heard the white army last night within a few miles of them. I now began to fear that the whites would come up with my people, and kill them, before they could get across. I had determined to go and join the Chippewa; but reflecting that by this I could only save myself, I concluded to return, and die with my people, if the Great Spirit would not give us another victory! During our stay in the thicket, a party of whites came close by us, but passed on without discovering us!

Early in the morning a party of whites, being in advance of the army, came upon our people, who were attempting to cross the Mississippi. They tried to give themselves up — the whites paid no attention to their entreaties — but commenced slaughtering them! Our braves, but few in number, finding that the enemy paid no regard to age or sex, and seeing that they were murdering helpless women and little children, determined to fight until they were killed! As many women as could, commenced swimming the Mississippi, with their children on their backs. A number of them drowned, and some shot, before they could reach the opposite shore. [General Winfield Scott later apologized to the Indians for killing women and children. However, in his official report he stated, "Some of (the women and children), in the different battles, were in the bushes and high grass, with their warriors, and were hurt or killed unavoidably, infinitely to the regret of our soldiers."]

One of my braves, who gave me this information, piled up some saddles before him — when the fight commenced —to shield himself from the enemy's fire, and killed three white men! But seeing that the whites were coming too close to him, he crawled to the bank of the river, without being perceived, and hid himself under it, until the enemy retired. He then came to me and told me what had been done. After hearing this sorrowful news, I started, with my little party, to the Winnebago village at Prairie La Cross. On my arrival there, I entered the lodge of one of the chiefs, and told him that I wished him to go with me to his father — that I intended to give myself up to the American war chief, and die, if the Great Spirit saw proper! He said he would go with me. I then took my medicine bag, and addressed the chief. I told him that it was "the soul of the Sac nation — that it never had been dishonored in any battle — take it, it is my life — dearer than life — and give it to the American chief!" He said he would keep it, and take care of it, and if I was suffered to live, he would send it to me.

During my stay at the village, the squaws made me a white dress of deerskin. I then started, with several Winnebago, and went to their agent, at Prairie du Chien, and gave myself up. [As a reward for bringing Black Hawk in, the Winnebago were given 20 horses and $100 ($2,500).]

On my arrival there, I found to my sorrow, that a large body of Sioux had pursued, and killed, a number of our women and children, who had got safely across the Mississippi. The whites ought not to have permitted such conduct — and none but cowards would ever have been guilty of such cruelty — which has always been practiced on our nation by the Sioux.

The massacre, which terminated the war, lasted about two hours. Our loss in killed, was about sixty, besides a number that were drowned. My braves could not ascertain the loss of the enemy exactly, but they think that they killed about sixteen during the action.

Of the more than 1,000 Indians who had entered Illinois less than four months earlier searching for summer quarters, as many as 600 were killed. In addition to the 12 militiamen that Abraham Lincoln helped bury at Stillman's Run, 58 soldiers and squatters lost their lives. Governor Reynolds wrote in his 1855 autobiography, *My Own Times*, of the white man's view of the war:

> General Gaines was a brave and stern warrior, who aided much in raising the Army of the United States to the glory and grandeur it so deservedly possesses, yet his heart responded in the kindest manner to the distresses of human nature. The unfortunate women and children, pertaining to the band of Black Hawk, were camped on the bank of the river, where they had nothing to eat or nothing to cover them from the inclemency of the weather. They had been deluded and ruined by the bad counsels and worse conduct of Black Hawk and other leaders of the tribe, but the helpless part of the band could not avoid it, they were in the hands of the chiefs and were ruined. Their distressed condition made a strong impression on General Gaines and myself.
>
> I know well my feelings for these deluded people were strong. I recollect well the argument I used to General Gaines — although, perhaps, he had as much benevolence at heart as I had — I observed, that I presumed this was the last time the Government would have any trouble with these Indians; the women and children were not so much to blame, they were starving, and that a support for them for one summer was nothing to the United States; that the Government possessed their fine country, and I could not be satisfied to leave them starving.
>
> We gave them more provisions than they would have raised on the fields they had left, and had it delivered to them at certain periods. But they are a race of people who will not observe the least economy or prudence, and I presume they did not take care of the provisions, and they were in want toward fall and winter. Our treaty was ridiculed by the volunteers. It was called a corn treaty. It was said we gave them food when it ought to have been lead. The army was disbanded, and returned home in good order. According to my recollection, not a man was killed by accident, or died of disease, during the campaign. All returned home with the best spirits, knowing we had done our duty.

After resigning as governor to fill a U.S. House of Representatives seat, Reynolds, who became known as "Old Ranger," would go on to serve five terms in the House. In *My Own Times*, he describes the land that he helped the squatters drive the Sauk and Meskwaki from:

> The scenery around Rock Island is not surpassed by any in the whole length of the Mississippi. It seems as though nature had made an effort in forming this beautiful and picturesque country. Rock Island itself presents a grand and imposing appearance, rising out of the waters of the Mississippi a solid rock, with many feet elevation. It is several miles long and three-fourths

of a mile wide. The rocks are covered with a fertile soil, at one time with a dense forest. The river washes around its base with a rapid current of pure and limpid water, and Rock River, a few miles south, is seen in the distance, forcing its way with great rapidity over the rocky rapids, into the father of waters.

The country around is interspersed with beautiful groves of timber, which gives to the scene a sweetness and beauty that is rarely equaled. The blue hills in the distance, directing the course of the river, are seen on the north and south to rise with gentle slopes from the water to considerable elevations, and the valley between, embracing the river, is some miles in extent, presenting a variety of surface and beauty of landscape never surpassed.

Another perspective of the Black Hawk War is the description of John Spencer's participation found in the *Biographical History of Rock Island, Illinois*:

During the Black Hawk War, [Spencer] was one of the organizers of the "Rock River Rangers," in which company he held the rank of first lieutenant ... He saw the chief [Black Hawk] and his people come again, and in common with other settlers, knew the purpose of their coming; he knew the possibilities of their discontent, and feared that the Indian was bent upon revenge. He noted the first out-break of their savage insubordination; saw the culmination of their ferocity as it rose in lurid lights from burning cabins, and disturbed the elements with the screams of butchered women and children. He saw the swift-footed pioneers as they pursued the savage destroyers, and saw the strong arm of the Government as it descended upon the wily Sac and his warriors at Bad Axe, and he saw peace reign supreme in the valley of the Mississippi.

At Fort Armstrong, George Davenport was one of the few who understood the Indians and their culture, and he was one of the most trusted and liked men on the frontier. He also understood the inevitable push of westward settlement, and in the five years before the Black Hawk War, he had urged the Indian clans on the east side of the Mississippi River to stake claims to land in the Iowa Territory. His position on this issue strained his relationship with Black Hawk, and he was greatly saddened to see the senseless conflict in the summer of 1832. During the Black Hawk War, Davenport was appointed quartermaster general with the rank of colonel, and thereafter he introduced himself as "Colonel Davenport."

One of the more controversial figures of the Black Hawk War was militia officer, James M. Strode who was a volunteer in the 1827 Winnebago uprising north of Galena that arose when Galena miners encroached on Winnebago territory west of the Mississippi. Strode remained active in the Illinois militia and was at the Battle of Stillman's Run, which he later said he attended "just for fun." After the battle, he was promoted to colonel of the militia and was given the command of the fort at Galena. Most of the regular army officers were disdainful of the untrained militia and their undisciplined, roguish ways. Davenport was particularly critical of Strode who stood by and watched as his men brutally annihilated women and children of Black Hawk's band

and shot warriors who advanced under a flag of truce. Historian Patrick Jung described the last engagement as "less of a battle and more of a massacre." The Black Hawk War was the last major Indian Removal action east of the Mississippi in the Midwest.

Black Hawk and The Prophet were taken to Prairie du Chien by the Winnebago and remanded to Lieutenant Colonel Zachary Taylor, the same officer who 18 years earlier Black Hawk had ignominiously driven back to Fort St. Louis from the Rock Island Rapids. Black Hawk and ten war chiefs and high-ranking warriors were taken to Fort Armstrong where they were treated well by the regular army. Their kind treatment continued when a 25-year-old West Point graduate from Mississippi, Second Lieutenant Jefferson Davis, escorted them to Jefferson Barracks just south of St. Louis. Black Hawk said of Davis, "He is a good and brave young chief, with whose conduct I was much pleased."

While at Jefferson Barracks, it was decided that six of the captive Indian leaders should be brought to Washington to meet with President Jackson and to demonstrate to the press and the public the effectiveness of Old Hickory's Indian Removal plan. In mid-March 1833, Secretary of War, Lewis Cass, sent word to Jefferson Barracks that Black Hawk and five others should be immediately sent to Washington. In addition to Black Hawk, his eldest son, Whirling Thunder; The Prophet and his adopted son; the Broth, a wily and reportedly treacherous Sauk brave; and Fast Swimming Fish, a Sauk warrior, were dispatched the next month to Washington. Black Hawk's biographical account of his journey east gives a fine account of American settlement in 1833 between the Ohio Valley and the East Coast:

> On our arrival at Wheeling, the streets and river's banks were crowded with people, who flocked from every direction to see us. While we remained here, many called on us, and treated us with kindness — no one offering to molest or misuse us. This village is quite a pretty village.
>
> We left the steamboat here, having traveled a long distance on the prettiest river (except our Mississippi,) that I ever saw — and took the stage. Being unaccustomed to this mode of traveling, we soon got tired, and wished ourselves seated in a canoe on one of our own rivers, that we might return to our friends. We had traveled but a short distance, before our carriage turned over, from which I received a slight injury, and the soldier had one arm broken. I was sorry for this accident, as the young man had behaved well.
>
> We had a rough and mountainous country for several days, but had a good trail for our carriage. It is astonishing to see what labor and pains the white people have had to make this road, as it passes over an immense number of mountains, which are generally covered with rocks and timber; yet it has been made smooth, and easy to travel upon. Rough and mountainous as is this country, there are many wigwams [houses and cabins] and small villages standing on the roadside. I could see nothing in the country to induce the people to live in it and was astonished to find so many whites living on the hills!
>
> We passed through several small villages on the way to Fredericktown, but I have forgotten their names. This last is a large and

beautiful village. The people treat us well, as they did at all the other villages where we stopped. Here we came to another road, much more wonderful than that through the mountains. They call it a railroad! I examined it carefully, but need not describe it, as the whites know all about it. It is the most astonishing sight I ever saw.

The Indians had not been told of the plans for them, and Black Hawk believed that the meeting with the President was a courtesy and that after the meeting they would return to their tribes. He was astonished when Jackson was brusque, warned them against future rebellion, and told them that they would be further detained at Fort Monroe outside of Washington. However, after meeting with the Indians, Cass and the Army officers decided that there was no further purpose in detaining them. They continued to be treated with kindness during six more weeks of detention while their return home was arranged.

The return trip to Rock Island took two months. To demonstrate to the press and public how well Indian removal was going and how pacified the Indians had become, they were paraded on an exposition through the East Coast's principal cities. From the time they left Fort Monroe, where the officers' wives showered them with presents and artists painted their portraits, through their journeys to Baltimore, Philadelphia, and New York City, they were treated as celebrities and stayed at the finest hotels, visited the best entertainments, and were received and honored at the largest theaters — and to convince them of the folly of any future rebellious notions, they were also shown every armory and military installation along the route.

Dressed in buckskins, sporting a colorful blanket over his shoulders, and with the feathered skin of a sparrow hawk for which he was named hanging at his waist, the 66-year-old, hollow-cheeked Black Hawk was the man the people came to see, but his son stole the show. Nasheaskuk (Whirling Thunder) fulfilled the image of the noble warrior. He was large and handsome, and as one journalist described him, "the perfect Apollo." The Indians were unaccustomed to the food and lifestyle and were occasionally ill and often fatigued; however, they all reveled in the attention. By the time they arrived in Albany, Black Hawk had exchanged his buckskins for a "short blue frock coat, white hat, and red leggings tied around below the knee with garters." And Whirling Thunder had acquired the affectations of "making great use of a silver toothpick" and wore "many ornaments about him and little bells that jingled as he walked." In his biography, Black Hawk wrote of his New York experience:

> On our arrival near the wharf, we saw a large collection of people gathered at Castle-Garden. We had seen many wonderful sights in our way — large villages, the great national road over the mountains, the railroads, steam carriages, ships, steamboats, and many other things; but we were now about to witness a sight more surprising than any of these. We were told that a man was going up into the air in a balloon! We watched with anxiety to see if it

could be true; and to our utter astonishment, saw him ascend in the air until the eye could no longer perceive him. Our people were all surprised, and one of our young men asked The Prophet if he was going up to see the Great Spirit?

After the ascension of the balloon, we landed, and got into a carriage, to go to the house that had been provided for our reception. We had proceeded but a short distance, before the street was so crowded that it was impossible for the carriage to pass. The war chief then directed the coachman to take another street, and stop at a different house from the one he had intended. On our arrival here, we were waited upon by a number of gentlemen, who seemed much pleased to see us. We were furnished with good rooms, good provisions, and everything necessary for our comfort.

The chiefs of this big village, being desirous that all their people should have an opportunity to see us, fitted up their great council-house for this purpose, where we saw an immense number of people; all of whom treated us with friendship, and many with great generosity. The chiefs were particular in showing us everything that they thought would be pleasing or gratifying to us. We went with them to Castle-Garden to see the fireworks, which was quite an agreeable entertainment — but to the whites who witnessed it, less magnificent than the sight of one of our large prairies would be when on fire.

We visited all the public buildings and places of amusement, which to us were truly astonishing, yet very gratifying. Everybody treated us with friendship, and many with great liberality. The squaws presented us many handsome little presents that are said to be valuable. They were very kind, very good, and very pretty — for pale faces.

When they left the coastal cities and moved inland, the attitude of the citizens became less kindly towards the Indians. Upon reaching Albany, newspaper accounts describe that thousands of curious onlookers lined the shores to catch a glimpse of the celebrity Indians, but the official account by the Indians' escort, Major John Garland, to the Secretary of War describes a somewhat different scene:

Since I took charge of the Indian prisoners at Fort Monroe, I met with kind and hospitable people, until my arrival at Albany, where, for the first time, the party was unduly assailed, by a mob assembled to witness the landing of Black Hawk. The sight was really appalling both from the number of the mob and its ruffian like appearance. I fortunately met with some few gentlemen with whose assistance the party reached a carriage in safety, the driver, however, was pelted with brick bats in trying to force his way through the crowd. I determined under all the circumstances of the case to make a speedy retreat and accordingly drove, under cover of the dark, to Schenectady, where we arrived with whole bones and empty pockets for in passing through the crowd of Albany ruffians, my wallet containing $100 ($2,500) was extracted from its hiding place by some dexterous cut purse. This unpleasant affair caused me to move more rapidly through the country than I had intended to do. The people of the towns and villages do not appear satisfied with the rapidity of my movement. The fact is, both the Indians and myself are heartily tired of the crowds.

Apparently unaware of the actual situation, Black Hawk wrote of the Albany stop in his autobiography:

On arriving at Albany, the people were so anxious to see us, that they crowded the street and wharves, where the steamboat landed, so much, that it was almost impossible for us to pass to the hotel which had been provided for our reception. We remained here but a short time, and then started for Detroit.

From Detroit it took but a few days to reach Prairie du Chien, and then down the Mississippi River to Rock Island. As he proceeded down the river, Black Hawk became despondent when he saw that within a year's time white settlements had sprung up on the west bank. The Mississippi was the promised dividing line between Indian and white territories. Black Hawk wrote, "I am very much afraid, that in a few years, they will begin to drive and abuse our people, as they have formerly done. I may not live to see it, but I feel certain that the day is not distant."

The morning after reaching Fort Armstrong, Black Hawk was delivered into the custody of Keokuk and told to "be governed by his counsel in all things." Although he later regretted it, he was indignant and said so. Disconsolate from losing his heritage and being exiled to Iowa under Keokuk's supervision, Black Hawk lived with his wife, two sons, and a daughter in a lodge of peeled bark near the Iowa River. He returned to Washington in 1836 with Keokuk to legitimatize another land cession of more than a million acres. Although not lionized as he was on his first trip, he was still the subject of great attention. Shortly before his death, Black Hawk moved into a new home on the Des Moines River in southeast Iowa. He died there after a short illness on October 3, 1838. There are conflicting stories of what happened to Black Hawk's remains. The most credible is that he was traditionally buried above ground in a small log mausoleum, and that his grave was looted. The remains that weren't stolen were deposited at Burlington's Geological and Historical Society and were destroyed when the building burned in 1855. There is a marker for him in the Iowaville Cemetery, but it is unknown if any of his remains are there.

After the Black Hawk War, the greatly diminished Sauk and Meskwaki tribes were disbursed to reservations west of the Mississippi, first in northwestern Iowa and southern Minnesota, and later as that land became desirable for farming, most were relocated to other Iowa locations and to Kansas and Nebraska. In several transactions over a five-year period ending in 1842, Keokuk sold most of Iowa to the U.S. Government for an average of 11¢ an acre (about two hour's wages at the time). It is impossible to know if Keokuk was an autocratic despot who had little concern for future generations of Sauk and Meskwaki or if he was a wise man who saw the inevitability of the destruction of his people's culture and merely chose to party on until the feast was over — but there is no question that he was a terrible negotiator.

As a speaker, Keokuk was described "as more magnificent than any other Indian chief" and "a greater orator than the best in the Unites States Senate." When Black Hawk stopped to recruit warriors from Keokuk's tribe in the summer of 1832, he delivered an impassioned speech that won over many of Keokuk's braves. Waiting for the frenzy that Black Hawk stirred up to subside, the practical, smooth-talking Keokuk delivered a response that rivaled Mark Antony's speech to the Forum. He began by building a case to take the warpath against the white squatters and settlers. He concluded by saying, "Let us first put our women and children to eternal sleep, for we cannot leave them and we cannot take them with us; we know they must die. Let us go to war, knowing that all of us must die." None of his warriors joined Black Hawk, and many of Black Hawk's braves chose to stay behind.

The land ruled by Black Hawk and Keokuk encompassed northwestern Illinois, southwestern Wisconsin, and eventually most of Iowa. At the time, Keokuk, the political leader who carried the white mark, was possibly the most eloquent Indian. Black Hawk, the warrior who carried the black mark, was possibly the most moral and intelligent Indian. Both of these polar-opposite leaders were born at Saukenuk and called the region of the Rock Island Rapids home. Within three years after Keokuk sold the last acre of Iowa, the Sauk and Meskwaki nations had become a scattered, dispirited clan of "government pensioners." In 1887 the last of the desirable Indian lands were confiscated by the U.S. Government. A series of Congressional acts were implemented, and over the next two decades, U.S Government policy destroyed tribal structures and placed administration of tribal land under the federal government. But proving that you can't keep a good people down, in 1934 after the Franklin Roosevelt Administration created a "New Deal" for Indians under the Indian Reorganization Act, the Sauk and Meskwaki nations re-formed, and today there are 11 distinct clans.

The fragmented Iowa clans reorganized as the Sac and Fox Tribe of the Mississippi in Iowa (Meskwaki). In 2012 they had a tribal census of 1,300, oversaw 7,000 acres of land near Tama, Iowa, and operated the Meskwaki Bingo Casino, the Midwest's largest casino with 1,500 slot machines and 30 table games. In 1937 the Kansas clans reorganized in the northeast corner of Kansas near Reserve as the Sac and Fox Nation of Missouri in Kansas and Nebraska (Nemahahaki). The 400-member tribe operates the 800-slot machine Sac and Fox Casino and a museum and tribal research center that celebrate the history of the Sauk and Meskwaki people. With 3,400 members, the largest of the three Sac and Fox Nation tribes is the Sac and Fox Nation in Oklahoma (Sakiwaki), which reorganized in 1937. The tribe grants membership to everyone who is a great grandchild (one eighth bloodline) of a Sauk or Meskwaki who was listed as a tribal member in 1893 and their descendants. Today the tribe operates two casinos. In one of the few Native American legal victories against the federal government or a state, the Sakiwaki won a lawsuit against the State of Oklahoma — the U.S. Supreme Court decision allows Indian tribes to issue their own license plates.

Chapter 7

Crossroads of the Nation

A pioneer destroys things and calls it civilization. ~ Charles Marion "Kid" Russell, Western artist and author

DURING THE CONSTRUCTION OF FORT ARMSTRONG, George Davenport built a trading post near the fort on Rock Island. Davenport and his family lived and worked out of a large log cabin, supplying and trading with soldiers, settlers, trappers, and Indians. Davenport was a tough man who worked hard. In 1818 he turned his attention fulltime to fur trading. Working independently, he initially traded with the Winnebago who trapped wolves, fox, muskrat, and beaver along the streams and creeks that flowed into the Mississippi and Rock Rivers. The Sauk and Meskwaki and most of the other tribes in the Upper Mississippi region sold their pelts to agents of John Jacob Astor's American Fur Company. But Davenport, traveling by himself during the winters, roamed the prairies of Illinois and Iowa visiting the tribes and paying top-dollar for their best furs. In this way he was able to corner the quality pelts. In the spring, the Indians would stop first at his trading post on Rock Island to leave the furs he had selected and marked and then take the bulk of their pelts to the French traders who had spent their winter on Credit Island drinking whiskey and playing cards.

Before the adventuresome Davenport moved to the western frontier and became the first permanent white settler in Rock Island, his future partner, Russel Farnham, had already traveled around the world. Like Davenport, Farnham was tough and fearless. Leaving his birth state of Massachusetts at age 24, he went to work as a clerk for the American Fur Company. In 1810 Farnham was dispatched to the Pacific Northwest to join the Wilson P. Hunt expedition, which had followed the route west that Lewis and Clarke mapped six years earlier and was in search of fur trading opportunities. Farnham was part of a support group of 16 who sailed with supplies for the trading venture on the *Tonquin* from New York around Cape Horn. Under Captain Jonathan Thorn, the party stopped at the Hawaiian Islands, where they "recruited" 12 Hawaiians to do the heavy work, and then sailed on to the mouth of the Columbia River where they met Hunt's party.

Since he was among the few who weren't "drinking in the morning, drunk at noon and dead drunk at night," Farnham soon became one of Hunt's most trusted agents. Little is recorded of the private trading expeditions to the Pacific Northwest, but author and historian, Washington Irving, wrote that Farnham was ordered to execute an Indian who had been caught stealing a silver cup from one of the trapping camps. He hung the Indian from a sapling on June 1, 1813. Irving recorded that the incident caused great hostility between Hunt's trading community and the local tribe. Irving also wrote of men like Farnham that "were removed for years from civilized society, leading a life almost as wild and precarious as the savages around him, exposed to the severities of a northern winter, often suffering from scarcity of food, and sometimes destitute for a long time of both bread and salt."

The enterprise to the Pacific Northwest was wildly successful, and in the spring of 1814, Farnham was entrusted with £40,000 ($2 million) in sterling notes from the sale of the Astoria trading post to the British North-West Company and sent by Hunt to deliver the bills to John Jacob Astor in New York. Fearing that Indians or thieves might intercept and rob him if he were to travel east across the width of North America, Farnham traveled west alone. After being dropped off on the coast of the Kamchatka Peninsula in northeast Russia with the notes and a single backpack of provisions, he soon suffered from exposure and malnutrition. Hunting and foraging for food and resorting to eat the tops of his boots to survive, he walked across Russia to St. Petersburg. After presumably buying new boots, he continued his hike and walked to Denmark. A three-day passport that was issued to the handsome Farnham in Copenhagen, described him as "32 years of age, born in America, speaks English, is tall of stature and medium build, has light curly hair, brown eyes." Farnham eventually arrived in New York, and his journey was the first documented circumnavigation of the world by an American. At the time, the trip went unnoted.

After returning to the States, Farnham was placed in charge of the Great Lakes Region of the American Fur Company. In 1817 he was arrested by the U.S. Army near Saukenuk. A Colonel Chambers had reported that Farnham and another Astor employee "appeared to be hardened rascals." Under guard, Fort Armstrong's commander had the men escorted to Fort St. Louis. Upset, John Jacob Astor sued the Army and was awarded $5,000 ($85,000) in damages. It seems that during this fiasco Farnham met George Davenport. The men became friends and business partners and built a series of scattered trading posts up and down the Mississippi River. Soon they became the most influential men in the area and the second largest private employer after the American Fur Company. Their French Canadian employees were hired for three years and paid $125 per year ($2,000). This was a princely sum for self-sufficient men who built their own shelters, lived off the land, and had few social or personal grooming expenses.

Davenport and Farnham's men appear to have made out financially better than their bosses, especially in the last years of their partnership. In an 1831 report filed at the Secretary of War's request, the men stated, "Most of our sales have been on credit to [the Indians] in the Fall of the year for the purpose of enabling them to make a Hunt and support their families during their absence. ... Our credits to these Indians for the last seven years have amounted to $136,768.82 [$3.4 million in 2012 dollars], and we have collected the sum of $83,498.74 [$2.1 million in 2012 dollars]. ... This balance we do not consider yet desperate because the Indians have obligated themselves and promised to pay whenever enabled to do so." A year later when the Army expelled the Indians from Illinois, and the debt situation with the Indians became desperate.

Spread by soldiers, a cholera epidemic struck Fort Armstrong during the summer of the Black Hawk war, and Davenport became more concerned with his health than his finances. He wrote to his partner and friend, "If I do not see you again, God Bless you, my account you will find correct. I now [sic] you will do justice." Davenport survived, but Farnham didn't. He died of cholera less than two months after Davenport wrote to him of his fears. He was 48. When he died, Farnham was living with his Métis wife, Susan Bosseron, in St. Louis with their young son, Charles Russel. Susan died the same year. The estate passed to the control of Susan's mother, a full-blooded Indian, who was Charles' guardian. The estate included land tracts that extended from present day 15th Street in Moline to 19th Street in East Moline. The estate was also enriched by $20,000 ($500,000), Farnham's share of monies that the U.S. Government withheld from Iowa land sales that Keokuk made to pay their debts to Davenport and Farnham. After his 18th birthday, Charles Farnham died of consumption (tuberculosis). Susan's mother sold the land, and there is no record of her whereabouts after the sale.

In 1826, six years before Farnham died and 143 years after Marquette and Jolliet discovered Rock Island, Farnham, Davenport, and John Barrell, a relative of Davenport's, built a large, well-designed log building near where the railroad tracks now cross to the Rock Island Arsenal. The John Barrell House became the first "public house [for] men to transact Rock Island County business." In addition to being his home, John Barrell's house served as the first county court house, post office, and inn. The scattered cabins and shops built on high land along the river, north of what is now 5th Avenue and west of 27th Street, created the Town of Farnhamsburg. After mining lead and coal, Barrell operated a ferry from Farnhamsburg to Iowa. Born in 1830, John Barrell's son, George William, was the first recorded white baby born in Farnhamsburg.

John Barrell was one of six ferryboat operators licensed by the Rock Island County commissioners in 1835, the year the county was incorporated. Ten years earlier, George Davenport had established the first commercial ferry service to Iowa, when on an as-needed basis, he transported traders and their furs from Credit Island to his trading post and the occasional pioneer who was heading west into the wilderness. Another of the six ferry operators was Antoine LeClaire who in 1837 sold his operation to John Wilson. The Wilson family continuously operated The Rock Island-Davenport Ferry Company between the two cities for 88 years. In 1904 the Wilsons had the Kahlke Boatyard build a three-deck ferry for them. The Government Bridge had opened eight years before, but for a nickel ($1.25) passengers could ride the *Davenport* between Rock Island and Davenport every 15 minutes between 6:30 a.m. and 10 p.m. and listen or dance to jazz bands, play penny and nickel slot machines, and have a meal or a beer or pop — most who boarded the ferryboat after 6 p.m. in Rock Island never stepped foot in Davenport. In 1925 William J. Quinlan purchased the *Davenport* and renamed it the *WJ Quinlan*. The boat operated for another two decades before it was forced to dry-dock at the Mill Street Kahlke Boatyard, where it remained a riverfront landmark until it burned in a spectacular 1967 fire.

Entrepreneurial speed skater and Farnhamsburg's first resident, John Spencer was the first judge of the Rock Island County Court, and in 1836 Judge Spencer was awarded the contract to build a two-story, 22-foot by 22-foot log jail — wisely, brick cells were added three years later. Two years before the jail contract and eight years after Barrell built his house, John Buford opened the first Farnhamsburg mercantile store on the levee. The son of a Revolutionary War hero and prominent Kentucky politician, grief-stricken after the death of two wives from cholera, Buford sold his 10,000-acre plantation, horse farm, and his slaves and moved to Farnhamsburg with his four sons, Napoleon Bonaparte, John Jr., Thomas Jefferson, and James Madison. He immediately became one on the region's leading citizens.

John Buford was a large, powerful man with a genteel nature. He had elaborately painted the high façade on his small wooden-frame store to look like granite. One day he said to a customer, "It looks like a man clothed in a ruffled shirt and nothing else." A close friend of Andrew Jackson, Buford was active in Democratic politics and served in the Illinois Senate where he often butted heads with a Whig legislator, Abraham Lincoln, who didn't agree with Buford's` Southern views and sensibilities. John Buford's boys did well. Napoleon and John Junior graduated from West Point, and both rose to the rank of Brigadier General in the U.S. Army. Thomas and James started an iron foundry in Rock Island. Thomas was commander of the Rock

Island home guards, and James, whose primary profession was banking, was city treasurer for 12 years. Thomas and James were both Rock Island mayors.

The man who possibly witnessed Rock Island's early history more than anyone else was Antoine LeClaire, a literate Métis who was born in St. Joseph, Michigan and had a French Canadian father and a Potawatomi mother. LeClaire served as an Army interpreter at Fort Armstrong in 1818, but when the garrison was reduced to fewer than 100 troops, he moved to Peoria until he returned to Rock Island in 1827. LeClaire and his Métis wife, Marguerite La Page, were present as the government's interpreters at the treaty signing where the land from the Black Hawk Purchase was divvied up. LeClaire spoke English, French, Spanish, and 14 Algonquin dialects. Other than his wife who spoke English, French, and Meskwaki, LeClaire was the only person at the treaty signing and forced sale of the Sauk and Meskwaki lands who was fluently bilingual. Unarguably, the treaty negotiations ended with the interpreters leaving as the biggest winners.

At the negotiations, Keokuk donated a large tract of land to the charming Marguerite, who was the granddaughter of another Sauk chief, Acoqua. The enigmatic Keokuk donated the land on the condition that Antoine and Marguerite build their home on the exact location where the treaty was signed. Consequently, the land that would become Davenport, Iowa, was transferred to the LeClaire's. As compensation for having to live in Iowa, Keokuk's deal was sweetened by the Potawatomi who agreed to endow the LeClaires with even more desirable land on the Illinois side of the Mississippi where most of Moline now stands. In the spring of 1833, Antoine LeClaire began work on an 18 by 18-foot log cabin at the site of the signing — which hardly seems adequate for a wealthy man, who weighed more than 300 pounds, and his wife.

At that time, the right of a woman to vote in federal elections, much less own land in a territory (single women could own slaves) was still almost a century away. As a consequence, Marguerite did not own the land she was given, and building her home on the treaty site caused more than 50,000 acres of former Sauk and Meskwaki land straddling the Mississippi River to be transferred to her husband for his fine work at the treaty negotiations — and for his agreement to live in Iowa. Even though it was the only legal structure in the county, upon completion of his house, LeClaire was made U.S. Postmaster of the newly vested Scott County. (A Wikipedia article states that "Claim House," the Treaty House, "was built in 1832 or 1833 by George L. Davenport, son of Colonel George Davenport, when he was fifteen years old. It was built as a claim on his property, and is thought to be the oldest structure in the city of Davenport.")

Later that same summer, as LeClaire was building the Treaty House, U.S. Army Doctor John Emerson was assigned to Fort Armstrong. His slave, Dred Scott, accompanied Emerson and lived with him until the garrison was closed. In 1846, after Emerson's death, Scott sued Emerson's widow for his freedom, claiming that he had been a resident of a free state while living in Rock Island. The U.S. Supreme Court ruled against Scott, essentially saying that regardless of country of birth or state law, the U.S. Constitution did not recognize African American slaves as U.S. citizens. The Supreme Court's decision is arguably one of the most momentous court decisions in the history of the United States. Scott had won his case in the lower state court and the Missouri Supreme Court reversed the lower court. The case was argued before the U.S. Supreme Court early in 1856, an election year in which slavery was the primary issue. Realizing that the decision would probably influence the vote, the Supreme Court waited until two days after the inaugural address of James Buchanan, a Democratic Southern sympathizer who had garnered only 45 percent of the popular vote, before revealing the longest and most controversial opinion the Court ever delivered. It is unfortunate the Court didn't hand down its decision earlier; it may have saved the nation from four years of the man who most historians view as the second worst president in the country's history. Buchanan tried to appease the North and South and failed at both.

The Court declared that Dred Scott not only remained a slave ("Scott was not made free by being taken to Rock Island in the state of Illinois."), but also that Negroes had no constitutional rights, and that the Missouri Compromise was unconstitutional. The Missouri Compromise had excluded slavery north of the 36°30' parallel (the southern boundary of Missouri) except within the limits of the proposed state of Missouri. In other words, the U.S. Constitution did not allow for the restriction of slavery. The decision polarized the nation and created a political tempest that hadn't been seen before or since over a Court decision. The Court's opinion fractured the Democratic Party between pro-slavery and abolitionist factions, rocketed Abraham Lincoln to the forefront of U.S. politics, and assured that there would be civil war.

Lost in the commotion of the decision was what happened to the principals. Emerson died 13 years before the Court's ruling, and his will bequeathed Dred Scott to his one-month-old daughter. Emerson's widow, Irene Sanford, married Charles Chaffee, a prominent anti-slavery U.S. Congressman. Chaffee was politically embarrassed by the connection to Dred Scott, and he had ownership of Scott transferred to Irene's brother. A year after the Court's decision, the sons of Peter Blow, Scott's first owner, purchased emancipation for Scott and his family. Scott worked in a St. Louis hotel until he died 18 months after the decision.

The spring after Dred Scott was taken to Fort Armstrong, and LeClaire was appointed Scott County postmaster, the opportunistic LeClaire established the first regular ferry service across the rapids between Iowa and Illinois. Two years after completing the "Treaty House," he met with a group of businessmen including Davenport to discuss the formation of a new town on his Iowa property. The group formed a company, and within a year the site of the town of Davenport was surveyed. Five years later, L'oste Davenport, in partnership with his father and LeClaire, opened the town's first store on Front and Main Streets — it was billed as "the largest store in the West." In 1995, after standing for 149 years, the building was demolished.

At the end of the Black Hawk War, the War Between the States was still almost three decades away and an ambitious, recently-discharged Illinois militia captain, Abraham "Honest Abe" Lincoln, began an adult life that would be filled with disappointments in love and many failures, including being denied entry into law school, losing eight public elections, twice failing in business, and understandably suffering a nervous breakdown before being elected the 16th President of the United States — and then things were to get worse.

While serving under Major John Stuart during the Black Hawk War, Lincoln struck up a friendship with Stuart, an accomplished lawyer from Springfield who was two years his senior. Stuart encouraged Lincoln to study law, which Lincoln eventually did after failing at several other pursuits. He mustered out as a private in an "independent spy company" (Indian reconnaissance) at the end of the war — this is one of the rare instances in U.S. military history where a soldier began his military career as a captain and retired as a private — and he returned to New Salem, Illinois, to begin a career. Stuart returned to Springfield where he resumed his law practice and successfully ran for the state legislature. Casting about for several years, Lincoln unsuccessfully tried his hand at managing a general store and running for the Illinois General Assembly. Additionally, he served as New Salem's postmaster and later as county surveyor. Studying the law by reading Blackstone's *Commentaries on the Laws of England*, in 1836 Lincoln was admitted to the bar. Of his law training, Lincoln said, "I studied with nobody." On his second attempt, he was elected to the state legislature, and moved to Springfield where he worked for Stuart. Three years later he met Stuart's cousin, Mary Todd who was from a wealthy slave-owning family in Lexington, Kentucky. They were married a year later.

The same year Lincoln passed the Illinois bar, the few remaining troops at Fort Armstrong were withdrawn for lack of Indians to subdue. For two years the garrison was the Indian Agency and was under the command of General Joseph Street. After the Indian Agency was moved to Iowa, Davenport was placed in charge of the island until an arms depot was established there; then the U.S. Army retook control. The year before the soldiers left, a large section of privately owned land on the mainland had been incorporated as Rock Island. It did not include any of the government-owned island that had the same name. To avoid confusion with the new city, the military-owned land was renamed "Government Island." The name changed again in 1862 when Congress created a national arsenal for the "deposit and repair of munitions," and the island became known as the Rock Island Arsenal.

The summer after the Black Hawk War, Davenport built one of the grandest mansions on the Upper Mississippi River on Rock Island. After retiring from the fur trade at age 50 and owning vast tracts of land, he built the first house made of sawed lumber in the region. Moving his family into their solid oak home on the north side of the island only a short walk from the garrison, Davenport retired from public life and became Rock Island's elder statesman. He advised and guided businessmen and politicians in their building of the frontier's most fascinating city. After suffering through almost four decades of Midwest winters, he spent his last winters in St. Louis and Washington D.C., where because of his jovial disposition, endless stories, and amusing anecdotes, he was invited to the finest dinners and parties.

Davenport was 62 when on the 4th of July, his wife and children went to the mainland to celebrate Independence Day. Staying behind to avoid the commotion, he was severely beaten when burglars robbed him and were angered when they found that the $100,000 ($2,500,000) rumored to be in Davenport's safe was only $400. Before dying of "blood stains" in a second-floor bedroom, Davenport lived long enough to describe his assailants. Eight men from a gang known as the "Banditti of the Prairie" were arrested; five were confined in Rock Island's newly erected brick jail; three were found guilty and executed for Davenport's murder, including the gang's leader, John Long, and his brother, Aaron. At the time the Banditti was the most notorious gang in the Midwest — they had terrorized settlers in six states.

October 29, 1845 was set as execution day, and because of Davenport's prominence and the Banditti's notoriety, the eyes of the nation were on Rock Island. The execution turned into a barbarous fiasco. At the time, Rock Island's population was only 1,660 and more than 5,000 came to watch the hangings. The entire event took on the air of a medieval fair. A gallows was constructed half a block south of the Court House. At 10:00 a.m. the sheriff paraded the condemned men through the downtown streets behind a ragtag collection of musicians who called themselves The Green Mountain Boys Band. At 12:30 the band struck up a solemn dirge as 130 guards escorted the three prisoners to the scaffold. Then the speeches started. The Rev. F. A. Haney of the Methodist church led off, and was followed by John Long, who spoke at length about the innocence of the other two condemned Banditti. Then Long's two accomplices spoke about Long's innocence. And finally after prayers by various clergy and a hymn played by The Green Mountain Boys — five and a half hours after being paraded from the jail — the prisoners were led to the gallows. Then chaos broke loose. A Galena journalist reported on the minutes leading up to the hangings:

> No one can describe or imagine the scene as it was at the time. [Someone cried] "Rescue!" Foremost were some four or five Sauk Indians running under full headway. Women were screaming, horses were running, and wagons upsetting. It was absolutely wonderful that none was killed or injured. The whole mass was running, some being trampled underfoot. As soon as the guard was brought to order, they were ordered to outward face, and again the crowd started — some ran to the river, some to the extreme upper end of the town, but I would not have you infer that your humble servant was one of the number, as I was captain of the Invincibles.

After the hysteria died, The Green Mountain Boys played a funeral dirge, and the gallows trap was sprung. Then the improbable happened. The noose around Aaron Long's neck broke. One woman related, the "rope broke and he said, 'don't choke a man and then hang him.' They gave him a drink and then hanged him again."

Davenport's mansion has been called "the cradle of the Quad Cities." The house became the center for County Government; the first elections were held there; and it was the seat of the County and Circuit Courts until 1835. It was there Judge John Spencer performed the county's first marriage ceremony. Probably at Mrs. Davenport's urging, in July 1835 Davenport and Russell Farnham purchased 62 acres from the federal government to build permanent county buildings and for residential and commercial sites. Several public and private buildings originally constructed on the large tract still stand. The oldest is the Rock Island County Jail, which was built in 1857. A contract with Jonah Case for $1,600 ($40,000) to furnish 200,000 bricks got the project under way. Thirty years later one of the grandest county courthouses in the country was contracted to Charles Larkin for $125,000 ($3.3 million).

Although not as ruggedly romantic sounding as "Rock Island," the city should have been named "Davenport," and if the locals had had their way, it would have been. The land Davenport and Farnham purchased for the civic center and their private development was adjacent to and west of Farnhamsburg, and during high water was an island. The Mississippi flowed to the north, and during the spring as the river rose, a slough developed to the south of the property, turning it into an island until late summer when the river fell again. Davenport and Farnham had observed the cycle for years, and after acquiring the property for a good price, they built a clay dike at the head of the sometime slough and began to backfill the lowland with logs, brush, and debris. Since Farnham already had a village named after him, the popular and logical choice for the name of the new acreage was "Davenport."

However, James Strode, who became a state senator from Chicago and who represented virtually all of Illinois north of Peoria, actively objected. Still smarting from

Davenport's criticism of his conduct during the Black Hawk War, Strode insisted on naming the property obtained from the federal government after a family friend, Benjamin Stephenson, a former Illinois militiaman and state politician. Virtually unknown in northern Illinois, Stephenson was best known for building what was then a magnificent brick home for himself in Edwardsville. He died shortly after his four-room mansion was completed and twelve years before the Black Hawk War. Strode's political influence prevailed, and the new village was called "Stephenson."

Chapter 8

Engineers and Businessmen

The military engineers have taken upon their shoulders the job of making the Mississippi over again — a job transcended in size by only the original job of creating it. ~ Mark Twain, *Life on the Mississippi*

THE ARMY CORPS OF ENGINEERS was created 1775 by General George Washington to oversee the building of fortifications. The Corps consisted of a chief engineer and two assistants. Twenty-five years later, the engineers were ordered to establish a military academy at West Point, New York, to train more engineers and Army officers in the art of war. It wasn't until the War of 1812 that the noncombatant engineers received backdoor authority over waterways when they were ordered to fortify the city of New Orleans. From there, a series of short steps expanded their authority to mapping the country, designing and constructing federal civil works, building and manning lighthouses, surveying land, and clearing navigational routes for warships.

After the British Band of Sauk defeated the U.S. Army in War of 1812 battles on the Upper Mississippi River, Congress thought it was militarily important to create canals around the Des Moines and Rock Island Rapids, opening the river to large gunboats between St. Louis and Fort St. Paul. The General Survey Act of 1824 authorized Mississippi River improvements, and instead of building canals with locks around the pair of rapids, an unknown Army engineer suggested that it would be simpler and less expensive to dredge a navigation channel — this suggestion may have been the most costly engineering error in history. Five years later, John Buford, Sr.'s oldest son, Lieutenant Napoleon Buford, surveyed the rapids and recommended that the river channel be widened and straightened. Unwittingly, a bright military man from Rock Island began the formal destruction of North America's most magnificent stretch of river. Eight years later the Corps selected a highly regarded engineer to plan the job: Robert E. Lee, a cadet who had graduated from West Point two years after Buford.

Lee had entered the Military Academy over the objections of his mother — later, he often said that he should have listened to her — and refined his civil engineering skills while working on fortification projects at Cockspur Island, Georgia, and Fort Monroe and Fort Wool, Virginia. After proving himself a first-rate designer and project manager, Lee was ordered to re-survey the straight, 75-mile long portion of the border between Ohio and Michigan. At first this appeared to be a mundane assignment, but Lee and his boss, Captain Andrew Talcott, were given a hornet's nest of a job. The survey had been done twice before, and blood would be spilled before they were relieved from their engineering assignment.

In an early example of Congressional oversight, the language establishing the southern boundary of the Michigan Territory of the Northwest Territory differed from gerrymandered language submitted by the Ohio Constitutional Convention in its application to become a state. Erroneously, Congress accepted the language provided by Ohio when statehood was granted in 1803. Two surveys, separated by 16 years, were done under the boundary language in the two Congressional Acts, and of course different results were obtained. The differing state lines resulted in a 468 square mile strip of land that was hotly disputed for 30 years and culminated in the 1835 Michigan-Ohio War, often referred to as the Toledo War.

To include the thriving Toledo community in the new state, when they submitted their petition for statehood, the Ohio Constitutional Convention changed the language of the survey benchmarks of the northern Ohio state line from the Congressional Act that originally created the Michigan Territory. Toledoites knew they lived in the Michigan Territory, but they liked the idea and the advantages of living in a state instead of a territory, so they went along with Ohio's deceit. Fifteen years after Ohio purloined part of Michigan, fiery 22-year-old Territorial Governor, Stevens Mason, became proactive about reclaiming the lost land. Only seven-years-old when Ohio stole Toledo, Mason quietly went about reclaiming the lost city. He started by developing roads within the disputed strip of land and then taxing the citizens who lived in "The Strip" as if they were Michiganders. The clever Mason had friends in high places, many of whom encouraged and fueled his high-spirited righteousness. After becoming familiar with the border dispute facts, former President John Quincy Adams backed Mason's claims and said, "Never in the course of my life have I known a controversy of which all the right is so clearly on one side and all the power so overwhelmingly on the other."

When the Ohio legislature set up county governments in The Strip, Mason responded by ramrodding the passage of the Pains and Penalties Act through Congress. The act made it a federal criminal offense for Ohioans to perform governmental actions in the disputed strip of land under penalty of up to a $1,000 fine and/or five years imprisonment at hard labor. Acting as commander-in-chief of the Michigan Territory, Mason appointed Brigadier-General Joseph Brown to head the territorial militia and ordered him to arrest Ohio law enforcement officers who were out of their jurisdiction. The Ohio governor formed a militia — and the War began.

On March 31, 1835, acting as commander-in-chief, the governor and 600 fully armed Ohio militiamen, set up camp on undisputed Ohio land ten miles southwest of Toledo. Governor Mason and General Brown occupied Toledo proper with 1,000 men. In a desperate attempt to prevent an armed battle, President Andrew Jackson asked his Attorney General for an emergency determination of the boundary. Jackson believed that because Ohio was a state with 19 influential Congressional votes and Michigan a territory with only Mason's single non-voting representation, the opinion would grant The Strip to Ohio. His hopes were dashed — he was told that the land belonged to Michigan.

Jackson held off the conflict between militias by dispatching U.S. Army Captain Andrew Talcott to protect Second Lieutenant Robert E. Lee's survey party while they again determined the boundary. All went well until an April Sabbath Day morning. Unhappy with where Lee's surveyors were laying the boundary, General Brown attacked the survey party with 50 militiamen who fired musket shots over the surveyors' heads. Lee's men ducked for cover, and the Ohio militia, who were on the south side of the recently surveyed boundary line, fired back into the air over the Michigan militias' heads. Both sides shouted insults at each other, and the Ohio militia retreated.

The battle stirred up the locals even more. The Ohio legislature approved a $300,000 budget ($7.5 million) to defend its borders, and Michigan countered by approving $315,000. Ohio had 10,000 men enlist to fight for Toledo's 1,200 residents. The *Michigan Territorial Press* dared the Ohio militiamen to enter The Strip by welcoming them "to hospitable graves." Through the early summer, both sides harassed each other with taunts, pushing and shoving matches, and arrests of trespassers by posses of militia.

In mid-July tensions overflowed and the conflict became bloody. A Michigan deputy sheriff arrested an Ohio militiaman, Major Benjamin Stickney, and his creatively named sons, One and Two, in Toledo. During the arrest, the major's second son, Two stabbed the deputy with a penknife and fled back to Ohio to avoid arrest. The deputy survived, but Old Hickory was beside himself — and unwisely removed the popular Mason as Territorial Governor. When the new governor arrived at the state capital, he was burned in effigy and pelted with rotten vegetables. Even though Congress had not authorized them to do so, in October Michigan voters passed a state constitution, and at the same time elected the now 23-year-old Mason state governor — the youngest governor in U.S. history.

Over the winter, passions cooled, and in the spring Jackson offered a compromise. On June 15, 1836 he signed a bill that granted statehood to Michigan on the condition that The Strip was ceded to Ohio. As a deal sweetener, Jackson also included most of the "Upper Peninsula" of the Michigan Territory, land that had originally been planned for Wisconsin — about 12,000 square miles of timber, iron ore, ski trails, and vacation home sites — in exchange for 468 square miles of prairie and Toledo. A special convention of Michiganders rejected the offer. Only because Michigan ran out of money to maintain their militia and because they were not going to receive a surplus distribution from the U.S. Treasury, it's not "Toledo, Michigan" today. On December 14, 1836 Michigan folded and took the Upper Peninsula and the money, and the next month the Wolverine State was admitted to the Union.

Freed from the perils of the Toledo War and surveying the meaningless state line, Robert E. Lee was promoted to First Lieutenant and transferred to St. Louis to supervise engineering work on the Upper Mississippi. In the summer of 1837, Lee picked up where Napoleon Buford left off eight years earlier. He surveyed and drew reconstruction plans for the Des Moines and Rock Island Rapids, and with engineering precision that his West Point instructors would be proud of, Lee's plans called for creating a channel 100 feet wide and 4 feet deep to be dredged and cut through the Rock Island Rapids. He estimated the cost to be $154,658 ($35,149,550). Lee was promoted to captain.

After the Sauk were driven from their land in the early 1830s, settlers staked out scattered farms and supported meager livelihoods by hunting and fishing along the bluffs on the shale riverbank where the Mississippi bent south before forming marshy backwaters at the confluence with the Rock River. Later, the riverbank became choice property for mills, factories, and warehouses, especially sawmills and lumber storage yards, and became Rock Island's first industrial area. Settlers' cabins and small vegetable farms and orchards to supply the growing town spread south along Camden Road (9th Street). The year before Lee surveyed the Rock Island Rapids, at the south end of Camden Road a town named "Rock Island City" was laid out and surveyed. Existing only on paper, the proposed community encompassed 608 acres of land located on the Rock River. The property, which was several times larger than Stephenson, extended north from the river in a nine-block-wide swath for 18 blocks. The charred remains of Saukenuk village were within the city's boundaries and became a marketing feature for the bold real estate venture.

Levi Turner, a New York lawyer, was the primary agent for the sale of parcels on land purchased from George Davenport. The development plan was visionary, and Davenport retained one quarter of Rock Island City for himself. The ephemeral city was designed to front the Rock River. A Rock River to Mississippi canal was designed to allow boats to bypass the treacherous stretch of rapids from Rock Island to Port Byron.

The canal was to be dug from the landing at Vandruff Island at the foot of the Rock River up to Campbell's Island at the head of the rapids. The well-conceived canal would allow boats to unload and receive cargo at the Rock Island City docks on the Rock River, and then to proceed up the canal through a series of locks, allowing safe access to the Upper Mississippi.

One of Turner's eight investors was statesman, Daniel Webster, a conservative, New England banker, lawyer, and politician. The famous Webster was called the "wisest man of his age and the worst businessman of all ages." Using other people's money, one of America's most highly acclaimed lawyers thought he bought all of Rock Island City. Webster was actually deeded 90 acres, for which he paid Davenport $666 ($18,000) an acre — about ten times their actual value.

The future Secretary of State and presidential candidate was then considered to be a sound economist and was the chairman of the Senate Finance Committee; however, Webster's own finances were so convoluted that his biographers were unable to track his dealings with either banks or individuals. Showing how a slick-talking attorney can convince almost anyone of anything, Webster recklessly borrowed, leveraged, and bartered his way to wealth. As counsel to the Bank of the United States, he had easy access to powerful men and their money. Using his banking connections, Webster borrowed $93,361.31 (approximately $2,400,000) against loans he had made, of which $60,000 went to Davenport for Webster's interest in Rock Island City. But Rock Island City development abruptly ceased when the frontier land bubble burst with the Panic of 1837. Soon, 20 years of litigation over Rock Island City's land ownership and its liabilities began.

The Illinois legislature had helped to facilitate the development plan of Rock Island City by committing to finance the Mississippi-Rock River Canal. But the last ray of hope of realizing Turner's vision faded in 1839 when the State of Illinois halted all public improvements after completing but a quarter-mile of the canal. If the proposed canal had been built and a similar canal built between Nauvoo and Hamilton, Illinois, the Mississippi River might today be a clear, fast running current that floods less often, and supports river transport, recreation, and the teeming natural wildlife that once lived in its waters and along its banks. When Rock Island City failed, Stephenson was a thriving frontier town of 600 residents and living in "175 neatly built houses." There were three doctors, and disturbingly, four lawyers — one for each tavern.

In order to satisfy other debts and a decade after buying land he never saw, Webster sold his interest in Rock Island City for $20,000 — a third of what he had paid for the property. A year later, demonstrating that he was a much better lawyer than realtor, as a U.S. Senator Webster introduced an amendment to the Mexican Cession

Treaty that would have excluded the acquisition of California and New Mexico in the treaty ending the Mexican-American War. Webster cited the financial liability and added governance responsibility as reasons not to acquire the western lands. Fortunately, his reputation as a savvy deal maker preceded him.

The year after Rock Island City went into foreclosure, Silas Reed decided to locate his homeopathic practice in Stephenson instead of Chicago, because at the time "Chicago was a swamp with only one brick building." (Five years earlier, the Town of Chicago had been organized with a population of approximately 200, about the same size as Stephenson). Setting up his practice and living on Bachelor's Row, which was located on Illinois (2nd) Avenue, Reed wrote a continuous stream of letters to East Coast bankers and capitalists extolling Stephenson and promoting its development potential. In 1840 Reed wrote a letter to the editor of the *Rock Island Argus* saying:

> Stephenson ought, by the way, be called "Rock Island City." I cannot for the life of me conceive what possible objection the proprietors of that name, on the Rock River side, of some five or six houses, can have to Stephenson's assuming that name.
>
> The time will come when this city will extend from river to river; then Rock Island City on Rock River will be a suburb. The responsibility rests upon us and demands words of truth and soberness. The time will come when the government will establish a national armory and arsenal on Rock Island and when a railroad will reach the Mississippi first here. To confine the name "Rock Island City" to so inconsiderable a place as that on the Rock River side seems inappropriate and unwise, against the fitness of things and against the interest of all. Stephenson, the future Lyons of the west, deserves the appropriate and dignified name of "Rock Island City."

Because the prophetic Reed didn't like the sound of the name "Stephenson" and had no familiarity with the man, and because his Eastern friends were more familiar with Rock Island, the site of Fort Armstrong, the proposed name change became an active cause with him, and he instigated public support for the change. He received overwhelming backing. On his way to Washington to see William Henry Harrison inaugurated, he stopped by Springfield to petition the legislature to change the name. On February 27, 1841 they did. President Harrison appointed Reed surveyor general of Illinois and Missouri. Although he is said to have once passed through Rock Island on the Rock Island Line without bothering to get off, he never again set foot on the city he named. Reed is believed to have died in Boston.

William Henry Harrison had parlayed his reputation as a crafty land negotiator and a tough Indian fighter into a long political career. After leading the U.S. Army to victory in the Northeast and killing Tecumseh during the War of 1812, Harrison slid into the six months remaining in the term of a deceased U.S. Representative from Ohio. He later won a Senate seat, and running as the Northern Whig — the only time a political party nominated two candidates — Harrison was defeated for the presidency in 1836. But he ran again in 1840 with vice presidential candidate John Tyler. They rode the snappy political slogan of *Tippecanoe and Tyler Too* and the enduringly campy campaign song *Tip and Ty* to a landslide victory. Until 68-year-old Ronald "The Gipper" Reagan, Harrison was the oldest president. He was a vain man, and to demonstrate his robustness and common-man approach, on a cold and rainy March day he took the oath of office and delivered his inaugural speech, which lasted more than two hours, while wearing neither a hat nor coat. Contracting pneumonia, Harrison died 31 days later — a record for the shortest presidency that may forever go unbroken.

Having no money and serious deflation issues after the Panic of 1837, Congress had set aside all public works until times improved. Fifteen years later, they had the money, and the project to reengineer the Mississippi was restarted when Congress allocated $100,000 to begin work on the Rock Island Rapids. Although it was unfortunate the project was restarted, the delay proved to be financially prudent. The nation had experienced 20 percent deflation during the depression that followed the financial panic, and Robert E. Lee's estimated cost to improve the rapids had decreased to $123,023.

In 1837, the same summer that Lee was surveying the Rock Island Rapids and Michiganders were celebrating their first summer of statehood, David Sears built a 600-foot stone and wooden dam and bridge from Rock Island across Sylvan Slough onto Illinois land that he purchased from Antoine LeClaire. Jack-of-all-trades John Spencer and two others assisted Sears. The dam and bridge connected Sylvan Island to a point just west of the present Rock Island city limits and gave access from the east end of the island to the mainland and provided waterpower for Sears' mills where he carded wool and ground corn and wheat. Significantly, he also built a sawmill, which initiated a seventy-year period where Rock Island was America's "lumber capital." On Rock Island, where the mills were located, a community of factories and houses sprang up, including the Dimock and Gould Tub and Pail factory, Atkinson's Sash and Blind factory, a bed factory, and a shingle shop. The small prosperous community started by Sears, which was about two miles upriver from Fort Armstrong, was called "Rock Island Village." Soon, a dingy cluster of small factories and cabins for Sears' workers sprang up along the shoreline across from Rock Island Village. They, too, wanted a piece of the fine name, and in 1843 "Rock Island Mills" was platted.

The Rock Island gentry had had enough, and they put pressure on the scruffy clump of buildings that comprised Rock Island Mills to change the name of their sooty factory settlement. The workers reluctantly agreed, and in what must have been a clever deceit, an erudite Rock Island surveyor, P.H. Ogilvie, suggested the French name "Moulin," meaning "mill" and "Hesperia," the Greek goddess of the evening star. The uneducated laborers, who couldn't make it in Rock Island, liked the fancy French name and bit on the suggestion. Unfortunately, Ogilvie didn't tell them how to pronounce "Moulin," and the town's residents called their scatter "Moline." Except for a tiny farm town in southeast Kansas that was founded by a man from Moline, no other U.S. municipality carries the same name.

In 1848 Moline was incorporated, and the same year John Deere, the inventor of the self-scouring steel plow, relocated his company there. At the time, there were only a few hundred residents, most of whom worked for Sears in his mills. As Deere established and expanded his plow factory, Moline also grew. Exploiting cheap immigrant labor, by 1857 Deere was turning out 1,000 farm implements a month — then the 1858 recession nearly wiped him out. He sold his interests to his son Charles and his son-in-law Christopher Weber, and although he served as president until his death, after the sale, he was not actively involved in the company's management. Just as Sears was the first to strategically position Rock Island as the home of the nation's lumber industry, John Deere one-upped him by positioning the Tri-City Area as the "farm implement capital of the world."

The year before Moline was incorporated, 65-year-old James Brackett, moved his family to Rock Island. Brackett was a Dartmouth classmate of Daniel Webster and an attorney for the failed Rock Island City development. Brackett's move from Cherry Valley, New York, was apparently precipitated by the necessity to unravel the Rock Island City property claims and to protect his personal interests. Brackett had five grown boys, two who were also lawyers and all who lived at various times in Rock Island and contributed to the city's progress. Brackett's oldest son, John Ely, was a West Point graduate who had a distinguished military career and rose to the rank of major general — he is buried in Rock Island's Chippiannock Cemetery. His second son, Joseph Warren, was an attorney and moved to Rock Island with his father to establish a law office together. Except for the years Joseph served in the 9th Illinois Cavalry during the Civil War, he maintained the family law practice in Rock Island until his death in 1894. James W., the third son, was a surgeon at the Confederate Prison on Arsenal Island during the Civil War. After the war he moved to Rochester, Indiana, where he practiced medicine. He retired to Rock Island and is also buried in Chippiannock Cemetery. Son number four, William, was a Harvard College and Law School graduate, and became a partner in the Brackett's Rock Island law office until 1852, when he moved to Chicago.

After mustering out of the Army at the end of the Mexican-American War, Albert Gallatin Brackett, the youngest of the five brothers, joined his family in Rock Island. In 1851 he became editor of the *Rock Island Advertiser*. While running the newspaper, Albert became the region's first historian. He assembled and published the first in-depth accounts of Black Hawk and the times in which he lived and the history of Fort Armstrong. When the Civil War broke out, he reenlisted and was made a Colonel in the 9th Illinois Cavalry. After the war he remained in the Army as a Colonel in the 3rd Cavalry, and he continued to write while he fought the Great Plains Indians for the next 13 years. He published two books about his army experiences, *General Lane's Brigade in Central Mexico* and the *History of the United States Cavalry*.

In 1853, six years after James Brackett moved to Rock Island to check on his real estate investments, the region was anxiously awaiting the arrival of the Rock Island and Chicago Railroad. John Locke Scripps, the publisher of the *Chicago Democratic Press*, which later merged with the *Chicago Tribune*, wrote a series of 12 articles about the area. One article gave Scripps' impression of the ill-fated Rock Island City property that brought the Bracketts to Rock Island and Milan, which was then called Camden Mills. After extolling the beautiful scenery along Camden Road (9th Street), he wrote:

> From this highland [the plateau above 12th Street that is now part of the Watch Hill neighborhood] may be seen the few straggling houses which mark the site of the town of Rock Island City. It lies upon the bank of Rock River, near the foot of the rapids, around which the state government in a wild scheme of improvement undertook to build a canal.
>
> Here existed one of the most magnificent of all the paper cities of that era. Some half dozen crazy tenements and the bitter remembrance of money squandered for "water and corner lots" are now its sole remaining monuments
>
> What the majority of the people living there do for a livelihood I am at a loss to conceive. A few of them, however, make their vocations known to passersby, as I noticed scrawled on the broad side of one of the houses — "Pork BarLes and MeAt TuBs' and on another "Cakes, Beer, and Cicars."

From 1850 to 1855, Rock Island was a booming frontier town and a favored Mississippi River crossing point. Thousands of westward bound migrants stayed to help build the city that, next to St. Louis, was the busiest congregation point for wagon trains headed west and for Mississippi riverboat traffic. In 1855, *The Rock Islander* said about those ferried across the river to start their westward journeys:

> Hundreds of muslin-covered wagons, bearing wives and children and household goods, and driven by stalwart men, seeking a new home in the mighty west, cross the Mississippi at this point weekly. It is a tide, which knows no ebb, but still keeps flowing, ever flowing, onward toward the rich prairies of Nebraska and the setting sun.

Throughout the 1850's, ferries were busy day and night hauling emigrants across the Mississippi River, and the Rock Island to Iowa ferry was the busiest on the river. *The Rock Island News* wrote:

> The Davenport levee presents an unusually stirring appearance to an eyewitness on the Rock Island shore. We counted no less than 25 white-

tented wagons ranged round near the ferry, while some 20 farm wagons stood here and there among a sea of reposing cattle. All the way up Brady Street was a row of these wheeled tents, while some half-dozen were visible on the steamer *Davenport,* just then crossing the river.

While Rock Island was riding out the depression that followed the 1837 Panic, the rest of the nation was not faring as well. Martin "The Red Fox" Van Buren, a staunch and influential supporter of Andrew Jackson had been rewarded with the vice presidency during Jackson's second term. Van Buren was a feisty, diminutive red-haired New Yorker, and piggybacking on Jackson's popularity and using his East Coast connections, he was elected to the Presidency in 1836. But Van Buren was doomed to unpopularity and a single term by the depression that followed the 1837 Panic and the resulting collapse of an overextended economy. Land speculation and public debt caused uncontrollable inflation that led to the Panic of 1837, during which 343 of the nation's 850 banks closed. In a single week beginning on April Fools' Day, there were more than 100 major business failures in New York City alone. Five foreign money and exchange brokers, 30 dry-goods jobbers, 16 commission houses, 28 real-estate speculators, eight stockbrokers, and many other New York City enterprises failed. A five-year depression ensued.

Van Buren's most lasting contribution to American culture was the popularization of the acronym "OK." One of the many Van Buren nicknames used by his supporters was "Old Kinderhook" — the positive reference to the initials of his New York birthplace became a lasting part of the American lexicon, but positive references to Van Buren were hard to find after his presidential term. However, after sitting out two elections, the fiery New Yorker hoped that sentiments had calmed — that was not the case. Running as a third-party candidate in 1848, Van Buren received only ten percent of the popular vote. In all the Southern states, the abolitionist Northerner received only nine popular votes, and all were from Virginia. His supporters raised a cry of voter fraud. "Yes, fraud," said a Virginian, "and we are still looking for the son-of-a-bitch who voted nine times."

While the dream of Rock Island City evaporated, along with the loss of fortunes in the depression, a self-sufficient cluster of frontier farms and orchards on rich Illinois plains, enterprising merchants, and the country's western-most manufacturing center prospered on the banks of the Mississippi around Stephenson. The name change initiated by Silas Reed brought the concentration of pioneer residents and industry together in a single community. The consolidation of the diverse new city, named "Rock Island," included Stephenson, Farnhamsburg, and three other settlements. Because ownership interests were being litigated, the new city did not include Rock Island City.

In 1840, less than a year before Stephenson and Farnhamsburg were renamed Rock Island, rigidly objective newspaper publisher, Henry C. McGrew, wrote of the near-mystical qualities of the men of Stephenson (a trait Rock Island men retain to this day) and of their characteristics relative to those of their neighboring towns:

> The inhabitants of the town and its environs could not be surpassed, if equaled, by any city in the west, for men of intelligence — courteous and kind in everything. Our judiciary consisted of Judge Stone, who was very soon superseded by Judge Brown; our bar consisted of Joseph Knox, Joseph B. Wells, J. Wilson Drury, and H. G. Reynolds; the clerk of the court was an old bachelor, Joseph Conway, brother of Miles Conway, who, with a Mr. Cooper, composed the magistracy of the village; while our medical department was represented by Doctor Gregg alone, a man eminent in his profession.
>
> There were three stores in the place, kept by John Meller, Lemuel Andrews and a Mr. Kauffman. Two more came afterwards, viz: Mr. Bond and Mr. Moore. There was one tinning establishment, Lee & Chamberlin's; one saddler shop, J. M. Frizzell's; one cabinet maker's and one gunsmith's shop; three taverns, Mr. Bently's on the river bank; Buffum's, back of the Court House Square; and the Rock Island House on Main Street, kept by VanCourt & Brothers. This was the leading hotel at that day. There was one restaurant, and one other, called a saloon for the want of a more appropriate name. One minister of the gospel (Presbyterian), Reverent Mr. Stewart, preached in a little schoolhouse back of Doctor Gregg's residence on Main Street — our only church, lyceum, and town hall. The Powers family, Guernsey's and old Mr. Vandruff, who lived on the island in Rock River, and kept a ferry at the Rapids, and something for the inner man, were among the first settlers of Rock Island.
>
> There were but few places of any note above Quincy, Illinois. Where Keokuk now stands there was a trading post kept by a half-breed, who sold liquor to the Sac and Fox Indians, and engaged in towing barges over the rapids with horses, to Fort Montrose. At the east side of the Mississippi, at the head of the rapids, at a place then called Commerce, was situated a stone warehouse, where passing steamers discharged freight for the surrounding country.
>
> The Mormons had a short time previously been driven out of Missouri, and they encamped on the west bank of the river, awaiting transportation to the Illinois side to build the City of Nauvoo, and their wagons and equipages presented the appearance of an army encamped. The town of Burlington, Iowa, had but few houses. Bloomington, now Muscatine, contained about six houses, and had the appearance of being a very sickly place, if I could judge from the looks of the citizens who came aboard the steamer.

One of Rock Island's remarkable citizens in 1840 was Cadwallader Colden Washburn. One of seven brothers, as a 21-year-old in 1839, C.C. — as he had the good sense to call himself — was employed by the geological survey and relocated from Maine to Rock Island. In his first year as a Rock Islander, he ran for county surveyor against P.H. Ogilvie, the man who had given Moline its name. In an early demonstration of "every vote counts," Washburn won by a single vote. Ogilvie, a hardheaded Scotsman, contested the election. In an attempt by both sides to demonstrate illegal votes by the opposition, the election was reduced to a hopeless muddle. The candidates agreed to draw lots for the position, and Washburn won again.

The popular and lucky 21-year-old Washburn became a busy man. During the three years he lived in Rock Island, he also clerked in a store, taught at the log schoolhouse, and studied law. In 1842, after passing the bar, C.C. moved to Wisconsin where he forged a career in politics and business. His political career peaked in 1872 when he became governor of Wisconsin. Two years older than C.C., his brother Elihu Washburne (the only brother to spell the family name with a concluding "e") was the more accomplished politician. Apparently on his younger brother's advice, Elihu bought land in Rock Island County but was a resident of Galena. He was a career politician who represented most of northern Illinois, including Rock Island County, in the U.S. House of Representatives from 1853 until 1869, when he resigned to become U.S. Grant's Secretary of State. Twelve days after being confirmed, he resigned that position (the shortest term ever for a U.S. Secretary of State) to become Ambassador to Paris.

Oldest brother, Israel Washington, Jr., stayed at home in Maine where he served five terms in the U.S. House of Representatives and then a term as Maine's governor. Seventeen years younger than Israel, William was the youngest of the notable brothers. Following C.C. to Minneapolis after he retired from Wisconsin politics, William went to work for C.C.'s flour milling company. He later branched out into lumber and railroading and served as the president of the Soo Line Railroad for eight years. Amassing a large fortune, William founded his own flour milling company, the Pillsbury Company, which 150 years later was acquired by C.C.'s company, General Mills. William was a one-term U.S. Senator from Minnesota. The brothers Israel, Elihu, C.C., and William became the only set of four brothers to be U.S. Congressmen while representing different states. Three were members of the House of Representatives at the same time — another record — and together they served 42 years in Congress.

Chapter 9

First Amendment Rights

In God We Trust ~ United States motto that replaced *E Pluribus Unum* (Out of many, one) in 1956

IN 1840 as Rock Island's first newspaperman Henry C. McGrew wrote, even the much-persecuted and well-traveled Church of Jesus Christ of Latter-day Saints (LDS, Saints, or Mormons) could hardly wait to get out of Iowa and relocate in Illinois. Twenty years earlier in a small grove of trees near Palmyra, New York, 14-year-old Joseph Smith, Jr. "saw two Personages, whose brightness and glory defy all description, standing above me in the air. One of them spake unto me, calling me by name and said, pointing to the other 'this is My Beloved Son. Hear Him!" Then a few years later, an angel named "Moroni" appeared to the handsome young man and told him the location of a book of golden pages inscribed with teachings and a religious history of ancient Americans. Smith described the book: "Each plate was six inches wide and eight inches long, and not quite so thick as common tin. They were filled with engravings, in Egyptian characters and bound together in a volume as the leaves of a book, with three rings running through the whole. The volume was something near six inches in thickness, a part of which was sealed."

Through his teens, Smith helped support his family's meager farm income by "treasure-digging," the art of finding lost valuables and precious metals. In 1826 he was tried for pretending to find lost treasure, and the following year he eloped with Emma Hale, the first of his 33 wives documented by Mormon historian, Todd Compton. Eleven of Smith's wives were teenagers when they married and the youngest were two 14-years olds. Even though Emma legally attested to the marriage of Smith to his second wife, Fanny Alger, Emma denied to her deathbed that Smith had plural wives. She bore Smith eleven children. Because Smith also denied that he had plural marriages, the number of children he fathered is unknown; however, several of his non-wives told their children that Smith was their father.

Before he eloped with Emma Hale, Smith began using a "seer stone" to translate the golden book. The stone Smith possessed was a "chocolate-colored, somewhat egg-shaped stone that he found while digging a well in company with his brother Hyrum." By using this stone, "Joseph was able to translate the characters engraved on the plates." Eight years later he finished the translation, which was delayed when Moroni took back the golden pages after investors in the translation demanded to see the golden book. Fortunately, Moroni later returned the book to Smith so that he could finish his assignment from God. The Book of Mormon was completed in March of 1830, when Smith said that Moroni took back the plates a final time. The next month declaring himself a prophet, the same as Jesus, Smith organized The Church of Christ — the first lasting American-founded religion.

Smith gathered a flock of believers, but also met with strong opposition from skeptics who remembered his days as a treasure-digger. Soon after forming his church, Smith performed an exorcism and was arrested and tried as a "disorderly person." His acquittal along with his assertion that God had told him that "all churches are false" caused some bad feelings among locals of other faiths, and Smith was forced to flee New York. Thus began his odyssey from New York to the Illinois banks of the Mississippi River, similar to the route of the Sauk nation generations earlier.

In January 1831, telling his congregation that Kirtland, Ohio was the eastern boundary of the New Jerusalem, Smith moved his church there. Along the way, he attracted hundreds of converts, who came to be called "Latter-day Saints." Accompanying a group of the newly converted to Jackson County, Missouri to establish a holy city of "Zion," he expanded the church — and animosities. Incensed by the Saints' proselytized political positions, social views, and religious teachings, Smith was beaten unconscious and tarred and feathered when he stopped to preach on a journey from Ohio to Missouri. The discontent fomented and in 1833 mobs of Missouri settlers began to attack the Mormons. The Missouri state militia quelled the attacks and then confiscated the Mormon's land to pay for the expense of protecting them.

Many of the foreclosed returned to Kirtland, others left the church or dispersed to safer havens in Iowa and western Illinois, and some moved farther west beyond the frontier, to establish a Mormon community in northwest Missouri called Far West — which at the time it was indeed. Except for internal disputes among church leaders that centered on the theological issues of exclusive polygamy rights for the church's prophet, affairs remained relatively stable in Kirtland until 1837 when Smith established a bank to pay the Mormon community's debts. The bank failed a month after opening, and Smith was charged with bank fraud. To avoid prosecution, Smith fled to Far West.

In 1839, the steady influx of Mormons into northwest Missouri again stirred up the locals. After a Mormon leader declared in a well-publicized 4th of July speech that Mormons would establish their "religion by the sword" and that Smith would be "a second Mohammed," the locals burned Mormon barns. In retaliation, the Mormons unwisely attacked the state militia. Governor Lilburn Boggs issued an "extermination order" that essentially gave Latter-day Saints their choice of leaving the state or dying. Surrendering to the militia, Smith and five other Mormon leaders were jailed. Many Mormons fled to Iowa, and it this group whose "wagons and equipages presented the appearance of an army encamped" on the Iowa shoreline that Henry C. McGrew described in his tribute to the men of Rock Island.

North of the Mormon encampment, pioneer farmers started to buy Antoine LeClaire's inexpensive, rich farmland surrounding Davenport. In the summer of 1840, the same year Davenport was incorporated, Isaac Cody, a Quaker who had been widowed twice, moved to the new municipality with a daughter by his first marriage and with his new wife, Mary Ann Laycock. Cody was a successful Indian trader, and the next year he bought a house in the town of LeClaire and filed a claim on a site two miles west of town where he built a large four-room log cabin. The Codys had six children, and their third was a boy named William Frederick. The family called the baby, Will, but he would later become more grandly known by the rest of the nation as Buffalo Bill.

The same year the Codys moved to Iowa, one hundred miles downriver at the head of the Des Moines Rapids, a rising young Mormon convert, Brigham Young, led a large number of Mormons, who had been driven from the Missouri Territory, to the tiny ramshackle town of Commerce on the Illinois side of the Mississippi. Sixteen years earlier the land where Commerce stood was called Quashquema, after the chief of the Sauk village located there. Quashquema had 500 lodges and was second only to Saukenuk in size and importance to the Sauk nation. To clear the way for white settlement, in 1823 the U.S. Government sold the Indian village to Captain James White. The displaced Sauk moved across the Mississippi to the head of the rapids where they moved in with another Sauk tribe.

Four months after his imprisonment in Missouri, Joseph Smith bribed a sheriff, who was transferring him to a different jail, and escaped to rejoin his flock in Commerce. He soon purchased Commerce and surrounding land. During seven weeks of instruction from an Oberlin College professor hired to teach Hebrew to 40 Mormon "scholars," the class was told that "nauvoo" meant "beautiful site" in Hebrew, and Smith renamed Commerce to Nauvoo. Reassuming control of his church, Smith sent Brigham Young, who was sick with malaria, and several other young Mormon men on missions to England, where they successfully converted poor British factory workers and enticed them to come to America with descriptions of abundant opportunity, plentiful food, land ownership, and a place in heaven.

The impoverished British workers were easily convinced. At their expense, the Industrial Revolution had created a wealthy social class of merchants and industrialists in England and France that rivaled that of the nobility and country gentry. Starting in Great Britain, in the later part of the 18th century Central Europe's agrarian, manual labor, and draft-animal-based economy had slowly transitioned to urban, machine-based manufacturing. The mechanization of the textile industry, improvement of steel-making methods, and the increased use of coal for heat and power created a demand for factory workers and miners. Industrial specialization drove the expansion of trade and correspondingly created a need for road improvements, canals, and railways. The opportunity for economic independence drove thousands of peasants living in serfdom from tenanted farms and villages to the cities, and soon an over-supply of unskilled labor resulted in the bottom tier of the social classes experiencing oppressive living conditions.

Chronic hunger and malnutrition were the norm, and in England and France disease and malnutrition dropped life expectancies to about 35 years. By the mid-18th century, Western European workers dreamed of escaping to America, the "land of opportunity." After the Midwest Indian wars, frontier farmland and timber for building materials were inexpensive or for the taking. Compared to Europe, opportunity was bountiful, and, for everyone except Native Americans who were dying from plagues of European diseases, life expectancies were ten to 15 years greater in America. When Mormon missionaries told London slum dwellers of the magnificent life that awaited them in the New World, hoards of poor British workers fought for an opportunity to convert to Mormonism and grab their ticket to New Jerusalem.

In Nauvoo, Joseph Smith began work on a magnificent temple (the original was destroyed by arson and a faithful reproduction was dedicated in 2002) on the bluffs above the low, swampy woodland, and he went about restructuring and updating the church's doctrines and creating a grand plan to establish theocratic rule over the earth. While publicly and repeatedly denying that he advocated or practiced polygamy, Smith kept "The Doctrine of Plurality of Wives" secret, revealing it only to potential wives and a few Mormon leaders. His secret marriage to his third wife in April 1841 opened a marital floodgate, and over the next 30 months, he averaged a marriage a month and the secret doctrine started getting out.

It didn't take long for things to unravel for Smith. Disillusioned by contradictory and ever-changing doctrine, within a year disharmony reigned in Nauvoo. More left the church than became Saints, and many were openly critical of Smith, characterizing him as a "fallen prophet." Undeterred, in 1843 Smith focused his attentions on political remedies and petitioned Congress to make Nauvoo an independent territory. He also announced his candidacy for the U.S. Presidency. Smith ran on a platform of redeeming slaves by using money raised by selling public lands; decreasing salaries of U.S.

Congressmen; closing prisons; annexing Texas, Oregon, and parts of Canada; securing international rights on the high seas; free trade; and re-establishing a national bank.

In March of the following year and in preparation for a future theocratic "Kingdom of God on earth," Smith gave authority to a secret, independent council to determine which national and state laws Mormons should obey. The Council of Fifty, which was given perpetual authority, was active for 40 years and was not officially terminated until the death of its last member more than a century later in 1945. The council's first act was to ordain Smith king of a "theodemocracy" designed by him — a position he would presumably retain if elected the 11th President of the United States.

Soon after Smith's ordination, William Law, a deeply devout and high-ranking Mormon, became upset that Smith continued to propose marriage to his wife after she repeatedly rebuked Smith's offers. Law spoke to others in Nauvoo about Smith's plural marriages, and when word got back to Smith that Law was opposing him, he stripped him of his position as a member of the LDS First Presidency, the church's highest ranking authority behind the Prophet. Because Smith had not followed proper procedures, Law appealed. Smith granted him a hearing — and then excommunicated him. Believing Smith was beyond redemption, Law formed a new church called The True Church of Jesus Christ of Latter-day Saints. Law published a newsletter, *The Nauvoo Expositor*, enumerating Smith's transgressions, and credibly exposing for the first time Smith's plural marriages. The Nauvoo City Council immediately destroyed Law's printing press. Finally finding a reason to arrest Smith, Illinois State authorities held Smith and his brother Hyrum in the Carthage jail on charges related to the destruction of the press and later on charges of treason. Less than five months before the presidential election of 1844, a mob broke into the jail and assassinated the presidential candidate and his brother. Five men were arrested for the murders but were later acquitted. Killed at age 38, Joseph Smith became a martyr to his followers.

Left without a chain of succession after Joseph Smith's death, many sought to lead the LDS church. When Brigham Young made a pitch to the congregation on his own behalf, Church elders noted that he sounded like Joseph Smith, and this was a sign that God meant for him to lead the church. Young emulated Smith in many ways, not the least of which was his enthusiastic support for the Doctrine of Plurality of Wives for the LDS Prophet. Young had 55 wives, and 16 of them bore him 56 children — birth records and parentage of children of the other 39 wives are muddled. (Among Young's direct descendants are Susa Young Gates, a notable women's rights advocate during the early 1900's, and Steve Young, a San Francisco 49er Hall of Fame quarterback.)

Holding the church together with a promise of better things to come, in 1845 Young shunned the idea of seeking safe refuge on the Iowa frontier and set his sights on land west of the Rockies that was outside U.S. borders and in Mexican Territory. The following summer, Young led 2,500 faithful from Nauvoo to a site on government-controlled Oto and Omaha tribal lands that were just north of present day Omaha, Nebraska. The Mormons obtained the land by providing a battalion of men to fight in the Mexican-American war that had broken out in the wake of the annexation of Texas. Young intended the site to be a jumping off point for a Mormon exodus to the Far West, and during the first summer, 800 log cabins and sod huts were built. The camp was called Winter Quarters.

The 500 volunteers who formed the Mormon Battalion served one year from July 1846 to the following June. Regular army officers commanded the battalion, but the troops and company commanders were exclusively LDS, and the unit was the only religiously based brigade in U.S. military history. While Winfield Scott led 7,000 others on a grueling march through Mexico, the Mormon Battalion marched from Winter Quarters to San Diego. Mormon historians point out that the Battalion was instrumental in securing southern California for the United States and played a significant role in establishing a southern wagon trail to California. After reaching San Diego, many of the Mormon Battalion did not return to Winter Quarters.

In the spring of 1847 with the Great Basin as his intended destination, Young led an advance party of 73 wagons, 143 men, three women, two children, and assorted livestock west from Winter Quarters. It took six weeks to cross the present state of Nebraska. Upon arriving at Fort Laramie, the wagon train was joined by a group of the Mormon Battalion, who had fallen ill before the prior year's march to California and was forced to spend the winter in Pueblo, Colorado. A party of Mormons from Mississippi also joined them, and the merged groups followed the well-traveled Oregon Trail to Fort Bridger. A careful and methodical planner, Young met with Jim Bridger, the famed mountain man, at the fort named after him. They discussed routes to the Salt Lake Valley and settlement options in the valleys of the Great Basin, which satisfied Young's primary requirement that they settle outside U.S. jurisdiction. Since Young did not intend to cross the Salt Flats or the seven Nevada Mountain ranges or the 40-mile Desert, he chose the same route the Ill-fated Donner Party had taken the prior year. This route later became a western segment of the Lincoln Highway or U.S. 40, which later became Interstate 80.

The party split into three groups. The first group was a small scouting party that was sent ahead to map the best route for the primary group. Brigham Young was in the last party, a small group that suffered from mountain fever, a disease caused by wood ticks. Scouts first entered the Salt Lake Valley on July 21. Three days later, Young first saw the valley from a "sick wagon." He immediately declared, "This is the right place, drive on." The next month Young and a few members of the scouting party returned to the eastern settlements to report their find. By the end of the year, 2,000 Mormons had completed the journey to the Salt Lake Valley. And within four years, 12,000 Saints had traveled the Mormon Trail to the Utah Territory. Young built two large Salt Lake City mansions for his wives, the Lion House and the Beehive House. There "each wife [had] an establishment of her own, consisting of parlor, bedroom, and a front door, the key of which she [kept] in her pocket."

Young was able to support his families through tithing to the church. He wrote, "We are not our own, we are bought with a price, we are the Lord's; our time, our talents, our gold and silver, our wheat and fine flour, our wine and our oil, our cattle, and all there is on this earth that we have in our possession is the Lord's, and he requires one-tenth of this for the building up of his Kingdom. Whether we have much or little, one-tenth should be paid in for tithing." Young enthusiastically and efficiently organized the collection of the Lord's ten percent. Also to help pay additional personal expenses, Young granted divorces to unhappy plural wives and then required their husbands to pay him a $10 ($265) fee. In 1858 alone, Young issued 1,600 certificates of divorce to unhappy wives in polygamous marriages (grossing $425,000).

Called the "Mormon Moses" for rounding up the U.S. Mormons and trekking them off to the Utah Territory, Young is rightfully credited with making the Church of Jesus Christ of Latter-day Saints the institution it is today. When he assumed the presidency of the church in December 1847, Nauvoo's population had swollen to 12,000, rivaling the size of Chicago and was four times that of Rock Island. Today, Nauvoo's population hovers around 1,000. (In 2012 there were 13.8 million baptized Mormons of which approximately a third was active in the church and one who was the Republican candidate for U.S. President. And the Fundamentalist Church of Jesus Christ of Latter Day Saints, which in defiance of state and federal laws continues to practice polygamy and "marry" girls as young as 14, was estimated to have as many as 10,000 members.)

Other than his practice and support of polygamy, Young's most controversial theological stance was his position on interracial marriage. In response to a Mormon elder's question about whether interracial marriage was permissible, Young replied, "Shall I tell you the law of God in regard to the African race? If the white man who belongs to the chosen seed mixes his blood with the seed of Cain, the penalty, under the law of God, is death [of the spirit] on the spot. This will always be so." This was the official Mormon position on interracial marriage until 1978 — when apparently God changed his mind and told Spencer W. Kimble, the twelfth President and Prophet of the Mormon Church that it might be politically expedient to get with the times.

Seven years after Brigham Young relocated the center of Mormonism from Nauvoo to the Utah Territory, another religious sect moved to the frontier of Eastern Iowa. Almost a century earlier, Lutherans founded the Community of True Inspiration in Hesse, Germany. Similar to the Mormons, the Lutheran splinter group believed that God communicated through inspired individuals, as he had through the Prophets. Seventy years later, to avoid persecution by church leaders and German officials, two of those inspired individuals fled to America with 350 faithful followers.

Naming their community that had grown to 1,200, Ebenezer, the immigrant-farmers settled in upstate New York and set up communal farms formed around six self-contained villages of about 200 people each. Each village physically resembled every other similar-sized American village with two notable exceptions: there was only one church and the houses had no kitchens. All of the farmers' food was stored in communal barns, and what wasn't prepared and served in the communes' dining halls was taken to market in Buffalo, where tools and nails were purchased in order to build new community-owned homes and barns.

By 1854 the Buffalo area had boomed and land prices were inflated. Seeking to flee encroaching materialism and find more remote and less expensive farmland to practice their ascetic lifestyle, the Community of True Inspiration purchased 18,000 acres on the Iowa River that was formerly occupied by the Sauk and Meskwaki and sold by Keokuk to the U.S. Government. The six New York villages were sold, and the community moved to the frontier where they established six similar villages. Three years later, a seventh village, Homewood, was purchased because it had a station on the Rock Island Line. The seven communes incorporated under the name of "Amana Society." This community existed for over seventy years as a religious society operating without profit while providing free public services, schooling, and food and housing for its members who worked on the community farms, labored in the mills and shops, and ate in communal kitchens.

The church-centric Amana Society lived cooperatively and with humility and dignity. Their religious tradition was based on a blend of Lutheran and Old Testament Jewish beliefs and customs. The communal dining rooms, where groups of 30 to 60 ate, exemplified their goals. Each kitchen had a woman Kuechenbass (kitchen boss) who supervised the garden and the preparation and serving of the meals, which were eaten in contemplative silence beginning at 6:00 a.m., 11:30 a.m., and 6:30 p.m., when it was believed that if God had something to say to you, he would speak then. Everyone, including the children, worked and was paid in credits that could be redeemed at the Amana shops and stores. Women had eight jobs to choose from, ranging from laundress to Kuechenbass; men had 39 jobs ranging from machine shop laborer to doctor.

Then when civilization reached into Iowa's heartland during the 1920s, young people in the socially restrictive Amana Society became restless — they wanted to chat during meals, have more control over their material lives, dress and wear their hair as they wished, and play baseball after chores were done. In 1932 a combination of the discontent among the young people and fires that extensively damaged the woolen mill and destroyed the flour mill caused severe economic stress and precipitated what is still called "The Great Change." The community voted to retain the traditional church but to abandon communalism. A joint-stock company was formed and the hardworking, German-heritage Midwesterners went into business.

The most successful enterprise that emerged was Amana Refrigeration. Two years after The Great Change, a businessman in Iowa City designed the first beverage cooler, and a craftsman from the Middle Amana colony built out the design. In 1947 Amana manufactured the first upright home freezer, and two years later added a side-by-side refrigerator/freezer. In 1949 the company was sold to a group of investors that included its founding members. In 1954 the corporation began making air conditioners, and the same year it turned out the first commercial microwave ovens, which were marketed under the brand name, Radarange. In 1997 Maytag acquired the company, and it is now a part of the Whirlpool Corporation.

At the same time the Mormons were preparing to leave Kirtland, Ohio, for good, in October 1836 American and Mexican settlers in Texas declared their independence and fought a 6-month land war against Mexico. The war was won when, in the most farcical proof of "you snooze, you lose" military conduct, Sam Houston and 909 Texans snuck up on Santa Anna and his Mexican force of 1,360 while they were taking their afternoon siesta. The battle raged for 18 minutes, and when the smoke cleared, Houston's forces had killed 630 Mexicans and captured the other 730 including Santa Anna. The Texans lost 9 men and 30 were wounded, including Houston whose ankle was shattered by a bullet.

A month later, Santa Anna, Mexico's president and military leader, signed two treaties — one public and one secret — allowing his men to return to Mexico and promising not to come back. The independent Republic of Texas received diplomatic recognition from the United States, France, Belgium, the Netherlands, and the Republic of Yucatán, and Sam Houston was elected its first president. In spite of Santa Anna's treaties, Mexico maintained its claims on Texas, and when on December 29, 1845 Texas was admitted as the 28th state, war was certain. The following April, a 2,000-strong Mexican cavalry detachment attacked a 70-man U.S Cavalry unit north of the Rio Grande. Sixteen U.S. soldiers were killed, and the Mexican-American War was on.

In the months before the attack on the cavalry unit, on behalf of the U.S. Government, John C. Frémont and a group of rugged mountain men that included Kit Carson and "Broken Hand" Fitzpatrick took a leisurely ride through Mexican-held Northern California. Frémont and his men had spent the prior four years scouting and surveying Northern California for Frémont's father-in-law, ardent expansionist U.S Senator Thomas Benton. Benton led a Congressional group that strongly supported the concept of Manifest Destiny and viewed California as the ultimate land grab. The year before, the scouting party had become the first white men to view Lake Tahoe and to inhale the air that Mark Twain described as "the same the angels breathe." After telling the Mexican governor that he and his men were traveling in the Mexican Territory to buy supplies on their way to Oregon, Frémont instead detoured south through the Salinas Valley to the Pacific beach town of Santa Cruz. When confronted by Mexican authorities, he said he was looking for a seaside home for his mother. His report to Washington was favorable, and in November 1845 the United States offered to buy Mexican territory north of the Rio Grande for $25 million ($670 billion). Mexico didn't respond to the offer, but they should have taken it. Three years later, after suffering about 50,000 casualties, they received $18 million for the same property that now constitutes most of the states of California, Nevada, Utah, Colorado, Arizona, and New Mexico.

One man clearly understood the American expansionist mentality at the time. Although only 49-years-old, dark-horse Democratic presidential candidate, James "The Plodder" Polk, had pledged that if he won the 1844 election, he would only serve one term. Running on the single issue to annex Texas and to balance the annexation of the slave state with Northerners by acquiring all or part of the Oregon Territory, Polk won. He kept his promises — he annexed Texas and did not seek reelection. A descendent of John Knox, the Scottish religious reformer, Polk was a righteous man from South Carolina who, as a young teenager, moved with his family to the frontier of Tennessee. There, he became the exceptionally unusual Tennessee politician who didn't drink, chew, or gamble. Although he didn't drink liquor, he was familiar with the medicinal effects of alcohol. As a 17-year-old, he was operated on to remove painful urinary stones. Polk was awake during the operation with nothing but brandy for an anesthetic. The surgery was successful but may have left Polk sterile, as he didn't father any children.

When he moved into the White House, Polk stepped up his war on fun by banning dancing and card playing. Fellow Tennessee political opponent, Sam Houston, said that the only problem with Polk was that he drank too much water. Always thin and frail, three months after leaving office, Polk died of cholera at age 53, adding credence to the observation that living a healthy lifestyle doesn't always translate to a longer life. During his presidency, Polk also issued the first postage stamps, which came in sheets without perforations. And because he brought Texas into the Union, some from the Lone Star State have called him "the least known consequential president."

The Whig Party had vigorously opposed Polk who was a slave owner. However, freshman Whig U.S. Representative Abraham Lincoln was atypically ambivalent and illogical about annexing Texas, which was to be admitted to the Union as a slave state and where English and Spanish were spoken equally. Lincoln said of the issue:

> But I will argue farther. I perhaps ought to say that individually I never was much interested in the Texas question. I never could see much good to come of annexation; inasmuch, as they were already a free republican people on our own model; on the other hand, I never could very clearly see how the annexation would augment the evil of slavery. It always seemed to me that slaves would be taken there in about equal numbers, with or without annexation. And if more were taken because of annexation, still there would be just so many the fewer left, where they were taken from. It is possibly true, to some extent, that with annexation, some slaves may be sent to Texas and continued in slavery, that otherwise might have been liberated. To whatever extent this may be true, I think annexation an evil.

Many Texans and most Northerners were agreeable to Texas remaining independent. The Whigs considered the annexation to be imperialistic and compared it to England's posture towards the original colonies. However, Democrats and most in the South thought annexing the huge neighboring republic with Southern sensibilities was a fine idea. Mexico said Texas was still theirs, and they would fight to keep it. After Congress declared war on Mexico, Polk immediately sent U.S. Army forces there. Major General Winfield Scott led the troops that rolled south through the country and captured Mexico City. The victory coerced Mexico into history's largest forced real estate sale. The United States almost doubled its size by acquiring the territories that would later comprise most of the Western States. One of General Scott's officers was a Captain of Engineers, Robert E. Lee. Lee's duties were to position troops and field artillery, which proved to be a good learning experience for his later military combat commands. His fine logistical work earned him a distinguished service commendation, and during the march to Mexico City, Lee first met fellow West Point alum, Ulysses S. Grant, a quartermaster who was 15 years his junior.

Polk was succeeded as president by a newcomer to the Whig Party, Zachary "Old Rough and Ready" Taylor, a 40-year career military man, who despite his ignominious defeat by Black Hawk during the War of 1812 had risen to the rank of general. Taylor was an apolitical man who had never voted until he cast a vote for himself to be the nation's 12th President. Even though Taylor was a Louisiana slave owner, Abraham Lincoln backed his party's candidate against the Democratic nominee,

Lewis Cass, and the Free Soil candidate, Martin Van Buren, who was returning to politics eight years after serving one disastrous term as president. Cass, whose Army exploits had been exaggerated by his supporters, had served honorably but without distinction during the War of 1812, and after his nomination, Lincoln made a speech in Congress mocking Cass and his military service. Lincoln said, "By the way, Mr. Speaker, did you know I am a military hero? Yes sir, in the days of the Black Hawk War I fought, bled — and came away. General Cass' career reminds me of my own. Like him I saw the [battlefield] — very soon afterwards. ... If General Cass went in advance of me in picking whortleberries, I guess I surpassed him in charges on the wild onions. If he saw any live, fighting Indians, it was more than I did, but I had a good many bloody struggles — with mosquitoes. ... Mr. Speaker, if my friends should ever take me up as their candidate for the presidency, I protest they shall not make fun of me, as they have of General Cass, by attempting to write me into a military hero."

Taylor won, but not because of his popularity or because of Lincoln's speech, but because third-party candidate, Martin Van Buren, siphoned off votes from Cass. Taylor and Cass each won 15 states; however, Van Buren potentially cost Cass four states that went to Taylor. Taylor set two notable "lasts" while in office. He was the last president to own slaves while in office, and he was the last Whig to win a presidential election. Old Rough and Ready died suddenly and mysteriously of gastroenteritis, thought to have been brought on by the deadly combination of eating a bowl of cherries and drinking a glass of milk on a hot summer day. Millard Fillmore, who regrettably had no snappy nickname, succeeded Taylor, who was only 16 months into his term.

During his 32 months as president, Fillmore's strong defense of Hawaii, when Napoleon III tried to annex it, and of Cuba, when the British invaded it, were not enough to overcome the criticism he received from the majority of his party for opposing to keep slavery out of the territories. Fillmore's presidency unfortunately can be summarized by the story told of his shopping for a new presidential carriage. After spending the better part of a day looking at new carriages, an aide spotted a slightly used one that seemed to satisfy the president's demanding requirements. Fillmore agreed that it was handsome and well-made, but then plaintively asked, "How would it do, sir, for the President of the United States to ride around in a secondhand carriage?" The exasperated aide reassuringly replied, "But sir, Your Excellency is only a secondhand president."

The Whigs knew they had a loser and passed over Fillmore for their presidential candidate in 1852 in favor of the popular war hero, Winfield Scott, who had retired from the Army after 47 years and who still holds the record for the longest tenure for an active U.S. Army general. Following a pattern of the electorate losing confidence in a party when a sitting president is not nominated for a second term, Scott lost to Franklin Pierce. Ten years earlier after he had succeeded the 31-day wonder, William Henry Harrison, the Whigs had kicked John "His Accidency" Tyler out of the party during his presidency because he opposed Whig Congressional programs, and the party leaders didn't like that he often put the country first and broke the party line. The Whigs were a righteously inflexible group, and in 1844 they had run Henry Clay against James Polk — Clay lost. Some historians believe Clay was victimized by timing and that if he had been nominated four years earlier instead of Harrison, he would have easily won and that today's two major parties would be the Democrats and the Whigs. When Clay ran against Polk, it was Clay's third shot at the presidency. The preeminent statesman of his time, Clay didn't fit neatly into any party — he was at various times a Democratic-Republican, a National Republican, and a Whig — and he was defeated for the top office by John Quincy Adams, Andrew Jackson, and Polk.

Always at odds with each other over the question of slavery, after the Fillmore fiasco, the Whigs, a party that took its name from an English political party that favored reforms and parliamentary authority and was identified with the opposition of tyranny, became irrelevant and dissolved. In the end, two Whigs were elected president, and both William Henry Harrison and Zachary Taylor died well before midterm elections — one of the dominant parties of its time, Whigs held the presidency only 17 months. Lincoln ran for the U.S. Senate as a Whig in 1854, but by then the Whigs were in serious decline, and he lost. At the time, Lincoln wrote, "I think I am a Whig, but others say there are no Whigs, and that I am an abolitionist, even though I do no more than oppose the extension of slavery." Helping to assemble the remnants of the Whig, Free Soil, Liberty, and Democratic parties, Lincoln was instrumental in forming the new Republican Party. At the Republican convention in 1856, he placed a distant second behind William Dayton to become John Frémont's running mate.

Chapter 10

Prosperity

"Go West, young man!" ~ John Babson Lane Soule, *Terre Haute Express,* 1851

LESS THAN 100 MILES up the Mississippi River from Nauvoo and at the time Joseph Smith and his followers were being run out of Kirtland, Rock Island was bustling and showing signs of its future prominence. The Rock Island House opened with fireworks and a grand ball on the 4th of July in 1837. The luxurious hotel sheltered the community's new arrivals in a style not seen west of the city — New Orleans and St. Louis are east of Rock Island. Prior to its opening, travelers stayed at John Barrell's house or in rooms over Jonah Case's tavern that had been licensed as a hotel four years earlier. For almost two decades, the Rock Island House operated as the city's premier hotel, stage office, and horse stable. When the railroad got to Tiskilwa in Bureau County, a hack operated by Indian Town Joe Barnett completed travelers' journeys to the Rock Island House, which was located at the northeast corner of Buffalo (16th) Street and Illinois (2nd) Avenue, Rock Island's main commercial artery.

Judge John Spencer and Jonah Case, owners of a square block of land bordered by Jefferson (19th) and Madison (20th) Streets and Illinois and Orleans (3rd) Avenue, made the property available for churches of any denomination -- as long as they were Protestant. There were three takers for the free land. In 1843 the Methodists moved their services from John Spencer's home where they had met since 1836 and built the first Rock Island church on the corner of Illinois and Jefferson on what was then called Union Square. But after the Presbyterians claimed a second corner and the Baptists staked out another, the locals started calling the block "Church Square." The block of churches that was visited only on Sundays was an often-flooded lowland, mostly hidden behind a six-foot whitewashed wooden fence. Spencer and Case had quarried the property for its limestone, and the resulting swamp was a summertime mosquito sanctuary. In 1850 Judge Spencer donated the property to the city of Rock Island, with the restriction in perpetuity that it would be used for the public good.

Education thrived in Rock Island. In 1837, a private, boys-only academy opened in a one-room log cabin near the riverfront. Classes were taught by an eccentric West Point graduate who, at the end of the school day, returned to a river-cave where he lived as a hermit. In 1839 Mr. and Mrs. Joseph Gerard opened a private school.

Unfortunately, it closed the next year after Mr. Gerard was convicted of murdering Z. Mayhew with an axe. In the spring of 1841, Miss Adelia Lowell advertised in the *Argus* that she would be arriving by steamboat from Quincy to instruct students in the various branches of ordinary English education, including plain and ornamental sewing. Miss Lowell accepted scholars from 4 to 8-years-old at 20 cents ($5) a week, those from 8 to 12 were 25 cents, and those over 12 were 30 cents. A practical woman, Miss Lowell accepted "articles of merchandise, produce, and mechanical production in payment of tuition." Later that year, P.H. Ogilvie, the surveyor who named Moline, opened a private school that offered the "usual classical and mathematical branches." Evening classes were also offered, but students were requested "to furnish their own lights."

In 1853 M. R. Kelly announced that he would take no more students because his classroom was "only large enough for 80 and 110 were enrolled, with more coming each day." Clearly, something had to be done, and Rock Islanders rose to the challenge. Five public school districts were formed. District One built a one-room schoolhouse on the southeast corner of Orleans (3rd) Avenue and Pearl (7th) Street that was "a miserable old shell not warm enough to keep the children half comfortable (The drafty building was replaced with a series of sturdier schools, and in 1907 a classic three-level redbrick schoolhouse opened on the sight. Hawthorne School served Rock Island's most historically diverse neighborhood until 1961 when it merged with Irving School in a new building.) District Two stepped up and built a brick school on Orleans Avenue and Beaver (13th) Street. District Three built a small brick school on Union Square. District Four bought an acre of land but built no school. And District Five had no school, no property, no contracts, and no debts. Mothers demanded their husbands to work out a better system — they did.

On February 18, 1857, the Illinois legislature granted Rock Island a unique school charter that created a single district for the city and vested ownership of school property in an elected board of directors. Twenty years later the *Argus* editorialized, "Few cities in Illinois provided at so early a day so ample provisions for the education of their youth. The present prosperity of the schools of Rock Island demonstrates the foresight and wisdom of her citizens in obtaining the enactment of this charter." The first school the school board built was No. 3. Replacing the Union Square School, the large schoolhouse at Jefferson (19th) Street and Canal Street (5th Avenue) had 339 elementary and 42 high school students when it opened in 1857. Bailey Davenport's wife, Mary Grace, was one of three teachers without a credential hired to teach at the new school, because her "character and qualifications are well known to this community."

The school board was active and semi-progressive. At a time when Southern blacks were forbidden to learn to read and write, the board appointed a committee to ascertain "the number of coloured children in the district and whether a coloured teacher could be procured." The committee reported that there were "thirty-two scholars between the ages of five and twenty years, twenty-three of whom would attend school," and that "a coloured lady was expected in a few weeks who would be willing and competent to take charge of such a school" — then, a classroom was called a school.

Monthly salaries in 1858 were $55 ($1,450) for male grammar school principals, $30 for female principals, $35 for female assistants (teachers) at the high school (about the same as male laborers and railroad workers were making), and $22 for female assistants in the grammar schools. Gender pay inequality in the school system remained in place for more than a century — in 1949, the Illinois Equal Pay Law was enacted. Pay inequality between teachers and administrators is still an issue. In the days before teacher contracts, one teacher asked for a $3 salary increase, and the school board granted it. When another asked for the same, she was informed that her "services would be dispensed with at the end of the month." In 1863 the school board passed a resolution to remove assistants who "habitually attend balls and theaters" because those "amusements distract the mind, make habits irregular, and consequently unfit a person for teaching." The same conduct code made the use of tobacco a cause for immediate termination.

One of the consolidated school board's first major accomplishments was the authorization of the building of a public high school. Christopher Atkinson, Rock Island's first large-scale commercial builder, was given the contract, and in the spring of 1858, he started construction of Rock Island's first high school. The school was to be a brick, three-story building on the northwest corner of Spencer (7th) Avenue and Dock (22nd) Street, but on the evening of July 4, an unexplained fire burned the unfinished school to the ground. After clearing the rubble, on the same location Atkinson immediately began to construct Rock Island's second high school. The school opened for the 1859 school year, and five women comprised the first graduating class. Frederick Denkmann delivered the commencement address to an audience of 700. All five graduates went to work in Rock Island as school assistants. The high school lasted until 1886 when a larger high school was built diagonally across that block on the southeast corner of Commercial (6th) Avenue and Adams (21st) Street. The third Rock Island High School burned in 1901 after 15 years of use.

Even after the first churches were built, for 37 years the Union Square block remained a fenced eyesore of quarry tailings and ramshackle buildings. In 1887 a group of citizens filled and graded the quarry and artistically landscape the lot with broad promenade walkways that diagonally crossed the square. The delightfully renovated block featured an elevated, cut-stone gazebo and fountain at its center; later a magnificent statue of Black Hawk was added near the corner of Madison (20th) Street and Orleans (3rd) Avenue. The charming green was renamed Spencer Square, and for three generations, it served as a meeting place for old men who watched over bored boys whose mothers left them to play there while they shopped in Rock Island's bustling downtown district. Arguably in violation of Judge Spencer's deed restriction, in 1954, the U.S. Postal Service bought "the grandest [square] in Illinois, if not the United States, for its size" and built one of the most unimaginatively designed public buildings in Illinois, if not the United States. Black Hawk's statue was moved to the state park that bears his name.

A block north of Spencer Square, the German Lutheran Church, formally called Emanuel Lutheran Church, was the spiritual, educational, and social center for Rock Island's large German-speaking community. From 1856 until 2009 when the Lutheran congregation moved into a new building, the site was home not only to Rock Island's oldest Lutheran church, but also to one of its few non-Catholic parochial schools. Thousands of children attended the grammar school that eventually held 150 students. After 100 years of operating a school on the downtown site, in 1957 a new school opened on 24th Street south of 31st Avenue. It was forced to close in 2010 because of declining enrollment. On warm nights, the Gothic Revival-styled downtown church entertained generations of passersby when, from the church's open basement windows, the noise of rolling bowling balls and the crash of tenpins were occasionally punctuated by boisterous cheers and blasphemous curses.

Not allowed to build a church at Church Square, Rock Island's Catholics built separate churches to accommodate their English and German speaking congregations In the 1840's Fr. John George Alleman traveled the Upper Midwest, establishing congregations and schools. For the decade before 1852 when St. James Catholic Church was built at Rock River (4th) Avenue and Dock (22nd) Street, Mass was offered at Beierlein's Cooper Shop. A beer barrel manufacturer, John Beierlein was a devout Lutheran, but each Sunday he made room in his warehouse for his German-speaking Catholic friends. The German Catholic congregation outgrew the warehouse, and with considerable financial assistance from Antoine LeClaire, who was a devout Catholic, St. James, a 61-foot by 30-foot church, was dedicated in 1852. The church was rebuilt and improved over the next half-century, and in 1874 St. James' congregation split, and a large segment of its English-speaking membership formed a new parish, St. Joseph's, in the Old Town Chicago District.

By this time, a second generation had descended from German settlers and had grown up speaking English. The older parishioners were joined by a large number of Irish who settled in the neighborhood around St. James. When St. Joseph's was formed, the Irish, who have an unusually strong devotion to the mother of Jesus, changed its name to St. Mary's, and soon masses were said only in English. In 1875 St. Mary's built a one-story schoolhouse that was replaced in 1890 by a $10,000 ($285,000) eight-classroom brick school. For 78 years children daily entered St. Mary's school through an arched entrance with the inscription, "For God, Our Country and Our Children."

The St. Joseph's congregation purchased the First Presbyterian building on Deer (14th) Street and Illinois (2nd) Avenue, and the Presbyterians moved into a spectacular new Gothic-style church on the south side of Spencer (7th) Avenue at Dock (22nd) Street in the Broadway Neighborhood. In 1877 Reverend Thomas Mackin was named pastor of St. Joseph's and immediately established a school. In 1885 both a new grade school and a high school were opened next to the church. During the 28 years that Fr. Mackin served as pastor, he established St. Anthony's Hospital and oversaw the incorporation of Calvary Catholic Cemetery — at the time it wasn't proper for Catholics and Protestants to be buried side-by-side. He also spearheaded the extensive rebuilding of the church when it was severely damaged by a sanctuary fire in 1900. When Fr. Mackin died in 1905, the church's congregation had grown to 2,600 — more than ten percent of Rock Island's population. In 2007 parishes were consolidated, and the immense spired cathedral was demolished. For 64 years Catholic secondary students attended school and served mass at St. Joseph's; then in 1949, Alleman High School opened with 571 students. The new high school was built on the south side of 11th Avenue across from Lincoln Park and arguably has one of the finest campus settings of any high school in the country.

About the same time the Catholics moved their services from Beierlein's Cooper Shop to St. James church, Reverend Louderback began holding Episcopal services in Rock Island. It's unknown how much the notoriously tight-fisted Bailey Davenport donated to the construction of the first Holy Trinity Church, but he is listed among its original members. Thirteen years later, the spectacularly ornate Trinity Episcopal Church (now named Trinity Anglican Church) was completed at a cost of $16,000 ($320,000) on Pleasant (6th) Avenue between Washington (18th) and Jefferson (19th) Streets. In 1884 Trinity's pastor, Reverend R.F. Sweet, and the Trinity Ladies Guild rented a building on 2nd Avenue and 9th Street and opened St. Luke's Cottage Hospital.

Rock Island's first hospital struggled but provided incalculable services until forced to close in 1890. Three years later, the Franciscan Sisters opened a 10-room hospital at the crest of the hill on 30th Street. St. Anthony's Hospital prospered, and two years after opening, a new 35-bed facility replaced the original building that burned. In 1899 a nursing school was added, and for the next 73 years, the hospital and nursing school admirably served the community. When the Franciscan Medical Center opened in 1972, St. Anthony's was converted to a Continuing Care Center for the elderly. In 1977, 1,300 nurses graduated in the school's last class.

While Rock Island was building a rock-solid infrastructure during the middle decades of the 19th century, discoveries of precious metals and dreams of California living conspired to slow Midwest growth and push the frontier towards the Pacific Coast. The discovery of gold in California in 1848 and a decade later of gold and silver in the eastern foothills of the Sierra Nevada drove high-spirited, adventuresome young men, newly-arrived European immigrants, and Missouri-born Samuel Clemens to cross the continent in search of instant wealth. Three years later, Horace Greeley, the editor of the *New York Tribune*, America's most influential newspaper, stole a memorable line from a Terre Haute, Indiana newspaperman, and advised, "Go West, young man" — many did. Greeley's purloined advice and glowing reports of California's Central Valley — a flat fertile plain that has a year-round growing season and runs for a stretch of 450 miles between the Sierra Nevada and Coastal mountain ranges — caused thousands of Ohio River Valley farmers to reconsider where to locate their fields. Sacramento became the country's most popular destination, and San Francisco quickly became the largest city west of St. Louis.

The freethinking Greeley, who was one of the founders of the Liberal Republican party, opposed slavery, espoused social reforms, and promoted progressive causes ranging from vegetarianism to socialism. It was Greeley who came up with the name for the Republican Party. He suggested "some simple name like 'Republican' [that] would more fitly designate those who had united to restore the Union to its true mission of champion and promulgator of Liberty rather than propagandist of slavery." To illustrate how much the party he named has evolved in 150 years, Greeley was notoriously secular and opposed faith-based charity. Once, when asking for a donation to a Christian charity, a solicitor said, "Your money will save millions from going to hell." "Then I'll not give a damn cent," retorted Greeley. "Not half enough of them go there now."

Rock Island was spared the economic turbulence of the mid-19th century that plagued most of the nation, especially the communities that lay between the Appalachians and the Rocky Mountains. With the linking of the Upper Mississippi to Chicago and the East by the completion of the Chicago & Rock Island Railroad in February 1854, a vital transportation artery pumped economic lifeblood into the region. Known as the Rock Island Line, the railroad was the final spoke in a transportation hub that linked Mississippi riverboat traffic, overland trails, and rail transport; only New Orleans and St. Louis surpassed Rock Island as a Mississippi River port. When the railroad came to Rock Island, the town had 595 dwellings with most clustered in the flat plain below the river bluffs that now comprise the downtown district. The arrival of the railroad spiked Rock Island's economy, and nearly 100 houses were under construction near the new depot at Dock (22nd) Street and another 100 were being built in the town's west end. At a time when the rest of the nation was in the middle of a ten-year span with no inflation or deflation, real estate in Rock Island jumped from 88¢ an acre to as much as $10 ($250) an acre in one year's time, and land fronting Illinois (2nd) Avenue sold for as much as $75 ($1,875) a foot. As outrageous as land prices were, wages matched them. Railroads paid up to $1 ($25) a day for the backbreaking jobs of grading railways and laying track. Young Irish men who had emigrated during the Potato Famine of 1845 to 1852 rushed to Rock Island to swing picks and sledge hammers during 12-hour shifts.

From February 1854 to April 1856 when the first railroad bridge to cross the Mississippi was opened, Rock Island was the westernmost outpost of civilization before crossing into the Wild West. The combination of ideal location, natural resources, as well as rail and river transportation fueled job growth and caused Rock Island's population to exponentially soar from 1,711 in 1850 to 3,475 in 1852 to 5,337 in 1854 to 10,140 in 1857 — a six-fold increase in only seven years. A trickle-down effect spurred growth in the surrounding communities, and the completion of the railroad bridge and frequent ferry service gave ready access to Antoine LeClaire's inexpensive land across the river. In an 1853 articles for the *Chicago Democratic Press*, John Locke Scripps wrote:

> A vast amount of business will ultimately concentrate at this crossing of the Mississippi and whether it will be mostly on the Illinois side (as some think) or on the Iowa side, property must always bear an equalized value ... Illinois Street, the second one from the river, is the principal street. Lots on this street sell for $75 per front foot. The Chicago & Rock Island Railroad purchased its way into the city all along the bank of the river, as far west as Madison [20th] Street. Lots 60x150 from the east edge of town to Dock Street cost an average of $800 [$23,000 in 2012 dollars] each ... Brick houses close to the business section are for sale at $1,700 [$50,000] to $4,500 [$130,000].
>
> When capital begins to seek western industrial investment, Rock Island will be able to present many inducements. The population of the three cities is estimated at 11,200 [At the time, Rock Island was larger than Davenport and Moline combined.]

Scripps was prophetic. The same year that John Spencer and Jonah Case donated their downtown block of swampland to the public welfare, Ben Harper, an entrepreneurial Philadelphian who had migrated first to Ohio and then Missouri, where he became wealthy in the meat packing business, blew into Rock Island seeking to make even more money in one of the nation's hottest opportunity spots. It is a mystery how historians know, but in 1850 Harper is reported to have arrived in Rock Island with $80,000 ($2.2 million). A dapper man with a neatly trimmed goatee, he brought with him an East Coast "style," and within four years, the urbane gentleman built a magnificent Greek Rival style home on Canal Street (5th Avenue) between Howard (27th) and Columbia (29th) Streets, invested heavily in real estate, and was elected Rock Island's third mayor. Another example of entrepreneurial businessmen seeing the obvious and having the money to capitalize on it was in 1857 when Philemon Mitchell and Philander Cable came to town from Louisville with an amount of cash equal to what Harper had arrived with. The two men bought three Rock Island banks that had failed in the Panic of 1837 and opened the First National Bank of Rock Island.

In contrast to bustling Rock Island, a newspaper article in the *Moline Workman* noted of Moline that a "much duller town could not be scared up this side of Sleepy Hollow." Initially platted in an orderly grid of sixteen square blocks with streets named after the primary landowners, indicative of their no-nonsense nature, the industrialists who planned "The City of Mills" chose not to install a town common or park along the river because they thought the space would be better used for industrial purposes. Led by John Deere, the city fathers set the bar low and envisioned a "Lowell on the Mississippi" designed after a planned industrial city in Massachusetts, and Moline was marketed to both investors and immigrant workers as the "Lowell of the West."

Prior to the Civil War, Rock Island was the glamour city of the frontier and the *Moline Workman* began advocating a consolidation of the two cities. Fearful that uniting with Moline would drive down property values and dull the town's image, most Rock Islanders were not keen on the idea. A few from Rock Island proposed annexing Moline, but to the relief of Rock Island's future generations, the union was never made. Another sticking point with Rock Islanders was that many of the Swedish, Belgium, and German immigrants, who got off the Rock Island Line to work in "John Deere's Town," were God-fearing, community-oriented workers, and Moline became home to temperance societies and other reform organizations and social movements that had few adherents in Rock Island. Moline's founding fathers were stoic immigrants seeking a better life or ambitious New Englanders, who brought a stern work ethic and a controlled civic life to the Midwest. Unlike their western neighbor, Moline was not a socially tolerant, fun-loving, rambunctious river-town.

In 1848 a few Swedish families established a fishing camp at the Moline end of Government Island, and two years later, A.J. Swanson became the first Norseman to move to Rock Island. The Swedish cobbler set up shop in the same block where John Buford had opened his grocery. Another of those attracted by Rock Island's charms was a wealthy Kentucky farm owner and relative of John Buford, Charles Buford. In 1853 he moved his wife, ten children, and a herd of purebred cattle to Rock Island. As John Buford had done a generation earlier, Charles Buford became active in a broad spectrum of community affairs. A Yale graduate, he was highly accomplished in mathematics and mechanics. He founded the Buford Plow Company, which was later sold to the J.I. Case Company, and keeping his priorities in order, he found time to become one of the most accomplished sport fishermen along the Rock Island Rapids.

Upon arriving in Rock Island, Buford purchased 10 acres to the southeast of the city's center for $100 an acre. At a cost of $10,000 ($265,000), he built a magnificent 18-room antebellum mansion at the head of Washington (18th) Street on Spenser (7th) Avenue (today 1804 7th Avenue). Carefully situated to allow an unobstructed view of the Mississippi River, the magnificent home became the social gathering place for Rock Island's crème de la crème and hosted many prominent out of town visitors — very probably including Abraham Lincoln. After Buford's death in 1866, his widow, Lucy, lived in the home for another three decades. Then after her death, the 12-bedroom mansion became a boarding house. One of the boarders was Levi McCabe, the founder of McCabe's Department Store, who later purchased the room he boarded in along with the rest of the house for his home. The building became home to the Tri-City Jewish Center in 1936. In 1951, an addition was built that housed the sanctuary and gymnasium, and an entrance was added on the west side of the building, which bore Hebrew script that mystified the young gentiles who visited there. A new Jewish Center was completed in 1981, and the following year, the Buford home became the headquarters of the Word of Life Christian Center. Charles Buford also developed two blocks of commercial buildings between Buffalo (16th) and Washington (18th) Streets on Illinois (2nd) Avenue.

Twenty years after buying and converting the Buford mansion, the congregation of the Tri-City Jewish Center saved another of Rock Island's fabulous mansions. In 1958 a new convent for the nuns at St. Joseph's was built and they moved out of an 18-room Gothic style mansion on 6th Avenue at the head of 19th Street. Built by Morris Rosenfield on the same site where John Spencer had built his cabin 70 years earlier — after Black Hawk evicted him from Saukenuk — the spectacular home features a three-story turret that affords an unobstructed view down 19th Street to the river. The mansion was completed in 1893, the same year Lincoln School was built, at a cost of $50,000 ($1,250,000) — $3,000 more than the school. Rosenfield was born in Germany and had become wealthy building wagons. The nuns had lovingly cared for the home for 40 years before it became the Tri-City Jewish Center's Educational Center. The Jews maintained the house as well as the nuns, and after the Tri-City Jewish Center moved to its present Street location in the late 1970s, Coventry Apartments used the home for offices and to house the maintenance manager.

Down the street from John Spencer's house, major competition to the 16-year-old Rock Island House arose with the 1854 opening of the four-story, 100-room Island City Hotel, located on the west side of Jefferson (19th) Street across from the Union Square swamp. Compared to the Harper House hotel that would be built on the same site 17 years later, the new hotel was modestly appointed. Larger and more modern and upscale than the Rock Island House, the wooden-structure Island City became Rock Island's crown jewel — for two years. Then Rock Island's Farnham House became the city's third 100-room hotel at a time when most hotels had 20 rooms or less. Favorably located across the street from the Court House, the new hotel matched the Island City's floors and sleeping rooms, and was the first hotel within 150 miles to be constructed of brick. Unable to compete with the Farnham House's sturdy, upscale style, the Island City went honky-tonk and built a dance hall and saloon next to the hotel, which became part rooming house and part brothel. The Island City Hotel burned to the ground in 1870, but for another half-dozen years the Island City Saloon remained one of the city's favorite watering holes and its adjoining hall was a primary gathering spot for meetings, dances, plays, and lectures.

The Farnham House's opening was timed to accommodate the influx of travelers and emigrants who arrived on the Rock Island Line. On April 22, 1856 citizens lined the riverfronts in Rock Island and Davenport and cheered as three engines pulled eight passenger cars across the first railroad bridge to span the Mississippi. Located a quarter-mile upriver from the present day railroad bridge, the wooden, single-track bridge opened the way for the settlement of Iowa. With little fanfare Iowa had entered the Union as the 29th state a decade before. Two weeks after the bridge was completed, a steamboat, the *Effie Afton,* ran into it, burning the boat and one bridge span. The following year, Abraham Lincoln — now a lawyer — was back in Rock Island to defend the Chicago & Rock Island Railroad in a lawsuit brought by steamboat owners.

The steamboat owners were accurately afraid that railroads would dramatically reduce their business, and their motivation was more to create competitive barriers than a concern for public safety. Lincoln argued that bridge construction across navigable waters was a good thing. In what, on the surface, should have been an easy argument to win, the lawsuit ended in a hung jury. In 1859 in response to a lawsuit brought by a St. Louis steamboat operator, an Iowa judge declared the railroad bridge "a common and public nuisance," and displaying the type of insular logic and provincial partisanship that Iowa was to become famous for, he decreed the removal of "the three piers and their superstructure which lay in the State of Iowa." Predictably, the bridge's owners appealed to the U.S. Supreme Court, where in 1862, with Lincoln then in the White House and William Stanton representing the railroad, the bridge builders prevailed. Stanton later became Lincoln's Secretary of War during the Civil War.

While Lincoln was arguing with Iowa over whether trains from the East should be allowed into their state, John Spencer's son, Edward, performed a heroic feat that made international news and was remembered by a generation of Americans. While attending Northwestern University, on a fiercely stormy September 1860 night, the Rock Island native and a number of his classmates were among the first to the site of a 2:30 a.m. collision of the Great Lakes steamer, the *Lady Elgin*, with the schooner, *Augusta*. There were 317 passengers on the *Lady Elgin*, which was returning to Milwaukee from Chicago.

Rammed by the *Augusta*, within 20 minutes the *Lady Elgin* broke apart and sank. At a time when many did not know how to swim and few were strong swimmers, of 400 passengers and crew, all but 98 died. Unable to break through the surge of the fierce shoreline breakers, many perished in view of those who lined the fog-shrouded Evanston shore. Only one from the shore, Edward Spencer, was strong enough to dive through the breakers to aid the stranded. Over a six-hour period, the robust Spencer swam to 17 who clung to debris and pulled them one-by-one to safety. His courageous efforts ended when he fell unconscious from exhaustion and hypothermia. The injuries that he sustained from being battered by waves against the rocky shore hospitalized him for weeks and left him an invalid for life. From his delirium in the hospital, he continually asked, "Did I do my best?" Spencer's heroics were the only bright spot in the greatest loss of life on open water in the history of the United States, and "Did I do my best?" became an American catch phrase of the time.

A half century later, in Los Angeles Spencer and some friends went to a sermon by a renowned evangelist of the day. The theme of the sermon was "Did I do my Best?" and unaware that Spencer was in the audience, the preacher retold his fearless deeds on that foggy Chicago night. After the sermon, a companion of Spencer's rose and said, "Ed Spencer is here now." Called to the pulpit, Spencer refused to elaborate on his heroism and modestly said, "It happened 48 years ago." Northwestern conferred Spencer an A.B degree retroactive to the year he would have graduated if his health had not prevented it. A plaque that is still displayed in the Northwestern library was placed on campus by the Class of 1898 to commemorate his life-saving bravery.

Three years after Edward Spencer's heroics, Henry Dart moved his family to Rock Island from Pennsylvania. Dart opened a grocery on Washington (18th) Street, and in 1864 he built a three-story brick building on the corner of Illinois (2nd) Avenue and

Washington Street to house his thriving grocery business. The *Argus* reported, "The foundations are being laid for five new stores on Illinois Street near the Island City Hotel. ... [The builders] will finish the second story of their block into a fine hall for public use. The hall will be 40 by 116 feet and furnished with all the improvements of a modern stage, raised seats, anterooms, etc."

Three years later the *Argus* reported, "The splendid 3-story brick block ... housing Hein's Billiard Saloon, Copp's livery stable, and Babcock's Hall has been sold to Henry Dart's Sons for $15,500 ($230,000). The building adjoins Darts' fine 3-story grocery. The public soon can listen to lectures, concerts and operas without the noise and annoyances, which have been so common there. The young Darts are just the men to run the corner as it ought to be run." Dart Hall quickly supplanted the Island City Hall as Rock Island's social and entertainment center, and the *Argus*' prophecy was fulfilled when celebrated choruses, symphonies, and operas performed there and Ralph Waldo Emerson, Wendell Phillips, Schuyler Colfax, Carl Schurz, Clara Barton, and many other celebrities spoke there. Clara Barton was paid the princely sum of $75 ($1,200) to describe her search for missing soldiers.

In 1866 when Emerson spoke at the hall, his speech was said to be "the most scholarly lecture Rock Island has heard." A decade earlier, Emerson had delivered a series of speeches in Rock Island and Davenport. He, of course, stayed in Rock Island and three times walked across the frozen river and back in the futile attempt to transport culture to Iowa. He wrote in his journal, "In Rock Island I am advertised as 'the celebrated metaphysician,' in Davenport as 'the essayist and poet." He added, "Soft coal comes to Rock Island from about 12 miles, sells for 16 cents ($4) a bushel; wood at $6 ($150) per cord. They talk quarter sections. 'I will take a quarter of that pie."

Although none stayed at the Farnham House, among the first passengers to get their "ticket at the station of the Rock Island Line" were thousands of poor immigrant Mormons, who in the first two years of the railroad's operation, spent a layover night in Rock Island on their journey to the Salt Lake Valley. Until the Mississippi River railroad bridge was completed, the Latter-day Saints camped a night on the Rock Island levee and then ferried across the Mississippi to begin their walk down the Mormon Trail to Utah. This walk became 50 miles shorter in 1856 when the Rock Island Line reached Iowa City and even shorter the next year when it reached Council Bluffs. As many as fifteen thousand Mormons bought one-way, west-bound tickets on the Rock Island Line, which ended at the start of the arduous last leg of a difficult journey. With visions of a better life, 3,000 poor British Mormon converts booked steerage accommodations for the ocean voyage from Liverpool to New York City and then boarded a train for a ride that ended at the western terminus of the Rock Island Line. There they were outfitted with supplies and provided handcarts designed by Brigham Young.

The handcarts resembled a Chinese rickshaw. Built of hickory or oak, the cart's two wheels were five feet in diameter with a single axle, four and a half feet wide. Running along each side were seven-foot shafts with a three-foot crossbar at the front. The crossbar allowed the carts to be pushed or pulled. Cargo was carried in a 3-foot by 4-foot by 8-inch box. In later years the wooden carts were reinforced with steel joints. Before beginning their 1,200-mile trek from Rock Island to the Great Basin, the immigrants assembled their own carts, and the handcart trains were rigidly organized to Young's specifications. Five people were assigned to each handcart, and each person was limited to 17 pounds of clothing and bedding. A tent captain oversaw five, round teepee-style tents that each housed 20 occupants. The tents and other group tools and equipment were carried in an ox wagon, which was driven by the captain — everyone else walked. One immigrant journaled, "People made fun of us as we walked, pulling our handcarts, but the weather was fine and the roads were excellent, and although I was sick, and we were very tired at night, I still thought it was a glorious way to go to Zion."

Two of the handcart companies, which left from Iowa City, did not encounter fine weather and smooth going. After getting a late start, the two parties, totaling almost a thousand immigrants, were snowed in near present day Casper, Wyoming in November. Young formed a rescue effort, but 210 immigrants died of starvation or exposure. The greatest western migration of Mormons occurred during the three-year period after Brigham Young reached the Salt Lake Valley. Mormons, who tend to be obsessive record keepers, have engraved on the Pioneer Memorial in Nauvoo the names of 2,000 who died on the trail to the Salt Lake Valley. It is believed that these and another 4,000 of about 60,000 Mormons died before reaching "the right place."

Even though they did not cross Nevada's waterless 40-mile Desert or the Sierra Nevada Mountains, which is where most Western immigrants perished, Mormons experienced a ten percent death rate while traveling west. This is more than double that estimated by early historians for all migrants who traveled the Oregon Trail to California. The high death rate is partially explained by Mormons' strong belief in Agency (predetermination), and because they often flaunted conventional wisdom and took unnecessary risks or started their journey too late in the summer. More probably, the higher Mormon mortality rate resulted from their being already weakened by the journey to the Mississippi and being under-prepared and ill-equipped for the challenging trip. One writer commented about a Mormon immigrant party saying that they "looked more like the population of the poor farm on a picnic than like pioneers about to cross the plains." Thousands of LDS Saints who traveled the Mormon Trail did not settle in the Salt Lake Valley. Building on town sites carefully chosen by Mormon leaders, immigrants settled throughout the Great Basin near canyon mouths that afforded access to streams and timber. Mormons founded more than 600 Western communities from Canada to Mexico, and are credited with spearheading the settlement of the Great Basin — the most barren land in America.

Other than handcarts, there were several other pre-Civil War travel options. For men traveling alone or in small groups, horses were the best choice. Those pioneers who wanted to go to California but bypass the inhospitable terrain between the Mississippi River and the Sierra Nevada Mountains could do so by traveling by schooner around Cape Horn. Those who weren't enchanted by an adventure at sea and wanted to travel in relative comfort and leave the driving and animal husbandry to others could take a stagecoach. The fastest clipper ships could sail from New York to San Francisco in four months. Passage was $150 ($4,000) for a stateroom and a five-cubic-foot storage locker. Stagecoaches were comparably priced to early clipper cruises and took less time but were excruciatingly cramped and luggage was usually limited to a single footlocker. Covered wagons offered the best value for families traveling together, but were the slowest and riskiest way to California, and wagon masters tended to downplay mortality rates on their wagon trains. Whereas clipper ships and stagecoaches were operated by companies that made large capital investments, wagon trains were usually organized by a two or three-man company consisting of a wagon master and a scout or two. But when the Rock Island Line bridged the Mississippi, all of these transportation modes soon became quaint relics of the past.

Chapter 11

A Divided Nation

One section of our country believes slavery is right and ought to be extended, while the other believes it is wrong and ought not to be extended. This is the only substantial dispute. ~ Abraham Lincoln (First Inaugural Speech)

Our new government [the Confederacy] is founded on exactly the opposite Idea: its foundations are laid; its cornerstone rests upon the great truth that the Negro is not equal to the white man; that slavery, subordination to the superior race, is his natural and normal condition. ~ Alexander Stephens, Confederate Vice President

SLAVE TRADERS SHIPPED 12 million Africans to the Americas, of which about 5 percent were sold in the United States. Because many poor British immigrants, who themselves had been servants or indentured servants, settled the northern colonies along with others who came to America seeking religious and personal freedoms, slavery was an ethical and moral issue from their arrival. In the United States, except for Catholics, Mormons, Muslims, and Jews, religious ideology generally was not a cause for discrimination. However, racial intolerance remains a national issue, and along with this, the systematic elimination of Native North and South Americans during the Colonial Period and Indian Removal program can accurately be described as the greatest and longest instance of genocide in recorded history. Similarly, the white population's attitude towards black African Americans was for the most part despicable until after World War II — and then it improved slightly. In the most prestigious history textbook of its time, W.E. Woodward wrote:

> The slave system ... did incalculable harm to the white people of the South, and benefited nobody but the Negro, in that it served as a vast training school for African savages. Though the regime of the slave plantations was strict, it was, on the whole, a kindly one by comparison with what the imported slave had experienced in his own land. It taught him discipline, cleanliness and a conception of moral standards. ~ *New American History* (1936)

It is estimated that more than 2 million Africans died while being shipped to the Americas. Those sold to Caribbean and South American plantations were conditioned or "seasoned" for a year or more to the hard labor and conditions they would endure after they were sold. Since about a third of all new slaves died from diseases or living conditions during their first year of acclimation in the Americas, the market value of seasoned slaves was about 50 percent more than the unseasoned. In North America, African slaves were auctioned as they came off the ship, and 645,000 were sold in the United States. The other 9 million who survived the voyage were sold in the Caribbean and South America where they labored on sugar, cotton, and coffee plantations. As oppressive as slave conditions were in the South, they were significantly better than in the Caribbean and South America.

Slaves were valuable, and their price reflected their value. Prior to the Civil War, a black man in the prime of life was worth $1,600 (about $45,000). By the war, the number of American slaves had almost tripled to approximately 1,775,000, and slaves south of the Mason-Dixon Line had a total economic value of about $70 billion in current dollars. The Emancipation Proclamation was issued in September 1862 with an effective date of January 1, 1863, but it had little effect on the slaves whose lives were tied to the plantations they lived and worked on. In Texas it took 18 months before anyone told them they were free. That happened on June 18, 1865, when General Gordon Granger and 2,000 Union troops arrived in Galveston to announce the emancipation. The next day, Granger read an order that began, "The people of Texas are informed that, in accordance with a proclamation from the Executive of the United States, all slaves are free." The day is now celebrated annually as Juneteenth Day. When the Emancipation Proclamation deflated the economic value of slaves, plantation owners' animosity hardened and their resolve deepened — many had more than 100 slaves and they knew they could not productively farm their plantations without them. To protect their investment and way of life, slave owners, which encompassed nearly all whites of means in the South, were left without recourse.

Because of the emotional division over slavery, civil war had been simmering for decades before armies at Fort Sumter fired the first shots in April 1861. The writing of the Constitution had been an exercise in compromise between politicians from the North and South. The Constitution's durability, checks and balances, strength and resiliency, and ability to allow populist change reflect the deep social and political differences and the mutual distrusts of the men who wrote it. James Madison observed, "It seems now to be pretty well understood that the real difference of interests lies not between the large and small but between the Northern and Southern states. The institution of slavery and its consequences form the line."

In 1820, the Missouri Compromise had created a latitudinal boundary where the Missouri-Arkansas border is drawn and where the northern boundary of the Texas panhandle extends. In the territory acquired by the Louisiana Purchase, slavery was prohibited north of this latitude with the compromise exception of Missouri, where a majority favored slavery and which was admitted to the Union as a slave state and tipped the balance from free states to slave states by one. That appeased the South for a while, and political balance continued to tilt the slave states until California was admitted to the Union in 1850. Fearing the loss of congressional control, Southern congressmen made efforts to acquire Cuba and annex Nicaragua. Five intricate congressional bills, called the Compromise of 1850, were intended to protect the interests of the North and South, but only heightened tensions and solidified opposing positions between the free and slave states. Four years later, the poorly conceived Kansas-Nebraska Act permitted settlers, who had spent the previous generation pushing Indians farther west, the right to decide whether they would be a free state or not. This set the stage for a four-year brutal free-for-all between pro-slavery and anti-slavery settlers in the Kansas Territory. The conflict is generally known as "Bloody Kansas."

One of the first settlers to stake a homestead in the Kansas Territory after it opened for settlement was Isaac Cody and his family. Claiming farmland northwest of Fort Leavenworth in the Salt Creek Valley, in 1854 Cody built a log cabin for his family. A devout Quaker, Cody was a fervent abolitionist in a highly politicized region that was mostly populated by pro-slavery advocates. In September after putting in his first hay crop to get his stock through the winter, he made an impassioned speech for the Free Soil Movement, which opposed the extension of slavery in the western territories. Taking issue with Cody's cause, a pro-slavery fanatic stabbed him through one lung. His eight-year old son, Will, helped drag Cody to safety, but he never fully recovered and died three years later "after suffering a chill."

The year his father was stabbed, Will was given his first horse. An older cousin, who was a horseman and had been a circus showman , taught him the riding tricks that would help make him famous, and after his father's death, to support his mother and siblings, the tall and athletic 11-year-old got a job as a wagon train messenger. He was paid well to carry messages along the wagon train, and when not working for the wagon train company, he trapped beaver for their pelts and hunted game for meat for his family. As a 12-year-old, Cody got a job as a scout to guide the U.S. Army into the Utah Territory where they established Fort Crittenden. It was on this expedition that his reputation as an Indian fighter began. In his autobiography, *Buffalo Bill's Own Story*, Cody wrote:

> Presently the moon rose, dead ahead of me; and painted boldly across its face was the figure of an Indian. He wore this war-bonnet of the Sioux, at his shoulder was a rifle pointed at someone in the river-bottom 30 feet (9 m) below; in another second he would drop one of my friends. I raised my old muzzle-loader and fired. The figure collapsed, tumbled down the bank and landed with a splash in the water. 'What is it?' called McCarthy, as he hurried

back. 'It's over there in the water.' 'Hi!' he cried. 'Little Billy's killed an Indian all by himself!' So began my career as an Indian fighter.

When he returned home from Fort Crittenden, Cody found that his oldest sister had died and his mother was in failing health. Will and his other older sister, Julia, were left to care for the family. The two siblings tended the farm and cared for the younger children, and to make extra money, Will worked as a bullwhacker (a wagon driver) and rounded up stray horses for the U.S. Army. After hearing of the fabulous wealth coming out of the Colorado goldfields, a 14-year-old Cody saddled up and headed west to strike it rich. On his way to Colorado, he met an agent who was recruiting riders for the newly formed Pony Express. After first helping to build the stations and corrals, he became one of the 140 men who rode for the Pony Express. Will Cody made the longest non-stop Pony Express ride; his remarkable ride of 322 miles took only 21 hours and 40 minutes and required 20 changes of horses (there is no record of covering anywhere near a comparable distance on horseback in less than a day): He wrote:

> The next day [Jack Slade] assigned me to duty on the road from Red Buttes on the North Platte, to the Three Crossings of the Sweetwater — a distance of seventy-six miles — and I began riding at once.
>
> One day when I galloped into Three Crossings, my home station, I found that the rider who was expected to take the trip out on my arrival had got into a drunken row the night before and had been killed; and that there was no one to fill his place. I did not hesitate for a moment to undertake an extra ride of eighty-five miles to Rocky Ridge, and I arrived at the latter place on time. I then turned back and rode to Red Buttes, my starting place, accomplishing on the round trip a distance of 322 miles.
>
> Slade heard of this feat of mine, and one day as he was passing on a coach he sang out to me, 'My boy, you're a brick, and no mistake. That was a good run you made when you rode your own and Miller's routes, and I'll see that you get extra pay for it.'
>
> Slade, although rough at times and always a dangerous character — having killed many a man — was always kind to me. During the two years that I worked for him as pony-express-rider and stage-driver, he never spoke an angry word to me.

The nearly 2,000-mile Pony Express route from Sacramento to St. Joseph operated for only 18 months. The ten-day trip to transport messages 2,000 miles over rough and hostile terrain cost $5 ($130) a half-ounce (the weight of four pages of this book) and was cut to a matter of minutes, when crews, working from the east and the west on the transcontinental telegraph, met at Fort Bridger — obsolescing overnight one of the world's most romantic enterprises. After working as a stagecoach driver for Jack Slade once the Pony Express closed down, Cody was forced to return home to help tend to his ailing mother. When he returned to his Kansas farm, the nation east of the Western frontier had become as violently and irreparably split over the slavery issue as was the new state of Kansas.

At the opposite end of the philosophical spectrum from the pro-slavery thugs in Kansas were the transcendentalist philosophers in the Northeast who believed that man was inherently good and that skin color had nothing to do with anything. They believed that society and its institutions — particularly organized religion and political parties — ultimately corrupted the essential honor of the individual, that mankind is at its best when people are self-reliant and independent, and that communities are at their best when they are composed of individuals who believe the same. The movement grew out of a reaction against 18th century rationalism that stated God was uninvolved in the affairs of man, and it was the opposite of New England Calvinism that believed that God "freely and unchangeably ordained whatsoever comes to pass."

No person better expressed or lived the transcendental philosophy than Henry David Thoreau, a Harvard educated author and poet who was an abolitionist, naturalist, historian, and social critic. Thoreau wrote, "If a man does not keep pace with his companions, perhaps it is because he hears a different drummer. Let him step to the music which he hears, however measured or far away." At the time, he was far away from the music of others. He is best known for his book *Walden*, a reflection upon simple living, and his essay *Civil Disobedience*, an argument against slavery and his disgust of war. Jailed for a night for not paying six years of Massachusetts poll taxes, his friend Ralph Waldo Emerson visited him in jail and asked why he was there. "Waldo, why are you not here?" Thoreau replied.

Although not as truculent as Thoreau, Emerson also lived and preached the transcendental philosophy, and was responsible for drawing together a community of like-minded people. Over extended periods of time, John Muir, Margaret Fuller, Elizabeth Palmer, Walt Whitman, Louisa May Alcott, and Amos Bronson Alcott lived near Emerson's home in Concord, Massachusetts, and were frequent visitors. All were members, along with a dozen other New England intellectuals, of the loosely formed Transcendental Club that believed as Emerson that "A foolish consistency is the hobgoblin of little minds." In addition to his fine house, Emerson was "landlord and waterlord of 14 acres, more or less" of a small rustic lake called Walden Pond where Thoreau lived for two years. Thoreau detailed his experiences and contemplations in *Walden*, and in contemporary times Garry Trudeau has kept the spirit of Walden Pond alive in his *Doonesbury Chronicles*.

Emerson was the most well-known intellectual of his time, and Oliver Wendell Holmes said of his essay, *Nature*, in which he defines transcendentalism, that it was the "Intellectual Declaration of Independence." Emerson handsomely supported himself and spread the transcendentalism gospel by giving more than 1,500 public lectures at top fees across the country. He was well received when he spoke in Davenport, but his presentations seem to have had little effect on the city's cultural awareness and were probably appreciated in the same way as that of the Boston scrubwoman who regularly attended his lectures. When asked if she understood Mr. Emerson, she replied, "Not at all, but I like to go and see him stand up there and look as though he thought everyone was as good as he." Rock Islanders and others of refined sensibilities were challenged and moved by the man's insights, perceptions, and judgments. Transcendentalism's practical ideas and theories are often compared to the more radical writings of the European existentialists who were forming remarkably similar philosophical ideas on religion and free will at the time.

From the same period Thoreau published *Walden* until 1900, politics was one of the nation's primary forms of participatory entertainment. Always fortified with free beer, political show business featured torch-lit parades, "jollification" barbecues, mudslinging (literally), and debates that often ended in fistfights between the audience and duels between the debaters. Political partisanship had a tribal identity that was not unlike the Sauk's black and white markings, voter turnout was the highest in American history, and politics was not left to only the politicians, most of whom encouraged their constituencies to become actively involved. Abraham Lincoln created a plan for a rowdy, disruptive Whig Rough and Ready Club that would rile up all the "shrewd, wild boys about town." In 1854, the same year Lincoln made an anti-slavery speech in Peoria, U.S. Senator David Rice Atchison of Missouri led a pro-slavery gang of 800 wild boys against the anti-slavery town of Lawrence in the Kansas Territory. Although laying waste to the abolitionist community and their two printing presses, only one fatality occurred, and that was when a dynamited masonry wall fell on one of the rebels. After the town's destruction, Atchison declared, "Boys, this is the happiest day of my life," that will teach "the damned abolitionists a Southern lesson that they will remember until the day they die."

Violence was not confined to the frontier. The same month that pro-slavery rebels trashed Lawrence, Senator Charles Sumner of Massachusetts was beaten unconscious on the floor of the Senate with a cane wielded by a South Carolina congressman who was incensed by an abolitionist speech Sumner delivered. News of Sumner's beating set off John Brown, who with his four sons and a small band of men, randomly captured five Kansas pro-slavery settlers and hacked them to death with swords. Three years later in an elaborate attempt to acquire munitions to arm the slaves, the radical Free-Soiler, Brown, led a raid on the armory in Harpers Ferry, Virginia.

With 15 white men and five black men, Brown's plan was to kidnap locally prominent pro-slavery advocates and hold them captive inside the Harpers Ferry arsenal as "protection" from Southern militia and make time for word of the insurrection to spread throughout the region. Brown believed that in addition to a flood of white abolitionists, 200-500 blacks would immediately join him at the arsenal. When a sufficient armed force was gathered, he envisioned marching into the heart of the South, freeing and arming slaves along the way. The plan started well and by the end of the first day, Brown had accomplished his first objectives: Brown's men captured Lewis Washington, George Washington's great grandnephew, and several of Washington's slaves. Then the activist-kidnappers captured several watchmen and townspeople in Harpers Ferry and cut the town's telegraph lines. Finally, the raiders captured the armory and seized a passing train. Then, things started to go wrong.

Ironically, a freed slave, who was a baggage handler on the train, confronted the raiders — they shot and killed him. Additionally, the support Brown expected from the abolitionist and black communities didn't materialize — in fact, no one showed up. Angered, the local militia and townspeople cut off all avenues of escape and started randomly firing on Brown's renegade band. The raiders took their hostages and moved into the armory's engine house. One of Brown's men panicked, bolted, and tried swimming across the Potomac River. Drunken townspeople made target practice of him until he sank below the surface.

When President James "Old Buck" Buchanan found out what was happening, he called on an engineer — Robert E. Lee — to retake the arsenal. Arriving with 88 U.S. Marines, Lee offered the local militia the first opportunity to storm the engine house. When they declined, he sent in the Marines who were led by Israel Greene. After battering down the door with a ladder, Greene was the first in the engine house. He described what transpired:

> Quicker than thought I brought my saber down with all my strength upon [Brown's] head. He was moving as the blow fell, and I suppose I did not strike him where I intended, for he received a deep saber cut in the back of the neck. He fell senseless on his side and then rolled over on his back. He had in his hand a short Sharpe's cavalry carbine. I think he had just fired as I reached Colonel Washington, for the Marine who followed me into the aperture made by the ladder received a bullet in the abdomen, from which he died in a few minutes. The shot might have been fired by someone else in the insurgent party, but I think it was from Brown. Instinctively as Brown fell I gave him a saber thrust in the left breast. The sword I carried was a light uniform weapon, and, either not having a point or striking something hard in Brown's accouterments did not penetrate. The blade bent double.

One marine was killed in the charge and one was wounded. Ten of Brown's men were killed, seven were captured, and four escaped. Brown was found guilty of treason and hung. To many in the North, Brown was a martyr. Henry David Thoreau said of him, "He has a spark of divinity in him." But to those in the South, Brown was a murderer who wanted to take their property. *De Bow's Review* said, "The North has sanctioned and applauded theft, murder, and treason." The brazen actions of white men from the frontier in genteel Virginia terrified many in the South, and they began to train militias for a feared invasion by the North.

Instead, taking the offensive on Christmas Eve only two months after Abraham Lincoln was elected president, South Carolina seceded from the Union. Quickly, six more of the "cotton states" voted to pass secession ordinances and the Confederate States of America was formed. Two weeks before Lincoln was sworn into office, Jefferson Davis, the man who transported Black Hawk from Prairie du Chien to Jefferson Barracks, was appointed Provisional President of the Confederacy.

Declaring their sovereignty, South Carolina ordered the United States to abandon all federal property in Charleston Harbor. The Union declined and moved their Army into Fort Sumter, a strategic fortification that controlled the entrance to the harbor. The South Carolina militia cut off the delivery of supplies to the fort, and the rebels began a three-month long siege. On April 12, Confederate troops began bombardment of the fortifications, and after 34 hours of continuous shelling, the Union commander agreed to evacuate. There was no loss of life until the surrender ceremonies when a gun exploded and killed two Union soldiers. President Lincoln put out an immediate call for 75,000 volunteers. The bloodiest war in U.S. history had begun.

Capturing Fort Sumter boosted Southern moral and began two years of heady times for the rebel nation. The Southern States were economically sounder than the North and had stronger European ties. Economics forged strange alliances, and because of European demand for cotton and tobacco and an ambivalent attitude towards slavery, Great Britain's sympathies ran to the South. And because they despised the U.S. Army, a majority of the more than 28,000 American Indians that fought in the war sided with the Confederacy. In particular, the Choctaw had a highly vested interest in the war's outcome — they had almost 6,000 Africans living in their villages, most of whom were treated only slightly better than they were on the plantations. Most important to the South's opening advantage was that they had more at stake. Whereas the North was fighting for principles — and even then, dying for one's principles was not a popular notion — the South was fighting for their lifestyle and livelihoods. The South had the more disciplined and better-trained military leaders, and their political leaders were equal to the North's. The North's only advantages were its industrial capabilities and greater numbers of young men.

Typical of the South's leadership was Confederate President Jefferson Davis. The youngest of ten children, Jefferson Davis grew up on a Mississippi cotton plantation. As a child, he was the only Protestant student at St. Thomas Catholic School. Then as a teenager, he attended Mississippi's Jefferson College and Transylvania University in Kentucky. Davis entered West Point as a 17-year-old, where he was a high-spirited but unremarkable cadet. His greatest notoriety at the academy was his role in the December 1826 Eggnog Riot when Cadets smuggled whiskey and rum into the Academy's North Barracks to make eggnog for a Christmas Day party. After warming up at holiday parties in town at Martin's and Benny's Taverns, cadets from the North Barracks returned to their rooms to make eggnog. Miffed at not being invited to the festivities, some cadets from the South Barracks crashed the all-night eggnog preparation party.

At 6:05 reveille sounded on Christmas morning, and many cadets fell in while still drunk; others slept in. Of the 70 who partied hardy, 22 were placed under house arrest pending disciplinary action. Even though Davis had gone to bed early and missed most of the holiday reverie, he was placed under house arrest because he had been observed as a "malefactor." Nineteen cadets were court-martialed — Davis and two others had their charges dismissed. Seventeen were found guilty, and ten were expelled from the Academy.

In spite of his alleged unruly behavior, Davis graduated 23rd in a class of 33. (Before the Civil War, fewer than half of those who entered West Point graduated.) While serving under Zachary Taylor in the Black Hawk War, Davis met and fell in love with Taylor's daughter, Sarah. Possibly because of his rowdy reputation, the colonel did not approve of Davis. Confronted with an unhappy boss and father-in-law, Davis resigned his commission to marry Sarah. Tragically three months after marrying, while visiting Davis' oldest sister in Louisiana, both newlyweds contracted malaria and Sarah died. Davis became reclusive for eight years and lived on his brother's plantation where he spent his days reading history and discussing politics.

Coming out of seclusion in 1844, Davis won a Mississippi seat in the U.S. House of Representatives. The following year he married Varina Howell, the granddaughter of a New Jersey governor, whom he met on a Natchez plantation. When the Mexican-American War began, Davis resigned his Congressional seat and became a colonel of a volunteer unit called the Mississippi Rifles. He distinguished himself during the war. Afterwards, Commanding General Zachary Taylor reconciled with his son-in-law saying, "My daughter, sir, was a better judge of men than I was." Elected to a U.S. Senate seat, Davis was made chairman of the Committee on Military Affairs. A tireless supporter of slavery, he introduced an amendment to annex most of northeast Mexico. Failing at that, he declared, "Cuba must be ours [to] increase the number of slaveholding constituencies."

In 1853 Franklin "Handsome Frank" Pierce appointed Davis Secretary of War. Pierce had run as a Democrat for the presidency under the slogan, "We Polked you in 1844; we shall Pierce you in 1852!" and easily defeated General Winfield Scott, a Whig who ran a poor campaign. Pierce appointed Davis during a period of U.S. international tranquility. Pierce was known as a "doughface," a man from the North with Southern sympathies — Davis and Pierce got along exceptionally well. After being returned to the Senate in 1858, Davis immediately resigned when Mississippi adopted an ordinance of secession in January 1861.

Four months after Mississippi seceded and after the Union defeat at Fort Sumter, Lincoln put out the call for volunteers and Illinoisans hastened to answer. One of the first to step forward was Hiram Ulysses Grant, a West Point graduate who had served under General Zachary Taylor and with many U.S. Military Academy graduates, including Jefferson Davis, during the Mexican-American War. At age 17, Hiram Ulysses Grant was nominated to the Academy under the name of Ulysses S. Grant — a mistake he never bothered to correct. At West Point, Grant was nicknamed "Sam" since his initials, U.S., were commonly used to designate Uncle Sam, the personification of the U.S. Government. Grant excelled as a horseman, and for 25 years he held the Academy's equestrian high jump record. Graduating 21st in a class of 39, he served as a supply and equipment quartermaster under General Taylor. After the war, he tried his hand at different businesses in the St. Louis area and failed at each. Disheartened, he moved to Galena where he worked as an assistant in his father's tanning company.

Galena had exploded into a bustling town of 14,000 and at the time was producing 80 percent of the lead ore in the United States. One dark and stormy night, Grant, who was a heavy drinker, dragged himself into an inn in Galena. A number of lawyers, who were in town for a court session, were gathered in front of the fireplace. One looked up as Grant approached and said, "Here's a stranger, gentlemen, and by the looks of him he's traveled through hell itself to get here."

"That's right," Grant cheerfully said.

"And how did you find things down there?"

"Just like here," replied Grant, "lawyers all closest to the fire."

Elated to return to the Army, Grant answered Lincoln's call for volunteers and rounded up a tough, unruly company of Illinois miners and settlers that he led into Springfield while astride his white mare, Methuselah. He was appointed to train and command the company. Described by Major General John Frémont, as "a man of dogged persistence and iron will," through relentless enthusiasm and with the staunch support of Lincoln, Grant was ultimately promoted to Commanding General of the Union Army.

In February 1862, shortly after his promotion to Major General, after five days of besieging Confederate-held Fort Donelson in Tennessee, the fort's commander sent a message suggesting an armistice. Grant replied, "No terms except unconditional and immediate surrender can be accepted. I propose to move upon your works." The terms of surrender were accepted. Capturing Fort Donelson was a major Union victory and again incorporating his initials, Grant became known to his superiors and troops as "Unconditional Surrender." He later revealed that a rebel deserter had told him that troops at the fort had been given six days' rations. Knowing that "troops do not have six days' rations served out to them in a fort if they mean to stay there" led to Grant's uncompromising position.

Moving southeast along the Tennessee River, two months later Grant's Army was attacked by equally strong Confederate forces at Shiloh. After falling back the first day, Grant took the offensive and scored another decisive Union victory on the second day. He was apparently drunk for most of the engagement, and advisors urged President Lincoln to relieve him of his command. Given the relative incompetence of his other generals, Lincoln responded, "I can't spare this man — he fights." When the complaints persisted, out of exasperation Lincoln exclaimed, "If I knew what brand of whiskey he drinks, I would send a barrel or so to my other generals!"

Grant's military Confederate counterpart, Robert E. Lee, was born at Stratford Hall plantation in Westmoreland County, Virginia — the same county where George Washington and James Monroe were born. Lee's ancestors arrived at Jamestown in the early 1600's, and his father was Major General Henry "Light Horse Harry" Lee III. Light Horse Harry served as a cavalry officer in the American Revolution and was later Governor of Virginia. Before entering the U.S. Military Academy at age 18, Lee attended Eastern View, "a school for young gentlemen," and Alexandria Academy.

Graduating second in a class of 45, Lee was commissioned a second lieutenant in the Corps of Engineers. The summer after graduating from West Point, he began courting a childhood friend, Mary Custis, a great granddaughter of Martha Washington by her first marriage. Two years later, they married. The Lee's had seven children — their three boys all served the Confederacy as high-ranking officers during the Civil War. The male Lee siblings survived into the 20th century and became accomplished educators, politicians, and businessmen, and they all fostered a close friendship with their grandniece, Helen Keller.

After serving as a civil engineer and developing the plan for taming the Rock Island Rapids and later as the Superintendent of West Point for three years, 26 years after graduating from the Academy, Lee was given his first combat command. Second-in-command of the 2nd Cavalry regiment in Texas, his mission was to protect settlers from Apache and Comanche attacks. Prior to the Civil War, Lee's only other combat command was at Harpers Ferry. Two weeks before Fort Sumter, Winfield Scott, the commanding general of the Union Army told Lincoln, who had just been sworn in, that he wanted Lee for a top command — Lee accepted a promotion to colonel.

A short time earlier Lee had been asked by one of his lieutenants if he intended to fight for the Confederacy or the Union, to which Lee replied, "I shall never bear arms against the Union, but it may be necessary for me to carry a musket in the defense of my native state, Virginia. In which case, I shall not prove recreant to my duty." After Fort Sumter, Lee asked General Scott if he could remain in the U.S. Army but not participate in the war. To which Scott replied, "I have no place in my army for equivocal men." Two days later Lee resigned his commission, and three days after that he took command of the Virginia militia. It appears Winfield Scott's abrupt dismissal of Lee's request to stay at the edge of the conflict tipped the scales in his decision. He was devoted to his country, Virginia, and his profession, and he had spent his adult life as an Army engineer and a military administrator. He was not a warrior, but he was an imposing figure who was loved by his men and respected by all. A soldier wrote upon seeing him for the first time at Fort Sumter:

> Glancing round we saw approaching us the then commander of the fort, accompanied by several of his captains and lieutenants; and, in the middle of the group, topping the tallest by half a head, was, perhaps, the most striking figure we had ever encountered, the figure of a man seemingly about fifty-six or fifty-eight years of age, erect as a poplar, yet lithe and graceful, with broad shoulders well thrown back, a fine, justly-proportioned head posed in unconscious dignity, clear, deep, thoughtful eyes, and the quiet, dauntless step of one every inch the gentleman and soldier. ... And this superb soldier, the glamour of the antique days about him, was no other than Robert E. Lee, just commissioned by the President [Jefferson Davis], after his unfortunate campaign in Western Virginia, to travel southward and examine the condition of our coast fortifications and seaboard defenses in general.

Before Scott's response to his request, Lee was torn by his allegiances, and he denounced secession as "revolution" and "betrayal" of the nation's founders. He wrote to his son, "I can anticipate no greater calamity for the country than dissolution of the Union." His wife, to whom Lee was devoted, favored the Union, and Lee's decision to fight for the South astounded her. His sons followed him to the Confederacy; however, many other close friends and relatives remained loyal to the Union. Virginia was intensely proud of its heritage, its founding patriots, and its leadership and countless contributions to the formation of the young nation. It was a momentous loyalty struggle for all of Virginia's citizens, and nearly as many of the Old Dominion State's U.S. Army regulars fought for the North as well as the South.

Lee's conscience was equally torn over slavery, and historians still argue whether he was pro- or anti-slavery. The reality is that he may have been as conflicted over that issue as he was over his allegiance to the United States or to Virginia. While fighting in Bloody Kansas, Lee wrote to his wife:

> In this enlightened age, there are few I believe, but what will acknowledge, that slavery as an institution, is a moral & political evil in any Country. It is useless to expatiate on its disadvantages. I think it however a greater evil to the white man than to the black race, & while my feelings are strongly enlisted in behalf of the latter, my sympathies are more strong for the former. The blacks are immeasurably better off here than in Africa, morally, socially & physically. The painful discipline they are undergoing is necessary for their instruction as a race, & I hope will prepare & lead them to better things. How long their subjugation may be necessary is known & ordered by a wise Merciful Providence.

It would be more than a century before mainstream white America believed differently.

Chapter 12

The War at Home

The war was an unnecessary condition of affairs, and might have been avoided if forbearance and wisdom had been practiced on both sides. ~ Robert E. Lee

AT THE START OF THE CIVIL WAR, the town of Davenport was designated Iowa's Union headquarters. No major military battles were fought there; however, Iowans contributed to the war effort by growing grain and raising livestock to feed the Union troops and by joining the Army. Of the 76,242 Iowans who served in the Union Army, 13,001 died of wounds or disease — of these, 277 were from Scott County. Many Iowans were pro-slavery and anti-Lincoln Confederate sympathizers. It is unclear how many Iowans served the Confederacy, but there were several raids by Confederate guerillas, known as "bushwhackers," into southern Iowa where they were provided safe haven by locals. The first from Scott County to give his life for the Union was Augustus Wentz, a 34-year-old German immigrant, who was Davenport's constable before assembling 50 volunteers shortly after the war broke out. Most of Wentz' recruits were from the local German Turner Society, a gymnastics organization. He was made captain of Company G of the 1st Iowa Infantry, and within a few months Wentz was promoted to lieutenant colonel and his unit was merged into "Iowa's Gallant Seventh," part of a force led by an obscure newly-appointed general, Ulysses S. Grant.

Just three months after leaving Davenport, Wentz' wife Rebecka and several other soldiers' wives journeyed to southern Missouri to visit their husbands. After arriving, the wives waited behind the lines of a skirmish that broke out at Bird's Point, Missouri, across the Mississippi from the Illinois-Kentucky state line. During the battle Wentz was shot from his horse and while dying, his last words were reported to be, "Let me alone, boys. I want to die on the battlefield." Tragically, two days later Rebecka found his body stripped of its clothing and possessions. Wentz was transported to Davenport by train where he lay in state at City Hall. Sixteen years later a memorial service was held for him, and most of Davenport turned out to witness the funeral parade to Oakdale Cemetery.

The Civil War drained Rock Island County of its able-bodied young men who were old enough to fight — everyone 18 or those who didn't work at the Rock Island Arsenal or for the railroad joined the Union Army. (It is estimated that more than 100,000 boys 15 and under served the Union in non-combat positions, that more than 400 women hid their gender and fought, that the youngest "soldier" was a 9-year-old Union drummer boy, that the youngest casualty was 12, and that there was a gray-beard division of men over age 45.) Of the 2,199 names of those from Rock Island County engraved on the Civil War monument that stands in front of the Rock Island County Court House "who served their country during the great rebellion and died that the nation might live," one name is carved in larger letters and literally stands above the rest. It is that of John Buford, Jr.

The second of John Buford's four boys, John, Jr., was a handsome and athletic young man who was described as, "a splendid horseman, an unerring rifle shot, and a person of wonderful nerve and composure." After attending Cincinnati College (now the University of Cincinnati) for a year, Buford returned to Illinois and briefly enrolled in Knox Manual Labor College (now Knox College) in Galesburg, before being accepted into West Point where he graduated 16th in a class of 38. Union General John Gibbon said of him, although "rather slow in speech, he was quick enough in thought and apt at repartee. He was not especially distinguished in his studies, but his course in the Academy was marked by a steady progress, the best evidence of character and determination." After graduation in 1848, Buford served in the West where he was first sent to Bloody Kansas to help quiet the anti-slavery and pro-slavery factions. He then fought the Sioux in Texas and the Mormons in the Utah Territory.

In 1850, President Fillmore had appointed Brigham Young Territorial Governor, essentially creating a theocracy in the Utah Territory. Mormons were virtually the only people living in the settlements that lined the Wasatch Front of the Great Basin, and under Young, polygamous marriage had become such the rage that it was estimated to encompass a third to a half of all Utah Territory women. Responding to Protestant outrage in the East, In 1857 President James Buchanan dismissed Young as governor. When he refused to step down, Buchanan sent in the troops. Under the command of Albert Sidney Johnson, who became the highest-ranking Confederate officer, John Buford was deployed to Utah to help quell what became known as the Mormon Rebellion.

With no apparent motives other than greed, orneriness, resentment of the government meddling in their marital affairs, and revenge for firing Brigham Young, the Latter-day Saints had engaged in some very unholy acts. The most egregious was the slaughter of a wagon train of 120 men, women, and children by the Utah Territorial

Militia in what is known as the Mountain Meadows Massacre. The well-stocked and well-managed wagon train of families from Arkansas had headed south from Salt Lake City to catch the Old Spanish Trail into southern California. After leaving Salt Lake City, the immigrants were advised by a Mormon frontiersman to graze their livestock and to rest in a southern Utah meadow before crossing the desert. While they were preparing for the grueling desert crossing, militiamen disguised as Paiute Indians attacked the immigrants in the meadow. The Arkansans fought back and a five-day battle ensued. Fear spread among the Mormon Militia that their disguises had been discovered. To quiet his troops' paranoia, the militia commander ordered the annihilation of the emigrants.

Because they were running low on water, the wagon master allowed a party of militiamen to enter their camp. Assured by the envoy that they would be unharmed, a group of leaders from the wagon train were led from the circled wagons to meet with the militia commander. Then making certain there would be no witnesses, the Mormon Militia slaughtered the unsuspecting camp, sparing only 17 children who were all younger than seven. The children were disbursed to local families and the wagons, provisions, and victims' possessions were auctioned to local buyers. Most of the emigrants' large herds of oxen and cattle were driven to Salt Lake City where they received a higher price. The 103 dead bodies were left as carrion for coyotes and other prairie scavengers.

Norman Klingensmith, a Mormon bishop and militia private and apparently a man with a conscience, was at the massacre. After leaving the church, Klingensmith turned state's evidence against his fellow militiamen. Nine men were indicted. After two trials, the militia commander was convicted and executed. A jury of their peers found the others not guilty. The month following this massacre, six wealthy Californians traveling through the Utah Territory were arrested by the Mormon Militia as U.S. Army spies. After their release, the men were robbed of their cattle and $25,000 ($625,000) before being killed. No one was indicted for the murders.

After Bloody Kansas, fighting the Sioux, and his three-year stint at Utah's Fort Crittenden, John Buford, Jr. was prepared for the atrocities he would experience in the Civil War. When Buford received word by Pony Express that war had broken out, like many of his West Point classmates, he was immediately pressured to pick a side — North or South. Before moving to Rock Island, he had spent the first eight years of his life on a Kentucky horse farm with black servants and slaves, and many of his classmates, friends, and relatives chose to fight with the South.

General Gibbon recalled, "One night after the arrival of the mail we were in [Buford's] room, talking over the news...when Buford said in his slow and deliberate way, 'I got a letter by the last mail from home with a message in it from the Governor of Kentucky. He sends me word to come to Kentucky at once, and I shall have anything I want.' With a good deal of anxiety, I asked, 'what did you answer, John?' and my relief was great when he replied, 'I sent him word I was a captain in the United States Army, and I intend to remain one."

Andrew Humphreys was a West Point graduate, who like Buford was steadfast in his loyalty to the Union. Humphreys was an underclassman when Robert E. Lee was a senior at the academy, and like Lee, Humphreys had a long career in the Army Corps of Engineers before the Civil War. He was an academic, whereas his professional peers in the private sector were men of engineering intuition and experience. Professionally, Humphreys was disliked because of his arrogance and because he used his education and Army commission to bully his way into prominent engineering positions.

In 1850 Congress had appropriated funds to determine why the Mississippi River recurrently flooded and why sandbars formed at the river's mouth. The 40-year-old Humphreys was assigned the task. Recognizing a boondoggle project when he saw one and sensing a career breakthrough, the opportunistic engineer organized three teams of engineers to collect data to substantiate what the engineers and river men already knew: more water than the riverbed could hold caused the river to flood and fast-moving water excavated troughs in the sand around big rocks and ledges, creating sandbars. Humphreys began what became the authoritative work of the time and for decades to come defining the hydraulics of the Mississippi River.

To Humphreys' initial distress, the Civil War interrupted his data gathering. The native Philadelphian and 30-year career officer stuck with the Union and began to make the best of a bad situation. He threw himself fully into his war assignments and found that he greatly liked battle. Called "Old Goggle Eyes" because he wore glasses, he was a strict disciplinarian and was disliked by his men and superiors alike. Charles Dana, the Assistant Secretary of War, called him a man of "distinguished and brilliant profanity." Humphreys' first major military action was at Fredericksburg, an early battle where the Union Army came up against Robert E. Lee. It was a bloodbath — more than 12,000 Union soldiers were killed compared to 5,000 Confederate losses.

General Lee's forces held a fortified ridge, and General Ambrose E. Burnside foolishly sent wave after wave of Union troops in frontal attacks against them. Humphreys commanded 5,000 men, and when his turn came to charge the ridge within five to ten minutes, he lost 1,000 men. After the battle a fellow officer wrote of him, "I do like to see a brave man, but when a man goes out for the express purpose of getting shot at, he seems to me in the way of a maniac." The clueless Humphreys was exhilarated by the carnage and wrote to a friend, "I felt like a young girl of sixteen at her first ball ... I felt more like a god than a man." To his wife he wrote, "The excitement grew, oh, it was sublime."

While Humphreys was commanding field troops during the war's first year, John Buford, Jr. was serving in Washington as an assistant to the Inspector General. He was soon promoted to Brigadier General of Volunteers. An excellent horseman, he was given a brigade of cavalry (about 3,000 men) and served with distinction until being wounded in the knee at the Second Battle of Bull Run. After recovering from his wound, Buford was promoted to brigadier general and given command of the 1st Division of the newly formed Cavalry Corps. (A division is two or more brigades.) It was in this position that Buford rode with his division towards the small town of Gettysburg in south-central Pennsylvania on June 30, 1863.

General Robert E. Lee, who was thought by most from the South and many from the North to be a brilliant strategist and nearly invincible, was concentrating his Confederate armies to move the war out of the South and into the North. Seventy thousand Confederate soldiers had moved into the hills of northern Maryland and southern Pennsylvania, and 90,000 Union troops under Major General George G. Meade were ready to engage them when they moved north into Pennsylvania. One of Lee's forces occupied the small town of Cashtown, eight miles west of Gettysburg. On June 30, a brigade from Cashtown was sent to Gettysburg to confiscate supplies — especially shoes and boots. The Confederates reached Gettysburg to see Buford's cavalry unit approaching the village. The Confederate brigade returned to Cashtown.

The previous day while overlooking the Cumberland Valley, Buford said, "Within forty-eight hours, the concentration of both armies will take place on some field within view, and a great battle will be fought." Buford positioned his cavalry in the high ground northwest of Gettysburg. Soon joined by Union infantry, the combined troops were the first to engage the Confederate forces when they attacked early the next morning. Forces from both sides converged in the wooded hills and grassy fields surrounding the town. Battles raged throughout the Gettysburg area for three days, and finally on the 4th of July, General Lee retreated. Although the significance of the Union victory was not fully appreciated at the time and the war would continue for two more years, historians mark the Battle of Gettysburg and the repulsion of Lee's forces as the turning point of the Civil War.

The three-day devastation of property and life at Gettysburg is hard to comprehend. Of the 46,000 casualties 7,800 were killed, 27,000 were wounded, and 11,000 were captured or missing. By comparison, the total Allied and German forces killed, wounded, and captured or missing at the World War II Normandy landings were less than a third of Gettysburg's. One Civil War historian wrote, "The town of

Gettysburg looked as if some universal moving day had been interrupted by catastrophe." Miraculously, only one civilian was killed during the battle — 20-year-old Ginnie Wade was hit by a stray bullet while baking bread in her kitchen.

Buford was an energetic man who was described by a superior early in the war as "never looking after his own comfort, untiring on the march and in the supervision of his command, quiet and unassuming in his manners." Three months after Gettysburg, another Union general said of Buford:

> He is one of the best officers of [the Union cavalry] and is a singular-looking party...a compactly built man of middle height with a tawny mustache and a little triangular gray eye, whose expression is determined, not to say sinister. His ancient corduroys are tucked into a pair of ordinary cowhide boots and his blue blouse is ornamented with holes; from one pocket thereof peeps a huge pipe, while the other is fat with a tobacco pouch. Notwithstanding this get-up, he is a very soldierly looking man. He is of a good-natured disposition, but not to be trifled with. Caught a notorious spy last winter and hung him to the next tree, with this inscription: "This man is to hang three days; he who cuts him down before shall hang the remaining time."

The war rapidly aged men beyond their years. After Gettysburg, Buford, whose men called him "Old Steadfast," led his division to victory in two more battles, but his health deteriorated badly. A fellow officer said of the 37-year-old Buford, "He suffered terribly from rheumatism, and for days together could not mount a horse without help, but once mounted, he would remain in the saddle all day." In late November after Gettysburg, Buford contracted typhoid and died within a month. He is buried at West Point. Twelve major generals served as his pallbearers.

Six months after the Battle at Gettysburg and two years after becoming the Rock Island Arsenal, the formerly sacred grounds of the Sauk became the largest Union prison. Between December 1863 and July 1865, more than 12,400 Confederate soldiers were detained there. In the military cemetery, white marble stones mark the graves of 1,964 prisoners and 125 Union guards. In a separate section of the cemetery are 49 graves of soldiers from the 108th Regiment of United States Colored Troops. Most of the prison deaths were from smallpox, dysentery, scurvy, pneumonia, and exposure.

In her epic Civil War novel, *Gone with the Wind*, Margaret Mitchell wrote, "at no place were conditions worse than at Rock Island [the island prison, not the city]." The novel's fictional character Ashley Wilkes was imprisoned at Rock Island, the "hellhole of the north." In January 1960, Sam Chilton, Rock Island High School's first swim team coach, was spending his first full winter in the North. Accepting the coaching position after graduating from the University of Mississippi and upon returning by school bus from a December meet in Cedar Rapids, Iowa, Coach Chilton looked out over desolate, snow-covered Iowa fields shrouded by gray skies and parroted Margaret Mitchell when he turned to two swimmers and drawled, "If I didn't see it with my own eyes, I would never have believed hell could freeze over."

Although there had been intense animosities and wide divisions over the slavery issue, Kansas was admitted into the Union as a free state on January 29, 1861, only three months before the Civil War's opening battle at Fort Sumter. When war broke out, 15-year-old Will Cody, along with 20,000 other Kansans, rushed to enlist in the U.S. Army but was denied because of his age. Instead he worked as a teamster, delivering Union supplies. When old enough, Cody enlisted in the 7th Kansas Cavalry and served until he was discharged at the war's end. Although the spark that ignited the war was lit in Kansas, during the war only a handful of minor skirmishes were fought there, and they were all waged along the Missouri border.

During the war, Texas' economic interests were aligned with the South's. After voting 166 to 7 to secede and overriding Governor Sam Houston's veto at a special convention, the state legislators voted themselves expense money and supplies and adjourned. Houston refused to take an oath of allegiance to the Confederate States of America, and the previously immensely popular governor was relieved of his elected duties. Although many from the Lone Star State fought for the Confederacy, most were content to stay at home and supply Southern forces with horses, cattle, and cotton. When Union forces began to intercept Texans and their products at the Mississippi River and blockaded the port of Galveston, most quietly waited out the war.

After passing the Ordinance of Secession in February of 1861, the Texas legislature appointed four men as "commissioners of public safety" to negotiate with the Federal government for the safe transfer of military installations and bases in Texas to the Confederates. The commissioners met with U.S. Army General David E. Twigs, a 70-year-old soldier from Georgia who during his 50-year career had fought in the War of 1812, the Seminole Wars, and the Black Hawk War. After the Mexican-American War, Twigs was appointed Brevet Major General of the Department of Texas.

Two weeks after the vote to secede, while meeting with three of the Texas Public Safety commissioners, General Twigs surrendered his entire command and its equipment, which included 10,000 rifled muskets that were stored at the Alamo, to the State of Texas. As soon as his superiors heard of his treason, they sent a replacement to relieve him of his command. Warned of the Army's intent, Twigs deserted and was commissioned a general in the Confederate Army. Unfortunately, his health failed before he could do more damage to the Union Army he had served for fifty years, and he died that fall. When U.S. Army Colonel Robert E. Lee, who was serving in San Antonio at the time, heard of Twigs treachery, he lamented, "Has it come to this so soon?"

Ironically, California was less involved in the American Civil War than England. Two thousand miles and a two-month-long stage coach ride from the action, most Californians passed the war rooting from afar for the region they had emigrated from. While the rest of the nation was tearing itself apart, California prospered, and a few Confederacy sympathizers from Southern California cashed in on the war by privateering for the South. Then after the war, California became a magnet for Southerners whose lives and property had been devastated by the conflict. California's wartime political power resided with their powerful mining, shipping, banking, and financial interests. And the significantly greater population in the northern half of the state drove the state's popular and electoral vote. In 1861 Democratic San Franciscans, apparently believing that everyone east of the Rockies was too preoccupied to notice or care, initiated their own secession attempt to separate California and Oregon from the rest of the nation. Republican businessmen, who had commercial ties to the Federal government and Eastern business interests, quickly squashed that idea.

To induce entrepreneurs to finish building a railroad through unsettled and inhospitable territory and to connect California's vast resources to America's transportation crossroads at Rock Island, the U.S. Government loaned $130 million ($3 billion) and gave massive tracts of land to four California businessmen and politicians. The "Big Four" or the "Associates" as they preferred to be called — Charles Crocker, Mark Hopkins, Collis Huntington, and Leland Stanford — joined the Eastern fraternity of Railroad Robber Barons, and the four Republican men dominated West Coast business and California politics for more than two decades.

Back in Washington, when the Emancipation Proclamation was presented to Lincoln at noon on New Year's Day, 1863, he twice picked up his pen to sign it and twice put it back down. To the secretary of state he said, "I have been shaking hands all morning, and my arm is almost paralyzed. If my name ever goes into history, it will be for this act, and my whole soul is in it. If my hand trembles when I sign the Proclamation, all who examine it hereafter will say, 'He hesitated.'" Lincoln then slowly picked up the pen and firmly wrote his name.

Because of the superior number of Northern forces, Lincoln's generals fought similarly as European generals had for centuries. In battles that resembled massive football games, waves of men would charge at each other trying to push the other side back, or in the best of cases, break through the defensive line and capture the supply lines behind them. The Civil War was a war of attrition that because of the North's greater numbers and because it was mostly fought south of the Mason-Dixon Line always favored the North. Both sides put "the cause" above personal and family considerations. Honor was foremost, and for Northerners not to believe that one should "die so that the nation might live" was an act of cowardice. In the South, it soon became apparent that the North was as committed to victory as they were and Southerners took comfort in their motto, *Deo Vindice* — under God our protector.

Lieutenant General Ulysses S. Grant was general-in-chief of all Union armies and directed the war's concluding campaign against General Robert E. Lee. Begun in early May 1864, with a series of major battles and eight weeks of intense warfare in northern Virginia, Grant succeeded in moving his armies into a battle line that eventually extended 30 miles to the east of Petersburg and Richmond, the Confederate capital. Grant's "Overland Campaign" was the bloodiest of the war. In the North, 55,000 Union casualties caused widespread criticism of Lincoln and his war effort, whereas the South's proportionately greater losses relative to its population of 32,000 and its seemingly desperate situation, only strengthened Southern resolve and support for the rebel cause.

In the second battle of the Overland Campaign, Lee met Grant in a standoff that demonstrated Lee's superior tactical skills. Receiving reports that Grant had lost legions of men in the campaign's first battle and was preparing to retreat, General John Gordon was surprised when Lee ordered him to move his troops to Spotsylvania Courthouse, a village away from Grant's forces. Having great respect for Grant's military instincts — which were a blend of superior intuition, a knack for surprise, and fearlessness — Lee had reasoned that in retreat Grant would take the most expedient route that offered the greatest protection, a route that would take him through Spotsylvania. Lee told Gordon, "That is his best maneuver, and he will do what is best. I am so sure of it that I have had a short road cut to that point, and you will move by that route." Grant's troops arrived at Spotsylvania to find Gordon's forces waiting for him.

For nine months, Grant engaged in a combination of classic siege and moving trench warfare as he launched repeated attacks on the critical supply lines and munitions depots of Petersburg and the seat of power of the Confederacy. During November and December, while Grant was assaulting the Petersburg region, General William Tecumseh Sherman made his infamous "March to the Sea" from Atlanta to Savanna, Georgia, in which he burned and destroyed by his estimate $100 million ($1.4 billion) of property.

Sherman estimated one fifth of what his forces destroyed was of strategic value, while the "remainder [was] simple waste and destruction." Sherman, who believed as many other Northerners did that blacks were inferior to whites, wouldn't allow slaves to join the march, although thousands followed in miles-long columns behind the Union troops. Because they suffered nearly equal hardships, Georgia's black slaves were as outraged as their owners at the destruction of their homes, barns, and crops that fed their families and because they felt betrayed by Sherman, many freed slaves remained with their prior owners after the war to work the land they were tied to. Although hailed at the time as devastating to the South's psychology and morale, Sherman's pernicious march served minor military purpose and increased Southern resentment of the North.

In April of 1865, Grant stepped up the pressure on Petersburg, and Lee abandoned both Petersburg and Richmond — at that point it became only a matter of time. Knowing that he had to fight to the end, retreating west and hoping to join his army with Confederate forces in North Carolina and believing that the Union Army which pursued him was composed of only cavalry troops, Lee made a frontal attack on Grant's Army at Appomattox Court House, Virginia, a village of about 20 buildings. When he discovered a battalion of infantry backed up Grant's cavalry, Lee had no choice but to surrender.

Grant sent a message to Lee allowing him the unusual courtesy of picking the time and place for the formal surrender. Lee selected a substantial brick home of a man who had retired to Appomattox Court House to escape the war. Meeting for the first time in the nearly twenty years since they served side-by-side in the Mexican-American War, Lee arrived impeccably dressed in Confederate gray. Grant wore a government-issue flannel shirt under a dirty blue Union uniform with his trousers tucked into muddy boots. He wore no sidearm and his rank was displayed only by his tarnished shoulder straps.

Recovering from a migraine headache, Grant was overcome with a profound sadness. The generals discussed the time when they had served together, and finally Lee directed the conversation to the issues at hand. Grant's terms for Lee to lay down his arms were generous. They provided that Lee and his men would not be imprisoned or prosecuted for treason, and they allowed Lee's troops to keep their horses and mules, enabling them to do the spring planting. As a final conciliatory gesture, he provided Lee with food for his starving Army. Lee was graciously appreciative and said that Grant's generosity would do much toward reconciling the country. Lee never forgot Grant's magnanimity, and for the rest of his life he would not tolerate an unkind word about Grant, who was generally as hated by Southerners as Lincoln.

After Lee's surrender at Appomattox Court House a Northern newspaper wrote:

> General Lee looked very much jaded and worn, but nevertheless presented the same magnificent physique for which he has always been noted. He was neatly dressed in gray cloth, without embroidery or any insignia of rank, except the three stars worn on the turned portion of his coat-collar. His cheeks were very much bronzed by exposure, but still shone ruddy underneath it all. He is growing quite bald, and wears one of the side locks of

his hair thrown across the upper portion of his forehead, which is as white and fair as a woman's. He stands fully six feet one inch in height, and weighs something over two hundred pounds, without being burdened with a pound of superfluous flesh. During the whole interview he was retired and dignified to a degree bordering on taciturnity, but was free from all exhibition of temper or mortification. His demeanor was that of a thoroughly possessed gentleman who had a very disagreeable duty to perform, but was determined to get through it as well and as soon as he could.

When Union General George G. Meade heard of Lee's surrender, he reportedly shouted, "It's all over." Although 175,000 Confederate troops remained in the field, as word spread of Lee's surrender, Meade proved correct, and the fighting ground to a finish. A month after Appomattox, the last battle was fought at Palmito Ranch, Texas, on the Rio Grande about 12 miles west of Brownsville. Since both sides knew of the South's capitulation, the reason for the battle remains somewhat a mystery. It appears that a young Union commander without previous battle experience, whose forces outnumbered the Confederates by 1,700 to 300, wanted to earn his stripes before he ran out of wartime opportunities. It also appears that 2,000 bales of contraband cotton stored in Brownsville may have played into the motive.

The Palmito Ranch Battle was unquestionably the most egalitarian of all the American Civil War battles: the fighting involved white and Indian Union and Confederate troops, blacks from the North's 87th and 62nd Colored Division, 100 plus Mexicans who were fighting with the South to protect their smuggling trade and the contraband cotton, and French forces who took time out from fighting in the "French Intervention" — an action where France sent troops to collect Mexico's war debts when they stopped paying. All joined with the Confederates in this final battle against the Union. The ragtag skirmish was without focus or passion, and ostensibly after killing four Union soldiers, wounding 12, and capturing 101, while suffering only five wounded and three captured, the greatly outnumbered Confederates won the last battle but lost the war.

Six months after he surrendered, Lee was appointed president of Washington College (now Washington and Lee University) in Lexington, Virginia. He held the position for five years until his death from a stroke. At Washington College, Lee repeatedly expelled white students for attacks on local blacks; he established state-funded schools for blacks; and he privately chastised Jefferson Davis and other ex-Confederates for their public outbursts against perceived Northern post-war injustices.

Shortly after the war, he had written to a magazine editor: "It should be the object of all to avoid controversy, to allay passion, give full scope to reason and to every kindly feeling. By doing this and encouraging our citizens to engage in the duties of life with all their heart and mind, with a determination not to be turned aside by thoughts of the past and fears of the future, our country will not only be restored in material prosperity, but will be advanced in science, in virtue, and in religion." When asked to write his memoirs, Lee declined by saying, "I should be trading on the blood of my men." Before his death, Lee said to a colleague that his greatest regret was not to have heeded his mother's advice to decline a military education.

Although brought up as a practicing Episcopalian, strangely Lee was not confirmed until he was 46-years-old. Not long after his surrender at Appomattox, a black man entered a fashionable Richmond, Virginia Episcopalian church for Sunday mass. The tension in the church escalated when the black man walked down the aisle and knelt at the altar for Communion. The thought of drinking the blood of our Lord from the same chalice as a black man was sacrilegious to the Southern parishioners. Then a distinguished layman stood, walked to the altar, and knelt beside the lone man. In a clear loud voice, Robert E. Lee said, "All men are brothers in Christ. Have we not all one Father?" One by one the congregation moved to the Communion rail.

"Unconditional Surrender" Grant could just as appropriately been called "Lucky." Often at the front line of battle and usually perched on his favorite steed, Cincinnati, he presented a prized target for the duration of the war. Unlike the 620,000 who lost their lives and an equivalent number who were wounded, Grant caught barely so much as a sniffle during the four years he led the Union forces.

After the war, Grant's luck continued to hold. Invited to see *Our American Cousin* at the Ford Theater with the president and first lady, Mary Todd Lincoln, Grant deferred because his wife and Mrs. Lincoln did not get along well and instead took a train trip with his wife to Philadelphia. Grant had been included in the assassination plot, and while in route to Philadelphia porters on the train thwarted an assailant trying to break into his railroad car. At Lincoln's funeral Grant stood alone and wept openly, and later said of Lincoln, "He was incontestably the greatest man I've ever known."

A Nation Rebuilds

Race remains America's unresolved dilemma ~ Bill Bradley, Rhodes Scholar, NBA All-star, Author, U.S. Senator

WELL AWAY FROM THE CIVIL WAR'S BATTLES, the Union's prison-supply and construction contracts on Government Island, sharply spiked Rock Island's economy during the war. To bolster the war effort, 15 months after the Battle of Fort Sumter, Congress established three new arsenals — one, which was to be the "Harper's Ferry of the West," was the Rock Island Arsenal on Government Island. The fast-tracked project, which was designed by Army engineers in Washington, called for a 3-story, 180 by 60-foot brick or stone storehouse with a full basement and attic. Congress allocated $100,000 ($2.5 million) for the storage building and the 34-foot square, 97-foot high tower that was capped by a bell and clock tower. A year after the funds were appropriated, the Arsenal's first commander arrived to supervise the storehouse's construction. A year later, work began. After another year and almost completing the first story and spending 60 percent of the Congressional allocation, the commander quit. The next spring, the war ended, as did the sense of urgency to complete the building.

At the Watertown Arsenal in Massachusetts, General Thomas Rodman, the arsenal's commander had spent the last three years of the Civil War designing a 20-inch 160,000-pound cannon that was never fired. (The world's largest gun was Germany's World War II Gustav Gun at 31.4 inches — it took a 500-man crew to move, position, and load the massive cannon — it fired a total of 330 shells.) Rodman's cannon was described by the *Pittsburgh Gazette* as being suitable for "a good sized family including ma and pa, to find shelter in the gun and it would be a capital place to hide in case of a bombardment." Rodman's wartime efforts came to the attention of Congress, and he was investigated because he "neglected to join officially in the observance of expression of joy at the surrender of the rebel General Lee, and of the sorrow at the death of President Lincoln. He was also accused of employing disloyal men; of interfering with the right to petition by refusing to allow female employees to circulate a petition in the laboratory and afterwards discharging 19 of them for doing so; of retaining an employee who had twice been found under the influence of liquor; of employing 57 foreigners out of 98 enlisted men; and of excessive spending in the building of the new commanding officer's quarters." The house he built for himself cost $63,478.65 ($1.3 million). After more than 100 witnesses testified against him, the results of the investigation were sealed, and he was assigned to complete the storehouse on the Rock Island Arsenal.

The Army had found the right man for the job. Rodman arrived with even more ambitious plans than had been originally approved, and two years after the war ended, with the efforts of a 400-man workforce, the storehouse was completed in 1867 at a total cost of $257,297 ($4.1 million). The *Argus* heralded the completion of the Clock Tower Building by declaring that the open third floor would be "a splendid room for a dance on opening the building." The bell for the clock weighed 3,538 pounds and cost $1,662.36 ($32,000). The clock's 4-wooden faces had grown from three feet to 12 feet in diameter, and the clock became a steal at only $5,000 ($75,000). Unfortunately, the clock only kept time for the Arsenal (one of the more than 100 U.S. time zones in 1867), which ran on "sun time" — a $10 sundial would have been as useful — whereas, Rock Island and its surrounding communities operated on Chicago railroad time.

The majority of the rest of the country didn't survive the Civil War as well as Rock Island did. Second only to the Indian Wars, the Civil War was America's most devastating conflict. The losses of life and property were staggering, and the social and cultural chasms that opened between the North and the Deep South have yet to be fully bridged 150 years later. The numbers only start to tell the story: 625,000 soldiers from both sides died with a total of more than a million casualties, 18 percent of the men from the Confederate States died in a four year span, income per person in the South dropped to 40 percent compared to those in the North, and the financial cost of the four-year war was an astounding $6.2 billion ($100 billion) — all at a time when the U.S. population was less than one tenth of today's. Although history books date the Reconstruction Era from the Emancipation Proclamation in 1863 to the withdrawal of federal troops from the South in 1877, arguably the South is still recovering from the war's destruction. It was not until the last decades of the 20th century that the South regained relevance in U.S. national politics, and its per capita income has made up less than half the gap created by the Civil War. Even today while driving down a Georgia, Mississippi, Alabama, or Louisiana secondary road, a driver with Northern license plates is still met with stares of contempt.

After Lincoln's assassination, Vice President Andrew "The Tennessee Taylor" Johnson appeared to be the best man to lead the mending of the nation. A U.S. Senator from Tennessee, Johnson was the only Southern senator not to resign his seat when the war began, and he was the most prominent War Democrat from the South. Lincoln appointed Johnson military governor of occupied Tennessee, where he effectively quelled the rebellion and implemented Lincoln's Reconstruction policies during the remainder of the war. Having served as vice president for only six weeks, Johnson tried to maintain Lincoln's conciliatory policies and approach to rebuilding the South, but hardline Radical Republicans in the North opposed his every move, and those in the South saw him as a turncoat. His appointments of new Southern governors were resented by almost everyone, and the governors were nearly powerless. Stating that the war's objectives of national unity and the end of slavery had been achieved, Johnson declared that Reconstruction was complete. But the Radical Republican Party vehemently disagreed. They believed that the South should be punished and that white Southerners were neither worthy nor capable of governing themselves.

Before the war, the self-described Radical Republicans were a loosely affiliated, ultra-conservative group within the Republican Party, and they had uniformly opposed Lincoln and his moderate policies. During the war, as the horrors mounted and the loss of loved ones reached staggering numbers, most of the Northern moderates joined their ranks. After the war, the Radical Republicans gave voice to the anger that Northerners felt over having fought a senseless war, and they demanded harsh reconstruction provisions. Winning complete control of Congress in the 1866-midterm elections, Radical Republicans were able to override Johnson's vetoes, and implemented what became known as the "Radical Reconstruction." Congress removed the civilian governments that Johnson had put into place and put the U.S. Army in control of the former Confederacy. New elections were held in which freed slaves could vote and former Confederate elected government officials could not run for office — Southern resentment deepened and hardened.

Post-war political attitudes in Rock Island ranged from those of the moderate Johnsonian Republicans to the Radical Republicans. Rock Island's most prominent cultural club, the Young Men's Literary Association, was instrumental in bringing a series of controversial Radical Republican speakers to Dart Hall. Formed in 1855 to prevent juvenile delinquency, the YMLA promoted cultural and Christian spiritual development, and they created the first public library in Illinois. The same year the YMLA was formed, a group of citizens including Thomas Buford, Stephen Velie, and Ben Harper met in the basement of the First Presbyterian Church to organize the Rock Island Library and Reading Association. An advertisement was placed in the *Rock Island Advertiser* for "an intelligent youth or elderly person, wishing a situation whose duties are light and easily performed" to act as librarian. The police magistrate's son got the job. The library opened on the third floor of a building on Illinois (2nd) Avenue with about 1,000 books.

Six years after the library opened, most of the YMLA went off to save the Union and library operations were suspended. Toward the end of the war, 500 books that had been kept in the homes of YMLA members were reassembled in a room of one of Ben Harper's buildings on Illinois (2nd) Avenue and Buffalo (16th) Street. And in 1868 a new library that operated every day except Sunday hired 15-year-old Ellen Gale as its librarian — an exceptionally progressive hiring for the day. In 1872 the YMLA donated their collection of books that had grown to more than 2,000 to the city, and Gale and the books she cherished moved into a room in the post office, establishing Illinois' first public library. Gale's salary was raised from $35 a month to $50 ($900). For an annual fee of $3 ($50), any citizen could check out books. Hired during Ulysses S. Grants' first term, the extraordinarily dedicated Gale competently filled her position for 64 years and catalogued books while 14 U.S. Presidents served; she retired during Franklin Roosevelt's first term. Gale's was the longest tenure ever for a U.S. librarian. (The record for longest service of any public employee goes to Harold "Bruno" Magnum who died in 2008 while still employed by the U.S. Department of Agriculture. Magnum had served for 71 years — he had 6,000 hours of unused sick leave when he died.)

Most of the young men who were members of the YMLA before the Civil War served in the Union Army. Understandably, after the war many held deep resentments towards the South. This was evidenced by the speakers they brought to Dart Hall, which included Wendell Phillips, an abolitionist leader and an early advocate of woman's suffrage; Congressman Schuyler Colfax, who was to become Grant's vice president; and Carl Schurz, an accomplished journalist, Union general, and U.S. Senator. He is well remembered for first saying, "My country, right or wrong;" but is less well remembered for the remainder of his quote, "if right, to be kept right; and if wrong, to be set right."

Many of the YMLA's speakers had been hardline abolitionists and advocated severe reconstruction policies for the South. Although the speakers were prominent men who contributed greatly to America's post-war growth, many of Rock Island's city fathers and their families had emigrated from the South and still had Southern ties and family who had suffered terribly during the war. Offended and disagreeing with the harsh Reconstruction positions of the speakers, dozens cancelled their ticket subscriptions. From then on the YMLA avoided controversial political speakers and concentrated on literary or inspirational speakers, such as Ralph Waldo Emerson and Clara Barton, the organizer of the American Red Cross. The YMLA also brought to Rock Island the nation's best musicians, including Ole Bull, a Norwegian violinist who received the standard YMLA performance fee of $75 ($1,200) per performance, and they presented popular plays, such as *Uncle Tom's Cabin*.

In most of the north, General Grant did not suffer from the same criticism for his harsh reconstruction policies as those of similar opinion did in Rock Island. Grant was the most popular man north of the Mason-Dixon Line – except with Jews. Out of necessity, during the war Lincoln had allowed limited trade with the South for cotton to make tents and uniforms in the Northern mills. A license was required to trade in cotton, and as commander of Tennessee, Grant was in charge of issuing licenses for his area. A burgeoning black market for cotton developed and a handful of the illegal traders were Jewish. In a knee-jerk reaction, Grant expelled all Jews from Kentucky, Tennessee, and Mississippi. Lincoln quickly reacted to the public outcry and reinstated the traders, but Grant had been labeled as anti-Semitic.

When he ran for the presidency in 1868, Grant repeatedly apologized for his wartime indiscretion and wooed the Jewish vote, ultimately winning more than half. Supporting the tough-line Reconstruction policies of the Radical Republicans, Grant narrowly won the popular vote over the little-remembered New York Governor, Horatio Seymour, who had successfully united the conservative Hunkers and liberal Barnburners factions of the Democratic Party. The Hunkers, who were named for someone who "hunkers" (hankers) for political power, favored state banks, improving the federal infrastructure, and minimizing slavery issues. The radical Barnburners were named for a person who would burn down his own barn to get rid of a rat infestation, and the name alluded to those who would destroy the banks and large corporations to get rid of their abuses. Seymour was a more skilled politician and administrator than Grant and his moderate Reconstruction views closely matched those of Lincoln and Johnson. Although he received almost half of the popular vote, he was soundly defeated in the electoral vote.

Four years later, Liberal Republican New York newspaperman, Horace Greeley, opposed Grant in his reelection bid. Although backed by the nation's most influential newspaper, in one of the most lopsided popular votes ever, the erudite Greeley received only 44 percent of the vote versus Grant's — the common man's favorite — 56 percent. Ironically, it was Greeley who championed workers' rights, government sponsored infrastructure, protective tariffs, suffrage, and a federal bank; he opposed government railroad support, monopolies, and the massive accumulation of wealth by a few. After the election, it got even stranger.

Shortly after Greeley cast his vote, his wife Margaret Cheney Greeley died. She was a spiritualist who believed that one of her sons, who had died at age five, was in constant communication with an 11-year-old medium she hired to live with her. Understandably, Greeley spent much time away from home and lived mainly in a rooming house. Within a few weeks after Margaret's death, the 61-year-old Greeley, who had been in fine health before the election, died of "madness." Released from their commitments, the electors who were pledged to Greeley voted for four different presidential candidates and eight different vice-presidential candidates, and to show their undying support for Greeley, three electors voted for their man posthumously.

Understanding where the political power was, Grant embraced the Radical Republicans and gave free reign to carpetbaggers and scalawags. Carpetbaggers were Northern opportunists cashing in on Reconstruction programs, while scalawags were self-interested, white Southerners who joined with the carpetbaggers and freedmen (freed slaves) to take control of state legislatures and the federal money that flowed to federal Reconstruction projects in the South. Although despised by the pre-war Southern aristocracy, the Radical Republican-backed carpetbaggers, scalawags, and freedmen accomplished many progressive objectives. After raising historically low taxes, they founded public schools in Confederate states that previously had only private schools. They established charitable institutions, and they subsidized industry, especially railroads. However, bribery, kickbacks, and favoritism were generally accepted as part of the deal, and as corruption became embedded in the Southern political landscape, it crept its way into all levels of Grant's Administration.

The carpetbaggers and widespread resentment of freedmen holding political office stoked Southern hatreds, and local vigilante groups formed to obstruct Northern Reconstruction efforts. Southern opposition grew as the South's plantation society was left in ashes, and a wide, disparate network of disenfranchised Southern men, many of whom were former Confederate soldiers, morphed into the well-structured and powerful Ku Klux Klan. In 1871 President Grant officially closed down the Klan, which drove the KKK underground and, of course, greatly increased its membership and power.

Soon after Grant began his second term, Otto von Bismarck took Germany off the silver standard and demanded a large retribution in gold from France, losers of the Franco-Prussian War. The action intensified the two-decade long European economic depression, which then spread to America where the post-war economy had boomed. The U.S. economy, driven by Reconstruction, had also been ramped-up by speculative railroad and manufacturing projects. Large amounts of capital had been invested in economic sectors that offered only long-term returns, and an economic downturn developed into a banking crisis. Called the Panic of 1873, many railroad projects and other economic programs in the South collapsed; Grant and the Radical Republicans took the heat. In a reaction to the recession, heavy-handed politics, and rampant corruption, Democrats crushed Republicans in the 1874 midterm elections and won back the House of Representatives. Immediately after the elections, Thomas Nast published a political cartoon in *Harper's Weekly*, in which he used a rampaging elephant as a symbol for the Republican Party. Republicans adopted the elephant as their party symbol. Oddly, in the cartoon the elephant was used in a derogatory way, but apparently the Grand Old Party didn't get the joke. (It was not until 2000, when the major broadcast networks used the color red to symbolize the states won by Republican George W. Bush that red became the party's unofficial color.)

Suffering from a poor economy and failed Reconstruction programs, Grant's second term was further marred by nepotism and scandal in the White House. More than 40 Grant family members fed well at the public trough, corruption of high-level public officials was rampant, and 11 major federal financial scandals were exposed during his two terms. At the end of his second term, Grant wrote to Congress, "Failures have been errors of judgment, not of intent." But the damage was done and Grant's chances for a third term nomination were ruined.

After leaving office, Grant went on a world tour that included stops in Europe, Russia, Egypt, the Holy Land, China, Thailand, Burma, and Japan. He was received enthusiastically, but he depleted his savings and then was financially bankrupted by poor investments at home. Restored by Congress to General of the Army with full retirement pay, Grant recovered financially, and he received a generous advance from Mark Twain to write his memoirs, which Twain finished only a few days before Grant's death from throat cancer at age 63. While dying, Grant was attended by a prominent Methodist minister, who prayed and sprinkled water over the unconscious man who was known for his lack of faith. The minister then announced to the press that Grant had been converted and baptized. A little later the doctor in charge succeeded in temporarily reviving his patient. When the minister was informed of this rally, he proclaimed, "It is Providence; it is Providence!" "Not at all," said the doctor, "it was the brandy."

Although many historians consider the 2000 presidential election results, in which George "Dubya" Bush defeated Al Gore, as the most suspect of the 55 elections held through 2008, the 1876 election to succeed Grant might have topped it. Samuel J. Tilden, a New York Democrat, outpolled Republican Rutherford B. Hayes by 250,000 popular votes. Weeks after the election and with the last 20 electoral votes from three Southern states still to be determined, Tilden led Hayes by 19 votes. Initial counts in Florida, Louisiana, and South Carolina showed Tilden to be the narrow winner in each state. Republicans in all three states contested the results, and ballot recounts were initiated.

To help illiterate voters, the ballots contained drawings of the candidates' faces, party symbols, or even a picture of Republican Abraham Lincoln to assist the freedmen in keeping their loyalties straight. Because of their hatred of Lincoln, white Southerners were overwhelmingly Democrats. Unquestionably, there were rampant Election Day and vote-tallying abuses by both parties and a fair determination of the winner may have been impossible. Almost three months after the election, Congress passed a law appointing a 15-member Electoral Commission with five members from each house and five Supreme Court Justices. It is generally believed that a deal was brokered by the Republican Party's counsel. The Republicans agreed to withdraw federal troops from the South and to end Federal Reconstruction, if the Democrats rolled over on their candidate and conceded the election — they did. Known as the "Corrupt Bargain" at the time, history books now call it the Compromise of 1877. The deal ended federal involvement in state racial matters for almost a century and ushered in state and local Jim Crow laws that created *de jure* segregation throughout the South and *de facto* segregation in most of the rest of the country — and Rutherford B. "His Fraudulency" Hayes became president.

De jure racial segregation, or segregation by law, was instituted in the Southern states after the Compromise of 1877. Jim Crow laws were enacted by state and local governments and were created around public policy of "separate but equal" status for black Americans in all public affairs and facilities. This quickly became a hypocritical policy that led to black mistreatment and public accommodations that were usually inferior to those of whites and systematized economic, educational, and social disadvantages for blacks. Jim Crow laws allowed for the segregation of everything from drinking fountains and restrooms to transportation and schools. It was not until the 1954 Supreme Court ruling that "separate educational facilities are inherently unequal" that de jure segregation was banned. The unanimous Court decision paved the way for the Civil Rights Act a decade later and the Voting Rights Act a year after that, which swept away the legal impediments to equal access and rights for all races.

"Jim Crow" was a pejorative expression that referred to a song-and-dance caricature, Jump Jim Crow. Performed by Thomas "Daddy" Rice, a popular white actor in blackface, the minstrel show entertainer popularized the term in skits that satirized Andrew Johnson and his moderate Reconstruction policies. The term "Jim Crow law" did not appear until the early 1900s. In the North, de facto segregation, or segregation in fact, was often more insidious than de jure segregation in the South where blacks could at least live in the same town as whites — but where black men did run the risk of being lynched if they so much as talked to white women or stepped out of their "place." Whereas in the North, there were hundreds of "sundown towns," such as Cicero and Naperville, Illinois; Appleton, Wisconsin; Creston, Iowa; Edina, Minnesota; and Ironwood, Michigan, that actively discouraged blacks from living there or even staying overnight. And although there were no laws on the books that prohibited blacks, signs such as the one at the city limits of Hawthorne, California, that read "Nigger, Don't Let The Sun Set On YOU In Hawthorne" lasted into the 1950s and made it clear that there were no local services, lodging, or facilities available for black Americans.

It is clear that the federal government didn't champion integration and racial equality. In the military, where it would have been just and logical to create true equality, it took 80 years before black soldiers were integrated with whites. During the Civil War, 186,097 freemen and runaway slaves fought for the Union Army. In World War I, 367,710 blacks were drafted into the Army, and in World War II, 909,000 served — except for those who performed service jobs, all were in segregated units. In 1948 President Harry Truman passed an Executive Order that integrated the U.S. Armed Forces and allowed black and white citizens to fight side by side to protect American rights and freedoms.

After the Civil War, Rock Island again boomed, and while the much of the country east of the Mississippi struggled, life was good in the West. In 1862 before establishing the prison on Rock Island, the Army condemned the private land and kicked all civilians off the island and out of Rock Island Village, including David Sears who had lived and operated his mills there for 27 years. In 1865 the federal government compensated Sears $145,175 ($2.2 million) for his property. Then two years later, Sears used the money to buy more than 500 acres south of Rock Island on the north Rock River shore and on the west end of Vandruff Island near the confluence with the Mississippi. Sears built a brick two-story house in the present Black Hawk State Historic Site (for many years the park's caretaker resided in the century-old home). Between the west end of Vandruff Island and just east of the Camden Road Bridge, which was 100 yards east of the current Milan Bridge, Sears built a dam and power plant to supply electricity to his new sawmill.

Sears built a cotton mill, which he sold to Graham Cotton Factory from Rockford. He attracted a paper mill and other manufacturing operations to his property, including the National Clay Manufacturing Company, which occupied a six-square-block area below the bluff at the south end of the village, where they made hundreds of thousands of bricks to pave Rock Island streets. A canning company employed dozens of seasonal workers who processed fruit and vegetables from the orchards and farms along Camden Road and on Big Island, a fertile highland south of the Rock River at its confluence with the Mississippi. And Bailey Davenport's Black Hawk Coal Mines were along the bluffs that are now in the state park and were east of Sears' property. Soon, Searstown was more prosperous than Milan, and houses sprouted up along Tower Street that ran north of the Rock River. Sears School opened, and two general stores competed for customers. The Sears Post Office and Town Hall sat across the street from each other at the foot of present day 11th Street. In 1884 the area was incorporated as Searstown, and three decades later was annexed by Rock Island.

One of the businesses that located on Vandruff Island was a watch works. The three-story brick building opened in 1871, and legend has it that on the day of its opening 4,000 men and boys, who hoped to escape hard factory labor and farm work, applied for jobs at the plant. The community was so supportive of the operation that Camden Mills changed its name to Milan in order to give the watch a sophisticated Italian name — regretfully, like their neighbors in Moline they didn't pronounce their new name correctly, but they did get the spelling right. Unfortunately, the business soon failed and the building then housed a furniture factory and later a wagon plant. From 1905 to 1912, it was used to build the Artista Piano Player, an innovative devise that was mounted on a piano keyboard and hammered out a variety of tunes.

A hardworking entrepreneur, Sears may have been additionally motivated to succeed in order to support his family — he had seven children with his first wife and six with his second. Sears' first eight children were girls. His oldest son, David, was the first white child born in Moline, and as an adult, ran his father's businesses in Searstown. David Sears, Jr. was civically involved. He served as Searstown's mayor for three terms, was Chairman of the Searstown Board of Trustees for three terms, and was Superintendent of the South Rock Island District for nine years. A 1925 *Argus* article about David Sears, Jr. gives an insight into how some Searstown and Milan men spent their evenings between 1860 and 1925 — David Sears, Jr. was 87 at the time of the article:

> Sears is an active member of the Rock Island County Old Settlers' association, and was president for one term. He has been a member of Eureka lodge, No. 65, Masons, of Milan for more than 50 years. Mr. Sears was the last master of the lodge of the Ancient Order of United Workmen at Milan and was also a member of the now extinct branch in Milan of the Ancient Order of Druids.
>
> He has been an active Republican all his life and votes at every election. Mr. Sears used the privilege of voting for the first time in the first campaign of Abraham Lincoln. He voted for him again four years later and asserts that if Lincoln still lived, he would still give him his vote.

The 1925 *Argus* article also reveals how some Searstown men viewed the women of their time. Sears, a man who grew up with nine sisters, said, "The pioneer women were much superior to those of this age. She [sic] was independent and self-supporting, an entirely different woman from the woman of today."

When Sears' father built the area's first sawmill in 1838, most timber was hauled to his mill by 2-wheeled oxcarts that had wheels 12 feet in diameter and held a single log suspended under the cart's axel. By 1860 more than a dozen sawmills had sprung up in the region on the Mississippi and Rock River banks. One of the sawmills was a failing operation that had partially burned. Located in the west end of Rock Island, the derelict mill was purchased and renovated by brothers-in-law, Frederick Carl August Denkmann, who was called Carl by his friends and is usually referred to by his Initials "F.C.A.," and Friedrich Weyerhaeuser.

Denkmann was the youngest son of a prosperous landowner and manufacturer. As a young child in Salzwedel, Germany, the Napoleonic Wars depleted his family's fortune and destroyed his father's business. His father died a broken man, and Frederick was left to care for his impoverished mother. At age 14, Denkmann was apprenticed to a machine shop; mechanically gifted, he learned his trade well and quickly advanced to become a well-paid machinist. The deplorable social and living conditions in Europe that were ignited by the Industrial Revolution and inflamed by near-constant wars drove middle-class Europeans to America throughout the 19th century. In 1848 Denkmann joined the wave of European emigrants who sailed to the New World seeking a better life. Settling near Erie, Pennsylvania, it is said that when Denkmann applied for his first machinist position, the plant foreman asked him what he could do. Denkmann replied, "The work of those three men over there."

By the end of his first year in America, Denkmann had not only found a good job, but also a wife. He married 18-year-old Catherine Bloedel, who also had recently emigrated with her family from Germany. Two years after their marriage and the death of an infant son, the Denkmanns moved to Moline, which they quickly abandoned for Rock Island, where they lived the rest of their lives. During his first years in Rock Island, Denkmann worked as a machinist, and after frugally accumulating savings, he opened a grocery store in downtown Rock Island. He separated himself from his competition by always having the freshest and best produce. He would rise before dawn and make a circuit of the local farms, where before the farmers loaded their wagons to take their crops to town for other grocers, he would select their best available product for his customers.

When Catherine's 17-year-old sister, Sarah Elizabeth Bloedel, visited the Denkmann's in Rock Island in early 1857, the circumstances were laid not only for her future, but also for the advancement of the Denkmanns, Rock Island, and the nation's lumber industry. Introduced to Friedrich Weyerhaeuser an industrious 22-year-old man who was from her hometown of Neidersaulheim, Germany, Elizabeth fell in love with him, and six months later she married him. One of eleven siblings, only Friedrich (most written accounts Americanize his first name to "Frederick") and four of his sisters reached maturity. His father, one of the solid men in their western German village, owned a 15-acre farm and a three-acre vineyard. He died at age 52 when Frederick was 12. Forced to leave school when his father died, Frederick and the Weyerhaeuser women maintained the farm for five years. They then joined one of the older sisters, who with an aunt, had journeyed to America and settled in western Pennsylvania two years earlier.

Arriving in New York City in July of 1852, the Weyerhaeusers located where their sister and aunt had settled. Frederick became an apprentice brewer and within two years had worked his way up and doubled his salary to $9 a month ($225). Abandoning his plans to become a brew master, he left the honorable trade for a pay increase to $13 a month and hired on as a farm laborer. When the family farm in Germany sold in 1856, Weyerhaeuser took his share of the proceeds and moved to a thriving Rock Island, which had become known throughout the country as a destination of opportunity. He landed a construction job in the building of the Rock Island & Peoria Railway. Soon after that, he found a better job as a night shift fireman at the sawmill owned and operated by Mead, Smith, and Marsh Lumber Company. Two days after beginning his new job, the night shift was laid off; however, the new fireman had already impressed his employers, and he was retained and made a tallyman (shipping clerk). It was during this period that Weyerhaeuser met Elizabeth Bloedel.

In December 1857, Weyerhaeuser was put in charge of a new lumberyard that his employer opened in Coal Valley, a farming community 15 miles southeast of Rock Island. The year before, Ben Harper, S.S. Guyer, and David Hakes bought a large tract of land that contained coal deposits, started a mining operation, and constructed a railroad to get the coal to market — all done in one year's time without filing an environmental impact statement. The newly formed town was the terminus of the Rock Island & Peoria Railway, and with a railroad spur to Rock Island the community boomed.

Weyerhaeuser's lumberyard and hardware store rounded out a self-sufficient town similar to hundreds of other farm towns with stops on railroad lines. Over the next two generations, indistinguishable towns with a general store, grocery and meat market, hardware store and lumber yard, blacksmith, school, church or two, tavern or two with rooms for rent on the second story, silos for corn, soybeans, and wheat, and a railroad station sprouted up throughout the Upper Midwest. In Coal Valley, which was more prosperous than most farm towns, Weyerhaeuser Lumber was clustered with Herrick's General Store, Grant's Meat Market, and the Coal Valley House hotel operated by L. Evans. The blacksmith was David Rowland; the carpenters were John Petty, William Meyers, and the Callahan brothers; and seizing an opportunity to get out of Camden Mills, Dr. Thomas Martin moved his practice to Coal Valley.

Unfortunately, the Coal Valley operation was the only portion of the Mead, Smith, and Marsh Lumber Company that was profitable. The Panic of 1857 caused the failure of 5,000 businesses and distressed virtually all others. From his savings, Weyerhaeuser bought the assets of the Coal Valley operation and kept it in business. In addition to the severe economic downturn that affected all raw material suppliers, Mead, Smith and Marsh suffered several small destructive fires at their sawmill and were forced to close their operation on Rock River (4th) Avenue and Pike (1st) Street in the west end of Rock Island. Seeing an opportunity to own the milling and retail ends of a lumber company, Weyerhaeuser approached his friend, the 38-year-old Denkmann, and asked to partner with him and manage the Rock Island sawmill. Denkmann agreed, and for the last nine months of 1859, Weyerhaeuser's combined operations made $3,000 ($75,000) and $5,000 in 1860. After purchasing the first band saw in the West, the operation doubled the daily board feet milled from 8,000 to 16,000 in its first year of operation.

The partnership of Weyerhaeuser and Denkmann was a perfect fit. In addition to a common heritage and marrying sisters, the men were enterprising and incredibly hardworking; they were friends who shared common values and had complementary skills. Denkmann was a fine machinist and manager, who supervised the sawmill and oversaw the manufacture of the lumber. Weyerhaeuser, who was 12 years younger than Denkmann, was an entrepreneur who had strong interpersonal and organizational skills and was the company's spokesman. The partnership of Denkmann & Weyerhaeuser continued to buy mills in the Rock Island area, which they eventually consolidated into the Rock Island Lumber and Manufacturing Company, and together they launched the world's most successful soft lumber company.

At that time, dozens of sawmills dotted the Upper Mississippi River from its tributaries in north central Wisconsin and northern Minnesota to St. Louis. During the high-water period in the spring and early summer, the rivers were choked with logs. The logs were marked at their source and floated down the rivers to the sawmills that had purchased them. The resulting confusion, poaching, delays, and errors as the mills sorted out their logs were monumental. It was Weyerhaeuser who came up with a simple solution to the multiple problems.

He convinced the mill and timber owners that since there was little difference in the logs, it would be to everyone's advantage to abandon branding their logs and to take out of the river, not the same logs they put in, but an equivalent number. Weyerhaeuser also established an alliance of lumber interests, the Mississippi River Boom and Logging Company., which by 1872 handled all the logs on the Mississippi River. The alliance had more than a hundred partners, and none, except Weyerhaeuser, knew the number of logs owned by each partner. This arrangement created an honor system among the lumber barons that was unique to American industry. Weyerhaeuser brought efficiency and economy to a chaotic industry, but he was most respected for being scrupulously fair and honest.

Denkmann was a private man who seldom left Rock Island, and customarily he only entertained and socialized with family members. When Catherine and he celebrated their 50th wedding anniversary, a dinner at home was held and only immediate family members were invited. Fortunately, their home was large, because their children, grandchildren, and other close relatives pushed the table setting count to more than 60. Frederick died in March 1905 and Catherine died less than two years later. Both are buried in Chippiannock Cemetery.

Denkmann's friend and partner, Frederick Weyerhaeuser, is seldom listed with the titans of American industry, primarily because he was quick to pass praise to others and never sought personal acclaim, but it was also due to living in the Midwest away from the social and political pressures of his business contemporaries in the East. He was an extraordinarily private man, whose only pleasure, other than his work, was his family. In one of the few interviews he ever gave, Weyerhaeuser said of his tremendous success, "The secret lay simply in my will to work. I never watched the clock and never stopped before I had finished what I was working on."

In 1864, Weyerhaeuser began to buy tracts of Wisconsin timber, and in three years between 1880 and 1882 he bought 200,000 acres of Wisconsin's Northwood for $10 ($210) an acre. The purchase of timberland allowed him to control all the stages of the lumber industry from logging to transportation to milling to finished product distribution. He spent four decades growing his business, during which time he acquired millions of acres of the world's best timber. At age 65, he consolidated his business interests and founded the Weyerhaeuser Company. It was then the world's largest seller of soft timber and remains so today. Although Weyerhaeuser acquired a personal fortune of $75 billion in 2012 dollars, which in 2006 made him the eighth richest American ever, he was not overly motivated by money. He was altruistic, personally giving countless private and anonymous donations to charitable causes. His foundation continues today and has distributed more than $100 million. During a period of widespread business and banking greed and corruption and when the robber barons controlled American industry, Weyerhaeuser held socially liberal views and was more involved with and showed more concern for his workers than other industrial magnates. While his contemporaries were exploiting the nation's resources, he impressed upon his managers and workers the necessity of maintaining forest sustainability by protecting the small trees and foliage in the areas they harvested.

Frederick and Sarah Weyerhaeuser built a magnificent French-style red-brick home on the hill at 3052 10th Avenue, where they raised their family and lived into their sixties. Business demands relocated them to St. Paul, Minnesota, before they retired to Pasadena, California. However their daughter, Apollonia, and her husband continued to reside at the family home where they often threw lavish parties, an indulgence Frederick and Sarah never abided. In 1954 Apollonia donated the home to Augustana College. Upon Frederick Weyerhaeuser's death in 1914, railroad tycoon, James Hill, commented, "His place can never be filled. ... He was one of those national forces that helped build our country." Weyerhaeuser is buried in the family mausoleum in Rock Island's Chippiannock Cemetery. Today, there is little in Rock Island to remind people of him or his positive affect on the community — the Rock Island Weyerhaeuser office closed in 1945 — and it is difficult to quantify his contributions to Rock Island and the nation. But one thing is certain, contrary to the song's lyrics, prior to World War I neither livestock nor pig iron was the primary freight of the Rock Island Line — it was lumber.

The efficiencies that Weyerhaeuser brought to the lumber industry also helped create its demise on the Upper Mississippi. Even though he was a strong conservationist and reforesting advocate, the white pine forests that covered five sixths of Wisconsin during Black Hawk's life disappeared when trees were harvested faster than saplings could grow to maturity. At their peak in 1884, mills on the Rock Island Rapids, powered by the racing water, processed 741,837,000 logs that floated down the river.

Other than Frederick Weyerhaeuser, no one contributed more to the efficiencies of lumbering on the river than a man who grew up in Rock Island, Samuel Van Sant. Van Sant's father, John, was an expert New Jersey shipwright who came to Rock Island in 1837 and went to work at John Holt's boatyard at the foot of Dock (22nd) Street. Eight years later, John Van Sant opened his own boatyard at the other end of town at the foot of Canal Street (5th Avenue).

As a boy, Van Sant loved the river, and when he wasn't working for free for his father or for 50 cents ($12.50) a day for Frederick Denkmann at his lumber mill, he explored the river in his skiff or tested one of his father's boats or hung out on the docks listening to the stories of the riverboat hands. Once when he was 13, on a Sunday morning, he was at his father's boatyard and the mate in charge of the *Prairie State*, which was docked at the yard, asked Van Sant to tend the ship while he went downtown for lunch. The steamer, *Kentucky No. 2*, started to maneuver into the dock, and ignored the boy who was shouting, "You can't land here." The steamer struck the

Prairie State, and both boats burned, as did a portion of a nearby sawmill — which was purchased by Weyerhaeuser and Denkmann later that summer.

After graduating from Rock Island High School, Van Sant attended Knox College for two years, until the Civil War interrupted his studies. During the war, he rode with Company A of the 9th Illinois Cavalry where he served with Joseph Brackett. Returning to Rock Island after the war, he designed a more powerful and easier to maneuver steamboat to push log rafts along the river. As more logs were dumped into the river, it became advantageous to create timber rafts of hundreds of logs instead of "driving" individual logs downriver. The rafts were made by chaining a rectangle "fence" of single logs together to make a frame that was typically 300-feet long by 90-feet wide, and then free-floating logs were allowed to drift inside the frame. Paddlewheel steamboats then shepherded the rafts in the same manner as they did barges.

Because log rafts were flexible, the wash from the paddlewheel restricted the boats to only work from behind and to one side of the rafts. Consequently, towboats had to work with the steam ferries in order to pilot the rafts to their destinations. It was Van Sant's idea to move the paddlewheel from the side to the stern of the towboat and minimize the effect of the wash. In addition to relocating the paddlewheel, he beefed-up the engines and engineered a complicated but brilliant system of steering cables. In May 1869 in the same week he celebrated his 25th birthday, Van Sant took his former boss, Frederick Weyerhaeuser, on a demonstration cruise of his redesigned towboat — within a few years, there were more than 70 stern wheel towboats pushing timber rafts down the Upper Mississippi to Rock Island's sawmills. The new towboats allowed rafts to be increased from 300 feet to 900 feet in length, and they eventually grew to 1,500 feet.

Van Sant was richly rewarded for his ingenuity, and after building towboats in LeClaire, Iowa, for 13 years, he moved his business to Winona, Minnesota. Running as a Republican in a then solidly Republican state, Van Sant was elected alderman. Ten years after arriving in Minnesota, he was elected to the state legislature. Because his sensibilities more closely aligned with the Democratic Party, Van Sant switched parties when he ran for a second term in the State House. When he was elected, the Democrats nominated him for house speaker. He also received every Republican vote and was unanimously elected. After failing twice in bids for governor, Van Sant was elected in 1900, defeating "Honest" John Lind. He then took on railroad baron James Hill, who was demanding a consolidation of railroad lines that would further increase his power. Although Republican voters publicly backed Hill and his candidates, Van Sant was reelected. He passed away at age 92 and is buried in LeClaire.

Two others who were richly rewarded for Van Sant's ingenuity were John and Peter Kahlke. The same year Samuel Van Sant demonstrated his unique riverboat designs to Frederick Weyerhaeuser, the brothers, who had been born on the Elbe River in Hamburg, Germany, opened a boatyard on Mill Street. The Kahlke Brothers Boatyard soon became one of the largest on the Mississippi and employed a large contingent of workers who performed not only new-boat construction, but also steamboat and barge storing, caulking, and short notice repairs for the steady stream of boats that were damaged while negotiating the rapids. The *1876 Holland's Rock Island Directory* stated that the brothers had worked in boat construction and repair "in different parts of the country, including New Orleans, where they owned extensive floating dry docks, and did an immense business."

In 1852, the same year Frederick Weyerhaeuser arrived in New York and took his first job as a brewer, 26-year-old Ignatz Huber started work at a Rock Island brewery. Huber was raised in Bavaria, where his father taught him the fine art of brewing quality beer. After arriving in America, he worked for three years in Ohio breweries before moving on to brew beer and ales for discriminating Rock Island palates. After his first month at the brewery, he purchased a small ownership interest. Within two years, he owned the brewery. In 1893 he consolidated his brewery with the city's two other breweries to form the Rock Island Brewing Company. His business became one of Rock Island's most important, and he became one of the city's most respected citizens. He was vice-president of the People's National Bank, served three terms as an alderman, was Captain of the Rock Island Rifle Company, and owned large tracts of property in each of the Tri-Cities.

There is no record why Huber was in Fort Madison, Iowa, in the summer of the same year he bought his brewery, nor is there any record why the Lutheran parents of the vivacious 22-year-old Cathariana Koehler allowed her to marry a Catholic, but he was and they did. Two years earlier, the Koehler family had emigrated from Stozback, Germany, and Catherine, as she called herself in America, was stranded in central Iowa. Escaping to Rock Island with Huber, she found a lifestyle that fit her personality, and she became exceptionally active in social groups and gave much of Huber's money to various charities. She mothered six children, and three, Otto, Amelia, and Lillie, lived to adulthood. After graduating from Rocky, Otto went to the University of Illinois and then spent two years at the Institute of Technology near Munich, Germany. He graduated in 1889 and began following in his professional father's footsteps.

Otto Huber was active in the formation of the Rock Island Brewing Company, and he later spread fine Rock Island brewing techniques across the nation. He organized the Seattle Brewing and Malting Company and the Des Moines Brewing

Company. He also followed his father into banking and became president of the People's National Bank in 1903 and president of the German Trust and Savings Bank in 1912. Neither he nor his sisters married, but following in his mother's footsteps, he was active in several social groups, including the Rock Island Club, the Davenport Commercial Club, the Chicago Athletic Association, and the Elks Lodge, and he held a lifetime membership in the Rock Island Arsenal Golf Club. In 1909, his mother and sister, Amelia, were seriously injured when the gas tank of their limousine exploded. His sister fully recovered, but his mother's health steadily declined until her death in 1917. His father died at the age of 84 less than a year after the explosion.

On 25 acres of densely wooded property located at the crest of the hill between 24th and 30th Streets, in the spring of 1914 Otto Huber began construction of a 35-room mansion for his ailing mother and his two single sisters. Tragically, six months after starting the home, he suffered a massive cerebral hemorrhage and died. He was 48. Amelia and Lillie lived together in the sprawling mansion until Lillie died in 1935. Neither sister was professionally or socially active, but they did their part to keep Rock Islanders employed during the Depression. The two women hired six servants to look after them and the house. After Amelia died in 1948 at the age of 86, with no Huber survivors, the home was given to St. Anthony's Hospital, located on the opposite side of 30th Street from the estate. The Franciscan Sisters operated a retirement home in the mansion until 1986, when it became uneconomical to maintain, and they obtained a permit to demolish the 70-year-old building.

With an 1870 population of 8,000, Rock Island was twice the size of Moline and approached the size of Davenport (11,000), which had flourished because land prices on the Iowa side of the river were less than half of those in Rock Island. Davenport closely rivaled Des Moines as Iowa's largest city, and piggybacking onto Rock Island's glowing national reputation, the residents of the region surrounding Rock Island started calling the urban area the "Tri-Cities." Business was booming in Rock Island, where many Davenport residents commuted to work, and industry was also progressing in Moline. In 1868 the *Rock Island Union* facetiously noted that "the laboring men of Moline are among the most prosperous to be found in the country. Instead of spending their spare earnings in saloons and dram shops [saloons], they carefully hoard them and in a few years a little home of their own is the result." The diverse cultural range of the adjacent cities straddling the Mississippi provided a spectrum of lifestyles that left no one without a choice of occupation, religious practice, political adherence, recreational pursuit, pastime, or debauchery that could not be satisfied.

As the United States slowly worked its way through the recovery from the Civil War, at America's crossroads Rock Island became one of the most cosmopolitan and prosperous cities in the country. Government subsidized and underwritten projects such as the Rock Island Line, Rock Island & Peoria Railway, Rock Island Arsenal weapons and vehicle manufacturing, and Mississippi River improvements created jobs that attracted skilled labor and pumped new money into a flourishing local economy. Coupled with the entrepreneurial efforts of men such as David Sears, John Deere, the Washburn brothers, Samuel Van Sant, F.C.A. Denkmann, and Frederick Weyerhaeuser, Rock Island County grew as if on economic steroids. The period from pre-Civil War through post-Reconstruction may have been Rock Island's grandest time on the world stage.

Chapter 14

Taming the West

Success in almost any field depends more on energy and drive than it does on intelligence. This explains why we have so many stupid leaders. ~ Sloan Wilson, author

AFTER THE CIVIL WAR, with the Union preserved and eastern Indians subdued and driven west of the Mississippi, the U.S. Army turned its attention to opening the plains to settlers and the entire Mississippi River system to navigation. During the 19th century, the Missouri-Mississippi-Ohio trident of rivers that feeds the Lower Mississippi efficiently transported logs, barges filled with ores and grains, and people, but the U.S. Army believed the rivers that Congress put under their control were too dangerous for commercial use — it was apparent that the inland rivers were no longer of military importance. Never mind that Mother Nature built her system of rivers more than 100,000 years before the first Indian saw her work of art, and that the purpose of the magnificent web of rivers, streams, and creeks that feed the three primary arteries that flow into the Lower Mississippi provided a consummately effective drainage system for land extending from the Appalachians to the Rocky Mountains and from Canada to the Gulf of Mexico — an area that covers all or part of 31 states and drains more than two-fifths of the continental United States. The dynamic river system was extremely flexible, and about every 1,000 years or so Mother Nature adjusted its course to keep up with her whims. The Upper Mississippi ran as pure as a mountain stream and there is no record of spring floods disturbing Saukenuk or Rock Island's residents — then engineers went about making it better.

In the entire country, the most treacherous stretch of steamboat-navigable river was the Falls of the Ohio near Louisville. Prior to 1830, 300 steamboats were destroyed in the three-mile run of Ohio River rapids. In that year, a two-mile-long, privately-built canal opened, and no more steamboats were lost. Using horse and oxen-drawn scrapers and carts, during low water the canal eliminated the necessity of dropping off passengers and freight at one end of the rapids and transporting them over land to the opposite end to another steamboat. The canal's three-lock system created a total lift of 26 feet over two miles. (The total lift of the proposed Rock River to

Mississippi River canal to bypass the Rock Island Rapids was 29 feet over ten miles.) In an excellent example of how government should not involve itself with commerce, beyond its regulation, the Louisville-Portland Canal was built with private money and favorably competed against railroads, road transport, and steamboat shipping that required a two-mile drayage. In less than a decade's time the canal was transporting 300,000 tons of cargo annually.

The canal was hugely successful and profitable for its investors, so of course, the U.S. Government condemned the canal, took over its operation and maintenance, and in 1867 put it under the supervision of the Army Corps of Engineers. Congress eliminated the tolls, but even without them, within a decade's time, railroad shipping rates fell dramatically and rail became significantly less expensive than river transport. The Corps didn't keep the canal up to date or adequately maintained, and when new steamboats and barges grew too large for the canal, the politicians' perk to farmers and manufacturers became meaningless. Not letting economics and financial sense get in their way, the Corp of Engineers lobbied to create a locks and dams' system on the Ohio River, and in 1885 the first of 53 Ohio River locks and dams were completed — 44 years later, the 53rd was completed. Today, the Corps oversees 23 locks and dams on the Allegheny, Monongahela, and Ohio Rivers. So instead of enlarging one previously proven canal to bypass the trouble spot, the Corps successfully lobbied to build locks and dams along the 920-mile length of the Ohio River to once and for all eliminate the Falls of the Ohio and remove other rapids and difficult stretches.

What is seldom mentioned in any of the Army's justifications for dredging, damming, and diking the Upper Mississippi to facilitate commercial navigation is that for almost half of the year, the river is unnavigable due to ice, and transport is reliant on rail and roads. Even Army engineers weren't up to solving winter's problems, but they believed they were capable of resolving the river's warm-weather issues, which are described in the U.S. Army Corps of Engineers' history, *Gateways to Commerce*:

> Once, the Upper Mississippi River flowed freely. From its headwaters in upper Minnesota, there were no locks and dams to obstruct the river's path as it flowed through the forests and fields of the Upper Midwest. But the river was also temperamental. Compared to the Lower Mississippi, that stretch of the river below St. Louis made mighty by the combined waters of the Missouri and the Ohio Rivers, the Upper Mississippi River was unreliable. During times of flood, the Upper Mississippi was deep flowing, but turbulent. More frequently, long dry spells made the river too shallow to navigate. The river's uncharted shoals and sand bars presented a constant danger. Equally dangerous were the "snags," trees that storms had washed from the river's banks into its waters. The Upper Mississippi was a challenge to all who plied its waters.

In 1867 at the same time Frederick Weyerhaeuser was organizing the lumber barons to effectively process the 740 million logs they floated down the Upper Mississippi each year, the Corps was dealing with sandbars and the occasional snag. Andrew Humphreys, who was still basking in the glory of his Civil War heroics at the Battle of Fredericksburg, was promoted to Chief of Engineers of the U.S. Army Corps of Engineers, and 16 years after he started the 500-page treatise, he finished the *Report on the Physics and Hydraulics of the Mississippi River.* The report was a masterpiece in its detailed definitions of the Mississippi's water mechanics, but its recommendations as how to beneficially alter the river's hydraulics were woefully shortsighted and wrongheaded. The report is a classic example of getting most of the details right, but totally missing how the parts affect the whole. In a relatively short time, it was apparent that Humphreys made the tragic engineering mistake of using selected facts to justify preconceived premises.

Forceful in his opinions and using engineering terms and arcane technical language to support conclusions that at the time few understood, Humphreys postulated that the best way to tame the mighty river was to straighten its channels, construct levees to prevent flooding, and to dredge a deep channel at the river's mouth and confluences to prevent sandbars. Then, many considered him brilliant — since then, not quite as much. And because engineers are slow to admit to, much less reverse, expensive mistakes, Humphreys' errors were repeated and built upon until they became irreversible, and now millions of people living along the banks of the Midwest's rivers deal annually with Humphreys' errors, and disappointingly, Army engineers continue to compound them. Never have the errors of one engineer been so devastatingly expensive and destructive to the environment.

Humphreys was not solely responsible for the devastation of the rivers — he had a legion of engineers to help and a foil that goaded him to extremes. When there were few engineering schools and the only formal technical education focused on mechanics, surveying, and railroad construction, the Army Corps of Engineers had sole oversight of navigation routes to assure that U.S. Naval ships didn't run aground. In East Coast harbors, the Corps completed dozens of projects that advanced both military and commercial interests. But it was on the Mississippi River that Humphreys roiled the waters.

For a generation after the *Effie Afton* ran into the Rock Island Railroad Bridge, riverboat captains and bridge builders battled over whose priorities came first. A self-educated engineer and inventor from St. Louis, James Eads, was the most respected private engineer on the river. Out of jealousy and arrogance, in 1873 Humphreys insisted Eads build a canal around the St. Louis Bridge — the first steel bridge to span the Mississippi — that he had designed and built and bears his name. The steamboat owners thought it was a fine idea, but Eads was outraged and looked to President Grant for relief. Grant sided with him and the canal was never built. Humphreys was left smarting from the loss of face inflicted by his Commander In Chief, and he initiated a vendetta against Eads — and the river.

Engineers are taught that virtually everything can be improved, and that with enough money and resources all improvements are possible. What they have only learned in recent years is that all "improvements" are not necessarily good, and that is especially true when they adversely affect the environment and habitat. Using Humphreys' report as a blueprint and under his direction, Army engineers set about destroying beaver dams, cleaning up debris, breaking up rocks and shelves, and dredging a navigational channel. Except for the beavers, those improvements were unquestionably good for all. Unfortunately the plan also called for building levees, wing-dams, and jetties to maintain the channel and protect riverfronts and farmland that encroached on floodplains and were susceptible to spring flooding.

As every Rock Island school kid knows who built snow dams and dikes around street gutters, small increases in dam elevations will back up snowmelt into driveways well down the street, and if there are no driveways, water will flood over the curb into yards. Unfortunately, early levee builders lived in the South and didn't have snow dam-building experience nor did they anticipate that cities in the North would learn to build levees too — requiring those downriver to build higher levees, creating an ever-increasing problem as upriver levees were also built higher. The levees transformed tens of thousands of acres of natural floodplains into farmland and home lots, and also dramatically narrowed the rivers. When Robert E. Lee surveyed the Mississippi in 1837, the channel at St. Louis was almost a mile wide — today it is less than half that.

As the Mississippi meanders 670 miles (3,538,000 feet) from St. Paul, Minnesota to Alton, Illinois, it drops only 220 feet. This means that if the size of the river channel and the volume of the river's flow are constant, an Upper Mississippi River dam one foot above natural surface level will back up water more than three miles upstream, and if the riverbanks aren't evenly tapered from one foot above natural surface level over the three-mile stretch, or if more water flows than the channel can hold, water will flood into yards. Of course, riverbanks aren't evenly tapered. Fifty years after Andrew Humphreys' death and two generations before computer modeling would have shown the fallacy of their plans, the Army Corps of Engineers built 26 dams and hundreds of miles of floodwalls the length of the Upper Mississippi.

After the acquisition of New Orleans in the Louisiana Purchase, keeping the Emerald City dry became a primary objective of Army engineers. With portions of New Orleans as much as eight feet below sea level, this was no easy task. Most of southern Louisiana is a natural, swampy floodplain, and the Army eagerly took on the job of creating a protective bowl around the unwisely located city. In the 300 years after Hernando de Soto noted that Indian maze fields on the banks of the Arkansas River were flooded, there were only six Mississippi floods that caused property or crop damage of note. Three of the floods affected only New Orleans, and one was caused by a hurricane. It wasn't until farmers started planting cotton in the floodplains that spring floods became an issue, and it wasn't until steamboat captains started complaining about rocks and bridges that river navigation was problematic. To resolve both manmade problems, the Army Corps of Engineers arrogantly set off to tame the nation's rivers.

Encouraged by their early successes in keeping New Orleans dry, the Army engineers marched up the river constructing levees along the Louisiana and Mississippi riverbanks, converting swampy floodplains into farmland. Southerners felt smug about what they had so easily taken from Mother Nature, until the flood of 1858-59 overflowed the levees, and she reclaimed much of her lost land and washed away most of the engineers' first efforts to control her. The Army fought back and built higher and stronger levees. And today flooding problems continue to compound, as city dwellers and farmers from the Gulf of Mexico to the rivers' headwaters build higher walls between the rivers and their front doors — and experience greater flood damage. Humphreys' plan created the levee system, and some Louisiana levees built on Humphreys' watch stood until the surge from Hurricane Katrina defeated them 150 years later. Mark Twain, who grew up on the river's banks in Hannibal, Missouri, knew the folly that Humphreys' engineers undertook and concluded that they "might as well bully the comets in their courses and undertake to make them behave, as try to bully the Mississippi into right and reasonable conduct."

No place on the Mississippi better illustrates the engineers' errors than Twain's hometown. Engineers rate flood severity by the frequency that specific heights above flood stage are exceeded. (Flood stage is somewhat arbitrarily defined as the "water level that causes damage;" the "height" of flood stage is measured from an average depth from the bottom of the channel.) Logically, based on historical water level data, engineers expect depths to exceed the "10-year floodplain" once every ten years. What is not factored into the determination of flood stages are the progressive manmade changes to the river channel. The 10-year flood stage at Hannibal was the same when Mark Twain was born in 1835 as it was more than a century later after the Corps finished building 26 dams across the river and hundreds of miles of floodwalls along its banks.

During Twain's 74-year lifetime, Hannibal should have expected to experience six to nine 10-year floods. It experienced nine. In the 25 years preceding 2011, Hannibal improbably experienced a 10-year flood every two years. And astoundingly, four 100-year floods have hit the Mississippi River in the 20 years preceding 2012, and three of the once-in-a-century floods have already struck in the first 12 years of the 21st century. This anomaly is statistically nearly impossible. Because their design criteria is no longer useful, the Corps of Engineers now designs dams and floodwalls for floods projected to happen in tens or even hundreds of thousands of years. (Stampede Dam near Truckee, California is currently designed to withstand a once in 75,000 year flood. Recently, $30 million was approved to upgrade the dam for a once in 250,000 year flood.) Incomprehensibly, instead of admitting that they have made a mess of the rivers system and redefining their criteria and objectives, the Corps stubbornly sticks to engineering practices dating back to Andrew Humphreys. The extraordinary flooding in recent decades may have been caused in small part by climate change, but unarguably, building levees that wall off natural floodplains leaves runoff from spring snowmelt and heavy rainfall nowhere to go, and the Corps' continuing reengineering of the rivers system to accommodate anachronistic river transport and decrease property and crop damage has done the opposite and abnormally increased flooding throughout the Midwest.

Ironically, the land along the Mississippi River that farmers claimed from Mother Nature to plant in cotton helped spread their greatest enemy — boll weevils. By claiming broad natural floodplains that each spring were scoured of the nasty beetles' larvae and presented wide barriers to their migration, boll weevils were able to traipse from Mexico through Texas into the Deep South because of the endless pathway of cotton fields. Since the 1950s, the primary method of controlling the pesky weevils has been to repeatedly spray cotton plants with insecticides. The deadly chemicals run off and accumulate in the water systems of the Mississippi Delta and flow to the Gulf of Mexico, killing fish and aquatic life along the way. It gets worse; because Delta soils no longer receive natural refertilization from spring flooding, ever-greater quantities of chemical fertilizers are spread on fields to artificially complete the cycle and relentlessly escalate environmental damage.

As much destruction as boll weevils did to the Southern economy, it is nothing compared to what the abolition of slavery did — it was not until after World War II that mechanical cotton pickers became viable. Before the Civil War, the economy of the Deep South was based on plantation farming, and giving 40 acres and a mule to 10,000 freedmen was not even a good start to transition the South into a different way of life. Although political and cultural differences separated other regions of the United States, the national unity that had been created by the Revolution was destroyed by the slavery issue.

In the Deep South those that stayed and didn't flee to Texas, California, or the Western Plains after the Civil War were as distanced from the rest of the United States as the British were from the French. Unlike the South, in the Northeast, plants that had produced Civil War uniforms and munitions quickly converted to manufacturing civilian clothes and tools, carriages, and wagons to supply the new stream of immigrants on their way West. In the Midwest, farmers returned to till their land with John Deere plows. People from outside Illinois no longer referred to the state as the Sucker State, but instead called it the "Prairie State" — most from Illinois referred to their home as the "Land of Lincoln." (In 1955 "Land of Lincoln" became the official state motto, and since then it has been etched on every license plate.) And across the plains' states, a web of railroad tracks were laid down from Canada to the Gulf of Mexico to connect the East and West Coasts and to carry grain and livestock east to feed the cities. The post-Civil War westward push moved the frontier across the Mississippi and ended Rock Island's reign as the West's most romantic outpost.

During the post-war period, the concept of Manifest Destiny, which stated it was a God-given right for the United States to extend across the continent, was championed by nearly everyone. Plains Indians and those that had been herded west were an irritating obstacle to white settlers as they moved onto every arable acre between the Mississippi River and the Rocky Mountains, and further removal of Indians to Oklahoma reservations was another task the U.S. Army eagerly took on. The Civil War had created a class of young, unmarried men who were often physically and emotionally damaged and knew an adult life of only hardship and violence. There was no shortage of socially misfit soldiers who were willing to fight and kill Indians on the plains. One of the most infamous misfits was George Armstrong Custer.

Best known for his "last stand" at Little Bighorn, the career soldier's ignominious end was predictable. After nearly being expelled several times from West Point for misconduct, Custer graduated last in his 1861 class, and instead of being assigned to a remote frontier outpost as he would have been during peacetime and because of the Civil War, he fortuitously spent the war in a series of assignments that somehow managed to keep him out of harm's way and at the front of the action. His most important contribution to the Union's war effort may have occurred when General Joseph Johnson was reconnoitering a potential crossing point on the Chickahominy River. Captain Custer overheard General Johnston mutter, "I wish I knew how deep it is." Brilliantly, Custer raced his horse to the middle of the river and shouted triumphantly to the astonished general, "That's how deep it is, Mr. General!" He was also present at the First Battle of Bull Run, and after rising to the rank of major general, he was present at Robert E. Lee's surrender at Appomattox. After the war, Custer's rank was reduced to captain, and he was assigned to fight Indians in the West.

The son of a Monroe, Michigan, blacksmith, Custer was smitten as a boy by Elizabeth "Lizzie" Bacon, but was not given permission to court her by her prominent father until he was promoted to major general, a rank, it is presumed, that Lizzie's father never thought he would attain. After being reduced in rank, Custer was made Chief of Cavalry in Texas. The "Eastern dandy" was considered vain and arrogant and generally despised by his troops, and his six-month Reconstruction duties in Texas were marred by continuous friction and desertions. After his regiment was mustered out in November of 1865, members of the Wisconsin Cavalry hatched a plot to assassinate him. Warned the night before the planned attempt, he avoided the attack. Two months later Custer took an extended leave, and over the next year explored business opportunities in New York and an opportunity to be a mercenary in Mexico. Nothing worked out, and he accepted an invitation to accompany President Andrew Johnson on a goodwill tour of the Midwest. In early 1867 after completing the tour, Custer was restored to active duty with the rank of lieutenant colonel and placed in charge of the 7th Cavalry Regiment at Fort Riley, Kansas, which was the Army's central outpost for launching attacks against the Plains Indians. Soon after taking his position, Custer was discovered to have sneaked away from his post to visit Lizzie. In a month-long court martial, Custer was found guilty of five of 11 charges including being AWOL and of conduct prejudicial to good order and military conduct — he was suspended from duty for one year.

The Indian battles were fought because the Indians refused to go to Oklahoma, the Dakota Territory, and the Southwest deserts where they had been again allotted new land. First the Colorado Gold Rush in the early 1860s and then the Black Hills Gold Rush a decade later created a torrent of white men flooding into inhospitable territory where Eastern Indians had been shuttled off before the Civil War. Coupled with the farmers and ranchers who settled on buffalo grazing lands, within a generation, the Plains Indians saw their ancestral lands first invaded by Eastern tribes forced west and then by white settlers protected by state militias and the U.S. Army.

In an early effort to protect settlers' routes through the Great Basin, General Patrick Conner told three columns of California Militia, "You will not receive overtures of peace or submission from the Indians, but will attack and kill every male Indian over 12 years of age." In a January 1863 attack on the Shoshone at their Bear River encampment near the Utah/Idaho border, a Conner-led regiment slaughtered approximately 300 warriors, women, and children, many while trying to swim across the ice-encrusted river. Eighteen months later, Connor's column destroyed an Arapaho village at Tongue River, Wyoming, killing 54. Most of the young braves were on a hunt, and only a few had been left behind to protect the women, children, and elderly. After taking the village, Conner's regiment proceeded to kill over 1,000 Indian ponies and destroy the tribe's winter food supply, tents, and clothing.

A secondary and only slightly more humane strategy to rid the plains of Indians was to kill the buffalo, which were the Indians' primary source of food and also provided virtually everything the Plains Indians needed for survival. In a PBS interview, Donald Fixico, an Indian history professor said:

> The enormous area of the Great Plains, Southwest, Pacific Northwest, and Great Basin area represented the homelands of many Indian communities. At least 28 tribes might be called Plains Indians. Trade alliances existed among these peoples, and protecting hunting domains was important to their economy, depending on the food resources of the environment, which included antelope and smaller game. North American Indians shared their world with two types of buffalo (plains and wood), eight species of bear, three primary species of wolves, 59 species of eagle, 150 species of antelope and 38 species of deer.
>
> Plains tribes had figured out how to use the buffalo in 52 different ways for food, supplies, war, and hunting implements ... the hooves, for example, are boiled to use as glue. The hump back is ... really kind of sturdy, and so it's used for making shields and the hides for making a teepee. It took about 12 to 14 hides to do that. The buffalo was plentiful and was the most important natural resource to the Plains Indians.

It was a U.S. Army maxim that to kill a buffalo was to kill an Indian. They well knew that when the buffalo were killed off that they would effectively destroy the Plains Indians. There were about 60 million buffalo when white men arrived on the Great Plains — less than a century later, by 1899 there were less than 1,000 free-roaming buffalo.

The Indian wars had not gone well in Kansas in 1867, and in early 1868 the Army needed a conscience-less and daring officer to establish a western supply camp in Oklahoma in the heart of Indian Territory. Custer's suspension was cut short, and he and the 7th Cavalry were sent to the Oklahoma Territory to fight the Cheyenne. The manically insecure Custer reveled in the opportunity to prove himself, and he quickly fulfilled his superiors' expectations. Using the charging cavalry attack-style commonly portrayed in 1950's movies, Custer reported killing 103 warriors and "some women and children" at the November 1868 Battle of Washita River. (The Cheyenne estimated their casualties to be substantially lower — 11 warriors plus 19 women and children.) After subduing the Cheyenne, Custer had his men shoot 875 Indian ponies. The battle was instrumental in forcing the Cheyenne onto a reservation, and Custer gained national exposure for his heroics.

Over the next five years, Custer divided his time between his command of the 7th Cavalry and Eastern political and social engagements and wrote his autobiography, *My Life on the Plains*. Reacting to the raging conflicts between the Plains Indians and white settlers and gold prospectors who had flooded the Black Hills, in 1874 President Grant directed that all free Plains Indians were to reside on their assigned reservations by the end of January 1876 or they would be considered "hostile." In May 1876, Custer's 7th Cavalry left Fort Lincoln, North Dakota, to round up the Indians who didn't get the message. Meanwhile, Sitting Bull, a Lakota Sioux chief, called together a gathering of Plains Indians on the Little Bighorn River in Montana to discuss what to do about the whites.

Six weeks out of Fort Lincoln, Custer encountered the largest concentration of American Indians ever assembled in one place. He divided his 600-man regiment into four detachments and attacked between 2,500 and 4,000 Indian warriors led by Crazy Horse, a war leader of the Oglala Lakota. Custer's detachment, which included his brother and three other relatives, charged one end of the three-mile long Indian encampment. His other detachments made a stand on a hilltop four miles from Custer—they were eventually rescued by cavalry reinforcements. Custer's detachment was surrounded, and in less than an hour's time every one of his 210 men was killed.

Democratic newspapers seized on Custer's defeat at the Little Bighorn as a signal of the catastrophic failure of Republican policies and corruption among the government Indian agents who had been appointed by Grant's administration. Grant told the press that he regarded "Custer's massacre as a sacrifice of troops, brought on by Custer himself that was wholly unnecessary." However, the *New York Herald* placed the blame squarely on the commander-in-chief: "The deplorable truth is that President Grant is chiefly responsible for the appalling miscarriages which have attended this disastrous campaign against the Sioux."

After the death of her 36-year-old husband, Lizzie Custer supported herself and promoted his memory by writing three books and delivering hundreds of speeches in which she glorified his life and confused the facts. She never had children and said that her greatest regret was that she didn't have a son to bear her husband's honored name. However, after an 1868 routing by Custer and his troops of Cheyenne and Arapaho in western Kansas, he is alleged to have fathered a child by the daughter of Chief Little Rock who was killed an attack Custer led. America's most engrained image of "Custer's Last Stand" is an 1896 Otto Becker lithograph that was commissioned by the Anheuser-Busch Company and was distributed as a free framed print to saloons and taverns across the country. The painting depicts a flowing-maned, red-scarved, saber-swinging Custer standing in front of his troops with hapless Indians cowering around — it still hangs in some bars today.

The last major battle with the Plains Indians was fought in 1890 at the Bad Lands of South Dakota. The encounter was more massacre than battle. To coerce the Lakota Sioux into signing away more of their lands, the U.S. Government sent the 7th Cavalry to subdue 350 Indians, most who were women and children. After the Calvary intercepted the Indians, they told them through an interpreter that they could keep their weapons and would not be harmed if they were peaceful. They complied and were escorted five miles to a camp on Wounded Knee Creek. During the night, 500 cavalry surrounded the encampment. Four rapid-fire revolving canons were set in place on all sides, and at daybreak the Indians were ordered to surrender their weapons. It is unclear what triggered the massacre, but when the rapid-fire canons ceased firing, 153 of the Lakota Sioux were dead and 51 were wounded — 25 cavalry were killed, most by the fire from the unwisely placed canons.

By this time, the Plains Indians' culture had been destroyed by the slaughter of the buffalo. Further, Congress had failed to keep its treaty promises to protect reservation lands from encroachment by settlers and gold miners, and white Indian agents, who were mere figureheads, did little to provide even the promised essentials exchanged in treaties for Indian lands. The Plains Indians were the last Native Americans to have their culture destroyed, and they were relocated to the most arid and least desirable regions in the United States. Today, Indians own 2.3 percent of the land they did when Columbus discovered them, and since then the Native American population has been reduced from more than 50 million to less than 3 million and virtually all of them have European bloodlines.

At the same time that Custer was sent to Texas to help Reconstruction efforts, Will Cody mustered out of the Union Army and returned to his family farm and married — he fathered four children. For a five-year period beginning in 1868, he scouted and hunted buffalo for the U.S. Army. In addition to the Army's efforts to eradicate the Plains Indians, the buffalo provided meat for the workers building the Kansas Pacific Railroad, and Cody was paid for 4,280 buffalo by the railroad. It was during this period that Will Cody took on the dashing moniker, "Buffalo Bill." But it was not until Cody defeated "Medicine Bill" Comstock in a buffalo shooting contest that the nickname name became well known. It is often written that the exclusive use of the name, "Buffalo Bill," was the winner's reward in an eight-hour buffalo shooting contest, but that is not so. The contest was the result of a $500 ($10,000) wager between supporters of the two men. At the time of the contest, Comstock was the more famous of the two.

Writing in the November 1875 issue of *Harper's New Monthly Magazine*, W.E. Webb recalls the first time he saw Comstock when he was standing in the doorway of a west Kansas stagecoach station, "He leveled those shining eyes at me with the precision a man would have used with field-glasses... I felt that I had been photographed and could be hunted the world over by him did he ever have occasion." A soldier in the 2nd U.S. Cavalry told how Comstock got his nickname: "One day a young Sioux squaw, while trying to catch a rattle snake, got bit on the finger. Bill, who was standing close by, without a moment's hesitation, grabbed the wounded finger and bit it off, slick and clean. From this time he was called Medicine Bill."

Comstock and Cody were two of the cavalry's most trusted scouts, and when they weren't scouting Indians, they were killing buffalo for as much as $5 ($100) a buffalo (tanneries paid $3.00 a skin and $.25 for a tongue and usually the meat was left to rot). By the 1880's there were as many as 5,000 hunters and skinners roaming the plains. When the Texas Legislature discussed a bill to protect buffalo, General Phillip Sheridan defended the buffalo hunters by saying, "These men have done more in the last two years, and will do more in the next year, to settle the vexed Indian question, than the entire regular army has done in the last forty years. They are destroying the Indian's commissary."

In his book Cody wrote, Billy Comstock "had the reputation, for a long time, of being a most successful buffalo hunter, and the [Army] officers in particular, who had seen him kill buffaloes, were very desirous of backing him in a match against me." A special excursion train carrying more than 100 spectators from St. Louis was taken to a spot about two miles west of Monument, Kansas, for the contest. Comstock killed 46 buffalo; Cody killed 69, and his career as a glib storyteller and ruggedly handsome showman was launched.

In 1866 at the same time Buffalo Bill started hunting buffalo and when Ralph Waldo Emerson gave his second series of speeches at Dart Hall, the first post-war step to gain control over the Upper Mississippi was taken when the U.S. Army Corps of Engineers created the Rock Island District. Before the war, using Robert E. Lee's 17-year-old design plans, work had begun at the chain of rapids west of Campbell's Island to create a navigable channel through the Rock Island Rapids. Records are unclear what was accomplished during the five years of work, but the Civil War distracted everyone from Mississippi River improvements.

Also in 1866, even before Andrew Humphreys' report on the river was published, the Army Corps of Engineers recommended making over the river. Ignoring what river men knew, what was intuitive to most laymen, and what Mark Twain sagely expressed when he said, "The Mississippi River will always have its own way. No engineering skill can persuade it to do otherwise," the Corps of Engineers created the challenge of improving the river. Again using the military stratagem as justification, the Army said that the Civil War clearly demonstrated the necessity of a navigable Upper Mississippi River. In their justification, the Army engineers ignored the fact that a railroad bridge passed through the Rock Island Arsenal, and they left out any projections of how much impact the burgeoning railroad system would have on the army's logistical needs. Most importantly, the military justification ignored that it was highly unlikely that the South would rise again to take on the U.S. Army, and just as unlikely that the Mississippi River would be important in any foreign wars. The financial costs of the river makeover ultimately exceeded that of the Civil War.

No longer trusting the surveys of the Des Moines and Rock Island Rapids signed by the defeated and consequently discredited Robert E. Lee, the surveys were redone. The updated design recommended making virtually the same improvements to the river that Lee had specced three decades earlier — the channel was to be dredged to Lee's specification of a width of 200 feet; however, the new survey added an extra half foot to Lee's proposed channel depth of four feet. The Corps estimated the project would cost just over $800,000. In the fall of 1867, using chisel dredges, cofferdams to allow river bottom excavation, and underwater blasting to clear a channel through the bedrock river floor, work began at the Duck Creek chain of rapids in the middle section of the Rock Island Rapids.

Two years after work on the rapids began, the most challenging project was undertaken. A huge rock in the main channel was situated at the north end of Campbell's Island and at low water was but a foot under water. To safely pass "Campbell's Rock," an arc of 20 feet had to be steered in the swirling waters. Scores of steamboats, keels, flats, barges, and riverboats had not successfully navigated past the rock, and the Corps' edict to destroy it was a good one. However, it was the application of some elementary science and some engineering astuteness by a private contractor that rid the Mississippi of the treacherous obstacle. Boys and engineers like to blow things up, and the January 1, 1870 *Argus* describes the engineering feat:

> Campbell's rock, which must have been part of the earth's surface at the creation and been trod over by monstrous antediluvian creatures before the trickling rivulet from a mountain lake became the mighty river which flows the whole length of our land, is now no more. Campbell's rock is broken into pieces hardly larger than eggs and scattered over the bed of the Mississippi River.
>
> That huge, protruding tooth of original earth was so very hard that innumerable drills of the finest tempered steel, along with the patience of the contractors, would have been worn out before the rock could have been

removed in the ordinary way. (The first cofferdam was being built to jut out three blocks [approximately 2,000 feet] from the head of Campbell's Island and the dam builders were obliged to remove Campbell's Rock.)

  A little human ingenuity was set to work on this flinty subject and resulted in the following efficacious device: Cordwood was piled all over the rock several feet high and a fire started. In a short time the rock was in a white heat. A crowd of men, stationed around the rock with buckets, deluged the hot rock with cold water. The sudden contraction split the rock from end to end. A couple of sand blasts were then put in the fissure and the rock was blown into atoms. It would be hard to discover now where Campbell's rock once stood.

  Twenty years after work began at the Duck Creek Chain of Rapids, the Rock Island Rapids were now more navigable for steamboats and barges; however, the engineering improvements created faster currents through the dolomite-bottomed channel and the 14-mile downriver trip from Port Byron to Rock Island was still a treacherous adventure and did not open the river for significantly larger river craft — that was a navigation and engineering problem to be dealt with later. Although not meeting riverboat captains' expectations, the Corps took great pride in their accomplishment — at just eight times the cost of Robert E. Lee's estimate and less than fifty years after first conceiving of the idea, engineers believed they had started to tame what Mother Nature had let go wild 20,000 years before.

  While they were tidying up the Rock Island Rapids, the Corps also was assigned the task of upgrading the six-year-old, wooden railroad bridge that had replaced the original bridge. The second bridge had used the same piers that had caused the *Effie Afton* so much trouble, but was built of sturdier timber and allowed heavier trainloads. While the Corps was at it, in order to maximize the usable area on Arsenal Island they moved the location of the third bridge 500 yards downstream to the westernmost end of the island. Constructed of steel and using the same truss design found in a child's erector set, the third bridge was a double-decker with a single rail line on the top deck and a roadway and passenger walk on the lower deck. Because the federal government shared the bridge's cost and use with the railroad, it was smartly named the Government Bridge. Whereas the first two railroad bridges lasted only 16 years, the first Government Bridge made it from 1872 to 1896 when it was replaced with a similar architecturally pleasing steel structure wide enough to allow for two train tracks. More than a century later, the inelegant, but durable bridge is still in use and retains its original name. Unfortunately, the river it spans is unrecognizable to the river it spanned in 1896.

  A blend of powerful special interests, Army engineers, flimsy justification, taxpayers' money, and generations of time are the only ingredients necessary for a boondoggle. At the same time the State of Illinois was starting the Mississippi-Rock River Canal at Rock Island City, in 1834 the Army Corps of Engineers began working on a much grander project — a 75-mile canal to connect the Illinois River to the Mississippi. With strong backing from Illinois farmers who were promised by politicians that the Illinois and Mississippi Canal would reduce shipping costs and open up grain markets in the East, Army Engineers were directed to design the canal. The Panic of 1837 halted the Corps' plans before they got off the drawing board. However a generation later in the years before the Civil War, the Corps resurrected the idea and finished the plans, but they were filed away when the Army's attention turned to holding the country together. When Illinoisan Ulysses S. Grant became president in 1869, the pork-barrel project was again dusted off. The next year, using the irrefutable logic that a 75-mile-long canal would shorten the waterway distance from Hennepin, Illinois, to Rock Island, the Corps did a land survey for the canal along the ancient Mississippi riverbed. Thirty-three years after its inception the project was finally off the drawing board.

  Eleven years later, farmers were again enraged over high railroad shipping rates and an angry committee of 400 men from seven Midwestern states assembled in Davenport to discuss what should be done. As with most large, financially self-interested committees, no logical plans were put forth. However, it was agreed that the canal may help lower railroad rates, and Republican politicians saw a way to diffuse their constituents anger and win votes. Another land survey was done, and after the War Department selected the route of the feeder canal from the Rock River, the project was shovel-ready. Seven more years passed before Congress approved $500,000 ($12.5 million) of the total estimated cost of $6,925,900 ($175 million) to build the first five miles of the canal. In that same year, Grover Cleveland signed into law the 1887 Interstate Commerce Act, and railroad shipping rates started to descend to their lowest historical levels. But 53 years after its initial proposal, the waterway now called the Hennepin Canal was under construction. Sadly for taxpayers, central Illinois had changed a lot during the last half of the 19th century, and there were eight railroad and 67 highway bridges that were unplanned for and had to be built over the canal.

  Time and money (considerable research could not uncover how much money) solved those problems, and 16 years after construction started, a boatload of dignitaries including Rock Island's most famous engineer, Samuel Van Sant, broke through October ice to make the 75-mile trip to Rock Island. The steamer's victory lap took six days to pass through the canal's 32 locks — the dignitaries could have taken the train or driven the distance in less than six hours. In the 73 years from the canal's inception to its operation in 1907, due to competition between railroads, shipping rates had stabilized at low levels, and there was no longer any economic advantage to ship by barge. But most disturbingly — and someone must have noticed during the 20 years it took to build the canal — the standard size of barges had grown much larger and new barges were too big for the canal's locks. However, the dutiful soldiers of the Army Corp of Engineers had faithfully carried out the orders they instigated and completed the fiasco. So, over the next 40 years, very little grain — or anything else — made its way to the Mississippi River via the Hennepin Canal.

However, the families of the 50 men who were given government housing and were employed year round — even though the canal only operated from April to October — benefited greatly. Because the lock operators and maintenance crews had nothing to do in the winter, until the late 1920s when electric refrigerators put them out of business, the canal workers created a thriving second business to supplement their government incomes by cutting ice on the canal and selling it to the locals. In 1948, when not a single barge traveled the canal during the entire shipping season, the Corps begrudgingly acknowledged that the Hennepin Canal was no longer a good idea and put it on a limited service basis. Three years later, after still no more barges floated the canal, they finally terminated all the canal's employees except a maintenance crew; a generation later in 1970 the Corps washed their hands of the canal and gave it to the Illinois Department of Conservation. Even though most of the abandoned canal is inaccessible because it runs through private property and is filled with brackish water, it is now an Illinois State Park that sports some informational signage and is creatively called the Hennepin Canal Parkway.

Not all Army Corps of Engineer projects end as pointless money sinks or are devastatingly destructive to the environment. The Rock Island Line benefited tremendously from the Corps-designed, government subsidized, two-track Government Bridge. Eventually reaching west into Nebraska, Kansas, Colorado, Oklahoma, Texas, and New Mexico, south into Missouri, Arkansas, and Louisiana, and north into Minnesota and South Dakota, the Rock Island Line was indeed "the road to ride" to any destination in the central United States. But it was the Chicago to Rock Island to Council Bluffs section of the Chicago & Rock Island Railroad that was linked to the Central Pacific Railroad of California in 1869 and became part of the transcontinental "Pacific Railroad" that carved a special place in history for the Rock Island Line.

The completion of the Pacific Railroad made those, who had risked their lives to travel from the East to California by wagon train, stagecoach, or clippership, appear impetuously foolish. A $65 ($1,000) Pacific Railroad ticket bought passage from New York to San Francisco. If only the Donner Party, Mormons, Forty-niners, and early Western pioneers had waited a decade or two, they would have completed in a relatively safe and comfortable eight days what had taken them a perilous half-year —

and saved 30,000 lives. Just as telegraph technology shut down the Pony Express in 1861, eight years later railway technology drove stagecoach, wagon train, and clipper ship transportation companies out of business.

With more than 2,000 miles of track, the renamed Chicago, Rock Island & Pacific Railroad Company made Rock Island a "last chance" jumping-off point for settlers, salesmen, and tradesmen before they crossed the Mississippi and ventured into the bleak Plains States to help fulfill the destiny God intended for the nation. Rock Island became a bustling transportation hub and the most raucously high-class entertainment destination east of Chicago — restaurants, taverns, saloons, dance halls, theaters, brothels, and hotels sprang up in the downtown district. Many ambitious young men, who were headed west to seek their fortunes, got off the train at Rock Island and ventured no farther — accurately sensing that life could get no better.

In 1871 Ben Harper opened the luxury, five-story 100-room Harper House Hotel on the former site of the Island City Hotel at the southwest corner of Illinois (2nd) Avenue and Jefferson (19th) Streets. The elegant new hotel brought national attention to Rock Island and the "picturesque Tri-Cities," and newspapers across the country acclaimed the hotel and its amenities that were found nowhere else between Chicago and San Francisco. The extravagances included Turkish baths, a music store, a spacious fine-dining restaurant, and an authentically decorated Oriental parlor. The Harper House also bragged of being "the first hotel in the West with a fire escape."

Six years after his hotel opened, Harper announced plans to build an elegant opera house at 16th Street and 2nd Avenue. Harper's 851-seat theater was to be as grand as his hotel. The first level of the building was retail space, and the three-story theater soared above the stores. The immense stage was 26 feet by 57 feet, the parquet had 185 upholstered opera chairs, there were 250 seats in the dress circle, 61 seats in the side balconies, and the rear balcony sat 355 comfortably on fine upholstered seats. Along with the plush seating for all patrons, the theater featured steam heating, gaslights, and fresh-air ventilation — all exceptional amenities for the time. Renowned soprano Marie Rose opened the opera house in 1878, and the nation's most popular and famous performers graced its stage over the next two decades: the Tom Thumb troupe of the famous company of Lilliputians, Mark Twain, Sara Bernhardt, Lily Langtry, John Drew, "hometown boy" Buffalo Bill Cody who starred in a melodrama, and Jay Rial's Company who performed *Uncle Tom's Cabin*. After Harper's death in 1887, the quality of performances declined, and the opera house closed four years later. One of its tenants who built furniture in the basement and operated a small store on the first floor bought the building.

The furniture manufacturer built the world's first "easy chair." The chair's inventor was C.C. Knell, a Swiss Canadian who became a one-trick-pony, but it was a heck of trick. With a crew of nine, Knell made the opera house seats for Harper, and then after the theater opened, he began manufacturing his "reclining chair" in the theater's basement, where he had set up his shop for Harper. He sold the chair from a small storefront on the theater's first level and by mail order. He made a well-padded, upholstered reclining chair whose back, while sitting, could be adjusted to different levels with a hand lever. The chair had broad armrests and an adjustable footrest. His patented invention was the first design improvement for a chair since Benjamin Franklin invented the rocking chair a century earlier. And Franklin's invention was the first chair improvement since backs were put on benches. Knell's reclining chair sold for $10 ($350), prepaid in cash. Greenbacks floated in from around the world, and Knell soon became one of the wealthiest men in Rock Island.

Knell's friend, Ben Harper, asked him to manage his opera house, and soon after taking over the theater's management, Knell became hopelessly star-struck with the beautiful Lillian Lewis, one of the many famous actresses who performed at the theater. Smitten, Knell left his thriving business and followed her on the road. When he returned, he was ill and soon died of typhoid fever. His doctor attributed it to "breathing the poisonous air left by theater audiences." Knell was 41. Hans Clemann, Knell's sales manager, and the company's manufacturing manager, Louis Salzmann, bought the profitable business from Knell's estate. Clemann and Salzmann also bought the opera house and maintained the furniture business until the Great Depression. After the patents ran out, the chair was quickly copied and variations of "dad's easy chair" populated dens and living rooms throughout the civilized world. The firm of Clemann & Salzmann must have continued to prosper, because Clemann supported 11 children and Salzmann eight.

The year before the Harper Opera House opened, in an attempt to keep up with the city's cutting-edge, modern image, an 1877 ordinance replaced Rock Island's 67 elegantly named streets and avenues with numbers — old street signs were torn down and new signs were erected with digits instead of letters for the street numbers. The ordinance specified:

> The streets of this city, unless otherwise specially designated, shall be named and designated as follows:
> The streets running north and south shall be called 'Streets' and shall be numbered from one upward, commencing at First Street as the extreme western street in the city and numbering towards the east.
> The streets running east and west shall be called 'Avenues' and shall be numbered from one upward, commencing at First Avenue as the avenue bordering on the Mississippi River and numbering toward the south.

Not anticipating electronic mail sorters and 9-digit zip codes, to the presumed satisfaction of generations of postal workers, Rock Island set the standard for simplified numbered streets and addresses for Midwestern cities and towns, and overnight people living on streets charmingly named Rock River, Orleans, Highland, Green Grove, and Indian Boundary found themselves living on 3rd, 4th, 5th, 6th, and 9th Avenues. Creating 8th Avenue was a service to all — along its modest length, it had had six different names: Union, South, Guyer, Eighth, Edgewood Park, and Barnard.

Chapter 15

Play Ball!

Almost every time we score three touchdowns and hold the other team to less than three, we'll win. ~ Adrian Book, Rock Island Central Junior High School football coach

THE LAST HALF OF THE 19TH CENTURY saw the rise of American sports, and baseball became the national pastime, a title it would hold for a century. A hundred years before the first baseball game with published rules was played in 1846, similar games were played in many variations and with rules made up to fit the number of players and the field it was played on. (Even through the 1950s fair balls popped over Longfellow School's short right field fence were an out.) Although baseball's green fields were uniquely suited to America's pastoral nature, millions have played it on New York streets and California beaches. It's a myth that Union General Abner Doubleday, who fired the Civil War's first shot at Fort Sumter, invented the game; it evolved from a number of English folk games, including stoolball, trap ball, and cricket. Then, two decades after the first baseball game was played with codified rules in Hoboken, New Jersey, on November 6, 1869, Rutgers and Princeton squared off 30 miles down the road in New Brunswick, New Jersey, to play the first game of gridiron football, a game that evolved from rugby and association football (soccer).

The one major sport that was invented by an American and that had no predecessor was born in December 1891 when James Naismith hung a single peach basket from an elevated running track 10 feet above the floor of the International Young Men's Christian Association Training School (now Springfield College). The professor tossed out an association football and said the winner was the first team to throw the ball into the basket. Incredibly, peach baskets were used for fifteen years until replaced by metal rings, and it's unclear when someone figured out that it was easier to cut the bottoms out of the baskets instead of poking the ball out with a long pole thrust through a hole in the bottom of the basket. The first official basketball game was played at the Albany, New York YMCA less than a month after Naismith bounced out the first ball. With nine men to a side, the rough and tumble game that resembled indoor rugby mercifully ended when someone tossed in a 25-foot shot — fouls and free throws were introduced later.

Always looking for an excuse to avoid classes and beat an Illinois team, the University of Iowa invited the University of Chicago to play in the first five-on-five intercollegiate basketball game on January 18, 1896. Chicago's football coach and athletic director, Amos Alonzo Stagg, showed up with players from his talented football team and muscled the Monsters of the Midway to a 15 to 12 win over the Iowa Hawkeyes. Four years before Iowa played Chicago, in 1892 Sendra Berenson, a physical education instructor at all-women Smith College read about Naismith's new game in a YMCA publication, *Physical Education*, and introduced the game to Smith College women. Berenson believed Naismith's rules were too unrefined for women and modified them. She divided the court into three regions (home, center, and guard), with three players from each team in the three regions. Players were prohibited from leaving their assigned region, could not dribble more than three times, could not hold the ball for more than three seconds, or snatch the ball away from an opponent. Berenson, who apparently was a non-aggressive sort and had something for the number "3," was a Lithuanian immigrant who was a nonathletic child who preferred music, literature, and art. She also introduced volleyball to Smith, and "the mother of basketball" helped develop Smith's gymnastics, field hockey, fencing programs, and folk dancing. There's no record that she suggested playing football.

California girls immediately took to Berenson's version of basketball, and on April 4 of the same spring that Iowa lost to Chicago, the *San Francisco Chronicle* reported that the Stanford women "ran with twinkling feet" past Cal's women in the first-ever intercollegiate woman's game. In their first glorious win, the Stanford Cardinal doubled the Golden Bears score 2 to 1 and through 2012 they would beat Cal 60 more times while only losing 17 games. The first game of intercollegiate basketball's longest running rivalry was played in front of 700 women — presumably because of the titillation factor, men were barred from watching the game. Eight months later, the first interscholastic contest between girls was played between Chicago's Austin High and Oak Park High.

Four years after Naismith invented basketball, a former student of his, William Morgan, invented volleyball. Morgan was the director of physical education at the Holyoke, Massachusetts YMCA, and was troubled by the brutish physicality of basketball. He wanted to design a game that rewarded teamwork and athleticism and could be played by any number of men of any age. Suspending a tennis net 6 feet 6 inches high from the sidewalls of the Y's gymnasium, Morgan demonstrated the game in an exhibition match at the YMCA Training Center only 10 miles up the road in Springfield. When an observer at the exhibition commented on the volleying nature of the game that Morgan called "Mintonette," the name was changed to "volley ball." The

Training Center raised the height of the net, refined the rules, and spread the game throughout the world.

During the rise of organized sports, unquestionably, the YMCA was a primary influence on the European and American spurt of interest in sports that occurred between 1870 and 1930. Founded in London in 1844 to get idle English boys off the streets and teach them Christian morality, the first Y in the United States opened in Boston in December 1851, and after the Civil War, Ys rapidly spread west. Rock Island's first Y was representative of the model that was developed in the East. Designed by E.S. Hammatt, who also designed Lincoln School and many of Rock Island's other early schools, the Romanesque square-towered building housed the gymnasium in a windowed basement; a large hall for group activities, dances, and productions; and rooms for meetings and offices on the second story. Gabled rooms looked out of the top floor over downtown Rock Island from their perch on the southwest corner of 3rd Avenue and 19th Street.

The attractive building, which was constructed solely from donations, had a short life. Designed for gymnastics, boxing, and wrestling, Naismith and Morgan's new games couldn't be played in the Rock Island Y's basement gym. And when swimming was included in the first Modern Olympic Games in Athens in 1896, new YMCA buildings were designed with a swimming pool in the basement and a high-ceiling gymnasium on ground level. Although swimming events at the first four Olympics were held on open water, the quadrennial event spiked interest in swimming as a competitive sport. Since open water swimming was not a year-round option in most U.S. cities, the Y stepped in to groom decades of Olympic swimmers and to teach water safety to all its young members.

Staying at the athletic forefront, in 1913 a new YMCA was opened on the southwest corner of 19th Street and 5th Avenue. For a half century, the new Y was the indoor playground for thousands of Rock Island boys and hosted noon and evening basketball and volleyball games for their dads. The new Y was a boy's paradise. Except once a month on Saturday nights, when escorted by a high school Hi-Y member to a dance, girls were not allowed in the building — even to visit the single men who lived on the Y's top two floors. The YMCA Residence had a separate entrance on 20th Street, and non-residents were forbidden beyond the lobby, which was fine with the boys who played ping-pong, shuffleboard, chess, and checkers in the rec rooms, and crowded into the small theater to sit on the floor and watch black and white Three Stooges movies before they were "buzzed down" to the locker rooms through a door with an electronic lock for a glorious hour in the gymnasium followed by another hour in the four-lane, 20-yard swimming pool.

For grade school boys, the gym fulfilled their every dream. They played spirited games of dodge ball, ball tag, and basketball on the gym floor, while others raced around the balcony track that could only be accessed by a two-story ladder that required a tricky and scary lunge from the ladder to the track. Although no one knew the kid's name, legend had it that sometime in the hazy past, a seven-year-old — the youngest age allowed at the Y — had missed the leap and creamed himself on the gym floor below. Best of all, the track could only be exited by sliding down a fire pole to the spectators' balcony, and then sliding down a second pole to the gym. Junior high school boys were allowed to use the three handball courts, jump on the trampoline, box in the ring, work out with free weights, and after donning masks and pads, thrash at each other with fencing sabers. Before World War II, the Y sported Rock Island's only crushed-rock tennis courts.

Until the Y moved sports indoors, the field games of baseball and football ruled the playgrounds, and horseracing was the largest spectator sport. Baseball was already America's favorite sport when professional baseball came to Rock Island in 1877. However in Rock Island, as in the rest of the country, legions had played variations of the sport for the love of the game years before teams were formed that charged admission to watch them play. Boys and girls of all ages played the game on farm pastures and vacant city lots throughout the country. An 1828 Maryland newspaper article described the game's attraction:

> Then comes a sun-burnt gipsy of six, beginning to grow tall and thin and to find the cares of the world gathering about her; with a pitcher in one hand, a mop in the other, an old straw bonnet of ambiguous shape, half hiding her tangled hair; a tattered stiff petticoat once green, hanging below an equally tattered cotton frock, once purple; her longing eyes fixed on a game of base ball at the corner of the green till she reaches the cottage door, flings down the mop and pitcher and darts off to her companions quite regardless of the storm of scolding with which the mother follows her runaway steps.

Before a challenge game against Davenport in the summer of 1866, the *Argus* obligingly published the rules for the game that was to be played on one of Bailey Davenport's pastures bordering Spenser (7th) Avenue. For novices to the nuances of the sport, the *Argus* informed that there were "four bases and the player must touch them all" to score. The Rock Island nine, who called themselves the Wapello Base Ball Club after a Meskwaki chief, was composed of young businessmen who were nattily uniformed in white linen shirts, blue Turkish pants (knickers) held up by belts embroidered with "WAPELLO BBC," and blue caps trimmed with red and topped with a white button. Baseball gloves were not yet popular, and until Albert Spalding, a catcher from Byron, Illinois, who played for the Chicago White Stockings (later renamed the

Cubs), started wearing a glove to protect his catching hand, gloves were for wimps. The glove idea caught on, and Spalding made a fortune selling them.

The game, of course, came naturally to the athletic men from Rock Island, and on August 25th in the first organized game in the area, they beat Davenport 118 to 7. After dominating teams from the neighboring cities, in October in what most probably was a predecessor to the World Series, the Wapellos journeyed to Peoria to play for the championship. In the final game, the Wapellos crushed the hometown favorite, Peoria Enterprise, 85 to 54. Arriving back in Rock Island with the $100 ($1,500) winners' take, the team was greeted at the train station by a cheering throng that had been notified by telegraph of the team's victory and had been pumped up during the wait for their heroes by several local bands. The players were paraded to the Island City Hotel where they celebrated their championship and shared their largesse well into the night. The Wapellos were undefeated for four years, and the humiliation of their first loss was so dispiriting the team disbanded and never played another game. The teams' first baseman was a professional photographer, and he took 4 by 2½-inch full-length individual photographs of his 13 uniformed teammates. The early-version Wapello baseball cards sold at auction in 2001 for $18,000.

For seven years after the Wapellos loss, little baseball news is recorded on the pages of the *Argus*. Then in 1877, after a suitable mourning period, the game burst back into the sporting spotlight. That summer a team of Rock Island's "members of the bar" challenged the local doctors. There were many more lawyers than doctors, and they had much more time for practice, and predictably the lawyers won 43 to 24. The same summer, the *Argus* reported that the Island City Base Ball Club defeated a team of railroad men 42 to 4, and another game between two Rock Island teams ended with the Acrobats defeating the White Stockings 42 to 26. Suddenly, everyone was playing baseball on the old fairgrounds on Otter (12th) Street, and in the summer of 1884 Rock Island secured a franchise in the professional Northwestern League. Over the next dozen seasons pro teams came and went, but amateur teams thrived. In 1897 the Rock Island Islanders joined the professional Western Association, and two seasons later the Islanders swept the previous champion, Cedar Rapids Bunnies, to win the league championship.

In 1901 the Rock Island Islanders were one of the eight teams to join the Three-I League, formally the Illinois, Indiana, Iowa League, for the league's inaugural season. In the same year the American League was formed, the Islanders finished ahead of only the last place Decatur Commodores and 27 games behind the champion Terre Haute Hottentots. The team steadily improved, and in 1907 after winning 86 games over the 132-game schedule, the Islanders beat out the Commodores for the Three-I title — the

Three-I League was the nation's best minor league and annually lost many of its players to the National and American Leagues. The Three-I Davenport team, who had changed their name from River Rats to Riversides before settling on Knickerbockers, had finished last in the league and folded the season before Rock Island won the championship — depriving Rock Island of even more regional bragging rights.

The Islanders became the hottest ticket in town and larger facilities were needed to accommodate their faithful "kranks" — the term then used for baseball fans, but whose etymology is unclear. ("Fance" were those who followed or "fancied" boxing. Fance was shortened to "fans," and its use was reinforced by its connection to the word "fanatics.") A 3-block long field of dreams was laid out to the north of 18th Avenue between 9th and 10th Streets. The splendid new ball field was built on a spacious swath of Bailey Davenport's pastureland and named Douglas Park. The Islanders' kranks were some of the most loyal and the most emotional in the league, and the field on the old fairgrounds had no barriers to them from mobbing their heroes in victory or assaulting the opposition and umpires in defeat. The *Argus* described one ninth inning rally that led to a win: The crowd, "which had almost abandoned hope, cheered the boys long and loud. Cushions were hurled in the air, hats were tossed up and umbrellas waved, the spectators actually mad from joy." In one defeat the kranks spilled onto the field and "attacked the umpire with pop bottles, cushions, and other missiles." In a later game, the ump got his revenge when kranks charged the field — he knocked out six. Douglas Park was a state-of-the art ballpark when it was finished in time for the 1905 season. It featured an elevated, covered grandstand to protect spectators from the rain and covered dugouts to protect the players from thrown projectiles.

The 1907 championship was the Islanders' apex, and as the 16 major league teams, especially the Cubs, supplanted interest in local teams, the Islanders eventually fell to the minor leagues' middle tier. After completing the 1937 season in the Class A Western League, the Islanders hung up their uniforms forever when the league suspended operations. Except for the occasional touring professional team that would take on local all-stars, Douglas Park would never again see the quality of play that it did in the first three decades of the 20th century. In 1966 Satchel Paige, who at age 42 was the oldest Major League Baseball rookie ever and the first player from the Negro Leagues to be inducted into the Baseball Hall of Fame, pitched an exhibition game at Douglas Park in his last professional year playing ball — he was 59-years-old.

In 1931, the year after lights were installed at Douglas Park, Davenport one-upped Rock Island when it built one of minor league baseball's classic stadiums. Named at the top of the best minor league parks on every list of historical baseball fields ever compiled, Municipal Stadium (now Modern Woodman Field) permanently moved professional baseball from Douglas Park across the river to Iowa. Douglas Park then became one of the country's best amateur baseball parks and most notable softball venues. From 1961 to 1970, the women's World Tournament of Softball was held at Douglas Park. And during a post-World War II period when men's fastpitch softball was played in most cities in the country, the International Softball Congress' World Fastpitch Softball Tournament was held at Douglas Park. Men and women's softball had immense fan interest, and one of the area's most anticipated events was the annual game between The King and His Court, which featured Eddie Feigner — the greatest softball pitcher to ever live — and the local Hamm's Beer nine, which finished third or better in the ISC Championship four times. The King and his four fielders always dominated.

The playing fields at Douglas Park, which lends its name to the neighborhood it still graces, hosted many notable sports' firsts, national championship games, and world-class athletes, and the park is one of the most history-rich ball fields in the United States. Until the 15,000-seat Rock Island High School football stadium was opened in 1929, Douglas Park was home to the city's major football games. Rock Island city records first list the official inclusion of Douglas Park as a public facility in 1904, but its name and use as sporting fields were in place years before that. Both the University of Illinois and University of Iowa sports' history records verify that on Thanksgiving Day in 1899 an undefeated Iowa Hawkeye team and the University of Illinois' Fighting Illini met each other for the first time at Douglas Park. Iowa students had played intramural and club football since 1872 and against other colleges since 1882. The early years of Iowa football were undistinguished — in 1889 Iowa fielded their first varsity team and one of their losses was to Grinnell, 24-0. In 1896 the Hawkeyes played a 9-game schedule and finished at 7-1-1, winning the Western Interstate University Football Association championship. The 4-team conference also included Missouri, Kansas, and Nebraska. In 1899 Iowa became an Independent and took off on a remarkable streak without a loss.

For the Thanksgiving Day game, the teams met on an Illinois field that was only an hour's train ride from Iowa City, and where most local fans were for Iowa. Because travel was difficult at that time, few from Rock Island attended the University of Illinois, and most Rock Island High School graduates who didn't attend Augustana or Saint Ambrose took the Rock Island Line to Knox College, Northwestern, the University of Chicago, or the University of Iowa. Illinois opened the 1899 season with wins over Illinois Wesleyan and Knox, but then lost the next four out of five with the fifth game against their alumni ending in a tie. However, the Illini were flying high after vanquishing St. Louis University 29-0 only four days before taking the train to Rock

Island for the holiday game. Iowa entered the season's final game with a 7-0-1 record — the Hawkeyes' only blemish, a 5-5 tie with the powerful Monsters of the Midway on the University of Chicago's home field. At the time, the team with the strongest punter and kicker usually won. In some games no passes were thrown, and at a time when it only took 5 yards to make a first down, few were achieved. Field goals and touchdowns counted 5 points, conversions 1, and safeties 2.

Of the 43 colleges that played intercollegiate football in 1899, Chicago was considered the nation's strongest team and compiled a record of 16-0-2. During the season, Chicago scored an incredible 505 points while giving up 28 against a schedule that included Notre Dame (23-6), Purdue (44-0), Northwestern (76-0), Minnesota (29-0), Brown (17-6), and Wisconsin (17-0). Curiously, but possibly an indication of the quality of Illinois high school football, Chicago's lowest scoring game was an opening game victory over Englewood High by a score of 2-0. Arguably, Iowa was as strong defensively as Chicago — and almost as powerful as Englewood High School. The field goal Chicago scored was the only points Iowa had given up all season, while scoring 115 points through only eight games. When the confident, leather-helmeted Illini strode into Douglas Park, they were met with enthusiastic applause and cheers of encouragement from a small but lusty contingent of fans and a chorus of raucous boos from the throng behind the Iowa side. Accounts of the game are sketchy, and there are no reports of their fans' reaction when the Illini slinked out of Douglas Park to enjoy their Thanksgiving dinner at the Harper House after being humiliated 58 to 0.

The next year, Iowa was invited to join the Western Conference — now the Big Ten. Through the first half of their eight-game schedule, the Hawkeyes outscored four Iowa colleges 198 to zip, but their fifth game was at the University of Chicago. The Monsters of the Midway were playing their twelfth game and injuries had decimated the team. After shutting out Englewood High 18-0 and Hyde Park High 5-0, Chicago rolled over six colleges by a combined 122-10 score before being tied 6-6 by Minnesota. Then disaster; in successive weeks they lost their first games in two years, 6-11 to Brown and 0-41 to Penn. Chicago was never in the game as Iowa trounced them 17-0. Instead of returning to Iowa City for a victory celebration, the Hawkeyes took the train to Detroit, where they were scheduled to play Michigan the next Saturday.

Iowa holed up in a resort outside of Detroit for a week of intensive preparation against one of football's strongest teams. The undefeated Wolverines had demolished their first six opponents, scoring 99 points while giving up only 12, and they were thought to be the class of the Western Conference. Michigan's Maize and Blue might have been looking ahead to their next games against Notre Dame and Ohio State and taken the "pony sized" Hawkeyes too lightly — all of Iowa's starting eleven were 5'10" or less and their average weight was only 177 pounds. During the week, Iowa added new plays and defensive formations, and on Saturday they ran past the unsuspecting Wolverines 28-6. When they returned to Iowa City, one player wrote, "The things that happened that night are written in the books. When our train reached Iowa City, every person in town was there. ... There was a bonfire on the field. The boys pulled President MacLean and faculty out of their buggies and carried them in a dance around the fire. The president's hair was singed."

The following Friday afternoon, the heroes of Iowa City barely broke a sweat when they beat the Grinnell Pioneers 63-0. Only Northwestern stood in the way of a perfect record, and a second undefeated season. The Hawkeyes had two weeks to catch up on studies and prepare for the Thanksgiving Day game at their home away from home field at Douglas Park. Rock Island had fallen in love with the Hawkeyes and was ready to put the city's famous hospitality on display. Douglas Park's seating was almost tripled when an extra 3,300 seats were added, bringing the stadium to an unbelievable capacity of 4,628 — and there still weren't enough seats. After reserved seating sold out at $1.50 ($37.50) a ticket and general admission for a $1, standing room tickets pushed the crowd to almost 6,000 for the 2:30 game. Leather-bound souvenir programs sold for a dime.

The Hawkeyes, who were undefeated over two seasons, were supremely confident of running past the Chicago North Shore school that was coming off a shutout loss to Minnesota and were 7-2-2 on the season. Still giddy from the Michigan game, Iowa fans were ready for a second consecutive Turkey Day roasting of an Illinois university. Surpassing Rock Island's commonly spectacular fall days, a perfect football day dawned that was sunny and warm. Other than one-upmanship and building crowd anticipation, there was no explanation for the Hawkeye's late arrival at 2:40. Led by their mascot, a dog — Herky didn't arrive until 1948 — the Iowa team ran onto the field to what the *Davenport Daily Times* reported as "vociferous cheers."

The game was a scoreless defensive struggle until late in the first half when Northwestern fumbled at midfield, and an Iowa player scooped up the ball and sprinted 45 yards for a touchdown. The Times reported, "The crowd broke loose with yells of every description and immediately Northwestern seemed to put more 'ginger' in the playing." Midway through the 35-minute second half, Northwestern kicked a field goal to even the score, and that's the way the game ended. Iowa opened the 1901 season with wins over Northern Iowa, Drake, and Iowa State before traveling to Minnesota and losing for the first time in three years.

After the turn of the century, college football became more popular and rougher, and a few schools temporarily dropped it, but many more picked it up. After some rule changes, by 1920 virtually every college fielded a team. It didn't take long for businessmen to see the game's commercial possibilities, and soon city teams were paying players, charging high admissions, and forming competitive leagues. Little heralded at the time, in 1920 the National Football League's first game was played at Douglas Park. A crowd of 800 watched the Rock Island Independents defeat the St. Paul Ideals 48-0 on September 26th. From their inception 13 years earlier, the Independents were one of the country's elite professional football teams. In 1919 under the ownership of Walter Flanagan, the 18-man squad charged to a 9-1-1 record, scoring 266 points while giving up only 12, and claimed to be "Champions of the USA." The Canton Bulldogs, who were champions of the powerful Ohio League and were led by the phenomenal Jim Thorpe, loudly contested the Independents' title claim. Guaranteeing a $5,000 ($60,000) appearance fee to the Bulldogs, Flanagan challenged the Ohio champions to a showdown at Douglas Park. Flanagan planned to pay the guarantee by selling 5,000 tickets at $2 each. When Thorpe, who was a very intelligent man, heard that only 1,700 had attended the Independents' previous game, he telegraphed back that the Bulldogs season had concluded.

The next year the Independents banded with four teams from the Ohio League and nine other teams to form a new league, the American Professional Football Conference — two years later the APFC renamed itself the National Football League. Thorpe was named president of the APFC and played for the Bulldogs. During the league's inaugural season, the Independents tied the Chicago Cardinals (now Arizona Cardinals) for fourth place. The league expanded to 21 teams in 1921 and the Independents finished fifth. One of the new teams in 1921 was the Green Bay Packers who finished their first season two places behind the Independents.

The Decatur Staleys, a league powerhouse that struggled financially, moved to Chicago in 1921. Augustus Staley gave his team to George Halas, who only two years before had been the New York Yankees' right fielder. Halas lost his summertime job in New York when the Yankees acquired Babe Ruth. Disillusioned by being shoved out of baseball by a mediocre pitcher with some hitting potential, Halas devoted himself to football. Despite a 10-0-1 record, the 1920 Staleys lost money in Decatur. At a time when players were often on the field for every play of the game, the 26-year-old owner/coach (a dual position he held for the next 47 years) also played wide receiver and defensive end for the Staleys — in addition to managing the team's administration and ticket sales. The Independents only 1921 losses were by scores of 14-10 and 3-0 to Halas' Staleys.

For the 1922 season, Halas renamed the team the Bears in tribute to the Chicago Cubs, who allowed them to play their games at Cubs Park — four years later the ballpark was renamed Wrigley Field. The Bears would play their home games there for 50 years. The Independents' two 1921 losses to the Staleys had been played in Chicago, and a frenzied crowd of 4,749 was on hand when the newly named Bears rolled into Rock Island for the season's second game. Fresh off an opening Sunday 19-14 victory over Green Bay, the Independents played the Bears tough but finally succumbed 10-6. Going into the 1922 season's final game against the Bears at Cubs Park, the Independents only other blemish on their season was when the Packers held them to a scoreless tie in front of 8,000 at Hagemeister Park in Green Bay. For the second year in a row, the Staley/Bears again sent the Independents home for the winter with a 3-0 loss. The Independents finished fifth in the league that had shrunk to 18 teams, but three positions ahead of the Packers.

After warming up for the 1923 season with an exhibition win over the politically incorrect Moline Indians, the Independents played the Bears in their first league game at Douglas Park — and won 3-0. That year the Independents were a strong offensive team that scored almost twice as many points as they gave up, but an early loss to the Milwaukee Badgers and two late season losses to the Bears in Chicago dropped them to 12th place, well behind the Canton Bulldogs, who were undefeated for the second straight year. Clearly, the team needed to make a major move if they were to return to the top of the NFL. New team owner, Dale Johnson, was up to the challenge — he brought Jim Thorpe to Rock Island.

Called "The World's Greatest Athlete," Thorpe had dominated the sports pages for two decades. Born of a Métis mother and a Sauk/Irish father, Thorpe had starred in four sports for Carlisle Indian Industrial School. Playing for Pop Warner in the first year of modern football scoring, he led Carlisle to the National Collegiate Football Championship in 1912. Thorpe also won the 1912 Intercollegiate Ballroom Dancing Championship and competed in baseball and track and field. Carlisle's championship season included a 27-6 win over Army, a game in which Dwight Eisenhower blew out his knee while trying to tackle Thorpe. Eisenhower later said of Thorpe, "Here and there, there are some men who are supremely endowed [It is believed that the future U.S. President spoke of Thorpe's football prowess]. My memory goes back to Jim Thorpe. He never practiced in his life, and he could do anything better than any other football player I ever saw." At the 1916 Stockholm Olympics, Thorpe won gold medals in the Decathlon and the Pentathlon. When presenting a special award for best athlete, Sweden's King Gustav said, "You sir are the greatest athlete in the world." To which Thorpe replied, "Thanks, King."

According to a widespread myth, Thorpe was said to be a descendent of Black Hawk. However in later years, Thorpe's daughter, Grace, ruined a perfectly good story when she related that through his mother, her father was descended from the "Thunder Clan," the same as Black Hawk, but that he had no direct relationship to the famous Sauk warrior. Grace said her father had told her that being descended from the same clan as Black Hawk made him as proud as did his Olympic gold medals.

Thorpe's Major League Baseball career spanned seven seasons with three teams, but his primary sport was football. He played professionally from 1915 to 1928. The 1924 Independents did not achieve the results that Johnson hoped for — the Cleveland Bulldogs, who were a merged team of the Cleveland Indians and the Canton Bulldogs, again won the championship. The Thorpe-led Rock Island eleven had a strong 5-2-2 league record with the two ties coming in defensive struggles with the Bears — the first game at Douglas Park ended scoreless and the second game saw each team score a field goal at Cubs Park.

During the 1924 season, the 36-year-old Thorpe and his teammates, Joe Little Twig (also from Carlisle) and Frank DeClerk lived at DeClerk's cottage on the Rock River, a mile east of where the main Saukenuk village had stood. After the regular season and completion of a 6-0 exhibition tour, including an Independents' 7-6 win over the Bears at Wrigley Field, the men returned to cut ice on the river for DeClerk's ice delivery business. While staying at the cottage, Little Twig and Thorpe befriended DeClerk's 12-year-old nephew, Hod Urie, who was also living with DeClerk while recovering from rheumatic fever. Urie later said of the pair, "Little Twig was a nice man; he played catch with me whenever I asked — even though I wasn't supposed to throw." And of Thorpe, "I knew he was a famous athlete, but that was only because Frank told me so. He drank a lot and wasn't around much. He rarely talked to me, and when he did, it wasn't to tell me sports stories." Fifty years later while serving as president of the Downtown Davenport Association, with marathoner John Hudetz, Urie organized the first Bix 7 Road Race as an adjunct to the 4-year-old Bix Beiderbecke Jazz Festival. The race featured world-class runner, Steve Hoag who three months earlier had finished second in the Boston Marathon. (One hundred tee-shirts were ordered for the first race. The 13 undistributed shirts were given to Urie's daughter Gail Nimrick, who ended up using all but one of the collectors' item shirts for rags.)

Thorpe was one of the few athletes of the time who was able to support himself by playing ball, and he was one of the first athletes to be exploited for his athletic skills. He died broke in California at age 64. Reportedly because Johnson refused to meet his salary demand, Thorpe left the Independents before the 1925 season. Johnny Armstrong, a 5'8" quarterback, led the team to a 5-3-3 record — splitting wins with the Packers and losing to and tying the Bears. The next season the Independents moved to the newly formed American Football League. During the Independents' six NFL seasons, they were 2-5-3 against the Bears and 3-1-1 against the Packers — in later years, both rivals would do well in the NFL.

The American Football League had acquired Red Grange, who after graduating from the University of Illinois had played the 1925 season for the Chicago Bears. "The Galloping Ghost" was a sensational athlete and the nation's best-known football player. He left the Bears over a contract dispute and was instrumental in founding the AFL. Dale Johnson believed the University of Illinois star would attract more paying fans to Douglas Park, and he followed Grange to the new league. But the AFL folded after one year and the Independents went with it. Today's Quad City Area football fans can only imagine what a modern day NFL team in the football-crazed heart of America may have become in a metropolitan area that has more than three times the population of Green Bay, Wisconsin — and had a winning football team when the Independents left the NFL.

Chapter 16

The Gilded Age

We are born in a Pullman house. We are fed from a Pullman shop, taught in a Pullman school, catechized in the Pullman church and when we die we shall be buried in a Pullman cemetery and go to a Pullman hell. ~ Pullman employee on life in Pullman, Illinois, circa 1885

BEFORE THE CIVIL WAR, most immigrants to the Americas came from England, France, Spain, Germany, Scandinavia, and Ireland. After the war, emigration to the Americas shifted from Western and Central Europe to Southern and Eastern Europe. Poor economic conditions, war, and religious persecution brought Southern and Eastern Europeans, especially Italians, Greeks, Russians, and Poles to the "Land of Opportunity" along with more immigrants from traditional European origins. Typically unskilled and often illiterate, a huge number of arriving immigrants settled in like-speaking ghettos in the Northeastern cities. Working long hours at subsistence wages in factories, mills, and mines, most non-English speaking arrivals found that the "American Dream" was for them only marginally better than the nightmare they had left in Europe — but they all understood that freed from economic, educational, and language barriers, their children would have it much better.

Two social barriers that were not left behind by America's white, early arrivals were racial and religious prejudices. "Nativists," who were American-born Protestant Anglo-Saxons, placed great value on rural ways of life, property ownership, and literacy and met the new wave of immigrants with resentment and discrimination — especially against poor Catholics and Jews. In the South, the strongest Nativist organization was the Ku Klux Klan. Although Jews and Catholics were unwelcome, they were not as low on the list of threats to the "American Way of Life" as blacks. There, the Klan focused their social purification efforts on easier to identify blacks and moved them to the top of Southerners list of un-American people.

As hard as Nativists worked to hold back the surge of non-Protestant Anglo-Saxons, the flood of Irish and Southern and Eastern Europeans continued. Historians estimate that less than a million and possibly as few as 400,000 Europeans crossed the Atlantic during the entire 17th and 18th centuries. In 1892 when the Ellis Island immigrant inspection station in New York Harbor opened, 450,000 European immigrants were processed during its first year. Immigration continued to soar, and between 1900 and 1910 nearly 9 million immigrants entered the United States. Fearing that immigration threatened to transform the republic into a non-Protestant nation of cities breeding disease, poverty, and crime, Nativists successfully lobbied the federal government for immigration reforms and restrictions.

In 1907 a staggering 1,285,349 "new Americans" officially entered the country. The same year, the Immigration Act was passed that prohibited the entry of aliens who were over 16 years of age and were illiterate. The first quota law was passed in 1921 and was a capitulation to bigotry. Warren Harding caved in to pressure from the Immigration Restriction League when he limited the annual number of immigrants to 3 percent of the number of foreign-born persons living in the USA in 1910. The law was aimed directly at limiting the number of Eastern and Southern Europeans, groups that were predominately non-Protestant. Ethnic immigration quotas in immigration remained in place until 1965.

The socially tumultuous period, dating from the 1879 recovery from the Panic of 1873 until the Bankers' Panic of 1907, is called the "Gilded Age." Brought on when Germany abandoned the silver standard at the end of the Franco-Prussian War and contributed to by President Grant's lack of economic leadership, the Panic of 1873 ended Reconstruction projects and started the "Long Depression," which lasted for 65 months until 1879. The period of economic contraction is the longest in U.S. history, eclipsing that of 43 months during the Great Depression of the 1930s. When the Long Depression ended, and boosted by inexpensive immigrant labor, the economy exploded at the fastest rate in U.S. history. The three-decade period draws its name from the process of coating an object with a superficial layer of gold. Although the two decades at the end of the 19th century and the first decade of the 20th century saw the birth of the modern industrial economy, income disparity during America's Gilded Age was the greatest it has ever been, and the nation's wealth was concentrated in the hands of a few. Entrepreneurial industrialists and bankers that included John D. Rockefeller, Andrew Mellon, Henry Flagler, Henry Rogers, J.P. Morgan, Cornelius Vanderbilt, the Astor family, Frederick Weyerhaeuser, and Andrew Carnegie led a free-enterprise revolution that forever changed the world's economics.

Given its name by Mark Twain in his satirical book, *The Gilded Age: A Tale of Today*, Twain and coauthor, Dudley Warner, mocked the often reckless and ostentatious lifestyles of those made wealthy by mining, manufacturing, railroading, distribution, and banking. It was not the entrepreneurial pioneers at the top of the economic pyramid that Twain ridiculed, but their managers, bankers, partners, suppliers, and associates who created a pretentious class of nouveau riche that he parodied. Many of those who were made wealthy by the business titans were second or third generation Americans who came from humble beginnings, but were not constrained by the language and literacy barriers their parents and grandparents faced — nor did they have the same appreciation and respect as did their pioneer ancestors for the unregulated and unfettered freedoms they enjoyed.

Presiding over the end of Reconstruction, Rutherford B. Hayes was a tough man — he was wounded five times during the Civil War — and a resolute reformer who kept his campaign promises. He helped guide the United States out of the Long Depression and into the "Second Industrial Revolution" and the Gilded Age. He cleaned up the rampant civil service abuses that fomented during Grant's terms and laid the groundwork for reforms that gained steam through the remainder of the century. He tried to reconcile the social and political divisions that had led to Civil War, but neither side was interested and his efforts were unsuccessful. And as he promised, he didn't seek a second term. He retired to his home state of Ohio and became a strong advocate for education reform and equal treatment for all men, regardless of race. Although Hayes periodically attended an Episcopal church, he never became a member, and after marrying Lucy Webb, a devout teetotalling Methodist, his views changed in regards to alcohol but not religion. During his presidency, he banned liquor and tobacco from the White House. After an official dinner, his Secretary of State commented, "It was a brilliant affair, water flowed like champagne."

The Gilded Age saw not only the accumulation of massive fortunes by a few, but also the rise of organized labor and a greatly increased awareness of the political process and a more involved electorate. The pervasive corruption during President Grant's administration, rampant scandals during the Reconstruction era, political payoffs and bribes by the wealthy, and massive fraud by big-city political machines gave everyone someone in politics to take issue with. Starting with the Corrupt Bargain in 1877 that slid Hayes into the presidency, the elections were hard fought and closely contested, and nearly every eligible voting man's politics became emotionally polarized with the result that voter turnout in some elections often exceeded 90 percent.

After the contentiously disputed election of 1876, the election of 1880 was essentially a referendum on Hayes and the Republicans' closure of Reconstruction. In the closest popular vote in presidential election history, out of 8,890,418 votes cast, Republican James "Boatman Jim" Garfield narrowly beat his Democratic opponent, Civil War General Winfield Scott Hancock, by 1,878 popular votes. Each candidate carried 19 states, but Garfield won by the huge margin of 69 electoral votes. Although not a resounding mandate for the Republican agenda, the compromise candidate, Garfield, picked up where Hayes left off. He rid the Postal Service of corruption, which at the time was seen as a near miracle. He named a Supreme Court Justice, revitalized the U.S. Navy, skillfully managed a national debt crisis, and named several African Americans to prominent federal positions — all in 200 days. Then an unknown religious fanatic, Charles Guiteau, assassinated Garfield because he was not appointed ambassador to Paris. Although certainly insane, Guiteau was hanged.

Not much was expected of Garfield's vice president. Chester "The Dude" Arthur wasn't elected to public office until he ran for the nation's second highest elected position. His résumé started with being principal of North Pownal Academy in Vermont and advanced to political appointments that included Engineer-In-Chief, Inspector-General, and Quartermaster-General of the New York State Militia, and Collector of the Port of New York. A political puppet of wealthy New Yorkers, initially Arthur didn't disappoint his critics. Before moving into the White House, he insisted that it be remodeled. Sparing no taxpayer expense, he hired a team of designers, including world-renowned stained glass artisan, Louis Comfort Tiffany. After having 24 wagonloads of furniture, draperies, and portraits hauled from the White House and sold at auction, and apparently feeling more comfortable in his remodeled rooms, Arthur set about handling the country's business.

Then Arthur started disappointing his Republican patrons and shocking his Democratic critics. He took his job seriously and did it well. A career civil servant, he continued the reforms that Hayes and Garfield began. Bucking Republican doctrine, Arthur championed the lowering of protective tariffs and joined with Democrats to pass legislation that banned salary kickbacks, mandated that new employees begin their service at entry levels and advance only by merit exams, and to the disappointment of his New York supporters, distributed federal appointments evenly among the states. Ironically, a lifelong public employee with no elected political experience ended the federal government's embedded "spoils system." After he left office, Mark Twain said of Arthur's partial term, "It would be hard indeed to better President Arthur's administration." Known as the "forgotten" president, he transcended the office by promoting the general good over partisan politics. And journalist/historian Alexander McClure wrote of him, "No man ever entered the presidency so profoundly and widely distrusted, and no one ever retired more generally respected."

Arthur sought a second term in 1884, but the Republicans, who were put off by his refusal to place party politics ahead of national interests, nominated Secretary of State James Blaine of Maine. Although bitterly opposed by Tammany Hall, the New York Democratic political machine, Grover Cleveland, a New Yorker, won the Democratic nomination when a Wisconsin delegate roused the convention with a stirring seconding speech for him. He said of Tammany Hall, which was resented by Democrats outside of New York, "They love him, gentlemen, and they respect him, not only for himself, for his character, for his integrity and judgment and iron will, but they love him most of all for the enemies he has made." Cleveland narrowly beat Blaine in the general election. He earned his nickname "The Hangman of Buffalo" while he was sheriff of Erie County, New York. As sheriff, he could designate hangings to deputies or collect the $10 fee himself — Cleveland made an extra $20 during his term as sheriff.

The Gilded Age is encompassed within the period historians refer to as the "Age of Technology" or the "Second Industrial Revolution." The began with the invention of the Bessemer steel manufacturing process in the early 1850s and ran to the start of World War I in 1914, which began the "Modern Manufacturing Era" in Western Europe and the Northeastern United States. The ability to make stronger, higher-quality steel affected everything from the production of watches and engines to the construction of bridges and high-rise buildings. The United States didn't actively join the technology age until the completion of the transcontinental railroad in 1869, but then it quickly caught up with Western Europe and took the worldwide lead in steel production and manufacturing. Having the perfect blend of raw materials, undeveloped land, cultural disposition, political structure, and abundant labor to manufacture and build at unprecedented rates, the world's first free enterprise economy quickly catapulted America to the forefront of international commerce and industry. Iron ore from the Mesabi Range in Minnesota and the Marquette and Menominee Ranges on Michigan's Upper Peninsula filled a steady stream of ore boats that sailed to the steel mills in the industrial cities that rimmed the southern shorelines of the Great Lakes. From the steel mills of Gary, Indiana; Detroit, Michigan; and Pittsburgh, Pennsylvania steel ingots, rails, beams, and girders were shipped east and west to build a steel-framed national infrastructure.

No person better demonstrated the "class-free" advantages of America's unique, free enterprise system and its unprecedented economic advantages during the late 19th century than a Scottish immigrant, Andrew Carnegie. Leading a life with remarkable parallels to Frederick Weyerhaeuser's, Carnegie's rags to riches story began in Dunfermline, Scotland, where he was born into an upper-middle class family. He was home schooled until he was eight, and then attended school for four years in a one-room schoolhouse. When Andrew was 12, his father, who had operated a successful handloom company, was driven out of business by the new mechanized looms. An economic fatality of the Industrial Revolution and nearly destitute, the family borrowed money for passage and immigrated to Allegheny, Pennsylvania in 1848.

Upon arriving in Pennsylvania, the 13-year-old Andrew went to work as a bobbin boy, changing spools of thread 12 hours a day, six days a week in a cotton mill. His starting wage was $1.20 ($34) a week. His father also worked at the mill, and his mother earned money by binding shoes. Two years later, Andrew left home and more than doubled his weekly wage when he became a telegraph messenger in Pittsburgh. Personable and hardworking, the charming young Carnegie made a point of remembering the names of the businessmen he delivered messages to, and then would cheerfully greet them by name whenever he passed them on the street. Soon, most of the businessmen and politicos in Pittsburgh considered the teenaged messenger boy a friend. In a late-life interview, Carnegie quoted the Disciple Paul when he said, "There is no sweeter sound to a man's ear than the sound of his own name." One of the prominent men he met was Colonel James Anderson, who each Saturday night opened his personal library of 400 volumes to working boys. Carnegie became a consistent book borrower, and when he wasn't working, he read.

The most financially beneficial contact Carnegie made on his message delivery rounds was that of Thomas Scott, the superintendent of the Western Division of the Pennsylvania Railroad Company. Scott stole the 18-year-old messenger and made him a telegraph operator at a weekly salary of $4, and when Carnegie became only one of three men who could interpret telegraphs by ear, he was quickly promoted as Scott's personal secretary at a salary of $35 ($875) per month. Scott introduced Carnegie to J. Edgar Thompson, president of the Pennsylvania Railroad Company, and the three men became life-long business associates and personal friends.

Scott also introduced Carnegie to the world of investments. Borrowing $500 ($12,500) against his widowed mother's $700 home and investing in inside stock tips given to him by Scott, Carnegie soon parlayed Scott's information into a modest fortune. In 1859 Scott was promoted to company superintendent, and Carnegie was appointed to Scott's former position. By the age of 24, Carnegie had reached an undreamt of professional station and financial status for a young man who only 11 years earlier was living in poverty in Europe — Carnegie's wealth would progressively escalate over the next 40 years.

Before the Civil War, Carnegie arranged a merger between T.T. Woodruff's railroad car company and that of George M. Pullman, the designer of the railroad sleeping car. The investment proved a great success and was profitable for Woodruff and Carnegie. During the war, Scott was appointed Assistant Secretary of War in charge of military transportation, and throughout the war, Carnegie assisted him with Union supply and troop transport. Carnegie later joked that he was "the first casualty of the war," when shortly before the battle of Bull Run, he received a scar on his cheek when he was slashed by a trapped telegraph wire that he freed.

After the Civil War, Carnegie left the Pennsylvania Railroad Company and purchased a large portion of the Pacific & Atlantic Telegraph Company, which he sold two years later to Western Union. In 1868 Carnegie was worth approximately $400,000 ($10 million). With the profits from the sale of Pacific & Atlantic Telegraph, Carnegie bought the Keystone Bridge Works and the Union Ironworks. During the war, Pittsburgh had become a center for wartime materials production, and Carnegie had astutely invested in the iron and steel industry. The acquisitions of Keystone Bridge and Union Ironworks launched his steel industry ventures, which ultimately led to his control of the U.S. steel industry.

By the late 1880s, Carnegie Steel was the largest manufacturer of pig iron, steel rails, and coke in the world. The integration of two manufacturing processes and a keen understanding of finance had propelled Carnegie's success. The first process was his companies' cheap and efficient mass production of steel by converting to the Bessemer method, and the second was vertical integration of raw materials' suppliers into the manufacturing process. As a result he was able to drop his price of steel, and soon Carnegie Steel became the primary supplier of railway rails and girders for bridges and buildings.

From 1860 to 1885, Carnegie was arguably the nation's most eligible bachelor. Handsome, glib, humorous, and unfathomably wealthy, the affable Scotsman was often seen in the company of America's most glamorous women. Once when a female admirer, who he had taken an interest in, turned her affections to another man, Carnegie said, "If anybody else in the world can win her, I don't want her." When he was 51, Carnegie married 30-year-old Louise Whitfield. For a wedding gift, he gave her a mansion, formerly owned by Collis Huntington, and an annual allowance of $800,000 ($20 million). When he was 61, she bore him his only child, Margaret.

The Carnegie's were generous patrons of the arts and among their beneficiaries was the New York Philharmonic Society whose debts they annually underwrote. One year as Carnegie was about to write a check for $60,000 ($1,500,000) to the society's secretary, he paused and said, "No, I've changed my mind. Surely there are other people who like music enough to help with their own money." He then told the secretary to seek half of the amount needed from others, and he would match the contribution. The next day the secretary was back and proudly announced that he had raised the first half. As Carnegie handed over his check for $30,000, he said, "Would you mind telling me who gave the other half?" Smiling, the secretary said, "Not at all — Mrs. Carnegie."

In 1901 at the age of 65, Carnegie retired from business. He sold his holdings for 12 times their annual earnings to J.P. Morgan, a financier, for $480 million ($12 billion). Using Carnegie's steel mills as his foundation, Morgan formed the United States Steel Company. Carnegie had been brought up in a household that strongly believed in the Chartist movement, an English philosophy that advocated building a utopian society and that, among other socially progressive ideas, believed that the advantaged should provide for the disadvantaged. From childhood Carnegie held strong egalitarian beliefs and was an avowed socialist and atheist; today he would be called a "Humanist." He said, "I don't believe in God. My god is patriotism. Teach a man to be a good citizen and you have solved the problem of life. "

In the two decades before his retirement, Carnegie became a political activist. He purchased several newspapers in England and then turned their editorial positions to advocate the abolition of the monarchy and to establish a "British Republic." Aided by his personal charm and financial power, Carnegie was befriended by many of England's Labor Party politicians, and he was instrumental in advancing their causes. Carnegie wrote dozens of articles for American and English magazines and published several books, including the radical *Triumphant Democracy* in which he idealized the American republican system and criticized the British monarchical system.

In 1889 Carnegie published "Wealth" in the June issue of the *North American Review*. In it, he argued that the life of a successful man should be comprised of two parts. The first was the creation of wealth through productive enterprise; the second was the distribution of his earned wealth to benevolent causes, because philanthropy was key to making a man's life worthwhile. Carnegie lived his philosophy, and after his retirement, he spent the 18 years until his death giving away his entire fortune to worthy institutions. He donated most of his money to establishing libraries, schools, and universities in the United States, the United Kingdom, and Canada. He built Carnegie Hall, founded the Carnegie Corporation of New York, Carnegie Mellon University, Carnegie Endowment for International Peace, Carnegie Institution of Washington, and the Carnegie Museums of Pittsburgh.

Although Carnegie underwrote the cost of building 2,509 public libraries, the Rock Island Library is not one of them. Reportedly when approached by Rock Island fundraisers, Carnegie said, "Any town that has Friedrich Weyerhaeuser need not ask for a library from me" (actually, Weyerhaeuser had recently moved to St. Paul). Weyerhaeuser and Frederick Denkmann did, in fact, make large donations to the library, and Weyerhaeuser contributed $10,000 and loaned $50,000 to start construction. The total building cost was $90,500 ($2,250,000) of which Weyerhaeuser donated $17,859.32.

Known as the "Star-Spangled Scotsman," there is no evidence that Carnegie ever became a U.S. citizen. He died on August 11, 1919 of bronchial pneumonia. Incredibly, by then he had given away all but $30 million of his fortune, and then after his death, the last one percent of his money was distributed to charitable foundations. He was buried at Sleepy Hollow Cemetery in North Tarrytown, New York — only a few yards away from the organizer of the American Federation of Labor, Samuel Gompers.

Andrew Carnegie was the second richest man in America, and after giving away all of his money, he was still only history's second largest philanthropist. The man who surpassed him in both wealth and charitable giving was John D. Rockefeller. Their financial success and their altruism is where similarities in the two men end. Whereas Carnegie grew up in a hardworking, happy, and loving family that believed that a person should be good for the sake of mankind, Rockefeller grew up in a dysfunctional family, where his mother believed that a person should be good or upon judgment of a vengeful God, they would burn in hell. Known as "Devil Bill," his father was a philanderer who earned his money as a conman, and spent little time at home with his four sons and two daughters. Devil Bill summarized his views on child rearing by saying, "I cheat my boys every chance I get. I want to make 'em sharp." In John D.'s case, it worked.

Demonstrating that opposites attract, Rockefeller's mother was a devout Baptist, who taught her children that "willful waste makes woeful want." He was a serious and studious boy who showed an aptitude towards math. His classmates described him as reserved, earnest, religious, methodical, discreet, and precise. Why he didn't turn out to be an engineer is anyone's guess, but he took his first job at 16 as an assistant bookkeeper for a produce company. He made 50¢ a day of which he donated 5¢ to the Baptist Church. At age 20, he partnered with a friend in brokering produce, and they did exceptionally well. After hiring a replacement to avoid serving in the Civil War draft, Rockefeller bought into an oil refinery in Cleveland and capitalized on wartime contracts. In early 1865 he bought out his partners, and his future was determined. He was well-positioned to take advantage of the post-war prosperity and of the emerging oil business. He reinvested his profits and bought out competitors as fast as they appeared. Forming Standard Oil in 1870, two years later over a four month period, the company absorbed 22 of its 26 Cleveland competitors. Then, Standard Oil's growth became a function of how fast the market for oil products grew, and it boomed.

By the end of the 1870s, Standard Oil was refining more than 90 percent of the U.S. oil. In 1879 the Commonwealth of Pennsylvania indicted Rockefeller on charges of monopolizing the oil trade. According to the *New York World*, Standard Oil was "the most cruel, impudent, pitiless, and grasping monopoly that ever fastened upon a country." The accusation was true. When questioned about his business practices and obscene wealth, Rockefeller unapologetically said, "God gave me money" — a justification that is difficult to argue. For three decades after Pennsylvania indicted Rockefeller, Standard Oil fought anti-trust actions. The company was hated by the public, politicians, and envious businessmen. In 1911 the U.S. Supreme Court found Standard Oil Company in violation of the Sherman Antitrust Act. The company still held 70 percent of the refined oil market, and the court ordered the company to be broken up into 34 new companies. These included Continental Oil (Conoco), Standard of Indiana (Amoco), Standard of California (Chevron), Standard of New Jersey (Exxon), Standard of New York (Mobil), Standard of Ohio (Sohio), and Pennzoil.

Rockefeller had retired at age 63, ten years before the Supreme Court decision. He had accumulated a fortune that may never be matched by an American businessperson. He gave away half of his wealth to education, health science, the arts, and Baptist Church related charities. His giving was in part to silence his critics, to buy high-level support, and to appease state and federal courts. Biographer Ron Chernow wrote of Rockefeller, "What makes him problematic — and why he continues to inspire ambivalent reactions — is that his good side was every bit as good as his bad side was bad. Seldom has history produced such a contradictory figure." Rockefeller believed in a moderate life style; he didn't party; he ate healthy food; he went to bed early; he never drank or smoked; and it paid off — he died at age 97.

Rockefeller's altruism was not equal to Carnegie's, but his benevolence was exceptional for the super-rich of his time. The dramatically uneven distribution of wealth and the arrogance of many rich industrialists created widespread resentment among the working classes that often exploded in violence. At the bottom of the wealth pyramid were the coal miners of the Ohio Valley that lived in wrenching squalor. In eastern Pennsylvania and West Virginia, 30,000 Molly Maguires (Mollies) worked in the coalmines. The name "Molly Maguires" was taken from a famous widow who headed a tenant protest in Ireland in the 1840s. Eighty-five percent of the miners were Irish Catholic immigrants who came to the United States during the potato famines.

Fearing reprisals from the mine owners and their superintendents, the mostly illiterate Mollies became a quasi-secret society made up of miners, saloonkeepers, and low-level politicians. Banding together to protect workers and community interests during the Long Depression, the Mollies were paid subsistence wages for long hours and labored under oppressive conditions. During the 1863 to 1869 depression, 20 percent of all Americans were unemployed, and another 60 percent worked part-time. As the Long Depression wound down, the miners' working conditions improved only minimally. A radicalized union offshoot of the Mollies, the Workingmen's Benevolent

Association (WBA) struck during the winter of 1869-70. The Anthracite Board of Trade, an association of mine owners, called on Franklin Gowen, a first-generation Irish lawyer, to help settle the strike. Gowen not only owned extensive mining interests but also was chief counsel and later president of the Reading Railroad, which transported most of the region's coal. Gowen mediated the first U.S. union agreement.

Under the pact, Gowen cleverly tied wages to coal prices. By artificially driving down the price of coal while raising the cost to transport it on his railroad, Gowen was able to increase profits for mine owners at the expense of the miners, and watched his profits from mining and shipping soar. A decade of strife ensued with Gowen and his managers the focal point of the miners' wrath. Vandalism and murder became common methods of Mollie retribution. Then Gowen, who controlled the police and courts, struck back. A skilled lawyer, he often represented himself in court and then stayed at the bar to examine union witnesses. Portraying Mollies as members of secret, murderous societies and as Communists, Gowen succeeded in prosecuting and hanging 19 Mollies and WBA members for murder in Schuylkill County and adjoining Carbon County. The charges against the Mollies and the WBA were not unfounded. There were continuous acts of destructive vandalism against the mines and the railroads that transported the coal, and in Schuylkill County alone there were over 50 unsolved murders of non-Mollies during the Long Depression.

Afraid of losing control of his workers, in a December 1874 show of power Gowen organized the Pennsylvania mine owners, and together they announced a 20 percent across-the-board wage cut. The Mollies immediately went on a strike, which lasted for six months before it was finally broken, and the human toll was horrific. One historian wrote, "Hundreds of families rose in the morning to breakfast on a crust of bread and a glass of water, who did not know where a bite of dinner was to come from. Day after day, men, women, and children went to the adjoining woods to dig roots and pick herbs to keep body and soul together." Schuylkill County was one of the most desperate areas in the country. From there a striker wrote to a friend, "Since I last saw you, I have buried my youngest child, and on the day before its death there was not one bit of victuals in the house with six children."

A union leader was murdered in March 1875. Another unionist was shot and killed by a mine superintendent. A mine boss fired into a group of miners, and according to a later boast by Gowen, as the miners "fled they left a long trail of blood behind them." National Detective Agency owner Allan Pinkerton sided with the mine owners' disdain and strong-arm tactics towards their workers when he wrote to his superintendent in Schuylkill County, "The M.M.'s [Molly Maguires] are a species of Thugs. Let [agent] Linden get up a vigilance committee. It will not do to get many men, but let him get those who are prepared to take fearful revenge on the M.M.'s. I think it would open the eyes of all the people, and then the M.M.'s would meet with their just deserts." A Pinkerton spy, James McParlan, infiltrated the Mollies and identified several leaders to Gowen. Based on McParlan's information, vigilantes attacked and killed three Mollie leaders and the wife of another.

Expecting retaliation from the strikers, Gowen took the initiative and brought in the state militia and private police forces to patrol the district. The union leaders were "denounced by the press and from the pulpit," and 26 union officials were arrested on a charge of conspiracy. The judge instructed the jury that, "any agreement, combination or confederation to increase or depress the price of any vendible commodity, whether labor, merchandise, or anything else, is indictable as a conspiracy under the laws of Pennsylvania." Using the law enacted to prevent the collusion of Gowen and other railroad robber barons, when he sentenced two of the union officials, the judge said, "I find you, Joyce, to be president of the union, and you, Maloney, to be secretary, and therefore I sentence you to one year's imprisonment."

The violently divisive struggle between owners and labor was not confined to the coalfields of Pennsylvania. Violence broke out in dozens of communities from the East Coast to California. In the Midwest, where working conditions were better than in the East, in 1877 federal troops killed 30 strikers in Chicago. In 1885 Chicago police killed four unionists during a peaceful march. The unionists retaliated by throwing a bomb at the police, killing seven — four unionists were hanged for the murders of the policemen. The next year in Milwaukee, police randomly shot into a crowd of 2,000 Polish workers who had gathered to protest working conditions — six men and a child were killed. The *Milwaukee Journal* congratulated the governor and the police on their decisive action.

The extraordinary wealth that accrued to less than one-tenth of one percent of the population created a political heft that allowed the super-rich to control government, state militias, local police, and the judiciary. No place was this truer than in Pullman, Illinois, a company town built in 1880. Erected on 4,000 acres south of Chicago, every structure in town, including the churches, was company-owned. To work for the manufacturer of railroad sleeping cars, employees and their families had to live in Pullman, even though less expensive rentals could be found in adjoining communities. With the single exception of his magnificent hotel where he entertained his guests and visitors, George Pullman prohibited alcohol inside the town limits. For 18 years, Pullman operated his Illinois fiefdom; then in 1898 the Illinois Supreme Court required that he sell off the town, which was annexed into Chicago. Today it is a historic Chicago neighborhood.

While many bright young immigrants seized the economic opportunities that their new country offered and put into practice their belief that a man's free enterprise success helped all, other smart newcomers recognized that most did not have the personal skills or abilities to manage a small business much less a major enterprise. This was especially true of the illiterate and those who didn't speak English well. One man who devoted his life to preventing exploitation of working men and their families was Samuel Gompers. Similar to the Carnegie's in Scotland, the Gompers' lives and philosophies were shaped by the deprivations of the industrial revolution. One of five brothers, Gompers was born in 1850 after his Jewish parents immigrated to London from Amsterdam. Living in harsh conditions in a South London ghetto, Gompers entered the Jewish Free School as a six-year-old, but forced to help support his impoverished family, after four years of schooling he was apprenticed to a cigar maker. When he was 13, his family immigrated to America and settled on Manhattan's Lower East Side. He assisted his father in making cigars until the day after his 17th birthday when he married a co-worker, 16-year-old Sophia Julian.

After going to work for David Hirsch & Company, a "high-class union shop where only the most skilled workmen were employed," Gompers received his first exposure to the union movement. Hirsch was a German émigré and a socialist. Karl Laurrell, a co-worker and secretary of the International Workingmen's Association, was an early mentor of Gompers and was responsible for moving him away from the socialist political movement and towards the trade unionism movement. In 1875 the 25-year-old Gompers was elected president of Cigarmakers' International Union Local 144. The Cigarmakers' Union nearly collapsed in the 1877 financial crisis when workers across the country willingly took a job to earn any wages. Introducing a high dues structure to subsidize the out-of-work and sick and death benefits for union members, Gompers' Local 144 became a model for all future trades unions. Telling his members, "the time has come when we must assert our rights as workingmen. Every one present has the sad experience, that we are powerless in an isolated condition, while the capitalists are united; therefore it is the duty of every cigar maker to join the organization. One of the main objects of the organization," he concluded, "is the elevation of the lowest paid worker to the standard of the highest, and in time we may secure for every person in the trade an existence worthy of human beings."

Four years later, Gompers was instrumental in founding the Federation of Organized Trades and Labor Unions, "a coalition of like-minded unions," and in 1886 it was reorganized into the American Federation of Labor. Gompers was elected president and remained president for 41 years until his death in 1924. During his four decades of leadership, the AFL focused on higher wages and job security and fought against socialism and the American Socialist Party, which gained increasingly stronger footholds in the East's large industrial cities. Because early strikes attempted to establish a single voice for workers in their contract negotiations with owners, it was important for workers in different trades to support other unions in the same company. Gompers understood the importance of worker unity, and it was the brotherhood and solidarity that he brought to members of local trade unions that gave the AFL its negotiating power and changed the face and fortunes of America's labor force.

While miners and factory and mill workers east of the Great Lakes experienced grave economic hardships and social strife during the Gilded Age, Rock Islanders and those in its neighboring communities lived in relative prosperity and harmony. Because of an economically stabilizing mix of farming, manufacturing, milling, river transport, and railroading, the region did not experience the turmoil of those living to the east Rock Island's high level of prosperity was reflected by modern amenities and social services that were enjoyed by few urbanites at that time. In 1882 gas street lamps were replaced with electric lights, and telephone subscribers totaled more than 100. Paid firemen and policemen replaced volunteers and deputies, and six years later mail delivery was made free of charge — a service few other Midwest communities enjoyed. In 1893 a 10-room hospital opened and was followed three years later by an orphanage.

Bailey Davenport was an enterprising businessman and civil leader who helped improve the city. When he was mayor of Rock Island during the Civil War years, he had started a push for public transportation, and in 1868, under his ownership, the first horse-drawn streetcar was introduced to the Tri-Cities. The predecessor company of the Rock Island and Milan Steam and Horse Railway was in business. The first streetcars slowly hauled passengers from Milan to Rock Island. In addition to serving Milan residents looking for an escape to Rock Island, Davenport also used his streetcars to haul coal from his mines along the bluffs of the Rock River where Saukenuk had stood. As important as coal was to the local economy, the entrepreneurial Davenport found an even more valuable use for his extensive land holdings and one that simultaneously jacked up streetcar ridership to unimagined levels — he built an amusement park on the bluffs overlooking the Rock River and Searstown.

Davenport's 208-acre amusement and nature park on Black Hawk's former home site opened in 1882. Initially, the Watch Tower Amusement Park sported a summer pavilion, picnic tables, walking trails, fishing, boating, bathing, and a spring, which had "medicinal properties." A decade later a Chicagoan bought the park and replaced the horse-drawn cars with electric streetcars, and on summer weekends several thousand people rode the streetcars, which left every ten minutes from both downtown and the train depot to the park — a 25¢ ($6.00) round-trip fare included park admission. Operated daily from May 15 to September 15, amusement rides and attractions included a 1,000-foot, four-loop, figure 8 roller coaster with one amazing loop that skied 60-feet high; a merry-go-round and calliope; a tunnel-of-love; a house of mirrors; and the world-famous, J.P. Newberg's invented-in-Rock Island Shoot the Chutes toboggan slide. Opened as a "Not Suitable for Ladies" thrill ride, women and children soon clamored for seats in the boats that screamed 500 feet down the steep river bluff on greased oak tracks. Reaching a timed speed of 80 miles per hour, the passenger sled was designed similarly to a roller coaster car, and with riders dressed in their Sunday finest and simultaneously holding on to their hats and the sled's rails, it hit the Rock River, skipped 25 to 50 feet through the air, threw up a 150-foot long rooster tail spray, and skimmed across the river's surface. (A hundred years later, the City of Rock Island removed teeter-totters and merry-go-rounds from city parks because they were deemed too dangerous.)

Watch Tower Park soon became the largest amusement park west of Chicago. Hot air balloon ascensions, target shooting, billiards, and bowling were added. Summer weekend and holidays featured fireworks, and band and orchestra concerts, plays, vaudeville, opera, and outdoor silent movies were presented from a magnificent two-story band shell that sat 1,000 people on its amphitheater benches for evening performances and weekend matinees. A Museum of Wonders offered "a regular 'old curiosity shop,' where the visitor may see thousands of relics, freaks, curiosities, animals, birds and wonders from every part of the world, [and] a thoroughly competent lecturer entertains and explains the multitude of interesting objects to be seen." The park's centerpiece was a grand inn that offered formal dining and had large porches that encircled the Queen Anne-design building. The inn burned only four years after its 1892 opening. Immediately, an even grander three-story inn was built that featured an ice cream parlor, café, second-floor ballroom for Saturday night dancing, and magnificent dining rooms that sat 1,000 and opened onto sweeping verandas that overlooked the Rock River. The second inn reigned over the park's heydays between 1897 and 1916 when it too burned. A third inn was built in the colonnaded Classical Revival style popular at the time, and although it also featured first floor dining and a ballroom on the second level, it never recaptured the grandeur of the park at the turn of the century.

After a visit to the park, William Sherman, the Civil War general who had seen amazing sights including spectacular fires in the Atlanta area, remarked that in his extensive travels he had never met its equal. Many accounts have been written about the excitement and thrills at Watch Tower Park, but none fully offers an explanation, other than "declining attendance," as to why in 1927 when lesser amusement parks were thriving throughout the country, the State of Illinois was induced by John Hauberg to purchase the park, tear down the amusement rides, drain the medicinal spring, create a nature preserve, and build a museum for Hauberg's Indian relics. When the State of Illinois acquired the site of the former Saukenuk village, it was renamed Black Hawk State Park and is now the Black Hawk State Historic Site. One can only imagine the sorrowful irony Black Hawk would feel while visiting the park's fine Watch Tower Museum exhibits, erected to honor him and his people only a century after driving them from their birthplace and burning their village. Similarly ironic is the world's second largest concrete statue. The 50-foot high, 100-ton Black Hawk statue in Illinois' Lowden State Park bears no physical resemblance to Black Hawk and is the sculptor's generic representation of a Native American.

Black Hawk would also probably be saddened to see what the U.S. Army did to the sacred island where the great, winged guardian spirit lived. After the Rock Island Confederate Soldier prison was shut down and Sears' mills were purchased, the Federal Government found itself with a prime piece of improved commercial real estate. Putting their newly acquired manufacturing capacity to good use, the Arsenal began turning out uniforms and leather military accoutrements and toward the end of the century, started producing military ordnance, including guns and ammunition, military vehicles, and field equipment. The military installation should have stuck to making uniforms and saddles, but in 1903 the Rock Island Arsenal started to produce the M1903 model of the famous 30-03 Springfield rifle. However unlike those rifles made by Remington Arms or at the Springfield, Massachusetts Armory, collectors are advised: "DO NOT fire this rifle; they can explode." To provide officers with recreation and to utilize the landscape architectural design skills of the Army Corps of Engineers, one of the world's flattest golf courses opened for play on Arsenal Island in 1898. In 2010 the private golf club that was built on public land and whose operating costs were partially underwritten by taxpayer dollars was opened to the public.

Seven years before Bailey Davenport turned Black Hawks' birthplace into an amusement park, in 1875 the Lutheran Scandinavian Augustana Synod Seminary and College moved to Rock Island in order to better serve its Midwest community. During the last half of the 19th century, drawn by the opportunity to plant on rich soil and by a six-month growing season, Scandinavian farmers flocked to the Upper Midwest. Swedish city dwellers, enchanted with the relatively mild climate and economic opportunities moved to Minnesota and northern Illinois cities, and by the end of the century Chicago had the second largest Swedish urban population behind Stockholm.

Augusta College was founded in 1860 in Chicago, but realizing that the campus would be more centralized and accessible to its northern Midwestern community by moving to the Midwest's transportation crossroads, in 1875 the college and seminary moved to Rock Island. Opening in time for fall classes, a single, three-story red-brick building housed the students and faculty, their classrooms, library, and chapel on a 16-acre site (presently expanded to 115 acres) purchased for $10,000 ($170,000). Organized to serve the Swedish community, all six of the first graduating class in 1877 were born of Swedish parents and two students had been born in Sweden.

Patterned after the main building at Sweden's Uppsala University and constructed of sandstone from the LeClaire quarry, Augustana's second campus building, "Old Main," was begun in 1879 and completed ten years later. During its construction, city water and electricity were extended to the campus. The bluish-domed 40,000 square-foot building housed classrooms, the Theological Seminary, and a 600-seat chapel with a $2,600 ($65,000) pipe organ; the original building became a dormitory. The center of campus activity for nearly a century, in 1975 the iconic building was placed on the National Register of Historic Places.

At that time, only Moline (5th) Avenue connected those from the City of Mills to their upscale neighbors to the east, and a dirt lane wound from Elm (30th) Street over the hill through "picturesque bluff land" nestled among forests, pastures, and orchards to the college's entrance. The 1882-83 Augustana Catalog boasted, "Few locations combine, in a more eminent degree, the advantage of accessibility, healthfulness, beautiful surroundings, and quietness for the purpose of study." Over the next several decades, the dirt lane was straightened and transformed into Rock Island's grandest boulevard. Extending for ten blocks east from the top of the 7th Avenue Hill to 44th Street, after plunging down the hill in front of Old Main, the elm and oak-lined brick road passed by the archetypal, two-story red-brick Longfellow Grade School (which held its first class two years before the completion of Old Main) and ended two blocks short of Moline. The single lanes of the elegant two-way, 70-foot wide tree-lined boulevard were separated by six-foot wide flower gardens.

Of most interest to Longfellow boys were the immaculate Augie playing fields only three blocks west of their barren schoolyard. Located in the far northeast corner of Augustana's campus were the Vikings' tennis courts, baseball field, and football and track stadium. The football stadium was named after Charles Ericson who, after moving to America from Sweden when he was 12, played and hunted on the site that he would donate to Augustana after his death in 1910. Through 2011 the 3,500-seat stadium was home to 253 football victories against only 85 defeats. And of the thousands of student-athletes who have played on the hallowed turf of Ericson Field, none became more famous than two-sport star, Kenny Anderson.

Recruited by Augie to play basketball at the non-athletic scholarship school and instead given a grant for mathematics excellence, Anderson scored more than 1,000 points during his four-year basketball career. After receiving permission from the basketball coach, Anderson was also allowed to play football. He still holds every passing record at the Division III school. Anderson was drafted by the Cincinnati Bengal's on the recommendation of Bill Walsh, an assistant coach, who was sent to scout him in 1970. Walsh later said of his trip to Augie, "There wasn't any doubt who Kenny was. He was bigger than anybody on the field. But what impressed me most was that early in the game Kenny got a major hip pointer and could barely walk. At that level they generally cart the guy off. But Kenny came back and played the whole game. That convinced me he could play in the NFL." Eleven years later, Anderson led the Bengal's against the future Hall of Fame coach's San Francisco 49ers in Super Bowl XXIII. Earlier in the season, Walsh had said of Anderson, "Ken Anderson is the greatest quarterback in football today" — Walsh's quarterback at the time was Joe Montana.

Until Augustana opened its doors in 1877, the area from the west side of the 7th Avenue Hill to Moline, almost three miles to the east, was woodland, dotted with pastures, vegetable gardens, orchards, and an occasional farmhouse. A Quaker farmer, Welcome Robbins, owned the land north of the campus that ran up to the factories and houses along the riverbanks, where Charles Ericson played as a child. A decade after Augustana held its first class, Edward Guyer, the son of a Rock Island pioneer who was a county sheriff and a judge, launched a dream to develop the land east of the campus. A life-long Rock Island resident who practiced law there for more than 50 years, Guyer developed a relationship with William E. Brooks, one of the area's largest landowners. Born in the Broadway district seven years before the start of the Civil War, Guyer was one of the Tri-Cities first real estate developers, and probably its largest ever. He was instrumental in developing 14 additions from Milan to Silvis. One of his additions was on land east of Moline that included a parcel that had been owned by Bailey Davenport and was the site of Rock Island Junction, a stop on the Rock Island Line. In September 1895, Guyer held a residential lot sale that attracted more than 8,000 people to a barbecue featuring free food, music, and entertainment. The planned village included a harbor, parks, schools, a library, an artesian well, and a bridge across the Mississippi. Of the 8,000 people who attended the barbecue, five bought lots. In 1903 Rock Island Junction was incorporated as the Village of East Moline, and four years later, the rapidly growing community of about 1,500 dropped the "Village" designation.

Guyer's most grandiose development was the KeyStone area east of Augustana, which began at 38th Street and ran the length of the steep river bluff to where Rock Island's eastern border now lies. On the huge but isolated tract of land located midway between the Rock Island and Moline downtowns, Guyer and Brooks, the grandson of the property's original owner who shared his name, planned to co-develop a futuristic, self-contained neighborhood. Guyer envisioned a modernistic, pre-planned district with its own commercial area of markets and shops, a train depot, and a theater, all to be constructed around the newly built Longfellow School. Brooks had donated the school site to Rock Island on the condition that it would only be used for a school.

Shortly after his arrival from New Hampshire in 1835, Brooks' grandfather purchased the undeveloped timberland that would become the KeyStone neighborhood. The Brooks' property was more than a square mile in area and comprised most of the land that ran from Robbins (38th) Street to what would become the western boundary of Moline 13 years later. It was bordered by the road on the north side of the property that would be named Moline (5th) Avenue and to the south by the current 14th Avenue. The first William E. Brooks' son-in-law, in a book of reminiscences published in 1893, told the story of how most of the northeast corner of Rock Island was purchased:

> Wm. Brooks, before starting to Galena to enter this land, learned that John H. Sullivan, a much younger man, intended to go on the first boat to Galena to enter the same piece of land. The boat was due in the morning and Mr. Brooks knew that in the race up the steep bank at Galena to Bench Street, where the land office was situated, Sullivan would outrun him. He consulted with Charles Eames, his brother-in-law, and they concluded that Mr. Eames should start that night on a good horse they had and try to beat the boat, and that Mr. Brooks should go on the boat, taking the specie along with him to enter the land.
>
> Mr. Eames started in the afternoon, stopping at Port Byron that night. His next stop was at Mr. Pierce's, at Savanna, who gave him a fresh horse to continue his night ride. The little rugged city came into view at 9 o'clock in the morning. As he rode down the steep hill in east Galena, he saw in the distance the smoke of a steamboat. He soon reached the land office and made application for the land, telling the officers that his brother-in-law would be on the first boat with the money.
>
> As Eames came down the hill he met Sullivan on the keen run. When Sullivan went into the office and found that the land was entered, he would not believe it at first until he saw Mr. Brooks come in with the money and pay for the land. They had made the voyage together and talked of everything except that one piece of land. [Sullivan, the loser, returned home and started an Iowa town named Rockingham, now West Davenport.]
>
> A few years after this, Mr. Brooks put up a substantial farmhouse. He obtained some apple seeds from a barrel of rotten apples and started a nursery from which he set out a large orchard of some 15 acres. He told his children that they would see the day when this land, lying between the two towns, would be worth $500 per acre. [Brooks bought the land for $1.25 ($30)

per acre. Fifty years later, the land where Lincoln Park is located was purchased for $1,500 ($34,000) per acre from Brooks' son.]

When the first William E. Brooks died in 1864, except for the newly laid railroad tracks and the road to Moline that paralleled the tracks on their north side, the three miles of land between the downtown districts of Rock Island and Moline were separated by forested land where Black Hawk would still have felt at home. The same year that Brooks acquired his chunk of Rock Island, Alanson Sinnet and his son Frank purchased 55 acres north of Brooks' land along the Sylvan Slough in what is now the northeast corner of Rock Island. After farming and profitably quarrying the land for more than three decades, Frank Sinnet laid out his farm acreage north of the tracks into town lots for the workers in John Sears' mills and for civilian laborers on Arsenal Island. Instead factories and taverns sprang up among a few houses.

The riverbanks from Sinnet's property through Moline were lined with an assortment of factories, many of which supplied tools, parts, and accessories to John Deere's plow works, the area's largest employer. For convenience, those who lived and worked in the unincorporated area attended Moline schools and churches and shopped at Moline stores. However, the week before Thanksgiving in 1872 the Rock Island Council quietly met and enacted an ordinance that annexed Sinnet's and Brooks' properties. Afraid that they might be forced to become Moliners, the landowners had petitioned to be attached to Rock Island. Furious and feeling "badly used," Moline countered by annexing all of the remaining unattached land to the west up to the existing Rock Island city limits. Although no blood was spilled and though not remotely equivalent to the uncivilized Toledo War between Michigan and Ohio, Rock Island old-timers, who are mostly a remarkably tolerant bunch, still resent all things Moline. To this day, the Moline City Clerk has yet to produce the landowners' petition that would make the illegal annexation legal.

For eight years after the annexation battles of 1872-73, children who lived in the KeyStone addition continued to go to Moline schools. In 1880 Moline demanded either taxes or tuition, so a four-room school was hastily built on the land donated by William Brooks. A decade later Longfellow School, the quintessential neighborhood school, replaced the interim school. Over the years, Brooks' land was subdivided and became seven different Rock Island additions. The most ambitious was the "Columbia Park addition to the city of Rock Island." Most of the land north of 7th Avenue and east of 38th Street is in the Columbia Park addition, which was where a spectacularly ambitious exposition in honor of the 400th anniversary of Christopher Columbus' discovery of North America was planned.

After acquiring 55 acres from William Brooks, in 1891 preparations for the exposition began, 5th Avenue was paved with bricks, and 7th Avenue was graded. By the addition of only four bridges over creeks and streams, 7th Avenue became "usable," and work began on the fair grounds. The land was graded and sculpted, a racetrack started, a bandstand and Roman theater and a circular loop-road, which wound through the exposition grounds, were surveyed and laid out. But when it became apparent that the Columbian World's Fair in Chicago would greatly eclipse Rock Island's plans, enthusiasm for completing the exposition grounds waned and good sense prevailed. Instead a spectacular 4th of July celebration was promoted for 1893 — it was rained out.

The same year 7th Avenue was graded, a small church called "Svenska Kapell" (Swedish Chapel) was built on the corner of 7th Avenue and 45th Street. The chapel was constructed because Grace Lutheran Church, which was a block to the west, said their services in English and the Swedish immigrants wanted to hear their services in their native tongue. Soon the church was overflowing, and in 1907 a new $18,000 ($450,000) church was designed by Olof Cervin and opened as Zion Swedish Evangelical Lutheran Church. The majestic new Lutheran church attracted the Grace parishioners, and they sold their building to the Knights of Pythias, a secret fraternal organization of men over the age of 18 who take an oath not to be professional gamblers, sell illegal drugs or alcohol, join Communist or Fascist organizations, and believe in a Supreme Being. In 2003 there were approximately 50,000 Knights of Pythias worldwide.

On the other side of the 7th Avenue Hill, Irish immigrants, who worked on the railroad and in the factories that lined the riverbanks, clustered their homes together in an area east of the Broadway District where a north/south ridge rises east of 28th Street. Anti-Catholic and anti-Irish sentiment served to bond the first and second generation Irish Americans together. Less than a half-mile to the east of the heart of the Irish neighborhood known as Greenbush, on Sunday the devout at St. Mary's Church overflowed into the vestibule, even though Sunday masses were said hourly from 5 a.m. until noon. Unable to seat all the faithful from the burgeoning Catholic families that crammed into the church to fulfill their Sunday obligation, in 1898 a new parish was formed to serve the Greenbush neighborhood. On Christmas Eve three years later, Sacred Heart, Rock Island's third magnificent Catholic Church was finished in time for midnight mass. Built on the block north of 5th Avenue between 28th and 29th Streets, the new church cost $36,000 ($900,000), and was on the same block where Ben Harper built his stately brick home a half-century earlier. Harper's first Rock Island house became the church rectory, and the beautiful brick building is believed to be Rock Island's oldest standing home.

When the Sacred Heart Parrish was established, a group of Visitation Sisters came to Rock Island from Maysville, Kentucky, to establish a school. The elementary school became Rock Island's largest K-8 parochial school and operated for more than a century until it merged with the Jordan Catholic School, which currently serves Rock Island's Catholic children. Encouraged by the instant success of Sacred Heart School, the Visitation Sisters opened a girls' boarding school, named the Villa de Chantal, on 14 acres of wooded land called Ball's Bluff at the crest of the 20th Street Hill. The august Gothic Revival main building and dormitories housed 60 boarders and a large number of day students from the Tri-Cities area. From its opening until 1929, the Villa expanded rapidly adding a chaplain's cottage, classrooms, library, and gymnasium. The school closed its doors in 1978, and sat vacant until a fire tragically destroyed most of the main building in 2005. Today the beautiful acreage is the site of a Rock Island School System magnet school, the Rock Island Center for Math & Science.

Sacred Heart Parish also served Catholics in the remote KeyStone neighborhood a mile to the east, where its students competed on the playgrounds and occasionally fought in the vacant lots with the public-schoolers from Longfellow. Kids from both schools played side-by-side, but seldom together, on the exquisite grounds at Lincoln Park. In 1909, 23 acres of the "Columbia Park" exposition land was purchased by the city and named Lincoln Park in honor of Abraham Lincoln's birth 100 years earlier. For a decade the parkland remained unimproved, and its primary feature was a large pond that formed when a planned exposition attraction was graded but not built. In 1920 Augustana College offered to buy the property, and a lively community debate began over whether the city should sell the dormant parkland. Edward Guyer weighed in saying, "Lincoln Park was acquired by popular subscription and in reality belongs to the people and any effort to deprive the people of it should be strenuously resisted." He did not add that the undeveloped land that his partner had received $1,500 an acre for would be more attractive for future lot sales of his private land holdings as a public park than a cluster of seminary buildings. Augustana's offer was turned down, and their campus expanded to the south and west.

At the time Augustana's bid for Lincoln Park was rebuffed, the parkland was so remote that Rock Island Mayor, Harry Shriver, admitted that he had never been there. Guyer developed the remaining 32 acres of the exposition grounds that were not sold to the city. The lots Guyer laid out for homes were eventually purchased for about half of what the syndicate formed to develop the exposition paid Brooks. The variety of American Foursquare architectural-style homes built in the KeyStone addition created a distinctive neighborhood that curls around Lincoln Park with Longfellow School at its center. More naturally a part of Moline, the city's remote northeast corner remains Rock Island's most isolated neighborhood.

The grid of streets in the KeyStone neighborhood was paved with "paving bricks," as were most of Rock Island's streets during this time. Over the years, many of the city's elegant brick streets have been patched or replaced with asphalt or concrete. Although costly to renovate, brick pavement is more eco-friendly than its impervious pavement competitors, and as their 100-plus-year life attests, more durable than other pavements. Under an insightful 1988 plan produced by the Rock Island Preservation Commission, many of the city's beautiful and historical brick streets are being preserved and renovated, and Rock Island's Brick Streets Plan has become a model for cities throughout the country.

"Soft brick" homes and buildings, which provided a level of fire safety not found in wooden structures, became popular among the affluent during the early 19th century. Rock Island's first brick structure was built in 1837 on the east side of Courthouse Square and housed a general store on the first floor and a social hall on the second. In 1850 an Englishman from Yorkshire, Christopher Atkinson, founded the Energy Brick Company on a six-acre site on Cemetery Road (12th Street). The Energy site was unusual in that it had a consistent 13-foot layer of good brick clay that covered the entire field. Atkinson fired over six million bricks, and his bricks built a majority of Rock Island's fine homes, schools, and commercial buildings.

The ancient riverbed of the Mississippi River that the Hennepin Canal follows contains layers of clay that are ideal for brick making. Especially large clay deposits are found in the Galesburg area, and in 1849 Henry Grosscup, a German stonemason, started a brick factory there. He acquired 90 acres of high-grade clay from Knox College by trading bricks he produced from the land to build two campus buildings. Other brick factories opened around Galesburg, and when durable paving bricks were first used for road construction in the 1890s, Galesburg became "the brick capital of America," a distinction it retained until huge deposits of red Arkansas clay pulled many of the large brick manufacturers to "The Natural State."

Before automobiles made road paving essential, except for the use of cobblestones in Eastern cities, any road surface other than dirt, gravel, or macadam was considered an unnecessary public extravagance. Although there were several brickyards in Knox County, most of the Galesburg factories produced the soft bricks used in building construction. One company that saw the future was East Galesburg's Purington Paving Brick Company. Purington became the world's largest manufacturer of paving bricks and shipped them all over the world. The one thing that streets in Rock

Island have in common with streets in Chicago; Deadwood, South Dakota; Paris; Panama City; and the Bazaar in Bombay is that they all still have bricks stamped with the name of the long defunct Purington Paving Brick Company.

Until the turn of the century, most of Rock Island's residences and businesses were clustered in a three-mile by three-quarter-mile wide natural basin that wound below the bluffs carved by the Mississippi and was roughly bounded by 30th Street to the east, 9th Avenue south and the river to the north and west. The hill formed by the bluffs south of town was so formidable to transportation and commuting that an *Argus* article reported that before 1900 there were only three non-farmhouses on "The Hill." Then, as now, the Downtown District extended south from the riverfront between 15th and 20th Streets with 2nd Avenue the primary business artery.

A half-century before, in the days of Farnhamsburg and Stevenson, residences were mixed among shops and taverns and often shopkeepers and tavern proprietors lived above their businesses. The first cluster of homes in Stephenson was built west of the commercial area and later was given the name Old Town. In 1836 a second plat was filed on land west of Old Town and called the Chicago Addition. Today the two neighborhoods comprise the Old Town Chicago Neighborhood, which is Rock Island's oldest residential area and was home to some of its finest residences.

Reflecting Rock Island's general prosperity during the Gilded Age, a graceful neighborhood of grand homes were built in Colonial Revival, Queen Anne, and Italianate architectural styles south of downtown between 17th and 23rd (Broadway) Streets and up to the hill's sharp rise at 12th Avenue. The quality of the homes in this area, built from 1890 until the beginning of World War I, is reflected in the fact that more than 500 houses from this period remain, and many have been restored to their original grandeur. At a time when it is often economically more viable to bulldoze old homes and buildings, the Broadway District is one of the country's finest examples of how caring and involved citizens can restore and preserve their neighborhood and its heritage. The Broadway Historic District is listed on the National Register of Historic Places and is the second largest preservation district in the country.

The northern edge of the Broadway District between 20th and 22nd Streets was the site of Rock Island high schools for 78 years. It was also the site of Rock Island's most iconic elementary school for 86 years. Located in the southeast corner of the school grounds, in 1894 P.S. No. 4 opened. Three years later when the school board decided to name schools instead of numbering them, it became Lincoln School. Until its closure in 1980, the grade school was annually attended by an average of 600 students and was the formative school for generations of Rock Island's children. Costing $46,900 ($1,175,000), Lincoln's Romanesque style became a model for future Rock Island schools. Large windowed classrooms lined the exterior walls of the two-story building that rose above a high, windowed basement, and a wide split staircase opened to spacious hallways leading to the classrooms. The architecture was praised in a 1905 *Argus* article: "The great center halls of the building have proved to be one of the most satisfactory arrangements in the schools of the city. The [school] buildings erected later than 1892 have halls patterned largely after the plan of the Lincoln building." Now used sparingly for non-classroom purposes, the magnificently ornate building is awaiting restoration for a new use in its second century.

In 1905 most days were big days in Rock Island, but November 18th was particularly monumental. The *Argus* reported that the first brick-paved street on the top of the hill reached Moline when a stretch of 14th Avenue was completed to 45th Street. A guest scientist spoke at Augustana and predicted that by the year 2000 "wireless telegraphy would send messages across the nation and to ships at sea" and "housewives would have electric ovens in which the heat would be controlled by thermometers." The best news was that the Rock Island Rocks steamrolled the Moline Maroons in football 4 to zip. And a back page blurb said that the last timber raft of the season arrived in Rock Island. Although no one knew it at the time, it would be the last log raft to float the Mississippi to Rock Island. The dearth of harvestable trees in Wisconsin, giant stands of redwoods in California, and immense forests of mixed evergreens and hardwoods in the Pacific Northwest moved the nation's lumber center from Rock Island to the Pacific coast.

Over the next generation, the loss of the lumber industry dramatically shifted Rock Island's economic base from relatively clean lumber milling to manufacturing. The Mississippi River ceased to be a source of sawmill power and became a sewer for the factories that moved onto the land where the mills had stood. Starting at the Twin Cities and continuing to New Orleans, towns along the river had dumped raw sewage, garbage, and waste into the Mississippi ever since French lead miners started dumping their tailings in the river at Galena in the 1690s. Many towns, such as Minneapolis, didn't even bother to settle out the solids before flushing their effluent into the river. In 1924 International Harvester bought Moline Plow Works and expanded the operation to manufacture Farmall tractors. Thirteen years later J.I. Case bought Rock Island Plow Works and expanded their factory operations. Both firms joined with Deere & Company and discarded their industrial waste into the Mississippi, and swimming in the river became somewhat less desirable. Not until the 1967 Clean Air Act and the 1969 Environmental Policy Act did the factories lining the Mississippi stop dumping their manufacturing waste chemicals directly into the river and spewing their gaseous soot into the air above Rock Island. Until then one of the jobs given to new Farmall workers was to cart spent hydrochloric acid from the "pickling" room where paint fixtures were cleaned to a platform above the river, and while the acid and lead-based paint mixture drained into the Mississippi, the young worker could watch fishermen a few hundred yards downstream hoping to land a catfish.

One of the environmental legacies left by the sawmills was the hills of sawdust that rose as high as a hundred feet. Besides being an "attractive nuisance" for young boys practicing back flips and leaps of great distance, the sawdust mounds were a constant fire hazard. Whereas lumber scrap such as defective woodcuts and short boards were left for all takers and were quickly snatched up, much more sawdust was produced than was needed to fill ponds and sloughs. All the mills had fire crews, and daily they extinguished fires. After the mills closed there were still daily fires, and the Rock Island Fire Department spent more time extinguishing sawdust fires than all other fires combined. One Rock Island assistant fire chief who lost his job at the mills when they closed said:

> In the summers and late into the fall, we could expect one to three sawdust fire calls every day. Some fires were half a block square. We got so used to the ways of sawdust fires that putting them out was as natural as eating. We had fun looking for openings to underground fire caves and shooting a blast of water into them. When the water hit the flames in the hole, there would be a good explosion. Finally, the chief decided to just let the stuff burn out. Much ground sank to its old levels. I remember one fire hydrant, which was left so high in the air we had to build a platform around it and some steps.

The underground fires burned for a half century and caused one tragic death. In 1940 a sleeping man who was camped in the "hobo jungle" on the river at the Y in the railroad tracks at 27th Street fell into a fiery crater. The man had the misfortune of laying his blanket on a warm patch of land, and while he slept, a sawdust fire turned his thermo-bed into a funeral pyre.

During the boom years of Rock Island's lumber milling, the city may have grown even faster, except that George Davenport's son, Bailey, who inherited huge tracts of land in the Tri-City Area including 2,200 acres (20 percent) of land in present day Rock Island, refused to sell any of the property for private development. However, in 1877 he magnanimously sold his "best piece of ground" to the school board to build School No. 6. In 1891 a fire destroyed the school that was located at 9th Avenue and 12th Street, and for two years, the children attended classes in Davenport's mansion. When the new school opened in 1893, it was still called School No. 6, but in 1897 when all the schools were given names, it became Irving School.

There are no ethnic enrollment records for Irving from that time, but it is very probable that a large percentage of the students were of Swedish ancestry. Drawn to the area to work in the lumber mills, in 1905 it is estimated that 3,500 of Rock Island's 19,500 residents were Swedish. First Lutheran Church was built in the block west of Irving School in 1870 and listed its membership as "80 plus 24 children." Surprisingly, First Lutheran was not the first Swedish-speaking church in Rock Island. Almost three decades earlier, in the late summer of 1852 America's first Swedish Baptist Church was organized by preacher Gustaf Palmquist and three founding members. For three years the Swedish Baptists held Sunday morning services in the schoolhouse on Church Square, and then in 1855 a church was built on Canal Street (5th Avenue) between Madison (20th) and Adams (21st) Streets.

Some locals blamed Bailey Davenport's undeveloped "pastures" that rimmed Rock Island for raising land prices to a point that it became desirable to live in Iowa and walk across the Government Bridge to work in Rock Island. Others say that is nonsense because living in Moline was much preferable to Davenport, and Moline land was as inexpensive. Not until Davenport's death in 1890 and the subsequent auction of his undeveloped pastures and orchards was the acreage west of the Broadway neighborhood developed. Thomas Robinson, Morris Rosenfield, Charles Deere, and Frederick Weyerhaeuser purchased much of the property with the intent of holding it and altruistically selling it at no profit in order to facilitate the orderly development of Rock Island. A steep 39-acre hillside tract bordering the 17th Street side of Davenport's land was not desirable for home construction. The four businessmen designated the site to be a public water supply reservoir. But when it was determined that the flat area at the top of the hill was not large enough for the reservoir, Rock Island Mayor Thomas Medill proposed using the land for a city park. In 1897 the land was donated to the city with two restrictions: that it would always be used for a public park and that liquor would never be sold there. (For size perspective, less than 2 percent of Davenport's Rock Island land holdings comprised the city's largest park.)

A group of local Sauk was asked to name the city's first park. They declined, saying that they had no interest in proposing a name for land that should still be called Saukenuk. The name "Long View" was selected from residents' suggestions. The land was fenced, and except for grazing cattle, sat vacant for five years. In 1902 an unpaid park commissioner was appointed and renowned Chicago "landscape gardener" Ossian Cole Simonds was retained to design the park. Two months after seeing the parkland for the first time, Simonds submitted the design to the City Council. It was accepted and built. One hundred and ninety citizens donated $12,500 ($315,000), and their contributions were matched by the city. Over the next six years, the land was cleared, graded, and landscaped; a spring-fed, winding brook connected two lagoons with fountain sprays; a rustic bridge spanned a waterfall that fell from the upper lagoon; a "monkey island" was built on the lower lagoon (the island was removed before World War II, but the lagoon was used for ice skating until the 1960s); a grand entrance from 17th Street accessed a drive that wove through the park; walkways and picnic areas were constructed throughout; and a bandstand that had public flush toilets — a convenience, which many Rock Islanders saw there for the first time — was built near the upper lagoon (in 1954 the lagoon and bandstand were replaced by an Olympic-size swimming pool and is now home to a water park). Fifteen thousand people attended the July 10, 1908 dedication that started at 8:00 a.m. and ended with fireworks.

With the mature Old Town Chicago neighborhood on its north side and the elegant Broadway neighborhood to the east, the Longview property was quickly developed over the new century's first decades. Built out during a period when the rest of the nation was experiencing extremely lean times, the highly desirable property was populated with modest but often ornate homes. And virtually all had large front porches to enjoy summer evening breezes and to watch children and make sure that they didn't get in the way of the horse-drawn wagons or the occasional newfangled automobiles that chugged down the streets. There are no classic architectural styles of the period that cannot be found today in the Longview neighborhood.

In 1911 Fred Boetje, another enterprising Rock Islander, began making Dutch-style mustard at his Longview neighborhood home. Using a recipe from his father, Boetje's simple ingredients included mustard seeds, sugar, salt, vinegar, and water. He also made horseradish, but contrary to what most believe, he put none in his mustard. The business thrived, and he had to move his operations to a larger plant across the street from Farmall, where twice a week, Boetje started the process of making a batch of 550 cases of bottled mustard by pouring distilled vinegar into his wooden 55,000-gallon vat; he added many pounds of rough-ground mustard seeds, a large dash of sugar, a big pinch of salt, and lots of cups of water. He stirred and let the goop marinate for three days, when it was pumped over a revolving stone, ground, stirred, and placed in holding tanks for bottling, sealing, and labeling. The office manager/shipping clerk then hand-packed each case for shipment. In 2008 Boetje's won the blue ribbon in the Coarse Grained grouping at the World Wide Mustard Festival in Napa, California.

Chapter 17

The Progressive Era

Every reform movement has a lunatic fringe. ~ Theodore Roosevelt

OVERLAPPING THE GILDED AGE and the beginning of Prohibition, a righteous period of social activism and political reform flourished from the 1890s to the early 1920s. Called by historians "The Progressive Era" (most of the faith-based progressive objectives of the time would be considered conservative today), the far-reaching movement included teachers, educated women, professionals, and Protestant clergy. Curiously, the political parties did not neatly align along Progressive ideals. Leading Progressive Republicans included Theodore Roosevelt, Robert M. La Follette, and Herbert Hoover; leading Democratic Progressives were William Jennings Bryan, Woodrow Wilson, and Al Smith. The high-minded politicians and their crusading followers backed Prohibition, women's suffrage, political reform, and greater regulation of banking and business. Virtually all Progressives were Protestant, from the upper classes, and neither they nor their parents were immigrants. The diverse group of reformers supported the application of scientific and structured methods to government, economics, banking, industry, education, health care, psychology, theology, and the family. What began as a movement for badly-needed government reform mushroomed into "purifying" anything that was perceived to be detrimental to a puritanical, Protestant-oriented society and attracted everyone with a social cause.

In a time before polling, it's fairly certain that if asked, most white Americans would say they were a Progressive. However when it came time for the men to vote, business and financial interests, sexism, racism, and the thought of life without booze got in the way of sweeping Progressive candidates into office. Immigration was the stickiest issue for Progressives. Unskilled, low-paid workers were needed in the mines, factories, and mills; however, most of the immigrant labor after 1890 was Catholic or Jewish, and poor Catholics and Jews didn't fit into the Northeast's social style, threatened rural Midwestern religious ideals, didn't match the South's profile of a "true American," and ran afoul of Prohibitionists and political reformers because Irish

Catholics, in particular, liked to gather in pubs and discuss which rascals they could next throw out of office.

From the time of writing the Constitution, one societal objective that all agreed upon was the value of an English speaking, literate, and informed electorate. However, education became another area that deeply divided Progressives. Religion-based educators and conservative proponents of traditional education believed that the purpose of public schooling was to communicate skills, facts, and standards of moral conduct that were deemed necessary to the material and social success of the next generation, and that this transfer of knowledge was based on elementary proficiency in the "Three R's" of reading, writing, and arithmetic. They were opposed by educators, who believed that in addition to learning rote skills, problem solving and critical thinking along with social skills were important in the development of young people. Usually, the Three R's backers believed those competencies were best learned at home and in church.

At the start of the Progressive Era, two medical discoveries radically changed how Americans viewed public health and medicine. An understanding of germs and their role in the cause of infections and spread of disease gave birth to the development of sanitary methods and antiseptics and started a steady rise in life expectancy. Coupled with the development of general anesthesia for pain control, doctors and pharmacists gained respectability and modern medicine was on its way.

Because a majority of immigrants could not speak English and many were not even literate in their native language, making education freely available to all children so that they could read and write and do simple arithmetic was a lofty and laudable goal. American public schools of the 19th century were spectacularly successful in raising the literacy rate of men and women, and the ability to learn to read and write English was at the core of the American dream the working classes held for their children — graduation from the eighth grade was a mark of high achievement. But high schools were generally thought of as college preparatory schools for young men from the upper class and as professional training schools for those few women who were headed into the specialized fields of teaching and nursing. Before the Civil War, it was illegal in the South to teach an African American to read and write, and educationally, white women didn't fare much better. At the start of the Progressive Era, almost 90 percent of Northern white men born in America could read and write — only half as many native-born, white women could.

By the 1880s, all states had public elementary schools and most required a two-year teaching credential that was often obtained at "normal colleges." By the end of the Progressive Era, many of the state-operated teachers colleges had become four-year institutions. Although Americans agreed with the Faber College motto, "Knowledge Is Good," they disagreed on the best way to impart that knowledge. University of Chicago professor, John Dewey, was the leading educational theorist of the time. He believed that schools should not only teach "content knowledge" or facts, but also how to apply that knowledge to everyday life. He also believed that there was a great deal to learn from understanding the classical philosophers and reading great literature from all ages.

Dewey was adamant that education was the key to social evolution and reform, and large segments of academic theorists, professional educators, and public school teachers agreed with him and applauded his ideas. However, they were never implemented on a large scale. Religious leaders who believed they should teach morality and ethics and bureaucrats and school administrators who pointed to the successes of the American public education system blocked the implementation of Dewey's ideas then, and many who favor traditional education continue to do so. In the century since he proposed his ideas, except in small experimental schools Dewey's concepts of experiential and corroborative learning with emphasis on critical thinking have not been widely implemented, and often when they have been tried, discipline and basic skills acquisition have been sacrificed.

Politically, the Progressive Movement began at local levels and later expanded into state and national politics. Starting in the big cities, Progressives set out to dismantle the political machines that controlled party-line votes. They first sought to destroy the power of local political bosses who ran their precincts from saloons and bought votes for as little as a shot and a beer. The anti-political machine movement was soon joined by Prohibitionists who sought to eliminate the evils of liquor from their communities and by Suffragettes who had endured long enough without a political voice. Backed by Protestant clergy who stirred nationwide anti-Catholic and anti-Semitic sentiment, white Protestant women took up the issues of prohibition and suffrage, fused the causes together, and encouraged virtuous politicians to seek legislative reforms.

One of the most outspoken early women's rights activists was Susan B. Anthony, who began her life as a political campaigner as a teenager, when prior to the Civil War, she collected two boxes of petitions opposing slavery. After the war, she expanded her horizons and began publishing the week journal *The Revolution*. The journal's motto was "The true republic — men, their rights and nothing more; women, their rights and nothing less." *The Revolution* espoused women's and African-American's right to suffrage, equal pay for equal work, more liberal divorce laws, and it goaded Protestant clergy to be more proactive on women's issues. Anthony wouldn't accept advertisements for alcohol or morphine-laden medicines and was one of the early voices for temperance. She got President Andrew Johnson to subscribe to her journal before she published the first edition.

The Progressive Movement was aided by the Panic of 1893, which threw the nation into a serious economic depression. Speculative railroad building had pumped up a financial bubble that burst when the Philadelphia and Reading Railroad declared bankruptcy. That started a chain reaction of railroad bankruptcies followed by bank closures. Unemployment rocketed nationally from three percent in 1892 to 12% the following year and stayed above that level for the next five years. Progressives were quick to point out that it was time for new ideas and dramatic change.

The latter years of the Gilded Age, and the beginning years of the Progressive Era, were golden for only the extremely wealthy. The depression that engulfed the country, except in the Far West, led to deflation and widespread discontent among the working class. Historians blame the depression on the laissez-faire policies of Republican President, Benjamin "The Human Iceberg" Harrison, and reckless government spending, which for the first time drove the Federal Budget to more than one billion dollars. The grandson of William Henry Harrison was also known as "Kid Gloves" Harrison because of his hands-off business policies and because he actually wore kid gloves to protect his hands from infections and allergic reactions.

After Harrison's ineffective four years, in 1892 Grover "Uncle Jumbo" Cleveland (his weight ballooned to 250 pounds during his semi-retirement after his first term) became the only president to be elected to two non-consecutive terms. The Democratic president inherited a run-amok economy that had been over-stimulated by unregulated industrial and real estate speculation, and the fiscally tough Cleveland totally alienated himself with protectivist Republicans by rolling back tariffs and opposing subsidies to businesses, farmers, and veterans. As a result of Harrison's lack of financial regulation, gold-standard currency value fell to dangerously low levels, and Cleveland was forced to go to Wall Street and borrow $65 million ($1.6 billion) of gold from banker J.P. Morgan. Republicans ridiculed Cleveland and his policies as ineffective. And Morgan, the nation's leading financier, arguably took away Cleveland's position as the most powerful man in the country. During Cleveland's term, Morgan lastingly redefined political conservatism in terms of America-first, business-centric financial prowess coupled with the ever-popular strong commitment to religion.

Known as "Populists," the People's Party sprouted up with regional support from disgruntled poor Southerners, Texans, and northern plains wheat farmers. By blaming the Democrats for the state of the economy, the Populists and the Republicans swept the 1894 mid-term elections and led Congress in repealing Cleveland's fiscal policies and reinstituted the tariffs and subsidies he had repealed — and financial conditions worsened. The Populists faded, Cleveland took the heat for the financial crisis, and J.P. Morgan-backed William "The Napoleon of Protection" McKinley gained back the White House for Republicans in 1896.

McKinley defeated the great liberal orator, William Jennings Bryan, who ran on a single issue of "free silver" and money policy. Free silver advocates favored an inflationary monetary policy using the "free coinage of silver" as opposed to the less inflationary Gold Standard. McKinley was a protectionist who favored high tariffs and "cultural pluralism," a social philosophy that advocated maintaining cultural identities along ethnic and religious lines, and that all citizens be accepted and treated equally throughout the nation's larger society. The depression dragged on through the first years of McKinley's administration, and the political dissensions that emerged during the Progressive Era caused a realignment of political interests between the industrial Northeast and the rest of the country. This polarization remained in place until Franklin Delano Roosevelt's election in 1932. Also because Abraham Lincoln was a Republican, the "Solid South" had supported Democratic Party candidates since the Civil War and was a major faction of the Democratic Party until the 1960s when the party split over civil rights issues, and blue states quickly turned red.

Midwestern farmers had little time for Progressive politics or causes. When untilled Northern Illinois farmland became scarce, new immigrants settled on inexpensive quarter-section parcels of rich prairie in the former Indian Territory west of the Mississippi River. The self-supporting farms of the Upper Mississippi Valley became the foundation of the Midwest's economy until the 1970s. Because of inexpensive land across the river in Iowa, Rock Island County's population grew slowly from 38,302 in 1880 to 41,917 in 1890. Whereas immigration had swelled the nation's population by 25 percent during the 1880's, Rock Island County grew by only nine percent. Although the rest of the nation was reeling from social issues and a poor economy, Rock Island County's controlled growth and balanced economy helped make the Gay 90's much gayer than in most of the country. And although the rest of the nation was recovering from the Panic of 1893, Northern Illinois enjoyed a temporary economic boon — and a giant boost was given to the Rock Island Line with the May 1893 opening of the Chicago World's Fair.

Burnt to the ground by Catherine O'Leary's cow less than twenty years before, in 1890 Chicago beat out the favorite, New York City, and also-rans, St. Louis and Washington D.C., for Congress' designation as the official exposition site to honor Christopher Columbus' discoveries 400 years earlier. Officially named the World's Columbian Exposition, Chicago raised $5 million ($110 million) to present their case.

And when Congress awarded the city the right to hold the fair if they paid another $5 million to the U.S. Treasury, they quickly bought the official designation.

Located along the Lake Michigan shoreline on a square-mile (more than ten times the size of the planned Rock Island expo) of mostly swampy land where Jackson Park and the Chicago neighborhoods of South Shore, Jackson Park Highlands, Hyde Park, and Woodlawn are now located, 40,000 workmen filled, graded, and landscaped the entire fairgrounds and constructed 200 exposition halls and attractions in only 20 months. Three thousand people a week paid 25¢ ($5.00) just to watch the construction. Besides bolstering the regional economy and Chicago's self-image, the fair also had a profound effect on architecture and the arts and on science and industry. The fair's most lasting industrial contribution was the awarding of the electrical contract to the Westinghouse Company, whose bid of $399,000 ($10 million) for alternating electric current to power the fair spectacularly undercut Thomas Edison's General Electric Company's bid of $1,800,000 for direct current. (Rock Island was one of the avant-garde cities lit by direct current electric power from its Edison General Electric generators in Searstown.) By demonstrating inexpensive, wide-scale electric lighting, George Westinghouse not only set the worldwide standard for delivering electric power with alternating current but also hooked the public on the benefits of inexpensive indoor and outdoor lighting.

When completed, the fabulously landscaped grounds were crisscrossed by canals traversed by passenger steamboats and featured a zoo, an immense swimming pool, a giant fun house and house of mirrors, and dozens of amusement rides that included a smaller version of J.P. Newberg's Watch Tower Park, Shoot the Chutes toboggan slide. The white stucco exteriors of 14 neoclassical buildings in the Court of Honor were extensively lit at night by spotlights and gave the fair its popular name — The White City. The fair's surrealistic night image is said to have inspired L. Frank Baum's Land of Oz and Walt Disney's theme parks. And when in early July, a Wellesley College English professor, Katharine Lee Bates, visited the fair, The White City later inspired the reference to "alabaster cities" in her poem *America the Beautiful.*

Exhibit pavilions were constructed by 46 nations. The pavilions featured cultural exhibits, served cuisine from the exhibiting country, and featured indigenous musical and dance extravaganzas. One of the fair's most popular attractions was a "Street in Cairo," starring a provocative belly dancer known as Little Egypt who danced the "hootchy-kootchy." Possibly the most lucrative of the fair's attractions was not inside the fair's majestic gates, but outside. Denied an exhibit spot, Buffalo Bill Cody set up his Wild West Show, which featured Annie Oakley, on leased land across the street from the fair and siphoned off tens of thousands of dollars from the fair's organizers who had spurned his application. Paid attendance for the six-month run was almost 27 million people, and on one day 716,881 passed through the turnstiles, setting a world record that still stands for a single day's paid admissions to an event. The signature attraction of the fair was a 25-story high rotating wheel that had 36 enclosed gondola cars, each seating 60 people and providing food and beverage service. Designed by George Ferris as a challenge to surpass the elegant tower designed by Gustave Eiffel for the 1889 Paris Exposition, the Ferris Wheel became the exposition's iconic symbol, and in only four months of operation it made $395,000 ($10 million) for Ferris' company.

Other notable inventions introduced at the fair included the zipper, picture post cards, and florescent and neon lights. And no single event in the history of the world inspired more culinary delights than the 1893 fair, which changed the eating habits of a nation and introduced packaged, processed food. In addition to exotic foreign foods at the international pavilions, foodies were treated for the first time to such all-American treats as Cracker Jacks, Hershey Bars, and Juicy Fruit Gum, to breakfast fare including Cream of Wheat, Quaker Oats, and Shredded Wheat, and to the cornerstone menu item for all future fast food restaurants — hamburgers. Although it is unclear who awarded it, a blue ribbon was given to Milwaukee's Pabst Brewing Company for the best beer. Most of the fair's 200 pavilions along the mile-long amusement midway were torn or burned down immediately after the fair closed at the end of October. Today only the Museum of Science and Industry and the Palace of Fine Arts buildings remain, and Jackson Park, one of the world's truly great urban parks, still preserves a large portion of the Exposition's landscaping.

The year before the fair, the University of Chicago opened on East 57th Street a mile west of the Museum of Science and Industry. The school had been chartered as a coeducational, secular institution in 1890 by the American Baptist Education Society. The new university was underwritten by John D. Rockefeller on land donated by Marshall Field, the Chicagoan who became wealthy by selling "the lady what she wants." The school's first classes were held on October 1, 1892, and that afternoon, Amos Alonzo Stagg held the football team's first practice. In its inaugural season, Chicago rolled to an 8-4-1 record. Without a nickname during their improbably strong first year, Chicago appropriately named themselves "The Monsters of the Midway" after the wildly successful fair that was a short walk from their campus. When Chicago dropped football in 1939, the Chicago Bears picked up the moniker.

One of the founding members of the Western Conference, which later changed its name to the Big Ten, Chicago won six conference football championships between 1899 and 1924. Coached from 1892 to 1932 by Amos Alonzo Stagg, The Monsters of the Midway achieved a remarkable .682 winning percentage (275-121-42) under Stagg and produced the first Heisman Trophy winner when Jay Berwanger was awarded the iconic statue. However, after Stagg's retirement Chicago's gridiron fortunes faded and the university concentrated on maintaining their rigorous academic standards. In 1969 the football program was resurrected and joined the academically prestigious DIII University Athletic Association. In 2011 the more aptly named University of Chicago Maroons won their fourth conference football title.

By the start of the 20th century the glow of the Gilded Age had started to fade. America had joined the European powers in throwing its weight around internationally. Angered over Spanish atrocities in Cuba, in ten weeks' time during the summer of 1898, U.S. naval power drove out the Spanish and secured Cuban independence. Ironically, the next year found American forces fighting Philippine insurgents seeking independence from the United States. In response to America's moral schism, Mark Twain published a bitter *Salutation-Speech from the Nineteenth Century to the Twentieth*. "I bring you the stately matron named Christendom," he wrote, "returning bedraggled, besmirched and dishonored from pirate-raids in Kiao-Chow, Manchuria, South Africa, and the Philippines, with her soul full of meanness, her pocket full of boodle, and her mouth full of pious hypocrisies. Give her soap and a towel, but hide the looking-glass."

Twain's ridicule of American hypocrisy did little to curb the moral righteousness that became rampant across the country, and reformers got serious about their divinely inspired missions. Temperance societies that had encouraged moderation in alcohol consumption were formed in New England during the late 16th century, but until the 1826 formation of the American Temperance Society there was no national organization to unify the cause. Though they called themselves a "temperance" society, the requirement for membership in the ATS was a pledge to "abstain" from drinking distilled beverages. Sparked by fiery sermons from 19th century preachers, like the Reverend Lyman Beecher, a Presbyterian minister (and father of Harriet Beecher Stowe), and backed by pietistic religious denominations, especially Methodists, within ten years there were 8,000 ATS chapters, and more than 1.5 million people had "taken the pledge."

One of the ATS' most influential ministers was Seattle's, Reverend Mark Matthews. Along with scores of other Progressive ministers, in order to gain broader support for abstaining from alcohol, Matthews wrapped alcohol abuse in with other vices. The anti-suffrage minister was quoted as intemperately saying, "The saloon is the most fiendish, corrupt, hell-soaked institution that ever crawled out of the slime of the eternal pit. It takes your sweet innocent daughter, robs her of her virtue, and transforms her into a brazen, wanton harlot. It is the open sore of this land." However, saloon patrons of the time were more inclined to justify their hours spent imbibing at the bar by quoting English author Samuel Johnson that was often stenciled on barroom mirrors, "There is nothing which has yet been contrived by man, by which so much happiness is produced as by a good tavern." (It was during the Progressive Era that Prohibitionists started calling taverns: "saloons," an anglicized form of "salon" which carried a derogatory connotation.)

The reality may well have been that neither the faith-based ATS position nor the attitude among the tipplers in the taverns, which were seldom visited by anyone's daughter, were as far apart as the two sides believed. Russian philosopher and anarchist, Mikhail Bakunin, may have spoken the truth when he said, "People go to church for the same reasons they go to a tavern: to stupefy themselves, to forget their misery, to imagine themselves, for a few minutes anyway, free and happy." Eventually, reason and the Civil War blunted the ATS' appeal, and the prohibition of alcohol in Maine (which was reputed to be the nation's drunkest state and the ATS' one great success) was repealed in 1856.

However in 1873, the Women's Christian Temperance Union was founded. Taking a different tact than the ATS and linking "the religious and the secular through concerted and far-reaching reform strategies based on applied Christianity," the WCTU took the core issue head-on by advocating the prohibition of alcohol as a method to prevent abuses by alcoholic husbands. To achieve that goal, the WCTU believed that if it could "get to the children," it could demonize liquor, which would lead to its prohibition. Frances Willard, the World WCTU president from 1879 to 1898, created a "union of women from all denominations, for the purpose of educating the young, forming a better public sentiment, reforming the drinking classes, transforming by the power of Divine grace those who are enslaved by alcohol, and removing the dram-shop from our streets by law."

Although she is most well-known for her crusade against the evils of alcohol, Willard was one of the Progressive Movement's earliest and most influential leaders. Her causes included labor organization rights, the eight-hour workday, federal aid to education, free school lunches, municipal sanitation, high community health standards, and strong rape and child abuse laws. In 1916 when both Woodrow Wilson and Charles Evans Hughes, the presidential candidates, chose to ignore the issue of Prohibition, a group of Rock Island PTA members made a political statement. Two years before, the Aiken Street School on 9th Street and 21st Avenue had been annexed to the city, and at a monthly meeting, the PTA voted to change the name to "Frances Willard School." Twenty years later, and three years after the repeal of Prohibition, a new school was built with Public Works Administration money, and the name was retained.

Taking a more direct approach than Willard, Carrie Nation shunned organized moderation and became a one-woman saloon wrecking crew. After God woke her on a June 1899 morning saying that he would "stand by her," Nation interpreted that to mean that what God meant to say was: "Take something in your hands, and throw at these [saloons] in Kiowa, [Kansas,] and smash them." Born of a mother who had delusions that she was Queen Victoria and from a family with a long history of mental disorders, after destroying Dobson's Saloon and two other bars in Kiowa the six-foot, 175-pound dynamo took off on a two-year bar-smashing tour.

Starting her rampage by throwing rocks through saloon windows and then breaking as many liquor bottles as she could, Nation moved on to a more effective device of destruction when her second husband — the first husband died of alcoholism after divorcing her after a year of marriage — jokingly suggested after an arrest in Wichita that she should use a hatchet next time for maximum damage. She thought that was a splendid idea and ratcheted up the fear factor in her crusade — he too soon divorced her. After being arrested more than 30 times and banned from several cities, the press and even her sympathizers started ridiculing her. Nation lost her mainstream Prohibitionist audience, and a standard barroom greeting sign of the time was "All nations welcome, except Carrie." No schools are named after Carrie Nation, but her home in Medicine Lodge, Kansas, is on the list of National Historic Landmarks.

One progressive cause of the time that most Progressives did not embrace was Margaret Sanger's on abortion and contraception. A nurse on New York City's Lower East Side, Sanger had helplessly watched a mother of three die from blood poisoning, the result of a self-inflicted abortion. Sanger was married, Irish-Catholic, and a mother of three. She defiantly began her illegal, grassroots campaign by distributing birth control information in New York's poor sections. In violation of the Comstock laws, which forbade the distribution of "erotic" materials" and which included medical and educational information on abortion and contraceptive devices, Sanger was forced to flee to London when a warrant, punishable by up to 40 years in prison, was issued for her arrest. The charges were dismissed, and a year later Sanger returned to New York. She began an association with other social activists, including Upton Sinclair and Emma Goldman, and in 1916 she opened the first birth control clinic in the United States. Her arrest and subsequent trial created newspaper headlines across the country, and to the dismay of her critics, she generated enormous support. It is said that letters addressed to Margaret Sanger, New York City, and to Santa Clause were among the few that weren't returned to sender for more address information.

Considered the founder of the modern birth control movement, Sanger organized the first birth control clinic staffed by all-female doctors and a clinic in

Harlem staffed by African-American doctors. In 1921 she founded the American Birth Control League, which became the Planned Parenthood Federation. Sanger remained active in the birth control movement throughout her life and was president of the International Planned Parent Federation throughout the 1950s. She died at age 86 in 1966 — five years after the Federal Drug Administration approved the birth control pill.

Absolutist causes such as the prohibition of liquor, labor organization, racial equality, and women's suffrage polarized organizations and communities during the Progressive Era. But of all the far-reaching political, social, and religious issues, none was as politically charged as Prohibition, and as new immigrants flooded into the cities, Prohibition became an ethnic issue as well. American-born, Anglo-Saxon Progressives did not understand the deep cultural use of alcohol that new immigrants brought with them. It was common in the old country for English and Scottish mill and factory workers and Irish miners and German laborers to receive beer and ale allotments as part of their wages, and for immigrants from the northern Mediterranean regions to sip wine from the noon meal until bedtime.

Because women had no political voice and alcohol abuse was predominantly a male problem, Prohibition also became a suffrage and gender issue. While people who lived in the cities were mostly unsupportive of Prohibition, people who lived in rural areas and Southerners were among the movement's greatest advocates — interestingly, many in both demographics made their own hooch. Will Rogers joked about Southern Prohibitionists saying, "The South is dry and will vote dry. That is, everybody sober enough to stagger to the polls." And above all, the battle to rid the country of demon alcohol was considered a moral issue with the sides for and against Prohibition aligning along religious lines. Eastern European Jews, Irish, and southern European Catholics comprised the bulk of new immigrants and surprisingly found themselves on the same side of the political fence, united in their libertarian position against Progressives.

Regardless of origin of birth or religious denomination, the average American considered beer, wine, and hard cider to be outside the intended bounds of Prohibition, and until Progressives included punishing Germans for starting the First World War, those beverages were not the targets of the temperance movement. The assassination of Archduke Franz Ferdinand of Austria triggered one of the bloodiest wars in history. Imperialistic designs and resentments between the Triple Entente of Great Britain, France, and Russia and the Prussian empires forced the world to choose sides, and America stuck by her English-speaking ancestors.

Wealthy and powerful American brewers, including Eberhard Anheuser, Adolphus Busch, Joseph Schlitz, Valentin Blatz, Theodore Hamm, Jacob Leinenkugel, Frederick Pabst, and Frederick Miller (Müller) — all were born in Germany — owned breweries, corner saloons, and big city politicians across the country. The German-American brewers were predominately Lutherans and Catholics, who as Ken Burns noted in his series on Prohibition, "worshiped God in secret and drank openly, while Methodists and Baptists worshiped God openly and drank in secret." It is doubtful that many late 19th century Germans would have immigrated to the United States had they known the hatred they would face — and that beer would become illegal. The Eighteenth Amendment gained enough traction to tip public sentiment only because "The Great War" incited such strong anti-German feelings that Progressives were able to turn hatred of Germany directly on the German-born brewers.

Hatred of Kaiser Wilhelm also caused a nationwide prohibition of German education throughout the country, and Rock Island's three private German schools were closed and their Lutheran and Catholic students were transferred to public schools. Because of their wealth and because many of the city's first generation immigrants spoke only broken English and seldom participated in citywide functions, resentment of Rock Island's large and prosperous German community had simmered for years. The German neighborhood in Rock Island's West End could just as easily have been a village along the Rhine River. It was as common to hear market proprietors and shopkeepers named Shultz, Krueger, Zimmer, Mueller, Keller, Bauer, and Koch talk to their customers in German as wall as English.

However, two second-generation German-Americans, Robert Wagner and Otto Huber, were venerated by almost every man in Rock Island and the surrounding region. Robert Wagner was the son of George Wagner, the founder of The Atlantic Brewing Company. Atlantic Brewing was Rock Island's first major brewery and was said to be "one of the largest breweries west of Chicago, producing [250 barrels a day of] a lager beer which has a national reputation." Wagner attended the University of Iowa and the United States Brewer's Academy in New York, and he was most responsible for merging Atlantic Brewing with their fierce competitor, City Brewery to form the Rock Island Brewing Company.

In 1893 Robert Wagner brokered a deal with Otto Huber, Ignatz' son, to merge their fathers' breweries. Wagner became the first president of Rock Island Brewing, and Huber was its secretary-treasurer. Huber remained a lifelong Rock Island resident but went on to establish breweries as far west as Seattle. Consolidating the operations on rural land that the Huber family owned south of 7th Avenue and 30th Street, Rock Island Brewing Company built a huge operation that included stables and pastureland for the teams of imported Clydesdales that pulled their elegant beer wagons. Although Lillie Beer, named after Huber's younger sister, became the region's best-selling near beer, Prohibition was the death knell for the Rock Island Brewing Company.

On 5th Avenue, a block north of the 30th Street brewery was Rock Island's largest and most popular beer garden. Another German immigrant, Joseph Huber, who was unrelated to the brewmeisters, opened a green, wooden pavilion that became the primary streetcar stop between Moline and Rock Island. Playing beneath strings of colored lights, oompah bands continuously pumped out brassy tunes while couples danced summer nights away to waltzes and polkas that annoyed no one, since there were no neighbors within a half-mile. When the Rock Island Arsenal commander invoked wartime regulations and made all liquor establishments within three miles of the Arsenal off-limits — a limitation that conveniently covered all of The District in Rock Island and temporarily made Milan a destination — because of its remoteness and difficulty to police, Huber's Beer Garden was one of the few places where a soldier could quench his thirst.

Chapter 18

Trouble Comes to River City

The first big step on the road
To the depths of deg-ra-day--
I say, first, medicinal wine from a teaspoon,
Then beer from a bottle.
An' the next thing ya know,
Your son is playin' for money
In a pinch-back suit.
~ "Ya Got Trouble," from *The Music Man,* Meredith Wilson

FROM THE TIME JOHN BARREL built its first tavern, Rock Island was a libertarian-leaning microcosm of the country. For decades its community of German brewers had kept the region well-supplied with strong stouts, cask ales, and pale pilsners — even Frederick Weyerhaeuser had tried his hand as a brewer before turning to other pursuits — and although the bustling river town had many churches, it had many more saloons. Progressives found Moliners to be more receptive to their message, while Davenport was a hellhole that even hard-core reformers thought was better left alone or even visit — in part, because until the completion of the Iowa-Illinois Memorial Bridge in 1935, Moliners had to travel through Rock Island to get to Davenport. Rock Island filled the broad expanse between the social extremes, and a native of Buffalo, Iowa, journalist, wine purveyor, and author of *The Quad Cities and The People,* Jim Renkes observed, "Rock Island, I think, is the Quad-City with the most history and personality."

During the last decades of the 19th century, Moline caught the overflow from Rock Island's prosperity, and Davenport was where Rock Islanders went slumming. The year before Rock Island replaced their downtown gas street lamps with electric lights, Deere & Company installed 16 electric streetlights outside their factory. Moline grew to the east along the Mississippi riverbanks from where it had hunkered up next to the Rock Island city limits and pushed to the south until the river bluffs presented a formidable barrier to horse-drawn wagons and carriages. Wikipedia says of the city at the time:

> Moline was a successful, if somewhat boring, turn-of-the-20th-century city. It was clean, well maintained, and prosperous, and unlike Rock Island and Davenport, contained no slums, congestion, or red-light districts. Despite the occasional conflicts between native-born and immigrant leaders, the

Puritanical, serious temperament of the city had not changed in the half-century since Moline's founding. The city became known as "Proud Moline" to its neighbors, a somewhat derisive nickname that touched on Moliners' sometimes haughty, holier-than-thou attitude.

In 1890 Moline's population of 12,000 approached Rock Island's only slightly larger, but infinitely more urbane census of 13,000. Again Moline initiated consolidation talks; again they failed.

Preferring the amenities and lifestyle of the town where he grew up, Bailey Davenport eschewed living across the river in Davenport, the deepening moral cesspool that was forming on the land Antoine LeClaire named after his father. A saloonkeeper of the era described the city and its Bucktown district at the turn of the century:

> I'll tell you about a town so tough it made Chicago look like an old-people's home. It was called "Bucktown" — six blocks of unadulterated sin, right at the foot of the Arsenal's Government Bridge. The *New York Tribune* said it was the "worst town in America, bar none. New York is a milk town compared to Davenport." There's Perl Galvin's bar known as the ultimate of sin. Naughty girls hung umbrellas and panties over the back bar of old Perly's place. If you got out of there still a virgin, it was a miracle.
>
> There were over 200 saloons in Davenport and most were located in Bucktown, running wide-open 24 hours a day, 7 days a week. Some of them dumps didn't own keys for the doors. Most of them had wine rooms in the rear of the saloon for con men, thieves, and whores to make deals with the suckers. Along with the saloons and sporting houses were sleazy theaters, real low-life burlesque acts, women whispering in men's ears making propositions to them, and lewd acts were held at some of the back-alley places. The Bijou, The Standards, The Orpheum, and the biggest of all was The Pavillion, owned by the King of Bucktown, Brick Monroe. He would entertain a thousand people on a single night. He had a gold mine.
>
> Davenport's gambling houses were famous all over the nation. The Eldorado, The Senator, The Saratoga, and the Ozark had poker games running three or four days a week. Bert Smith was the bookmaker who promoted most of the games. He hung out at The Hot Springs, a wild place. Slot machines were everywhere — cigar stores, pool halls, dance halls, whorehouses, and I saw some in bathrooms. ~ *Citadel of Sin*

On the rolling farmland above Bucktown, community-minded Davenporters slogged forward, especially making strong progress in post-secondary education. Seven years after Augustana College moved to Rock Island, in 1882 Saint Ambrose College was founded as a Catholic seminary and school of commerce for young men, and 50 years later the Diocese of Davenport stepped up and provided equivalent education for young women when it opened Marycrest College. In 1897 David Daniel Palmer opened the Palmer School of Chiropractic — the first chiropractic school in the world. Gary Farr tells in the online *Chiropractic History Time Line* how D.D. Palmer invented chiropractic medicine:

It was there, along the lush banks of the Mississippi River, amidst the wagons and buggies of late 19th century Davenport, that chiropractic was born on September 18, 1895. For it was on this day that D.D. Palmer made the first chiropractic adjustment on a janitor who worked in his office building. David Daniel Palmer had opened an office, devoted to magnetic healing, in 1887. In Palmer's building was a janitorial service, owned by Harvey Lillard. Lillard, who had been deaf for 17 years, was asked by Palmer how he had become deaf. He replied that one day, when he had strained his back, he heard something "pop" in his back.

Palmer examined Lillard's back and found a spinal vertebra out of position. Reasoning that this was the cause of his deafness, Palmer thrust the vertebrae back into place. And, as he expected, Lillard's hearing improved.

Palmer was sure he was on to something. He began developing a theory of what he later called "chiropractic", meaning "done by hand". Palmer theorized that decreased nerve flow may be the cause of disease, and that misplaced spinal vertebrae may cause pressure on the nerves. Thus, he reasoned, if the spinal column were correctly positioned, the body would be healthy.

Palmer decided to open a chiropractic school in 1897. By 1902, 15 people had graduated from the Palmer Infirmary and Chiropractic Institute, which was renamed the Palmer School of Chiropractic (PSC) in 1907. One of these graduates was Palmer's son, Bartlett Joshua (B.J.) Palmer, who would become as memorable a figure in chiropractic history as his father.

Similar to towns and cities throughout the rest of the country, the financial, educational, religious, and cultural differences that separated the citizens of the Tri-Cities created suspicions and resentments between established residents and those that hopped off the train looking for a place to settle. Fortunately, between the three cities there were welcoming arms for everyone. At the turn of the century, Moline provided a respectable home base for earnest, solid citizens looking for honest work. Davenport offered inexpensive housing and a permissive, restriction-free refuge for scofflaws, the eccentric, and misfits. And because they had been the first to arrive, Rock Islanders had claimed the prime real estate and built a thriving, diverse community when Moline was still a sooty factory town and Davenport a slum.

It was into this eclectic bi-state community that in 1885 an 18-year-old, second-generation Irishman arrived on the train from his home in the "Kerry Patch," the Irish neighborhood in Ottawa, Illinois. John Looney, the new arrival, had learned telegraphy at the age of 15 working at the Western Union office, and after serving as the night operator for three years, he was promoted to manager of the telegraph station in Rock Island. The relocation would dramatically change his life and the history and image of Rock Island. The primary city of the Tri-Cities, Rock Island was a modern, model city and had a superior infrastructure with a waterworks and sewer system that routed waste to the Mississippi River, a well-organized police force and fire department, paved sidewalks and roads lit by electric lights, a disproportionately high number of quality stores and markets, and a flourishing night-life that offered something for everyone's tastes. And as one righteous reformer (probably from Moline) described it, "If Davenport is hell, Rock Island is the chimney."

If that were the case, the crossroads of the nation passed through hell. Daily, five railroads loaded and unloaded freight and passengers in Rock Island, making it the railroad center of the region, while on the docks at the foot of 23rd Street, laborers unloaded tons of raw materials and coal every day but the Sabbath. Eastbound freight trains carried out lumber, bricks, and finished-goods that included plows, wagons, and carriages that were manufactured using the abundant power supplied by the rapids that raced past the factories lining the riverbanks. Looney's new home offered prosperity and vibrancy unmatched by any like-sized city. Slowly integrating into the community, Looney determined that a law career was the quickest route to prominence. Before his 23rd birthday, the gregarious Looney had befriended many of Rock Island's most influential men and had climbed the social and political ladders. He was elected president of the Fifth Ward Democratic Club and controlled several precincts in a Democratic town. At 5'8" tall and 125 pounds, Looney was small in physical stature but becoming a big man.

Specializing in criminal defense, Looney began his law career in January 1891. He quickly became one of the area's most sought-out defense lawyers and was soon defending most of the cases of poor Irishmen that went before the court. His leisure pursuits included membership in a literary club, and in the same month he began his law career, he wrote, produced, and acted the lead in a play that was presented at the Harper Opera House. The *Argus* gave him good reviews and said that the play's ending speech was magnificent.

Raised by a tough, but attentive Irish-immigrant father and a controlling mother in the rough, Irish section of Ottawa, Looney was introduced to hard work early in life. From age 12, after school he helped his father deliver drayage arriving on the Rock Island Line. Growing up next to the tracks, the wiry boy with wavy black hair, dark penetrating eyes, and an impish smirk on his lips learned to fearlessly fight at first for what he needed and later for what he wanted. When he got off the train in Rock Island, he began leading a double life. In Rock Island, Looney was a flashy young lawyer with political ambitions, and in Ottawa, where he returned most weekends, he was the dutiful son.

When he was 27, his mother pushed Looney into marrying Nora O'Connor, his sister's partner in a successful Ottawa millinery store and a friend of his mother. For seven years after the wedding, the Looneys lived in Ottawa — John continued to work in Rock Island and returned home on weekends — and Nora bore him two girls, Kathleen and Ursula Mary. A son, John Connor, was born in November 1900 in Rock

Island, where his wife and daughters had finally relocated. Looney moved his family into a 6,000-square foot Queen Anne home with five fireplaces at 1635 20th Street (the house's exterior is virtually unchanged today). Soon after she moved to Rock Island, Nora contracted spinal cancer and spent most of her last months in Chicago. She died in May of 1903, and John was left to raise the children. He did a terrible job.

Before his marriage, Looney had socialized with Rock Island's elite at night and defended the city's low-life by day. He was equally at home with the well-heeled at Broadway house parties or in the company of criminals in the downtown saloons. Consciously accumulating chits that he would cash in later, he often defended criminals for no fee, and his door was always open for free legal advice to the poor. He learned how to manipulate the law and people to his benefit, and he began to do both exceedingly well. One of Looney's first marks was a prominent German-born contractor, Matthias Schnell, who built more than 100 hospitals and churches across the country. His most notable building is the state capitol in Austin, Texas. As a young man, Schnell had moved from New York City with his Irish wife to Rock Island, where he operated his nationwide business. The accomplished Schnell was enamored with the much younger Looney and praised him to his friends and associates as one of the most brilliant men in the Tri-Cities. It was Schnell who gave Looney the credibility and early boost that allowed him to move forward with his ambitions.

Schnell financially backed Looney in several ventures. One was the 1897 construction of the 24th Street storm sewer. Looney cut corners by not building to specifications and using inferior materials, and he and five others including his law partner and Schnell were convicted of fraud. Looney fought the conviction for ten years and eventually had the case overturned. Although he was probably uninvolved in the scheme, the *Argus* ravaged Schnell as a Looney co-conspirator. The degrading publicity ruined him, and he never recovered professionally or psychologically. Schnell died a broken man while living alone in a Rock Island apartment. Looney seemed to be professionally invigorated by the conviction, and he launched two new careers: newspaperman and gangster.

The newspaper that destroyed the legitimate reputations of John Looney and Matthias Schnell had published its first daily papers almost a half-century earlier in 1853. Founded by a resolute Democrat, Colonel J.B. Danforth, the conservative *Rock Island Argus* was the region's largest paper, in part because it staunchly opposed the liberal views espoused by Whig/Republican Abraham Lincoln. The paper had many competitors and few equals over the 30 years Danforth was publisher. The editorial position of the paper became even more conservative when John Potter bought it in 1882 when its daily circulation was 500. When Potter died in 1898, his wife Minnie took over the paper's operations. Minnie was a conservative Progressive, and it was under her stewardship that the *Argus* picked up the mantle of righteous causes and rooting out the evil-doers — John Looney became her favorite target. Looney was a quick study, and he fully understood that by alienating Minnie Potter, his professional and social status among the Broadway District crowd was destroyed.

Instead of slinking out of town, Looney brought his two younger brothers Bill and Jerry to town and started his own newspaper, *The Rock Island News* — Bill had been a reporter for an Ottawa newspaper and Jerry was a typesetter. Looney later explained his decision to go into the newspaper business:

> As most lawyers are, I was forced into politics. I happened to get under the shadow of the ill will of what we call the money element in Rock Island, Illinois, very early in my political career. On every possible occasion the *Argus* would write me up, and on several occasions when I carried conventions, it would put in belting conversations against me and create disturbances, which always, however, ended in a tribute to me.

The battle of the dueling newspapers began. Each had their faithful readers, and arguably Looney had the entertainment advantage because he never let the truth get in the way of his stories.

Looney bought the finest club in the Tri-Cities, the Mirror Lounge at 1819 2nd Avenue. He located his law offices on the second floor, and behind the ornate bar and restaurant, he housed the offices of the *Rock Island News*. He would later operate card games and run prostitutes from the basement. Newspapers were the only distributor of the news in 1905 — Rock Island's first radio broadcast was still 20 years off — and less than two-thirds of America's adults could read English. It was common for men to congregate at the end of the workday in Rock Island's saloons and read the papers aloud to contrast the news stories against the facts that were observed or "known" to be credible — and a picture, of course, was worth a thousand words. Newspapers of the time were more like today's supermarket tabloids than to the *New York Times*. News, entertainment, and editorial comment were liberally mixed together in a stew of hyperbolic writing where facts that got in the way of the story were often left out. Although certainly more precise and truthful than Looney's yellow journalism, Minnie Potter's reporters were not above exaggerating events and circumstances to inform, entertain, and retain the Argus' readership, and news that was damaging to business leaders and advertisers and prominent citizens was fluffed up or completely omitted.

There's no journal that reveals when Looney decided to become a gangster, but until Nora's death in August 1903, he was at least publicly a functional part of the community. Without Nora's moderating influence, Looney become manic, and he began living the life of a gangster, although it is unclear what illegal vices he was indulging in and to what extent. Six months after burying Nora, he purchased 37 acres of secluded woodland bordering the Rock River. At the end of a gated lane that wound to the river from Black Hawk Road (approximately where 30th Street now ends), he first built a two-story "barn" with 18-inch thick stone walls that had a basement with ceilings high enough for carriages to drive in to. The upper two floors were devoted to a gym and guest rooms. When the barn was completed, he built a three-level house made of limestone overlooking Rock River. The extravagant home was connected to the garage with a secret tunnel. Called Bel Aire, the mansion's third-story ballroom is reputed to have hosted some of the underworld's most ostentatious and degenerate parties. Having the accoutrements of a gangland chieftain, Looney set out to become one.

Involved in gambling, prostitution, and extortion rackets during this period, Looney's law practice, bar and restaurant, and newspaper were his primary businesses — and possibly from a lack of focus, he wasn't particularly successful at any of them. A petty blackmail scheme of his was to have one of his prostitutes approach a prominent man in a bar, throw her arms around him while a *News* photographer snapped the picture, and then for a "kill fee" Looney wouldn't publish the picture. Always looking for another scheme to pay his debts, in November 1908 he turned to arson. A mysterious blast ruined the Mirror Lounge's bar, and after refusing a $7,000 ($170,000) insurance settlement, a second blast did more damage to the building.

Among Rock Island's respectable citizens, Looney was liked by few, avoided by most, and hated by some — and he was the target of several assassination attempts. One of the men who hated him was W. William Wilmerton, a wealthy farmer. In 1908 Looney thought he had suckered Wilmerton into buying the *News,* while he still managed the paper and retained control of its content. The night after Wilmerton acquired the paper and seized control of the *News* from Looney, mysteriously, the printing press blew up, putting the paper out of business.

A year later Wilmerton and Looney engaged in a shootout that had the elements of a Hollywood western/comedy. Late, on a cold February afternoon, the sun had fallen behind the buildings that backed up to the alley between 2nd and 3rd Avenues. Except for the occasional rat that scurried between garbage barrels, the icy alleyway was empty until two men stealthily approached from opposite directions. When Wilmerton and Looney got to within 20 to 25 feet of each other, they started shooting. The showdown was spontaneous, but both men had entered the alley armed with pistols and were prepared to kill the other; however, they didn't have the skills. Looney fired five times, one shot breaking an office window and scaring the bejesus out of a young female worker. Hiding behind a telephone pole, Wilmerton fired four times, grazing

Looney in the side with one shot. The gunfight ended with the men firing insults at each other. Both were arrested and released.

This was not the first time Looney was fired upon. After the *News'* printing press was blown up, Looney was shot while riding in a horse-drawn buggy — he fell out of the carriage with a minor wound. Later while gazing out his dining room window at his Bel Aire mansion, a man jumped out from behind a tree and shot at him through the window — again wounding him slightly. In June after the gunfight in the alley, Looney was returning home in his buggy about 10:00 p.m. on a Saturday night. He was shot at by an assailant who used a "breech loading gun loaded with heavy BB shot with a heavy charge of powder" — one BB penetrated Looney's left arm, another his hat. In each attempt, he claimed the assailant was Wilmerton.

Within a year after selling the newspaper to Wilmerton, Looney started the *News* up again at a house on 16th Avenue just west of 20th Street. As irascibly truculent as ever, he went too far in March 1912 when he published a 2-inch, front-page headline in the *News* that screamed "SCHRIVER'S SHAME" and the sub-headline read "Night and Day in Peoria in Filthy Debauch with Ethel." (Ethel was a Peoria prostitute that *News* readers came to know on a first name basis). An attorney and the son of a police captain, new Mayor Harry Schriver, who never married, had been at odds with Looney since the preceding September when the *News* reported that he and his friends, the Ramser's, were running a resort on the Rock River where men and women swam in the nude in the plain view of children. Jake Ramser, a prominent jeweler, hadn't taken well to the first *News* story, and in a barbershop confrontation shortly after the libelous story, he wrestled Looney's .32 Colt revolver from him when Looney drew and aimed at him and ordered him out of the barbershop. After knocking the gun from Looney, Ramser aimed it at Looney's head and repeatedly pulled the trigger and would have killed him if he had known to release the safety. Instead he beat Looney bloody with the butt of the gun.

Looney's scurrilous attack on Schriver resulted because the mayor declined to terminate prosecution of a Looney lieutenant on gambling charges. Schriver was forewarned of the slanderous *News* attack, and at 10:00am on the morning the paper came out, Looney was arrested on 2nd Avenue and taken to the police station. Released into a locked room with only Shriver present, no one knows exactly what followed, but Looney was heard to scream, "Murder, murder, he's murdering me!" Looney was hospitalized with a broken nose, deep wounds to the head, and blood streaming from his right ear. The *Argus* reported, "Driven beyond the limit of human endurance by a libelous, defaming, and besmirching attack which appeared the morning in John

Looney's *News*, Mayor H.M. Schriver stopped, to a certain degree, the sale of the sheet, caused the arrest of 18 newsboys who were offering it for sale, and of Looney himself."

Four days after the Looney licking, political opponents of Mayor Schriver and those beholding to Looney gathered in Market Square — the triangle of land framed by 16½ and 17th Streets between 1st and 2nd Avenues — with the expressed intent of fomenting a riot. An opening speech by E.E. Gardner, editor of the *Tri-City Labor Review* and a Socialist candidate for supervisor, enraged the crowd that gathered in part out of curiosity and in part out of anger over the abuse of First Amendment rights and the police brutality directed at a defenseless citizen who had done nothing more than possibly slander the mayor. Looney's cohorts incited the mob of 3,000 to 4,000 to storm the police station. Then things got out of hand.

When a plea for order from Commissioner Archie Hart at the station's entrance was met with a barrage of bricks and rocks, the police fired over the heads of the crowd — and random fire was returned. Over the next half-hour, the mob ebbed and flowed downtown as reports and rumors of attacks and violence elsewhere diverted them. But when the mob returned en masse to the station, the police again fired a volley overhead, and the mob went wild, again throwing rocks and bricks and firing at the station. The next volley was into — not over — the crowd's heads; two were killed and nine were injured. Although the *Argus* claimed that most in the mob were from out of town, seven of the nine seriously injured were from Rock Island; many others than those hospitalized were wounded and several were hit with birdshot. The two that were killed by police bullets were 36-year-old Frank Kellogg of Davenport who had come to Rock Island with his wife to see some excitement and 18-year-old Ray Swingle who "was downtown doing an errand for his mother. Before dying, he told his father that he was ignored by the crowds because they thought he was faking."

The sheriff contacted the Illinois governor, and martial law was declared. By the next morning, 100 National Guard troops were patrolling the streets and were soon reinforced with 700 more guardsmen. Citizens were warned to stay off the streets, and all gatherings were outlawed. For many, the most disturbing action was the mayor's order to close the saloons. Also, the brothels were raided, and 34 people were arrested over the next two days. The primary after-effects of the riot were that the red light district was closed down for a period — and Looney left town. By the weekend the saloons reopened, and by Monday the guardsmen went home. Although federal agents were reportedly seeking Looney, he was long gone — disappearing to Horse Lake Ranch near Chama, New Mexico, which three months earlier had become the 47th state.

At the time Looney was rising to prominence in Rock Island, in the presidential race of 1900, William McKinley was elected to a second term, again defeating William

Jennings Bryan. Less than a year after being reelected, following a speech at the Pan-American Exposition in Buffalo, New York, the president was greeting the public when an unemployed, self-described anarchist, Leon Czolgosz, approached McKinley with a .32 caliber pistol concealed in his bandaged hand. Czolgosz' first shot grazed McKinley's sternum; the second passed through his stomach, pancreas, and kidney and lodged in the muscles of his back.

Although the expo had thousands of electric lights to illuminate the buildings' exteriors, the emergency hospital had no interior lights, and the doctors were forced to operate by reflected sunlight. Unable to locate the bullet and fearful of doing more damage, they decided to sew the president up and see how he progressed. He did surprising well, and after a week he ate solid food. However, two days later he went into shock brought on by gangrene and died. (An aide had sent word to Thomas Edison to rush an X-ray machine to Buffalo to find the bullet. It arrived but wasn't used because the president appeared to be recovering and the doctors were uncertain of the machine's side effects.) The nation was outraged. For the third time in 36 years the president had been assassinated. In a two-day trial conducted nine days after McKinley died, it took the jury one hour to unanimously agree on the death penalty. Czolgosz, who didn't speak a word during his trial, was executed a month later.

Republican kingpins' worst fears had come true: no longer was Vice-president Theodore Roosevelt a heartbeat from the presidency — he was the president. Hugely popular with the people, Roosevelt was unpopular with party leaders who considered him a rogue. Also, he had not been the Republican elite's first choice as McKinley's running mate. During his first term, McKinley's vice-president, Garret Hobart, had died in office, and bowing to the clout of the Progressive Movement, Roosevelt, a left-leaning Progressive Republican from New York, was selected for the second spot in order to balance the ticket against Progressive Democrat William Jennings Bryan.

Probably no American ever was more suited to be president than Theodore Roosevelt. An asthmatic child, Roosevelt disregarded doctors' advice to avoid physical exertion, and with his father's encouragement, he became an exuberant sportsman and outdoorsman. Home schooled because of his health, his wealthy family supplemented his education with yearlong trips to Europe and Egypt when he was a young teenager. In 1880 Roosevelt graduated Phi Beta Kappa from Harvard where he edited the student magazine, rowed, and boxed — he was runner-up in the Harvard boxing championship. Marrying the month after graduating, Roosevelt enrolled at Columbia Law School but dropped out after a year to successfully run as a Republican candidate for the New York Legislature. A master at multi-tasking, Roosevelt, who had a photographic memory, quickly conquered all challenges and as quickly moved on to others. Began while at

Harvard, Roosevelt completed writing *The Naval War of 1812*, which is still the definitive history of the U.S. Navy during the War of 1812.

Roosevelt's "maverick" politics began at the end of his first legislative term. At the 1884 Republican national convention, he stood with the liberal "Mugwump" reformers, who bitterly fought the conservative "Stalwarts." The Mugwumps (from the Algonquin word "mugumquomp," meaning "war leader") lost the convention battle, and Grover Cleveland soundly defeated the Republican candidate in the general election when many Mugwumps joined the Democrats. Earlier that year, Roosevelt's wife died two days after delivering their only child. The pregnancy had masked a serious kidney disease, and in the same house earlier the same day, his mother died. Shaken by the deaths and disillusioned with politics, Roosevelt moved to a South Dakota cattle ranch he had purchased the previous year while on a buffalo hunt.

Three winters after Roosevelt began ranching, North America endured one of the longest, coldest winters on record. His cattle and his $60,000 ($1.4 million) investment were wiped out, and again doing a complete lifestyle reversal, he returned to New York where he built a home on Oyster Bay and ran for Mayor of New York City. He lost and went to London where he married his childhood sweetheart, Edith Kermit Carow — they had five children — and after climbing Mount Blanc while honeymooning in Europe, Roosevelt returned to New York.

Campaigning for Benjamin Harrison, in 1888 the president rewarded Roosevelt with a position on the Civil Service Commission. He attacked the public job so zealously that the *New York Sun* complimented him for being "irrepressible, belligerent, and enthusiastic" in his efforts to do the nearly impossible by reforming government. And despite his continued support of Harrison, Democratic President Grover Cleveland appointed him to the same post in 1892. During the seven years he served on the commission, he broke up a spoils system that had been in place since Andrew Jackson's presidency. His work done, Roosevelt left his federal position to take on a greater challenge and assumed the presidency of the New York City Board of Police Commissioners. The N.Y.P.D. was one of the most corrupt forces in the nation. Two years after Roosevelt took charge, the police were exemplary public servants. He implemented regular firearms inspections, annual physical exams for officers, appointed 1,600 recruits based on their qualifications and not on ethnic or political affiliation, and established a merit system. Having instituted lasting reforms in the New York City Police Department, he took the position of Assistant Secretary of the Navy.

Essentially running the Department of the Navy, Roosevelt wanted to test the U.S military in combat because they had not been in a major international conflict since the War of 1812, 85 years before. He said, "I should welcome almost any war, for I think this country needs one." He got his wish when the Spanish sank the U.S. battleship *Maine* in Cuba's Havana Harbor. Resigning his Navy post, Roosevelt assembled a volunteer cavalry regiment by recruiting a diverse group of friends and associates from his school days at Harvard, his time in the West, and his post with the N.Y.P.D. Dubbed the "Rough Riders" by New York newspapers, the brigade was made famous by their charge up San Juan Hill. But because the other steeds were left behind for the lack of transport ships, Roosevelt was the only Rough Rider to have a horse, and the cavalry actually walked and crawled up San Juan Hill. Roosevelt's forces were decimated by malaria and contributed little to the decisive U.S. victory. The war against Spain caused a rise in patriotism, and in Rock Island it was decided that the high school should change the school colors from red and yellow, the colors of Spain's flag to red, white, and blue. The new colors remained in place until the year after the war, when the bold colors of crimson and gold were adopted.

On returning to the states, Roosevelt was elected governor of New York in 1898. His national image was considered such a powerful campaign asset for the party that he was put at the forefront of the sticky issue of the annexation of the Philippines. William Jennings Bryan had supported the war against Spain, but argued that annexing the Philippines was imperialistic. Vigorously attacking Bryan, Roosevelt countered in a string of campaign speeches for McKinley, saying that it was the best thing for Philippine stability. The Philippine Republic didn't agree with Roosevelt — on June 2, 1899 they declared war against the United States. The war did not officially end until a year after Roosevelt was president. Roosevelt uttered his most memorable quote during the war, "Speak softly and carry a big stick, and you will go far."

Roosevelt attended church regularly, and he opposed including the motto "In God We Trust" on money. He wrote during his presidency, "It seems to me eminently unwise to cheapen such a motto by use on coins, just as it would be to cheapen it by use on postage stamps, or in advertisements." After hearing that the president wanted to abolish the motto, in a conversation with Mark Twain, Andrew Carnegie observed, "The name of God is used to being carried into improper places everywhere and all the time." "It was a beautiful motto," Twain said. "It is simple, direct, and gracefully phrased — In God We Trust. I don't believe it would sound any better if it were true."

Although Roosevelt often publicly came across as a righteous man, he was humble with his friends. When staying with his good friend the naturalist William Beebe, the two men would walk outside before retiring, search the night sky, and ritualistically say, "That is the Spiral Galaxy in Andromeda. It is as large as our Milky Way. It is one of a hundred million galaxies. It consists of one hundred billion suns, each larger than our sun." Then Roosevelt would turn to Beebe and say, "Now I think we are small enough. Let's go to bed."

At the age of 42, Roosevelt was the youngest U.S. president in history, and the teetotalling reformer and political centrist was the perfect man for his time. He was a social liberal hiding in the skin of a GOP elephant, and he coined the phrase "Square Deal" to describe his administration's domestic agenda that emphasized protecting the average American. His governance plan emphasized three basic concepts: conservation of natural resources, consumer protection, and corporate control and regulation. Aimed at advancing the welfare of the growing middle class, over his nearly two full terms he had legislation passed that gave the government control over public land use, restricted railroad freight rates, created the Interstate Commerce Commission, passed the Pure Food and Drug and the Meat Inspection Acts, leveled the playing field between labor and management, and initiated 44 anti-trust suits against major corporations. He promoted the conservation movement and was the impetus behind the construction of the Panama Canal. Roosevelt's only significant failure was his inability to lead the Republican Party toward the Progressive goals of greater business and banking regulation. The rebuff by his own party would come back to bite the Republicans and the nation 20 years later when the securities bubble popped, markets tanked, and the world plunged into the Great Depression. Roosevelt is considered one of the most effective presidents and was the first American to win a Nobel Prize.

William Howard Taft, another Republican, rode into office in 1908 on Roosevelt's popularity and his promise not to seek a second term. "Big Bill" was a wrestling champion and Phi Beta Kappa from Yale and was smart enough to know not to change strategy in a winning game. He continued Roosevelt's civil reform efforts, busted trusts, and took up the ever-popular crusade to improve postal efficiency. He endorsed Booker T. Washington's plan for the advancement of African Americans and encouraged black education and entrepreneurship. A supporter of free immigration, he vetoed a law backed by labor unions that would have restricted unskilled immigrants by imposing a literacy test on them. An uncompromising, results-oriented president, Taft managed to alienate constituencies to his political left and right.

Taft was a large man who weighed an estimated 350 pounds. He was once stranded at a small country railroad station where he was told that the next train through would only stop if there were a large party of people to board. Taft sent a telegraph to the station before his stop saying, "Stop at Hicksville. Large party waiting to catch train." When the train rolled to a stop, only Taft was on the platform. He eyed the conductor, and said, "I'm the large party." When Taft left the White House, he was offered a Chair of Law at Yale. He thanked the university and said that he believed a

"Sofa of Law would be more appropriate." He signed into law the Sixteenth Amendment that gave the Federal Government the right to impose an income tax, which was also a popular Progressive cause. A decade after serving a single term as president, Taft was appointed Chief Justice of the U.S. Supreme Court. He enjoyed his years on the court and was respected by his peers. Although usually given average marks as a president, Justice Felix Frankfurter once remarked to Justice Louis Brandeis that it was "difficult for me to understand why a man who is so good a Chief Justice could have been so bad as President."

The 1912 election made politics fun again, and in his bid for reelection, Taft barely defeated Roosevelt for the Republican nomination — Roosevelt said he meant "three consecutive terms." When he lost the nomination to his former good friend who he had groomed to be his successor, Roosevelt formed the Progressive Party, better known as the Bull Moose Party. (Its name came from the time when Roosevelt was asked if he was fit to be president, and he thumped his chest and said he was as "fit as a bull moose.") The Democrats ran Woodrow Wilson, and to completely fill out the political spectrum, the Socialists ran convicted felon, Eugene V. Debs, for the fourth time. As a leader of the American Railway Union, Debs was imprisoned for failing to obey an injunction to stop a strike against the Pullman Palace Car Company over pay cuts. Eight years later, Debs would be in jail again for the 1920 election, and would run from his prison cell for a fifth shot at the presidency. He was serving a 10-year sentence for breaking laws under the 1917 Espionage Act, which apparently trumped the First Amendment — he had given speeches denouncing American participation in World War I. Receiving a presidential pardon a year later and upon being released, Debs defiantly exclaimed, "It is the government that should ask me for a pardon." He died of heart disease in 1926, less than two years after being nominated for the Nobel Peace Prize.

Three weeks before the election, while Roosevelt was campaigning in Milwaukee, a saloonkeeper named John Schrank shot him. After penetrating his steel eyeglass case and passing through the 50 pages of a folded copy of the speech he was to deliver, the bullet lodged in Roosevelt's chest. Roosevelt and his doctors concluded that since he wasn't coughing blood he must be okay. He began the 90-minute speech by saying, "Friends, I shall ask you to be as quiet as possible. I don't know whether you fully understand that I have just been shot; but it takes more than that to kill a Bull Moose." Papers found on Shrank indicated that he was advised in a dream by the ghost of William McKinley to avenge his death. The ghost pointed to a picture of Roosevelt. Schrank spent the last 29 years of his life in the Central State Mental Hospital in

Waupun, Wisconsin. With no further complications, Roosevelt carried the bullet in his chest for the rest of his life.

Out of a sense of fairness or maybe because they were tired, Taft and Wilson suspended their campaigns until Roosevelt recovered from his wound — he gave two more speeches. Roosevelt beat Taft by five percent of the popular vote, but with a whopping 42 percent of the popular vote in the three-man race, the Democrat, Wilson, skated into the White House. When asked to comment on his crushing defeat, Taft eloquently said, "Well, I have one consolation; no candidate was ever elected ex-president by such a large majority." Wilson had been a virtual unknown going into the Democrat's 1912 convention, which remained deadlocked after 40 ballots. Publisher William Randolph Hearst supported a far left candidate, and William Jennings Bryan who had been the party nominee three times previously backed a moderate. The two powerful men conferred and the Princeton president emerged as the party's compromise candidate. Shortly after taking his oath of office, Wilson visited an elderly aunt who he had not seen for a long time. When she asked what he had been doing of late, he replied, "I've just been elected president." "Oh, yes, president of what?" she inquired. "Of the United States." "Don't be silly," she snorted.

The former Princeton president was a leader of the Progressive Movement. The only president ever with a Ph.D., Wilson presided over the contentious time that saw the enactment of the Seventeenth (election of senators by popular vote), Eighteenth (Prohibition), and Nineteenth (women's suffrage) Amendments and the culmination of the Progressive agenda. He was president during all of World War I, and in 1919 he received the Nobel Peace Prize for his strident advocacy of the League of Nations. Wilson hated his pacifist-Socialist challenger Debs, who received almost a million popular votes, and wrote of him, "While the flower of American youth was pouring out its blood to vindicate the cause of civilization, this man, Debs, stood behind the lines sniping, attacking, and denouncing them. ... This man was a traitor to his country and he will never be pardoned during my administration."

Ironically, Wilson had narrowly defeated Chief Justice Charles Evans Hughes, a Republican, for reelection in 1916, and historians credit his campaign slogan of "He kept us out of war" as making the difference. When a German U-boat sank the British liner *Lusitania* in 1915 and 128 Americans perished, Wilson had proclaimed, "America is too proud to fight." Three months after his inauguration for his second term, the sinking of seven U.S. merchant ships by German submarines gave Wilson the excuse to call for war, and he mustered 4.4 million American troops for the last 18 months of the 4-year European conflict. By the summer of 1918, the United States was sending 10,000 troops a day to France. American casualties totaled 323,000, which were a pittance compared to the 22.7 million suffered by British, French, and Russian allies and the 15.4 million that the Germanic allies incurred. Of the 8.5 million who lost their lives in a war that saw great technological advances in firepower without corresponding advances in mobility, 116,516 were Americans.

As he began his second term in 1917, Wilson required 250,000 first-generation German-Americans to register with the Department of Justice. After interrogation and investigation, 2,048 were incarcerated in internment camps until the end of the war. The Enemy Alien Registration Section was headed by 23-year-old J. Edgar Hoover. Showing a disregard for common sense, a disdain for the arts community, and a pathological paranoia that would mark the remainder of his professional life, Hoover had 29 musicians and the director of the Boston Symphony Orchestra interned. Apparently also detecting a subversive element among German-American orchestra directors, Hoover jailed the Cincinnati Symphony Orchestra director. Memorable concerts were held at the Fort Oglethorpe Internment Camp, where frequently, audiences of internees and their jailers listened to some of America's finest music.

The loss of lives during World War I military actions were a pittance compared to those who died from the flu. Ten months before the war ended, a severe influenza was observed in Haskell County, Kansas. Two months later, 522 men at Fort Riley, Kansas, were stricken with a flu that seemed to affect young adults more than children and older adults. (Modern analysis of the deadly virus has shown that the flu fed upon and ravaged the stronger immune systems of young adults.) Spread by the mass transportation of soldiers, a more virulent second strain of the virus reached France in August. The more deadly second wave of flu was attributed to sick American soldiers who were shipped to Europe to fight. Unlike normal situations where flu victims stay home, on the battlefront the mild flu cases stayed to fight and multitudes more were infected, while the very sick were put on crowded troop trains and sent to overflowing hospitals where even more were exposed.

Named the "Spanish Flu" because Spain was a neutral country and accurately reported its deaths, it appeared that the death rate was especially high in Spain. The warring countries, which were all the other European powers, were reluctant to let the enemy know how sick they were. The virus spread amazingly quickly around the world, even infecting the few people who were in Antarctica. One area was left untouched — Marajo, a small island in Brazil's Amazon River Delta reported no flu cases. No fewer than 50 million people and as many as 100 million died — by comparison, over the duration of the 14th century between 75 million and 150 million died from the Black Death. Although the Spanish Flu lasted until December of 1920, it peaked during the fall of 1918 and had mutated to less viral strains by November. At least five times as many people died from the war-fed flu in the summer and fall of 1918 as died in combat. Crowded out of the public's consciousness by time and the devastation of World War I, the 1918 Spanish flu is often called the "forgotten pandemic."

The 1920 election was between two dark horse Ohio newspaper publishers: Democrat, James M. Cox and Republican, Warren G. Harding. Europe and Russia were devastated, and the United States was a mess. The wartime economic boom that pushed Wilson into the final months of his term had collapsed, and no experienced national politicians stepped forward to take on the seemingly impossible job of cleaning it up. There were deadly strikes in the steel and meatpacking industries, terrorist attacks on Wall Street, race riots in Chicago, and thanks to Prohibition, mobsters were running the big cities and paying cops and judges more than they were making from their government jobs. With a promise of a return to "normalcy," Harding was elected with more than 60 percent of the popular vote, and the last shovel-full of dirt was thrown on the grave of the Progressive Movement.

Chapter 19

Great Migrations

The white man's happiness cannot be purchased by the black man's misery.
~ Frederick Douglass

FROM 1915 TO 1970 more than 5 million African Americans fled the South to live anywhere in America except there. During the two decades after 1910, 1.5 million black citizens moved from the South to the cities of the Northeast and Great Lakes Region. The trickle of Southern blacks to the North during Reconstruction became a torrent when Jim Crow laws were tightened during the 1890s. Between 1890 and 1910 all the Southern states wrote new constitutions that disenfranchised blacks and made it nearly impossible for them to vote. Although lynching blacks was popular sport in Mississippi until the 1960s, it was at its height at the turn of the century — between James Garfield's presidency and the Civil Rights Act of 1964, at least 3,300 black men and 160 black women were lynched in the South. Blacks could not go north fast enough.

Established black neighborhoods in New York's Harlem District, North Philadelphia, Detroit's Hastings Street and Frederick Avenue neighborhoods, and the "Black Belt" chain of neighborhoods on Chicago's South Side were safe harbors. Carl Sandburg wrote of the destination cities that each became a "receiving station and port of refuge." Small towns and rural areas were not nearly as welcoming, and although Davenport and Moline were not small towns, they were as white as the rural areas outside their city limits. Rock Island was the regional exception. Railroad, factory, dock, and domestic workers and occasional musicians from Memphis and St. Louis found a relatively warm welcome there.

In 1884 a white man, John Streckfus, helped create a black port of refuge when he sold his Rock Island grocery to J.M. Schaab and bought a small steamboat to cart produce to Rock Island from Andalusia, eight miles downriver. The previous fall, the Army Corps of Engineers completed dredging the 4 1/2-foot channel from the mouth of the rapids to the Rock Island docks. Streckfus saw the efficiencies of using the river to transport goods and the advantage of being in the right place at the right time. He began the first daily freight service from Andalusia to Rock Island. When the channel work was completed three years later, Streckfus was the first to offer daily roundtrip riverboat service between Rock Island and Clinton. Black laborers were hard workers and wise to the ways of the river, and Streckfus was quick to hire them.

Streckfus purchased a larger two-deck steamboat to haul small freight and mail and to ferry passengers on the Rock Island-Clinton run. With a speed of 13 knots on still water, Streckfus had the fastest boat in the region. Making six stops along the way, the *Verne Swain* went upstream to Clinton in six hours and returned home in four. When business grew, Streckfus added an even larger third boat to his fleet, which he used for the stretch from Rock Island to LeClaire where passengers disembarked and boarded the *Verne Swain* for the second half of the trip to Clinton. Providing morning and afternoon runs to Clinton, Streckfus monopolized the passenger trade from the Tri-Cities north.

In 1901 Streckfus acquired the *J.S.*, the first paddle wheeler designed exclusively for excursions and passenger travel. A crew of 45 transported and serviced as many as 2,000 passengers at a time in luxurious style as she cruised from New Orleans to Saint Paul. When the *J.S.* burned, Streckfus replaced her with the even more extravagant *J.S. Deluxe*, which because of her grander size operated from New Orleans but only as far north as St. Louis where the Des Moines Rapids posed a navigational barrier to super-sized paddle wheelers. Entertainment on the *J.S.* was provided by men who paid a concession fee for the right to deal poker games, which ran 24-hours a day, and by black musicians from Louisiana, who played an improvisational music called jazz. The music was born in New Orleans but grew up along the river. Theories abound as to the etymology of "jazz," but the least obscene and least romantic is that when black musicians were asked what kind of music they were playing, they slurred "*J.S.*," the name of the boat they were working on. Originally, jazz was spelled "jas," later "jass," and finally "jazz."

In 1911 Streckfus moved his family of seven children from their home on 7th Avenue and 23rd Street to St. Louis, which was the hub of his Streckfus Steamers Company operations. His four boys became active in the business and ran the company's operations from New Orleans to St. Paul. In 1929 Streckfus Steamers purchased the *President*, which became their flagship. Advertised as the "New 5 Deck Luxury Super Steamer, Biggest and Finest on the Upper Mississippi," she tramped with no fixed schedule or published ports of call until 1941, hosting riverboat gamblers and those who enjoyed fine wine, liquor, and good music and who sought a rollicking Saturday night, get-away weekend, or a vacation on the Mississippi.

Throughout the Great Depression riverboat travel remained one of the primary amusements for those who could afford it. In 1938 Streckfus Steamers set out on the world's most ambitious excursion riverboat project. Completed in 1940, the *S.S.*

Admiral cost more than $1 million ($15.6 million). In her initial years during World War II, her travel was greatly restricted due to gas rationing. Operating out of St. Louis, the five-deck, silver-metal excursion boat could easily pass as an art deco object. She accommodated 4,400 passengers and was lavishly appointed — she even had air conditioning, which at the time was an outrageous guest perk. After the war, she became a popular daytime cruise and nighttime club destination, and when casino gambling came to Missouri in the early 1990's, the *Admiral* was refurbished with 1,200 slot machines and 60 card tables. Then in 2010, she was taken out of commission and sold for scrap metal.

After World War II, the *President* was taken to New Orleans where she operated as a popular nightspot until she was given a second life as a riverboat casino. In 1991 Iowa legalized riverboat gambling, and after having her smokestacks removed so that she could pass under the railroad bridge south of Rock Island, the President reopened in Davenport with 27,000 square feet of casino space. She was the nation's second riverboat casino. Thirty minutes before the first gambler boarded her, Bernie Goldstein, a longtime Davenport scrap iron dealer who had a prime riverfront location, opened the *Diamond Lady* in Bettendorf.

As the new century began, jazz moved north on the paddle wheelers up the Mississippi and Ohio Rivers and up the Missouri River as far as Kansas City. The complex, improvisational musical form, which arrived with African slaves, is held together by a distinctive West African drumbeat. Using European instruments, black New Orleans marching bands imitated the beats and music they brought with them from Africa and merged ragtime piano and blues notes and beats to create an American music that is as indigenous as baseball.

The music transcended racial and social lines and was embraced by everyone. Leon Bismark Beiderbecke, a white kid from Davenport, became one of the genre's geniuses. In 1907 as a four-year-old, "Bickie" was playing music he heard on the street on the family piano. Three years later, the Davenport Daily Democrat proclaimed: "Seven-year-old boy musical wonder! Little Bickie Beiderbecke plays any selection he hears." The music he heard was ragtime and jazz. It poured out of saloons and brothels onto the streets of Davenport and Rock Island, and some say it was so pervasive it was occasionally heard in Moline. By age ten, little Bickie was sneaking off to play piano and calliope with the black musicians on the riverboats when they tied up at the docks. At age 18, he moved to Chicago where he started going by the name "Bix." Playing improvisational piano and cornet, Beiderbecke formed an ensemble he named the Wolverines, and at age 21, he made his first of dozens of recordings.

At the same time young Beiderbecke was jamming on the docks with the jazz pioneers, a migration of Eastern European Jews began. Pushed out of czarist Russia by growing anti-Semitism, the United States offered unprecedented opportunity for social and economic freedoms that Jews hadn't known since Moses led them to the Promised Land. Between 1880 and 1920, 3.4 million Jews immigrated to the United States and of that number almost three quarters were from Russia. For $34 ($850) per adult or child, one-way steerage tickets could be purchased to the land of milk and honey. Steerage passage was an economic invention of German-Jewish shipmaster, Albert Ballin. Freighters from America bound for Europe typically carried heavy materials such as lumber from Weyerhaeuser sawmills or high-grade steel ingots from Carnegie mills, and had less cargo for the return trip. Instead of filling the holds of his ships with ballast, Ballin hit on the idea of using people. He fitted his empty cargo holds with rudimentary beds, and for three weeks his passengers didn't see the light of day until they reached New York Harbor. The shiploads of Jewish cargo that Ballin transported soon became a concern of the established second and third-generation New York Jews who were primarily from Central Europe and who had carved out a successful economic niche in the city. They were acutely aware that the penniless, Yiddish-speaking Russian immigrants would create an anti-Semitic backlash, not unlike what they escaped in Eastern Europe.

Always looking for another social issue to resolve, President Theodore Roosevelt approached his friend Jacob Schiff, a prominent Jewish financier and philanthropist. In one of their frequent conversations, Roosevelt observed that dense urban ghettos like New York's could only serve as a major provocation to immigration restrictionists, and asked if dispersing the new immigrants throughout the country wouldn't make good sense. Schiff rose to the challenge and pledged $500,000 ($12.5 million) to create a network that would transport European Jews to America's heartland. Distributing literature, written in Yiddish, throughout Eastern Europe that promoted the opportunities in America's West, Schiff selected Galveston, Texas, as his port of entry over New Orleans because he felt that the small town on a sandbar in the Gulf had few things to commend it as a permanent home.

What Galveston did have was the southern terminus of the Texas spur of the Rock Island Line, which had feeder lines throughout the Midwest. Starting in 1907 and lasting until World War I brought the "Galveston Movement" to an unfortunate conclusion, 12,000 Jews bypassed Ellis Island and rode the Rock Island Line directly to better lives. Writer and humorist/foodie Calvin Trillin describes his Uncle Benny Daynovsky's incredible journey from Kiev to Missouri by saying, "When I was a child I didn't realize that there was anything out of the ordinary in getting on a boat in darkest Europe, getting off in Galveston, Texas, and going straight to St. Joseph, Missouri."

No one knows how many Jews from Galveston stayed on the Rock Island Line until they reached the line's namesake, but those who did found a sizeable Jewish community already spread about in Rock Island's West End. By 1856 there had been enough Rock Island Jewish males to form the Young Men's Hebrew Association, and the Sons of Israel had organized in 1875. Opened in a fine brick building in 1902, Beth Israel Synagogue on 3rd Avenue was the region's first synagogue, and a decade later a second Jewish congregation purchased the Methodist Mission on 12th Avenue and opened the B'nai Jacob Synagogue.

Blacks who migrated north for better opportunities matched the numbers of newly arriving Jews. They settled into homes in Rock Island's West End that became available when German, Belgian, Swedish, and Jewish families started to move to the top of the hill after the first streetcar climbed 30th Street in 1891. The newly-arrived black migrants worked in menial jobs as house servants and janitors, they rode the trains as porters and baggage handlers, and they worked the docks and in the foundries and factories, where young, strong black males were able to land jobs that the Irish regarded as too hard or too dangerous.

In the large industrial cities rimming the Great Lakes, fierce competition for lowest-cost labor opened opportunities for blacks that were not available in Rock Island. Because black laborers depressed wages, intense resentments formed within communities of recent European immigrants who found that their tenuous grasp on the American dream threatened by blacks that understood English and were used to hard work. As a result, in most big cities, the working class immigrants defended their housing and work territories by strong-arm means. But despite the bigotry, blacks made substantial gains in the steel, automobile, shipbuilding, and meatpacking industries. In the decade after 1910, blacks employed in industry nearly doubled from 500,000 to 900,000. Rock Island did not see this same percentage increase in black population or employment, but it also did not see the racial violence and overt discrimination found in the big cities.

In 1920 a bumper cotton crop turned into an economic failure when prices fell from 42¢ a pound to less than 10¢. The next year prices recovered, but drought and boll weevil destruction ruined the crop. Within two years, cotton production in South Carolina fell by two-thirds, leaving blacks with no source of income, and the northern migration picked up in intensity. Then Mother Nature and the ever-growing levee system on the Lower Mississippi added to a northerly flow of black families. In the spring and summer of 1926 heavy rains pounded the Mississippi Basin. By September, at the time that the Mississippi and its tributaries are usually at their lowest levels, rivers in Kansas and Iowa had swollen and been backed up to capacity. Rains continued through the fall, and on Christmas Day, 1926, the Cumberland River at Nashville crested at a record level. Four months later, 15 inches of rain fell on New Orleans in 18 hours. The next month, the Mississippi River below Memphis reached a phenomenal width of 60 miles. Black men were conscripted at gunpoint to build levees and dikes, and unlike whites who were rescued and taken to refugee camps, black women and children were left to fend for themselves. Then after the floodwaters began to recede, blacks were forced to work on cleanup crews and provide free labor or were paid extremely low-wages for relief work. One black man was shot by a white police officer when he refused to unload a relief boat. To escape the wave of oppressive treatment, tens of thousands of blacks moved north, especially to Chicago.

Sociologist E. Franklin Frazier wrote of the black migrants that fled the South for Chicago, "Masses of ignorant, uncouth, and impoverished migrants flooded the city and changed the whole structure of the Negro community." Sadie Mossell, the first black woman to receive a Ph.D. in the United States and the first woman to receive a law degree from the University of Pennsylvania wrote that the Southern migrants "crushed and stagnated the progress of Negro life, early in the migration to Philadelphia." They might be right, but statistics show that like all first generation immigrants and migrants, Southern blacks that migrated North earned higher incomes than Northern blacks and were less likely to be on welfare; they were also more likely to be married and raise their children in two-parent households.

Although flood control techniques were not among them, the 20th century ushered in a wave of stunning technology. Thomas "The Wizard of Menlo Park" Edison invented the phonograph, the motion picture camera, and the long-lasting electric light bulb. He was one of the world's most prolific scientists and engineers and became a multi-millionaire from his flagship company, General Electric, and the 13 other companies he founded to produce his inventions — amazing accomplishments for a kid who was described as "addled" at age seven by his teacher during the three months of the only formal schooling he would receive. The youngest of seven children, Edison was home schooled by his mother and gained almost all the knowledge to satisfy his insatiable curiosity by reading and through trial and error experimentation. He taught himself virtually everything he knew about his passions in science, technology, and business, and he credited his mother's encouragement, confidence, and guidance as the reason for his success. He was once asked to sign a guest book that, in addition to the usual columns for name and address, also had a line for "Interested in." Edison entered a single word, "Everything."

As an adult, Edison developed strong opinions about education and believed that most schools taught children only to memorize facts. He thought that students should observe nature and make things with their hands. "I like the Montessori method," he said. "It teaches through play. It makes learning a pleasure. It follows the natural instincts of the human being. ... The present system casts the brain into a mold. It does not encourage original thought or reasoning."

Edison's business acumen emerged before his talent for invention. Hearing-impaired from a bout of scarlet fever, the young Edison sold candy and newspapers on the Grand Trunk Railway between his home in Port Huron, Michigan, and Detroit. As a 12-year-old, he started the first newspaper printed on a train, *The Grand Trunk Herald*, and distributed it daily along with his other papers. As a reward for saving the stationmaster's three-year-old son from being struck by a runaway train, he was given a job as a telegraph operator. This responsible position later led to several communication inventions, including the stock ticker.

At the age of 19, Edison moved to Louisville, Kentucky, where as a Western Union employee, he worked the Associated Press bureau news wire. To allow more time to read and experiment, he requested the night shift. Three years later, he received his first patent (he would receive 1,092 more) for the electric vote recorder. There was nothing Edison enjoyed more than working in his lab, and it was said that the only days he did not spend some time in it were Christmas and the 4th of July — but he did find time to father six children. He despised social events, and one time at an exceptionally tedious affair, he was maneuvering into position to escape from the formal dinner when the host intercepted him at the door and said, "It certainly is a delight to see you, Mr. Edison. What are you working on now?" "My exit," he replied.

Although Edison's inventions headed the list of technological breakthroughs of the first decade of the new century, they were not alone. The Brownie Camera (1900), radio (1901) electric typewriter (1901), air conditioning (1902), airplane (1903), player piano (1904), tractor tracks (1904), tandem-wing gliders (1905), jukebox (1906), color film (1907), photocopier (1907), dictation machine (1907), and plastic (1909) all took their places in the Technology Hall of Fame. The "auto-mobile" had been around since 1672 when a Jesuit missionary, Ferdinand Verbiest, built the first steam-powered vehicle. (The next year fellow Jesuit, Jacques Marquette, discovered the Rock Island Rapids.) Designed as a toy for the Chinese Emperor, Verbiest's auto-mobile was unable to carry a person but was the first steam-powered vehicle. And 231 years after the auto-mobile was invented, Mary Anderson invented the windshield wiper.

During the last decade of the 19th century, workshop engineers and mechanics designed scores of automobiles. Since no one had any idea what a motorized carriage should look like or what the most efficient design was, every motorcar was unique, and devices as obvious as the windshield wiper and the steering wheel were slow to become universal. When automobile windshield wipers were first installed, engineers were still making up their minds if steam, electricity, or gasoline should propel cars. And there was much controversy among engineers whether aviator's sticks, dual handles, or steering wheels were preferable for guiding automobiles around potholes. Henry Ford put to rest the engineers' arguments.

Ford was a bright lad who was born on a farm outside of Detroit. His father was from County Cork, Ireland, and his mother was born in Belgium. Henry was the oldest of five children, and all the siblings were raised as hard-working, devout Episcopalians. Young Henry hated farm work, and as a 16-year-old he went to work as an apprentice machinist in Detroit. While servicing steam engines for Westinghouse, he studied accounting at night. In 1888 when he was 25, he married Clara Ala Bryant, and five years later they had their only child who they named Edsel for the German word meaning "noble." In 1891 Ford went to work for Thomas Edison. Within two years he was promoted to Chief Engineer of Edison Illuminating Company, which gave him enough time and money to work on his own engineering projects. Three years later in a tiny workshop behind his home, Ford produced the "Quadricycle," a one-of-a-kind ethanol-powered motorcar with a 2-cylinder engine that generated four horsepower and a top speed of 20 MPH. It was so named because it rode on four bicycle tires.

In his spare time, Ford continued to dabble in automobile design and to build prototypes. Backed by financial partners, in 1899 he formed the Detroit Automobile Company, but because the cars were costly and inferior, the company folded within two years. With new investors, in October 1901 the Henry Ford Company built and successfully raced a deluxe 26-horsepower automobile. At the time, racing was the fastest way to prove a car's worth. The auto's instant success caused a rift between the financial partners; Ford left the company; and it was renamed the Cadillac Automobile Company. When Ford was designing the first Cadillacs, the best-selling car in America was the Jeffery Company's Rambler. In 1902 1,500 Ramblers were sold — they represented one-sixth of all U.S. cars.

The next year, Horatio Nelson Jackson, invented the road trip. In a heated discussion at San Francisco's University Club about whether the mechanically temperamental automobile was a passing fad, Jackson bet $50 ($1,200) that a four-wheeled machine could be driven across the country. The 31-year-old Jackson was planning a train trip with his wife, Bertha, in a few days to visit his family in Vermont. So also inventing the "you go ahead, and I'll bring the car" ploy, Jackson sent his wife on the train, while he drove. Since he didn't own a car or know how to drive, he must have been one smooth-talking son-of-a-gun. He also had no mechanical experience, so he hired Sewall Crocker, a young chauffer and mechanic, to teach him to drive and ride shotgun on his cross-country adventure. Jackson bought a used snazzy-red, two-cylinder, 20-horsepower, two-seater Winton and donning a dashing white canvas driving suit and goggles, five days after making his bet, Jackson left San Francisco for New York in an all-out attempt to collect his wager.

The daring young duo had no maps, but Jackson must have read his history, because he avoided the trail over the Sierra Nevada that the Donner Party had blazed only 56 years earlier, and he took the longer but easier and more northerly Oregon Trail. An excerpted chronology of their journey includes most of the same mundane things that all ill-prepared men encounter on roadtrips. Some highlights:

- 15 miles outside of San Francisco, they replaced the first of many blowouts with the only spare tire they could find before leaving.
- Outside of Sacramento, a woman misdirected them by 108 miles, so that some or her relatives could see their first car. (Since then, knowledgeable men have wisely refused to ask anyone for directions.)
- After getting back on track, an entrepreneurial farmer charged them a $4 ($100) toll to pass down the road that ran through his property.
- When they ran out of spare tubes and tires, they tied ropes around the wheels. (Supplies, spare tubes, tires, and parts were sent by train along the way.)
- After running out of gas in southern Oregon, Jackson bicycled 25 miles to fill a gas can. A tire on the bike blew out on the way back and he had to walk.
- Outside of Vale, Oregon, they ran out of oil. Jackson walked back to the last town to get more, only to find out that Vale was around the next bend.
- Near Caldwell, Idaho, a bulldog they named "Bud" joined them. Bud was fitted with goggles because road dust in the roofless, windshield-less auto bothered his eyes.
- As their progress was wired ahead, they became national celebrities, and they were enthusiastically greeted at every town.
- Jackson lost his coat with his money in it and had to wire home for more.
- Near Cheyenne, Wyoming, wheel bearings burned out, and Crocker had to talk a farmer out of the bearings from his mowing machine.
- After reaching Omaha, seven weeks after starting, the roads improved and the trip became less adventuresome.
- Two weeks later, they arrived to cheering throngs in New York City — and a very perturbed Mrs. Jackson.

- The two men completed the first cross-country automobile trip in 63 days, 12 hours, and 30 minutes. (In 1982 Lon Haldeman won the first Great American Bicycle Race from Santa Monica to the Empire State Building in 9 days, 20 hours, 2 minutes.)
- With logic that only adventuresome young men understand, Jackson spent $8,000 ($192,000) to collect a $50 bet — and for a lifetime of barroom stories.
- Joined by his two brothers who drove their cars to meet him for the victory lap to his family's home in Vermont, his brothers' cars broke down.
- As he pulled up to his house, the Winton's drive chain snapped.
- Not wanting to listen to Bertha's complaints on the drive back to San Francisco, Jackson settled in Burlington, Vermont, with Bud and her.
- Jackson became a successful businessman and was one of the founders of the American Legion.
- The Winton is in the Smithsonian.

The same year that 1,500 Ramblers were sold and Jackson established transcontinental motoring, Henry Ford received major financial backing from John and Horace Dodge to design an 80 horsepower muscle car. Learning from his marketing failures with his initial attempts, in 1902 Ford sponsored Barney Oldfield — the first man to drive a car 60 MPH — to attempt to set a world speed record in his Ford 999. On a frozen Michigan Lake, they succeeded in reaching the outrageous speed of 91.3 MPH. Ford then hired Oldfield to tour Ford dealerships that were being established from coast to coast and eventually were on every continent but Antarctica. Four years later, the Stanley Steamer smashed the land speed record at 127.7 MPH at Daytona Beach, and steam engines were the hot rodders' choice for the next few years. Twins Francis and Freeland Stanley had been made wealthy by the sale of their photographic dry plate business to Eastman Kodak, and the twins were among the first "car nuts." From 1897 until 1911, when General Motors engineers replaced hand cranks with starter motors on Cadillacs, their crankless automobile held a top position in the world of cars. Francis Stanley died in 1918 when, while racing down a country road, he drove his car into a woodpile trying to avoid horse-drawn farm wagons traveling side by side.

During the first decade of the 20th century, (much as today) five topics dominated Midwest male conversations — politics, women, technology, cars, and the Chicago Cubs. The Cubs were Major League Baseball's dominate team. The same year that the Stanley Steamer was setting speed records, the Cubs were setting baseball records. Finishing 20 games ahead of the New York Giants in the National League standings, the Cubs fell in the World Series to Chicago's American League team, the White Sox, 4 games to 2. Although they finished only 17 games ahead of the Pittsburgh

Pirates in 1907, the Cubs swept the Detroit Tigers 4 to zip in the World Series. To finish out the Senior Circuit three-peat, the Cubs nosed out the Giants and Pirates by a game for the 1908 Pennant and again drubbed the Tigers, 4 games to 1, for back-to-back World Championships — starting cries from the rest of baseball to break up the Cubs.

Three of the nation's most famous men were Joe Tinker, Johnny Evers, and Frank Chance. The graceful precision of the Cubs' double play combination during their Championship years made women swoon, men cry, and inspired great poetry by a forlorn New York Giants writer:

> These are the saddest of possible words:
> "Tinker to Evers to Chance."
> Trio of bear cubs, and fleeter than birds,
> Tinker and Evers and Chance.
> Ruthlessly pricking our gonfalon bubble,
> Making a Giant hit into a double –
> Words that are heavy with nothing but trouble:
> "Tinker to Evers to Chance."

Although most of the country was focused on the fabulous Cubs during the first decade of the 20th century, literary critics were praising Joseph Conrad's *Heart of Darkness* and Lucy Maude Montgomery's *House of Green Gables*, but real men were reading Jack London's *Call of the Wild* and Conrad's *Secret Agent*. Physicists were wrestling with Albert Einstein's Special Theory of Relativity, and the art world was selling their Art Nouveau and buying Art Deco and wondering what this Pablo Picasso guy was doing to fine art — subjects and subtleties lost on most Midwestern males.

In 1908, the last year the Cubs were to win a World Championship for a while, Ford introduced the Model T, which was one of the first automobiles to have the steering wheel moved from the center of the car to the left side. Other notable Model T firsts were that both the engine and transmission were enclosed; the four cylinders were cast in a solid block; the suspension used two semi-elliptic springs; the car was easy to drive and repair; and best of all, it was inexpensive to own. Unlike Benjamin Franklin and Thomas Edison who were inventors and scientists, Ford was a skilled engineer who invented little. He studied which designs produced the most efficient results, were the most durable, and provided the greatest value, then he implemented the best of what he found, and by systematizing the production process, he became the father of industrial engineering. As with most engineers, he was not overly into style and famously said, "Any customer can have a car painted any color he wants — so long as it is black."

By 1910 most of the automobile's functional design issues were worked out, and the gasoline-powered internal-combustion engine prevailed as the best source of propulsion. Fiercely intense competition sprang up among car manufacturers, and parallel-manufacturing companies across the continent jumped into the race against Detroit, which was establishing itself as Motor City, USA.

In the Tri-cities, spotting an emerging trend, Charles Deere — John's son and Deere & Company's second president — directed the company to diversify. At the Moline plant, during a fourteen-month period between 1906 and 1907, the company knocked out 100 handmade Deere Gentleman's Roadsters, which were as ruggedly reliable as a tractor and were of equally utilitarian design. Charles Deere died the same year Deere roadsters did, and in 1911 under Deere & Company's third president, William Butterworth, six noncompeting farm equipment companies were brought into the Deere organization, establishing the company as a full-line manufacturer of farm equipment. In 1918, the company purchased the Waterloo Gasoline Traction Engine Company in Waterloo, Iowa, and tractors rounded out Deere's full line of farm machinery.

In addition to founding a solid, innovative manufacturing company and providing well-paying jobs for thousands of Tri-City families, one of John Deere's grandest legacies was he was buried at the feet of the Black Angel, a statue of a shapely angel wearing a long, flowing dress who held a wreath in one hand and with the other pointed to the heavens — where presumably John Deere had ascended. Placed on the hill in Moline's Riverside Cemetery in 1906, the year before Charles Deere was interred at the family plot, the angel weathered with age and blackened — possibly in part by soot from the nearby Deere factories. Atop a stone pedestal, the angel was visited during the day by young children who wandered up from the swimming pool in Riverside Park. At night their adventuresome teenage siblings, who were mostly from Rock Island (apparently Moline's timid teens were too afraid of the well-known consequences) arrived by the carload to mix with teenagers from other schools, drink beer, make out — and defy the spirits entombed there.

Bold adolescent boys would coolly saunter up to the Black Angel, defiantly slap her on the backside, and stroll back beyond the hedge that surrounded the graves. Terrifying stories abound of those who tried to get away with more. One tale tells of a luckless young man from Iowa who wrapped his arms around the angel's shapely shoulders, planted a kiss on her black lips, and died on the spot. Another story regards a perverted Moline boy who squeezed her stone-cold breast and whose hand was completely severed the next week in shop class. It was also said that the angel could prophesize if a young person was doomed to eternal damnation. Supposedly, if you visited the statue by yourself after midnight and if you were not going to be joining John Deere in heaven after your death, the Black Angel would slowly turn and point to you and then to the ground. But these stories are unsubstantiated because few had the nerve to visit alone, and because there were no witnesses of those who did, their tales were not believed.

The story with the greatest credence, or at least the one that was most faithfully passed from high school class to high school class and was told to every first-time teenage visitor, was of the young woman, who as part of a sorority initiation, was tied to the statue one summer night and told that her prospective sisters would return in the morning to free her. After driving off and waiting for a suitably long time, the young women returned to free their pledge — only to find that they were murderers. Fatefully, the pledge hung in her bindings, a shriveled, white-haired and very dead old woman. Mercifully, the Deere family had the Black Angel removed from the family plot in the mid-1970s. Her present whereabouts is unknown.

By 1910 Deere's roadsters and dozens of other brands of handmade horseless carriages were chugging along the Midwest's muddy "auto trails" and automobiles quickly became the preferred means of private transportation for those who could afford them. East of the Mississippi River, autos were in high demand everywhere except in the big cities where traffic jams were ever-present and there was little parking. In 1912 Carl Graham, an Indianapolis headlight manufacturer and a principal investor in the Indianapolis Speedway was the first to promote the concept of an "ocean-to-ocean highway." The idea was put into action by the Lincoln Highway Association, and on July 1, 1913, the LHA "Trail-Blazer" tour headed west from Indianapolis in 17 cars and two supply trucks to scout the best route to California. To the cheers of thousands, 34 days later, they motored down San Francisco's Market Street.

Along the way, the LHA trailblazers were enthusiastically greeted in every town — it didn't take visionaries to see that being on the coast-to-coast highway would accrue similar economic benefits to those towns that benefited from having train depots on the transcontinental railroad. The LHA selected the Sauk Trail as the route for the Lincoln Highway through Illinois. Starting in the northwest corner of Indiana at Valparaiso, the ancient Indian trail ran northwest to Joliet, along the north bank of the Illinois River to Peru, and then crossed Central Illinois' checkerboard of farms to the Mississippi River. However instead of crossing the river on the Government Bridge, the association deviated from the traditional Sauk Trail and crossed on the two-lane, wooden-decked North Bridge that connected Fulton, Illinois, to Lyons, Iowa (originally called Little Rock Island and now the north section of Clinton), at the head of the Rock Island Rapids. The LHA's decision to cross the Mississippi at Clinton instead of Rock Island was a major chink in the city's title as the crossroads of the nation.

When the 13-state, 3,389-mile route of the Lincoln Highway was laid out and designated with distinctive red, white, and blue markers with a large "L," less than half of the transcontinental roadway was improved. The section of the Lincoln Highway from Atlantic City, New Jersey, to Salt Lake City, Utah, became the primary route of U.S Hwy 30 in 1926, when the system of U.S. Numbered Highways was created. The Lincoln Highway from Salt Lake City to Reno and over Donner Pass to San Francisco became an extension of U.S. Hwy 40. Six years after the Lincoln Highway was mapped, the U.S. Army dispatched 81 vehicles of every type of army transport including ambulances, motorcycles, and field kitchens to cross the country from Washington D.C. to San Francisco. Travelling over dirt roads from Illinois to California, the convoy of "24 officers, 15 Army observers, and 258 enlisted men" had 21 casualties on the 62-day, 3,250-mile excursion. (The Army completed the cross-country tour one day faster than Horatio Jackson had 16 years earlier when he made the first transcontinental trip.) No mention is made how the soldiers returned from San Francisco, but one of the officers, Lt. Col. Dwight Eisenhower, was so moved by the difficulties of transcontinental motoring that during his presidency 35 years later, he became the primary promoter of the Interstate Highway System.

To motor to the coasts or just about town, the automobile of choice for affluent Rock Islanders was the 3-on-the-floor, 334-cubic inch four-cylinder Velie 40, which was named after John Deere's grandson, Willard Velie. It came with a standard Splitdorf magneto and offered a choice of Hartford or Firestone tires — all for only $1,800 ($45,000). Believing that America's transportation future was in automobiles, not tractors, Velie started turning out hand-built cars in 1908 — the same year the Chicago Cubs won their second straight World Championship. Velie picked up where his uncle, Charles Deere, had failed. The Velie 40 was immediately successful, and Velie changed the name of the Velie Carriage Company to Velie Motor Vehicle Company. In 1910, 1,000 Velie 40's were sold, and a Velie truck line was started. A decade later annual car sales peaked at 9,000. The Velie line included the Velie Oakland and the Colt Runabout, which had a six-cylinder Continental engine, electric starter, Bosch dual ignition, glove box, dashboard light, and a speedometer that topped out at 50 MPH. In 1927 the company began producing aircraft, and in 1928 the Velie Company folded.

Custom-manufactured cars peaked in 1913, and at the February Tri-City Auto Show in Rock Island, 11 dealers showcased their new models. Then, Henry Ford changed manufacturing. Before his 1914 implementation of the concept of mass-producing interchangeable parts that were assembled on a moving production line, sticker prices ranged from $900 ($20,000) for 2-seat, low-end car models to $5,250 ($115,000) for an American Motor Company Traveler. Cars were not in the average

American's budget, and only one in 13 families owned one. By 1920, 240 automobile lines were competing for buyers; however, the following year the renamed Ford Motor Company reduced the price of the Model T to $310 ($3,900 in 2010 dollars — the 2010 price for a Model T restored to factory specs was $16,000 to $20,000). And in eight years, automobile ownership jumped to four out of five families. Unable to compete with the Model T price, Ford started the elimination of local auto manufacturers that the Great Depression finished off. When the United States entered World War II, only 17 automobile manufacturers remained, and their factories were soon converted to aircraft and military vehicle plants. Two of the companies, Ford and Willys, produced 643,000 Willys designed jeeps during the war.

Henry Ford's politics were high-profiled and exceptionally muddled — he was a Republican who embraced many Progressive ideals. He believed in "welfare capitalism," a form of industrial paternalism and social engineering where companies provided for all economic and social facets of their employees and their family's lives. In 1908 in a move that rocked Detroit, Ford offered a wage of $5 ($120) a day to all his workers who were with the company for longer than six months. The standard wage doubled what most of his employees were making. The idea was a stroke of genius. Ford Motor Company quickly garnered most of the sober, skilled labor in Detroit and created an intense loyalty to the company. However, the "profit sharing," as Ford called it, came with a catch: no labor union membership was allowed and each employee had to meet the standards of the Social Department, which frowned upon drinking (Ford thought it decreased productivity), gambling, and dead-beat dads. Fifty investigators, plus a support staff, were hired to keep tabs on the work force. But the social restrictions proved too arbitrary and difficult to enforce, and within a dozen years, Ford conceded that benevolent paternalism and control of workers' off-hours time had no place in industry.

Chapter 20

The Looney Years

Simplify, simplify, simplify! ~ Henry David Thoreau

WELL INTENTIONED, but misguided by their belief that they could change human nature for the better through good example and legislation, on January 16, 1919 Congress ratified the Eighteenth Amendment, which had been approved by the required 36 of 48 states and prohibited production of "intoxicating liquor." It was to go into effect one year later, and on October 28, 1919 Congress passed the Volstead Act, the enabling legislation for the Eighteenth Amendment and the common name for the National Prohibition Act. The act defined intoxicating liquor and listed the penalties for producing it.

That is the politically correct textbook version of the Progressive initiative to cleanse the nation of the socially debilitating effects of alcohol. Another view is that out of a confluence of a fear of blacks and immigrants, a hatred of Germans and their biermeisters brought on by World War I, rural resentment of big-city politics that increasingly dictated how federal tax dollars were spent, and a desire to rehabilitate the lifestyles of the working classes, crusading white women and supportive Protestant clergy, who wanted to make sure no one was having any fun anywhere, relentlessly pressured righteous politicians afraid to appear less than totally virtuous and ramrodded into place the only Constitutional amendment that was ever repealed.

The prohibition of alcohol production had no chance of success. Alcohol is as easy to make as baking bread, and about as popular with most adults. Religious factions of the Progressive Movement, who strongly believed they were implementing God's will and overcoming satanic influences, drove even deeper the wedge that had formed between themselves and the rest of society. Funded by donations, Prohibition leaders' three-generation crusade to outlaw alcohol had become an end unto itself, and Prohibitionists weren't prepared for a victory most thought they would never see. Little thought had been given and no planning had been done for its implementation. Supporters of the Amendment believed that once in place those who had opposed Prohibition would see the light and join them in championing the noble cause. One U.S. Senator summed up the Prohibitionists' view when he said, "There is as much chance of repealing the Eighteenth Amendment as there is for a humming-bird to fly to the planet Mars with the Washington Monument tied to its tail."

A belief that people would simply obey the law proved to be incredibly naïve, and the reality became the direct opposite of what Prohibitionists planned to achieve — few drinkers significantly reduced their alcohol consumption. Due to the closing of breweries, wineries, distilleries, and saloons, income tax decreased (six years earlier the Sixteenth Amendment had allowed the levy of an income tax); alcohol-related health issues and deaths increased due to alcohol poisoning from the consumption of rotgut alcohol and denatured spirits; state and federal revenues fell from the loss of tax revenue, and federal enforcement ballooned by a factor of five from a pre-Prohibition projection of $6 million per year to an actual $30 million ($385 million) in only three years. Saloons went underground and became speakeasies (New York alone had 30,000). Racketeering as a result of the unenforceable law was rampant and crime in the cities soared. Police corruption, which Progressives had been largely successful in cleaning up, exploded to unprecedented levels, and distilleries and breweries in Canada, Mexico, and the Caribbean flourished as did the fleets of boats and vessels that transported liquor across virtually unpatrolled border waters.

No government act in U.S. history generated as much crime as did Prohibition. It corrupted police forces and judiciaries to unimagined degrees, and produced criminal gangs that were organized in vertical integration from street thugs to prosecutors. Prohibition scofflaws were winked at, and some gangsters became cult heroes. Upscale speakeasies gained a high-society status that male-only saloons never enjoyed, and women flocked to the mobster-owned, private clubs that were safer than the streets outside them. And the risqué covertness of drinking forbidden whiskey and dancing to good music in private underground clubs jacked up the excitement factor.

Unlike Prohibition, women's suffrage was a long overdue concept that was gradually achieved over more than a century at state and local levels before the Nineteenth Amendment was ratified. The notion that women might be intellectually capable of casting an informed vote and should be included in the electoral process was first raised in the United States in 1756 when Lydia Chapin Taft was allowed to vote as a proxy for her recently deceased husband in Uxbridge, Massachusetts. Although no other woman was allowed to vote in a Massachusetts election for another twenty-three years, it was not lost on the citizens of Uxbridge that they had broken new ground and nothing terribly bad had happened. Another local, Abby Kelley Foster, who belonged to the Quaker Meeting at Uxbridge, led two budding suffragists, Susan B. Anthony and Lucy Stone, into the anti-slavery movement. And four years after Lydia Taft's death in 1778, America's first woman soldier, Deborah Sampson, enlisted in the Continental

Army. She was disguised as Robert Shurtlief of Uxbridge — irrefutably establishing Uxbridge as the cradle of women's rights.

No greater or more effective suffrage efforts were put forth than those by Alice Paul, Lucy Burns, and their National Women's Party. Paul was a remarkable woman. At age 16, she entered Swarthmore, a Quaker College founded by her grandfather, and after graduating with a B.S. in biology, she attended Columbia and then received an M.A. in sociology from the University of Pennsylvania. After studying in England at the Woodbrooke Settlement for Social Work, the University of Birmingham, and the London School of Economics, she returned to Penn and received a Ph.D. in sociology. While Paul was in London, she worked closely with Emmeline Pankhurst, the founder of the British suffrage movement. After being processed at a London police station for taking part in a suffrage demonstration at the entrance to Parliament, Paul met Lucy Burns, an equally impressive American who approached her when Burns saw an American flag pin on her lapel. Having attended Columbia, Vassar, and Yale, Burns was as well educated as Paul and as passionate about the cause of women's suffrage.

Taking Pankhurst's advice to "take the movement to the streets," the soul sisters (Burns was five years older than Paul), who were schooled by the world's best activists and experienced in the art of civil disobedience, returned to the United States and took their act to Washington where they joined the National American Women Suffrage Association as the leaders of its Congressional Committee. One historian wrote of Paul and Burns that they "were opposites in appearance and temperament ... Paul appeared fragile, Burns was tall and curvaceous, the picture of vigorous health. And unlike Paul, who was uncompromising and hard to get along with, Burns was pliable and willing to negotiate. Paul was the militant; Burns, the diplomat." Despite their stark differences, the couple worked together so effectively that their followers described them as having "one mind and spirit."

Before his narrow election victory in 1912, Progressive Woodrow Wilson told the NAWSA Congressional Committee that he supported their cause, and the NAWSA and their supporters limited their criticism of Wilson and the Democratic Party, which had given women's suffrage only marginally higher legislative priority than had their Republican counterparts. However on the eve of Wilson's inauguration in 1913, Paul organized a parade down Pennsylvania Avenue from the Capitol to the White House. Formed to draw attention to their cause and "in a spirit of protest against the present political organization of society, from which women are excluded" the march drew Helen Keller and more than 5,000 other women dressed in white, and included nine bands, four mounted brigades, and more than 20 floats.

District of Columbia Police were detached to provide a safe escort for the women, and a mostly male crowd of more than a half a million jeered and harassed them as they traveled the mile and a half route. The march took over six hours, and often the police turned their backs as the women were assaulted and even joined in on the mistreatment of the marchers. Pioneer female journalist, Nellie Bly, participated in the march and headlined her article "Suffragists are Men's Superiors." (Bly had become an international celebrity 25-years earlier when unescorted she beat by eight days Jules Verne's fictional circumnavigation of the world by Phileas Fogg in 80 days.) Senate hearings into the police misconduct resulted in the District of Columbia firing its police superintendent. Newspapers nationwide featured the stories and launched Paul and Burns' cause into national prominence.

More militant than the mainstream membership of the NAWSA, Paul and Burns split from the organization in early 1914 and formed the Congressional Union. Focusing on political support for pro-suffrage candidates, the Congressional Union claimed victory in unseating five incumbents in the November election. Gearing up for the 1916 elections, Paul formed a political party, the National Women's Party, to further draw attention to the cause. During the 1916 Congressional campaigns, issues such as suffrage and Prohibition lagged behind the primary issue of whether the U.S. should join World War I. Wilson opposed the war, was for Prohibition, and promised to support the goals of the NWP. Less than a month after his reelection, the Democratic president, who won because he kept the "nation out of war," gave a speech to a Democratic-controlled Congress praising their quick response to German submarines sinking U.S. freighters by entering World War I. In the initial Congressional speech of his second term, Wilson affirmed his support of Prohibition, but neglected to mention his promises to the women. When Paul, Burns, and a delegation from the NAWSA tried to meet with him to register their protest, he claimed to be ill. A few days later, he reneged on his vow to support suffrage and said he would not impose his private views on Congress.

Not to be trifled with, Paul took the fight back to the streets. Starting in January 1917, for two and a half years she and Burns and the Silent Sentinels, a group of more than 1,000 women, picketed the White House night and day except on Sundays. Although the placards the women carried were directed at Wilson and carried such inflammatory messages as "Mr. President, what will you do for woman suffrage?" and "We shall fight for the things which we have always carried nearest our hearts — for democracy, for the right of those who submit to authority to have a voice in their own governments," Wilson ignored the women. And in April 1917 when anger over entering World War I inexplicably broke out in verbal and physical abuse against the women, following the inaction of their Commander in Chief, the District of Columbia police did little to protect the protesters.

After ten weeks of escalating conflict, on June 22 police arrested two women picketers on charges of obstructing traffic. The charges were dropped. Then three days later, 12 women were arrested on the same charges. Each was sentenced to three days in jail or a $25 ($400) fine. To further focus public attention on their cause, they chose jail. Three weeks later, 16 more women were again arrested on the same charges. This time the judge upped the ante and sentenced the women to 60 days in jail or a $25 fine. Again, the women chose jail, and they were sent to Occoquan Workhouse in Virginia. In a major political faux pas, one of the women in the second arrest was Elizabeth Selden Rogers who was from an immensely powerful and conservative Massachusetts political family that dated back to John and Abigail Adams and had connections to almost every prominent New England politician since then. Three days after Rogers' arrest, Wilson pardoned the women.

For four months the harassment, arrests, and confinements continued, and then on November 15, 1917 all hell broke loose. Historian Barbara Leaming wrote:

> Under orders from W.H. Whittaker, superintendent of the Occoquan Workhouse, as many as forty guards with clubs went on a rampage, brutalizing thirty-three jailed suffragists. They beat Lucy Burns, chained her hands to the cell bars above her head, and left her there for the night. They hurled Dora Lewis into a dark cell, smashed her head against an iron bed, and knocked her out cold. Her cellmate, Alice Cosu, who believed Mrs. Lewis to be dead, suffered a heart attack. According to affidavits, other women were grabbed, dragged, beaten, choked, slammed, pinched, twisted, and kicked.

Burns and Paul led the women at Occoquan in hunger strikes and were painfully force-fed through their noses with feeding tubes. The press had a field day, and within two weeks all the women were released, and later the U.S. Appeals Court overturned their convictions. Altogether 68 Silent Sentinels were incarcerated at Occoquan — for obstructing traffic. Two months later, after the dust refused to settle, Wilson abruptly announced that women's suffrage was needed as a "war measure" (presumably, he meant World War I and not of the sexes). He urged his Democratic Congress to pass the legislation that was commonly known as the Susan B. Anthony amendment — Anthony and Elizabeth Cady Stanton had drafted the legislation 41 years earlier.

Two and a half years later the Nineteenth Amendment was ratified when Utah became the 38th state to vote for the constitutional amendment. Ten months earlier the Volstead Act had passed, and men were so angry that the price of beer had gone through the roof that it barely registered with them that "The right of citizens of the United States to vote shall not be denied or abridged by the United States or by any

State on account of sex." However disinterested as some men were, it is reported that women in speakeasies throughout the land raised a toast to sisters Anthony, Stanton, Paul, and Burns. The battle to pass the Nineteenth Amendment through Congress was not easily won. It had failed to pass the House of Representatives in January 1915, January 1918, and September 1918, but in each vote the opposition had narrowed. When suffrage legislation lost by a single vote in February 1919, victory was in sight. Four months later the amendment passed, and two months after that it was ratified by two thirds of the states. Although the law of the land for 50 years, the final states to ratify the Nineteenth Amendment were Georgia and North Carolina in 1970, Louisiana in 1971, South Carolina in 1973, and finally Mississippi in 1984.

Young women in the Northeast and in the big cities along the Mississippi and Ohio Rivers and those rimming the Great Lakes were already having a grand time as the '20s came roaring in. Men had returned victorious from four years of fighting the "Great War" in Europe, "normalcy" returned to politics as Progressives and their causes waned, the young discovered jazz, and "flappers" flaunted their sexuality and their new political and social freedoms by wearing short skirts, bobbing their hair, wearing makeup, driving automobiles, drinking and smoking — behavior that generally drove their mothers and grandmothers nuts and was not at all what they had in mind as they had grimly marched for suffrage and Prohibition.

During World War I, England and the United States were the only countries that didn't distribute condoms to their soldiers. As a result 400,000 American soldiers came home to their womenfolk with syphilis or gonorrhea — both diseases had less than effective cures at the time. Prior to the war, almost all condoms were made in Germany. However with the invention of penicillin still a decade off, even the Protestant and Catholic moral watchdogs that believed that STDs were God's punishment for sexual misbehavior turned a blind eye to the production and distribution of "rubbers" when their sons and daughters were swept into the epidemic. And in 1918, as the war concluded, a conviction against Margaret Sanger was overturned, and a federal judge ruled that condoms could be legally advertised and sold for the "prevention of disease only." To appease their righteous religious voters, a few states retained laws against buying and selling contraceptives, and advertising condoms as birth control devices remained illegal in all but 16 states.

Most religious crusaders believed that the cause of most immoral behavior was demon alcohol. However the Prohibition law that Progressives had fought so hard to enact was deeply flawed, and it will never be known if they were right. The Volstead Act did not prohibit the consumption of alcohol, so enormous quantities were stockpiled in the months before enactment, which smoothed the transition from legal to illegal liquor production. The act allowed up to 200 gallons of wine and fruit cider to be homemade annually — as if anyone was keeping track. To further punish German-Americans for emigrating from a militaristic nation, beer, even though lower in alcohol content than wine or cider, was not granted a homemade exemption. Physicians could prescribe pure grain alcohol for medicinal purposes, and they did so in astounding quantities. Two years after the law went into effect, Congress held hearings on the medicinal value of beer — few disputed its healing qualities, but prescribed dosages became an issue.

Semi-organized racketeers had influenced politics and ruled prostitution, drugs, and gambling in the big cities from the East Coast to Chicago since the Civil War, but Prohibition expanded organized crime to the West Coast and embedded it into heartland cities like Denver, Kansas City, St. Louis, Omaha, and Minneapolis where it had only a small presence before Prohibition. Overnight there was more than enough money from illicit liquor sales to spread around to all those willing to play by the underworld's rules. One of the first crime syndicates was the Jewish mob known as the Big Seven whose original members included Moe Dalitz of Cleveland, Longy Zwillman of New Jersey, Waxey Gordon (born Irving Wexler) and Nig Rosen of Philadelphia, Bugsy Siegel and Meyer Lansky from New York's Lower East Side, and Charles "King" Solomon from Boston's West End.

Jews did not have the same religious and cultural hang-ups about alcohol that goyim had. A leading Philadelphia rabbi at the time, Louis Wolsey, counseled, "The whole Prohibition question is a Protestant-Anglo-Saxon matter," and that Jews ought to avoid the whole mess. The Volstead Act also gave Jews a special dispensation to use wine for religious purposes, which gave Jews a kosher excuse to produce huge quantities of it — it's estimated that as many as half of the nation's bootleggers were Jewish — and for police on the take to overlook the great number of casks that were being used for sacramental purposes. The wine dispensation further exacerbated anti-Semitism, and Prohibitionists claimed that one of the chief sources of illicit liquor was Jewish religious wine that was "sold to Houlihans and Maguires" — there was some small truth in the exaggerated claims.

The mob's financial kingpin was New York's Arnold "The Brain" Rothstein. Called the Moses of gangsters, Rothstein gained notoriety and admiration among his gangland peers in the Black Sox scandal when he pulled off the impossible and fixed the 1919 World Series — the same month the Volstead Act passed. But his real influence lay in his organizational powers and his control over the financing he made available to those gangsters who played by his rules. Rothstein was the first to treat the rackets like big business, and he organized neighborhood gang leaders into cooperative business partners.

Prior to Prohibition, East Coast Sicilian-descended Mafioso co-existed peacefully with the Jewish mobs as each stayed within the bounds of their ethnic neighborhoods. Rothstein was the first to fully understand the enormous wealth to be made from Prohibition and how to capitalize on it. He envisioned expanding into all neighborhoods well beyond their ethnic borders, and he organized the gangs to implement his vision. Even before the Eighteenth Amendment passed, to head off territorial warfare, he had created a loose confederation between the Jewish mobs and New York City's Italian Broadway Mob headed by Joe Adonis and his henchmen Lucky Luciano and Frank Costello — Rothstein's brainchild evolved into the multi-ethnic (although mostly Jewish, Irish, and Italian) National Crime Syndicate which flourished into the 1950's.

Rothstein was a top-drawer guy. For a price, he supplied the Stork Club, the Silver Slipper, the 21 Club and every other upscale nightclub and speakeasy that insisted on quality whiskey and women with the best of both. While lesser clubs were fighting to get rotgut gin from bathtub distillers, Rothstein was supplying Canada's finest whiskeys. He bought into dozens of the high-class speakeasies he supplied, and he owned Manhattan, its politicians, and its police. He ruled the East Coast mobs until murdered in 1928 over a gambling debt that he had arrogantly reneged on. After his death, his understudies, Luciano and Lansky, took over the New York Syndicate, and after Prohibition they expanded their gambling operations into Havana and Las Vegas. New York never really took Prohibition seriously — although there are terrific pictures of well-dressed men being loaded into paddy wagons, of the first 4,000 arrests resulting from raids, there were only six convictions, and no one did jail time.

Chicago gangsters weren't as refined, as civil, or as organized as their Eastern counterparts. Instead they relied on brute force and intimidation tactics. In the two decades before Prohibition, the Market Street Gang (also known as the North Side Gang), which was centered in the Irish Near North Side neighborhood known as Little Hell, made their living as pickpockets, thieves, and labor sluggers. They expanded their menu of services when they worked both sides of the newspaper "circulation wars" between the *Chicago Tribune* and the *Chicago Examiner*, beating up newsstand owners who didn't carry both publications and then charging both the *Tribune* and the *Examiner* for their services.

Only 134 Federal Prohibition Unit agents were assigned to cover Illinois, Iowa, and Wisconsin. According to Chicago's Chief of Police, during Prohibition "sixty percent of my police were in the bootleg business." The Market Street Gang even had a well-organized apprentice division of juvenile delinquents called the Little Hellions who ran errands and collected numbers bets for the grownup hoods. One of the Hellions' graduates was Dean O'Banion who distinguished himself as the most powerful ward boss in Chicago and as the Italian South Side (also known as The Outfit) gang's chief rival in the Windy City's bootlegging business.

The organizer of the Chicago Outfit was Naples-born Giovanni "Papa Johnny" Torrio. Under Torrio's direction, Alphonse Capone, a smart, fearless thug from Brooklyn fought his way to the top of The Outfit. Capone, who was better known as "Scarface," ruled the gang, its customers, and the police with an iron hand — any dispute with Torrio's operation was certain to end in bloodshed caused by Capone and his lieutenants. Initially, the Irish Gang, who controlled gambling, prostitution, protection, and liquor north of the Loop, formed an uneasy alliance with the Italians on the South Side. But the working agreement deteriorated over territorial rights and finally disintegrated when O'Banion cheated Torrio out of $500,000 ($6.5 million) in a brewery deal. Although not his modus operandi, Torrio ordered O'Banion killed, and O'Banion was gunned down in his North Side flower shop. Of course, the Market Street Gang retaliated, and an assassination attempt on Torrio ended with Torrio near death, severely injured by five slugs to the body. He survived; and incredibly for a mob boss, he lived to the age of 75.

Leaving Chicago for the safer streets of New York, Torrio gave complete control of The Outfit to his protégé, Al Capone. Semi-retired, Torrio became a consigliore to Lucky Luciano who had moved on to establish the Genovese crime family. In Chicago, the brutal gangland war between The Outfit and the Northsiders boiled for several years. Although Capone ultimately won the bloody conflict, ruled Chicago's 10,000 speakeasies, and operated most of the Midwest's bootlegging operations, he was never freed from the threat of retaliation from his Chicago competitors or from the relentless pursuit by Bureau of Prohibition and revenue agents, who to most of the underworld's relief concentrated their enforcement efforts on Capone and Chicago.

One Midwest gangland operation Torrio and Capone never controlled was the Tri-Cities area and the Mississippi corridor north of St. Louis. That was in the tight grasp of John Looney. After fleeing to the fresh air at his 20,000 acre ranch in northern New Mexico, Looney had tired of the esthetic life and his spectacular failures as a rancher — one year he shipped in $100,000 ($1.7 million) of cattle, only to have them freeze and starve to death over the winter on his 7,500-foot-elevation ranch. The ranch was so remote that no one knew if Looney was ever there or not. He also started to wear disguises, but because of his diminutive build, ever-present sneer, and distinctive way of carrying himself, he was readily recognizable by anyone who had seen him only once.

After being run out of Rock Island by Mayor Harry Shriver when martial law was declared, five years later in 1917 Looney began sneaking back to civilization for short periods. World War I had spiked an already prosperous Rock Island economy by further stimulating Tri-Cities manufacturing, Arsenal munitions' production, and railroad and riverboat freight transportation. Also, higher factory wages, farm boys looking for a good time on Saturday night, and an influx of new workers stimulated Rock Island's building trades and the sprawl of saloons, brothels, dance halls, and cabarets. At the center of the 30-square-block Downtown District that extended between 2nd and 4th Avenues from 9th to 24th Street was the police station — possibly the most profitable business location of all — and sprinkled between the saloons and pleasure palaces were legitimate shops, markets, hotels, restaurants, and professional offices to take wages that didn't find their way to bartenders, card dealers, ladies of the night, and occasionally the collection plate.

Everyone was doing well. The lively red-light district — known simply as "The District" — thrummed non-stop along with saloon backroom card games, and the clang of bells and coins from Chicago's Mills slot machines drowned out the wail of losing gamblers. Policemen were everywhere. Paid on Mondays by saloonkeepers, madams, and card room managers, they served as on-duty security to control the drunks, protect the prostitutes, and break up fights. And they never had to buy a meal or a cup of Jo. Looney couldn't stay away.

After the riot that gutted the police station and the reputation of the force, former mayor William McConochie was returned to the mayorship in 1915. His first term had started in 1889, and the well-respected McConochie had served three non-consecutive terms prior to Shriver taking office. Hoping to reverse the wide-open, bawdy-town personality that Rock Island had assumed under Schriver and wresting the title of King of the Mississippi Honky-tonks away from Davenport, with the *Argus*' endorsement, McConochie took over a city that was hopelessly beyond the reform efforts of a part-time, 72-year-old mayor. Although apparently McConochie wasn't on the take during his fourth term, he may have been the only city official who wasn't. After four years of tilting at windmills, McConochie gave the mayor's gavel back to Shriver, which proved to be worse than putting the fox in charge of the hen house.

Mayor Shriver didn't suffer from the ethical compunctions of his predecessor, and knowing that he could control Looney, he welcomed him back to town with open palms. A strong case can be made that Shriver invited Looney back to town, and that Looney was simply a front man for a crooked city hall. Prohibition was a financial godsend for Looney, Shriver, his Chief of Police Thomas Cox, and most of the police force. If New York winked at Prohibition, it could be said that Rock Island rolled out the red carpet for the Eighteenth Amendment. Now everybody would share in the big money — there would be no liquor stamps to buy, and nationwide the price of a drink had doubled to 50¢ ($7) for well drinks and 75¢ for bonded liquor. The only losers were the working stiffs.

While the January 1920 passage of Prohibition threw most of the country into a paranoid state of hypocrisy, there were only minor changes in Rock Island's downtown saloons. The most noticeable was that liquor bottles were no longer displayed on the back bar but instead were kept under it. And because beer was stored in kegs, concealing it was an issue that drove the price of beer to the level of mixed drinks, turning beer drinkers to hard liquor. However, in Rock Island often the suds that came from the root beer or near beer taps tasted remarkably similar to the German lagers that had previously flowed from them.

From a historical perspective, unquestionably Shriver was the man in charge. He had a seasoned police chief and obliging puppet in Tom Cox who had worked his way up from patrolman and who was intensely faithful to the mayor. Shriver had handled Looney during his first term, and he knew full well what he was dealing with when he let Looney and his gang back into town. When Looney blasted back onto the scene only weeks after Shriver was returned to office, it was as if the calendar was rolled back to 1912 — with the exception that Mayor Shriver, Chief Cox, and Looney were on the same side of the law.

Whether by Intelligent Design or ironic coincidence, at the same time the Volstead Act passed, Billy Sunday, America's most celebrated and influential Christian evangelist was midway through a seven-week gig at a temporarily built tabernacle at the corner of 5th Avenue and 24th Street. Sunday had grown up in Davenport at Iowa Soldier's Orphans Home — just a leisurely walk up the hill from Bucktown. Having developed into an outstanding track athlete and baseball player, Sunday played eight seasons in the National League — five with the Chicago White Stockings — when it was the only major league. A lifetime .248 hitter from the leadoff spot, Sunday was known for his defensive play in the outfield and as a base stealer. In his final season in 1890 he stole 84 bases in 117 games. Immediately after leaving baseball, the dapper Sunday discovered the Lord and devoted the rest of his life to doing His work.

Developing his preaching skills as a "pulpit evangelist," Sunday toured the "kerosene circuit" (those towns without electricity) in Iowa and Illinois. After preaching stops of a month or two in more than 70 rural communities over a dozen years, Sunday was ready to take his frenetic act to the national stage. Managed by his wife Nell, he became a "nationally renowned phenomenon" with a traveling show of 26 advance men, support staff, musicians, chorus leader, and music director who auditioned and rehearsed local choirs and gospel singers to accompany Sunday.

Between 1915 and 1917, Sunday often teamed up with Virginia Healey Asher, a gospel singer and America's most famous female evangelist. Riding the Prohibition bandwagon, Sunday toured the East and captivated audiences in every major city. The press loved Sunday's traveling salvation show and often printed his sermons word for word, pushing World War I news to the second page. In his peak years from 1908 to 1920, Sunday reported a net income of more than a million dollars ($15 million) — all from donations left on the collection plate during his appearances. The Sundays lived a plain lifestyle and contributed large amounts to diverse Christian charities. Among his friends, Sunday counted John D. Rockefeller, Presidents Theodore Roosevelt, Woodrow Wilson, Herbert Hoover, and countless athletes, movie stars, and musicians.

When the evangelistic road show got off the train in Rock Island in September 1919, Sunday was at the height of his career. His crusade against alcohol was still radiating with success, and the vicious backlash that reformers would encounter when the realities of Prohibition set in had not yet fomented. Before leaving Chicago, Sunday announced that he was on his "way to kick the devil out of the Tri-Cities — Rock Island, Moline, and Davenport." Deeply tanned and immaculately dressed in a tailored suit that accentuated his athletic body, the handsome and charming Sunday met the throng that greeted his homecoming by saying, "Rock Island, that citadel of sin, is the wickedest city in the United States of America, bar none (apparently he didn't include his hometown in his survey). And the leader of that wickedness is John Patrick Looney."

Delivered in charismatic, rock star-style to predominantly female audiences that ranged from 6,000 to 12,000 — one "women only" sermon drew 11,000 — Sunday's fiery but folksy fundamentalist sermons focused on the devil's tools of male vices, booze, and Communism. During the nearly two months he preached in Rock Island, more than 10,000 pledged to convert and become Christians. The orphan from Davenport left town a hero to the righteous and $20,000 ($250,000) richer — his cut of the $48,923 dropped on the collection plate. This was at a time when the average Rock Island laborer was making about $1,000 a year. Sunday's parting words were, "I think some of the finest people in the country live here — and one or two of the meanest."

Down the street from Sunday's large, specially-built tabernacle, Helen Van Dale and Jenny Mills, Rock Island's cooperative and most successful madams, operated their houses on the meandering red-light strip. The difference in dress, manners, conduct, and somberness of the proper women who lined up to watch Sunday deliver his impassioned evangelical pitch and those that were working just down the street cannot be overstated. At the same time Sunday was warning the faithful of the eternal damnation that would befall the pleasure seekers who indulged in the devil's deeds, an estimated 150 saloons, gambling parlors, and brothels were actively engaging in the devil's work in the rollicking two-block wide corridor that roughly began at the steps of St. Mary's Catholic Church and ended at the door of St. Joseph's Catholic Church.

A recovered Catholic, Helen Van Dale boasted that she turned her first trick when she was 16. Born in Paris, Illinois, the nuns at Galesburg's St. Mary's School thought of her as a bright girl who was an avid reader and strong public speaker. Van Dale came to Rock Island as Katherine Helena Lee, and shortly after her arrival she went to work for Jennie Mills, who taught her the business side of her new profession. Mills was an established madam who ran an orderly brothel on the corner of 3rd Avenue and 22nd Street. She was one of the few operators from The District during Rock Island's "Crazy Years" of the 1920's, who survived. She conducted her business from the same location for more than 40 years until her death at age 87 in 1958 — she was a good-hearted woman who appeared to contribute more to charitable causes than she paid in police protection.

Starting as a lone wolf hooker before going to work for Mills, by the time the stunningly attractive Van Dale was 30, she was known as the "Queen of the Brothels" and had a stable of 300 high-class women working for her in a half dozen houses between Davenport and Rock Island. She was described by a government agent as "one of the most interesting madams in the annals of prostitution." Although Van Dale paid for Looney's protection in Rock Island, she also supplied women to mob-run clubs and brothels throughout the Midwest, including Papa Johnny Torrio's Chicago Outfit. Because of her reputation, women wanting to get into the trade sought her out, and for a fee she placed them in good hands — possibly becoming the region's first employment agent.

Until 1915 Davenport was unarguably more wide-open, low-class, and decadent than Rock Island. Because Iowa's economy was totally farm-based, Des Moines legislators from 89 rural counties gave little attention to the needs or regulation of the Mississippi River towns in the ten counties bordering Illinois. They had the votes to control the state, and they neither understood nor cared what the city-folk along the river were up to. Church-going farmers were disdainful of the sinful lifestyles they saw on their rare trips to the Eastern Iowa cities, and the concept of anyone objecting to closing bars after midnight was as foreign to them as paying ten times the price of a good horse for a fragile automobile that wouldn't last nearly as long.

In 1907 Davenport mayor Harry Phillips realized that if the city didn't clean itself up, the Feds would. T.H. Kemmerer, a low-level lawyer who represented the Ministerial Association, had pressured Phillips to enforce the laws or the Association would complain to their Congressmen. Davenport didn't have a large reform agenda, but on behalf of the Association, the lawyer pressured the mayor to issue a midnight closing order for saloons, which created a fabulous scam for Kemmerer and his high-profile law partner C.W. Neal. The con was simple: Kemmerer would issue a complaint against one of the 240 Scott County saloon owners. and his partner, Neal, would represent the saloon owner who paid court costs plus a $25 ($625) fine that was paid to the attorneys, enriching Kemmerer, Neal, and the city and giving city hall the appearance of respectability. The legal scam netted the attorneys $6,250 ($155,000) in fees in a single year.

At first the transparent hustle met with mild protest from some of Davenport's citizens, and most who cared saw the rip-off hurting no one but the saloon owners. However one indignant citizen, A Richter, rose up. Richter was the editor of the *German Demokrat*, and he was especially outraged by Neal and Kemmerer's shakedown and the tepid response his editorials had received from the public. On a chance meeting with Kemmerer on Brady Street, Richter imprudently broke his cane over Kemmerer's head. Kemmerer swore out a complaint with Neal appearing as his attorney. Arrested, Richter demanded a jury trial, and while the parties were hurling accusations at each other in the magistrate's office, outside on the street the simmering pot of moral correctness boiled over.

News of the arrest had quickly spread, and a crowd assembled. After an outraged citizen delivered an impassioned speech, a hat was passed to collect money for a new gold-headed cane for Richter. When Neal, who was the more prominent of the law partners, emerged from city hall, he was greeted with shouts of "kill him, hang him, tar and feather him, throw him in the river, take him to Rock Island!" Pulling his Colt automatic from his belt, Neal faced the crowd. They backed off, and he fled to his law office. After seeing Neal wave his gun about, another citizen went into the magistrate's office and swore out a complaint against him for carrying a concealed weapon. Neal was arrested, dragged into court, and fined $5 ($125), which enraged the throng that had flooded the courtroom to see justice served. After hiding out under police protection at the Masonic temple, the next day Neal was escorted by the police to the train depot, where to the accompaniment of a 20-piece band, he was bid good riddance. Neal died a few years later at a Soldiers' home in Seattle.

On January 1, 1908, Scott County had 240 licensed bars. During the previous year, Mayor Phillips was successful in shuttering Davenport's whorehouses and card rooms and removing slot machines from cigar stores. Though it wasn't until Richter made his stand for righteousness that reform-inclined residents banded together and formed the Civic Federation. One of their first accomplishments was enforcing the closing time for liquor service and sales that put a halt to "never-closed" saloons. The law was selectively enforced, weeding out the worst offenders and those that didn't pay for the police to turn a blind eye. After two years of closing-time enforcement, 26 of Scott County's 49 bars were shut down and 40 of the Davenport's 191 bars were closed. None of Bucktown's saloons were closed, but New Year's celebrations in 1909 found Davenporters without slot machines, card rooms, and whorehouses, and Mayor Phillips had done the improbable and made Bucktown even sleazier by crowding the gamblers and hookers into Bucktowns saloons' basements and attics.

In March 1909, representatives of Iowa farmers forced through a law that limited the number of licensed saloons to no more than one per 1,000 residents. Ironically, the law helped Davenport. Virtually unknown and of no real concern to the legislators in Des Moines, the towns of Dubuque and Davenport were chartered when Iowa was a territory and their charters exempted them from the law. Not to be outmaneuvered by foresighted city slickers, in 1913 a second restriction act was passed that even the two river towns fell under. Iowa's Prohibitionists were among the nation's most fervent, and in 1915 they were successful in repealing a state law that allowed the licensing of saloons, and by its repeal affected the prohibition of "alcohol, ale, wine, beer, spirituous vinous, and malt liquor" throughout the state. The law went into effect on New Year's Day 1916 and was immediately tested by three Davenport saloonkeepers, but the law was upheld by the Iowa courts.

Iowa suffered under some of the nation's most draconian liquor laws until 1987. To Rock Island's liquor stores benefit, after Prohibition ended in 1933, Iowa became a "control state" in which liquor was sold only through state-operated retail stores — and at a much higher price than in Illinois. When Iowa finally turned retail liquor stores over to private enterprise, it continued to maintain the role of middleman. And in 2010 the Iowa Alcoholic Beverage Division sold 4.4 million gallons of liquor worth $210 million to the state's almost 500 liquor stores and bars.

One of the bar owners most hurt by Iowa jumping the gun on Prohibition was Anthony Billburg. After moving across state to Davenport from Centerville, Iowa in 1905, Billburg, a monster of a man, worked as a bartender and bouncer in Bucktown. He was a rawboned Iowa farm boy who was big and strong, and he had a mean streak that was complemented by a hair-trigger temper. One of his saloon bosses said of him, "In a fight, I'll take Billburg — you can have five other guys." In addition to having the disposition of a cage fighter, he was a smart, hardworking businessman with a supportive wife, Margaret, who later became the madam in his Rock Island brothels. Billburg was also one of best poker players north of St. Louis. Always congenial as he raked in pots in the high-stakes games on Davenport's Pretzel Alley (the narrow alley between Main and Harrison that ran from 3rd to 4th Street), he made friends with the Tri-Cities' powerbrokers as he took their money.

When Mayor Phillips closed down the card rooms, Billburg and many of his pals moved their games across the river to Rock Island. He bought most of the block between 2nd and 3rd Avenues on 20th Street across from Spencer Square and opened a brothel and two saloons that fronted the city's highest stakes poker games. However his crowning glory occurred 1915 when on the corner of 3rd Avenue and 20th Street, he opened The New Billburg with "The Longest Bar in the World." The ornate, brick building that ran along 3rd Avenue housed a polished mahogany bar that was 117 feet long. Crystal chandeliers reflected light from the decorative tin ceiling, the cut glass shelves and whiskey bottles, and through the large beveled-glass windows facing 20th Street. Billburg added windows, so that everyone could see that he ran a clean, upscale, and honest business, and so that wives, who were forbidden to enter, could check on their husbands. The narrow saloon had a row of slot machines that ran along the wall opposite the bar and ended at a sumptuous carving station. Here for the cost of a nickel beer, customers dined on a "free lunch" of roast beef and ham.

The world's longest bar didn't have a single barstool. Billburg's philosophy was that when a patron could no longer stand at the bar, it was time to go home — and it allowed more customers to pack themselves into the always crowded saloon. Billburg's grandson told the story of how his grandfather had tossed a drunk that failed the sobriety test only to have him appear at the side door. Booted again, the drunk staggered down the block to the rear entrance where Billburg accosted him a third time. Shaking his head, the discouraged man muttered, "My God, man, do you run every saloon in town?" But then invoking wartime powers, in 1918 the Feds closed the high-class barroom and all other saloons within a three-mile radius of the Arsenal. Prohibition followed the war and the magnificent bar never reopened. In 1935 it was leveled and replaced by a used-car lot.

While Iowa Prohibitionists were cleaning up their state, James Mann, a U.S Representative from Chicago and a University of Illinois graduate, was successful in throwing a kink into Helen Van Dale's business operations. Passed in June of 1910, the White-Slave Traffic Act, better known as the Mann Act, prohibited interstate transport of females for "immoral purposes." Aimed directly at the Queen of the Brothels who was supplying women to a half dozen Midwest states, Van Dale was later charged by the Feds under James Mann's law. In addition to prosecuting prostitutes, the law's ambiguous language was selectively used until the 1980's to criminalize consensual sex between bigamists, especially in Utah, and interracial couples in the Deep South.

One of the first prosecuted under the law was black Heavyweight Boxing Champion, Jack Johnson. At a time when boxing was bigger than baseball, Johnson had an affair with a white prostitute, but the case was dropped when the prostitute — who later became his wife — refused to testify against him. Not to be thwarted by "the most famous black person on earth," less than a month later the government re-arrested Johnson for crossing a state line with another prostitute — an act that was committed before the Mann Act was passed. Before Federal Judge Kenesaw Mountain Landis, this prostitute testified against Johnson, and he was convicted and sentenced to the maximum penalty of a year and a day in prison.

Johnson was hated by whites. After winning the heavyweight title from Australian Tommy Burns in December 1908, Johnson defended his title against one "Great White Hope" after another. In 1910 former undefeated champion James Jeffries, saying that he felt "obligated to the sporting public at least to make an effort to reclaim the heavyweight championship for the white race," was enticed out of retirement for a reputed guarantee of $120,000 ($2.7 million) to fight Johnson. On the 4th of July 1910 in downtown Reno, Nevada, 20,000 people gathered to see "The Fight of the Century." In the 15th round, Johnson knocked Jeffries down for the first two times in his career. The referee stopped the fight, and after receiving the $65,000 ($1.5 million) purse, Johnson left Reno as one of the world's wealthiest black men. White men felt humiliated by the defeat, and there were race riots from Reno to New York.

One of the first celebrity athletes, Johnson earned incredible amounts of money through endorsements, exhibitions, and personal appearances. He once displayed his flamboyance and arrogance when he was pulled over speeding and peeled off a $100 bill ($1,500) for the $50 ticket. The arresting officer protested that he couldn't make change for a bill that large. Johnson told him to keep the change, as he was going to make his return trip at the same speed. In 1920 Johnson opened a nightclub in Harlem — he sold it three years later to a gangster who renamed it the Cotton Club.

The same year Johnson opened his nightclub, Kenesaw Mountain Landis was double dipping as a federal judge in Chicago and as the first Commissioner of Baseball. As commissioner, Judge Landis expelled eight Chicago White Sox from baseball for life because of their roles in the Black Sox scandal. Included in the expulsions was Joseph Jefferson "Shoeless Joe" Jackson, who over his 12-year career hit .356, the third ever-highest career average. Landis ruled baseball with an iron hand until his death in 1944 and was responsible for maintaining Major League Baseball's color line, which Jackie Robinson broke three seasons after Landis finally left his position when he died.

Illinois state law had made prostitution illegal, but brothels operated in the open in Rock Island, making it necessary, on a recurring basis, to randomly close them for short periods and to run the madams into court. This legal farce gave the *Argus* evidence of the positive results of their relentless editorializing to clean up The District and rid the city of sin. But while hearings were held and fines were levied, few were jailed and houses were seldom closed for more than a few days and never for a Saturday night. Because Helen Van Dale always had multiple brothels going 24/7 on both sides of the river, a raid of one of her houses had little effect on her operations — the women just packed an overnight bag with their cosmetics and teddies and walked down the block. Van Dale was a haughty crusader against hypocrisy. Once when she was going through the courtroom charade, the prosecuting attorney asked her if she had ever been a prostitute. She retorted, "You should know. You were in my house." Another time when testifying in a case brought against some of her employees, the prosecutor asked if she signed the register when she signed in a customer. She answered incredulously, "Of course, just like I did with you when you went there." The court soon learned to leave her alone.

There may have been no man in The District who was the quick-witted Van Dale's equal or who was as respected and beloved as an employer. She was a razor-sharp businesswoman who placed and incented her employees as if they were selling retail goods in a department store. The women who worked for her were continually graded on their looks and charms and on their ability to make money. Attractive women made $5 a trick plus tips, while their less seductive sisters made half that — the house kept half of the base fee, which was paid to the madam. It was common for an experienced, high-class prostitute to make $100 ($1,250) a week — five times as much as a Deere & Company laborer. One woman who left Chicago for a better life in Rock Island said, "Things is fixed in this here town of Rock Island. In Chicago, the coppers was always chasing us, but down here we're all setting pretty. A girl that knows her stuff can make money in Rock Island when The District is wide open."

For a short while, it was no more open to anyone than to John Looney. He assured that Mayor Shriver, Chief Cox, the beat cops, and the judges were paid well, which kept him politically secure and out of jail. And he was a master of intimidation, which kept him physically safe. He hired top "muscle" for his personal bodyguards, to collect his protection money, and to oversee his operations. Although he dabbled in gambling, stolen cars, and extortion, protection and bootlegging were his primary businesses. To run those operations he partnered with a huge black man, Emeal Davis, who came to Rock Island while working as a gandy dancer driving spikes for the Rock Island Line. Davis ran several black clubs and brothels of his own, and besides being an impressively big man, he was ruthless and violent. No job Looney gave him was too big or too vile for Davis. He kept Looney's enemies at bay, moved his stolen cars west, kept the Bel Aire arsenal stocked with knives, brass knuckles, and guns, but most importantly, he was in charge of collections and transportation of booze and women.

Unlike the railways, highways, and country roads, the Mississippi was solely under federal jurisdiction and was impossible to police. Black men worked the river's docks, and through his contacts, Davis was able to freely transport liquor and prostitutes from Missouri to Wisconsin. Looney owned a large freight launch, *Marithia*, which Davis used to haul flesh and kegs up and down the river. Bootlegging was not complex. Looney bought a gallon of drinkable whiskey from his distillers for $3. He sold it to the Tri-City saloons for $8, and saloon owners sold it by the drink for $30 a gallon — ten times what Looney had paid for it the day before. It's estimated that weekly $20,000 ($250,000) of untaxed liquor passed over Rock Island's bars.

All business was done on a cash basis and payment was due on delivery. There was no surer way to go instantly out of business than to miss a payment. To the unsophisticated Looney, the rackets seemed simple — no paperwork to keep track of and no taxes to pay. What Eastern mobsters, Arnold Rothstein, Meyer Lansky, and Lucky Luciano understood that the rube mob bosses in the Midwest didn't was that illicit profits had to be "legitimatized" and taxes had to be paid, or the government would put an end to the enterprise — Al Capone ended up spending almost as much time wearing prison garb for tax evasion as he did wearing silk shirts. The Northeast mob survived because they learned how to finance expansion and new operations, and they knew how to "launder" dirty money through legal businesses — and they got along.

Northeastern Jewish and Italian gangsters kept to what they knew, and they worked cooperatively. Their heritages and goals were complementary. They had arrived penniless at Ellis Island, they spoke languages that the natives couldn't understand and resented, they were brown-eyed and dark-skinned, and they were not Protestant Christians. They formed tight communities where godfathers and kvatters deferred to priests and rabbis, and they took care of their own. Their tight communities were a necessity, not a convenience, and they were steeped in customs and traditions that they weren't going to change because some blue-eyed cop with an aquiline nose said otherwise. Both of the late-to-arrive ethnic groups were family-centric, Jewish and Italian men respected their women and entrusted the raising of their children to their wives, and after puberty boys and girls married for life and propagated the millennium-old roles and traditions of their fathers and mothers.

To both ethnicities, America offered undreamed of freedoms, opportunities, and unimagined wealth that weren't available in the Old Country. They laughed at the grim Protestant ethic founded on the belief that God put man on earth to prove himself worthy of heaven. To believe that God rewarded a woman for not having sex, that a wager on a game of chance was immoral, and that the devil lived in a bottle of vino were foolishnesses that only presented opportunity — and they banded together and seized it. Jewish gangsters understood finance and human nature, and Catholic Italian Mafioso understood obedience and enforcement. Together, they were the perfect fit to capitalize on America's new rules — Jews managed the back office and Italians ran the streets. Jewish and Italian immigrants grew up with respect for authority; they strongly believed in God and tradition — and they were used to defending their beliefs. Importantly, they weren't greedy and they didn't flaunt their successes.

John Looney had none of the qualities of the Eastern bosses that he desperately wanted to be like. He was godless, brash, egotistic, insecure, unprincipled, and respected no one. In the final analysis, Looney may well have been nothing more than a mean-spirited little punk who got by on nothing more than chutzpah. Looney's second run at the rackets in Rock Island lasted for just over three years. One of his enterprises was a nationwide stolen-car ring. He used Rock Island as the collection hub for cars stolen by gangs throughout the Midwest. Often the cars were driven to Mexico, where the drivers would trade them for drugs that were brought back to Rock Island and fetched Looney a far greater return on his modest investment than the outright sale of the car.

Although not as high profile as the Volstead Act, another of the Progressives' political victories, the Harrison Narcotics Tax Act of 1914, made it illegal for anyone other than physicians to prescribe and pharmacists to sell products made from opium or coca leaves. Although more whites than blacks were addicted to opium and cocaine, the general attitude of the country reflected that of Christopher Koch of Pennsylvania's State Pharmacy Board when he testified that, "Most of the attacks upon the white women of the South are the direct result of a cocaine-crazed Negro brain." And just before Congress overwhelmingly passed the Harrison Act, the New York Times headlined an article by Edward Huntington Williams: "Negro Cocaine 'Fiends' Are New Southern Menace," with the sub-headline, "Murder and Insanity Increasing Among Lower-Class Blacks." The article reported that Southern sheriffs had increased the caliber of their weapons from .32 to .38 to bring down Negroes under the influence of cocaine. The Harrison Act opened up another source of revenue for Looney.

When still new to town in 1907, Anthony Billburg befriended John Looney. Billburg was shrewd enough to know that he was better off patronizing Looney than fighting him, and he lived by the Sun Tzu axiom: Keep your friends close, and your enemies closer. The men became associates of convenience, and as such, Billburg became Looney's first in command. After taking office for his first mayoral stint, Harry Shriver misjudged Billburg and initially harassed him instead of Looney with constant raids and closures of his 20th Street operations. Even though Billburg had a terrible temper when dealing with foolish men who crossed him, he kept his cool when money was involved, and he manipulated Looney into eventually taking the major heat from Mayor Shriver. After Looney was chased out of town following the 1912 riot, Billburg quietly became Rock Island's top crime boss — and he and The District prospered. Unlike Looney, Billburg was uninterested in the extortion rackets, and he left the collection of protection money up to the police, politicians, and judges.

For six years after the 1912 riot, which had greatly reduced the police's image and authority, and until Looney and his ego returned to town to live fulltime and revive his old newspaper, the *Rock Island News*, peace reigned in The District. With The New Billburg saloon as their centerpiece and Anthony Billburg as their boss, District businesses operated in a competitive environment free of violent crime. Not content to operate as an equal, Looney quickly stirred up the status quo by restarting his protection business with the low-end saloons and brothels. With the thinly covert cooperation of Mayor Shriver and Chief Cox, Looney rapidly moved up the pecking order, and when the Volstead Act went into effect, he vaulted once again to the top.

Looney controlled the regions' bootleg liquor, and if a saloon owner wanted to serve anything stronger than near beer, he had to deal with Looney. During the time of Looney's second reign, there were no speakeasies in Rock Island. Secrecy and privacy weren't required — at a high price, saloons operated without peepholes and passwords — they just didn't openly display their liquor. This probity helped lead to Looney's downfall. Obvious and easy prey for the woefully understaffed Bureau of Prohibition, Rock Island in general and John Looney in particular became targets of bureau agents. Looney also put himself in the cross hairs of local fellow gangsters who resented his monopoly of the bootlegging business and his protection scams.

In the 30 months between the passage of the Volstead Act and when it all unraveled for Looney, sides were clearly drawn. Looney was on one side with Mayor Shriver and Chief Cox and everyone else in The District was on the other. One of the saloon owners who balked at Looney's heavy-handed tactics was Bill Gabel. The former police officer operated one of The District's largest saloons, and when Looney upped his protection fee to $1,000 ($13,000) a month from $300, Gabel refused to pay. Looney was enraged and vowed he would collect, but Gabel had an ace in the hole.

Inexplicably, Looney had deviated from his cash-only policy and accepted 12 checks from Gabel who arranged to meet with a team of federal investigators at the Como Hotel on the night of July 31, 1922 to discuss the Looney-endorsed checks. Gabel never made it to bed that night. After the meeting as he was getting out of his car in front of his 4th Street saloon, he was shot at by at least two men. Five .38 caliber slugs hit him, and one passed through his heart killing him instantly. For days the *Argus* rhetorically asked, "Who Killed Bill Gabel?" Because no witnesses stepped forward, the question went unanswered, but almost everyone in The District believed that Looney lurked behind the killing.

One of the cardinal rules of gangsters at the time was to keep their families out of their business and out of harm's way. But Looney played by no rules. Of his three children, his oldest girl, Kathleen was the smartest. She not only was elected class president her junior and senior years at the Villa de Chantal, but had the good sense to join the convent after graduation. After taking vows to become a nun, she moved to a convent in St. Louis. Middle child, Ursula also attended the Villa, and before partially escaping her father by going away to college and later marrying, she was forced to write for the *Rock Island News*. She said of Looney, "My father would sell me, body and soul, for money." Both sisters hated their father.

Looney's son, Conner, was not as fortunate as his sisters. A Lincoln School classmate described Conner as a "nice kid" who was well mannered and good-looking. Conner had the same physical stature as his father and looked remarkably like him. Unlike his sisters who boarded at the Villa, which was less than 100 yards away from the family mansion, Conner lived with his father on the New Mexico ranch. After Conner returned to Rock Island with his father, he lived with him at the smallest of his father's three Rock Island houses, which was located at the top of the hill on 16th Avenue and 20th Street and was just around the corner from the mansion he grew up in. Called "the Roost," the house was where the *News* was published for a short time and where several of Looney's henchmen listed as their address. Conner was said to disapprove of his father and his lifestyle, but sadly after returning to Rock Island, he started working with him.

Shortly after the assassination of Bill Gabel, the *Argus* editorialized, "The thing for you to keep in mind, Mr. Good Citizen, is that the murder of Bill Gabel was unwritten notice to you and the other 35,000 residents of Rock Island that the price of interference with the activities of the local underworld is death." Goading the community for months, the *Argus* continued to indignantly editorialize on the need for citizens to demand that their public officials clean up the town. Meanwhile, Looney was circulating petitions for his candidacy for county judge.

Three months after Bill Gabel was done in, the house of cards collapsed. On October 6, 1922, less than three years after Prohibition became effective John and Conner Looney pulled up in front of the Sherman Hotel on 17th Street just south of Market Square. Lawrence Pedigo, the hotel's owner, pulled in behind them. As the Looneys were walking towards the hotel, John Looney spotted Anthony Billburg's black Maxwell parked down the block. He yelled to his son and started running toward the hotel as two convertibles pulled up outside the hotel. The cars' passengers rose and started firing at the Looneys. Conner went down, wounded by a bullet in the stomach. A man standing in front of the Argus Building watching the posting of World Series scores rushed to Conner's aid. He too was shot in the stomach. From the hotel, John Looney returned fire on the cars. After emptying their guns, the men sped away with police in pursuit. John Looney escaped without a scratch. Eight hours after the gunfight, Conner Looney died at St. Anthony's Hospital. He was 21-years-old.

The day after Looney's death, Edward L. Eagle, a Rock Island assistant state's attorney, issued this statement: "Everything we have found substantiates the theory that this was a war between two rival factions. Our evidence indicates that the men who manned the two cars from which the shooting came went out with the express purpose of killing Looney and his son, and perhaps Pedigo." Eagle would later assist in the prosecution of the case. Over the next week, The District erupted in gangland warfare. Eight more men were killed, including two policemen. Among the more prominent gangsters gunned down were Marcel Martinez, a pimp who also sold dope, and James "Dude" Bowen, king of Rock Island's gamblers. The war raged while a force of 25 government agents combed Rock Island gathering evidence in the murder of Conner Looney.

Although no evidence was uncovered to indicate anything different than Eagle's initial statement, there may have been much more behind the shootout, and Rock Island may have been the site of one of America's last condoned episodes of vigilantism. Prominent citizens raised $65,000 ($800,000) supposedly to prosecute the murderer — but it is nearly inconceivable that as hated as John Looney was by Rock Island's establishment that 65¢ could have been raised for the prosecution of the men who tried to rid the world of him. More remarkable was that an improbable number of influential men had coincidentally met on 17th Street at 2:00 p.m. on a muggy, 88-degree Friday afternoon to witness the shooting.

Among the witnesses to Conner Looney's murder were Rock Island's most substantial leaders: John W. Potter, Minnie Potter's son and publisher of the *Argus*; Fred Mueller, the *Argus*' advertising manager; Thomas Haege, clothier; J.L. Vernon, former president of the People's National Bank; Harry H. Cleveland, insurer; and Walter

Rosenfield, former chairman of the Republican State Central Committee and the next man to be Rock Island's mayor (he succeeded Harry Shriver the following year). Absent from the spontaneous block party of Rock Island's elite was anyone from city hall or law enforcement. Amazingly, all the high-minded citizens who witnessed Conner Looney's murder declined to appear before the grand jury.

Four men, who would not be greatly missed by Rock Island's legitimate business establishment, were charged with the murder: George "Crimps" Holsapple was arrested while adding water to his car's radiator only minutes after the shooting; George Buckley, a saloon owner; Dan Drost, an early editor of the *Rock Island News* but later a Looney rival; and Anthony Billburg. Jake Ramser, a prominent jeweler, was in one of the cars, but he was never charged. A grand jury was convened, and Billburg testified that Ramser called him to arrange a meeting with John Colligan, Potter, and Haege. He said that it was Haege who suggested that it was time to get rid of Looney, and that before he was killed, he should be tortured until he confessed to the murder of Bill Gabel. Billburg also said that he received a call from Ramser on the day of the shootings and was told that if he wanted to see some excitement, he should get some "friends to come down to Market Square. We are going to take Looney out and kill him."

Many believed Billburg's testimony, and that the city's leading citizens solicited him and the others to kill John Looney. After years of appealing to the community from church pulpits and on the *Argus'* editorial pages, it appeared that when Looney arrogantly thumbed his nose at the law and avoided prosecution or even investigation for Bill Gabel's murder, the city's leaders resorted to vigilante justice. Everyone knew that Rock Island's deeply-rooted vice and corruption would be sustained as long as Looney was in town, and after the gangland hit on Bill Gabel and the *Argus* repeatedly asking, "Who killed Bill Gabel?" without anyone venturing the obvious answer, apparently the influential core of Rock Island's community despaired of ever seeing the "proper channels" restore grandeur to the town they grew up in.

Taking a page from the Roman Senate's assassination of Caesar, it also appears that Rock Island's power brokers had a legally questionable but well-conceived plan. To divert blame from themselves and to keep the crime syndicate from re-forming, as it had when Looney was expelled eight years earlier, the civic leaders used The District's crime hierarchy's hatred of Looney to do the dirty work, and then abandoned their empty promise to protect the assassins. The situation was thorny. The twice-elected mayor was in cahoots with The District's kingpin; judges, prosecutors, and police were on the take from a consortium comprised of every saloon, gambling parlor, and brothel in The District; and to complete the circle of corruption, the Queen of The District had the chief of police totally under her spell. Looney was not only the kingpin, but the crime circle's linchpin.

Billburg testified before the grand jury that jewelry storeowner, Jake Ramser, was involved in the shooting, and that when he met with him after Conner Looney was shot, Ramser said, "If that boy dies, there is a murder charge against someone." Billburg later said that although a number of people who witnessed the shooting and Ramser's participation were called before the grand jury, all the questions of the witnesses were about him, Drost, Buckley, and Holsapple. It was generally believed in The District that John Potter and his friends reneged on their promised support, and threw the four men into the teeth of the state judicial system — very probably that was always the plan, and the only thing that changed was that Looney was still alive.

Later Crimps Holsapple testified to the grand jury, "These fellows had promised to help us. They were supposed to pay for all these legal expenses, and that we would never see the pen. It was supposed to be fixed that we were safe." In retrospect, if it wasn't the blue blood's plan to exploit the hatred of Looney by The District's business owners and turn it against them, Rock Island's leadership wasn't as proactive and as clever as they appeared. In whatever case, they were unquestionably hypocritical and unethical and very probably outside of the law, and it now appears that the community leaders resorted to the Biblical methods of extracting an eye for an eye — and then cast the den of thieves out of the citadel of sin.

It's unclear where the $65,000 went, but Billburg and Holsapple used their own money to hire Clarence Darrow, the nation's most famous lawyer, to defend them and the others. Brought up by a father who was known as the "village infidel" and a mother who was a leading suffragist and women's rights advocate, Darrow attended Allegheny College and Michigan Law School but graduated from neither. After passing the bar, he rapidly rose to become one of the nation's top labor lawyers and a prominent leader in the Democratic Party. A staunch opponent of the death penalty, at a time when few were, his first of 50 murder defendants was a deranged drifter who confessed to the murder. It was the only murder case he took that resulted in an execution. His brilliant elocution moved juries and even judges to tears, and he won many "unwinnable" cases.

Darrow was at the height of his career, when he presented the defense for Billburg and the others. In the year after their trial, he defended Nathan Leopold and Albert Loeb for their kidnapping and murder of 14-year-old Bobby Franks. There was no doubt about Leopold and Loeb's guilt in the gruesome premeditated killing of Franks, but in a moving 12-hour closing argument to the judge who heard the case, Darrow set legal precedence when he got life sentences for the two killers based on "mental disease."

The next year, the renowned religious agnostic squared off against devout Presbyterian and Progressive leader, William Jennings Bryan, in the "Scopes Monkey Trial," a case that pitted modernists against Christian Fundamentalists. A Tennessee law forbade the teaching of "any theory that denies the story of the Divine Creation of man as taught in the Bible, and to teach instead that man has descended from a lower order of animals." Setting up a test case, the fledgling American Civil Liberties Union engaged Darrow to take the side of John Scopes, a high school teacher, who had taught a chapter from a textbook that presented Charles Darwin's theory of evolution.

In the unusual situation of a prosecuting attorney taking the stand as a defense witness, Bryan agreed to testify as an expert on the Bible. Darrow skillfully set Bryan up and put him on the defensive. Their exchange began with the following:

Darrow: You have given considerable study to the Bible, haven't you, Mr. Bryan?
Bryan: Yes, sir; I have tried to.... But, of course, I have studied it more as I have become older than when I was a boy.
Darrow: Do you claim then that everything in the Bible should be literally interpreted?
Bryan: I believe that everything in the Bible should be accepted as it is given there; some of the Bible is given illustratively. For instance: 'Ye are the salt of the earth." I would not insist that man was actually salt, or that he had flesh of salt, but it is used in the sense of salt as saving God's people.

The examination lasted for two hours and centered on interpretation of the Book of Genesis. Darrow asked such questions as "Was Eve actually created from Adam's rib?" and "Where did Cain's wife come from?" (Bryan flippantly dodged that question by saying that he would "leave the agnostics to hunt for her.") Darrow used these examples to suggest that Biblical stories weren't scientific and should not be used in teaching science. But he spared no words when he told Bryan, "You insult every man of science and learning in the world because he does not believe in your fool religion." After an angry exchange over the temptation of Eve by the talking serpent, the judge banged his gavel and closed the testimony.

Bryan's righteous but bumbling answers to Darrow's questions were instrumental in swinging the press and public opinion to the modernists. However, the judge threw out all testimony that did not specifically address whether Scopes taught evolution, of which he was plainly guilty. Darrow lost the case and Scopes was forced to pay the minimum fine of $100. The verdict was overturned on a technicality, the ACLU got their $100 back, and the Tennessee Supreme Court refused to hear a defense appeal saying, "We see nothing to be gained by prolonging the life of this bizarre case."

But two years before Darrow frustrated himself with the devout fundamentalist arguments of William Jennings Bryan, he tackled an equally righteous prosecution of Anthony Billburg. The four men indicted for killing Conner Looney were tried together, and in their opening statement the prosecution stated what they believed to be Billburg's motive and deflected Darrow's planned defense of creating a probable cause that it was the community's leading citizens and Lawrence Pedigo, not its vice lords, that botched the execution of John Looney and killed his son. The prosecution began by brokering the reputation of the business leaders and discrediting Billburg when it said, "This was not a fight to rid the community of Looney, but to place Billburg back on the throne in that room, so that he could say, 'Come here. You pay $200 a month, and you pay $150, and you and you and you. That's the reason for the battle in Market Square that day. This was a battle that the underworld must again bow to King Billburg in his lust for the dirty money, the filthy lucre."

The 13-day trial ended with Darrow delivering an impassioned summation:

> Here are four men before you charged with killing John Conner Looney. I shall attempt to bring no tears as my friend Barbour (a prosecutor) did. There is no sorrow for John Conner Looney to be considered in this case. It is the facts that count, not the emotions. The question is, are they guilty or not guilty? I think without a reasonable doubt that they are innocent. ... [The prosecutors] base it all on this conspiracy, meaning that two or more men got together to come to an agreement to do an unlawful act. There is no evidence to show there was a conspiracy in existence. There was no intent. ... Now let's go further into the wonderful conspiracy that these men have spit out of their own brains as a spider weaves his web to catch flies, and then to try to show a motive. They say Billburg hated him. Who swears to that? Pedigo? ... Anyone else? Not one.
>
> What of Pedigo? Will you tell me why a man is under so many indictments in courts that he can't count them? Will you tell me why he has met and conferred with the detectives in this case, and the state's attorneys? There is just one answer — that he is thinking of himself and clemency for him. He is practically led into this courtroom by a halter. He is the associate and friend of John Looney, whose blood-red hands hang over this case, as for years they have hung like a shadow over this town.

The trial ended in a victory for the establishment. Anthony Billburg was convicted of murder and sentenced to life in prison. The other three received 14-year sentences. After serving seven years at Joliet State Penitentiary, Billburg was paroled and eventually received a full pardon. He returned to Rock Island, and died at his home on 20th Street in 1950. After serving his sentence, George Holsapple returned to Rock Island, where he died in 1966 at the age of 87. The city both men returned to was much different from the one they left. The Depression and the Twenty-First Amendment, which repealed Prohibition, had conspired with community leaders to clean up The District.

After Conner Looney's funeral mass that filled the massive St. Joseph's Catholic Church, John Looney disappeared, and in less than two weeks his saloons and brothels were closed, his bootleg stills demolished, and his Bel Aire arms cache was seized. Many of his lieutenants and associates were arrested and fined, and more damaging to

Looney was that they became state witnesses against him. He faced more than ten indictments, and the Pinkerton Detective Agency posted a $2,000 ($25,000) reward for his capture. His influence disappeared with him, and his crime syndicate folded.

Unsurprisingly, the indictments returned by the grand jury against Looney included one that also named Police Chief Thomas Cox; Lawrence Pedigo; Leonard "Fat" Walker, one of Emeal Davis' saloon manager's; and Joe "The Gadget" Richards for the murder of William Gabel. Another indictment named Mayor Harry Shriver, Cox, Pedigo, and Robert Kinner for conspiracy to furnish gambling equipment (punch boards and slot machines) and to provide "protection." In less than a month, Rock Island fell from the pinnacle of underworld power along the Upper Mississippi to become once again just another boisterous river town.

Before Thanksgiving a year after Looney disappeared, a Belen, New Mexico, rancher spotted a stranger sitting in the lobby of the town's hotel. The former deputy sheriff went to the post office to confirm that the man in the lobby was the same one he had seen on the Pinkerton wanted poster. He was, and John Looney's crime career was over. Rock Island's business leaders again rose to the occasion and raised $75,000 ($950,000) to finance the parade of witnesses that presented 30 days of testimony in the first of Looney's two trials. Among those who testified, the most damaging to Looney was the mercurial Lawrence Pedigo, and the most entertaining was Helen Van Dale.

When the still strikingly attractive and elegant Van Dale was called to the stand, women drew their jackets tightly to their chests, and men pointed and elbowed each other while carrying on like adolescent boys. When the prosecutor asked, "Mrs. Van Dale, you don't like John Looney, do you?" She replied, "I neither like, nor dislike him, I have no reason to." Van Dale was testifying while under charges of transporting women from Rock Island to Davenport. The charges were dropped after she testified against Looney in a later trial for the murder of Bill Gabel.

When pressed about why she was testifying against Looney, the ephemeral Van Dale said, "I really don't know how to answer that. After he blackmailed and bled so many people, I think he should have a little justice handed him." "I could hang him," she concluded. Her long testimony also detailed the love-struck attraction Chief Cox had developed for her and the affair she carried on with him. On cross-examination, when she was asked if she wasn't the "real chief of police," she coyly replied, "When Looney didn't prevent me, yes." After a year of rapidly deteriorating health, Thomas Cox died. Co-conspirator, Mayor Harry Shriver was also convicted. But another of Looney's indicted co-conspirators in his prostitution and gambling shakedowns, William Scott, was not convicted, and he moved on to a successful public law career in Rock Island.

Looney's trial for the murder of Bill Gabel was moved to Galesburg and again Pedigo and Van Dale were the star witnesses — both had been promised immunity for their testimony. Pedigo testified that in a conversation with John Looney the day after Gabel was killed, Looney said that it was good he had a strong alibi — he had been with a cop — because Looney knew they were going to throw suspicion towards him. Van Dale testified about discussions with Chief Cox and Conner Looney — both men were dead — when they told her "what Gabel was going to get." After a month of testimony by 57 witnesses, on only circumstantial evidence, the jury took five hours to find John Looney guilty of Bill Gabel's murder. He was sentenced to 14 years at the Joliet State Penitentiary.

At age 67, after serving eight years and in poor health during most of his sentence, Looney was given an early release. He died seven years later at the home of his daughter, Ursula Hamlin, near Falfurrias, Texas. Lawrence Pedigo left the rackets and the hotel business and became manager of Cram Field airport in Davenport. He also operated the Mississippi Valley Flying School from the airfield. He died at age 37. Helen Van Dale stayed in Rock Island for another three years after Looney was sent to Joliet, reportedly spending most of her time sitting on the customer side of the bar in Rock Island's new speakeasies. Looking for a different life, she met and married her fifth husband in LaSalle, Illinois, where they operated a sandwich shop. After her husband of 14 years was killed in a train wreck, Van Dale changed her name to Eula H. Wonders and lived in obscurity until her death in LaSalle, Illinois, at age 58.

There is no question that John Looney ruled Rock Island's rackets with extreme swagger for the first two and a half years of Prohibition, but to glamorize his life or his lifestyle would be a grave disservice to Eastern mobsters, many of whom became legendary because they openly defied senseless and unpopular laws regulating adult behavior and because they usually publicly behaved with better manners and more panache than the hypocritical, nouveau riche industrialists, bankers, and politicians they partied with. Al Capone's Outfit controlled bootlegging in most of the Midwest, but there is no record of him even visiting the Tri-Cities — avoiding Iowa and skipping straight-laced Moline is understandable. Rock Island was probably too much hassle for its relatively small market, and the community was still righteously recovering from Looney when Capone seized control of Chicago. Casting Paul Newman in *The Road to Perdition* to play the likeable and suave cinematic John Rooney (the last name was changed because it was thought a neurotic gangster named "Looney" was a bit much) may have been the most egregious stretch of artistic license in the history of historical film making.

Chapter 21

A Conservative Time

I'm not a member of any organized political party, I'm a Democrat! ~ Will Rogers, after the 1924 Democratic convention

AFTER EIGHT YEARS of prudish Democratic idealism under Woodrow Wilson and unrealistic Progressive public policy culminating in Prohibition, President Warren Harding's promise of a return to "normalcy" hinged on what Republicans considered "normal." Bolstered by his landslide victory, Harding quickly reestablished patronage at government's highest levels and appointed many of his political allies and campaign contributors to powerful positions that controlled the nation's finances and resources. Called the "Ohio Gang," in only two and a half years Harding's cronies orchestrated the selling of U.S. ships valued at $200 a ton for $30 a ton, siphoned off $225,000 ($2.8 million) from hospital construction for World War I vets, and sold nearly $1 million ($12 million) of alcohol permits meant for pharmacists to bootleggers. Then they flaunted their ill-gotten largesse by opening their own private speakeasy/clubhouse on Washington's K Street where poker games never ended and free confiscated liquor and beer always flowed.

Harry Daugherty, a Cleveland political boss and Harding's campaign manager, headed the clubhouse in Washington's Georgetown District. Harding had rewarded him for his hard work delivering the vote by making him U.S. Attorney General. One historian at the time described the Justice Department under Daugherty as "the den of a ward politician" and Harding's "White House [as] a nightclub." Daugherty made sure that his boss got the very best liquor his department confiscated, and Alice Longworth, daughter of President Theodore Roosevelt, claimed that trays "with bottles containing every imaginable brand of whiskey stood about" Harding's White House. At a time when the president was supposed to be enforcing Prohibition, he freely served alcohol to White House visitors, and Mrs. Harding mixed drinks for their dinner quests. When confronted by journalists about the White House parties, Harding said that there was no law against consuming alcohol and that drinking inside his residence was his own business. During his term Harding played poker twice a week — curiously, he always seemed to win and once he allegedly won a $4,000 ($50,000) pearl necktie pin in a pot.

Because he was U.S. Attorney General, there were only Daugherty's subordinates to investigate his crimes — an impeachment attempt failed — and Daugherty had the most envied mob job in the country. In addition to skimming off the best bootleg liquor for his pals, the attorney general and the Ohio Gang's scams and graft included selling pardons, patronage, single bid contracts, cronyism, kickbacks, and influence peddling. The most flagrant of the crimes was the work of Harding's Secretary of the Interior, Albert Fall.

After World War I, the importance and value of oil reserves for military purposes became increasingly clear. For a bribe of $385,000 ($4.8 million), Fall leased a teapot shaped Montana mountain on top of a plain full of oil to Edward Doheny's drilling company. Until the impeachment of Richard Nixon, the Teapot Dome Scandal was the benchmark for high profile U.S. political wrongdoing. A decade after the crime was exposed, Fall was sentenced to one year in prison for accepting the bribe. Paradoxically, Doheny was acquitted of paying the bribe. To add to the insult, Doheny foreclosed on Fall's home for not repaying loans he made to him. At the time, Ohioans were quick to point out that Fall was from New Mexico. Harding's ostentatious lifestyle and blatant disregard for the alcohol laws were viewed as a less than subtle public rebuke of the Prohibitionists and the Democrats who gave them power. Clearly, the Republican message was that Democrats were responsible for turning the big cities over to mobsters and creating a hypocritical social structure that was more corrupt, less accepted, and less popular than what the idealistic Woodrow Wilson inherited from his Republican predecessor.

Everywhere but in Ohio and New York, the press began to bash Harding and his administration. In order to restore the public's confidence and polish his image for his reelection, in June of 1923 Harding set out on a westbound "Voyage of Understanding" that had an initial schedule of 18 primary speeches to be given in major cities along the railroad trip. Accompanying Harding were an entourage of World War I heroes and those few popular political appointees he could round up — one was his relatively unknown Secretary of Commerce, Herbert Hoover. As he crossed the continent, the president's speeches increasingly departed from Republican dogma. In St. Louis he encouraged U.S. participation in the World Court, and by the time he reached Kansas City, he had given up drinking (possibly because of chest pains and advice from his doctor). In Denver he proclaimed that he hoped the Eighteenth Amendment would never be repealed. When he reached Tacoma, Washington, he totally spun off the party line and promoted an 8-hour workday. Harding confided in friends that he felt a spiritual change was influencing his stance on issues.

Then departing on the *USS Henderson*, a naval transport ship, he journeyed to the Alaskan Territory to promote colonization. After touring the immense territory for two weeks, Harding visited Vancouver, British Columbia, as he returned to the States. After a round of golf in Vancouver, he complained of exhaustion, severe chest and abdominal pains, and nausea. His doctor diagnosed the illness as food poisoning, and the next day Harding delivered a speech to 50,000 cheering Canadians. After entering Elliot Bay in Seattle, the *Henderson* rammed a U.S. destroyer in the fog — Harding was uninjured. In Seattle, he led 50,000 Boy Scouts in reciting the *Pledge of Allegiance*, and then feeling ill again, he rushed through a speech to 25,000 in the University of Washington's football stadium. Hoover wrote the speech that trumpeted his tour of the vast Alaskan wilderness and extolled the territory's "measureless oil resources." Feeling nauseous, Harding rushed from the podium without waiting for applause.

A scheduled speech in Portland was cancelled, and the presidential train proceeded to San Francisco. At a stop in Dunsmuir, California, Hoover, an Iowan who had gone to college in Northern California, sent a telegram to his personal physician asking him to examine the president when the party arrived at the Palace Hotel. There, Harding was diagnosed with pneumonia and given digitalis and caffeine. The medications seemed to help, and during the next day he perked up. But while his doctors were at dinner and while talking to his wife, in mid-sentence he shuddered and died. Mrs. Harding refused to have an autopsy, and even though his symptoms pointed to congestive heart failure, after some discussion, the doctors indicated the cause of death as "some brain evolvement, probably an apoplexy." Possibly, only his physicians were less professionally competent than he, and Harding is the consensus pick as the worst president in U.S. history. Vice President Calvin Coolidge, who was vacationing with his family at Plymouth Notch, Vermont, was sworn into office by his father, a Vermont notary public.

By the time "Cool Cal" became president, the "Twenties" were roaring in the big cities. The new entertainment technologies of phonographs and motion pictures enlivened Saturday nights, telephones and radio transformed communication, and above all, airplanes and automobiles revolutionized travel. "Modernity" did away with decorative frills in favor of practical design. In architecture Frank Lloyd Wright became the dominant designer. His stylish horizontal lines, flat or hipped roofs with broad over-hanging eaves, and large, well-placed windows opening onto integrated landscapes influenced the way Americans lived and worked. Modernism extended into new ways of thinking about philosophy (*The Concept of Time*, Heidegger, 1924), sociology (The rise of Marxism in Russia), psychology (*The Ego and the Id*, Freud, 1923), and religion (Scopes Monkey Trial, 1925). Sigmund Freud also expressed an increasingly common view held by intellectuals of the time on religion when he said, "The whole thing is so patently infantile, so foreign to reality, that to anyone with a friendly attitude to humanity it is painful to think that the great majority of mortals will never be able to rise above this view of life." D.H. Lawrence, George Bernard Shaw, Somerset Maugham, and James Joyce gave the country the best reads with *Sons and Lovers, Pygmalion, Of Human Bondage*, and *A Portrait of the Artist as a Young Man*. In the art world Cubism and Futurism flourished. In sports the 1916 Olympics were cancelled because of World War I, and worse, the Cubs descended into just being good.

The 1920s were also known as the "Jazz Age," and many jazz variations — ragtime, Dixieland, and swing — exploded throughout the cities. Flappers danced the Charleston, Lindy hop, shimmy, and foxtrot to Louis Armstrong and the Hot Five, Duke Ellington, Jelly Roll Morton and the Rhythm Kings, Earl Hines' Band in Chicago, and Bix Beiderbecke and The Wolverines. While some were dancing the '20s away, liberal writers and artists, disillusioned by the war and resultant post-war political conservatism and materialism, flocked to Paris to live its avant-garde lifestyle and to freely express themselves and their crafts. Best known of the wave of expatriated American intellectuals were Ernest Hemingway, Gertrude Stein, and F. Scott Fitzgerald. This cadre of Americans who fled to Paris after World War I to escape increasingly repressive social conditions imposed by the Progressives became known as "The Lost Generation."

Ernest Hemingway grew up in Oak Park, Illinois, a Chicago suburb that fellow resident and atheist Frank Lloyd Wright described as having "so many churches for so many good people to go to." After graduating from high school, Hemingway briefly worked for the *Kansas City Star* before becoming a World War I ambulance driver on the Italian front. His war experience before he was 19 provided the material for *A Farewell to Arms*, one of his seven novels. He also compiled six short story collections and wrote two works of nonfiction. Three years after recovering from shrapnel wounds to his legs that ended his war experience, the ruggedly handsome 22-year-old moved to Paris. There he was befriended and mentored by Gertrude Stein, who was 25 years older and had lived in Paris for 20 years.

Hemingway remained in Europe and lived in the expat arts community for the next decade. During that time he became friends with Pablo Picasso, Henri Matisse, Juan Gris, Ezra Pound, James Joyce, and F. Scott Fitzgerald, about whom he said, "We formed a friendship of admiration and hostility." During his first 20 months in Paris, Hemingway filed a story a month for the *Toronto Star*. After reading Fitzgerald's *The Great Gatsby*, he decided to write a novel — eight weeks later, he finished the first draft of *The Sun Also Rises*.

In 1954 Hemingway received the Nobel Prize for Literature, five years after it was awarded to William Faulkner. The two Nobel Laureates didn't have high opinions of each other's writing. Faulkner said that Hemingway "had never been known to use a word that might send the reader to the dictionary." Hemingway responded, "Poor Faulkner. Does he really think big emotions come from big words? He thinks I don't know ten-dollar words. I know them all right. But there are older and simpler and better words, and those are the ones I use." Hemingway succinctly expressed the sectarian beliefs of most Jazz Age artists when he said, "All thinking men are atheists," and Faulkner displayed his opposite beliefs when he wrote, "I believe that man will not merely endure. He will prevail. He is immortal, not because he alone among creatures has an inexhaustible voice, but because he has a soul, a spirit capable of compassion and sacrifice and endurance."

Hemingway's mentor, Gertrude Stein, was a remarkable woman who grew up in a wealthy German-Jewish home in Oakland, California. Her parents died when she was a teenager, and after four years at Radcliffe and two years in Johns Hopkins Medical School, she moved to Paris in 1903. Over the next decade, collecting the "geniuses, not the masters," she assembled the world's largest private collection of French Impressionist paintings. After disposing of most of her Impressionist pieces, she started collecting her friend, Pablo Picasso's, Cubist works. Although Hemingway popularized the name, "The Lost Generation," by using it in *The Sun Also Rises*, he admitted in *A Moveable Feast*, an autobiographical account of his time in Paris that was published after his death, that Stein coined the term. After being angered by the poor skills of a young French car mechanic, she asked the garage owner who had trained him. The owner told her that young men were easy to train, but that he found that the men who endured World War I were une génération perdue — a "lost generation"

While she collected art, Stein also wrote for publication. One reviewer of her rambling novel, *The Makings of Americans*, wrote, "In Gertrude Stein's writing every word lives and, apart from concept, it is so exquisitely rhythmical and cadenced that if we read it aloud and receive it as pure sound, it is like a kind of sensuous music." In 1907 on her first day in Paris, Alice B. Toklas, a 30-year-old San Franciscan, met Stein, and became her confidante, cook, secretary, editor, critic, and muse until Stein's death 38 years later. In 1954 Toklas published *The Alice B. Toklas Cookbook*, an autobiography and cookbook that provides a terrific recipe for haschich fudge, a mixture of fruit, nuts, spices, and cannabis sativa. Many believe Alice's brownies and her last name are the inspiration for the slang term, "toke."

Toklas said that F. Scott Fitzgerald wrote the "definitive portrait of his generation" and that he "had become a legend, and the epoch he created was history."

She was speaking of *The Great Gatsby*, which is at the top of every literary critic's list of great American novels. Set in New York City and the North Shore of Long Island during the summer of 1922, the classic novel is a tale of its generation, and gives a damning insight into the fascinatingly sad lives of the nouveau riche.

An Irish Catholic from St. Paul, Minnesota, Fitzgerald was a poor student at Princeton, and enlisted in World War I before he graduated, but the war ended before he could serve. Fitzgerald married Zelda Sayre, a bright, beautiful, and audacious Southern belle who was only two years out of high school and they moved to Europe where the couple lived and socialized with other expatriates. To support Zelda, who he described as "the first American flapper," Fitzgerald sold short stories to popular magazines, although his friend, Hemingway, criticized him for "whoring" himself by writing for money. An alcoholic from his days at Princeton, Fitzgerald wrote only four novels and died from heart failure at age 44. After his death, a *New York Times* editorial said that Fitzgerald "was better than he knew, for in fact and in the literary sense he invented a generation." Fitzgerald and Zelda had one child, Francis Scott, who was named after his father, who had been named for his distant relative Francis Scott Key. Fitzgerald was also related to Mary Surratt, who was hanged for conspiring to kill Abraham Lincoln. It was Fitzgerald who named the period the "Jazz Age."

While Fitzgerald was parodying the lifestyles of America's rich and famous, sports were becoming institutionalized, and elite professional baseball players were as well-known as movie stars and politicians. The post-World War I period was known as the "Golden Era of Baseball." The "dead ball era" of low-scoring games was blasted into the past when a Boston Red Sox pitcher named Babe Ruth was traded to the New York Yankees and moved to right field so he could play every day. Coming off two wins in the 1918 World Series when he pitched 29.2 scoreless innings, in 1919 his last year in Boston, The Bambino had a 9-5 pitching record with a 2.97 ERA. Unbelievably, The Babe not only threw 133.1 innings but also smashed a major league season record of 29 homeruns — the record lasted until the following year when he blasted 54 homers — while hitting .322 with a .456 on base percentage. Many baseball historians agree that Ruth's 1919 season was the most phenomenal year a player has ever had. He then demanded that his record-high annual salary of $10,000 ($125,000) be doubled.

When Boston balked at the outrageous salary demand, the Chicago White Sox offered Shoeless Joe Jackson and $60,000 for Ruth, but in an eleventh-hour deal, the Yankees, who were the third best and least popular team in New York behind the Dodgers and Giants, saw a way to hype interest in their moribund team and agreed to a $100,000 all-cash payment for the 24-year-old pitcher and slugging outfielder. Sox owner, Harry Frazee, took the Yankees' money, which he used in part to later finance the Broadway play *No, No, Nanette*. The Red Sox had won five World Series before selling Ruth — a deal that caused the "Curse of the Bambino" to descend on the franchise for 86-years. The drought of not winning a World Series lasted until 2004 when the Red Sox finally won their sixth World championship.

While Progressive and libertarian ideologies were clashing after World War I, America's working class was realizing a "golden age" of economic prosperity that was unprecedented in world history. The conflicting political philosophies and upward mobility of the classes were embodied in a single man: Henry Ford. In 1918, Woodrow Wilson asked Ford, a Republican, to run as a Democrat for a U.S. Senate seat from Michigan. Ford did run, but as a peace candidate and a strong supporter of the League of Nations. Wilson also supported this international organization, and after the war it became the United Nations. Without campaigning or spending one cent of his own money, Ford lost by one percent of the vote. Although his pacifist ideology may have been self-serving to protect his investment in European car manufacturers, the Republican businessman believed in women's suffrage, Prohibition, the 40-hour workweek, and he was a strong advocate for public education. Ford Motor Company was one of the first U.S. companies to hire large numbers of black workers, but at the other end of the social tolerance spectrum, from 1920 to 1927 Ford underwrote an anti-Semitic newspaper, *The Dearborn Independent*.

Although Ford claimed he was unaware of the Fascist content of the *Independent* that was published with his money and run by his closest aide, he defended the paper by saying that it "fit in with what is going on." The weekly publication had a circulation of 700,000, and whether he knew it or not, Ford's newspaper became a forum for right-wing extremism and Jewish prejudice. European Nazis frequently quoted the paper, and in Germany its eight years of publications were translated and republished in four volumes.

Ford is the only American mentioned in Adolph Hitler's *Mien Kampf*, and Hitler explained his reason for keeping Ford's life-size portrait next to his desk by saying that he regarded Ford as his "inspiration," and that he imitated Ford's business model and production techniques for building the Volkswagen. Whether he felt honored or not, in 1938 prior to the outbreak of war and on his 75th birthday Ford accepted the Grand Cross of the German Eagle, the highest honor Nazi Germany bestowed on a foreigner. Eighteen years earlier Ford helped earn his award by delivering what may have been the most illogical slur in the history of American sports when he wrote, "If fans wish to know the trouble with American baseball, they have it in three words — too much Jew."

Two years before Willard Velie started making airplanes, Henry Ford directed that just as the Model T was "everyman's vehicle," the Ford Flivver would become "everyman's aircraft." Before it ever flew, the single seat plane was a national sensation. Although he never flew one, Will Rogers posed with the Flivver for press photos. In August 1927, the same month he first visited Rock Island, Charles Lindbergh flew the Flivver, and after landing, he shakily announced that it was "one of the worst aircraft I've ever flown." Six months later, Ford's chief test pilot crashed into the Atlantic Ocean off the Florida coast, and Ford got out of the airplane business.

Although the wealthy were tooling about Rock Island's grid of brick streets in their Fords and Velies shortly after the turn of the century, for two generations Rock Islanders had ridden on the web of streetcar lines that blanketed the Tri-Cities. A decade after Bailey Davenport introduced horse-drawn streetcars to the area in 1868, steam-powered streetcars began to serve the cities, and a decade after that, one of the nation's early electric streetcar systems zipped amazed passengers up Davenport's Brady Street Hill. Lines spread rapidly throughout the cities and their surrounding areas, and by the late 1800s, 13 streetcar companies were shuttling factory workers, commuters, shoppers, and joy riders into Rock Island and its bordering communities. Between 1897 and 1912 the lines consolidated and were eventually merged into a single ownership. The result was that no longer were the cluster of communities autonomous, and the distinct personalities of the Tri-Cities and the rural nature of their surrounding towns began to blur. A nickel bought a visit to The District from anywhere within a ten-mile radius, and streetcars opened up residential development above the bluffs in all the cities.

In Rock Island, roads were improved and bricked simultaneously as streetcar tracks were laid down, which allowed the wealthy with automobiles to move to a secluded area called Hill Crest. Large lots on the flat plain to the north of Watch Tower Amusement Park were platted in 1918 and it quickly became Rock Island's most exclusive neighborhood. Unlike the grid of streets in the Broadway neighborhood, which Hill Crest soon supplanted as Rock Island's most prestigious addresses, the roads in the area that was popularly called "Watch Hill" followed the ridgelines and contours of the rolling hills where magnificent oak and elm trees shaded spacious lawns. From the construction of Tudor homes in the 1920s to modern contemporary-styled homes in the 1950s, the region's most elegant neighborhood developed.

At the time the first lots in Hill Crest were sold, most in Rock Island didn't have an auto much less the cash to buy an acre lot in the country. However, with the opening of a streetcar line that ran along Rock Island's 18th Avenue from the West End to Moline and north/south connections running up the steep brick-paved hills on 17th, 20th, 24th, and 30th Streets, the flat plain above the river bluffs was opened for family residential development. The area above the crest of the hill between 20th and 24th

Streets was developed first. Called the Highland Park District, the new neighborhood became Rock Island's most popular during the early 1900s. Perched above the commercial district but still only a short streetcar ride to work and the action in The District, the upscale neighborhood attracted many of Rock Island's professionals and businessmen. And soon, extending six blocks to the east of Highland Park between 14th and 18th Avenues, a delightful neighborhood of family homes bursting with children sprang up. The four-block-wide and 20-block-long Hilltop District eventually stretched east to Moline and absorbed four clusters of 200 homes built between 1918 and 1919 by the Federal Private Housing Initiative to provide emergency housing for Arsenal workers during World War I. There were 17 different house designs, including side-by-side town homes. The homes were well built, and not one has been torn down to make way for new development.

The dense network of streetcar lines dropped off a continuous stream of adults seeking good entertainment and a good time into Rock Island's Downtown District. Because of the folklore and bigger-than-life images that gangsters and their speakeasies had during Prohibition, it is easy to overlook the high quality of live entertainment and legitimate theater that thrived in the big cities in the East, Chicago, and Rock Island. For amusements of all kinds, Rock Island was the entertainment destination for the tens of thousands of men and women who lived within fifty miles of The District — the popular name for the stretch of restaurants, saloons, dance halls, brothels, theaters, and hotels that snaked between the river and 3rd Avenue around the upscale shops and markets in Rock Island's downtown. (After World War II, the bars and brothels east of 20th Street along 2nd Avenue became known as "The Strip")

After John Looney was chased out of town, The District went legit. The city fathers understood that if the quality and style of the city's nightlife and entertainment wasn't ratcheted up a notch, The District would probably sink back into the muck that Looney had spread about. The business community pulled together, and in one-week's time in 1925, $450,000 ($5.8 million) of the $800,000 ($10.25 million) building cost of a luxury hotel was raised by public subscription. Called the Fort Armstrong, the nine-story, 160-room hotel on the block to the southeast of 19th Street and 3rd Avenue featured ten penthouse suites, a banquet room, three dining rooms, a bar and lounge, a bowling alley and billiard room, a barbershop, and seven storefronts. It was exactly the anchor needed to keep Rock Island from drifting back into the slimy days of early Prohibition. Name entertainers, including Ella Fitzgerald and Louis Armstrong, played the jazz clubs only a block or two away, but the new hotel missed an opportunity to break new social ground and refused to let the black celebrities stay in its rooms. The discriminatory policy stayed in effect into the late 1930s when Nat King Cole was also refused a room and had to stay at a black boarding house. Today, the hotel is a senior citizen's residence and reflects the ages and energy of its residents.

From before the turn of the century, out-of-towners had come to Rock Island to see the nation's premier performers, and virtually all of the famous stars of the time played the theaters and clubs in The District. Often, nationally famous headliners simultaneously competed for discerning audiences. The year after the Harper Opera House closed in 1891, the larger and even more modern Illinois Theatre opened to a packed house of 1,400. Built by the efforts of the Rock Island Club on the corner of 2nd Avenue and 16th Street, the sturdily constructed theater featured star performances by Norwegian conductor/composer Ole Olsen and renowned Shakespearian-actor, Otis Skinner. Next door to the Illinois Theatre was the upscale Cross Country Buffet, a tavern owned by Ignatz Huber who also owned the Rock Island Brewing Company. The theater and saloon were complementary enterprises that not only shared patrons but also the same restrooms. In the 1950s, the theater became home to Hyman's Furniture store and remained its home for more than a half century until its closure in 2011. Over the years, Hyman's owner, Stanley Goldman, methodically restored the building to much of its original luster, including the restoration of the molded-tin ceiling.

In 1911 the Empire Theater opened on 4th Avenue at 19th Street at the peak of vaudeville and featured many of its stars, including Fred and Adele Astaire, George Burns and Gracie Allen, The Marx Brothers, Sophie Tucker, Ted Lewis, Eddie Cantor, Minnie Palmer, Ed Wynn, Jack Benny, and W.C. Fields. Vaudeville was today's version of channel surfing. Typically, two shows were performed each night with matinees on weekends, and each performance was a series of separate and unrelated acts, which included something for everyone: musicians, singers, dancers, circus acts, female impersonators, acrobats, magicians, famous athletes and celebrities, and everyone's favorite — comedians.

Motion pictures killed vaudeville, but in 1948 CBS Television hired Ed Sullivan, a dour-faced, washed-up boxer, who was writing an entertainment column for *The New York Daily News,* to host a one-hour vaudeville show on Sunday night. "Toast of the Town" became must-see TV for the next 23 years. When Sullivan's live, primetime show debuted, network television was in its infancy and virtually all TV actors had already made a name for themselves on Broadway, in Hollywood, or on the vaudeville circuit. A frequent Sullivan guest was Tim Moore, an accomplished African American actor who had been one of vaudeville's greatest actor/comedians for 30 years before he appeared on television.

One of 13 children, Tim Moore, left school at age 11 — he later said the only thing he excelled in was recess — to work for a Rock Island medicine show on 2nd

Avenue and 19th Street. He was a smooth-talking improvisationalist who always had a broad smile on his face. Two years later he left Rock Island to travel to Europe with Cora Miskel and Her Gold Dust Twins. The next year, he was back in the States working for Doctor Mick's Traveling Medicine Show. He left Doctor Mick to ride as a professional jockey, a skill he picked up from his uncle, but he soon grew too big for the job and became a professional boxer. Fighting as "Kid Klondike," he won 80 of 104 fights, knocking out Australian Middle Weight Champion Jimmy Driscoll and Scotland's Jack Barker. After the Barker fight, Moore returned to show biz, saying "the footlights were easier on the eyes than boxing gloves." His vaudeville troop "Tim Moore's Chicago Follies" played the national circuit from 1916 to 1925. In 1917 *The Evening Post* praised Moore's one-man presentation of *Uncle Tom's Cabin*, where with white chalk applied to one side of his face he played Simon Legree, and after pivoting 180 degrees, he played Uncle Tom with burnt cork on the other half.

Moore moved to the Broadway stage where he starred in *Lucky Sambo*, a musical revue. He became a sensation and starred in *Blackbirds*, a Broadway musical revue featuring the song *I Can't Give You Anything But Love*. After 500 New York performances, the production moved to Paris' Moulin Rouge, where it was an even bigger hit, and then on to London for two seasons where command performances were given for the Duke of Windsor and the King of Siam. At the start of World War II, Moore returned to New York, where he wrote skits and performed in *Harlem Cavalcade* at the Apollo Theater. In his late 50s, Moore retired from the spotlights to Rock Island to fish with his brothers, but after returning to New York to do a *Toast of the Town* show, he stopped by the Apollo to see friends and perform some encore skits. Three years later, that "last" visit to the Apollo launched Moore to even greater stardom.

The popular *Amos 'n' Andy* radio comedy that was produced by and starred Freeman Gosden and Charles Correll was America's longest running serial. First airing in 1928 and every weekday night until 1943, after broadcasting an incredible 4,091 15-minute episodes, the two-man show backed off the nightly grind and became a half-hour weekly comedy for another 12 years. The show centered on the antics of "the Kingfish" who was always swindling his gullible fellow members, especially Andy, at the Knights of the Sea Lodge and was always in trouble with his wife, Sapphire, and her mother, Ramona. Gosden was the voice of George "Kingfish" Stevens, Brother Crawford, Lightning, and a dozen other male and female main characters. Correll narrated the show as Amos and did most of the bit parts. Together, over the show's first decade, the two white actors did more than 120 distinct black character voices. If ever there were radio actors whose faces didn't transition from radio to television, it was Gosden and Correll. But they still wanted to take their show to TV, and in 1948 while he was in New

York, they asked the 61-year-old Moore to star as the Kingfish on a CBS Sunday night television adaptation of the radio show. Moore declined, saying that he didn't want to do a live show because "Sunday is for church, not work." For three years, the white comedy duo looked for a suitable Kingfish. After 800 actors struck out, they wanted to ask Moore to reconsider, but they couldn't find him.

Finally after the Apollo's manager dug up Moore's Rock Island address, by dangling lots of money in front of him, the producers lured the famous catfish fisherman back to New York. Starting in 1951, Moore starred in 78 *Amos 'n' Andy Shows* that were written by the same writers, who six years later wrote *Leave It To Beaver*. From the radio show's early years, black media had criticized *Amos 'n' Andy* for racial stereotyping, mocking malapropisms, and derogatory characterizations. One black paper in particular, the *Pittsburgh Courier*, turned its editorial protest into a crusade, and although the NAACP didn't back the paper's protest of the radio show, when black actors starting saying the same lines Gosden and Correll had drawled for 23 years, the black organization protested and put pressure on Blatz Brewing to drop their sponsorship. After three seasons, the show quietly went off the air. In December 1958, after more than a half century of making people laugh, Moore died at the age of 71

In 1914 during the peak years of vaudeville, radio came to the Tri-Cities. Four years earlier in California, a geek tinkerer, Charles Herrold, started broadcasting to some other geeks who assembled their own primitive receivers. Herrold's station eventually became KCBS. A Rock Island electronics whiz, Robert Karlowa, was not only an accomplished engineer, but was also an entrepreneur. On an amateur wavelength, Karlowa started broadcasting weather, news, and sports scores, and played music when he ran out of things to say. Apparently, the format worked, because within a decade every radio station in the country was doing the same thing. Being way ahead of his time, Karlowa realized that if broadcasting were to be commercially viable, there would have to be a listening audience. So, he started making radios and selling them for $30 ($375) a pop. His regional newspaper ad was an early example of the technology salesman's creed of "If you can't dazzle them with brilliance, baffle them with bullshit:"

OH, BOY! BUT WE GOT SOME FISH!

Although, we won't "stake our bankroll in providing some of the stories about our catch, we will "shoot the whole works" and "bank" our reputation on the little K73. And we will sure give her our best 73's. Used her at our camp on a 50-foot single wire, average height about 30 feet, and among tall trees. A ground of one rod about two feet in sandy soil. All the area rolled in loud, NAA and NAJ ticked 'em off regular, NUR rattled the diaphragms at 200 miles, and the buzz of 200-meter dope was constant. She sure is good at 150 to 25000 meters. A wonder on music.

THE STORY that's about the new K73 tuner and detector.

THE PRICE IS ...... $30 Express Collect, Rock Island, Ill.

The illustration shows the first K73 manufactured, which took the fishing trip above mentioned. The later models are improved by the addition of an "A" battery potentio-meter, condenser, vernier attachment, smooth running panel rheostat, "A" potentio-meter, coil mount, two short wave coils, UV 200 bulb, "B" battery, and necessary fixed condensers, all in one cabinet 7 ½" inches square, and 8" deep.

Send 5¢ stamp for our 55-page catalog, 4¢ for our CW catalog, or 7¢ for both.

KARLOWA RADIO CO., 514 Best Bldg., Rock Island, Ill.

Apparently having become fabulously wealthy, in 1922 Karlowa sold his radio station to David Daniel Palmer's son, B.J., and disappeared. B.J. Palmer saw radio as a splendid way to spread the word about the medical techniques his father developed. Taking the call letters WOC, which he said stood for the "World of Chiropractic," and beaten by only KDKA in Pittsburgh, Palmer received the nation's second commercial radio license and the first west of the Mississippi. Three years after Palmer started WOC, a Rock Island businessman, Calvin Beardsley, set up a transmitter in the rear of his store. Using the call letters WHBF, which Beardsley said stood for "Where Heroic Blackhawk Fought," he blasted out his programming over a 100-watt transmitter. In 1932 Beardsley moved the station to the Harms Hotel, bumped the transmission to 5,000 watts, and sold the station to the Potter family, who with their ownership of the *Argus*, expanded their monopolization of Rock Island's media.

Downtown Rock Island was tamed in 1918 when the Feds restricted saloons from operating within three miles of the Arsenal and Prohibition became the law, and it was pacified when John Looney was run out of town in 1922. In a decade's time, The District's strip of saloons interspersed with brothels, casinos, and dancehalls converted to retail shops, light manufacturing, and warehousing. Saloons became taverns, restaurants, and cafes. Brothels were converted to offices, and dancehalls made fine hardware stores, five and dimes, and movie theaters. Along 9th Street, a commercial strip of shops, stores, and markets catered to Rock Island's most diverse neighborhood. Michael Brotman came to town to work as a painter and paperhanger, but when an opportunity opened in 1915 to buy Dreamland, a failing, rundown performance hall on a commercial strip between 6th and 7th Avenues, he jumped on it. Brotman slapped a coat of paint on the derelict hall and converted it to a movie theater — an easy conversion requiring only the installation of seats, a screen and projector — and took the first step in becoming the local movie house mogul.

Brotman's family members were the theater's only employees. Because early movie projectors were irritatingly noisy, theater owners hired organists, pianists, and sometimes in large theaters, full orchestras to play music to cover the projector noise. Initially musicians played extemporaneously to fit the mood of the film, but by the 1920s, most films came with sheet music scored for the production. With Isadore playing violin, Buster on drums, and Barney singing and playing the piano, Brotman's three sons drew crowds that often came only to hear them jam. After the performance, they always marched the audience out of the theater with appropriately clever tunes. But it was the boys' mother who was the most innovative entrepreneur. She had the novel idea of selling food and pop to the audience and introduced popcorn to Tri-City moviegoers. Six years after buying Dreamland, Brotman built the 600-seat Rialto on the same 9th Street block — the theater became the neighborhood's centerpiece. Later Brotman owned and operated numerous theaters throughout Rock Island and Moline, including the Ritz, one of the first neighborhood theaters on the hill.

Cinematic improvements and innovations moved quickly from grainy, two-reel black and white short movies to serials to fast-paced thrillers — audiences never tired of watching the beautiful heroine freed from the tracks before the train rolled around the bend — to sound and color in the late 1920s and finally to full length dramas, comedies, adventures, and epic films. Until television brought entertainment on-demand into homes in the 1950s, movie theaters were the coolest place in town. And from the early 1900s through World War II, Rock Island had a score of them: In the West End, at the foot of 18th Street was The Elite, later remodeled and renamed the Spencer, the Airdrome was a block away on 19th Street, the Blackhawk was on the corner of 13th Avenue and 11th Street, the Grand was on 12th Street, and the New Lion was on 6th Street. A block south of the Rialto on 8th Avenue was the West Side Hippodrome, and two blocks north of the Rialto on 4th Avenue stood the West Side Theater, and only a block farther north was the B&B on 3rd Avenue. Making a right turn onto 2nd Avenue, the Lyric, the Colonial, and the Princess lined up along Rock Island's main thoroughfare. Not surprisingly, the Fifth Avenue Theater was on 5th Avenue at the edge of the Broadway District. On the hill, competing with the Ritz, was the Best Theater on 14th Street, located just west of the present day purveyors of Harris "The World's Greatest" Pizza.

Pizza aficionados claim that Harris Pizza may indeed be the world's greatest, and for a generation the pizza's recipe was kept secret. As with all epicurean delights whose ingredients and preparation are undisclosed, foodies and envious competitors were able to eventually break the formula. Food scientists revealed that the unique hand-thrown, quarter-inch-thin dough has a spice mix that has an extra pinch of malt, giving it a nutty flavor, and that the spicy sauce contains both finely ground red chili and cayenne. Devotees, who disdain plebian pizza that tends toward pepperoni and globs of sausage, rave about the lean, twice-ground, fennel-flecked Italian sausage that is spread in an even blanket and topped with finest quality cheeses. The carefully prepared pizzas are cooked in specially-built gas ovens for 12 minutes and cut into narrow strips with scissors. Connoisseurs claim that "Quad City" pizza is a subtle improvement to world-renowned Chicago-style pizza, and are indebted to the master chefs at Harris Pizza.

Only a half-mile west of the original Harris Pizza is one of the first magnificent homes built on the hill. It was constructed by Susanne Denkmann, the youngest of Frederick Denkmann's seven children that survived to adulthood. In 1909 when Rock Island's most desirable bachelorette was 37, she began construction of a Prairie-style home with German half-timbering. The spectacular home was built on an elegantly landscaped ten-acre site at the crest of the hill west of 24th Street. The first social event held in the fabulous home was Denkmann's marriage to John Hauberg, a handsome 42-year-old man, who may have been the region's most eligible bachelor and almost certainly was its most solid citizen. Three years later, Susanne mothered Catherine, and in 1915, two-year-old Catherine had a little brother, John. Whereas Susanne Denkmann was born into a wealthy, well-established family, John Hauberg was born on a farm near the mouth of the Rock Island rapids. One of eight children, Hauberg attended school until he was 11, when he was forced to drop out to help with the farm, but his education didn't end. Insatiably curious and a constant reader, Hauberg left the farm when he was 20 and headed west to begin a life of thoughtful exploration and adventure. Over a three-year period, he worked on a railroad construction gang in Missouri and at an Arkansas sawmill. But it was his job as a ranch hand that captivated him and influenced the rest of his life. A decade after Theodore Roosevelt had satisfied his thirst for rugged adventure on ranches in North Dakota's badlands, the remarkably similar Hauberg, whose life and ideals had amazing parallels to Roosevelt's, did the same on a ranch in Chugwater, Wyoming. When he returned home, he enrolled in Duncan's Business College in Davenport. After his graduation in 1894, he headed east and enrolled in Northern Indiana Normal College (now Valparaiso University).

The college offered an accelerated program, where in 50 weeks of classes that began at 6:30 a.m. and ended at 9 p.m. and were uninterrupted by holidays, one could earn a bachelor's degree. The intense school days did afford time for Hauberg to play tennis, debate, perform with the military drill team, and sing in the choir. He received a

Bachelor of Science degree in 1896 and a Bachelor of Arts in 1897. He then moved to Ann Arbor and enrolled in the Law Department at the University of Michigan, all while working odd jobs to pay his way. During summer vacation after his first year of law school, Hauberg and a college friend bicycled from Ann Arbor to Washington D.C. and New York City and back. The more than 1,000 mile trip was done over rutted wagon trails, and his bicycle, which he named "Rocinante" after Don Quixote's steed, in no way resembled today's trail bikes.

After obtaining his LL.B, Hauberg rode Rocinante back to his family's farm, which he briefly visited before again heading east to work his way to Europe on a cattle ship. On the first of his several European tours, he lived in Berlin for a while, where he worked for an opera company so that he could attend performances for free. Three years before Gertrude Stein arrived in Europe and wrote about how educational and fashionable it was for young American college graduates to experience the Continent, he visited England, Holland, Belgium, Switzerland, Austria, and Germany.

Returning to the States, Hauberg established a law practice in Moline before moving it to Rock Island when he married Denkmann ten years later. He became involved in Lutheran Church and community work, and especially enjoyed working with children, who were drawn to him because he was an adult who loved doing what they too loved. He founded the United Sunday School Boys Band, a fife, drum, and bugle corps. Formed for the boys of the 7th Street Lutheran Mission, in its second year Hauberg opened the band to all, when boys of other denominations started to gather to listen and watch. His only requirement was that the boys weekly attend some church's Sunday school. Under Hauberg's direction the band thrived for 15 years, and hundreds of proud boys marched in parades and gave performances throughout the Tri-Cities.

A passionate outdoorsman and curious traveler, during the school year Hauberg planned weekend hikes for the boys, and in the summer a longer trip. The boys' "Big Hike" was an annual two-week long journey of hiking. Traveling by foot, but supported by wagons and later trucks, the boys and Hauberg hiked and climbed the hills and bluffs throughout Rock Island county, played their instruments, had ball games, cooked over campfires, and slept under the stars. After World War II, Hauberg turned the Big Hike over to the YMCA, and the hike turned into a road trip. Each summer Dale Holmgren, the Y manager, loaded several dozen boys into the back of a big, red cattle truck that was customized with wooden benches along the sides and covered by a roll-down canvas tarp in case of rain. Camping in parks along the way, the Y Truck covered America on road trips that would make Jack Kerouac envious.

For adults Hauberg organized the Black Hawk Prairie Club, which later changed its name to the Black Hawk Hiking Club. The group hiked year round, regardless of the weather — a hike was never cancelled. Hike guidelines included designating a leader to build a campfire at the end of the hike, make hot chocolate, and prepare a meal over the fire. And long before the Sierra Club popularized similar wilderness policy, Hauberg forbade the picking of wildflowers, nuts, or fruit on his hikes. "Big Hikes" for the adults took them from coast to coast and from Canada to Mexico, and once to Switzerland. Hauberg served as president of the Black Hawk Hiking Club for twenty years. A Prohibitionist, Hauberg did not allow liquor on his adventures.

His church involvement also included serving as president of the Luther League of Illinois for four years. He was superintendent of Sunday school at the 7th St. Lutheran Mission and president of the County Sunday School for ten years and its state president for two terms. He was a member of the Board of Trustees and Finance Committee of the International Council of Religious Education and represented Illinois at the World's Sunday School Convention in Glasgow, Scotland.

In the year before he married, Hauberg became the attorney for the Rock Island Law and Order League. By 1910 John Looney was operating outside of Rock Island's law, and there was little order in The District. Also, Looney had started to encroach on the more orderly liquor establishments in Moline by demanding payments from the beer and liquor wholesalers who supplied Moline's saloons, if they wished to sell their products in the lucrative Rock Island market. Few businessmen and politicians were up to the fight against Looney, but Hauberg led the small contingent that was. The Law and Order League hired investigators to gather evidence against Looney. The investigators were beaten up and jailed in Rock Island on trumped-up charges, and Looney's *Rock Island News* ran a stream of fictitious, but embarrassing, stories attacking Hauberg. The *News*, in an egregious distortion of First Amendment rights, filed libel suits against the League and Hauberg.

Hauberg was a guardsman and invested observer in 1912 when the National Guard was called in to quell the riots and drive Looney out of town. Recently married and now living in Rock Island, Hauberg joined the tepid fight to clean up The District, but the effort received little support. After Looney was banished to his New Mexico ranch, Rock Island breathed a collective sigh of relief, and even the *Argus* took The District off the front page. Hauberg took a broader view and became involved in Rock Island County's temperance movement and served as president of the Illinois Anti-Saloon League.

Locally, he started his Prohibition efforts in Moline by becoming chairman of a "local option" campaign to outlaw liquor in Moline. However, by the time the initiative reached the ballot in 1914, Looney had been gone for two years, and lawlessness in both cities had been dramatically reduced. The proposed ban became a referendum on

Prohibition, and even Moline would have no part of that nonsense. Hauberg suffered one of the few defeats in his life. Possibly Rock Island's most respected resident, Hauberg never tarnished his reputation by running for political office. (Hauberg was about the only prominent Rock Islander who was not present at the murder of Conner Looney.)

After marrying, Hauberg moved his law practice to Rock Island. But after three years of marriage, he closed his law books for good to focus on Denkmann's family's business interests. He served as vice-president of the Manufacturers Trust and Savings Bank of Rock Island, and as chairman of the board when the bank consolidated with the Rock Island Savings Bank and the Central Trust and Savings Bank. He also served as president of Weyerhaeuser & Denkmann Company, Rock Island Sash and Door Works, Rock Island Lumber Company, RILCO Laminated Products Company, Rock Island Millwork, Denkmann Paper Company, and Tallahala Lumber Company. He was vice-president of the Northern Lumber Company and Natalbany Lumber Company and was a director of the Rock Island Plow Company and Servus Rubber Company. Although an exceptionally adept businessman, all were positions that he felt duty-bound to fulfill to protect his wife's interests, and business was not his passion.

During this period of intense professional involvement, Hauberg's elevated sense of values never changed. He continued to put aside small chunks of time for travel with his family and to entertain friends and family in their fine home. Also, the Haubergs were extraordinarily philanthropic, especially with causes concerning education, the underprivileged, and children. Both were active with the YMCA and YWCA. John Hauberg served on the board of directors of the Moline and Rock Island YMCAs and as vice-president of the Illinois State Association of Young Men's Christian Associations. He was chairman of the Illinois Older Boys Conference, an annual event that drew thousands of boys together from around the state. In addition, the couple went to Helsingfors, Finland, to represent Illinois at the World Conference on Boys' Work in Young Men's Christian Associations. Susanne donated the land for Archie Allen, a Rock Island YWCA camp, and John donated land to the Moline and Rock Island YMCAs for Camp Hauberg — both camps were built on the Mississippi River close to where John had grown up on the Hauberg farm.

Before building her own home, Susanne Denkmann built the West End Settlement House at 7th Avenue and 5th Street. She had attended the National Kindergarten College in Chicago (now National-Louis University), where the importance of early education was stressed. While in Chicago, she visited the Hull House, "a community of university women" who were inspired by the charitable work of Jane Adams and whose main purpose was to provide social and educational opportunities for immigrants and working class people in the surrounding neighborhood. Hull House was the first of more than 500 of the country's "settlement houses." At a time when government was uninvolved in social work, Denkmann organized and paid for Rock Island's settlement house. After its construction, the Haubergs remained long-term joint directors of the West End Settlement House.

The couple also gave generously of their time and money to Augustana College. John served for 37 years, 19 as president, on the Augustana College and Theological Seminary Board of Directors and was vice-president of Augustana's Handel Oratorio Society. The college rewarded him with an honorary LL.D. degree. He was a trustee of Port Byron Academy, which he had briefly attended as a child; a board member of the Tri-City Symphony Orchestra; secretary of Bethany Protective Association, a voluntary child welfare agency in Moline; president of the Rock Island Rotary Club, the Chamber of Commerce, and the County Pioneer and Old Settlers' Association; secretary of Riverside Cemetery; president and director of the Chippiannock Cemetery Association; a sergeant in the 6th Illinois Infantry of the National Guard; a board member of the Rock Island Public Library; and president and curator of the Rock Island County Historical Society. For fun and to keep himself busy, the relentlessly energetic Hauberg joined the Outing Club of Davenport; the Tri-City Men's Rose Garden Club; the Press Club of Chicago; and the Chicago, Mississippi Valley, and Augustana Historical Societies; as well as the Iowa, Wisconsin, and Minnesota State Historical Societies.

Possibly because his legacy is so overwhelmingly broad and because he left a rich trove of historical writings and photography, Hauberg is thought of first as a historian — one of his lesser passions. His historical contributions were a result of satisfying his personal curiosity and sharing with others what he thought important. Probably, his most notable contribution to Rock Island was spearheading the drive to buy the land Saukenuk stood on from private parties and create Black Hawk State Park, now Black Hawk State Historic Site. He stated the argument for the public acquisition of the land in a 78-page pamphlet that he placed before the Illinois State Senate. After giving a persuasive presentation to the legislature, his proposal received unanimous approval. He then donated many of the Indian relics that were displayed in the museum that was later named after him.

Hauberg's interest in photography began when he was 19, and he purchased a $4.50 ($120) camera from the Montgomery Ward catalog. Over the next 65 years, he took more than 4,000 glass negatives, 3,000 lanternslides, 60,000 film negatives, and 1,000 35mm slides. His cameras were usually with him, and he took pictures of everything that interested him. He was in great demand to show his slides and tell stories about his travels and adventures, and it is estimated that he spoke to more than

300 different audiences about them. He interviewed and photographed 350 Tri-City area pioneers and recorded their oral histories. He authored nearly 150 unpublished volumes of Rock Island County and Illinois history, which he typed himself and then placed in binders with relevant photographs. He published many articles and booklets on Tri-City area and Illinois history and also a Hauberg family history and his German heritage, which he entitled *A Midwestern Family*. In 1953 Hauberg received the Award of Merit from the American Association for State and Local History for his contributions to historical writing.

Hauberg had established the Indian Pow-Wow at Black Hawk Park in 1940. To create an appreciation and respect for Native American culture, he brought the Meskwaki tribe from Tama, Iowa, to demonstrate their customs and dances. At the first pow-wow, Hauberg was elected an honorary chief of the tribe and named "Ah-be-chi-ne-ma-so-ta Ma-qua," or "Standing Bear." His last public appearance was in August 1955 when an audience of 3,000 honored him. Over the long Labor Day weekend, 57 family members gathered at the Eighth Hauberg Family Reunion at Archie Allen Camp to again honor him. He died nine days later on September 13, 1955 at the age of 85. The next year Susanne and John Hauberg's children donated their family home to the City of Rock Island. It is now the Hauberg Civic Center.

The year after Susanne and John Hauberg married, Audubon, a modest frame elementary school opened three blocks east of their estate on 27th Street and to the north on 18th Avenue. Within a decade, the first Audubon school was unable to accommodate the hordes of children from the new homes in the Hilltop District. In the fall of 1922, 324 students began the term at a majestic Georgian Rival style school that the *Argus* praised and noted, "Two rooms stood out as worthy of notice above all the others, one the library and the other the combination auditorium and gymnasium. The library is a large room and many windows on the east side furnish plenty of light. Something new has been worked out in the combination auditorium and gymnasium. The auditorium with the balcony will easily seat 500 people. When the auditorium is needed for a gymnasium, the front seats of the auditorium directly below the balcony to the stage are rolled under the stage out of the way with the result that part of the auditorium has been converted into a good sized gymnasium."

Audubon's new principal was Jane Wilcox. She had been a teacher in the Rock Island school district for 35 years, was a teacher at the first Audubon school for its entire ten years of operation, and had taught Catherine Hauberg and her younger brother John, Jr. Promoted to principal, she oversaw the opening of the new school. Her friendship with the Hauberg children's parents resulted in the gift of 20 John James Audubon bird prints to the school. Sadly, Wilcox died of a heart attack five months after the opening of the new school. Little was thought of the prints until 65 years later when a parent, who was rummaging through the school's attic looking for a storage box, found them and recognized their value. All but one of the prints (a whippoorwill, which was donated to Augustana) were sold to a Chicago art house for $15,289 ($29,300). The 45,000 square foot school was closed in June 2010 to make way for the new Rock Island Center for Math & Science, which opened the next fall on the site of the old Villa de Chantal.

In 1926 while John Hauberg was successfully helping guide Rock Island's burgeoning business community to new heights and the Deere heirs — to the temporary detriment of their plow and farm implement product line — were dabbling in automotive and airplane manufacturing, in 1926 International Harvester opened a tractor factory in Rock Island. Within four years, 100,000 Farmall tractors had been produced. Building a general-purpose tractor designed for the average family farmer, Farmall separated itself from its competition when it introduced the "tricycle" wheel configuration where two, small narrowly spaced tires tracked a single row. This design allowed for easier maneuvering and more accurate cultivation than the Deere or Ford tractors, and Farmall soon became farmers' first choice. By 1939 IH Farmall passed the combined annual tractor sales of Ford and Deere, a sales advantage they maintained for the next two decades, when they sold more than 400,000 tractors. The huge Farmall plant was located north of the railroad tracks in the far northeast corner of Rock Island and ran for a half mile along the Mississippi River banks up to the Moline city limits. The plant provided Rock Island an enviable source of well-paying jobs that was sustained into the 1970's.

The post-Prohibition population of East Moline — Moline's forgotten little stepsister — had swollen in the three decades preceding World War II. With no more farmland to annex and with the city boundaries of Rock Island and Moline constrained by the Mississippi to the north and west, the Rock River to the south, and each other to the east and west, inexpensive land for new commercial and residential development was squeezed northeasterly up the Mississippi into what is now East Moline and Silvis. Giving no forethought that the farmland that crested the bluffs above the factories would someday become highly-valuable real estate, in 1914 in an unwise community-image move, East Moline had annexed Watertown, the home of the Illinois State Mental Hospital. Located on the bluffs overlooking the Mississippi and housed in a Gothic mansion that was called "The Castle on the Mississippi," the mental hospital would become a weekend evening destination for decades of local high schoolers looking for creepy adventures. By 1944 the hospital complex was home to more than 2,200 mental patients, living in 43 separate buildings scattered on more than 600 manicured acres.

The institution's buildings included a 1,000-seat theater, a gymnasium, three bowling lanes, pool tables, a recreation hall that held 1,500, and arts and crafts and sewing rooms. Weekly concerts by local bands and orchestras in the magnificent assembly room allowed the residents to dance to the finest music the Tri-Cities had to offer — The Castle was unquestionably East Moline's finest address.

In the mid-1930s International Harvester expanded their tractor storage facility in the dingy industrial area that fronted East Moline's riverbanks and built a thresher factory. The housing needs for the hospital's staff, factory workers, and teachers for the recently constructed and smartly named United Township High School that drew students from farms and communities up to 20 miles away, had caused a prewar building boom on the bluffs above the factories. Although less than half the size of Moline, the smallest of the three Tri-Cities, but buoyed by rapid growth and a high school that competed in sports, albeit poorly, against the area's larger schools, towards the end of the Depression, East Moline started to say that it was one of the "Quad Cities."

Citing the confusion of being a suburb of a community that had the same name as a similarly-sized community in southeastern Washington, East Moline diplomatically suggested that the Tri-Cities would be enhanced by becoming the "Quad Cities," and that they would agree to be the fourth city. Most of the Illinois Tri-City residents didn't care what they were called as long as it didn't play up the Iowa connection. Because cosmopolitan Illinoisans resented being associated with rubes from Iowa, they saw an upside to the name "Quad Cities," in that Iowans would be minimized demographically and, of course, four is better than three. With yawning indifference from the other cities, East Moline stuck with the regional designation, and slowly, Tri-City citizens started to repaint their signage.

Across the river, a village that started as a cluster of homes conveniently built within a short walk of the Lillienthal Tavern merged with the village of Gilbert at the turn of the 20th century and gave two brothers, Joseph and William Bettendorf, 70 acres of riverfront land on the condition that they moved their wagon factory there — and they promised to rename the town after them if they did. Beaten to the public relations' punch and apparently jealous of East Moline's panache, Bettendorf, Iowa, objected to being left out of the renaming. They objected that they were a real city — not a mere township — were physically twice as large as East Moline, occasionally beat them in football and basketball and they were more deserving to be the fourth Quad City. During the critical years of the territorial battle of words, Bettendorf was distracted by a seven-year civil war with the Aluminum Company of America over whether the giant Bettendorf ALCOA plant that sat on 1,100 acres alongside the

Mississippi River was able to secede from Bettendorf. In February of 1950 the Iowa Supreme Court said they could and upheld the secession and incorporation of a new town, Riverdale.

After the smoke cleared, Bettendorf rejoined the naming battle and thought they had the solution when they suggested calling the megalopolis the "Quint Cities." Giving Iowa disk jockeys something to rant about, WOC Radio jumped on the bandwagon and starting calling themselves the "Quint Cities Favorite Radio Station." Totally miffed, Milan, which was settled when Black Hawk lived across the river at Saukenuk, suggested the "Sex Cities," but they were totally ignored. After a decade of general disinterest, Bettendorf backed off their proposed renaming and settled into being half of the fourth Quad City. Today, five cities comprise the Quad Cities and anchor a sprawling, mostly connected patchwork of 17 Iowa and 14 Illinois municipalities that hold a place in the Greater Quad City Area.

During this dynamic time of new businesses and neighborhoods along the south banks of the Rock Island Rapids, when the Tri-cities were the Farm Implement Capital of the World and the Cubs dominated conversations in the local speakeasies, Prohibition hung like black funeral crepe over the country. Within months of its implementation, cries for its repeal began, and the issue moved back onto the center stage of politics. With their growing Protestant and rural constituency — at the time, three-quarters of the U.S. economy was agrarian based — Republicans pledged themselves to the "dry" camp. On the other side of the aisle, the Democratic Party was sharply divided between its "wet" Northern, urban Jews and Catholics and its dry, Protestant Southerners who shared the same beliefs as Republicans but couldn't get over their hatred for anything associated with Abraham Lincoln.

Warren Harding's sudden death provided a serendipitous way for Republican leadership to cleanse the party of corruption, rid itself of the scandalous Ohio Gang, and introduce Calvin Coolidge to the nation. A fifth-generation, Protestant New Englander, Coolidge was the perfect Republican for the time. He was a popular, honest lawyer who believed in smaller government and had a feel for the country's needs. A biographer wrote of him, "He embodied the spirit and hopes of the middle class, could interpret their longings and express their opinions."

In 1924 the Democrats met in New York City, the center of illicit liquor, to select a worthy opponent for Coolidge. Party cultural differences immediately coalesced behind polar-opposite candidates. A Californian, William McAdoo, was a former Secretary of the Treasury and the son-in-law of Woodrow Wilson. Democratic "Drys" and those from the South, Far West, and the rural areas of the Midwest supported

McAdoo. The "Wets" and those from the East and the urban areas in the Midwest backed New York Governor, Al Smith.

Improbably, an unbridgeable chasm developed over the political legitimacy of the Ku Klux Klan. The Klan's popularity peaked at the time of the convention, and it had as many as 5 million members in chapters in all 48 states. Ignoring that a Klan member would never vote for a Republican, a brutal floor fight developed over whether the party should publicly condemn the Klan. McAdoo had a solid majority of the convention delegates; however, it took two-thirds to elect, and the liberals backing Smith would not back down. After two weeks and 100 ballots, delegates were running low on money and energy. Will Rogers joked that New York had invited the Democratic delegates to visit the city, not to live there. After the 100th ballot, McAdoo and Smith withdrew, and the Democrats conceded the election to the Republicans when they nominated an obscure former West Virginia congressman, John W. Davis.

Progressives were increasingly elitist, and Democratic egalitarians from Wisconsin were so disgruntled by the New York convention that they ran favorite son, Robert La Follette, under the defunct Progressive Party's name. La Follette was a Republican senator and only slightly better known than Davis. However, in the general election millions of Democrats bolted from the party and backed La Follette, who ended up carrying Wisconsin and received more than half of the popular vote that Davis received. When the vote was tallied, it was obvious that the Democrats never had a chance. In one of the biggest landslides in American presidential voting, "Cool Cal" Coolidge received 54 percent of the popular vote and 72 percent of the electoral vote. In an election that has been described as "the high water mark of American conservatism," both major party candidates were traditional conservatives who advocated less government. The Democrat, Davis, campaigned on the very un-Democratic platform of limited government, lower taxes, and less regulation. He didn't carry his home state of West Virginia, but he did carry the Solid South, Texas, and Oklahoma. The Progressive La Follette campaigned on the liberal platform of nationalizing cigarette factories and other large industries. He strongly supported increased taxation of the wealthy and the right of collective bargaining for factory workers. He carried his home state of Wisconsin.

Harding's was an easy act to follow, and without intervention from Coolidge, corruption in Washington slipped back behind closed doors. The country was at peace, post-war inflation was under control, and the economy was humming. Europeans were scratching their heads wondering why anyone would buy into Russia's Vladimir Lenin's party line encouraging workers of the world to unite when laissez-faire capitalism was giving U.S. workers the highest standard of living in the history of mankind — even if they couldn't legally buy a beer. Coolidge praised his party's economic success by proclaiming: "The requirements of existence have passed beyond the standard of necessity into the region of luxury."

Unlike many of his fellow lawyers turned politicians, Coolidge believed in an economy of words. After he vacated his position as Massachusetts' governor to become vice-president, he was approached by his successor Channing Cox and asked how he was able to see a long list of callers every day and yet leave the office by five, while Cox was often detained until nine. "How come the difference?" asked Cox. "You talk back," said Coolidge. Another time at dinner, a woman sitting next to him said, "I have made a bet that I could get more than two words out of you." "You lose," said Silent Cal. And on returning from church one Sunday, he was asked what the minister's sermon was about. "Sin," said Coolidge. "And what did he say about sin?" his questioner probed. "He was against it," the president replied.

Chapter 22

Serious Depression

The Great Depression, like most other periods of severe unemployment, was produced by government mismanagement rather than by any inherent instability of the private economy. ~ Milton Friedman, economist

The miserable failures of capitalist economies in the Great Depression were root causes of worldwide social and political disasters. ~ James Tobin, economist

WHEN BABE RUTH was told in 1930 that his salary was more than President Herbert "The Great Humanitarian" Hoover's, he said, "I know, but I had a better year" — and unarguably he did. The laissez-faire business and unregulated economic policies of Presidents Harding and Coolidge pumped up a stock speculation bubble that burst in Hoover's face. Economists argue whether economic depressions are part of natural economic cycles or are government failures. However, few argue that Hoover, who had been in office only seven months before the October 1929 Stock Market Crash, had much responsibility for the economic conditions and policies that led to the Great Depression — his stultifying inaction and policy decisions that worsened the Depression are a totally different argument.

Hoover was a complex man with simple tastes. The only president to be born in Iowa, his Quaker parents died before he was ten. Brought up by an uncle in Oregon, instead of going to high school, he worked in a land office during the day and studied bookkeeping and math at night school. Because Stanford University apparently had less restrictive admittance requirements than today, as a 17-year-old high school dropout, Hoover enrolled there in 1891, the college's first year and only year that tuition was not charged. By virtue of being the first student admitted into the school's first class, Hoover proudly proclaimed himself to be the university's "first student."

Hoover was Stanford's student manager for both the baseball and football teams. Because the school didn't have a football coach and there wasn't time to properly train for an autumn game during the school's first semester, the first Big Game with the University of California was put off until the following spring. Cal had been established 23 years earlier and had fielded a football team for the previous five seasons. Entering the game, the Golden Bears from Berkeley were confident of overwhelming the small first-year college on a horse farm in Palo Alto. Held on a field on Haight Street in San Francisco on March 19, the inaugural Big Game was further delayed because Hoover, and everyone else, forgot to bring a football. After finding a ball, Stanford easily humbled Cal 14-10 — establishing an athletic dominance over their primary rival that they would never relinquish. The next spring, when Hoover, who took his managerial and fiscal responsibilities seriously, discovered that Benjamin Harrison, who had left the presidency in March, had entered the ungated baseball field without paying, he personally hit him up for the 25¢ admission fee.

During his senior year, Hoover became enamored with Lou Henry, a freshman from Waterloo, Iowa, who was the only women in the geology school. Hoover graduated with a degree in geology, and three years later when he cabled a marriage proposal from Australia, she cabled back her acceptance. For the next two decades, the Hoovers traveled the world, and he became a highly respected mining engineer. (After World War II, detailed topographical maps of Russia's Kyshtym region that Hoover drew and gave with his papers to Stanford provided valuable Cold War intelligence on the location of the Soviet's first plutonium facility.) He was made wealthy by his mining career, and when World War I began, he led 500 volunteers in assisting the safe return of Americans from Europe. He later said, "I did not realize it at the moment, but on August 3, 1914, my career was over forever. I was on the slippery road of public life." When the U.S. entered the war, Hoover was appointed to head the Food Administration. After the war, he provided aid to Germany as well as relief to Bolshevik Russia. Criticized by fellow Republicans for helping the Bolshevik cause, Hoover retorted, "Twenty million people are starving. Whatever their politics, they shall be fed!" The *New York Times* named Hoover one of the Ten Most Important Living Americans.

In 1912 Hoover followed Theodore Roosevelt to the short-lived Bull Moose Party, and eight years later he rejected overtures from Democrats to join their party and stuck with the Republicans. After the election, Harding rewarded him for his loyalty by appointing him Secretary of Commerce. An engineer by training, Hoover was a proponent of the "Efficiency Movement," which was backed by philanthropic industrialists such as Andrew Carnegie and John D. Rockefeller, and held that government and the economy were rife with inefficiency and waste, which could be improved by experts who could identify and solve problems. Hoover envisioned the Commerce Department as the hub of the nation's economic growth and financial stability. Because Harding was inexperienced in business and finance, he gave Hoover an inordinate amount of power and allowed him to encroach on other departments' responsibilities. As one of the most visible men in the country, pundits referred to Hoover as the "Secretary of Commerce and Under-Secretary of Everything Else!"

The devastating Mississippi River floods during 1927 further boosted Secretary of Commerce Hoover, who was in charge of flood relief operations and favorably projected him into the national spotlight, setting the stage for his election to the presidency. Besides giving Hoover Midwestern and Southern exposure, the flood improbably helped contribute to his defeat four years later. White Southerners praised him for his handling of the refugee camps, but the treatment of blacks in those camps and during the year of flooding prompted him to promise the black community that significant reforms would be made if he were elected. In trade for the promises, the Colored Advisory Commission headed by Robert Russa Moton allowed the Republicans to suppress reports of the terrible situations in the refugee camps. After sweeping the 1928 election, the Republicans did nothing, and led by Moton, black political allegiance shifted from the Republican Party to the Democrats — improbably aligning blacks and white Dixiecrats against Republicans.

The flood created a great outpouring of emotion that was expressed in song and produced one good short story, "Old Man," by William Faulkner, which is about a prison break from Parchman Penitentiary. Along with many others, Charlie Patton, Barbecue Bob, and Bessie Smith wrote and sang songs about the flood. Kansas Joe McCoy and Memphis Minnie's *When the Levee Breaks* was reworked and released by Led Zeppelin in 1971 and became one of the British groups' most popular songs. Decades after the flood, songs continued to pour forth: Zachary Richard's *Big River*, Eric Bibb's *Flood Water*, and Randy Newman's *Louisiana 1927*.

Although Hoover sacrificed the black vote in 1928 because of his broken promises, he understood the math of getting elected, and this led to his development of the "Southern Strategy," a tactic that exploited Southern racism. Although whites in the Deep South remained solidly Democratic until Northerners in their party pushed through the Civil Rights Act of 1964, the electorates from states bordering the South — Tennessee, North Carolina, Florida, Virginia, and Texas — were torn over protecting their economic interests, which aligned them with the Republican Party, and their dislike of Protestant Northerners, who were also predominately Republicans. As a result, their racism usually won out. Hoover and the Republicans played to fears about black lawlessness, loss of states' rights, and economic inequalities and wooed votes from those swing states. Hoover became the first Republican presidential candidate to win Texas, and the Southern Strategy was locked into place until Deep South Dixiecrats finally forgot their Lincoln problem and split with the Democratic Party over civil rights issues during the 1960s.

Hoover clobbered Al Smith in 1928. Smith, an honest, anti-Prohibitionist, Roman Catholic from the Northeast, didn't have a chance. Even the solidly Democratic

Ku Klux Klan opposed the New Yorker and justified backing Hoover because the Catholic Church was an "un-American, alien culture" that opposed freedom and democracy. However, Hoover's half-year honeymoon with the populace ended abruptly over two days in October 1929 when the New York Stock Market tumbled 25 percent. The market had been on an incredible six-year run during Coolidge's entire presidency that saw market value rise five-fold. Starting at the end of the summer, a volatile market had taken huge swings, causing economist Irving Fisher to predict, "Stock prices have reached what looks like a permanently high plateau." Economists agree that unregulated trading fueled by brokers lending investors more than two-thirds the face value of stocks created an overheated, speculative market that led to the market's free-fall. However, today most economists view the Stock Market Crash as a symptom of a cluster of causes contributing to the Great Depression that followed The Crash. In 1998 the *Economist* succinctly stated, "Briefly, the Depression did not start with the Stock Market Crash."

One of the causes was Republican-backed tariff increases that were rammed through Congress in the Smoot-Hawley Tariff Act. During his campaign for reelection in 1828, Hoover promised beleaguered farmers, who were not enjoying the same level of economic prosperity that city laborers were, that he would bolster prices by increasing tariffs on agricultural products. The pledge bought Hoover votes he didn't need and assured large Republican majorities in the House and Senate. It also created an obligation to farmers, Hoover's strongest supporters that he felt he had to honor. As the tariff act made its way through Congress in the weeks leading to The Crash, it caused trading swings. After the House overwhelmingly passed the bill in May 1929 and the Senate began to deliberate its version, the market became unstable, teetered in late summer, and then fell over the edge in October. Displaying party loyalty over good economic legislation, the Senate passed their version of the bill in March 1930.

In May 1930, well after economic conditions had rapidly deteriorated, almost two thousand bi-partisan economists signed a petition asking Hoover to veto the legislation. Henry Ford called it "economic stupidity" and spent an evening with Hoover, pleading with him to veto the bill. J.P. Morgan's chief executive said he "almost went down on [his] knees to beg Herbert Hoover to veto the asinine Smoot-Hawley tariff." A man of his word, Hoover signed the bill, and over the next three years U.S. exports fell to a third of their 1929 totals, farmers' lives worsened, and unquestionably, the "asinine" tariffs accelerated and deepened the Depression. When Hoover lamented to Calvin Coolidge that his attempts to stimulate economic recovery seemed to be making little impact and that his critics were becoming increasingly vocal, Coolidge counseled, "You can't expect to see calves running in the field the day after you put the bull to the cows." The downcast president replied, "No, but at least I would expect to see contented cows."

In addition to the Smoot-Hawley Act, abuses by unregulated utility holding companies, widespread failures of commercial banks that had invested customer deposits in the stock market, a near total breakdown of international trade, and a failure by government to regulate interest rates and money supply contributed to the economic free-fall started by the Stock Market Crash. There were many other contributing factors, including the weather — drought from 1930 to 1936 and poor farming techniques turned the southern Great Plains into a "dust bowl." Also, once the panic set in and spread, the world fell into deflation, and the extremely wealthy understood that they were better off holding onto their cash, because when the economy grew again, as it surely would, their money would gain value. Hoarding cash and gold dried up credit, exacerbated the drop in demand, and fed the Depression.

An example of how long-term recession or depression doesn't hurt those who can afford to go years without new income is the construction of the Empire State Building. Built on a site that in the late 18th century was a pleasant farm with a stream running through it and then from the 1890s until 1930 became the site of the Waldorf-Astoria Hotel, on St. Patrick's Day, six months after the Stock Market Crash, construction began on the world's tallest building. Due to the deflation of the dollar, the cost of labor and materials plunged. Completed in only one year and 45 days, the final costs totaled $24.7 million ($373 million) instead of the estimated $43 million ($650 million). Twenty years after opening and weathering the Depression and World War II, the ownership syndicate headed by John Raskob and Pierre du Pont sold the building for $51 million ($439 million) and profited $225 million in 2012 dollars.

During the year after the Crash, bankers, businessmen, politicians, and the public anticipated that the stock market would rally, as it had in the year after the Panic of 1907, when the market fell almost 50 percent. The government predicted that after markets and prices stabilized, the recession would be similar to the one-year recession of 1907. The nation's powerbrokers also remembered the last recession's rapid recovery and they acted accordingly. In 1907 J.P. Morgan had plowed huge sums of money into shoring up the banking system and convinced other bankers to do the same. It worked, and as a result the Federal Reserve System (the U.S.'s privately managed central bank) was created to perform similar banking services in future economic crises. But in the early months following The Crash, the Fed didn't pump money into the economy, and it badly flunked its first major test.

In a 2000 PBS interview, Nobel Prize-winning economist Milton Friedman said:

> We have to distinguish between the recession of 1929, the early stages, and the conversion of that recession into a major catastrophe. The recession was an ordinary business cycle. We had repeated recessions over hundreds of years, but what converted [this one] into a major depression was bad monetary policy. The Federal Reserve System had been established to prevent what actually happened. It was set up to avoid a situation in which you would have to close down banks, in which you would have a banking crisis. And yet, under the Federal Reserve System, you had the worst banking crisis in the history of the United States. There's no other example I can think of, of a government measure, which produced so clearly the opposite of the results that were intended.
>
> And what happened is that [the Federal Reserve] followed policies which led to a decline in the quantity of money by a third. For every $100 in paper money, in deposits, in cash, in currency, in existence in 1929, by the time you got to 1933 there was only about $65, $66 left. And that extraordinary collapse in the banking system, with about a third of the banks failing from beginning to end, with millions of people having their savings essentially washed out, that decline was utterly unnecessary. At all times, the Federal Reserve had the power and the knowledge to have stopped that. And there were people at the time who were all the time urging them to do that. So it was, in my opinion, clearly a mistake of policy that led to the Great Depression.

A Friedman contemporary, James Tobin, who was also a Nobel prize winner in economics, served on the Council of Economic Advisors and later the Board of Governors of the Federal Reserve System, and taught at Harvard and Yale, postulated that the Great Depression was primarily the result of laissez-faire business practices and unregulated markets. It is certain that neither economist was totally correct — or totally wrong — and it is equally certain that as long as politicians control U.S fiscal policy and economics, the financial pendulum will swing from left to right between prosperity and recession. In June 2012, columnist Martin Wolf said in the *Financial Times*, "Before now, I had never really understood how the 1930s could happen. Now I do. All one needs are fragile economies, a rigid monetary regime, intense debate over what must be done, widespread belief that suffering is good, myopic politicians, an inability to co-operate, and failure to stay ahead of events."

It is now apparent the Fed erred on the side of fiscal conservatism, and Hoover and the public were stranded on a ruptured ship without a lifeboat. At the time, economists generally believed that economic swings were self-correcting. However in the years following the market's crash, conditions continued to worsen and the deepening downspin cast doubt on Republican policy that held fast to this view. Even though interest rates dropped to very low levels, unemployment increased; manufacturing and consumer prices declined; commodity prices plunged; and agriculture, logging, and mining spiraled downward. The period of social adventure and prosperity during the '20s roared to a halt, and Calvin Coolidge's boast that "the requirements of existence have passed beyond the standard of necessity into the region of luxury" was suddenly as empty as the nation's pantries.

The deprivations of the Great Depression formed the attitudes and shaped the ethic of the next two generations of North Americans and Europeans. It is difficult to overstate the dramatic fall in the nation's fortunes during Hoover's administration. And back-to-back readings of F. Scott Fitzgerald's *The Great Gatsby* and John Steinbeck's *The Grapes of Wrath*, a Pulitzer prizewinning novel about Oklahoma sharecroppers driven from their home by economic hardship during the Depression, challenges the reality that the writers were contemporaries who set their novels in the same country within a decade's time of each other.

The public and every sector of the economy pleaded for the government to respond, but each call for action was based on self-interest and every plan's advocate had many opponents. Hoover rejected federal relief programs, saying that a dole would be counterproductive and produce a welfare state that would destroy self-reliance. Instead, he promoted a nebulous public-private alliance to achieve long-term growth, and he appealed to his former friends among the business magnates not to lay off workers and to maintain wage levels. His unrealistic suggestions were ignored, and his ill-conceived policies and inaction contributed to the deteriorating economy. It is now agreed by virtually all economists that the best way to avoid a depression is to stimulate an economy that's in recession with government spending before it falls into depression. The primary opposition to that policy is from the mega-wealthy and high-income professionals who financially benefit from depression and have a disproportionate voice in creating public policy.

In an attempt to recapture the public's confidence, three weeks before the 1932 Democratic convention, Republicans reversed course and voted in a very un-Republican-like tax increase. An act of desperation, the Revenue Act of 1932 raised taxes to an unprecedented level. The income tax rate on the highest incomes shot from 25 percent to 63 percent, the estate tax was doubled, and corporate taxes were raised by 15 percent. To counter the backlash of criticism they received from their conservative constituencies, Hoover and Eastern Republican Congressmen said that the additional revenues would allow the government to stimulate the economy in areas where it would do the most good and happy days would return. It is unclear whether Hoover and his Wall Street cronies were admitting to their errors, were fiscally enlightened, or were frantically buying votes.

During Coolidge's administration, the unemployment rate had held consistently between 3 and 4 percent, but during Hoover's four years in office, unemployment soared to 24 percent. Moderate Republican leaders were correct, of course, in thinking that increased revenue from taxes, redirected towards creating jobs, would stimulate the economy. But the Depression was so severe, it would take eight years, not eight months, to show solid results. Naively, Hoover and Congress did not pluck the low-hanging fruit and seek an end to Prohibition, which everyone outside of Kansas, Utah, Iowa, the Deep South, and organized crime had grown to hate. Besides desperately needed revenues for federal, state, and local governments, the entire nation was in need of a good stiff drink.

In the irony of all ironies, gangster bootleggers gave the final shove to push Prohibition over the edge and end mob control of the big cities. Six months before the October Stock Market Crash and only a month after Herbert Hoover's inauguration, on April 14 Al Capone's Outfit brought in former members of St. Louis' Egan's Rats to assassinate George "Bugs" Moran, the boss of Chicago's North Side Gang. The plan was to lure Moran to a warehouse in his territory on North Clarke Street to receive a shipment of stolen whiskey supplied by Detroit's Purple Gang. A Capone lookout mistakenly reported that Moran was in the warehouse, but Moran had arrived late and saw a police car and two police officers enter the building. He had no idea that the officers were two of Egan's Rats dressed as police, and he slowly drove away as seven of his men were lined up against a wall and gunned down. The only survivor of those inside the warehouse was Highball, a neighbor's German Shepard.

The St. Valentine's Day Massacre drew massive national newspaper coverage and set off a Chicago mob war that forced Hoover to insist to his Secretary of the Treasury Andrew Mellon that Capone must be brought down. Under Mellon's direction, the government created a two-pronged attack against Capone. The first prong was the creation of a unit that was headed by Eliot Ness, a University of Chicago graduate in economics who had earned a master's degree from Chicago in criminology. Ness was a street-smart Chicago native from the Roseland District on the South Side, and because there was rampant corruption within the Chicago Police Department, he formed an elite squad of 10 "outsiders" that became successful in raiding Chicago stills and breweries. Ness claimed to have destroyed a total of more than $1 million ($13 million) of equipment and liquor. Even if his figure was accurate, this was a pittance compared to The Outfit's estimated weekly revenues of $1.5 million. Ness was expert at manipulating the press, and to illustrate his integrity and that of his men, he held a press conference to describe how he had been offered $2,000 ($25,000) a week to "take it easy," and how Capone's men attempted to bribe two of his agents by tossing an envelope of cash into their car, which they tossed back. The media dubbed the team "The Untouchables."

The second government unit was not as glamorous or as publicized as Ness' Untouchables, but was more effective. Working as an investigator for the Bureau of Internal Revenue, over a three-year period Frank Wilson gathered financial evidence by having federal agents infiltrate Capone's rackets and prosecuted him under a Supreme Court ruling that revenue from criminal activities were subject to income taxes. During the investigation, Wilson and his wife moved into Chicago's Sheridan Plaza Hotel disguised as tourists — even his wife didn't know he was investigating Capone. As Wilson diligently tracked down and interrogated Capone's accountants, Capone ordered a hit on him that was thwarted only when Johnny Torrio, who was Capone's mentor and understood the implications of public backlash, insisted that the assassination be called off. Capone reluctantly agreed. None of The Untouchables was killed, but to send a "message" to them, a personal friend of Ness was killed.

For 18 months after the St. Valentine's Day Massacre, Capone operated as a ruthless modern-day Robin Hood, giving extravagant amounts of money from his racketeering profits to Chicago charities. But his charitable contributions and virtual ownership of the Chicago Police Department and courts system weren't enough to prevent his federal conviction for tax evasion, and he was sentenced to 11 years imprisonment. He was never prosecuted for racketeering or Prohibition violations. He entered prison at the age of 32 and was paroled in poor health at age 40. Before his death by a stroke, eight years after his release, his physician, a Baltimore psychiatrist, diagnosed him as having the mental capacity of a 12-year-old — he suffered from acute neurosyphilis, the long-term brain damage resulting from untreated syphilis.

Capone's conviction forced Midwest gangland bosses to become more discrete and less ostentatious, but did little to slow the production and distribution of illegal alcohol in the final year of Prohibition. Arguably, a majority of the public never backed Prohibition, and it was only a dedicated, vocal righteous minority that got the Constitutional Amendment passed. In 1925 journalist H.L. Mencken wrote that the opposite of their predictions was realized:

> Five years of Prohibition have had, at least, this one benign effect: they have completely disposed of all the favorite arguments of the Prohibitionists. None of the great boons and usufructs that were to follow the passage of the Eighteenth Amendment has come to pass. There is not less drunkenness in the Republic, but more. There is not less crime, but more. There is not less insanity, but more. The cost of government is not smaller, but vastly greater. Respect for law has not increased, but diminished.

Speakeasies had become fashionable and unlike saloons, women were always welcome. Before the Eighteenth Amendment was adopted, alcohol consumption and the incidence of alcohol-related domestic violence had already started to decrease, and Progressive social scientists "were dismayed to find that child neglect and violence against children actually increased during the Prohibition era." Mothers also began to worry about what affect the glamorized lifestyles of gangsters and the allure of alcohol would have on their children.

Before the Volstead Act, some Prohibitionists such as Reverend Charles Stelzle claimed that Prohibition would eventually lead to reductions in taxes, since drinking "produced half the business" for institutions supported by tax dollars such as courts, jails, hospitals, almshouses, and insane asylums. He was wrong and, in fact, the Women's Organization for National Prohibition Reform estimated that $861 million ($15 billion) was lost in federal tax revenue from untaxed liquor and $40 million ($650 million) was spent annually on Prohibition enforcement. The loss of "sin tax" revenue and increased government costs as the economy was tanking was the final kicker. In 1932 the Democratic Party's platform included a plank for the repeal of Prohibition, and Franklin Roosevelt ran for president promising repeal of federal Prohibition laws.

While Chicago was a gangland playground during the 1920s, Rock Island became a model city. After the mess left by Mayor Harry Shriver and John Looney was cleaned up, The District returned to business as usual — but much more discretely than in prior years when prostitutes solicited from doorways and open windows and policemen hopped from bar to bar for free after-shift free shots and beers. In 1923, the same year Al Capone moved from his home in Brooklyn to head The Outfit, Walter Rosenfield, a smart 46-year-old World War I vet, was elected mayor. Rosenfield had been among the group of prominent citizens who witnessed the botched assassination of John Looney and the regretful murder of his son Conner. The son of Morris Rosenfield, Walter and his brother and sister grew up in the Gothic mansion at the head of 18th Street, the "handsomest home in the city" that later became the Sisters of Charity convent and the Jewish Center's Educational Center — at different times.

Rosenfield graduated from Rocky and enrolled in St. John's Military School at Manlius, New York. After graduation he returned to Rock Island and assumed the presidency of Moline Wagon Company, his father's business. Before he became an army major in the Great War, he sold the family home. Then when he returned from the war, he bought the plantation-style antebellum Buford mansion, across the street from where he grew up and lived there until 1928. Six years after Rosenfield left the mansion and after extensive remodeling, the Buford home became the Tri-City Jewish Center. Rosenfield added to the family's manufacturing, political, and cultural legacies when he became president and managing partner in Rock Island Bridge and Iron Works, a seven-time delegate from Illinois to the Republican National Convention — the first time in 1912 to nominate William Howard Taft and the last time in 1952 to send Dwight Eisenhower on his way to the White House — and as a cosmopolitan patron of the arts and the lead partner in building the Fort Armstrong Theatre.

After clearing away the first YMCA building, Rosenfield and his partners built their theater on the southwest corner of 3rd Avenue and 19th Street. The magnificent building, graced with a large performance stage and orchestra pit and side and rear balconies, opened in January 1921 to an enthusiastic packed house of 1,566. A ten-piece orchestra accompanied *Midsummer Madness*, a silent movie starring Lila Lee, who made a personal appearance on opening night. Before and after the movie, the audience was treated to a gala of musical and comedy acts, which assured that they received their 40¢ ($5) admission's worth. The theater opened as the golden age of vaudeville was giving way to the silver screen, and for a decade the stylish theater remained the region's finest until the 2,700-seat RKO Orpheum Theater opened in Davenport.

Also during the 1920s, Rock Island's young adults were drawn to dancehalls to jitterbug to live jazz and swing bands. American social dancing had progressed (some say, deteriorated) from the formal court minuet of the 16th and 17th centuries to the flowing waltz of the 18th and 19th centuries to swirling ballroom dance at the turn of the 20th century. But no one except the healthy and exuberantly young at heart was ready for the upbeat, heart-pumping, social defiance of dances like the Charleston and Lindy Hop. For a brief period, Rock Island's young adults flocked to the Palace Amusement Center, a converted warehouse on the northwest corner of 5th Avenue and 13th Street. Roofing contractor and entrepreneur, Herman "Babe" Brandle, put the warehouse that was being used as the Lighthouse Gospel Tabernacle to a more profitable use — he opened a dancehall. The cavernous building was also used for expositions, car shows, boxing matches, and roller-skating.

At the start of the Depression, an early form of survivor-genre reality shows swept the nation with the dance marathon craze, and Rock Island's youth, like those in the rest of the nation, had time on their hands and would do most anything to earn a buck. Dance marathon contests exploited the situation. In 1923 a risqué American girl in London had gained international attention when she danced for 27 straight hours with multiple partners. Predictably, the record became the target of promoters who charged admission to watch contestants dance for a cash prize. The fad exploded and "there were once fifteen thousand people — promoters, emcees, floor judges, trainers, nurses, cooks, janitors, cashiers, ticket-takers, publicity agents, promotion men, musicians, contestants and even a lawyer — whose main source of income over a number of years came from endurance [dance] shows."

In 1930 the Tri-Cities most notable dance marathon began on Wednesday night before Thanksgiving at Brandle's Palace Amusement Center. Fourteen couples began the contest, and after three days of dancing with only 15 minute hygiene and nap breaks every two hours, 3,000 perversely curious spectators paid to see nine remaining couples swing through the 100th hour on Sunday evening — two girls were dancing alone waiting to join a boy if his partner dropped out. It is difficult to imagine what morbid attraction would prompt people to spend money to watch exhausted couples, who had been hanging onto each other for a week, shuffle about, and apparently there weren't many that would. Eight days after the marathon began, the six remaining couples were moved into the Palace gymnasium, so that the main auditorium could be used for a boxing match. At the 200th hour, the *Argus* reported that another couple dropped out. Seemingly for lack of interest, the contest soon ended, and there are no accounts of who won or how long the dancers lasted. Many communities banned marathon dancing, and in 1931 Texas made it illegal to hold a dance marathon in the state.

Movies were the Depression's most popular form of entertainment, and films starring Rock Island's June Haver were sure to simultaneously pack the Fort Armstrong and the RKO Orpheum theaters. Named after the month she was born, on the 10th day of 1926, June Stovenour (she later took her stepfather, Bert Haver's, last name) was born in Rock Island. When Haver was seven, her family briefly moved to Cincinnati where she won a contest and a scholarship to the Cincinnati Conservatory of Music. After the precocious Haver, who had a strong voice, won a film test by imitating Greta Garbo and Katharine Hepburn, her mother, who was an accomplished actress, steered her away from childhood acting and toward music. Returning to Rock Island when she was ten, Haver gained notoriety when she sang with Rudy Vallée's band, and by the time she was 13, she was making $75 ($1,200) a week singing with Rock Island's best bands. The next year, she hosted a Saturday morning children's show on WHBF radio, but the stunningly attractive Haver had the talent, face, and figure for live performance. The following year when she signed a two-year contract for a cross-country tour with the Ted Fio-Rito orchestra, she was forced to abandon her goal of becoming a Rocky cheerleader.

The band took her to Hollywood, and while performing as the featured singer in two short musical films, Haver graduated from Hollywood High School where she acted in school plays. Discovered by a 20th Century Fox scout during her senior year, the 17-year-old signed a $3,500 ($40,000) a week movie contract. The same year she made her first feature film, *Home In Indiana*, which was followed by leads in the musicals, *Look For the Silver Lining, Wake Up and Dream, I Wonder Who's Kissing Her Now, Irish Eyes are Smiling,* and *Oh, You Beautiful Doll.* The year after she made her first feature film, she co-starred with Betty Grable in *The Dolly Sisters*.

Because of their striking physical similarities, Haver was called "Pocket Grable" — Grable was ten years older than Haver and an established star. The Hollywood tabloids created stories of a clash between the actresses, but Haver refuted the columns saying, "Betty is a big star, and I'm just starting. I try to be nice to her, and she reciprocates by being just as nice to me. It's silly to think two girls can't work together without quarreling. You see, I've two sisters. I'm the ham between the bread and butter — the middle sister — and I know girls pretty well. Betty likes to talk about her baby, so we talk about her baby." As an 18-year-old she co-starred with Fred MacMurray in *Where Do We Go from Here?* Eight years later she married MacMurray, who became better known as the dad on the *My Three Sons* television series. Haver left show business and raised their adopted twin girls on their ranch in the Russian River Valley in Northern California.

Rock Island's early movie theaters were converted halls or live performance theaters, but the Rocket Cinema, which opened on 19th Street in 1940, was designed as a movie theater and featured "love seats" which allowed teenage couples to take advantage of the darkened theater. Also, to compete with the larger and more elegant Fort Armstrong Theatre, which was just around the corner, the Rocket ran "double feature" afternoon matinees for kids. For a quarter — popcorn and a Coke deducted another dime from weekly allowances — a generation of unsupervised, pre-adolescent boys escaped sweltering summer afternoons to watch back-to-back variations of the same cowboys and Indians movie and to flick Jujubes at one another and clusters of pigtailed girls. The smell of slowly decomposing Jujubes mixed with spilled Coke and stale popcorn gave the cool air a pungent and unforgettable odor and covered the theater's floor with a sticky patina that grabbed the soles of sneakers and reluctantly released each step with a soft pop.

Chapter 23

Happy Days are Here Again

I believe that banking institutions are more dangerous to our liberties than standing armies. If the American people ever allow private banks to control the issue of their currency, first by inflation, then by deflation, the banks and corporations that will grow up around the banks will deprive the people of all property — until their children wake-up homeless on the continent their fathers conquered. ~ Thomas Jefferson, 1802

ALONG WITH MOST of his 1928 campaign promises, Herbert Hoover's pledge to bring about a new era of prosperity fell far short, and his prospects for reelection in 1932 were grim. The social issues of immigration, racism, women's rights, and even Prohibition repeal took a distant backseat to the economy, which was in the worst shape in generations and getting worse. The Democratic nomination went to the exceptionally popular governor of New York, Franklin Roosevelt. Voters remembered his cousin, Theodore Roosevelt, and the nation's prosperity during his presidential terms that had ended only 20 years earlier. For two centuries, the Roosevelt family name had been synonymous with wealth and public service, which began in the years immediately before 1750, when Claes Maartenszen van Rosenvelt, emigrated from the Netherlands to Nieuw Amsterdam and bought 48 acres of land. It is unknown what he paid for the land, but it was a good buy — the land lay roughly between what is now 5th Avenue and Lexington Avenue, and was bounded by 29th and 35th Streets in Midtown Manhattan.

Claes' only son, Nicholas, changed his surname to Roosevelt, which he passed on to his two sons. The older son, Johannes, was the great, great grandfather of Theodore Roosevelt, the uncle of Anna Eleanor Roosevelt, who always went by her middle name. Johannes' brother, Jacobus, was the great, great, great, grandfather of Franklin Roosevelt. At a White House reception that Theodore Roosevelt threw on New Year's Day in 1903, 18-year-old Eleanor met her fifth cousin, 20-year-old Franklin. They fell in love and became engaged over the objections of Franklin's extraordinarily controlling mother, Sara Delano Roosevelt. Eleanor was not on the elite list of young ladies that Mrs. Roosevelt had her eye on for Franklin. But on St. Patrick's Day 1905,

President Theodore Roosevelt gave his niece Eleanor away in marriage to Franklin, and the money stayed in the family.

After his nomination in 1932, Roosevelt, the extremely wealthy, liberal Yankee united the bizarrely divided cultural and political interests in the Democratic Party — even garnering support from the Ku Klux Klan that tepidly backed the Episcopalian candidate from New York. Roosevelt capped his march to the presidency by adopting the rousing, stick-in-your-mind campaign song *Happy Days Are Here Again*, which relentlessly reminded voters of what they were missing. Holding Hoover to less than 40 percent of the popular vote and capturing 42 of 48 states in one of the most lopsided presidential elections, Roosevelt moved into the White House with the country's high expectations weighing on him. He didn't disappoint.

Hoover had virtually conceded the election to Roosevelt before the campaign started, but he still mustered up enthusiasm for a cross-country "whistle-stop" tour. On October 4, 1932, without even bothering to stop as his train chugged through Moline, the president delivered a forgettable 15-minute speech to a Rock Island crowd that was comprised mostly of kids who had been let out of school so that someone would come to hear how the Republicans planned to fix the mess they created. One enterprising student planned to make the event worthwhile. Billy Baltzer described his fieldtrip to see the president:

> I really intended to get an autograph from Mr. Hoover, and I did. I was a student at St. Mary's in Rock Island and met the Hoover train. It was pulling out and I ran up to the back platform, yelling, "I want your autograph, please, please!" The nuns were running after me because the train was moving, but I got the autograph. I lost the pencil he used, and I don't know whatever happened to the autograph.

There was probably little sentimental or monetary value for Hoover's autograph at the time, but in 2012 when his autograph on a fan's New York Yankee program sold for $1,895, 96-year-old William Baltzer was still looking for his.

The economy progressively worsened during Hoover's four years and hit rock bottom in March 1933, the month of Roosevelt's inauguration, and as soon as he took office, it began to rebound. The 1932 election flipped Congress from Republican to Democratic, and in the first 100 days of the new administration, Roosevelt drove major public relief and banking reform legislation and issued a profusion of executive orders that created the eagerly anticipated New Deal. Government programs put the unemployed back to work, stimulated economic growth, and clamped regulations on run-amok Wall Street securities markets and commercial banks. The economy improved and continued to grow over the next four years. When Roosevelt took office, unemployment dropped from 25 percent to 22 percent during his first year, and then in the next three years to 20 percent, 17 percent, and finally 14 percent.

Besides proving an irrefutable model for how government programs can stimulate economic growth through the "3R's" of Relief, Recovery, and Reform, the New Deal's most lasting contributions to the American landscape were made by two relief programs: the Works Projects Administration (WPA), which hired unemployed and unskilled workers, and the confusingly similarly named Public Works Administration (PWA), which employed men to build roads, bridges, and public buildings in virtually every community in the country. WPA projects injected $11.4 billion ($200 billion) into the economy, and in addition to spending more than a third of the money on roads and highways, the WPA built such diverse projects as Doubleday Field in Cooperstown, New York, the Dock Street Theatre in Charleston, South Carolina, the Griffith Observatory in Los Angeles, and the Timberline Lodge on Oregon's Mt. Hood.

One of the WPA relief programs that conservative New Deal opponents attacked was hiring artists and craftsmen to create large art, drama, and literacy projects. The arts grants that comprised about 10 percent of the total WPA funding produced work that ranged in scope from John Augustus Walker's murals in Montgomery, Alabama to the Federal Writers' Project that employed more than 6,000 authors, playwrights, and poets, including Saul Bellow and Ralph Ellison. Fifteen percent of the WPA workers were single women who headed households or married women whose husbands were disabled. The women were taught to use sewing machines to make uniforms, clothing, bedding, and supplies for the military, hospitals, and orphanages.

PWA funding for public infrastructure improvements was more popular, and among the hundreds of projects it subsidized or paid for were the Florida Keys overseas highway, Chicago's water system, buildings at the University of Washington, New York's Lincoln Tunnel and LaGuardia Airport, and Rock Island High School. Another relief program, the Civilian Conservation Corps, was formed to employ young, single men to develop natural resources on government-owned lands. Segregated camps were established for blacks and Indians, but all CCC employees were paid $30 ($500) a month, of which $25 was mailed home to their parents.

As he put America back to work, Roosevelt also put reigns on Wall Street and the banking industry. In his inauguration address, he proclaimed:

> Practices of the unscrupulous moneychangers stand indicted in the court of public opinion, rejected by the hearts and minds of men. ... The moneychangers have fled from their high seats in the temple of our civilization.

Five days after his inauguration, Roosevelt sent the Emergency Banking Act to Congress. It was passed and signed into law the same day and provided for the reopening of banks under Treasury supervision. Within three days, three-fourth of the closed banks reopened and billions of stagnated and hoarded dollars flowed back into the banking system. The economy was jump-started, and most importantly, depositors, who had given up hope of seeing more than pennies on their invested dollars of savings, eventually received on average 86¢ on the dollar. The Federal Deposit Insurance Corporation (FDIC) was created, and by July 1, 1934 up to $5,000 ($80,000) of individual deposits in federal banks was insured. In what can only be called a bold act of economic genius, to deal with extreme deflation and over the loud wails of bankers and Republican businessmen, a month after taking office, Roosevelt signed an executive order that combined with legislation temporarily took the nation off the gold standard and allowed the dollar to float freely on foreign exchange markets. Stock and commodities markets rose dramatically for the first time in four years, and a year later the Gold Reserve Act fixed the price of gold at a significantly lower level than when the gold standard was suspended — except for those who had hoarded gold, Americans were unaffected.

The proof of insightful, effective legislation is the durability of a law or program that lasts through political administrations. In addition to the FDIC, the New Deal produced the Social Security Act, the U.S. Housing Authority, the Farm Security Administration, the Securities and Exchange Commission, and the Fair Labor Standards Act, which established maximum hours and minimum wages for most workers. The Depression also resulted in the involvement of the federal government in labor-management relations. The passage of the National Labor Relations Act (Wagner Act) of 1935 guaranteed the rights of workers to join labor unions and to bargain collectively with their employers. The impact of unionization on the wages and benefits of blue-collar workers in important manufacturing industries also spilled over into non-union workplaces and industries. Union membership rates, which had been about one in eight workers before the Depression, doubled to more than one in four, less than a decade later.

Roosevelt's New Deal cut deeply against the grain of America's 150-year-old views of self-reliance and unfettered capitalism and redefined political "liberals" and "conservatives." Conservatives became those who sought less government and opposed social programs and business and banking regulations — essentially opposing what Roosevelt and liberals espoused. In the 80 years since, the nation's views on national defense, welfare, and taxation policy have further separated the two political ideologies. However, by today's political measurements, Roosevelt would be considered a progressive moderate that leaned towards fiscal conservatism. He was often at odds with a Democratic Congress over economic issues and fiscal policy.

Ten days after his inauguration, the Economy Act, which called for a 15 percent cut in federal employee's wages and veterans' pensions, was signed. It saved $500 million ($8.3 billion). And in an unpopular move with Democratic Congressmen, before the 1936 election, Roosevelt vetoed a $1.5 billion ($25 billion) Bonus Bill for World War I veterans. Congress overrode his veto. Roosevelt believed in a balanced budget, and when deficits grew, he maintained that they were temporary and argued that his spending programs were necessary to restore the economy — they were and they did. He told Congress, which had become over-enamored with the popularity of their free-spending ways, "Let us have the courage to stop borrowing to meet continuing deficits. Stop the deficits."

Successfully running on a platform of "change," in 2008 Barak Obama stepped into a presidency that had grave economic problems similar to Roosevelt's. But unlike Roosevelt who inherited an economy that had spiraled downward for two years, the 2008 economy had just tanked, and the electorate was not yet embittered by the failed fiscal policies of the previous administration. However, the most significant difference between the Democratic presidencies was that in 1932 the Republican controlled Congress significantly raised income tax rates in the higher tax brackets, providing Roosevelt the financial cushion to implement his recovery and jobs programs, without running the national debt out of sight; whereas, Obama fought Congressional Republicans who banned together and pledged not to raise taxes.

In direct opposition to prevalent capitalistic economic theory at the start of Roosevelt's first term, John Maynard Keynes codified and championed the economics of the New Deal in his 1936 book, *The General Theory of Employment, Interest and Money*. Keynes argued that private sector actions sometimes lead to inefficient economic outcomes. And therefore proactive government policy responses are sometimes needed by the public sector, especially by the central bank, to stabilize the economy over the natural business cycle. From the end of World War I until "supply-side" economic theory was proposed 30 years later and provided a conservative alternative, as a herd, economists migrated towards Keynesian theory.

The opposing side to Keynesian economics was laissez-faire capitalism, as practiced under the administrations of Warren Harding, Calvin Coolidge, and Herbert Hoover. Ayn Rand, a Russian-American actress turned political novelist, carried the conservative capitalists' banner. Rand's economic theory/philosophy, which she called Objectivism, was introduced in her 1936 novel *We the Living*. In 1943 she published *The Fountainhead* and 14 years later *Atlas Shrugged*. The later books further promoted her philosophy, and both became bestsellers — over 13 million copies have been sold. Through relentlessly idealized situations, the exceptionally long works of fiction give improbable economic scenarios that portray their heroic leading characters as rugged, uncompromising individualists who achieve wealth through unwavering adherence to libertarian principles, disdain of government and welfare assistance, and hard work. *The New York Times* review of *The Fountainhead* said that Rand was "a writer of great power" who wrote "brilliantly, beautifully and bitterly," and stated that "you will not be able to read this masterful book without thinking through some of the basic concepts of our time." Another reviewer said of the atheistic Rand that her writing was "shrillness without reprieve."

The political right would worship Rand even more if it were not for her religious disbelief. She called God "a being whose only definition is that he is beyond man's power to conceive." However, her conservative advocates are more likely to spiel off Randisms such as, "Run for your life from any man who tells you that money is evil" and "The ladder of success is best climbed by stepping on the rungs of opportunity." She has influenced many powerful business leaders since World War II, but none was closer to her or more powerful than Alan Greenspan, the chairman of the Federal Reserve from 1987 to 2006. Greenspan was part of Rand's "inner circle" that read and critiqued *Atlas Shrugged* while she was writing it. Because of his sour demeanor, Rand nicknamed Greenspan "the undertaker" — since 2008, for different reasons, some economists feel that is a very appropriate nickname.

During the 1950s and 1960s, Greenspan was a proponent of Objectivism and wrote articles for Objectivist newsletters and contributed several essays for Rand's 1966 book *Capitalism: The Unknown Ideal*. Rand stood beside him at his 1974 swearing-in as chair of the Council of Economic Advisors. In October 2008, Greenspan stated before a Congressional hearing that his free-market ideology that shunned certain oversight regulations was flawed. However 18 months later in an interview, when asked about free markets and Rand's philosophy, he clarified his stance on laissez-faire capitalism and said that in a democratic society there could be no better alternative, and that the debt crisis and collapse of the real estate markets stemmed not from free market principles but from "assuming what the nature of risks would be" in competitive markets.

One group of extreme risk-takers during the Depression was the cadre of bank-robbing outlaws who terrorized Midwestern banks. They include Baby Face Nelson, who has the dubious distinction of killing more FBI agents than anyone else; Pretty Boy Floyd, who was sensationalized by FBI Director J. Edgar Hoover for his role in the Kansas City Massacre in which four law enforcement officers and Frank "Jelly" Nash, a successful bank robber, were killed attempting to free an escaped bank robber — Floyd swore he wasn't there; Bonny and Clyde who preferred the relative ease of knocking off grocery stores and gas stations (more than 100) to banks (about a dozen); and John Dillinger. All had their lives, and deaths, glamorized by the media during their criminal escapades and later on the silver screen.

Dillinger was the most daring of the Depression Era outlaws. He not only robbed two-dozen banks of more than $300,000 ($5 million) of their newly FDIC insured deposits, but also four police stations of their money, guns, and bulletproof vests. He escaped from jail twice and became a major embarrassment to the image-conscious FBI head. Hoover sicced his top agent, Melvin Purvis, on Dillinger, after Dillinger tried to go into semi-retirement, although he continued to finance several bootlegging operations. In the spring of 1934, Dillinger and Baby Face Nelson, who had hooked-up with Dillinger's gang, were hiding out at Little Bohemia Lodge in northern Wisconsin. The lodge's owner, who was constantly monitored by Nelson, managed to pass a letter on to the U.S. Attorney's office in Chicago. After Purvis and more than 20 agents surrounded the lodge, Dillinger and his gang were alerted when the agents mistakenly shot a local resident and two Civilian Conservation Corps workers as they drove away from the lodge. The bank robbers escaped unscathed, and Hoover, who resented the acclaim the press gave Purvis for his heroics and often took credit for his agents' accomplishments, did not take credit for shooting the two CCC workers.

A big-city boy from Indianapolis and a life-long, die-hard Cubs fan, Dillinger escaped to Chicago to hide out and to watch his team, which was on a hot streak. The Cubs were one of Dillinger's three passions — the other two were women and beer — and in Chicago he was able to indulge all three loves. With virtually the entire Chicago police force on the mobs' payroll, Dillinger and his gang felt safer in the city than in the Northwoods, and the friendly confines of Wrigley Field was one of Chicago's safest havens. When Dillinger got back into town in early June, the Cubs were battling St. Louis for first place. On June 7 after taking the last two games of a road series from the Cardinals, the Cubs were 11 games over .500. The FBI's Public Enemy #1 couldn't stay away from the ballpark, and the next day he caught the opening game of a home stand with the Phillies. He was back in the bleachers for a June 26th win over the Dodgers, and he saw his last games on a long July 8th afternoon when the Cubs wound up the home stand with a double header split against the Pirates.

Charlie Grimm's hard-hitting '34 squad was short on pitching, and after pounding the Phillies 14-6 on July 21st, the Cubs were 54 and 34 going into the final game of a road series with Philadelphia. They lost the get-away game by a run on the 22nd, and the season started to slip away as the overworked pitchers tired during the dog days of August. After the loss to the Phillies, the Northsiders played .500 ball the rest of the season. The same day the Cubs lost to the Phillies, Dillinger took in a movie. His date's madam was a Romanian immigrant who the FBI was threatening to deport because of "low moral character;" she instead brokered a deal with them — her citizenship for Dillinger's life. As Dillinger left the Biograph Theater in Chicago's Lincoln Park neighborhood, the 5'4" Melvin Purvis, whose appearance fit his name, lit a cigar and pointed to Dillinger with it. Dillinger spotted the signal and fled into an alley across Lincoln Avenue, where he was killed.

During the Depression, most everyone, who didn't rob banks or bootleg, had a financial story of woe to tell. Almost everyone was poor, and it was a time of constant fear. There were no safety nets, no insured savings, no unemployment checks and few job prospects for the unemployed, no social security or medical coverage for the retired or disabled, and at its depths — no beer. It was a time of survival, many went to bed hungry, and there were fewer and fewer real jobs. In the election year of 1932, Davenport's unemployment hit the national average of 25 percent. The next year before the New Deal kicked in, it exceeded 30 percent. In 1929 at Petersen's Department Store in Davenport, clerks made $14.80 ($210) a week, and in the year Hoover left office, their pay was cut 40 percent to $8.90 ($126) a week.

For heat, farmers found it cheaper to burn corn that sold for a dime a bushel than to buy coal. In Coal Valley a man mined coal in his backyard and sold it by the bucketful from a stand in his front yard. For food and rent, people did what they could. A renowned Iowa sculptor made large intricate art works in the sand under the Government Bridge for donations of pennies and an occasional nickel in his Karo Syrup can. A Bettendorf artist went from one used car lot to another pin-striping cars. He made 50¢ a car, and on his best days he did ten cars. Men, women, and children clammed along the riverfronts for the meat and then sold the shells to button shops — twelve shops in Andalusia alone punched "pearl buttons." A University of Iowa student arrived in Iowa City with a wagonload of potatoes and smoked hams. He sold them to Kellogg House and made enough money to pay for the semester.

On 9th Street in Rock Island, American Federation of Labor construction workers helped the Rauch's, a poor Jewish family, weather the Depression by building a small storefront on the front of their modest home. The sons of a paraplegic father, Lester and Albert Rauch helped their parents run the family grocery store when they weren't in classes at Rocky and later at Saint Ambrose College. Only a year apart in age, after graduation the inseparable boys stayed in the community and contributed to its growth. Al went to work for Deere & Company as a chemist, where he worked 48 years and became a Senior Scientist. Les was director of Food Services at St. Anthony's

Hospital and later at Franciscan Medical Center. When Les died in 1987, he left his assets to his brother, and two foundations were formed. The first provides annual grants to programs and activities that enhance the lives of Rock Island's citizens — in 2010, one Rauch Foundation gave grants ranging from $500 to $10,000 to more than 40 nonprofit organizations, and a second foundation gave more than $55,000 during the year to area youth and Jewish organizations.

Manufacturing was devastated during the Depression, but because Rock Island and Moline's industry was farm equipment and tractor-oriented, they weren't hit as hard as other larger Midwestern manufacturing centers such as Cincinnati, Detroit, and Cleveland. At the end of 1930, after the first year following The Crash, there were only seven farm implement manufacturers remaining in the country. Of the seven, Deere & Company and International Harvester were the two largest and their combined annual sales were greater than Minneapolis-Moline, J.I. Case, Allis-Chalmers, Oliver, and Massey-Harris combined. In 1931 an embezzlement of $1.2 million ($17 million) at People's Savings Bank in Moline nearly caused the bank's closure and threatened the loss of Deere employees' savings. Deere & Company wrote a check to cover the loss and saved the bank.

As the Depression hardened the following year, massive layoffs in the six Illinois Deere plants reduced their work force to 742, and the wages of the retained employees were cut and their hours shortened. A savings program, the Thrift Plan, eased the burden for some laid-off employees. Deere kept their unemployed workers on their insurance plan and lowered the rent in company housing. And while 50 other Tri-Cities companies closed their doors in 1933, Deere started "make work" projects for those they laid off. They sold their equipment to farmers on credit with minimum down payments and never repossessed a piece of equipment for nonpayment. Their understanding and generosity built trust and loyalty with employees and customers and paid huge long-term dividends. In 1937 while the rest of the country was still suffering, Deere & Company recorded sales of $100 million ($1.6 billion).

What little passenger travel and interstate freight shipping there was continued to flow through the transportation crossroads at Rock Island. Mississippi River steamboats and barges kept up a steady flow of goods, grains, coal, and passengers, as did major east/west highways, and the Rock Island Line. The Rock Island Arsenal retained many of its jobs, and although local manufacturing struggled, most Rock Island and Moline factories survived, which gave shaky support to local farmers and merchants. A benefit to those who had jobs, which were most in Rock Island, was that food and retail prices plummeted. At Geifman's Grocery Store, prime rib was 25¢ ($4.00) a pound and flour was 5¢ (80¢) a pound; downtown at McCabe's Department

Store, new dresses started at $1.88 ($30). Davenport, which had the least manufacturing and would not boom until after World War II, was the hardest hit of the Tri-Cities and suffered like the rest of the country.

The plight of Davenport and its banks is described in Bill Wundram's and the *Quad-City Times'* 1999 century celebration book, *A Time We Remember:*

> Davenport had two sturdy banks, among the strongest in the Midwest. American Savings Bank & Trust was easily the largest bank in Iowa. Union Savings Bank was next in line. But by the autumn of 1931, depositors were hounding the banks for their money.
>
> The run was most fierce on American, which borrowed $100,000 [$1,425,000 in 2010 dollars] from the Union on a frantic day in '31. By noon it was gone, and the bank closed with depositors pounding on the doors.
>
> Union would always be solvent, the thrifty Germans convinced themselves. They made up the bulk of the depositors, but most of the bank's resources were tied up in farmland, and the bottom was falling out of farm prices and land.
>
> Logic was not on anyone's mind. Depositors lined up, four abreast. Many were at Union's doors all night to be the first in line. Some brought market baskets, insisting they be paid off in small denominations. The baskets were for carrying off their cash.
>
> To soothe the panicky mass, a string quartet was hurriedly booked from the Tri-City Symphony. They played from the bank's balcony level, while a soprano, Ethel Baker Waterman, sang "Ah Sweet Memory of Life." It was a portent of times to come.
>
> E.P. Adler, publisher of the *Daily Times* (predecessor of the *Quad-City Times*) and a director of the Union Bank, rushed up and down the lines of the anxious depositors with his own passbook in hand. To encourage confidence in the bank, he wrote his personal guarantee of the amount on deposit — with the amount the individual sought to withdraw. But Union was at death's door, and it, too, ultimately closed. A moratorium was to come in 1933, temporarily closing all American banks.
>
> But before, Adler was making things happen, a hero of that day and many others. He was drafted to reorganize Davenport's American bank. Across the Midwest, all eyes were on him, for this could be a pattern for other reorganizations. On a chilly November night in 1931, 5,000 people jammed Davenport's Masonic Temple auditorium. There was not enough room, so they filled lodge rooms. Others sat on the long marble corridor floors. Loudspeakers broadcast the hopeful message of reorganizing the bank.
>
> Adler called for subscription of $1,500,000 [$21 million in 2010 dollars] in new capital stock, enabling the return of some cash to strapped depositors.
>
> The crowd was enthusiastic. They would be happy about anything that offered hope. One man questioned, "If we have a new bank, what'll it be called?"
>
> Adler, a shrewd and witty businessman, replied: "Don't you think we should have the baby before we name it?"
>
> A $25 [$350 in 2010 dollars] prize was offered in a naming contest, and C.F. Simmermaker of Tipton, Iowa, won. It would be Davenport Bank & Trust Co.
>
> The goal for the money was oversubscribed in 1932, and the city was so thrilled that factory whistles hooted and church bells rang. On the Davenport levee, Battery B of the National Guard set up field pieces and let go with a salute of 100 rounds.

The new Davenport Bank opened in July of '32 amid apprehension of another bank run. It didn't happen. Citizens had trust. One customer brought a flower for each teller window.

By the time of the national moratorium in 1933, Davenport's new bank already had more than $12 million [$200 million] in assets. The success of an Iowa town in getting a bank back on its feet claimed national attention. *Time Magazine* even told of "Davenport's success story."

A bank, yes. But the end of the Great Depression was a decade away.

Grim men walked the streets, many of them in neckties and clean-shaven. Their only shame was that they had no work to do.

When Davenport Bank & Trust Co. opened its doors, the New Deal was still eight months away and already thousands of Davenport residents were on public relief. A large shantytown had sprung up in Davenport's west end along the river near Credit Island, and disease and hunger plagued the sprawling city. On the other side of the river, Rock Island was weathering the Depression remarkably well. When one of the city's five banks teetered on failure, a consolidation of Manufacturer's Trust & Savings Bank, Rock Island Savings Bank, and Central Trust & Savings formed the Rock Island Bank & Trust Company, solidified the banks' assets, and saved depositor accounts. Throughout the 1930s, the city was a glowing bright spot on the bleak local landscape. With solid support from business leaders, Mayors John Bengston and Robert Galbraith surged ahead with public works projects that complemented what the federal government was doing nationally. Voters approved a tax to build a new city hall, a new sewage treatment plant, a modern sanitation system that was constructed along with new reservoirs, and miles of street paving. The forward-thinking projects stimulated jobs in the construction and housing sectors and attracted more skilled craftsmen and businessmen to the area.

Galbraith also saw an opportunity to again solidify Rock Island as the primary highway crossroads across the Mississippi River between St. Louis and the Twin Cities by building a 4-lane highway bridge between Rock Island and Davenport's downtown districts. The Army Corps of Engineers had redesigned the Government Bridge with a "swivel span" that opened every time a barge passed through their new Locks No. 15. In the spring of 1934, the revolving bridge began a game of traffic-delay roulette that continues today. Barges had the right-of-way regardless of the time of day, and a commuter problem was created that had to be remedied or there would be no incentive to ever go to Iowa. Davenport wanted to be part of the bridge construction but had no money, so when the State of Iowa backed out of the $1.75 million ($27 million) project, Galbraith had Rock Island build the first four-lane bridge to cross the Mississippi. The voters didn't object because the city collected a dime ($1.50) for every car and a nickel for each walker that crossed after its July 1940 opening. Before his daughter, Bonnie, cut the ribbon to open the bridge that was to be named after her father, Galbraith requested that the bridge be called the "Centennial Bridge" in honor of Rock Island's centennial, which had occurred five years earlier.

In the year of the Stock Market Crash, 56 new businesses opened in Rock Island, more than 30,000 conventioneers spent an estimated $400,000 ($6.5 million) in the city's hotels and The District, and 600 men played baseball in the summer leagues. An extremely savvy and proactive Chamber of Commerce anticipated that the nation's economy would continue its downward spiral and deftly moved to isolate Rock Island's economy. They promoted a "Buy Now" slogan to keep Rock Island's money circulating and needlessly encouraged its citizens to shop with city merchants — as if anyone was going to go to Moline or Davenport to shop. Also, Rock Island's citizens took care of their own, and similar to the Rauch's, modest investments in temporarily distressed residents paid back huge dividends later. During the 1930 Christmas season, $18,500 ($300,000) was raised by local charities to help the unemployed have happier holidays. While the Depression deepened in the rest of the country, Rock Island shrugged off the downturn and played ball games under the Chamber's optimistic new slogan: "Prosperity Always Comes Back." City baseball leagues tripled in number and expanded to 143 teams, and in 1933 the Parks & Recreation Department had to limit players to only playing on two teams. City officials claimed there was no city in the nation that had greater amateur athletic participation.

Rock Islanders' "What, me worry?" refusal to accept the financial plight the rest of the country was experiencing and business leaders' aggressive economic strategies worked beyond expectations. Although the convention business took a huge hit, during the increasingly lean years of the early 1930s, few, if any, cities in the country saw less of a drop in lifestyle than Rock Island, and by 1935, life was back to normal. In that year, in six months' time, families on relief dropped from 4,700 to 400 and business boomed again. Established businesses spent $385,000 ($6.4 million) to expand; IH Farmall, already the world's largest tractor factory, launched a $1 million dollar ($16.6 million) modernization program. Incredibly, a record number 93 new businesses opened their doors. Arthur J. Hause & Company announced the opening of their new department store and the hiring of 75 people with a parade down 2nd Avenue, and the Chamber of Commerce updated their slogan to the aggressively upbeat "Forward with Rock Island in 1936!" — which proved to be an understatement. After expanding the police force, buying a street sweeper to clean miles of newly bricked roads, modernizing the sewage treatment and water systems, and spending $35,000 ($580,000) on park improvements, the city still showed a $70,000 surplus. A housing shortage developed for out-of-towners who wanted to move to Rock Island and share in the prosperity, and 77 new homes were started — only Chicago and Cicero, the mobs' retirement community, had more 1936 housing starts in Illinois.

If ever there were a crucible for a live economics experiment, it was the Tri-Cities during the 1930s. Davenport panicked when the markets crashed, and then withered after its banks closed and savings were lost and assets expended. It sank into a pool of despair where it wallowed until it was dragged out by the giddy times of post-World War II prosperity. Moline's citizenry tightened their belts, hunkered down, and with the benevolent assistance of Deere & Company, its largest employer, stoically rode out the tough times. Rock Islanders shrugged their shoulders, recognized that Davenport's head-in-the-sand approach was futile and that Moline's face-up-to-the-grim-reality method wasn't any fun, and with an enlightened, proactive private/public partnership to stimulate business and create jobs and a "can-do" attitude, set out to get the Depression problem behind them as quickly as possible — the positive approach worked spectacularly well.

Chapter 24

Government Waste

I do think the patriotic thing to do is to critique my country. How else do you make a country better but by pointing out its flaws? ~ Bill Maher, political commentator and comedian

FEW ARGUE that government programs eased the pain of the Depression. But with the benefit of hindsight, some believe these programs were mismanaged and extravagantly wasteful and inefficient, and in some cases were incalculably destructive to the environment. Both the Work Projects Administration and Public Works Administration's primary objective was jobs' creation, which they accomplished, and to the Roosevelt Administration's credit they didn't hesitate to start "shovel ready" projects, and major undertakings that were approved prior to the formation of the PWA were accelerated. One was the construction of Boulder Dam on the Colorado River; another was the Upper Mississippi 9-Foot Channel Project. First proposed by Warren Harding's Administration to gain farmers' support and advanced by Calvin Coolidge's Administration, in 1926 a Republican Congress passed the bill to create a 9-foot deep navigation channel from St. Paul, Minnesota, to the Lower Mississippi River, but did not fund the project.

As proposed by Harding's Administration and passed by Coolidge's, the purpose of the massive project was to facilitate bigger barges and make river transport from the Upper Midwest more competitive with railroads. To solidify farm votes he already had, during his 1926 campaign, Herbert Hoover again brought attention to the project, and after winning the presidency, he authorized the Army Corps of Engineers to design the deeper channel, but Congress still did not fund its construction. The pork-barrel legislation was a boondoggle during prosperous times that almost everyone understood was a political nostrum that would never be funded. However, given the go-ahead, the Corps dutifully jumped right on it. The 4 ½-foot channel that had been straitened and dredged of obstructions served the nation well during the steamboat era. The Upper Mississippi River was a vibrant waterway that transported logs, grains, ore, materials, and people — and it had no dams. It synergistically supported almost 200 fish and mollusk species and more than 300 varieties of birds, and was home to dozens of species of wild animals. However, solely to accommodate larger barges and facilitate commercial navigation, in less than a decade, Army engineers demolished the delicate balance between nature and man that had evolved since white men started trapping beaver and determined that the depth of the river's channel should be doubled, and that it would take only 29 dams to do that. Fortunately, dam construction was prohibitively expensive, and the cost to create the 9-foot channel far exceeded the justification of potentially lowering freight costs that were already at historic low levels due to regulation under the Interstate Commerce Act and competition from a growing trucking industry. And it appeared that the project would remain a political hot-air balloon that would be floated as needed.

After three Republican presidents won their elections, the plans were filed away to gather more dust. But in 1934 when the Roosevelt Administration's call went out for public works projects that were ready to go, the U.S. Army stepped forward, and the fatal last battle against the Upper Mississippi River was waged. Admitting that their orders were politically driven and the "general good" was secondary to pandering to farmers, the project is described by the Army Corps of Engineers in their official history of the 9-Foot Channel Project that damned the Mississippi River:

> The Upper Mississippi River 9-Foot Channel Project was one of the largest and most ambitious river improvement projects ever constructed in the United States. From conception to completion, the massive undertaking reflected the changing political moods of the nation, spanning several presidential administrations and agendas. The project originated in the 1920s when it was promoted as a way to alleviate the Nation's worsening farm crisis. It was also aimed at allaying the inequities in commercial rail and water freight rates brought about by the 1914 opening of the Panama Canal. Although direct governmental aid was an anathema to the conservative Warren Harding and Calvin Coolidge administrations, waterway improvements were an acceptable way to promote the general good. The 9-Foot Channel Project was authorized by the Rivers and Harbors Act of 1930 during the presidency of Herbert Hoover, an engineer and strong waterway improvements advocate. During the Great Depression, the project was recast into a massive public employment project by the New Deal administration of President Franklin Roosevelt. As a result, much of the 9-Foot Channel Project was constructed during what might be called the U.S. Army Corps of Engineers' "Golden Age," the period of its greatest dam construction, organizational security, highest volume of work, largest area of responsibility, and maximum power.

In summary, the Army Corps of Engineers states that even though governmental aid was anathema to Republican presidents, during the Coolidge Administration, Republicans put aside their ideological beliefs and directed the Corps to design and plan the 9-Foot Channel Project to help farmers who were beleaguered by high freight rates. Then during the Hoover Administration, Republicans apparently switched their approach and advocated the 9-foot channel to equalize competition between rail and water shipping. No mention is made that at a time before economic and environmental studies were required for public works' projects, a massive network of railroads were outcompeting river transport for the shipping of Midwest grains, ore, and finished goods. Essentially, the project was a Republican pork-barrel promise to farmers to secure their votes and Democrats turned it into a make-work project for the unemployed. *Gateways to Commerce* describes with some pride how the system of dams works:

> The Upper Mississippi River 9-Foot Channel Project, which was designed and constructed by the U.S. Army Corps of Engineers between 1930 and 1940, has transformed the once free-flowing river into a slack-water navigation system. The system is often compared to a stairway. The "treads" are the slack-water lakes, or navigation pools, created by a series of dams across the river. The "risers" are the locks, which through their changing water levels carry the boats from one pool to the next. From the largest barge to the smallest raft, every vessel traveling the Upper Mississippi River has to navigate this system of locks and dams. While passage through the locks is time-consuming, it provides what the river in its natural state could not: a dependable 9-foot navigational depth on the Upper Mississippi.

What the Corps doesn't say is that given the green light and money, in less than a decade's time, in the midst of their Golden Age when they enjoyed their maximum power, they capped off what Andrew Humphreys had first envisioned 80 years earlier and turned a marvelously efficient, self-scouring 665-mile stretch of river that Mother Nature carefully sculpted over 130,000 years and that supported a wondrously diverse ecosystem and a spectacularly scenic river valley into a series of stagnant, brackish backwaters that spill over their banks virtually every spring. The flooding occurs because 29 ill-conceived dams and hundreds of wing dams force the river's flow into the fast-moving center channel, while significantly reducing the overall rate of flow. Since the Army Corps of Engineers first started messing with the Mississippi, they have compounded the river's problems by trying to fix them under the guise of improving the river for commercial transport — which has been in steady decline since the end of the 1950s. By building dams on every major Mississippi tributary, the river's natural flow has been further impeded, and the engineers are primarily responsible for the unprecedented floods in recent years to communities that are miles away from the Mississippi.

The disastrous Iowa floods in June 2008 are but one dramatic example. The 2008 floods exceeded the 500-year floodplain (the calculated extreme), which was also exceeded in Iowa only 15 years earlier (a probability that should happen once every 17,000 years), and covered ten square miles of Cedar Rapids, Iowa, under as much as eight feet of toxic water contaminated by raw sewage, farm chemicals, industrial waste, and oil products, and forced 83 of Iowa's 99 counties to be declared a federal disaster area. More than $65 billion dollars of destruction was done in Iowa alone. To put that number into perspective, $65 billion dollars is three times the amount of the value of all petroleum, coal, chemicals, and grain transported on the Upper Mississippi River System each year. In June 2008, record floods were also seen in four other states whose water flows into the Upper Mississippi River.

Insurance companies accepted the lawyers' definition that the 2008 floods were an "act of God." Some environmentalists attributed heavy spring rains to global warming, and the Iowa State Meteorologist explained away the floods by saying, "More than 80 percent of moisture that falls in the Midwest is from the Gulf of Mexico, and the primary cause of it coming here is the Bermuda high pressure. The pressure arrived very early and much stronger than usual by April and May this year." Whatever the reasons for the high amount of precipitation, the river system that the Army engineers redesigned and built to decrease flooding and aid commerce is extraordinarily expensive and woefully incapable of fulfilling Mother Nature's primary purposes, which were to efficiently drain the Upper Mississippi Valley and provide a healthy habitat. Incredibly, when the Mississippi again flooded two years later and Army engineers had to sacrifice 200 square miles of farmland and open up spillways in Louisiana, a Corps' spokesman, who apparently was uninformed of his employer's design history and record of flood control told *Time Magazine,* "The system is under the most stress it's been under since it was designed, and so far, it's working."

Calamities on the Mississippi are now more frequent. After a July 2008 collision between a tanker and a barge spilled 420,000 gallons of fuel north of New Orleans and caused the temporary closure of a 100-mile stretch of river, the Director of the Port of New Orleans direfully warned that a closure of the port could cost the U.S. economy $275 million a day — a claim that defies logic and mathematics — the port remained open. Less than 10 percent of the spilled fuel was cleaned up, and there are no public figures on the cost of the damage to the freighter and barge, loss of fuel, cleanup, and destruction to the ecosystem. Similar catastrophes do not happen with rail and highway transport. An increasing number of Midwestern farmers, who see their fields flooded more often, and city residents, who see their downtown and commercial areas inundated, now agree that it was unwise to seek lower transportation rates by damming the rivers. But even if it were possible to wave a magic wand and make the Army engineers' atrocities disappear, it would be unwise. Millions of people now live in the natural floodplains, so for the rest of mankind's time in the Missouri-Mississippi-Ohio Valleys, the best that can be done is to stop the expansion of a bad system, mitigate the damage, and restore as much natural flood plain and habitat as possible.

The river that Marquette and Jolliet paddled their canoes down, the river the Illiniwek named "The Father of Waters," and authors and poets of a bygone era called

"The Mighty Mississippi" is now commonly referred to as "The Muddy Mississippi" or "The Big Muddy." Rationalization for the hubristic engineering nightmare is partially explained and apparently justified by the Corps of Engineers in *Gateways to Commerce*:

> The 9-Foot Channel Project involves social, political, economic, military, environmental, and technological histories. It touches labor and ethnic issues, and portrays the end of the American Progressive Era and the beginnings of the New Deal. It involves the economics of the Upper Mississippi Valley, and vividly reflects the role of the military in domestic issues. The 9-Foot Channel Project's impact on the environment was of a magnitude rarely experienced since the famous Hetch Hetchy project of California in the second decade of the twentieth century [a project that naturalist John Muir fought to his dying breathe in 1914]. It demonstrates the evolution of technology and its impact on man and his environment. Unfortunately, the project's documents also reflect the history of the era selectively; women and minorities only appear as shadows in its saga when they appear at all. The 9-Foot Channel Project as built by the United States Army Corps of Engineers represents not only an astounding engineering feat—it accurately reflects the tenor of a nation and its feelings concerning society, politics, economics, labor, the military, technology, and the environment in those hard years before the Second World War.

The confluence of advanced civil engineering technology, improved construction equipment and techniques, and unlimited money and manpower allowed the Corps to accomplish what surely would have convulsed Andrew Humphreys into spasms of joy. The 9-Foot Channel Project irreversibly destroyed the natural ecology of the Upper Mississippi Basin and put all future generations of those who live at river's edge and their property at risk. By slowing the river's flow with dams, the project greatly compounded Humphreys' 70-year-old mistake of constricting the river's channel with levees that block the natural floodplains. It doesn't require a degree in hydraulic engineering to understand that if the main drainpipes and reservoirs of a system that drains the rainfall and snowmelt from 31 states and two Canadian provinces are reduced in size, like a partially clogged drain, it will take longer for the water to seep out of the basin, and if more water runs into the basin than drains out, it will overflow. However, this simple concept continues to be ignored by each generation of Army engineers, and the flooding problem is exacerbated. Sadly, it's not that the well-intentioned engineers don't understand the problems their predecessors created; it's that they are powerless to fix them, and continue to deny Mark Twain's advice that "ten thousand river commissions ... cannot tame that lawless stream, cannot curb it or confine it, cannot say to it, 'Go here,' or 'Go there,' and make it obey."

Locks and Dam No. 15 was constructed as one of the 29 dams in the 9-Foot Channel Project. It spans 1,209 feet between Rock Island and Davenport's riverbanks, about a third of the river's width when Marquette and Jolliet first walked Rock Island's shoreline. The quarter-mile long dam is the world's largest roller dam. It consists of 11,

109-foot roller gates and has two 110-foot wide locks — one of the locks is a backup. One reason it is the world's largest roller dam is because the dam's design was obsolete and rejected by the Corps of Engineers as soon as it was completed in 1934. In fact, Locks and Dam No. 15 was an expensive failed experiment in roller dam design and construction. Because they had never undertaken a similarly difficult task, the Army engineers tried out several design concepts in constructing the first of the 29 dams in the 9-Foot Channel Project.

Built at the doorstep of the U.S. Army Corps of Engineers, Rock Island District headquarters, which at the start of the Depression had moved into the vacant Clock Tower Building on Arsenal Island, Lock and Dam No. 15 is the only dam on the Mississippi that is not built perpendicular to the river's flow, has different sizes and types of roller gates, and has both non-overflow and overflow gates. The experimental roller gates proved to be more expensive to construct, harder to maintain, and much more dangerous than Tainter gates. Locks and Dam No. 15 has a short lipped-wall on its downriver side, and as water pours over the dam it hits the baffle and is reflected back toward the face of the dam, a continual "rolling" action is created at the foot of the dam; hence its name. The purpose of baffling the water after it falls is to dissipate energy from the fall; otherwise, the water would accelerate downstream at a greatly increased rate, creating turbulence that would erode the riverbed and riverbanks. The design partially worked.

Most of the 9-Foot Channel Project dams were built using the less expensive and more efficient Tainter gate design. Locks and Dam No. 15 cost $7.5 million ($125 million), and by comparison, Lock and Dam No. 14, three miles downstream from the head of the Rock Island Rapids, is a Tainter gate dam, which was completed in 1940 at 80 percent of the cost of its dangerous, ugly stepsister 11 miles downstream. As anyone who has viewed Locks and Dam No. 15 from the site of the old Draught House/American Legion Post on the Iowa side of the river can verify, roller dams create "washing machine of death" turbulence. Anything that goes over the top of the dam is caught in the rolling action at its base and may not be ejected from the "cycle" for days. Even very buoyant objects, such as rafts and life vests, can periodically be seen resurfacing near the downstream face every few seconds for several hours before finally escaping. (In what surely is a roller dam Guinness World Record, since 1960 16 people have died by drowning at the Fox River roller dam near Yorkville, Illinois.) Inexplicably, in 2004 the 68-year-old Rube Goldberg atrocity, Locks and Dam No. 15, was listed in the National Register of Historic Places.

Although the Army Corps of Engineers begrudgingly admits that engineers from previous generations overestimated their ability to tame the Mississippi, they continue to play the trump card that has kept them in the game for the last century by promoting the Mississippi River as critical to commercial transportation. As commercial river traffic decreases annually and environmental and property damage dramatically increase, the card is of diminishing value. Since 1990 annual cargo tonnage from the Upper Mississippi River decreased by 30 percent. Eight years earlier, the Corps projected that tonnage would double in volume over the same period. The outrageous estimate was made in order to justify replacing and rebuilding a failing dam and to build larger locks at Locks and Dam No. 26. The improvements were made, and annual freight tonnage at the new locks is about half of what the engineers projected and continues to decrease. The Corps maintains their near-perfect record on the Mississippi River of never getting it right.

After enlarging Locks and Dam No. 26, the new centerpiece on the Corps' river project's wish list became the $1.88 billion Upper Mississippi River and Illinois Waterway Project to build seven new 1,200-foot locks and double the size of five other 600-foot locks on the Upper Mississippi upriver of Locks and Dam No. 26. To put the cost of the UMR-IWW Project into perspective, adjusted for inflation, the proposed expansion of seven of the 29 Upper Mississippi locks would cost more than half the total cost of the 9-Foot Channel Project. The Corps justifies the proposed project by saying that the new locks will reduce barge delays resulting from "double-lockage" — the necessity for barges longer than 600 feet to pass twice through the locks. One project cost analysis shows that for every taxpayer dollar invested, the barge industry will save about 20¢ — the other 80¢ can be chalked up as wasted tax dollars.

A 2006 Congressional Research Service report, Upper Mississippi-Illinois Waterway Investments, chronicles the Corps' duplicity of mission:

> The Upper Mississippi River and Illinois Waterway (UMR-IWW) is at the center of a debate over the future of inland navigation, the restoration of rivers used for multiple purposes, and the reliability and completeness of the U.S. Army Corps of Engineers analyses justifying investments. ...The UMR-IWW is a 1,200-mile, 9-foot-deep navigation channel created by 37 lock-and-dam sites and thousands of channel training structures built beginning in 1822. The UMR-IWW makes commercial navigation possible between Minneapolis and St. Louis on the Mississippi River, and along the Illinois Waterway from Chicago to the Mississippi River. It permits Upper Midwestern states to benefit from low-cost barge transport. Since the 1980s, the system has experienced increasing traffic delays, purportedly reducing competitiveness of U.S. products in some global markets. The river is also losing the habitat diversity that has allowed it to support an unusually large number of species for a temperate river. This loss is partially attributable to changes in the distribution and movement of river water caused by navigation structures and operation of the 9-foot navigation channel. [Further, it is strongly argued that navigation structures and barge traffic are overwhelmingly the greatest cause of loss of habitat diversity and decline in

native species, and building more structures and subsidizing more barge traffic is extremely counterproductive.]

In their September 2009 report on the Upper Mississippi River System, the Corps says "the maintenance needs of the aging infrastructure are increasing at a rate much greater than the operations and maintenance funding provided for the system." However, to satisfy environmentalists who are opposed to further infrastructure improvements and those few who directly benefit from lower river transport costs, the Corps proposes to split the baby. Using the loss "of habitat diversity" caused by their dams, dikes, floodwalls, and levees as justification, the engineers propose to whitewash their ongoing errors by spending $1.46 billion on ecosystem restoration while spending $1.88 billion on larger locks, whose sole purpose is to decrease the transport time of barge traffic passing through them.

In a 2009 report Donald Sweeny, the former lead economist for the UMR-IWW feasibility study, wrote, "The existing seven 600-foot locks have had excess capacity of well more than 50 percent of their annual carrying capacity over the last five years and could accommodate significant increases in barge traffic. With lockage 'supply' already outstripping 'demand,' there is no justification for spending more than $2 billion to construct new 1,200-foot locks." Refusing to admit defeat and denying the obvious, the Corps has spent more than $50 million preparing more than 250 engineering and economic reports to justify the project. In a 2004 report evaluating the Corps' navigation expansion plan, the National Research Council stated that the Corps' plan "contains flaws serious enough to limit its credibility and value within the policy-making process."

To its credit, but without taking responsibility, the Corps states the obvious and candidly writes in its study of expanding navigation construction on the Upper Mississippi that the river's ecosystem is "significantly altered, is currently degraded, and is expected to get worse" — in fact, it is getting worse at an accelerating rate. Because of budget constraints, Army engineers are becoming increasingly sensitive to the public's growing environmental awareness and have changed strategies — they now ask Congress for roughly equal amounts of money to restore what they have previously destroyed, while spending the other half on new infrastructure. Accurately gauging the direction the political winds blow, they also ask for less money. In FY 2010, the Corps received $5.5 billion in budget allocation. In FY 2011, the Corps asked the Obama Administration for $4.9 billion, and in FY 2012, they asked for $4.6 billion. Of that budget, approximately 2 percent goes to the maintenance of the locks and dams included in the UMR-MWW Project — the cost of the proposed new locks would roughly pay for the maintenance of the entire system for 20 years. If the Corps were genuinely concerned about the public good, they would not hold badly-needed environmental restoration projects captive to construction projects, but, of course, there is little need or financial allocations for army construction engineers in wetland and floodplain restoration.

As the Army of Corps Engineers' profile and reputation shrinks, a persuasive argument asserts that in a time of general government reduction and consolidation, all non-military engineering projects and personnel should be removed from U.S. Army command, and that the civilian personnel who make up the world's largest public engineering, design, and construction management agency be placed under the Department of the Interior, and that more resources are directed from the public to the private engineering sector. Initially, the U.S. Army Corps of Engineers consisted of three soldiers who were organized to build fortifications for General George Washington at Bunker Hill, but now the Corps is a destructively wasteful and anachronistic bureaucracy that shouldn't be responsible for public projects, much less wetlands' management.

One of the line items in the UMR-IWW Project is the purchase of 35,000 acres (about 55 square miles or an area smaller than Davenport) of privately-owned farmland for environmental and natural habitat restoration and reclaimed floodplain. This is an insignificant step in the right direction. Whereas Upper Mississippi Valley farmland sells for more than $2,000 per acre, Mississippi Delta land for cotton farming sells at a tenth of that price. Extrapolating the cost of building seven new locks and expanding five others under the UMR-MWW Project (economists estimate cost overruns would be from 85 to 200 percent, and they are not included in the following calculation), if the money spent on the project was diverted to habitat restoration and floodplain expansion, a modest step of 1 million acres (1,500 square miles or an area larger than Rhode Island) of farmland in the Upper Mississippi Valley could be purchased or ten times that amount of land (an area larger than Maryland an about half the size of the land inundated by the 1927 Mississippi flood) could be acquired in the Mississippi Delta and returned to Mother Nature.

Another argument against building the locks and dams project is that barge transport is in part an unneeded and immensely expensive farm subsidy to provide grains at lower prices to foreign markets. Almost half of the barge tonnage on the Upper Mississippi is agricultural products destined for overseas markets. Selling corn to China and wheat to Russia is a good thing, but at what cost? Is it sensible to compromise the environment and further jeopardize city dwellers in the Upper Mississippi Valley each spring so that Midwest farmers are marginally more competitive in world markets? Just as U.S citizens pay what world oil producers sell their gasoline for, foreign citizens will pay what American farmers sell their grains for. And if grain prices go up due to less acreage planted, how does that hurt Midwest farmers? Paradoxically, today's conservative politicians fervently espouse free market values, just as those from the 1920s did, and they are the first to line up behind farm and transportation subsidies of all stripes and to champion the construction of more commercial "improvements" on the Upper Mississippi River.

Andrew Humphreys' concepts are now known to be outrageously wrongheaded, and in recent years, engineers' and environmentalists' understanding of waterway management has greatly increased. Returning floodplains to their natural state and restoring wetlands to increase natural wildlife habitats are two positive steps that can help reverse Army engineers' misguided attempts to control the Mississippi River. Shoreline protection, side-channel rehabilitation, island building, and backwater restoration are environmental engineering methods that enrich biodiversity, restore natural river hydrology, improve water quality, and enhance fish and wildlife habitats.

In their September 2009 report on the Upper Mississippi River System, the Army Corps of Engineers says that the UMRS "is a place for this and future generations to learn how to restore and maintain a 'living river' in the face of an ever growing human population. The lessons learned in more than a half century of study and application of large river function, form and restoration have provided us with the necessary tools, knowledge and experience to effectually protect, preserve and enhance environmental conditions necessary for ecological health and sustainability of this national treasure." Doubtful, and this hyperbolic statement, of course, begs the question of what lessons have the Corps learned that qualifies them to restore what they destroyed? There are few environmentalists or engineers that seriously believe that United States wetlands and river management should be entrusted to the U.S. Army. Fortunately, as with the ill-fated Hennepin Canal, obsolescence and economics will eventually end the engineering insanity in the Mississippi Valley. The only remaining question is how much more environmental damage will be done before control of the Mississippi is taken away from the U.S. Army?

Relative to the 9-Foot Channel Project, a much smaller but infinitely superior federal government Depression Era project in Rock Island was the Black Hawk Museum and Lodge. The state historic site's native limestone and rough-timber building was constructed in the mid-1930s by the Civilian Conservation Corps, which also built two small shelter houses that hosted wienie roasts for generations of hikers, scouts, and student outings. The main building houses the Hauberg Indian Museum and a CCC exhibit. The Indian Museum displays a large portion of John Hauberg's collection of Sauk and Meskwaki artifacts and dioramas with life-size figures that depict Indian life in Saukenuk. Two paintings by WPA artist, Otis Hake, have been restored and grace the Lodge's beautiful main room in the lower level. This story of finding one of the Museum's artifacts is from the Black Hawk State Historic Site's website:

> Imagine! It is the summer of 1934. You and your siblings, cousins, parents, aunts and uncles live in three summer cottages located on Big Island. Every day you and the other kids spend the entire day outdoors, playing in the woods and swimming in the river. The area is gripped by record heat. There is a drought. Every day the level of the Mississippi River drops a little more.
>
> One day you come home to hear your uncle complaining that when he was out on the river fishing, his boat kept hitting a log submerged just below the surface of the water. He asks you, your 10-year-old brother, and two of your cousins to help him remove the log. Out you go, dig the log out of the mud, bring it to the surface of the water ... only to discover it is a dugout canoe — one Indians probably made and used! Fiction? No, fact. The dugout canoe housed in the Hauberg Museum was found in just this way.

The money that the PWA contributed to build iconic Rock Island High School may have been the best-spent federal money in the history of the republic. The first four Rock Island high schools were built in the area near Lincoln School, and the last of the downtown high schools, which was designed for only 600 students but had almost 1,000, had become overcrowded. Keeping their priorities straight, the school district had completed the equally iconic 15,000-seat high school football stadium and running track seven years before construction began on the new high school. Built for $150,000 ($1,875,000), the classic bowl-shaped stadium was constructed on the site of an abandoned clay pit. On October 5, 1929 in the first game played in the stadium, a full house watched the Rocks overwhelm Grant High of Cedar Rapids, Iowa. After purchasing undeveloped land to the west of the stadium, in 1936 work began on the high school, which was designed for 1,600 students. In September 1937, the first classes were held in the august school whose spacious campus cost $1,250,000 ($20 million) of which 36 percent was paid for by a PWA grant. President Franklin Roosevelt was unable to attend any of the four dedication ceremonies, and he was one of the few invited dignitaries that didn't attend at least one.

Of even more national importance than the opening of the new Rock Island High School was the end of Prohibition. On April 8, 1933, in possibly the most famous presidential understatement ever, Roosevelt said, "I think this would be a good time for a beer." The occasion was the day after the Cullen-Harrison Act became law — a law which allowed the manufacture of wine and 3.2 beer. Anheuser-Busch Company delivered a case of beer to the White House by an ornate horse-drawn wagon pulled by a team of Clydesdales. Eight months later on December 5, 1933, the Eighteenth Amendment was repealed when the Twenty-First Amendment was ratified. Support for Prohibition had diminished, and virtually everyone who didn't live in the Bible Belt, including some of its strongest early supporters, believed it should be repealed. John D. Rockefeller Jr., a teetotaler and contributor to the Anti-Saloon League, announced his support for repeal because of the widespread problems he believed Prohibition had caused, as did Eleuthère Irénée du Pont of chemical company fame who led the Association Against the Prohibition Amendment.

Prohibition had started as a women's movement and later coupled itself with women's suffrage. However, after seeing their noble experiment in action, many of those who passionately led the crusade, admitted their error and became just as emotional in their efforts to repeal the amendment. Using women's prerogative to change their minds, they "had come to the painful conclusion that the destructiveness of alcohol was now embodied in Prohibition itself." Activist Pauline Sabin argued that repeal would protect families from the corruption, crime, and underground drinking that Prohibition had spawned. She formed the Women's Organization for National Prohibition Reform that numbered 1.5 million women when the repeal passed. Originally, Sabin supported the Eighteenth Amendment; however, after seeing its realities, she viewed Prohibition as both hypocritical and dangerous and recognized "the apparent decline of temperate drinking" and feared the rise of organized crime that developed around bootlegging. Additionally, she worried that children who witnessed the blatant disregard for Prohibition's laws would cease to recognize the sanctity of law itself. Finally, Sabin and the WONPR publicly took the libertarian stance that disapproved of government involvement in personal matters like drinking.

State conventions ratified the Twenty-First Amendment, which was the only time an amendment was ratified by state convention instead of by state assemblies. This alternate form of ratification was used to appease hypocritical elected officials, who didn't want to offend their conservative constituencies. Even after repeal, 38 percent of Americans still lived in areas where either state or local laws prevented the sale of alcohol. The last state to repeal Prohibition was Mississippi, which finally caved in 1966. One of the last major cities to repeal Prohibition was Evanston, Illinois, home of Northwestern University. When the college opened in 1855, the trustees petitioned the Illinois General Assembly to prohibit the sale of "spirituous, vinous or fermented liquors within four miles of the location of said University," a distance that included all of Evanston. In 1972 Evanston repealed their Prohibition law. Three years later, Northwestern students, who wanted to open a bar at Norris University Center, filed a lawsuit in Cook County Circuit Court to have equal access to liquor because they claimed the 120-year-old law was struck down when Evanston opted out — the students got their bar.

The repeal of Prohibition and the steady improvement in the economy gave Roosevelt one of the highest approval ratings of any president, and in 1936 he defeated Alf Landon even more soundly than he thumped Herbert Hoover four years earlier. The House and Senate remained solidly Democratic and both increased their seats. But smarting from the repeal of Prohibition and the wave of progressive New Deal legislation, Southern Democrats joined with Republicans to form the "conservative coalition," which would dominate Congress until 1963 and remained a force through the 1970s. The coalition successfully halted new legislation and stalled many New Deal relief programs. The country relapsed into a deep recession, and unemployment shot up to 19 percent.

With a conservatively recalcitrant Congress, economic recovery stagnated during Roosevelt's second term. So, he turned his attention to labor, which had significantly increased its political sway during his first term. John L. Lewis, the president of the United Mine Workers of America, became a driving force behind the Congress of Industrial Organizations and was one of Roosevelt's most powerful supporters, delivering millions of votes to the Democratic Party. Lewis was as tough as the miners and steel workers he represented, and he was as smart and smooth as the Washington Congressmen who sought his support. As he stole longtime American Federation of Labor unions, relations between the two organizations became bitter. And in 1937, after Lewis won collective bargaining contracts from General Motors and U.S. Steel, two of the nation's most powerful anti-union companies, the long-dominant AFL expelled the CIO. Labor disunity weakened both organizations and compromised their public support, causing Roosevelt to wish a "plague on both your houses." Democratic support for the unions also drove small businessmen and professionals to join rural America in supporting the Republican Party.

The grind of politics and its endless social functions created a blithe cynicism in Roosevelt. He maintained that often in meetings and at social functions his audience didn't listen to a word he said. And occasionally he would say outrageous things to noddingly agreeable guests to prove his point. Once to see if anyone was paying attention, he began an address to the Daughters of the American Revolution — an organization of women who can trace their ancestry to the Revolutionary War — by saying, "My fellow immigrants ..." At a White House reception, he said to a guest who didn't make eye contact, "I murdered my grandmother this morning." And was pleasantly surprised when the man diplomatically replied, "I'm sure she had it coming to her."

Roosevelt's second term saw the meteoric rise of a brazen international political star: Adolph Hitler. After the Treaty of Versailles ended World War I, Germany was left a humiliated and impotent nation without leadership. Hitler, an Austrian who was a devout Roman Catholic during his childhood and had considered joining the priesthood, seized on the vision of restoring Germany's prominence by playing on the country's lost pride and lost territory. In addition to severe military restrictions and reparation payments, the Versailles Treaty had ceded small portions of Germany to Denmark, Belgium, and Czechoslovakia, a larger amount to France, and a big portion to Poland. It was the loss of territory to Poland that was particularly galling to Germans. In his 1925 autobiography/political treatise, *Mein Kampf (My Struggle)*, Hitler glorified himself, defined his political ideology, spelled out his vision for eliminating Germany's twin foes of Judaism and Communism, and proclaimed the righteousness of restoring Germany's borders.

The worldwide Depression and the destruction of World War I exempted Germany from the giddy times the United States and Western Europe had enjoyed during the 1920s — what the French called the "Crazy Years." The 1929 Stock Market Crash devastated the fragile Germany economy faster and harder than the United States' economy, and Western Europe's failed economies directly resulted in Hitler's rise to power. Internally, he was able to cast blame on the failures of moderate German politicians, who had been in place since the end of World War I. In addition Germany's neighboring countries were too absorbed in their own problems to concern themselves with what Hitler was up to.

Germans were ready for an extreme solution, and Hitler would give them one. After shoving aristocratic, 85-year-old German President Paul von Hindenburg from power, in February of 1933, only a month after Roosevelt took office, Hitler established the Third Reich. The Nazi government issued a decree that suspended civil rights and created a state of emergency in which Hitler's decrees didn't require parliamentary confirmation. In the first days of Hitler's dictatorship, the Nazis instituted a policy of "coordination," which aligned individuals and institutions with Nazi goals. The arts, the economy, the law, education, and the church all came under Nazi autocratic control.

The Nazis also narrowly controlled sports. Two years before Hitler seized power, the International Olympic Committee had awarded the Summer Games of the XI Olympiad to Germany. In the previous Olympics, the Los Angeles Games were victims of the Depression, and even though L.A. made a million dollars ($16 million) on the games, only about half the number of athletes that participated in the 1928 Summer Olympics in Amsterdam attended the games four years later. In Los Angeles, U.S. female athletes had outshone the men. Babe Didrikson won gold medals in the javelin and hurdles and would have won the high jump but was disqualified for illegal form, and Helene Madison won three golds in swimming. Stanislawa Walasiewicz, a Polish immigrant who grew up in Cleveland, was unable to obtain U.S. citizenship, so she competed for Poland. She won the gold medal in the women's 100-meter dash. Four years later at the Berlin Games, as Stella Walsh, she won a second gold medal in the 100 meters for the U.S.A. During her athletic career, Walsh set 18 world records, and her European record for the 100-yard dash remains unbroken. In 1980 she was shot and killed as an innocent bystander in a bank robbery — she was 69. An autopsy revealed that she had male genitalia.

For the 1936 Summer Olympics, the Nazis built a 100,000-seat track and field stadium, six gymnasiums, and a host of smaller arenas for the minor sports. A closed-circuit television system was installed, which for many provided a first glimpse of TV, and a radio network broadcast to 41 countries. Dancer, movie star, and filmmaker Leni Riefenstahl personified what Hitler believed epitomized the perfect German female. German Olympic organizers commissioned the talented woman to film the games. Titled *Olympia*, the $7 million ($110 million) documentary film introduced many techniques now common to sports filming, including extreme close ups, abrupt cuts from one scene to another, overhead shots from cranes, multiple cameras shooting the same action, and tracking cameras on rails mounted next to the running track. *Olympia* appears on most of the "best-ever" film lists. The Olympic Torch Relay was devised for the Berlin Games, and Riefenstahl later staged the torch relay for her film. She also mixed staged film clips with actual event film from the major Olympic competitions, including famous footage of African-American Jesse Owens' victories.

Hitler had German athletes carefully selected, based not only on their athletic prowess, but also on their Aryan good looks. The lithe, black Owens did not fit Hitler's Aryan image of the "master race." However, he stole Hitler's show. Seventh of 11 children, James Cleveland Owens was born in Alabama in 1913. He was called J.C. until he was nine-years-old when the family migrated to Cleveland for better opportunities. When his teacher asked his name, he said "J.C.," but because of his strong Southern accent, she thought he said "Jesse," and that is what he was called for the rest of his life. Because he worked in a shoe shine and repair shop after school, his junior high school track coach practiced with him daily before classes, and Owens always attributed his athletic success to the encouragement of his early coach. At a time when track and field meets were as well attended as the fall football games that were played on the fields circled by quarter-mile running tracks, Owens became a national sensation when, at the National High School Championships, he equaled the world record of 9.4 seconds in the 100-yard dash.

After high school, Owens enrolled at the Ohio State University. He was not given a scholarship and had to work his way through college. He lived off campus with other black students. When he traveled with the team, he ate carryout or at blacks-only restaurants and stayed at blacks-only hotels. On May 25, 1935 at the Big Ten Championships, the Buckeye Bullet performed what has been called "the greatest athletic achievement in modern history." Owens set three world records and tied a fourth in the span of 45 minutes. He equaled his own, co-held world record for the 100-yard dash (9.4 seconds); set world records in the long jump (26' 8 1/4" — a record that would last 25 years); the 220-yard dash (20.3 seconds); and the 220-yard low hurdles (22.6 seconds, becoming the first to break 23 seconds). This was a prelude to his time on the world stage.

The next summer, Owens arrived in Berlin as half of an exceptionally strong pair of black U.S. sprinters. At the time, a Marquette University student, Ralph Metcalfe, was acknowledged as the "World's Fastest Human." Three years older than Owens, Metcalfe had been world record co-holder with Owens in the 100-yard dash at 9.4 seconds, and he later ran 9.3 several times. He also held the 200-meter world record. Running on the same 4x100 meter relay team with Owens, it was generally conceded that the baton would have to be dropped in the Olympic finals for the Americans to lose the gold medal — it wasn't. Metcalfe finished a close second to Owens in the final of the 100-meter dash as Owens claimed the mantle of World's Fastest Human — the closest German was a distant fifth. The next day Owens won the long jump, the day after that, the 200-meter sprint, and finally, as a member of the 4x100 meter relay team, he won his fourth gold medal — a stunning achievement. Hitler left the stadium before Owens received his gold medal for the 100-meters win, and when asked by the press if he felt snubbed, Owens graciously said, "Hitler had a certain time to come to the stadium and a certain time to leave. It happened he had to leave before the victory ceremony after the 100 meters. But before he left I was on my way to a broadcast and passed near his box. He waved at me and I waved back. I think it was bad taste to criticize the man of the hour in another country."

While in Europe, Owens and Metcalfe were allowed to travel with and stay and eat in the same hotels as their white teammates. After a ticker-tape parade down New York's Fifth Avenue in honor of his achievements, which were seen by the Western media as a slap in the face to Hitler, Owens had to ride the freight elevator at the Waldorf-Astoria to reach the reception honoring him. Owens later said, "Hitler didn't snub me — it was FDR who snubbed me. The president didn't even send me a telegram." On the other hand, Hitler sent Owens a commemorative inscribed photograph of himself. Owens was never invited to the White House, nor did Presidents Roosevelt or Truman honor him in any way.

After the Olympics, Metcalfe completed a master's degree at the University of Southern California. He joined the Army and served in World War II, and later coached track at Xavier University in Louisiana and became a successful Chicago businessman. Owens had a tougher time of it. While in Berlin, he had been visited in the Olympic village by Adi Dassler, the founder of the Adidas shoe company. Dassler persuaded him to use Adidas shoes, and Owens became the first African-American athlete to receive a shoe sponsorship — he received all of the track shoes he could wear, but no money.

After returning to the States, he tried to capitalize on his achievements, but he did not receive the anticipated financial rewards. To the anger of Ohio State University and most U.S. white men, he gave up his amateur status and joined Abe Saperstein, the owner of the already successful Harlem Globetrotters, in the formation of a Negro baseball league. Owens became a draw for the league, and between innings he raced horses and spotted fans a ten-yard head start in a race around the bases. He always won and the act became old. After working at odd jobs to support his wife and three daughters, in 1955 President Eisenhower finally honored Owens by making him an Ambassador of Sports. Over the last 25 years of his life, Owens provided for his wife and family by making public appearances and giving inspirational speeches to schools, including Rock Island High School, and businesses. He died in 1980 from lung cancer caused by smoking.

Chapter 25

Another Great War

I think a lot of women said, screw that noise. 'Cause they had a taste of freedom, they had a taste of making their own money, a taste of spending their own money, making their own decisions. I think the beginning of the women's movement had its seeds right there in World War Two. ~ Dellie Hahne, educator and World War II Red Cross worker

ON THE DAY FOLLOWING the attack on Pearl Harbor, aides, cabinet members, and top military brass surrounded Franklin Roosevelt, vying for his attention. As he moved from one group to another, he dictated to his secretary a speech for Congress, which she dutifully recorded word for word. The message began, "Yesterday, December 7, 1941 a date which will live in world history, the United States was suddenly and deliberately attacked by naval and air forces of the Empire of Japan." After typing the 500-word draft, she returned it to Roosevelt, who, while still multi-tasking, made only one change — he crossed out "world history" and replaced it with "infamy."

Conspiracy theorists, who believe that Roosevelt and other high administration officials were looking for any excuse to enter a war that many Americans thought was solely Europe's problem, claimed that Roosevelt knew well in advance that Japan was going to bomb Pearl Harbor. If their theory were true, he had days to compose his speech to Congress and the nation, and he knew exactly what he would say. But most serious World War II historians and scholars think that is highly improbable, and there is little solid evidence or even credible motives to advance this theory. As the United States entered the war, Roosevelt said, "More than an end to war, we want an end to the beginning of all wars - yes, an end to this brutal, inhuman, and thoroughly impractical method of settling the differences between governments."

That is not to say that the war didn't help cure the nation's financial woes, divert Roosevelt's critics, and launch the United States on a half-century run of social and economic dominance never before attained in the modern world — or that America's extraordinary post-war prosperity was worth the horrific price paid. America's accomplishments very probably would have been attained even if the United States didn't enter the war. However, it is unlikely that the European allies would have prevailed over the Axis nations without U.S. intervention. Japan had gained dominance in the East, and six months before Pearl Harbor was bombed, Germany had launched an aggressive attack against Russia. The previous year, Germany had overrun France and the Low Countries of Western Europe and pounded England in an air war conducted over Great Britain and France. The English had held out but were in a tenuous defensive position. Without American forces to help invade the Western Front and U.S. munitions and supplies to aid Russia and prop up the Eastern Front, the Axis allies of Germany, Hungary, Romania, Bulgaria, and Italy probably would not have been defeated on the ground.

What is beyond dispute is that Adolph Hitler duped central Europe into buying into his master race theory and was hell-bent on exterminating the world's non-Aryans, starting with the Jews and Gypsies — even though Gypsies are Aryan. Nine months before Germany invaded Poland in September 1939, Hitler said in a speech:

> In the course of my life I have very often been a prophet, and have usually been ridiculed for it. During the time of my struggle for power it was in the first instance only the Jewish race that received my prophecies with laughter when I said that I would one day take over the leadership of the State, and with it that of the whole nation, and that I would then among other things settle the Jewish problem. Their laughter was uproarious, but I think that for some time now they have been laughing on the other side of their face. Today I will once more be a prophet: if the international Jewish financiers in and outside Europe should succeed in plunging the nations once more into a world war, then the result will not be the Bolshevizing of the earth, and thus the victory of Jewry, but the annihilation of the Jewish race in Europe!

In a spectacular demonstration of self-fulfilling prophecy, Hitler very nearly annihilated the Jewish race in Europe. At one of the 35 "death camps, "Auschwitz-Birkenau, from early 1942 until late 1944 at least 1.1 million people, including Jehovah Witnesses (400), Soviet POWs (15,000), Gypsies (23,000), Poles (150,000), and Jews (all the rest) were marched through the gates famously inscribed "Arbeit macht frei" (Work sets you free). Another documented 3,151,500 people lost their lives in the other 34 extermination and concentration camps. The 231,800 Gypsies who died in death camps is a small number compared to the 5 to 6 million Jews (of which approximately 1.5 million were children), but it was a proportionately greater percentage of their entire race.

To this day, numerous groups of people deny that the Nazi government had an official policy or even an intention of exterminating Jews, and that the number of deaths claimed in the Holocaust is grossly exaggerated. They are partially right — it is an incomprehensible number that is as mind-numbing as the equal number of black Africans who were enslaved and died between the time they left Africa and celebrated their first anniversary in the Americas, or the minimum of 50 million indigenous North and South Americans who died fighting for their homes or from diseases white men gave them. The 73 million people that died in World War II made it even greater than the first Great War, where 68 million perished — if carnage measures wars' greatness.

One of the most glamorized figures from World War II is General George Patton, a Californian and West Point graduate. After the defeat of the Third Reich, Patton anticipated that our Russian allies might become a problem, and when Secretary of War Robert Patterson asked him what he would do with the Soviets, Patton replied: "I would have you tell the Red Army where their border is, and give them a limited time to get back across. Warn them that if they fail to do so, we will push them back across it." He explained his aggressive attitude toward the U.S. ally by saying, "The difficulty in understanding the Russian is that we do not take cognizance of the fact that he is not a European, but an Asiatic, and therefore thinks deviously. We can no more understand a Russian than a Chinese or a Japanese, and from what I have seen of them, I have no particular desire to understand them except to ascertain how much lead or iron it takes to kill them. In addition to his other amiable characteristics, the Russian has no regard for human life, and they are all out sons-of-bitches, barbarians, and chronic drunks."

Patton may have been a military genius, and his position toward the Russians may have been sound military advice, but he came up a bit short as a humanitarian. However, his rhetoric generally expressed the hubris of America's military leaders as they helped rescue the free world. Before the Normandy landings, Patton told his troops about his plans after D-Day: "We want to get the hell over there [Japan]. The quicker we clean up this goddamned mess, the quicker we can take a little jaunt against the ... Japs and clean out their next too ... before the goddamned Marines get all of the credit." It is unclear what he proposed to do with the 110,000 devious Japanese-American citizens and their next of kin who were interned in War Relocation Camps spread throughout the California desert and the Great Basin.

Patton's attitude towards the 125,000 African Americans, who served oversees during the war, changed depending on his audience. Of black soldiers, he said, "Individually they were good soldiers, but I expressed my belief at the time, and have never found the necessity of changing it, that a colored soldier cannot think fast enough to fight in armor." Later he said, "I don't give a damn who the man is. He can be a nigger or a Jew, but if he has the stuff and does his duty, he can have anything I've got. By God, I love him!" Then, when addressing a black armored tank unit, he said, "Men, you're the first Negro tankers to ever fight in the American Army. I would never have asked for you, if you weren't good. I have nothing but the best in my Army. I don't care what color you are as long as you go up there and kill those Kraut sons of bitches. Everyone has their eyes on you and is expecting great things from you. Most of all, your race is looking forward to you. Don't let them down, and damn you, don't let me down!"

Back home, Patton's racial attitudes were commonly held throughout white America; however, among the primary beliefs he was fighting to protect was that prejudices are constitutionally protected and the majority's opinion prevails, regardless of how uninformed it is. But what is also constitutionally protected is that the U.S. Military is responsible to the electorate, and the president is their Commander in Chief. It was unwise for Patton, when speaking to a group of reporters, to say that that being a Nazi in Germany was "like being a Democrat in the States." Roosevelt soon relieved him of his command.

Most Americans also wanted what Roosevelt wanted when he said, "We look forward to a world founded upon four essential human freedoms: freedom of speech and expression, freedom of every person to worship God in his own way, freedom from want, freedom from fear." Ironically, while black Americans were being drafted to fight for their country, Japanese Americans were being tagged for shipment to internment camps. Although pre-war prejudice against Asians didn't follow ethnicity lines, Chinese, Koreans, and Malaysians got a free pass from Americans because they hated the Japanese as much as white Americans did and had been fighting Japanese imperialism for more than a quarter century.

In July 1937, Japan invaded China, and over the next eight years the Japanese massacred 6 million Chinese, Indonesians, Filipinos, and Koreans. The invasion was a final stage of Japan's 25-year imperialistic expansion into the Asian mainland, which had begun in 1910, when Japan annexed Korea. The Japanese also controlled Formosa (now known as Taiwan), hundreds of South Pacific islands, Eastern Siberia, and Kamchatka. The preemptive strike on Pearl Harbor was not an invasion but an attempt to keep the United States from interfering in Japan's military conquests of Asia. By sinking four of the eight Pacific fleet battleships (two others were damaged beyond repair), three cruisers, three destroyers, and a minelayer, the Pacific fleet was dealt a crippling setback — but the attack woke a sleeping dog that should have been left undisturbed.

In fact, a year before Pearl Harbor, the U.S. Navy had adopted "Plan Dog," which was to fight a defensive war in the Pacific and to concentrate on helping U.S. allies defeat Hitler. The sneak attack that killed 2,402 Americans was bad strategy, and later Admiral Hara Tadaichi summed up the Japanese attack by saying, "We won a great tactical victory at Pearl Harbor and thereby lost the war." The resolve that was to bond the nation was expressed during the attack when a Navy chaplain, who was in a chain of men passing artillery shells from below the deck of a damaged cruiser to a gun mount, noticed the man next to him was giving out. He slapped the sailor on the shoulder and said, "Praise the Lord and pass the ammunition." The line of fatigued men picked up the chant, and it was often repeated for the next four years.

Although Pearl Harbor focused ethnic hatred on Japanese-Americans in the same way that World War I had on German-Americans, ugly underlying motives emerged for the relocation and imprisonment of U.S. Japanese, which was ostensibly done to prevent spying. During the attack on Pearl Harbor, a Japanese kamikaze pilot, who apparently chickened out, crash-landed on the small Hawaiian island of Ni'ihau. The island's natives were unaware of the attack, but when they realized its significance, they arrested the pilot. Communicating in Japanese, three Japanese Ni'ihau islanders helped the pilot escape — he was quickly found and killed. The Hawaiian Territorial governor rejected calls for the internment of Japanese in Hawaii, but the incident provoked hysteria in California.

The Roberts Commission Report, which was the official report prepared for Roosevelt and formulated the internment program, was met with this evaluation from award-winning columnist Henry McLemore:

> I am for the immediate removal of every Japanese on the West Coast to a point deep in the interior. I don't mean a nice part of the interior either. Herd 'em up, pack 'em off, and give 'em the inside room in the badlands. ... Personally, I hate the Japanese. And that goes for all of them.

A *Los Angeles Times* editorial said:

> A viper is nonetheless a viper wherever the egg is hatched. ...So, a Japanese American born of Japanese parents, nurtured upon Japanese traditions, living in a transplanted Japanese atmosphere... notwithstanding his nominal brand of accidental citizenship almost inevitably and with the rarest exceptions grows up to be a Japanese, and not an American. ... Thus, while it might cause injustice to a few to treat them all as potential enemies, I cannot escape the conclusion... that such treatment... should be accorded to each and all of them while we are at war with their race.

White California farmers were also slow to support their hardworking farmhands and neighbors. A spokesman for the Salinas Vegetable Grower-Shipper Association, told the *Saturday Evening Post*:

> We're charged with wanting to get rid of the Japs for selfish reasons. We do. It's a question of whether the white man lives on the Pacific Coast or the brown men. They came into this valley to work, and they stayed to take over. ... If all the Japs were removed tomorrow, we'd never miss them in two weeks, because the white farmers can take over and produce everything the Jap grows. And we do not want them back when the war ends, either.

When the United States entered the war, there were 92,000-Japanese, 315,000-German, and 695,000-Italian "enemy aliens" in the United States. Under the 1798 Alien Enemies Act, all were subject to arrest and imprisonment. However, it was impractical to jail 1.1 million students, merchant seamen, tourists, visiting relatives, and those that had simply snuck into the country years before because they wanted to live in America — an estimated 600,000 Italian immigrants were not naturalized. Also, there were large, influential German and Italian communities that had serious numbers of voters. So the Justice Department took the popular approach and sent most of the Japanese enemy aliens and all of the Japanese Americans living on the West Coast (110,000), 3.6 percent of the German enemy aliens (11,507), and 0.0003 percent of the Italian enemy aliens (231) to the internment camps. No records can be found of the number of Hungarians, Romanians, or Bulgarians that were interned.

War usually boosts industry, and as the Depression tenaciously hung on, entering a war that was being fought overseas provided a kick start to the United States' meteoric economic and political ascension. Rock Island had already emerged from the Depression before America entered the war, and during the 1930s, the city's population had grown by 11.5 percent, well ahead of the nation's and the region's other towns and cities. Public works projects driven by Mayors Bengston and Galbraith had created jobs, and while surrounding cities watched their infrastructures deteriorate, Rock Island's dramatically improved. Rock Island's business leaders followed the public sector's aggressive spending, and International Harvester led the way. In 1933 employment in all Tri-City industrial plants totaled 6,332. In 1939 employment at Rock Island's IH Farmall plant exceeded 5,000, and in October of the same year, 16,000 crammed into the high school stadium not to watch a football game but to attend the unveiling of Farmall's new M and H model tractors. Farmall wasn't the only Rock Island company that was thriving: J.I. Case employment was approaching 1,000 as was Servus Rubber, and Container Corporation of America was attracted to the progressive city and started turning out thousands of cardboard boxes. Well before Nazi tanks rolled into Poland in September 1939, Rock Island was positioned for the wartime boom.

As prepared as Rock Island was for the economic surge, it could not handle the deluge of workers and their families that arrived at the Rock Island train station. The federal government hastily built the Arsenal Courts, 305 low-cost apartments in Rock Island's West End, and by Pearl Harbor Day 1,200 people were living there. During the war years, 822 new homes were built in Rock Island, exceeding the number in both Moline and Davenport. Astonishingly, in less than a decade's time, manufacturing employment rose by a multiple of eight and by 1943 exceeded 50,000 in the Tri-Cities alone. Just as amazingly, women, who before the war were too frail to do factory work, held more than a third of the jobs.

Farmall, Case, Servus Rubber, American Container, Gellman Manufacturing, and Bertman Electric all received huge government contracts. Feltex Corporation moved to Rock Island to make ammunition containers, as did Blake Specialty Company to produce plumbing construction supplies. Farmall produced high-speed military tractors and continued to turn out rugged tractors for both American and U.S. allies' "lend-lease" farms. Case produced more than 3,000 tractors for the military and diversified into 500-pound bomb production, turning out 111,000 bombs to be dropped on the bad guys. Servus Rubber cranked out waterproof boots and tents by the thousands. After the war, Russian Premier Joseph Stalin magnanimously said, "Without American production, the United Nations never could have won the war." Obviously, Rock Island contributed its fair share to wartime production.

Of course, the Arsenal was ground zero for wartime manufacturing. In 1937 it was operating with a skeletal work force of 1,807. Feeling the winds of war, two years later when Germany attacked Poland, Arsenal employment had risen to more than 4,000, and the work force steadily grew until it peaked four years later at 18,467. During the war, 60,000 freight cars carrying tanks, trucks, machine guns, howitzers, gun carriages, and spare parts originated at the Arsenal and passed through Rock Island on their way to Europe and the South Pacific. The city's prosperity marginally increased, but the relief from financial woes was greatly outweighed by the anxiety over the 4,601 Rock Island men who were drafted.

In 1940 the first American peacetime draft was instituted. It contained a "one year" provision, stating that if an eligible man voluntarily signed up, he could return home at the end of a year. Many Rock Islanders took advantage of the one-year promise, and those that survived the war returned home five years later. As was the case in every war starting with the Civil War, compared to the surrounding region, Rock Island men disproportionately served their country. During World War II, Rock Island County sent 12,000 men to war. While sixty-two percent of the county's residents lived in Moline, East Moline, Milan and the other small towns in the strip of land along the Rock Island Rapids — more than half of those from the county who served were from Rock Island.

While the Rock Island Arsenal was feverishly manufacturing conventional weapons, in a handball court under abandoned stands at the University of Chicago's Amos Alonzo Field, Enrico Fermi, with assistance from every top American and British physicist, was busy assembling the world's first nuclear reactor. Encouraged by Albert Einstein, in June 1941 Franklin Roosevelt had funded research for using uranium to "provide a possible source of bombs with a destructiveness vastly greater than anything now known." Eighteen months later, the first controlled, self-sustaining nuclear chain reaction was initiated under the bleachers. When the nuclear reaction stopped after 28 minutes, a Fermi collaborator, Arthur Compton, excitedly called Harvard's Office of Scientific Research to announce the beginning of the Atomic Age by saying, "The Italian navigator has reached the New World." "And how did he find the natives?" came the response. "Very friendly," replied Compton.

While the United States was making a quantum leap in manufacturing weapons of mass destruction, Japan was launching "killer balloons" aimed at the United States. Over the course of the war, the Japanese launched 9,000 "wind ship weapons," balloons made of paper and rubberized-silk. The hydrogen filled balloons carried incendiary bombs, which ignited on ground contact, and were floated on wind currents to North America. More than 1,000 balloons hit their target, and one reached as far east as Michigan. The balloon bombs killed six Americans — five children and a pregnant woman who were picnicking on a beach in Oregon. Three years after Fermi created the first nuclear chain reaction, in the early morning hours of August 6, 1945, a bomb vastly more destructive than an incendiary balloon was dropped on Hiroshima, Japan.

Eleven days earlier, Harry "Give 'em Hell" Truman, English Prime Minister Winston Churchill, and Chairman of the Nationalist Government of China Chiang Kai-shek issued a joint ultimatum to Japan to unconditionally surrender or face "prompt and utter destruction." Very probably because he didn't know the level of utter destruction threatened, Japanese Prime Minister Kantarō Suzuki rejected the ultimatum. The United States was only slightly surer of what they threatened than Suzuki was. Only three weeks before, the first nuclear bomb was exploded at the New Mexico Alamogordo Bombing and Gunnery Range. Prior to the test, some physicists feared that an atomic bomb might trigger a nuclear reaction that turned the earth into a mini-sun.

For almost seventy years, the debate has continued as to whether or not it was a bit too harsh to bomb Hiroshima, and then when the Japanese didn't immediately raise the white flag, to bomb Nagasaki three days later — killing a total of about 140,000 civilians and a dozen American POWs. At the time of the two bombings, the Japanese military was in retreat and nearly impotent. Their army was spread out and stranded on dozens of islands throughout the South Pacific, and the naval fleet had been decimated by U.S submarines and warships and had little ability to supply the troops, much less attack. But with the help of 130,000 civilians, the scientists had "secretly" built three atomic bombs at a cost that was equivalent to less than ten days of wartime spending. U.S. Generals strongly believed that the demonstration of "The Gadget" would make conventional warfare obsolete, and they were not going to be denied the opportunity to demonstrate their new weapon.

The bombing of Nagasaki was a first test of an implosion-type atom bomb; whereas, the Hiroshima bomb was detonated with a "gun method" triggering device. Both bombs exceeded expectations, and surprisingly, in the wake of the first bombing,

Japanese military leaders hardened their positions, twice attempting to assassinate Suzuki, who had quickly come to his senses and encouraged surrender, and planning a military coup against Emperor of Japan Hirohito to block him from surrendering. Finally, six days after the bombing of Nagasaki, on August 15 in a recorded radio message, Hirohito announced Japan's surrender.

The superiority of atomic bombs over balloons had been demonstrated to the world, and world power would never again be defined in the same way. What the generals didn't foresee was that the rest of the world wouldn't quake in fear of U.S might, and that they would race to have their own atomic bombs. After stealing the U.S. design, it took the Russians only four years to develop their first atomic bomb, and today there are more than 12,000 nuclear warheads in the hands of countries that have political ideologies opposed to those of the United States — and each bomb has an explosive force at least 50 times greater than the bombs dropped on Japan. It is generally agreed that when a country has 20 nuclear weapons, it can destroy the world — in 2011 India had 75 and Pakistan had 90. Albert Einstein, who was born in Ulm, Germany, said a decade after the war, "I made one great mistake in my life, ... when I signed the letter to President Roosevelt recommending that atom bombs be made; but there was some justification — the danger that the Germans would make them."

Japan's formal surrender ceremony was held on September 2, 1945, aboard the U.S. Navy battleship Missouri, and World War II ended. As often happens in the military, not everyone got the word. Six months earlier, a Japanese intelligence officer, Hiroo Onoda, was put ashore on Lubang, a Philippine island. His orders were to coordinate the destruction of the island's airstrip and harbor pier to hamper an immanent invasion by U.S. Marines as they marched north from one Pacific island to the next — and under no circumstances was he to surrender or commit hara-kiri. The Japanese soldiers who occupied the island met Onoda, but their officers outranked him and the troops were told to ignore his orders. Within a month of Onoda's landing, the marines captured the island and all but Onoda and three other Japanese were killed or surrendered. The four soldiers took to the hills.

Although leaflets, written in Japanese, announcing the war's end were dropped on the island's jungles, the fugitive Japanese thought they were propaganda. Four years later, one of the men walked away from the others, and after foraging alone for six months, he surrendered to the Philippine Army. Five years after he surrendered, a party searching for the three rogue Japanese shot and killed one of them. Living off the land and periodically raiding small farms for rice and livestock, all went well for another 12 years until police officers killed Onoda's remaining comrade while he was burning stolen rice. A year later, a Japanese college dropout went looking for Onoda. He found him, and after befriending him, he took their picture together and returned to Japan alone when Onoda told him that he wouldn't quit his mission until ordered to do so by his commanding officer. Fortunately, his commander was alive and selling books in Tokyo. He flew to Lubang and relieved Onoda of his mission, fulfilling the promise he made 29 years earlier when he said, "Whatever happens we'll come back for you."

In the four years following the end of the war, the United States righteously prosecuted the war's miscreants and doled out $13 billion ($125 billion) under the Marshall Plan in economic and technical assistance to those European countries that were on the western side of the Iron Curtain. Winston Churchill coined the term "Iron Curtain" in a March 1946 speech when he said, "From Stettin in the Baltic to Trieste in the Adriatic an iron curtain has descended across the Continent. Behind that line lie all the capitals of the ancient states of Central and Eastern Europe: Warsaw, Berlin, Prague, Vienna, Budapest, Belgrade, Bucharest and Sofia." Post-war Europe became polarized between two political spheres: the democratic, capitalistic Western Bloc, and the authoritarian, communistic Eastern Bloc.

Although the United States lost 418,500 soldiers and civilians (0.32 percent of its population) to World War II, its human losses were dwarfed by the Soviet Union, which lost 23.4 million soldiers and citizens (13.88 percent of its population) — a staggering 40 times as many as the United States when compared to total population. The property loss and damage was infinitely greater. Whereas the United States had no damage on its home shores, the Nazis waged the bloodiest siege in world history in Eastern Russia. Roughly half the deaths that occurred during World War II were on the Eastern Front — more than 10 million Russian soldiers were killed and more than 20 million civilians died. In July 1943, history's greatest tank battle was waged between the Germans and Russians near Kursk, Russia. More than 3,600 tanks fought to a draw, but by repelling the German Panzers, the Russians turned the war's tides and softened the German forces, enabling the successful Normandy landings the following spring.

For four long years, Eastern Europe and Western Russia were ravaged by unprecedented brutality, wholesale destruction, and immense loss of life from combat, starvation, disease, genocide, and massacres. In a generation's time, Russia had overthrown the tsarist monarchy that had ruled the massive country since before the American Revolution and suffered the greatest losses in defending the world from Axis control. Four out five Russian males born in 1923 died before the war ended and never celebrated their 22nd birthday. It is not surprising that Russia's leaders felt left out of the raucous victory celebration that the Western Allies threw and isolated themselves and the countries they won from Germany during the war. They busied themselves repairing their war-devastated country, attempted a grand social experiment where property was held in common and wealth was distributed equally, and desperately fought to gain the world's respect.

As the war wound down and having liberated Latvia, Lithuania, Hungary, Rumania, Bulgaria, and the eastern Yugoslavia from Nazi rule, in late 1943 at a dinner meeting with Winston Churchill and Franklin Roosevelt, Soviet leader Joseph Stalin seriously proposed that they execute 50,000 to 100,000 German officers at the war's end. Roosevelt cavalierly joked that he thought 49,000 would be adequate, and Churchill righteously said that he'd rather be "taken out in the courtyard and shot" than to be part of such an action. In fact, Stalin may have had a better perspective on history's brutal genocides than his Western allies. At the Tehran Conference, when Churchill argued against an eastern front in France because of the potential of unnecessary deaths, Stalin replied, "When one man dies it is a tragedy. When thousands die it is a statistic."

Churchill did agree that punitive actions needed to be taken, and a tribunal of judges and prosecutors from Russia, Great Britain, France, and the United States tried 200 Nazis for war crimes at Nuremberg, Bavaria — ten of the Third Reich's top leaders were hung. Another 1,600 were prosecuted in traditional military courts, and many were convicted in absentia. The Mossad, Israel's intelligence organization for foreign activity, Western European governments, and independent Jewish organizations are still tracking down fugitive Nazi war criminals. In July 2012, 96-year-old Laszlo Csatary was nabbed in Budapest, Hungary. Csatary was convicted in 1948 of assisting in the murder of 15,700 Jews.

Possibly feeling guilty about blasting more than 100,000 people to death in three days — many took up to five years to painfully die from their wounds and radiation poisoning and tens of thousands were grotesquely disfigured for life — the United States did not aggressively pursue Japan's imperial family or top political leaders for war crimes after the country's surrender. A Japanese survivor described the human destruction:

> The appearance of people was ... well, they all had skin blackened by burns. ... They had no hair because their hair was burned, and at a glance you couldn't tell whether you were looking at them from in front or in back. ... They held their arms bent [forward] like this ... and their skin — not only on their hands, but on their faces and bodies too — hung down. ... If there had been only one or two such people ... perhaps I would not have had such a strong impression. But wherever I walked I met these people. ... Many of them died along the road. I can still picture them in my mind — like walking ghosts.

The Truman administration and General Douglas MacArthur, who had been the Pacific Supreme Commander during the war and oversaw the Japanese occupation through 1951, believed occupation reforms would be implemented more smoothly if they used Emperor Hirohito to legitimatize their authority. More than 50 top-level war crimes suspects were charged but released without going to trial. MacArthur has been criticized for his soft approach towards the Japanese, and one historian wrote, "MacArthur's truly extraordinary measures to save Hirohito from trial as a war criminal had a lasting and profoundly distorting impact on Japanese understanding of the lost war." As is often the case, it was the second tier of military command that took the fall. In 2,200 trials conducted between 1946 and 1951 before judges from most of the Allied countries, 5,600 were prosecuted for war crimes, 4,400 were found guilty, and more than 1,000 were executed.

To counteract the worldwide paranoia that developed after the bombing of Hiroshima and Nagasaki, the U.S. took a proactive, positive approach to nuclear energy. In 1949 U.S. Atomic Energy Commission chairman, David Lilienthal stated "atomic energy is not simply a search for new energy, but more significantly a beginning of human history in which faith in knowledge can vitalize man's whole life." Scientists, politicians, and the media jumped on board and soon it was commonly believed that nuclear power would replace fossil fuels as a sole source of power. In the early 1950s, the Chairman of the U.S. Atomic Energy Commission declared:

> Our children will enjoy in their homes electrical energy too cheap to meter. ... It is not too much to expect that our children will know of great periodic regional famines in the world only as matters of history, will travel effortlessly over the seas and under them and through the air with a minimum of danger and at great speeds, and will experience a lifespan far longer than ours, as disease yields and man comes to understand what causes him to age.

Ford Motor Company modeled a steam-powered car that used the same concepts as nuclear submarines. School children were taught that atomic energy would "provide the power needed to desalinate water for the thirsty, irrigate the deserts for the hungry, and fuel interstellar travel deep into outer space." The federal government spent $1.5 billion ($12 billion) researching nuclear-powered airplanes. Tykes wiggled their toes under shoe-fitting fluoroscopes, zapping their feet with enough radiation in a single visit to cause acute radiation poisoning. And best of all, it was thought that golf balls with a tiny speck of uranium in their core would never be lost because they could be found with a Geiger counter. Politicians and generals "believed that demonstrating the civilian applications of the atom would also affirm the American system of private enterprise, showcase the expertise of scientists, increase personal living standards, and defend the democratic lifestyle against communism." Then, in the same year that Lilienthal made his futuristic predictions, the struggle between the polarized politics of the East and West took a dark and paranoid turn for the worse, when in August 1949, the Soviets exploded a nuclear weapon.

Virtually all Americans believed to their core that democracy and capitalism were absolutely the best forms of government and national economics. At the other end of the political spectrum was the totalitarian Soviet Union that, after the war, renewed the cause of Communism with great gusto. Although most of the Eastern European countries that Russia liberated from German Fascism shared Russia's Marxist ideals, they didn't believe in Russia's methods of instituting the more extreme structure of Communism and chaffed at losing the Social Democratic Party and having their vote limited to a single Communist candidate — but working on a collective farm was much preferable to the gulag. The devastation of the war in the Soviet Union resulted in a massive recovery program to rebuild industrial plants, housing, and transportation, and there was work for all. Unfortunately, there was no food to buy with their equally distributed rubles. During the winter of 1946-1947, Soviets experienced the worst natural famine in the 20th century and the image of long lines and empty shelves became a continuing reality that the Soviet Union never got past. Even though Joseph Stalin was careful to consolidate power in the hands of Communist loyalists, except in Czechoslovakia, and especially in Poland and Hungary, the support for the Communist Party was less than enthusiastic.

Stalin was among the Bolshevik revolutionaries who brought about Russia's October Revolution in 1917 and his attitude toward civil liberties and human rights were well known. When a group of English dignitaries visited Russia in 1931, Lady Astor asked him, "How long are you going to go on killing people?" Stalin replied, "As long as necessary."

By 1947, the Cold War was in full swing. Stalin believed that capitalism was a hollow shell and would eventually crumble. He greatly underestimated the economic strength of the West and the power of innovation and profit motive. The West, which started at the guarded, barbed-wire boundaries of the Soviet Union and wrapped to the west around the world to Japan and South Korea, built a solid alliance to contain Soviet expansion. Expecting a quick conquest, in early 1950 Stalin gave the go-ahead for North Korea to invade South Korea. He was stunned when the Americans quickly came to the aid of their Asian ally and drove the North Koreans almost to the Soviet border. Stalin supplied military equipment and supported China's entry into the Korean War. The reinforced North Koreans were able to eventually reclaim their prewar boundaries, but the conflict greatly escalated East-West tensions. The United States understood that the world was not going to become democratic overnight and settled in for a long contest with the Soviets. The North Atlantic Treaty Organization was strengthened, and the nuclear arms race was on.

Chapter 26

Subversives

A subject for a great poet would be God's boredom after the seventh day of creation. ~ Friedrich Nietzsche

FOLLOWING THE SECOND GREAT WAR, Rock Island was like an elegant older lady who was born at the turn of the century and grew up with the advantages of a prosperous family. She lived life to the fullest during the Roaring Twenties; held on to what she had and rode out the Depression, praying for those who had it far worse; she was constantly worried while her boys were at war and was overjoyed when they returned home; and optimistically looked forward to her golden years — they would take longer to arrive and would not be as bright as she anticipated. Moline was a younger woman who hadn't frittered away her youth in the speakeasies and dancehalls, went to church regularly, worked hard, met an earnest young man, and they saved their money. She was ready to frugally fulfill the fruits of her hard-earned labors. Davenport was a penniless, worn-out old hag in need of major rehab.

Ironically, Moline and especially Davenport were better positioned for post-war prosperity than Rock Island. Unlike Rock Island that was constrained from new growth on three sides by the rivers and by Moline on the fourth, and was already subdivided and mostly built out, the two other cities had large tracts of undeveloped land where returning GI's could build a nice little starter house and middle-age couples that had built their first house in the '20s could finally build a comfortable new home. Rock Island was a small city that had the big-city problems of aging housing and a flight by families to new subdivisions beyond its borders. This reduced its tax base and left the core of the city to industry, the aged, and the poor.

Unlike its neighboring cities, Rock Island had maintained and improved its infrastructure during the Depression, but it was a solid foundation supporting a stately but antiquated structure. The post-war economic boom proved a boon to the cities and towns positioned for growth. The military had disciplined young men to seek the common good, accustomed them to hard work and long hours, and instilled confidence and a sense that anything could be achieved. The Quad City-combo of East Moline and Bettendorf also boomed, and the duo became similar to Moline and Davenport in temperament and lifestyle. From the opening of the Government Bridge in 1896 until the Iowa-Illinois Memorial Bridge between Moline and Bettendorf opened in 1935, the only way to walk or ride across the Rock Island Rapids was over the Government Bridge. When the Memorial Bridge opened, the preferred interstate crossing avoided Rock Island, and like an older stepsister, the senior city became isolated and politely ignored by her newly hip siblings.

Every city in the area except Rock Island built miles of new sewers and concrete streets to connect sprouting housing tracts to single-level, concrete bunker-style schools and expanding downtowns. In a knee-jerk travesty of misguided civic improvement, Rock Island replaced, covered, and patched miles of redbrick streets with asphalt, tore up the flowered boulevard that ran down the middle of 7th Avenue, and turned 4th and 5th Avenues into a broad expanse of four-lane, one-way concrete raceway that whisked no one to Moline and rivaled the Quad City Speedway for racetrack thrills. And unlike Rock Island and Moline, Davenport hadn't separated long stretches of its neighborhoods from the Mississippi with railroad tracks and factories and the ugly blight that accompany them. Combined with half-century-old neighborhoods below the hill, hastily constructed government housing for the influx of thousands of workers attracted to wartime Arsenal jobs and their subsequent abandonment when they returned to their hometowns, Rock Island had the air of a grand ballroom the morning after the New Year's Eve party. It was a hell of a party, and when the partiers sobered up, they set about cleaning it up, but Rock Island will never shine with the same luster it once did or achieve its former uniqueness.

Signs indicate to travelers when they cross from one Quad City Area municipality into another, but that is the only indication of difference. The contiguous cities have evolved into an amorphous urban sprawl that could easily be mistaken for a slice out of the Chicago suburbs. The riverfronts on both sides of the Mississippi have been carefully cleared of blight, and parks, office buildings, clean vacant lots, and parkways fill the space between a seldom-used, single railroad track and the river. On the Illinois side, a delightful bicycle path traverses what was once the shoreline of the Rock Island Rapids. The major cities have become cooperative, and the Quad Cities Chamber of Commerce, known as The Q, boasts of more than 2,000 member companies. Running every 30 minutes, glass roofed buses revolve around a 14-mile loop that shuttles residents and visitors across two bridges between the downtown districts of Rock Island, Moline, Bettendorf, and Davenport.

The "let's work together and make it better" attitude of Quad Citians began with the generation that returned from the Second World War. The war unified the nation, its regions, states, and cities. World War II soldiers were born of fathers who fought in the First Great War, started their school years in the prosperity of the Roaring '20s, graduated during the Great Depression, went to war, and returned victorious to an adoring nation. Armed with unbridled enthusiasm and a sense that anything was possible, they were supported by GI bills that paid for college educations and subsidized first homes to raise broods of pig-tailed girls and freckled-faced boys. The women they returned home to were the best educated in the history of the world, had almost the same rights as men, and had demonstrated during the war that often the best man for the job was a woman. However, as soon as the men returned, unless they were teachers, nurses, or nuns, women were again consigned to defining themselves as mothers and homemakers and their only path to upward mobility was through their husbands. So, high school and college sweethearts married and set out as committed couples to rebuild a redefined American Dream.

Small-town and farm boys from the Plains States who rode troop trains to Boston, New York City, Washington D.C., Charleston, Seattle, San Francisco, Los Angeles, and San Diego could not help but notice that on the coasts life was more vibrant, the girls more stylish, and the weather milder. When they returned from Europe and the South Pacific to the same ports and mustered out, many returned home to reunite with family and friends — and then caught the next train back to the coast. Many more who grew up in the urban ghettos and had already experienced fast times in the city were inclined to marry the girl next door and move into a new house on the rural fringes of the city where they grew up and where a quarter-acre of land was inexpensive.

Courtesy of Harry Truman and his Democratic Congress, vets could get a 4 percent GI Bill home loan and buy a two-bedroom, one-bath house that was about the same size as the apartment they were raised in but had a backyard for the dog. Even more vets, who took advantage of federally guaranteed loans, used the GI Bill to further their education, and by the time the bill expired in 1956, almost half of the 16 million World War II vets received advanced education. Incredibly, less than a decade removed from when a young white man was fortunate to have a job to pay his rent, with relative ease he could now go to college and buy a home through government subsidies and loans — dreams unimagined by his father's generation. Although the GI Bill was not discriminatory, the nation was. The bigotry and poverty blacks faced on returning home presented a nearly insurmountable barrier to their further education, and while more than 50 percent of white vets received GI Bill funded educations beyond high school, only 2 percent of black vets enrolled in college for so much as a semester.

Tragically, Franklin Roosevelt didn't live to see the fruits of his economic policies or the victorious end of World War II. At age 39, he had been stricken with Guillain-Barré syndrome and paralyzed below the waist. He refused to accept his physical limitations and pushed himself to extremes. The physical and psychological stresses of three full presidential terms starting at the beginning of the Depression and extending through the bleakest period of World War II, along with a lifetime of heavy smoking, appear to have simply worn him out. In March 1944, Roosevelt was examined at Bethesda Naval Hospital and the test results were shocking. He suffered from systemic arteriosclerosis, coronary artery disease, and hypertensive heart disease with congestive heart failure. Nevertheless, he ran for a fourth term and carried 36 of the 48 states on his way to an easy victory. Less than three months after his fourth inauguration and two weeks before Hitler's suicide, he died of a stroke.

Roosevelt had handpicked his third vice president, Harry Truman. In sharp contrast to Roosevelt's witty urbanity, Truman was a folksy, down-to-earth man from the Show Me State. Born on a Missouri farm, the only school he attended until he was eight was the Independence, Missouri, Presbyterian Sunday School. Then entering the public school system, in 1901 he graduated at age 17 from Independence High School — it was the last degree Truman earned. He enrolled for a semester at Spalding Commercial College and later attended some night school classes at Kansas City Law School. Truman is the only president since Grover Cleveland not to have a college education.

By memorizing the eye chart, the near-sighted Truman was able to enlist in the Missouri Army National Guard. Before going to France as a World War I artillery officer, he ran the Camp Doniphan canteen with Edward Jacobson, a Kansas City clothing clerk. On the last day of the war, his artillery unit fired some of the final shots of World War I. Demonstrating what war can do to a good man's attitude, after leaving the battlefield he wrote in a letter, "It is a shame we can't go in and devastate Germany and cut off a few of the Dutch kids' hands and feet and scalp a few of their old men." Despite those hateful, war-inspired words, he was a natural leader and eventually rose to the rank of colonel in the Army Reserves. After the war, he joined the Democratic Party and became part of the Kansas City political machine. In May 1919, a month before he married Bess Wallace, Truman and Jacobson opened a haberdashery in downtown Kansas City. The business failed two years later.

Even after their business failure, Truman and Jacobson, who was Jewish, remained close friends, and Jacobson counseled Truman throughout his career. At a time when cracks were appearing in the walls of racism and anti-Semitism — most men still conformed to racial stereotyping and good-ole-boy attitudes — many racial and anti-Semitic remarks were attributed to Truman. However, his actions belied his words. It is often written that in 1922 he submitted a $10 fee through a friend for membership in the Ku Klux Klan. What is seldom mentioned is that he came to his senses and asked for his money back after never attending a meeting. The same year he was elected a county administrative judge, a position similar to county commissioner. He followed that with several other elected county positions, and then in 1934 he vaulted into the U.S. Senate. Ten years later, he reluctantly replaced Vice President Henry Wallace as Roosevelt's running mate.

Truman had been vice president for 82 days when he was summoned to the White House. He was shown into Eleanor Roosevelt's sitting room, and she told him President Roosevelt was dead. After a stunned silence, Truman asked, "Is there anything I can do for you?" She shook her head and said, "No, is there anything we can do for you? For you are the one in trouble now." Truman was uninformed on the broader political issues of the war, and he had almost no knowledge of the Manhattan Project, which was nearing completion. However, he was not a pretentious man, and he readily admitted his ignorance. After being sworn in, he said to reporters, "Boys, if ever you pray, pray for me now."

Truman spent little time on state affairs that could be better handled by those with experience and almost no time on the social and public relations aspects of his new job. The White House decorator told the story that when he approached the President and First Lady about choosing their official china pattern, a selection that often took several meetings over many weeks' time, Truman said, "Just match the wallpaper." Once, when Truman referred to a public speech as "a bunch of horse manure," an aid suggested to Bess Truman that she counsel her husband on toning down his language. She replied, "You don't know how many years it took me to tone it down to that!"

Truman put aside much of the White House protocol that had become ingrained during the 12 years of Roosevelt's tenure. He held meetings as requested and needed, and he had an open-door policy for those he trusted and relied upon. One who had open access to the Oval Office was his old business partner, Edward Jacobson. In March 1948, on behalf of powerful American Jewish leaders, Jacobson persuaded Truman to meet with Chaim Weizmann, the leader of the Zionist movement. With typical Truman efficiency, two months later the United States became the first nation to recognize the new state of Israel — other nations quickly followed.

Compared to the economic problems and social issues that Roosevelt inherited from the three Republican presidents that preceded him and then facing a second World War started by German fanatics — some historians say that World War II was simply a continuation of World War I with time out to re-supply — the post-war issues Truman faced were a cakewalk. Times were changing, and citizens were made tough and self-reliant by the Depression and war and were not looking to Washington for answers. A general feeling of relief and optimism swept through the nation, and Truman was smart enough not to get in the way. The shuffling of the physical and economic demographics of the country not only fractured ethnic groups and mixed up the gene pool, but also changed social and political mores. No longer were Protestants disowned when they married Catholics — the couple just wasn't invited to dinner on Fridays. And although an atheist might still have been stoned to death in the Bible Belt, in the big cities and on Northern college campuses, it became fashionable for mature men, who had praised the Lord while passing the ammunition, to claim to be agnostic and to challenge literal interpretations of the Bible. But it would still be another generation before interracial marriage was even legal, much less condoned, and two generations before gays and lesbians would become open in their sexual preferences and marry.

In 1944 Roosevelt had soundly defeated Thomas Dewey, a liberal Republican New York governor with Clark Gable good looks. But Truman was not Roosevelt, and it was generally believed — even by Bess Truman — that because of Dewey's moderate views and assurance of carrying the populous Northeastern states, and because third party States Rights candidate, Strom Thurmond from South Carolina was certain to steal Democratic electoral votes from the Deep South — that Dewey would thump the vice president. Truman, however, believed in himself, and he claimed that the Tri-Cities was the place he started to believe that he could win reelection. When the *Truman Special* campaign train pulled into Rock Island early on a September 1948 morning, he was flabbergasted to be greeted by 4,000 cheering Rock Islanders. After a short speech, his next stop was the Rock Island Lines depot in Davenport where an even larger crowd met him. Still overwhelmed by the enthusiastic throng in Rock Island, he said from the platform at the end of the train, "I'm not surprised to see this many in Iowa — Iowans get up early — but I was surprised over in Illinois." On election night, Dewey and hundreds of well-healed supporters gathered at the Roosevelt Hotel in New York City to celebrate their predicted victory, while Truman had a ham sandwich and a glass of buttermilk at the Elms Hotel in Excelsior Springs, Missouri, and went to bed early.

The outcome was such a sure thing that before the polls closed in the West, the *Chicago Tribune* printed its first edition with an enormous banner headline, "DEWEY DEFEATS TRUMAN," and the next morning when Truman met a cheering crowd of supporters at St. Louis Union Station, the broad-smiling, newly-elected president held up the morning *Trib*. Syndicated political analyst, Arthur Henning, had predicted even before the Northeast states counted their votes that Dewey would win. Henning had accurately predicted the outcome in four of the previous five elections, which wasn't saying much since Roosevelt won four of them, and Henning whiffed on Roosevelt's first election. Even after the race narrowed, Henning stuck with his prediction well into the night and 150,000 Chicago papers carried the erroneous headline.

As it turned out, Truman beat Dewey by almost as many electoral votes as Roosevelt had. However, with only a few thousand more popular votes for Thurmond in the swing states of Ohio, Illinois, and California, Dewey would have won. The reason for the grossly inaccurate prediction is usually explained as bias of an East Coast media that wanted Dewey to win and missed a last minute wave of concern by Midwestern and Western voters who switched to Truman, fearing Republicans would return the country to pre-war depression. The 1912 price for pristine original copies of the 5¢ *Tribunes* announcing Dewey's win was $1,500.

After a brief but intense period of patriotism and national unity during Truman's first term, the nation returned to argue over the best way to assure that their children would never know the deprivations of a depression or have an atom bomb dropped on them. Republicans insisted that if private enterprise was unfettered by government intervention, it would take the country to undreamed of heights, that traditional, time-proven principles and methods were best, that an unwavering trust in God and His divine wisdom had ultimately prevailed and defeated Fascism, and that after 12 years of struggle under a near-Socialist president, American stick-to-itiveness had returned the nation to its earlier glory. Democrats pointed to the numerous successes of righting the ship after the course set by three Republican presidents who ran it aground, advocated that progressive principles and methods were the only way to save a world capable of destroying itself, and espoused that the greater the division between church and state the better. Both parties agreed that education was good and Communism was bad.

The only reason the United States and Russia were World War II allies was because Nazi Germany was more despicable and threatening to their political systems and social structures than they were to each other. As soon as Nazism died with Hitler in his Berlin bunker, the two massive, resource-rich nations whose politics were diametrically opposed locked themselves into a power struggle to prove their way was best. The two superpowers competed for domination and the world's attention in everything from Olympic events to reaching the moon. After demonstrating their military might at Hiroshima and Nagasaki, America grabbed the early lead, but Russia soon challenged with, "You may have dropped the first bomb, but our missile arsenal is bigger." America responded with "Mine's bigger," and so the Cold War went.

The Cold War was never much more than an expensive, military-incited, bluster-filled shouting match that wasn't more destructive than the war between Michigan and Ohio over who owned Toledo. However, the rancorous political battles over what was the best way to show off America's muscle and to denigrate the Soviet Union caused the political pendulum to swing from the New Deal's priorities on the economy and social issues to the more conservative goals of assuring that what had been won on the battlefield wasn't lost in an ideological race and what was discovered in the science labs wasn't stolen by spies. Since the United States Congress couldn't root the Communists out of Russia, they did the next best thing and kicked them out of the U.S. government, the military, and Hollywood.

The most famous postwar anti-Communist was Joe McCarthy, a Senator from Wisconsin, who piggybacked his career onto the infamous House Un-American Activities Committee (HUAC) and became the chairman of the confusingly named Senate's Permanent Subcommittee on Investigations of the Government Operations Committee. McCarthy was a career politician who grew up on a farm near Appleton, Wisconsin. Dropping out of school at age 16 to raise chickens, he returned to school after an exceptionally cold Wisconsin winter wiped out his flock. After cramming four years of high school work into one, he enrolled in Marquette University's School of Engineering. The 6-foot, 200-pounder was a heavyweight boxer at Marquette, but apparently spent more time in the ring than the library, and poor grades forced him to switch to law school. At the age of 25, he earned his law degree from Marquette.

Setting his sights on public service, through a combination of shameless self-promotion and lying, he reached the highest levels of public office and later became, along with J. Edgar Hoover, the nation's head watchdog against Communism. Running as a Democrat, McCarthy was defeated in an election for Appleton's District Attorney. Two years later, at age 29 he was elected to the nonpartisan circuit court judgeship — he was the youngest judge in Wisconsin. His incumbent opponent had held the position for 20 years, and expecting an easy victory, did not campaign. McCarthy visited every farm in the district, and by lying about his opponent's age and wealth, he started to perfect tactics that he would use throughout his career. After being narrowly elected, he ingratiated himself to his political supporters by granting quickie divorces, but the Wisconsin Supreme Court censured him when he destroyed crucial evidence in a price-fixing case.

Because he thought it would promote his political career, at age 33 he enlisted in the Marines and was commissioned a second lieutenant. He served as debriefing officer for a bomber squadron and flew 12 combat missions as an observer. After the war, he gave himself the nickname "Tail-Gunner Joe" and claimed that he entered the Marines as a buck private and rose to the rank of captain. As time passed, his combat missions steadily rose until they reached 32. Twenty-five missions were needed to qualify for the Distinguished Flying Cross, and eight years after he left the Marines, he requested the honor; sadly it was given to him. He publicized a war wound that he sometimes claimed was received in a plane crash and at other times from antiaircraft fire — actually it was incurred during a shipboard ceremony. He also proudly displayed a letter of commendation signed by Admiral Chester Nimitz — he wrote it himself. In an age when the art of self-promotion and trashing political opponents with half-truths was in its infancy, McCarthy broke new ground.

Another Wisconsinite, Robert La Follette, Jr. had succeeded his father, a U.S. Republican Senator, upon his death. Father and son were both well respected and honorably served the state for 22 consecutive years. A 1982 survey of historians ranked Robert La Follette in a tie for first with Henry Clay on their list of the "ten greatest Senators in the nation's history" based on "accomplishments in office" and "long-range impact on American history." McCarthy challenged La Follette Junior for his Senate seat in 1946, and savagely attacked the three-term senator for not enlisting in the war — La Follette was 46-years-old and serving in the Senate when Pearl Harbor was bombed. McCarthy accused La Follette of profiteering from the war, while he was earning the Distinguished Flying Cross fighting in the South Pacific. During the war, in addition to his Senate pay, La Follette had made $47,000 ($590,000) from his partial ownership of a radio station. In 1943 alone, McCarthy had made $42,000 ($530,000) from stock market investments — war profiteering was commonly thought to be the most unpatriotic act of an elected official. La Follette did not believe that his constituency would believe the trumped up accusations, but proving that you can fool a majority of the people most of the time, McCarthy sneaked past La Follette with a one-percentage point margin of victory. *Washington Times* columnist, Arnold Beichman, wrote that McCarthy "was elected to his first term in the Senate with support from the Communist-controlled United Electrical, Radio, and Machine Workers," which preferred McCarthy to the anti-Communist La Follette

In less than five years, his counterpart J. Edgar Hoover had springboarded from the 23-year-old head of the Enemy Alien Registration Section, to the top spot on the newly organized General Intelligence Division of the Bureau of Investigation, to become BOI deputy head and then to 29-year-old BOI Director. By 1924 Hoover was in charge of 650 employees of which 441 were special agents. In 1935 the BOI was renamed the Federal Bureau of Investigation. After the agency eliminated John Dillinger, Baby Face Nelson, Pretty Boy Floyd, Creepy Karpis, and Machine Gun Kelly, Hoover turned his attention to subversives. When he was a law student, Hoover had become fascinated with the methods and effectiveness of Anthony Comstock, the U.S. Postal Inspector who forced Margaret Sanger to flee the country and was able to stop the U.S. Postal Service from shipping "lewd" anatomy textbooks to medical students. Comstock boasted that he was responsible for 4,000 arrests, the destruction of 15 tons of books, and 4 million obscene pictures. Emma Goldman called Comstock the leader of America's "moral eunuchs."

Goldman, a Russian immigrant, had become a naturalized U.S. citizen. She and her husband were anarchists and women's rights activists. They were both jailed many times for "inciting to riot" and illegally distributing information about birth control. Using the 1918 Anarchist Exclusion Act, Hoover deported Goldman and 250 others to Russia in 1920. Hoover wrote, "Beyond doubt" Goldman and her husband were "two of the most dangerous anarchists in this country and [their] return to the community will result in undue harm." In 1940 when she died at age 70, the US Immigration and Naturalization Service permitted Goldman's remains to be returned to her hometown of Forest Park, Illinois, for internment.

Before Pearl Harbor, Walt Disney had popularized what would become one of America's most patriotic pursuits for the next two decades: "red baiting." Taking Disney's lead, the Daughters of the American Revolution invented the ultra-patriotic pastime in 1928. Righteously protecting their heritage, the D.A.R. created a "black list" of men and women who would not be welcome at their club as members or speakers. The list was composed of people accused of being Communists, Socialists, liberals, or pacifists and was circulated to all their chapters. But not all D.A.R. chapters agreed with the idea of a black list, and when a Stanford University president made the list, the Palo Alto, California, chapter resigned from the national organization. The conservative womens club's tactics of publicly identifying those whose politics they didn't agree with didn't initially attract much attention. Then right before Pearl Harbor, Walt Disney, who in addition to being a creative cartoonist was also a master promoter and publicist, took out an ad in *Variety* that declared that "Communist agitation" was behind a cartoonists' and animators' strike. Anti-Fascism, anti-Communism, and John Wayne-style patriotism became Hollywood's primary themes for four years.

After the war, Disney co-founded the Motion Picture Alliance for the Preservation of American Ideals, a political action group that issued a pamphlet advising producers to avoid "subtle communistic touches" in their films, and said: "Don't smear the free-enterprise system ... Don't smear industrialists ... Don't smear wealth ... Don't smear the profit motive ... Don't deify the 'common man' ... Don't glorify the collective." In late 1947, HUAC summoned a number of people in the film industry to appear before them. Disney and Ronald Reagan, the president of the Screen Actors Guild, testified that the threat of Communists in the film industry was a serious one. Popular film actor and "Best Dressed Man In America," Adolphe Menjou, testified, "I am a witch hunter if the witches are Communists. I am a red baiter. I would like to see them all back in Russia."

Not everyone in the industry felt the same, and many treated Menjou with open contempt, including four-time Academy Award winner for Best Actress, Katharine Hepburn. Hepburn appeared with Menjou in two of her films, *Stage Door* and *State of the Union*. The smart, sophisticated, and headstrong Hepburn strongly opposed the Motion Picture Alliance, and during the filming of *State of the Union*, she refused to speak to Menjou except when the script required her to. Knowing that their adoring audiences would not accept government harassment of mega-stars such as Hepburn, HUAC instead went after those whose names appeared in small type at the end of the credits; they cited ten screenwriters and directors for contempt of Congress for refusing to testify before the committee.

Called the Hollywood Ten, Ring Lardner, Jr., was the only recognizable name, and that was because of his famous father, who was a New York sports columnist and satirical short story writer. Lardner, along with 50,000 other Americans, had once given his party affiliation as a Communist, and HUAC used voter registration rolls to determine who was a Communist threat. Although the Communist candidate received more than 100,000 votes in the 1932 presidential election, its membership had fallen, as did the votes for a Communist president in the 1936 election. During his first term, Roosevelt accomplished many of the Marxist Party's labor goals, such as a minimum wage, time and a half for overtime, and child labor laws. Knowing that lawyers and used car salesmen were more popular than Communists, executives from the major motion picture studios stated, "We will forthwith discharge or suspend without compensation those in our employ, and we will not re-employ any of the ten until such time as he is acquitted or has purged himself of contempt and declares under oath that he is not a Communist."

Assisted by J. Edgar Hoover and his agents, the list of Hollywood subversives grew, and inclusion on the black list became a professional kiss of death. By 1950, 151 names were on the list, including Charlie Chaplin, who was once the world's most famous movie star, was in his sixties when he was included. The names on the list doubled and careers were ruined. In 1954 "screenwriter Louis Pollock, a man without any known political views or associations, suddenly had his career yanked out from under him because he was confused him with Louis Pollack, a California clothier, who had refused to cooperate with HUAC." Hollywood gossip columnists, Walter Winchell and Hedda Hopper, patriotically jumped to the aid of their country and published names in their columns that they felt HUAC should talk to — and HUAC did. An example of the Committee's interrogation techniques and due process is exemplified in an excerpt of the transcript of HUAC Chairman, J. Parnell Thomas' interrogation of screenwriter, John Howard Lawson:

>Thomas: Are you a member of the Communist Party or have you ever been a member of the Communist Party?
>
>Lawson: It's unfortunate and tragic that I have to teach this committee the basic principles of Americanism.
>
>Thomas: That's not the question. That's not the question. The question is — have you ever been a member of the Communist Party?
>
>Lawson: I am framing my answer in the only way in which any American citizen can frame his answer to...
>
>Thomas: Then you deny it?
>
>Lawson: ... a question that invades his ... absolutely invades his privacy.
>
>Thomas: Then you deny ... You refuse to answer that question, is that correct?
>
>Lawson: I have told you that I will offer my beliefs, my affiliations and everything else to the American public, and they will know where I stand as they do from what I have written.
>
>Thomas: Stand away from the stand...
>
>Lawson: I have written for Americanism for many years...
>
>Thomas: Stand away from the stand...
>
>Lawson: And I shall continue to fight for the Bill of Rights, which you are trying to destroy.
>
>Thomas: Officer, take this man away from the stand.

Similar to HUAC's list of Hollywood Communists, Joe McCarthy's list of State Department employees who were "members of the Communist Party and members of a spy ring" caused dismissals and destroyed reputations, while at every turn McCarthy proudly pointed to the Communists he "cleaned out of government." McCarthy floated his fabricated allegations on a sea of paranoia created by China's 1950 fall to Mao Tse-tung's Communist Party, the start of the Korean War, and the Soviet Union's development of the atomic bomb. A subcommittee was set up in February 1950 to conduct "a full and complete study and investigation as to whether persons who are disloyal to the United States are, or have been, employed by the Department of State."

Films of McCarthy in the early days of the hearings he chaired show he had a receding hairline that left behind a dime-sized island of hair that he grew long and combed back. When he got excited and started jabbing the air to make his points, it flopped distractingly above his eyebrows. His 200 pounds of muscle from his collegiate boxing days had turned to fat and were joined by additional pounds of flab, and he had the appearance of a man bloated by alcohol. In later films, he shaved the annoying tuff of hair, but retained a soft, pudgy look. Throughout the more than four months of hearings, McCarthy consistently used inflammatory and exaggerated rhetoric, and the media loved his sound bites, which made headlines on front pages throughout the country. McCarthy described one World War II State Department employee, Owen Lattimore, as "the top Russian espionage agent in the United States."

Lattimore, who was consulting with the State Department on Chinese affairs at the time, was born in America and raised in Tianjin, China, where his parents were English teachers at a Chinese university. He developed a lifelong academic interest in China, especially the Mongolian culture, and studied at Chinese universities and under Confucian scholars. In the 1930s, he was editor of *Pacific Affairs*, a journal published by the Institute of Pacific Relations, and then taught at Johns Hopkins University from 1938 to 1963. During World War II, Roosevelt had appointed Lattimore as a special liaison and advisor to the pro-Allies Chinese Nationalist leader Chiang Kai-shek.

McCarthy didn't prove his spy allegations against Professor Lattimore or any others called before the committee. A Senate report said that those examined were neither Communists nor pro-Communist, that McCarthy's charges were a "fraud and a hoax," and that McCarthy's actions "confused and divided the American people to a degree far beyond the hopes of the Communists themselves." Senate Republicans responded by stating that the report was guilty of "the most brazen whitewash of treasonable conspiracy in our history." The full Senate voted three times on whether to accept the report, and each time the voting was precisely divided along party lines. McCarthy achieved his purpose and became the most well-known Congressman and anti-Communist. He was reelected in 1952, when due to the controversial Korean War, Democrats abandoned Truman, and he chose not to run for a third term. Republican Dwight Eisenhower was elected the 34th president, and Republicans swept into control of both houses.

Communist hysteria had been further elevated in the year before the election by the media-sensationalized Rosenberg spy trial. In 1939 Julius Rosenberg had received an electrical engineering degree from City College of New York. He had also been a leader in the Young Communist League USA, where he met his wife, Ethel Greenglass. They had two children. After graduating, Julius worked at the Engineering Laboratories at Fort Monmouth, New Jersey, until 1945. In August 1950, a federal grand jury indicted the Rosenbergs; Ethel's brother, David Greenglass who was a machinist at Los Alamos National Laboratory during the Manhattan Project; and Anatoli Yakovlev, who was General Consul of the Soviet Union's delegation in New York City and a spymaster, on 11 counts of overt espionage acts.

At the trial in March 1951, David Greenglass, who turned state's evidence, stated that his sister Ethel typed notes containing U.S. nuclear secrets in her apartment. He also testified that he turned over to Julius Rosenberg a sketch of the cross-section of an implosion atom bomb of the type dropped on Nagasaki. The Rosenbergs refused to testify on grounds of self-incrimination, and Greenglass' testimony proved decisive. The Rosenbergs were convicted, and at sentencing, the judge said:

> I consider your crime worse than murder. ... I believe your conduct in putting into the hands of the Russians the A-Bomb years before our best scientists predicted Russia would perfect the bomb has already caused, in my opinion, the Communist aggression in Korea, with the resultant casualties exceeding 50,000 and who knows but that millions more of innocent people may pay the price of your treason. Indeed, by your betrayal you undoubtedly have altered the course of history to the disadvantage of our country. No one can say that we do not live in a constant state of tension. We have evidence of your treachery all around us every day for the civilian defense activities throughout the nation are aimed at preparing us for an atom bomb attack.

He sentenced them to death. Pope Pius XII appealed to President Eisenhower to spare the Jewish couple, but he refused, and all other appeals were also unsuccessful.

On June 19, 1953, the Rosenberg's were executed. Commentator and writer Bob Considine reported that Julius Rosenberg died after the first electric shock, but Ethel did not. After three electric shocks, attendants removed Ethel's strapping only to have doctors determine that her heart was still beating. Two more electric shocks were applied, and Considine said that smoke rose from her head in the chamber. The Rosenbergs' boys were ten and six at the time. Nobel Prize-winning French existentialist Jean-Paul Sartre called the trial "a legal lynching which smears with blood a whole nation. By killing the Rosenbergs, you have quite simply tried to halt the progress of science by human sacrifice. Magic, witch-hunts, autos-da-fé, sacrifices — we are here getting to the point: your country is sick with fear ... you are afraid of the shadow of your own bomb."

The Rosenberg's execution had a sobering effect on the country and dampened media support of McCarthy. When he began his second term, even Republicans were growing tired of his rhetoric. In response to his increasing irrelevancy, McCarthy's blusters became more reckless, and he started making gaffes. The first was when he hired J.B. Matthews as staff director of his House subcommittee. Matthews had recently taken a page from his boss' book and written an article titled "Reds And Our Churches," which opened with the sentence, "The largest single group supporting the Communist apparatus in the United States is composed of Protestant Clergymen." Eventually, Matthews was forced out, and McCarthy was embarrassed. So, he doubled-down and took on the U.S. Army.

McCarthy grabbed some headlines when he stated that there was a dangerous spy ring among Army researchers, but after weeks of hearings, no spies were found. Narrowing his focus, he then accused an Army dentist of subversive activities. When the dentist took the Fifth Amendment, McCarthy ordered the Secretary of the Army to have him court-martialed. The same day, the dentist asked to have his pending discharge effective immediately. His commanding officer, General Ralph Zwicker, complied and gave the dentist an honorable discharge. McCarthy lost what little restraint remained and summoned General Zwicker before his subcommittee. Zwicker vacillated on some answers, and McCarthy compared the general's intelligence to that of a "five-year-old" and said he was "not fit to wear that uniform" — ill-advised words.

Zwicker was a highly decorated World War II veteran, and Eisenhower, who despised McCarthy, had had enough. Previously, when approached by aides to silence him, Eisenhower said he believed such an action would divide the party and that, "I just will not — I refuse — to get into the gutter with that guy." Using one of McCarthy's own tactics and with the Commander In Chief's permission, the Army brought charges against the senator for actions unrelated to General Zwicker, and took him before his own committee. During the hearings, Edward R. Murrow's documentary series, *See It Now*, showed clips in which McCarthy accused the Democratic Party of "twenty years of treason," described the American Civil Liberties Union "as a front for, and doing the work of, the Communist Party," and showed McCarthy haranguing witnesses, including General Zwicker. In his conclusion, Murrow said of McCarthy:

> His primary achievement has been in confusing the public mind, as between the internal and the external threats of Communism. We must not confuse dissent with disloyalty. We must remember always that accusation is not proof and that conviction depends upon evidence and due process of law. We will not walk in fear, one of another. We will not be driven by fear into an age of unreason, if we dig deep in our history and our doctrine, and remember that we are not descended from fearful men. ... We proclaim ourselves, as indeed we are, the defenders of freedom, wherever it continues to exist in the world, but we cannot defend freedom abroad by deserting it at home. The actions of the junior Senator from Wisconsin have caused alarm and dismay amongst our allies abroad, and given considerable comfort to our enemies. And whose fault is that? Not really his. He didn't create this situation of fear; he merely exploited it — and rather successfully.

During World War II, live network radio broadcasts from war correspondents Alexander Kendrick, Ed Bliss, Eric Sevareid, and Edward Murrow had battled newspaper reports as America's source for war news. In March 1938, Murrow, flew from Poland, where he was arranging a broadcast of a children's chorus, to Vienna to cover the Hitler-led annexation of Austria by Nazi Germany. In the first live on-the-scene broadcast of the 29-year-olds' career, Murrow introduced himself in a measured, distinctive style that would become instantly recognizable to two generations of radio and television audiences. He began, "This is Edward Murrow speaking from Vienna. ... It's nearly 2:30 in the morning, and Herr Hitler has not yet arrived." At the request of CBS New York, Murrow orchestrated a live broadcast of European leaders, American diplomats, and newsmen to report the reaction of Germany's occupation. The broadcast came off flawlessly and became the basis for CBS' *World News Roundup*, a newscast that still airs. Murrow's live broadcasts of the London Blitz electrified U.S. listeners, and he became America's most respected and listened to newscaster.

Twenty million people watched 36 days of McCarthy's televised hearings before the committee he chaired. The committee's report was inconclusive, but he had trivialized his cause, and it was apparent to all that his witch hunts were over. Murrow graciously offered McCarthy a chance to rebut the *See It Now* accusations, and the senator seized the opportunity to clear his name by attacking the commentator. He said, "Murrow is a leader, and the cleverest of the jackal pack, which is always found at the throat of anyone who dares to expose individual Communist traitors. I am compelled by the fact to say to you that Mr. Edward R. Murrow as far back as 20 years ago was engaged in propaganda for Communist causes." That did it. All but the conservative radical fringe abandoned McCarthy, and his approval rating plummeted. Until then newspapers had treated McCarthy with kid gloves, but fearing further loss of credibility and threatened by the rise in popularity of TV personalities and the timeliness of their news, they ravaged him. And even better, newspapers became more responsible, slowly abandoned the muckraking tactics that they had used for more than a century to sell papers, and started to embrace Chicago journalist Finley Peter Dunne's admonition, "Comfort the afflicted, and afflict the comfortable." Republican Senators saw McCarthy as a liability and took the politically expedient solution — they washed their hands of him and censured him in December 1954. He remained in the Senate for two more years until May 1957, when he died from liver failure brought on by chronic alcoholism — he was 48.

A liberal backlash among the intelligentsia against the stifling conservatism and blatant materialism that swept the country after World War II grew out of New York's Greenwich Village coffee houses and leapt across the nation to San Francisco's Haight-Ashbury District. Stimulated by the open sexuality and free-thinking espoused in Allen Ginsberg's *Howl* (1956), Jack Kerouac's *On the Road* (1957), and William S. Burroughs's *Naked Lunch,* (1959) the Beat Generation attracted bohemians who celebrated non-conformity and creativity — and the scrutiny of J. Edgar Hoover's FBI and Dwight Eisenhower's Justice Department. In the mid-1960s, beatniks abandoned poetry readings for rock concerts, and beat hipsters were pushed aside by college-age hippies who rejected any convention accepted by those over 30, especially fighting Communist peasants in Southeast Asia.

Almost as threatening to McCarthy Era Fundamentalist Christians and conservative super patriots as Communism was a post-World War II revival of existentialism. Two French writers, Jean-Paul Sartre and Albert Camus, wrote best-selling novels that extolled a philosophy that includes the philosophical concept that existence precedes essence, or more plainly that an individual's life is what constitutes his or her "nature" instead of a created, predetermined essence — in practical terms, people determine if they are good or bad, not God or Satin.

A century before the McCarthy hearings, Søren Kierkegaard, who was a Christian philosopher and Lutheran theologian in the Church of Denmark, wrote: "Science and scholarship want to teach that becoming objective is the way [to enlightenment.] Christianity teaches that the way [to enlightenment] is to become a subject." As Galileo had challenged Catholics, Kierkegaard's writings challenged Christian dogma and not only confused them, but because non-Christians and atheists praised Kierkegaard, he was ridiculed and dismissed as a nonbeliever. The opposite was true, he strongly believed in the existence of God, and his message was in line with Christian morality.

Writing before Charles Darwin published *On the Origin of Species*, Kierkegaard challenged the commonly held concept of Christians that God "freely and unchangeably ordained whatsoever comes to pass." He rejected predestination, and believed that individuals should find the meaning of life through free will, choice, and personal responsibility. He said, "God is not like a human being; it is not important for God to have visible evidence so that he can see if his cause has been victorious or not; He sees in secret just as well. Moreover, it is so far from being the case that you should help God to learn anew that it is rather He who will help you to learn anew, so that you are weaned from the worldly point of view that insists on visible evidence." In the 1950's, this view of God greatly distressed most everyone.

Kierkegaard was a prolific writer, but his logic was complex and subtle, and he was greatly misunderstood; however, within a generation, Friedrich Nietzsche, an intellectual German poet, composer, and philosopher was able to simplify the message of existentialism. A contemporary of Charles Darwin, Nietzsche questioned just about everything including evolutionary theory — not that species evolved, but how. He said of Darwin's theory of natural selection, "Species do not evolve towards perfection: the weak always prevail over the strong — simply because they are the majority, and because they are also the craftier. Darwin forgot the intellect (that is so British!), the weak have more intellect. In order to acquire intellect, one must be in need of it. One loses it when one no longer needs it." Because of the absurd circular logic, ignoring the obvious that only man has an intellect, the digs at intellectuals and the Brits, scholars with a sense of humor and both theologians who possess one are convinced that Nietzsche was sarcastically parodying Darwin's critics.

In the last century, few Americans have not heard or drawn solace from Nietzsche's irrefutable logic, "What doesn't kill you, makes you stronger," and the image is immediately drawn of him doing a stage wink, and in his best Groucho Marx voice saying, "But why risk your life to get stronger?" And many get emotionally distressed with his chopped quote: "God is dead." Like Kierkegaard, Nietzsche believed in the existence of God, and his entire quote is: "God is dead. God remains dead. And we have killed him. How shall we comfort ourselves, the murderers of all murderers?" For a hundred years, clerics, atheists, philosophers, and millions of college students have argued over the ambiguous statement, but at least one existentialist believes Nietzsche meant that by defining God in human terms and codifying him through religion misses the point that to be able to define God requires a God-like essence. Absent that essence, it must be taken on faith the God carries on a dialogue with mankind through prophets or periodically manifests Himself in human form or sends angels to explain to men and women the meaning of their lives.

In his 1961 book, *The Death of God,* Syracuse University theology professor Gabriel Vahanian argued that modern culture has lost all sense of the sacred and of providence, and that God is dead in the cultural sense. Rabbi Richard Rubenstein wrote in *After Auschwitz* that in the wake of the Holocaust, Jews could no longer advocate the notion of an omnipotent God or that Jews were the chosen people. And the 1950s and '60s Wabash College and Emory University theologian Thomas Altizer exploited Nietzsche's words and premises and stated that God really died. Altizer has great credentials — he received undergraduate, masters, and doctoral degrees in theology from the University of Chicago — and through his degrees, books, and university positions, he built himself a reputable public pulpit. He is the leader of the many present day theologian/philosophers who label themselves as existentialists and created a pop culture around the "God is dead" congregation. Altizer says that God incarnated in Jesus and imparted his spirit to the world through Him. Altizer also says that he doesn't deserve the public scorn and death threats he has received, and that his presentation of evil as the absence of will, not predestination, is more legitimate than the devil made me do it belief of Killer, Geraldine Jones' boyfriend at Reverend Leroy's The Church of What's Happening Now.

Benefiting from Einstein forever separating physics and cosmology from metaphysics and religion, Sartre and Camus posited that, in relationship to the universe, humans are insignificant and will have miniscule effect on the totality of existence. Known as existential nihilism, this was a highly un-American belief, but since the philosophers lived in France, they were outside of Joe McCarthy's jurisdiction. And, of course, 350 years earlier an English playwright had much more eloquently stated the existential nihilist's perspective when he wrote in Macbeth's soliloquy:

> Tomorrow, and tomorrow, and tomorrow,
> Creeps in this petty pace from day to day,
> To the last syllable of recorded time;

And all our yesterdays have lighted fools
The way to dusty death. Out, out, brief candle!
Life's but a walking shadow, a poor player
That struts and frets his hour upon the stage
And then is heard no more. It is a tale
Told by an idiot, full of sound and fury
Signifying nothing.

Chapter 27

New Rules

American history is longer, larger, more various, more beautiful, and more terrible than anything anyone has ever said about it. ~ James Baldwin

AFTER THE WAR when the troops returned to Rock Island, most reintegrated into the community. However, in the surrounding farm regions the lyrics from "How Ya Gonna Keep 'Em Down on the Farm (after they've seen Paree)?" could not have been truer, and now that farm boys' fathers had new Deere and Farmall tractors and their mothers had the Sears Catalog, they and their sisters were no longer needed to work the fields and do homemaking chores. Thousands fled family farms and poured into the Quad Cities to work in the factories, enjoy big-city entertainments and recreations, and send their children to fine schools. Jobs were plentiful, and for men taking advantage of the GI Bill, Augustana offered a solid college education to those who wanted the joys and comforts of Rock Island but didn't want to travel to Iowa City, Chicago, Milwaukee, or Evanston, or deal with urban hassles.

Quad Cities' merchants prospered. After two decades of depression followed by wartime shortages and rationing, people had money and were in a buying mood, and new shops and stores sprang up. For four years, the war had kept new cars from rolling off Detroit's assembly lines, and now Ford, Chrysler, American Motors, and General Motors couldn't turn out sleek, brightly-colored, new models fast enough to satisfy demand. A generation that came of age during Prohibition, took any job they could find during the Depression, and fought in Europe and the South Pacific during World War II had seen it all and were still only in their 20s and 30s. They were ready to settle down and raise a family, and this they did with consummate skill and great enthusiasm. During the last years of the Depression, the American birthrate per woman had fallen to 2.0 children. By the late 1950s, it shot up and almost doubled to 3.8. With men returned home, finances no longer a constraint, and opportunity at new highs, the number of children under five sprouted from 11 million in 1940 to 16.4 million in 1950 and didn't peak until it hit 20 million a decade later when Depression Era women left their fertility years and "The Pill" was invented. The post-war wave of kids, called the Baby Boom, reshuffled the nation's demographics and cultural mores.

The post-war decade was also distinguished by innovation, entrepreneurial enterprise, and political conservatism. A decade and a half of depression followed by wartime economics had stifled new product development and stunted consumer product growth. Sitting atop the world's pecking order and having renewed confidence after defeating the Great Depression, winning big in two world wars while suffering relatively small losses, and having the conflicting security, responsibility, and fear that comes from knowing the secret to nuclear power, the nation was anxious to return to building the ephemeral American Dream. Fifteen years of doing without, fear of backsliding into recession, losing a job, and having unpayable debt was fresh in the minds of most. The national psyche was a confused mix of pride in wartime accomplishments, a heady desire for an unrestrained shot at wealth, and deeply ingrained fears and paranoia that prosperity could end in a flash. After 20 years of New Deal federal programs and wartime economics, Americans were weary of government controls and ready for less regulation, fewer restrictions, and smaller government.

Five-Star General and Supreme Commander of the Allied Forces in Europe Dwight David Eisenhower shared that assessment. Eisenhower had served as Chief of Staff under Harry Truman, and he was asked by both parties to run for president — he picked the Republicans. In 1950 the Korean Conflict became an undeclared war. Japan had controlled Korea since 1910, and after Korea's surrender, the country was arbitrarily divided at the 38th Parallel with the Soviet Union occupying the territory to the north and the Allies occupying the south. National elections were supposed to be held in 1948 but were ignored by North Korean Communists. Raids across the 38th Parallel became increasingly aggressive, and in June 1950 the Soviet-supplied North Korean Army invaded South Korea. At the time of the 1952 elections, a million U.S troops were in Korea and almost 30,000 U.S. soldiers had lost their lives fighting Korean Communists. Running against Eisenhower, Illinois Governor Adlai Stevenson was a liberal intellectual and powerful orator whose pacifist campaign pitch didn't resonate with Americans that wanted to hear that the Communists would be beaten back as the Fascists had been.

Eisenhower easily won the election, and six months after he took office an armistice was negotiated and a 2.5-mile wide demilitarized zone was created at the 38th Parallel, and Korea was divided in the middle — three generations later, tensions and Korean politics remain much as they were then. Eisenhower was the third of six boys who brought up in a frugal, hard-working and deeply religious home in Abilene, Kansas. Eisenhower's father worked as a mechanic and his mother and her sons tended their three-acre farm, which provided the family's food from a large vegetable garden, fruit trees, a cow or two and chickens. As a high school freshman, Eisenhower contracted a leg infection that caused him to miss a year of school, and he didn't graduate from Abilene High until he was almost 19.

Eisenhower and his older brother, Edgar who was called "Big Ike," both wanted to attend college and agreed to alternate school years while the other worked to earn tuition and support themselves. "Little Ike" worked the first year while Edgar attended the University of Michigan. When Big Ike asked his little brother if he could attend a consecutive year, Little Ike consented and continued to work to support his brother. A family friend suggested that Eisenhower apply to the Military Academy, and he received an appointment. A month before his 21st birthday, he entered West Point. His mother, who was a Jehovah's Witnesses minister, was strongly opposed to warfare, but did not overrule her 20-year-old son. Edgar graduated from Michigan, with a law degree and became a "shoot from the hip, ultra-conservative" that later "considered Roosevelt a work of the devil."

Based on his conservative, disciplined upbringing, it is surprising that Eisenhower, who entered the academy three years older than most plebes, was often reprimanded and graduated with a below average discipline rating. His class ranking was better than average but less than what would one would anticipate of the man who would rise to become the nation's top war-time military leader — he was 61st in a class of 164. Although apparently accident prone, he was fast and tough, and at West Point he became a jock. He started at halfback and linebacker until he broke his leg trying to tackle Jim Thorpe; then he switched to boxing and equestrian. After re-injuring his leg in a fall from his horse, he again switched to gymnastics and fencing. As a senior, he was a yell leader and JV football coach. He wasn't good enough to make the baseball team, and he said, "Not making the baseball team was one of the greatest disappointments in my life, maybe the greatest."

Graduating and commissioned in 1915, improbably, but to his mother's great delight, Eisenhower spent World War I stateside. He also spent the first year of World War II in Washington and gained the confidence of Roosevelt. In December 1943, the man who his brother believed personified the devil, surprisingly picked him over General George Marshall to be Supreme Commander of Operation Overlord, the invasion of Normandy. As the Allies marched through Europe, a newsman asked Eisenhower's mother if she were proud of her son. "Which one?" she asked.

Marshall may have been passed over for the war's most critical command because Roosevelt felt that he was derelict in passing on intelligence concerning the attack on Pearl Harbor. Post-war investigations exonerated him, and Truman appointed Marshall Secretary of State. For his role in directing the European Recovery Plan, more commonly known as the "Marshall Plan," he was named *Time's* Man of the

Year in 1947 and later received the Nobel Peace Prize for his work. As Secretary of State, he strongly opposed recognizing the State of Israel, telling President Truman that if he had a vote, "I would vote against you." After leaving office, when Truman was asked who he believed was the American who made the greatest contribution in the last 30 years, he unhesitatingly answered, "General Marshall."

While serving as Truman's Commander in Chief, Eisenhower was politically uncommitted. But in 1951, when Truman pressed him to run as a Democrat to be his successor, Eisenhower declared himself a Republican. He then served two terms as Commander in Chief. The Eisenhower years were a time of rampant materialism. Parents who had known the Depression's deprivations were obsessed in making sure their little Baby Boomers knew nothing of their earlier financial tribulations. An expanding middle class aspired to live in a new house in the suburbs, which wouldn't be complete without a crew-cut boy named Scooter or Terry and a dimpled girl named Mary or Nancy. Riding to the A&W in the backseat of the shiny new Chevy was the cat's meow, and a kitchen full of electronic gadgets, a basement rec room with a poker table for dad's Thursday night games and a ping pong table that was seldom played on because the "little lady of the house" needed it to fold her clothes when they came out of the new side-by-side washer and dryer and because the "man of the house" had half of it covered with unfinished home improvement projects were lifestyle status symbols that proved dad had "made it." Terry had a room with walls covered with team pennants and a mound of important stuff separating bunk beds. No one ever saw Nancy's room, but knew when she and her friends were there from the shrieks and screams that could be heard over the blare of scratchy Elvis Presley records. Living rooms were only lived in when company came, and the plastic see-through furniture covers were removed from the chairs and sofa and hidden in the hall closet. Then after introductions and a chuck on the shoulder, the kids were pushed out the door to ride bikes or play tag while the adults sipped martinis and Manhattans and talked in lowered voices about work, Joe McCarthy, the neighbors, and Hugh Hefner.

In 1949, Hefner, a smart and devilishly handsome 23-year-old World War II vet graduated from the University of Illinois in only 2 ½ years with a double degree in art and creative writing. After going to work for *Esquire Magazine* and being denied a request for a $5 raise, he decided to strike out on his own and start a competing magazine. Hefner scraped together $800 ($7,500) and borrowed $8,000 more from friends and family, including a grand from his mother, to start *Playboy* magazine. Hefner understood that the swimsuit clad, GI barracks pinup pictures of June Haver, Rita Hayworth, Betty Grable, and Jane Russell all had one thing in common: they were overdressed. So risking his whole stake on a single undated issue — he was afraid there wouldn't be a second — in December 1953 Hefner printed 54,000 copies with a cover price of 50¢ ($4.50). Copies were only sold at newsstands and sold out in weeks — Hefner was on his way to becoming one of the 20th century's iconic figures.

The image of the first *Playboy* "Sweetheart" centerfold was to become seared into the consciousness of two generations of males. Hefner purchased a picture of Marilyn Monroe for $200 ($1,600), which had been taken as a calendar photo months earlier, but was too hot for prospective buyers. Between the time Hefner purchased and published the photo, Monroe's breakthrough film, *Gentlemen Prefer Blondes*, was released. After replacing Betty Grable as co-lead, Monroe, America's sexiest comedic actress starred alongside her good friend Jane Russell. Marrying Joe DiMaggio the month after *Playboy* premiered at newsstands, the Yankees' centerfielder was sandwiched between Monroe's first marriage to a policeman classmate of Russell's and her third marriage to playwright Arthur Miller who converted her to Judaism. While dating Miller, Monroe's studio executives implored her to drop him when he was called before HUAC and charged with contempt of Congress for refusing to testify. Monroe called the execs "born cowards."

Monroe personified the philosophy and lifestyle espoused by Hefner and the Playboy Adviser. America's sexiest woman had affairs with numerous Hollywood actors, and when John Kennedy was forced to end their long affair, she became despondent and took up with his brother Bobby. Two months before her "probable suicide" by overdose, Monroe made her last public appearance when she seductively sang "Happy Birthday, Mr. President" to Kennedy who was seated next to Jacqueline at his 45th birthday celebration at Madison Square Garden. Mint condition copies of the first *Playboy*, which carried Monroe's picture on the cover, sell for $6,000; the dress that she wore during the awkward rendition of *Happy Birthday* sold at auction in 1999 for $1.26 million.

Playboy boosted the careers of hundreds of models, writers, humorists, actors, musicians, and film artists, but none more than that of Peruvian artist Alberto Vargas. Like most of *Playboy's* featured talents, Vargas was successful before his monthly pinup girl first appeared in 1960, but as the magazine's circulation surpassed 7 million in the early '70s, the value of Vargas' art soared. He was published monthly until 1974 when his model-business-manager-wife died, and he stopped painting. Today, original water color "Vargas Girl" pinups sell for $50,000. *Playboy's* format not only appealed to men's prurient interests, but the magazine also published virtually every popular and serious author of the last half of the 20th century; it featured in-depth interviews with celebrities, musicians, athletes, businessmen, politicians, actors, and one president; and published monthly lifestyle features, social commentary, and non-fiction along with sophisticated cartoons that were second only to the *New Yorker's*. At the end of the 20th century, most every man between the ages of 14 and 84 had a stash of *Playboys*, and contradicting the feminist notion that they were faithfully collected only because of their pictures, in 1970 *Playboy* started publishing issues in Braille.

Four months after the first *Playboy* started changing the world's social mores, Bill Haley and His Comets rocked the world's musical tastes with one of the first rock and roll recordings, "Rock Around the Clock." Combining elements of blues, jazz, swing, doo-wop, boogie-woogie, rhythm and blues, and traditional folk music, rock and roll evolved from "race music" improvised by Southern blacks beginning in the 1920s. No song can be called the first rock and roll song, and writer Nick Tosches said of the genre, "It is impossible to discern the first modern rock record, just as it is impossible to discern where blue becomes indigo in the spectrum." White audiences didn't generally know rock and roll until Cleveland radio disk jockey, Alan Freed, started playing it to mixed audiences in 1951. Louis "Moondog" Hardin sued Freed and forced him to stop calling his radio program Moondog Symphony. After a night of drinking with friends, Freed and his companions came up with the new name for the show, *The Rock and Roll Party*, to describe the music he was playing. Although some white singers like Johnnie Ray — who early radio audiences often mistook for a woman and always mistook for black — imitated black vocalists, the up-tempo music with a strong backbeat was exclusively constructed by black musicians and singers.

Bill Haley and His Comets were a band of seven white men in their late twenties who performed in "wild plaid dinner jackets" and bow ties. They were well known in the country music world before their breakthrough hit went to No.1 in both the United States and Great Britain. As hokie as Haley was with a spit curl hanging down his forehead, his music engaged America's teenagers, and even if their music wasn't, the Comets were "acceptable" to their parents. At a time when the best-selling tunes in the country were *Delicato* (Percy Faith and his Orchestra, 1952), *Doggie in the Window* (Patti Page, 1953), and *Oh! My Pa-Pa* (Eddie Fisher, 1954) there wasn't much competition for teenage record sales when *Rock Around the Clock* topped the charts in early 1955. Rock and roll pushed aside the aging music stars and their ballads and love songs in 1956 when Elvis Presley, a 21-year-old rockabilly singer and guitar player, burst onto the scene. Two years earlier, Memphis' Sun Records owner, Sam Phillips started looking for a "white man who had the Negro sound and the Negro feel" and discovered Elvis — the first recording artist known by a single name. The roguishly good-looking singer sported a variation of a slicked-back pompadour hairstyle that became known as a "duck's butt" and introduced a hip gyration move that every teenage boy of the '50s tried unsuccessfully to imitate. Elvis would be crowned the "King of Rock and Roll" and fulfill Phillips' every wish.

Elvis had a versatile voice, and two of the 1956 top three tunes were Elvis ballads, *Heartbreak Hotel* and *Don't Be Cruel,* but it was his No. 1 hit of the year, *Hound Dog* that drove teenage girls wild and their parents crazy. Elvis first performed *Hound Dog* on the *Milton Berle Show* on June 5, 1956. Forty million people tuned in for the performance, and many of the nation's parents and the press went ballistic. If Elvis' squeal-inducing, hip-gyrating moves had been performed by a black man, he would have been banned from television, but censors didn't know what to do with Elvis. Critics said he was an "influence on juvenile delinquency," and parents of teenaged girls agreed, but some of the more informed, who liked the music and recognized a budding talent, jokingly referred to him as "Elvis the Pelvis."

In the early days of network television, the Columbia Broadcasting Company and the National Broadcasting Company dominated the airwaves, and in most cities were the only stations available. The American Broadcasting Company didn't become relevant until 1961 when Jim McKay was hired to host *ABC's Wide World of Sports.* For 37 years, the 90-minute program opened with the melodramatic introduction, "Spanning the globe to bring you the constant variety of sport — the thrill of victory — and the agony of defeat [solemnly spoken over footage of a Slovenian ski jumper tumbling off the jump — the weekly replaying of "ultimate defeat" effectively killed ski jumping in the United States] ... This is ABC's Wide World of Sports!" By introducing to TV the Indianapolis 500, Wimbledon, the NCAA Basketball Championship, The Open, the U.S. Figure Skating Championship, the X-Games, and the Little League World Series, it was indeed a wide breadth of sports coverage. Aired on Saturdays at 5:00 p.m., *Wide World of Sports* became must-watch TV for dads and their sons — except if they were thankfully pushed off the couch by moms and their daughters when figure skating was aired.

Sunday evening was "family night" in front of the TV, and NBC's, *The Steve Allen Show,* vied with Ed Sullivan's more highly rated CBS program for primetime viewers. Allen's comedy-variety show avoided circus acts and slapstick comedians and was geared to adult viewing, whereas the awkward and fumbling Sullivan aired what his producers believed was a "family program." Although everyone with the sophistication of an eight-year-old preferred *The Steve Allen Show,* a decade of well-meaning parents forced their kids into becoming intimately familiar with The Flying Wallendas and Kate Smith. That changed for one night on July 1, 1956 when Allen invited Elvis. The word was out that the world's first rock star was going to sing *Hound Dog* again, and every kid in America solemnly promised that they wouldn't become a JD if they could watch just one more time. Most of their parents were equally curious, so for educational purposes, the nation tuned in.

The kids were sadly disappointed. The normally hip Allen hated rock and roll, and he dressed Elvis in a tuxedo and had him sing to a Basset Hound wearing a top hat. Ever the curmudgeon and even though Allen had trounced him in the ratings for one night, Sullivan said that Elvis would never appear on his show. In a way, he was right. Sullivan was seriously injured in a car accident, and on September 9, 1956, when he was recovering from the accident, Peter Laughton hosted *The Ed Sullivan Show* from Hollywood, where Elvis was filming *Love Me Tender*. In the first set, Elvis sang *Don't Be Cruel* and *Love Me Tender*, and then the wraps came off when he opened the second set with Little Richard's hard-driving *Ready Teddy*, and 60 million viewers watched Elvis finish with a shortened but unrestrained *Hound Dog*. Maintaining their highbrow image, the *New York Times* said that TV's most highly rated program ever (82.6 percent of the viewing audience), was "distasteful" and that Elvis' "over stimulating the physical impulses of the teenagers was a gross national disservice." The critics' fears were realized, and all the teenagers broke their promises and became juvenile delinquents.

Baby Boomers first rocked out to Elvis, and as the music matured, so did their tastes. (Inexplicably, rock and roll began to devolve in the mid-1970s when New York-based counterculture reacted against the music's domination and answered with disco music. Rock and roll further degenerated when, as a backlash against disco, the hip-hop genre that would feature "rapping," "scratching," and "breaking" eventually destroyed classic rock and roll.) Because of *American Bandstand,* when the first Boomers entered Rocky, they knew how the cool kids in Philadelphia danced, and from movies like *Suddenly, Last Summer; The Apartment; La Doce Vita;* and *Inherit the Wind* they knew that there was life beyond the Quad Cities, and that it wasn't always rosy. And because the media had become more competitive and sophisticated and world news was easily followed, it wasn't a shock when John F. Kennedy, a strikingly handsome Massachusetts' Senator who had received the 1960 Democratic presidential nomination, showed up to an overflowing Rocky gym in October. Kennedy spoke with a clipped-syllable Boston accent that only a few years before would have sounded like a foreign language to Quad Citians.

Kennedy's Irish Catholic parents were polar-opposites of Truman's straight-laced Presbyterian and Eisenhower's devout Jehovah's Witnesses' parents. His mother, Rose Fitzgerald, was the oldest child of John "Honey Fitz" Fitzgerald, a Boston mayor and three-time U.S. Representative. His Harvard-educated father, Joseph, was born into a wealthy Boston political family and added to his own fortune by prudent investments in the stock and commodities markets. After Prohibition, he also made prudent investments in real estate and liquor when he secured exclusive American distribution rights to Dewar's Scotch and Gordon's Gin. He was the first Chairman of the Securities and Exchange Commission and was ambassador to Great Britain during the first years of World War II. John Kennedy was not only financially advantaged and politically connected but also smart and good looking. He graduated cum laude in international affairs from Harvard in 1940, and wrote the bestseller *Why England Slept* as an undergraduate.

The next year after being medically disqualified from the Army, Kennedy joined the Navy. Two years later while commanding a patrol torpedo boat in the South Pacific, PT-109 was rammed by a Japanese destroyer and sunk. Gathering the surviving crew around him, he took a vote on surrendering or trying to swim to a nearby island after saying, "There's nothing in the book about a situation like this. A lot of you have families, and some of you have children. I have nothing to lose." They swam, and with a rope clenched between his teeth, Kennedy, who had been a varsity swimmer at Harvard, towed a badly injured man to safety. He received a breast pocket full of commendations, and later when asked about how he earned them, he joked, "It was easy. They cut my PT boat in half." Kennedy's older brother, Joe, was the family's designee to follow his father into politics, but when he was killed in action in 1944, John Kennedy was forced to give up his chosen career in journalism. Two years later, the 29-year-old won the first of three terms in the U.S. House of Representatives. Setting his sights on the U.S. Senate, in 1952 he defeated Henry Cabot Lodge, Jr., and to cap a good year, he married debutante Jacqueline Lee Bouvier. The month after his 43rd birthday, he became the Democrats' choice to take on Vice President Richard Nixon as Eisenhower's successor.

Before Kennedy spoke to more than 10,000 frenzied supporters in the new Rock Island gymnasium, he visited Davenport, where he stood on the trunk of a white convertible at the intersection of Second and Main Streets and delivered a short speech to a crowd almost equal in size to the one which awaited him in Rock Island. The Rocky gym filled beyond capacity two hours before Kennedy arrived, promptly at 9:00 p.m. on a school night. Although many of Rocky's students saw their hero in the Boy's Gym, the real action was in the Girl's Gym, which was packed with students who wished to avoid their parents and were as interested in each other as they were in the politician. After listening to the Pep Band repetitively play *When the Rocks Go Marching In* to the beat of a similarly named song and chanting, "Jack, Jack, Jack" until they were hoarse, they quieted enough to listen to Kennedy's speech over the school's tinny PA system — he was speaking live only a couple of hundred feet away. One of those who didn't hear Kennedy speak in either gym was the son of the boy who lost Herbert Hoover's autograph when he did his whistle-stop in Rock Island. Unlike his father, Terry Baltzer didn't plan far enough ahead to get the future president's signature and was stopped at an intersection on his way to the high school parking lot by Kennedy's motorcade, but as the senator rolled past, like his father, he got within arms' length of the future president.

Because his running mate, Lyndon "Bullshit" Johnson, was from Texas, Kennedy narrowly won the Lone Star State, and because fellow Irish Catholic and Democratic Chicago Mayor, Richard Daley, ruled Chicago's politics, Kennedy squeaked out a last minute Illinois victory. Daley held back final vote totals until late morning on the day after the election when all the other states had reported their totals. Amazingly, out of almost 5 million Illinois votes, Kennedy won the state by 9,000 — and arguably the most dynamic 1,000 days of a U.S. Presidency began. Between his election and death when a bullet fired by Lee Harvey Oswald ended his life, Kennedy presided over a nation in flux caused by the Cuban Bay of Pigs Invasion, a CIA directed and botched invasion to rid Cuba of Fidel Castro and Communism; the Cuban Missile Crisis, a toe-to-toe nuclear showdown with Russia; the Space Race with Russia, a Cold War tech contest to determine who had the best rocket technology and consequently the best nuclear bomb delivery system; the construction of the Berlin Wall, a heavily guarded barrier to keep Communists from fleeing their utopian state; the Civil Rights Movement; and the first phase of the Viet Nam War.

To America's youth, John Kennedy represented a break from the conservative repression of their parents' generation, and a segment of America's youth turned on and tuned out "the establishment." Raised with the background noise of McCarthyism, hiding under desks during air raid drills (Longfellow Grade School teachers told their students that the Arsenal made Rock Island one of the ten most likely places the Soviets would bomb), given silly rules for the sake of discipline, a near national belief that sex was only for procreation (indoctrinated by their mothers and threatened by their fathers, most teenage girls of the time denied that they liked to even be in the same room with boys unless, of course, they were dancing), and suspecting that joining the Navy wasn't the best way to see the world. Hearing hypocritical and racist attitudes expressed at the dinner table and from the pulpit led America's youth to question the ethics of their parents and the morality of their pastors, shoving sex into the closet with their dads' *Playboys* caused them to question whether they wanted to be virgins when they married for life and if an all-knowing and all-powerful God was really watching their every move and monitoring their every thought. When they arrived at college, the conventional joined the football team, a fraternity or sorority, ROTC, and the Young Republicans. The questioning joined the sailing club, the Poetry Society, the NAACP, and the Young Democrats. Those who believed both political parties were out of touch started a rock band, burned their bras, and occupied the administration building as a symbolic protest against unreasonable authority. The radical dropped out and moved to the corner of Haight and Ashbury in San Francisco. All but the Young Republicans drove their parents crazy.

No one was more offended by the youth movement away from traditional values than the nation's top cop, J. Edgar Hoover. Kennedy was the fourth president Hoover served under — he reported to no one and arguably wielded more domestic power than any of the presidents he ostensibly served. Starting with Franklin Roosevelt, Hoover made it known that there was nothing in any American's life that he felt was worth knowing that he hadn't documented. In the world's freest country with the most protected citizens, Hoover had a level of personal data on the nation's wealthy and powerful leaders that Communist premiers could only dream about. Only he and his personal secretary, Helen Gandy, had access to his files, and no one knew what Hoover did or didn't know. It is also unknown how much Hoover used his information to accomplish his objectives. Although he was certainly zealous in his pursuit of gangsters and Communists, it is unclear to what degree he violated civil liberties, and he is probably undeserving of the vilification he has received in recent books and movies.

However, proving that an unrevealed secret is the most powerful knowledge, because of their sexual peccadilloes, Kennedy and his brother Bobby, who he named Attorney General, were powerless to alter Hoover's agendas. Hoover waged war on political dissenters and activists, the Black Panther Party, the Youth International Party (Yippies) and Martin Luther King's Southern Christian Leadership Conference. Whether true or not — and no one will ever know if many of Hoover's carefully dropped accusations and scurrilous comments were true — Jacqueline Kennedy said that Hoover told her husband that King tried to arrange a sex party while in the capital for the March on Washington. Unquestionably, he did overstay his usefulness. He was appointed Director of the Bureau of Investigation as a 29-year-old, and because he manipulated the mandatory retirement age of 70, he was FBI director for 49 years — as many years as his most faithful Congressional supporter, Joe McCarthy, lived.

In May 1972 when President Richard "Tricky Dick" Nixon heard that Hoover died of a heart attack at his Washington D.C. home, it is said that he excitedly blurted out a very uncomplimentary expletive. At his funeral service, Nixon eulogized Hoover as "One of the giants ... a national symbol of courage, patriotism, and granite-like honesty and integrity." Two years later, Nixon became the only president to resign from office. He quit instead of facing impeachment for lying. After Hoover's death, it took his secretary weeks to destroy his personal files. Although the Bureau of Investigation hired women agents in the 1920s, none were hired during Hoover's tenure. He required female clerical workers to wear skirts or dresses, and unlike the males they served, they could not smoke at their desks, and undeniably, the FBI became more transparent and the civil rights movement picked up steam after his death.

African-American rights were less of an issue in Rock Island than elsewhere. Because of accessible jobs in the hotels, bars, and restaurants, railroad work, and work at the docks and in entertainment, a cluster of blacks started to settle in Rock Island following the Civil War. As other ethnic groups had, the black community grew slowly and formed its own economy west of downtown where the Mississippi river bends to the south. During the last decades of the 19th century and the first decades of the 20th, in the northwest corner of Rock Island, just as in the "Old Country," tight-knit German and Swedish neighborhoods formed, and soon an equally-bonded Belgian enclave sprang up west from 9th Street between 4th and 9th Avenues. The anchors of the Flemish-speaking community were the business district along 9th Street, the taverns and restaurants found on most corners, and the Belgian American Brotherhood that moved into the West End Settlement House. Susanne Denkmann's former home for immigrants was used for English lessons, Saturday night dances, rolle bolle (bocce ball) tournaments, and pigeon races. At St Paul's Catholic Church on 8 ½ Avenue, Father Culemans, a native of the Louvain in Belgium, said the mass in Flemish.

As the city's second-generation German and Belgian residents moved from the West End to the Broadway District and then to newer neighborhoods on the hill, blacks moved into their homes and businesses and formed a stable neighborhood with its own stores, shops, theaters, and churches which were marginally integrated into the neighborhoods to the south and east. Black and white children attended school and played afterward with each other. The downtown area stopped black neighborhood growth to the east, and until the mid-1960s the construction of a four-lane thoroughfare along 11th Street from the Milan Bridge to the Centennial Bridge the decade before, created a de facto boundary to the east of the black neighborhood. Segregated into the West End's northwest corner, the black community was out of sight and was mostly out of mind to most of Rock Island's citizens.

The students in the high school classes of 1962 were the last babies born before the Baby Boomers burst out in 1945. Those born in the last years before the Boomers arrived experienced the sharp cultural pivot from Depression Era parents and the "anything is possible" post-World War II generation. Rocky *Watchtower* yearbooks before the late 1960s reveal that rarely did black students participate in school-wide clubs, were selected as cheerleaders, or elected to class offices. Most Rocky students of that era have stories of racism that was not only tolerated but was unofficially endorsed by merchants, school officials, and law enforcement officers:

In 1958 after winning a choral competition, a group of Rocky girls were taken to Milan's Bringer Inn to celebrate. The black student piano player was told she would be served in the kitchen.

In 1959 after a Moline football game played in the rain, a Rocky girl asked a fellow band member if he would like a ride home. On the way, they were involved in a minor traffic accident. A Rock Island High School administrator, who was returning from the game, thoughtfully stopped to ask the girl if she needed help. The next Monday morning, the student was called into the dean's office and told that it was improper for her to be in a car with a black boy.

In the early 1960s, a white policeman's son got into a fight with a black student. They fought to an exhausted draw. The father's response when he heard about the fight was "Never let me hear that you got in a fight with a nigger and didn't win it."

In a recent email exchange, when it was mentioned that there were only 14 black 1962 Rocky graduates (six years earlier, in one classroom at Hawthorne 9 of 24 6th graders were black), four classmates told of racial attitudes during their school years:

> I remember getting in a fight in gym class with a black kid. He gave me a bloody nose before the gym teacher could break it up. The teacher, who knew my father very well, told me that if my dad knew that a black kid bloodied my nose he would be very upset. I didn't know that to be true, but that is what he said. Yes, there were some aspects of racism. I also recall issues in the West End when there was rioting, and it was dangerous to go down to 7th Avenue and 9th Street. My dad would drive that way down to Mill Street to go to work, and during that period of unrest, he carried a handgun with him. I can't remember the years that happened. ~ Carl Hinze

> I never understood the civil rights movement in the beginning because of the environment I was raised in. I didn't know there was a problem. I went to Hawthorne on 7th Street and 3rd Avenue, which had an inordinately strange mix of races, cultures, religions, etc. If you had asked me whether my friends were black or brown or white, I'm not sure I could have told you. The only ones that stand out in my mind were Alexandra, who moved to Rock Island from Russia, and a girl who was a Jehovah Witness and was not allowed to pledge to the flag.
> We all went to the Lifeline, which was a block from the school, and the guys played basketball, and the girls did crafts. It was run by an elderly couple, and I think sponsored by some faith-based organization, but there was never any preaching, at least I don't remember any. That's where Harvey, Teague, and the other guys learned to play ball together. My neighbors were Italian and spoke very little English. My Brownie troop leader was black and ran Brown's Funeral Home on 9th Street & 4th Avenue where we held our meetings. I knew nothing of racism nor anti-Semitism or that we were poor. My mother bought my Buster Brown shoes at Halpern's Department Store on 9th Street, where the Hebrew Temple was just across the street next to the

movie theater. It was like a little New York. If there were problems, the kids never knew it.

Junior high split some of us apart. Some went to Central and some to Franklin. Still, I had no problem, and we were still friends, but sometime in high school things changed. Some organization started holding meetings for the blacks that gave the black kids replies that they could use against racism. Apparently they were hearing of the horrendous things that were happening, not necessarily in Rock Island, but in other places. It was never the same after that. In the late sixties, I can't tell you how shocked I was on a trip through Alabama. I saw drinking fountains marked "White" and "Colored," and at a bar and restaurant I saw some black gentlemen refused carryout, by a man with a ball bat. I was outraged, but did nothing. It was then I started to understand.
~ Donna Dempsey Skowronski

Our Rock Island High School social/class experiences may be harder to reconstruct than our attitudes toward race, as the issues are more complex, and there were more examples of lines that were crossed other than racial lines. Race has been discussed or thought of by most, but the social/class issues of today's politics underscore this area of latent tension. Rock Island, in general, was a prosperous area with ample job opportunities to make enough money to not live in poverty. For most, the minimum job was in a factory, and it provided a decent living. Most blue-collar families were very hopeful, relative to today that they, or at least their kids, would break through by hard work and/or an education. There seemed to be enough for all.

Frankly, the black families I knew in the West End voiced the same publicly, but privately were not as confident. Many of these families were only one or two generations removed from the South themselves, and all had connections down there and knew exactly what was going on. Several of my black classmates and friends from Irving did not make it to their senior year at Rocky. Many of us didn't even have to search for summer jobs because they were found through parental or family connections. Not so for many of my black classmates who didn't venture too far from the West End. Sports were a great common experience, but after the games or practice, most returned to different neighborhoods.

Of course, then as now, the churches were the most segregated places in Rock Island. There were far more blue-collar whites in the West End than blacks, but perhaps no blacks above the hill, except maybe the Watts family who owned the garbage disposal business. I must say that at some level, I was aware of who left the school by the north or west door to walk home 'down the hill,' and who left by the south door to get in their car and drive home. Donna makes excellent points about the early years, but in all honesty, in high school I lived in two different worlds — school friends and neighborhood friends. Even playing tennis as a Westender was somewhat unusual. ~ Gene Utke

I grew up on the corner of 44th Street and 23rd Avenue — not far from the Gersick clan. No black folks in that neighborhood and certainly no large houses. Ours was about 900 sq. ft. with two bedrooms, one bath, small living room, and kitchen. I don't think many would tolerate that size for a family of four like we did. No wonder my sister and I were at odds! I was surprised by the number of blacks in our class! I know I didn't have an overwhelming memory of number, but 14? I went to Washington and before that Denkmann, in largely white neighborhoods, but I thought the high school was more diverse. What planet have I been on? A good friend of the family was a foreman at Frank's Foundry. There were a large number of Hispanics who worked there, most could not speak English. One guy, in particular, was called "Bicycle" because he was always running. I don't recall any Hispanic kids in high school. Where were they? ... I must have had my head in the sand. ~ Lorene Jensen Kowalsky

And one classmate who attended all-white elementary and junior high schools, succinctly commented on the discrimination he saw:

> I haven't looked, but there were probably no more than 14 Jews (all at the top of the class academically). Also, there was a fair amount of anti-Semitism going on back then. ~ John Birkeland

In Rock Island, Jews had a much easier go of it than blacks, and the primary social issues they faced were not being invited to join social clubs and race-based jealousy. Jews worshipped together, but unlike other tight-knit racial and ethnic groups who for a generation or more had their own well-defined neighborhoods, there was never a Jewish enclave in Rock Island. Most Jewish immigrants to the Tri-Cities first settled in Rock Island's West End, often in homes passed on by Jews who moved up the social scale to newer digs on the hill or to other cities. No ethnic group more exhibited the Midwestern work ethic than Jews. Most of the Jewish families were poor when they arrived during the first two decades of the 20th century, and with the help of other Jewish families that they met at Rock Island's West End temples, they quickly integrated themselves into the community. There were no enterprises that Jews did not compete and excel in. Their prices were usually the lowest, their quality and service usually the best, and no one worked harder and longer. They won the race for economic security, and by the 1950s, there were few downtown Rock Island shops and stores whose proprietors weren't Jewish.

Three of Rock Island's most enterprising Jews were Isador and Henry Finkelstein and A.L. "Al" Tunick. Twelve years after the first Dairy Queen opened in Joliet, Illinois, in 1940, but pre-dating the original McDonald's golden arches that debuted in 1955 in Des Plaines, Illinois and the first Colonel Sanders Kentucky Fried Chicken store that a 65-year-old failed restaurateur franchised the same year, the Finkelstein brothers created a novel twist to fast food — they deep fried whole chickens. The brothers bought a small local manufacturing plant that made pressure fryers, and then hired a cook from one of Rock Island's most popular restaurants, the Dutch Inn on 17th Street in downtown Rock Island. Using the Dutch Inn's "Chicken-In-The-Basket" recipe with a crispy batter coating, the brothers launched a takeout and delivery store named Chicken Delight on 18th Avenue that became immediately popular. (Colonel Harlan Sanders developed a similar method of pressure frying chicken and a "secret recipe" for his batter that most deep-fried chicken connoisseurs feel was inferior to the Dutch Inn's.)

Saddled with debt from acquiring the fryer plant and startup costs, the brothers sold their assets to Tunick, who had been hired to manage and promote the business. Tunick had a sensational idea — franchise the Finkelstein's concept. By supplying a terrific business model, preparation equipment, deep fryers, and the process, Tunick franchised a ready-to-go operation that created not only a market for his fryers but also provided a steady source of recurring revenue from franchise fees for recipes and promotion and from supplying ingredients and packaging supplies. Within ten years, the franchise grew to 750 stores nationwide, and Tunick had enhanced the takeout operation by adding fleets of white delivery vehicles that had huge plastic chickens mounted on their roofs. Throughout the country, strings of boys on bicycles chased after the chicken-topped delivery cars through suburban neighborhoods shouting the slogan conceived by Henry Finkelstein, "Don't Cook Tonight; Call Chicken Delight."

Ever the entrepreneurial innovator, for a short time Tunick partnered with the Mueller Brothers, who provided the only recorded instances of takeout meals delivered by airplane. Boxed meals attached to miniature paper parachutes were dropped from Mueller's planes to farmers and those living in the Tri-Cities outlying areas. The bill and a mail-in envelope were included for easy payment. In 1965 Tunick sold Chicken Delight to Consolidated Foods. After a brief and restless retirement, Tunick was back in business, franchising Karmelkorn and opening several of his own stores next to Rock Island theaters. When Tunick's health began to fail, he sold the Karmelkorn franchise to Dairy Queen.

Through the '50s, Chicken Delight was usually precariously balanced on spindly-legged TV trays in front of humongous RCA Victor, Magnavox, or Sylvania black and white, 21" televisions. On Friday nights, *Gillette's Cavalcade of Sports* televised boxing and had huge ratings in Rock Island, unless the Rocks were playing on the stadium turf or the gym's hardwood. Then KWQC, NBC's Quad City outlet, took a huge hit in viewers. Today, men brag that they haven't missed their college alma mater's rivalry game for 20 years or more. Before cable television started broadcasting sports on multiple channels 24/7, it was not uncommon to hear graying Rocky grads among the stadium's crowd of 10,000 or more recall dates, players, and stats from games when the Rocks rolled over Moline or Davenport decades before. Although many great Rocks brought glory on the gridiron, Don Nelson, a basketball player, is Rocky's most famous student-athlete.

As a ninth grader at Central Junior High, Nelson wasn't anything special, and possibly because of the high-level competition he encountered at Rocky, he didn't start fulltime until his senior year. When Wheaton College was the only out-of-area school to offer him a scholarship, it appeared that Nelson would stay at home and play for Augustana. During the summer, first year Iowa coach, Sharm Scheuerman, dipped back into his hometown's talent pool and offered Nelson a scholarship, which he eagerly accepted.

Scheuerman is arguably the best athlete to graduate from Rocky. He was a three-sport standout who grew up dreaming of playing centerfield for the Chicago Cubs. Heavily recruited and knowing he had all spring and summer to work on his baseball game, Scheuerman accepted a scholarship to play football and basketball at Iowa. He dumped football and was a four-year starter in baseball, but basketball became the heady point guard's primary sport. In his junior year, he led Iowa's "Fabulous Five" to the Final Four, and after a poor start to his senior season, Iowa reeled off 17 consecutive wins before Bill Russell, Casey Jones, and the University of San Francisco ended their season in the national championship game. Scheuerman had been recruited by basketball coach, Bucky O'Connor, who was so impressed by his abilities and knowledge of the game that he asked him to be his assistant after he graduated. For two years, Scheuerman continued to learn from his head coach, and then days after his 24th birthday, he was thrown into the top coaching spot when the 44-year-old O'Conner was tragically killed in an automobile accident.

Scheuerman coached Nelson for four years at Iowa, where Nelson grew another inch and put on 20 pounds of muscle. With hard work, he developed into a smart and rugged 6'6" center and averaged 21.1 points and 10.5 rebounds for his career. He received All-American honors his last two years, but the pros were still skeptical of the under-sized big man, and the Chicago Zephers didn't take him until Round 3 of the 1962 NBA Draft. The Zephyrs weren't high on him and sold the rookie to the Los Angeles Lakers after one season when the Chicago team moved on to become the Washington Wizards. After two nondescript years with the Lakers, he signed with the Boston Celtics. In his first season playing for legendary Red Auerbach, Nelson came off the bench to pick up Bill Russell's garbage and average 10.2 points and 5.4 rebounds a game. Nelson went from near-NBA miss to the Celtics' sixth man on five NBA Championship teams.

In Game 7 of the 1969 NBA Finals, Russell clinched his 11th championship ring when Nelson made one of the most memorable shots in NBA history. With less than a minute to go and the Celtics clinging to a 103-102 lead over his old Lakers team, Nelson shot a long jumper from the baseline corner; the ball hit the back rim and bounced several feet straight up before dropping cleanly through the hoop, securing Boston's 11th NBA title in 13 seasons. Nelson was the stabilizing key-player to transition from the Russell dynasty years to the Celtics return to dominance with a rounded team that also included Dave Cowan, Paul Silas, and Jo Jo White, and he picked up two more rings in 1974 and 1976. Nelson's most memorable basketball characteristic was his unique "hop" free throw. With a shooting motion he probably would have corrected when he coached, he balanced on his right foot with the ball in his right hand, and with his left leg trailing, after an excruciatingly long pause, he straightened his right leg in a hop and launched the ball to the basket. His free throws weren't fundamentally sound or pretty, but they worked. Nelson hit 76.5 percent from the line over his 14-season pro career.

In 1976, only months after retiring from the Celtics, Nelson took over the head-coaching and general manager's job with the Milwaukee Bucks. The year before, the Bucks had traded Kareem Abdul Jabbar to the Lakers and sorely needed rebuilding. Nelson was the man for the job. He traded Swen Nater for the third overall draft pick that turned into UCLA sensation, Marques Johnson, a player who was a near clone of Nelson. Nelson's Milwaukee teams with Johnson did well and won five consecutive division titles between 1980 and 1984, but unfortunately they were playing at the same time that Larry Bird was playing with the Celtics and Moses Malone and Doctor J. were with the Philadelphia 76ers. Nelson went on to coach the Golden State Warriors for 11 seasons over two stretches, the New York Knicks for a season, and the Dallas Mavericks for eight seasons. Known as "Nellie Ball," he devised a scrambling, up-tempo style of offense that combines the disciplined, selfless play he learned from Sharm Scheuerman and Red Auerbach with the speed and skills of today's players.

Nelson was a master at getting the most out of his teams; he made average players good, and as a player and a coach, he made every team he was with better. As a coach, he never had a dominating player and never won an NBA title. In a 2012 radio interview with Tom Tolbert, an average player he made solid enough to stick for seven years in the NBA, Nelson said of his teams, "We battled, we tried the best we could, and I thought I always got the best out of my ballclubs. That's what was important." Nelson was a winner, and after coaching his last game in 2010, he had battled hard enough to win an NBA record 1,335 games.

In March 2012, Nelson was voted into the Basketball Hall of Fame. "I was sitting on my back porch smoking a cigar, when I got the call," he said. "It was a great moment for me. I'm the luckiest man in the world. I've been involved with the game of basketball for over 60 years, and I've never had a bad day, even when we lost games. They've all been great days." In May 2012 Nelson graduated from the University of Iowa. He had left school in 1962 to play pro ball while ten credits short of graduation. The dream of most that played on Rock Island's driveways and concrete courts at Lincoln and Longview Parks was to ride the hoops high until he died. Nelson pulled it off. Most of Nelson's teammates tucked away their hoops dreams when they graduated, and so did he — but he was smart enough to prolong graduation for 50 years.

The month before Nelson got the call from the Hall of Fame, in a game between Stanford University and the University of Colorado, standout Stanford freshman Chasson Randle, a sensational guard who led Rocky to its first state basketball championship in 2011, and who may eclipse Nelson as Rock Island's most famous athlete, shot a long jumper; the ball hit the back rim and bounced several feet straight up before dropping cleanly through the hoop. Possibly the only person alive who could instantly make the connection to a similar shot that Don Nelson made 43 years earlier to clinch the 1969 NBA Championship is Marques Johnson. He was doing the television broadcast and said, "Whoa, soft shot, and a Don Nelson bounce! ... You know, they went to the same high school in Rock Island, Illinois."

Rock Island High School may be the ideal secondary school. Its faculty and facilities are phenomenal; however, what distinguishes the school is that Rock Island has only had a single public high school. So for more than a century and a half, most of the children of an extravagantly diverse community have sat side-by-side in the classroom, competed on the playing fields, and have mixed, befriended, and socialized with each other. Arguably, of the almost 2,000 Illinois municipalities, none is more representative of the state and its history than Rock Island. Illinois is considered by some demographers to be the most broadly representative state in the United States. By extension, Rock Island may be the archetypal microcosm of all American cities. It certainly has one of the richest histories and has produced an inordinate number of amazing people. Today, there is no one who can tell their grandchildren of when they caught trout in the pools and eddies of the Sylvan Slough and swam in cold racing water from sandbar to sandbar picking their way across the Mississippi from Rock Island to Davenport — but it's still the only place the Mississippi flows west and is one of America's most fascinating spots.

After Notes

On a hot summer afternoon in 1956, I followed the sound of squeaking sneakers, players' grunts, and a bouncing basketball up the backstairs to the Rock Island YMCA gym. I was hoping to find Bob Beale, a friend of my dads who would let me shoot hoops if no one was around to bust kids under 16 for being in the gym. Mr. Beale wasn't there, and I was surprised to see only two players — Don Nelson and a black kid whose name I now forget were going at each other in a game of one-on-one as if the Mississippi Valley Conference title were on the line. They were both leaving pools of sweat on the glossily varnished floor, and Nelson, who was entering his junior year at Rocky, seemed to be winning. He was a half-step slower and a tad softer — two playing traits that 7th grade boys knew to look for — but was playing harder. Seven years later, Nelson was playing in the NBA. His YMCA opponent, like so many other great black athletes of the time, faded into obscurity.

Fifty-three years after that YMCA game, at a summer shootaround at Rocky, nine Big Ten basketball coaches showed up to see if another Rock Island 16-year-old was as good as advertised. Chasson Randle was. Unlike Nelson, there was never a question that Randle would get a full ride to a quality university; it was just which one he would select. He chose Stanford, and what is most amazing is that if basketball didn't work out, Randle could have gone to Stanford on an academic scholarship. After receiving a B in the second grade, Randle swore that he wouldn't get another. He didn't and he was Rocky's 2011 co-valedictorian. Randle had a good freshman year at Stanford and was named to the Pac-12 All-Freshman team. When his basketball days are over, he plans on becoming an orthopedic surgeon.

It sounds trite and shouldn't have to be mentioned, but Randle is black. I graduated from Rocky four years after Nelson. The most talented athlete in my class was Ron Teague who was also black. Like Randle, he led the Rocks to the state basketball finals. And like Randle he was a good student, and he was an exceptional musician. Unlike Randle, he didn't receive the acclaim he deserved, and he didn't have the support of faculty and community to assure that he fulfilled his potential and was pushed to be his absolute best. It saddens me that minorities and women have been denied equal access and resources for most of America's history, but I am heartened when I see an amazing, fully developed talent like Randle come out of Rocky. Or as happened on a recent spring day, when I stopped by the Rocky baseball field to watch a game, I was surprised to hear cheers coming from the football stadium. After strolling across one of the nation's grandest high school campuses, when I peered into the massive bowl, I was amazed to see a sizeable, enthusiastic crowd watching a girls' soccer game. Rocky has come a long way, as has Rock Island and the nation.

The political rancor of the last decade seemed to be greater than what I remembered when white men over 50 were totally in charge of the country's institutions and government, and because I'm now solidly part of that demographic, a motivating factor during the research of this book was to understand, if in general, our nation really is more racist, misogynous, intolerant, belligerent, entitled, greedy, and flat-out rude than it has ever been. I was pleased to find that we are not. As a country, we've always been bigoted, sexist, fractious, contentious, self-interested, and selfish, and most of the time to a far greater degree than we are now. Maybe there was a time after World War II that the populous felt less entitled and was kinder and politer, but then we compensated for having better manners by being more intolerant and hypocritical. That is not to say that the great majority of Americans have not always been good and law-abiding citizens as judged by the conventions and laws of their times. However that's faint praise: until 1968 blacks were lynched under Jim Crow laws, and for 400 of the 500 years since Columbus landed, killing Native Americans was not only legal but also officially encouraged. Indian killers were heroes and received Congressional Medals of Honor. Today, they get life without parole.

Since the writing of the Constitution, the only group of Americans that has not felt the oppression of discrimination is white Anglo-Saxon Protestant men — the same demographic that is most responsible for shaping our country. WASP males have always been a minority — except at the ballot box and in the workplace — and we have fought hard over two and a half centuries to keep the odds in our favor. After we won the country from England, for the United States' first century Native Americans who weren't killed were systemically marginalized, blacks and women couldn't vote, and then for another half-century women still couldn't — that's one sure way to stack the odds. Then until the last generation, we denied women and people of color equal access to education and professional opportunity, and we still don't give them equal pay. It is not in mankind's nature to give up wealth and power easily, and America's white men are fighting to hold onto the edge we have. It's a losing battle. White people are becoming a minority, the playing field has leveled, and the rules have changed to fairly include all.

It is often said we are a nation of immigrants, but that distastefully ignores that there are 2.5 million Native Americans living in the United States, most of whom live in sovereign nations carved out on the most undesirable land within U.S. borders, and that we decimated the aboriginal population so that white people could live in the choicest spots with access to the greatest natural resources — it's not coincidental that Rock Island and Saukenuk are on the same spot. It is sobering to read the history of how America was colonized and to realize the expenditures of life and property and the length of time it has taken for a majority of our nation to accept the reality that all mankind is created equal and has an equal right to pursue happiness — and to individually define what makes them happy, so long as they don't infringe on another's rights. I believe the United States is closer to that ideal than it has ever been. And I also believe that, of course, old white men are more cantankerous now than when we controlled all of the money and power, and now that we control only the money, we are desperately fighting with each other to determine the best way to keep from losing it. I believe this bodes well for the generation of students at Longfellow Grade School — I think when they are grandparents, everyone will be playing by the same rules.

Bibliography

n.d.

Ander, Oscar Fitiof. *The Standing Bear.* Google Books, 1952.

Anonymous. *Historic Rock Island County.* Urbana, Illinois: University of Illinois, 1923.

Bartlette, John. *Bartlett's Book of Anecdotes.* Edited by Clifton Fadiman and Andre Bernard. New York: Little, Brown and Company, 1985.

—. *Familiar Quotations.* New York: Philosophical Library, Inc., 1965.

Beschloss, Michael. *Presidential Courage: Brave Leaders and How They Changed America 1789-1989.* New York: Simon & Schuster, 2007.

Black Hawk. *Black Hawk: An Autobiography.* Edited by Donald Jackson. University of Illinois Press, Champaign, Illinois, First Edition 1833.

Brinkley, Alan, Davis Dyer, and Editors. *The Reader's Companion to the American Presidency.* New York: Houghton Mifflin Company, 2000.

Catton, Bruce. *The American Heritage Picture History of the Civil War.* New York: Heritage Publishing Co., 1960.

Collins, David R., BJ Elsner, Rich J. Johnson, and Bessie J. Pierce. *Rock Island: All American City.* Charleston SC: Arcadia Publishing, 1999.

Coopman, David T. *Rock Island County.* Charleston SC: Arcadia Publishing, 2008.

—. *Watch Tower Amusement Park.* n.d. http://captainerniesshowboat.com/watchtoweramusementpark.

Davis, Marni. *Jews and Booze.* New York: New York University Press, 2012.

Efflandt, Lloyd H. *Lincoln and the Black Hawk War.* Rock Island: Rock Island Arsenal Historical Society, 1991.

—. *The Black Hawk War, Why?* Rock Island: Rock Island Arsenal Historical Society, 1986.

Elsner, BJ, ed. *Rock Island: Yesterday, Today & Tomorrow.* Rock Island: Rock Island History Book Committee, 1988.

Grunwald, Michael. "Who Controls the Mighty River?" *Time Magazine*, May 12, 2011.

Hamer, Richard and Ruthhart, Roger. *Citadel of Sin.* Moline: Moline Dispatch Publishing Company, L.L.C., 2007.

Jung, Patrick J. *The Black Hawk War of 1832.* University of Oklahoma Press, 2007.

King, David C. *First People.* New York: DK Publishing, 2008.

Leinicke, Will, Marion Lardner, and Ferrel Anderson. *Two Nations, One Land.* Rock Island: Citizens To Preserve Black Hawk Park Foundation, 1981.

Meese, William A., Editor. *Historic Rock Island County.* Rock Island: Kramer & Company, 1908.

O'Brien, William Patrick, Mary Yeater Rathbun, and Patrick O'Bannon. *Gateways to Commerce: The U.S. Army Corps of Engineers' 9-Foot Channel Project on the Upper Mississippi River.* Edited by Christine Whiteacre. Denver: U.S. Government Publication, 1992.

Oestreich, Diane. *Rock Island Preservation Society > Postcards From Home.* n.d. http://rockislandpreservation.org/index.php/postcardsfromhome.

Renkes, Jim. *The Quad-Cities and The People.* Helena, Montana: Unicorn Publishing, Inc., 1994.

Rock Island Preservation Society. n.d. http://www.rockislandpreservation.org/.

Rock Island, Il - Official Website. n.d. http://www.rigov.org/index.aspx?nid=90.

Seusy, Kathleen. "Rock Island History: A Companion to the Architectural Walking Tours." *Rock Island Preservation Commission.* 1992. http://www.rigov.org/DocumentCenter/Home/View/1135.

Tillinghast, Benjamin Franklin. *Rock Island Arsenal: In Peace and In War.* Rock Island: Kessingger Publishing Rare Reprints, 1898.

U.S. Army Corps of Engineers Mississippi Valley Division. "Upper Mississippi River -- Illinois Waterway System Locks & Dams." *U.S. Army Corps of Engineers.* September 2009. http://www.mvr.usace.army.mil/brochures/documents/UMRSLocksandDams.pdf.

Walker, Brad. *Big Price -- Little Benefit: Proposed Locks on the Upper Mississippi and Illinois Rivers Are Not Economically Viable.* Nicollet Island Coalition, 2010.

"Welcome Home Celebration to the Sauk and Meskwauki People." Citizens to Preserve Black Hawk Park Foundation, 2010.

Wickstrom, George W. *The Town Crier.* Rock Island: J.W. Potter Company, 1948.

Wikipedia. n.d. www.wikipedia.org.

Wilderson, Isabel. *The Warmth of Other Suns.* New York: Vintage Books, 2010.

Wundram, Bill. *A Time We Remember: Celebrating a Century in Our Quad Cities.* Davenport: The Quad City Times, 1999.

YouTube. *President Eisenhower warns against the rise of military industrial complex speech.* 1961. http://www.youtube.com/watch?v=8y06NSBBRtY.

—. *Joseph McCarthy Army Hearings.* n.d. http://www.youtube.com/watch?v=Po5GIFba5Yg.

—. *President Kennedy.* n.d. http://www.youtube.com/watch?v=xBGadsd_IG0.

—. *President Roosevelt Day of Infamy Speech.* n.d. http://www.youtube.com/watch?v=3VqQAf74fsE.

—. *President Truman on U.S. Policy on Communism Speech.* 1961. http://www.youtube.com/watch?v=-FfdsHP1UWU.

—. *See It Now, Edward R. Murrow/Joe McCarthy.* n.d. http://www.youtube.com/watch?v=e4LZsDqSSfk.

Index

1

108th Regiment of United States Colored Troops, 179
1905, November 18, 261
1919 World Series, 316
1927 Mississippi River flood, 300, 366, 398
1st Iowa Infantry, 174

2

20th Century Fox, 375
21 Club, 317
2nd Texas Cavalry, 171
2nd U.S. Cavalry, 216

4

40-mile Desert, 139, 159

7

7th Cavalry, 213, 214, 215
7th Kansas Cavalry, 180, 212

9

9-Foot Channel Project, 390, 391, 392, 394, 395, 399
9th Illinois Cavalry, 129, 130, 201

A

Abilene, Kansas, 440
Acadia, 43
Accomack, 33
Acoqua, 116
Act of God, 393
Adam and Eve, 335
Adams, Abigail Smith, 60, 61, 314
Adams, Henry, 84
Adams, Jane, 356
Adams, John, 53, 60, 61, 62, 63, 64, 67, 314
Adams, John Quincy, 61, 91, 92, 123, 146
Adams, Samuel, 57
Adidas, 406
Adler, E.P., 386
Aegir, 27
Africa, 9, 10, 15, 173, 272, 297, 408
African Americans, 117, 161, 240, 266, 290, 295, 409
  black men, 6, 300, 328, 451
  black women, 295, 300
  blacks, 44, 49, 61, 90, 149, 167, 173, 182, 184, 193, 194, 237, 295, 299, 300, 310, 329, 366, 379, 405, 422, 444, 450, 452, 453, 459
  freemen, 30, 59, 61
  slaves, 5, 28, 31, 32, 57, 75, 117, 162, 297
Age of Entitlement, 58
Age of Technology, 241
Agency, 159
Aguilera, Christina, 79
Alamo, 180
Alaskan Territory, 341
Albany, New York, 48, 107, 108, 109, 224
Alcott, Amos Bronson, 165
Alexander the Great, 8, 17, 18
Algonquin Language, 12, 40, 70, 87, 116, 288
Ali, Mohammed, 6
Alien Enemies Act, 411
Allegheny College, 334
Allegheny, Pennsylvania, 241
Alleman, John George, 150
Allen, Gracie, 348
Allen, Steve, 445, 446
Allis-Chalmers Company, 385
Altizer, Thomas, 437
Alton, Illinois, 208
Aluminum Company of America, 360
Amana Colonies, 141, 142
Amana Refrigeration, 142
Amana Society, 141, 142
American Bandstand, 446
American Baptist Education Society, 271
American Birth Control League, 275
American Broadcasting Company, 445
American Civil Liberties Union, 335, 434
American Dream, 237, 422, 440
American Federation of Labor, 236, 245, 249, 250, 384, 402
American Football League, 235
American Fur Company, 112, 113
American League, 228, 304
American Legion, 304, 395
American Motor Company, 308
American Professional Football Conference, 233
American Railway Union, 291
American Red Cross, 189
American Revolution, 5, 44, 45, 46, 49, 50, 52, 53, 54, 55, 56, 57, 59, 60, 61, 64, 66, 74, 80, 81, 115, 171, 196, 211, 239, 402, 416, 419
American Savings Bank & Trust, 386
American Socialist Party, 250
American Temperance Society, 272, 273
Amos Alonzo Field, 413
Amsterdam, Holland, 31, 249, 377, 403
Anastasia, 24
Ancient Dark Age, 15, 18
Ancient Near East, 14
Andalusia, Illinois, 295, 384
Anderson, James, 242
Anderson, Kenny, 254
Anheuser-Busch Company, 214, 400
Ann Arbor, Michigan, 354
Antarctica, 293, 304
Anthony, Susan B., 267, 311, 314
anti-Communists, 427, 428, 429, 432
anti-Facists, 429
Anti-Saloon League, 355, 401

Apache Indians, 172
Apollo Theater, 349, 350
Apostles, 20
Appalachian Mountains, 42, 44, 152, 205
Appleton, Wisconsin, 193, 427
Appomattox Court House, Virginia, 183, 184, 185, 212
Arabia, 18
Arabian Peninsula, 9
Arapaho Indians, 213, 214
Archie Allen, 356, 358
Aristotle, 17, 18
Arizona Cardinals, 233
Arkansas River, 40, 209
Armstrong, John, 84
Armstrong, Johnny, 235
Armstrong, Louis, 342, 347
Army engineers, 186, 206, 208, 209, 217, 391, 393, 394, 395, 397, 399
Arsenal Courts, 412
Arsenal Golf Club, 252
Arsenal Island, 129, 218, 252, 256, 395
Arthur, Chester, 240
Artic Circle, 10
Articles of Confederation, 48, 53, 56, 57
Artista Piano Player, 195
Asher, Virginia Healey, 321
Ashkenazic Jews, 31
Ashland, Wisconsin, 40
Asia, 6, 9, 10, 15, 16, 23, 24, 410
Asia Minor, 15
Astaire, Fred and Adele, 348
Astor, John Jacob, 112, 113
Atchison, David Rice, 166
Athens, Greece, 16, 17, 56, 226
Atkinson, Christopher, 149, 259
Atkinson, Henry, 100
Atlanta, 182, 251
Atlantic Brewing Company, 276
Atlantic City, New Jersey, 308
Atomic Age, 413
Attila the Hun, 8, 21
Audubon, John James, 358
Auerbach, Red, 455, 456
Augustana College, 2, 3, 71, 200, 230, 252, 253, 254, 255, 258, 261, 279, 357, 359, 439, 455
 Ericson Field, 254
 Old Main, 253
Augustana College and Theological Seminary, 357
Augustana Handel Oratorio Society, 357
Augustana Historical Society, 357
Auschwitz, 408, 437
Austin High School, Chicago, 225
Austria, 275, 354, 434
Axis nations, 407, 408, 416

B

Babcock's Hall, 158
Baby Boom, 439
Baby Boomers, 442, 446, 450
Babylon, 15
Babylonia, 14, 15
Bad Axe, 105

Bad Lands, 215
Baffin Island, 34
Bakunin, Mikhail, 273
Ballin, Albert, 298
Baltimore, 77, 79, 107
Balts, 22
Baltzer, Terry, 448
Baltzer, William, 378
Banditti of the Prairie, 119
Bankers Panic of 1907, 238, 368
Barbados, 47, 51
barbarians, 21, 409
Barbecue Bob, 366
Barker, Jack, 349
Barnburners, 190
Barnett, Indian Town Joe, 147
Barrell, John, 114, 115
Barton, Clara, 158, 189
Baseball Hall of Fame, 229
Basketball Hall of Fame, 456
Baton Rouge, Louisiana, 55
Battle of Bull Run, 212, 243
Battle of Corinth, 18
Battle of Fallen Timbers, 67, 72
Battle of Fredericksburg, 177, 207
Battle of Gettysburg, 178, 179
Battle of Little Bighorn, 214
Battle of Palmito Ranch, Texas, 184
Battle of Spotsylvania, 182
Battle of Stillman's Run, 100, 101, 104, 105
Battle of Stono Ferry, 64
Battle of Washita River, 213
Baum, Frank, 270
Bavaria, 202, 417
Bay of Bengal, 9
Bay of Pigs Invasion, 448
Bay State, 61
Bazaar in Bombay, 260
Beale, Bob, 458
Bear River, 212
Bear Valley, Arizona, 35
Beardsley, Calvin, 351
Beat Generation, 435
Becker, Otto, 214
Beebe, William, 289
Beecher, Lyman, 272
Beehive House, 140
Beichman, Arnold, 428
Beiderbecke, Leon "Bix", 297, 298, 342
Beierlein, John, 150
Beierlein's Cooper Shop, 150, 151
Bel Aire, 284, 285, 328, 336
Belen, New Mexico, 337
Belgian American Brotherhood, 450
Belgium, 78, 142, 154, 302, 354, 403, 450
Bellow, Saul, 379
Bengston, John, 387, 412
Benny, Jack, 348
Benton, Thomas, 143
Berenson, Sendra, 225
Bering Land Bridge, 10, 11
Berkeley, California, 364
Berle, Milton, 445
Berlin Wall, 448
Berlin, Germany, 354, 404, 405, 406, 416, 426

465

Bermuda, 35, 393
Bernhardt, Sara, 221
Berwanger, Jay, 272
Berwick, Scotland, 36
Bessemer steel process, 241, 243
Bethany Protective Association, 357
Bettendorf, Iowa, 297, 361, 384, 420
Bettendorf, Joseph, 360
Bettendorf, William, 360
Bibb, Eric, 366
Bible, 20, 37, 72, 94, 335, 400
Bible, King James Version, 9
Biblical Lands, 13
Big Four (Associates), 181
Big Freeze, 11, 13
Big Game, 364
Big Hikes, 354, 355
Big Island, 84, 194, 400
Big Seven, 316
Big Ten Conference, 231, 271, 405, 458
Bill of Rights, 58, 431
Billburg, Anthony, 324, 325, 329, 330, 332, 333, 334, 335, 336
Billburg, Margaret, 325
Biograph Theater, 384
Bird, Larry, 456
Bird's Point, Missouri, 174
Birkeland, John, 453
Bix 7 Road Race, 235
Bix Beiderbecke Jazz Festival, 235
Black Angel, 6, 306, 307
Black Belt, Chicago, 295
Black Death, 23, 27, 293
Black Hawk, 3, 70, 71, 76, 81–84, 87, 88, 89, 97–110, 114, 116, 119, 120, 130, 144, 145, 150, 155, 168, 169, 200, 234, 250, 252, 256, 284, 361
Black Hawk Coal Mines, 194
Black Hawk Hiking Club, 354
Black Hawk Museum and Lodge, 399
Black Hawk Pow-Wow, 358
Black Hawk Prairie Club, 354
Black Hawk State Historic Site, 12, 194, 252, 357, 400
Black Hawk State Park. *See* Black Hawk State Historic Site
Black Hawk War, 100, 101, 105, 109, 118, 121, 180
Black Hills Gold Rush, 212
black list, 430
Black Panther Party, 449
Black Sea, 16
Black Sox scandal, 316, 326
Bladensburg Races, 78
Blaine, James, 240
Blake Specialty Company, 412
Blatz Brewing, 350
Blatz, Valentin, 276
Bliss, Ed, 434
Bloody Kansas, 163, 173, 175, 176
Bloomington, Iowa, 132
Blow, Peter, 117
Bly, Nellie, 313
Boggs, Lilburn, 136
Boleyn, Anne, 29
boll weevils, 210

Bolsheviks, 365, 419
Bonaparte, Napoleon, 74, 77, 80, 125, 145
Bond, Thomas, 48
Bonny and Clyde, 383
Bonus Bill, 381
Book of Genesis, 9, 335
Bosporus, 16
Boston, 46, 51, 53, 60, 127, 166, 226, 293, 316, 344, 422, 446
Boston Celtics, 455, 456
Boston Marathon, 235
Boston Red Sox, 344, 345
Botticelli, 28
Boulder Dam, 390
Brackett, Albert Gallatin, 129
Brackett, James, 129, 130
Brackett, James W., 129
Brackett, John Ely, 129
Brackett, Joseph Warren, 129
Brackett, William, 129
Brandle, Herman "Babe", 374
Brant, Joseph, 66
Brewer's Academy in New York, 276
Brick Streets Plan, 259
Bridger, Jim, 139
Bringer Inn, 451
British Band, 44, 45, 76, 79, 81, 82, 84
British Columbia, 10
British Isles, 21, 22
British Loyalists, 44, 66, 74, 81
British Parliament, 49, 50, 312
British Republic, 244
Brock, Isaac, 74
Bronze Age, 14, 15
Brooklyn Dodgers, 344, 383
Brooklyn, New York, 373
Brooks, William, 256
Brooks, William E., 254, 255, 256
Broth, the, 106
Brotman, Buster, 352
Brotman, Isadore, 352
Brotman, Michael, 351
Brown University, 231
Brown, John, 166, 167
Brown, Joseph, 123
Brown's Funeral Home, 451
Brownsville, Texas, 184
Bryan, William Jennings, 265, 269, 287, 289, 292, 335
Bubonic Plague, 23
Buchanan, James, 117, 167, 175
Buckley, George, 333, 334
Bucktown, 279, 320, 324
Budapest, Hungary, 417
Buffalo, Iowa, 278
Buffalo, New York, 141, 287
Buford Plow Company, 155
Buford, Charles, 155
Buford, James, 115
Buford, James Madison, 115
Buford, John, 115, 122, 154, 155, 175
Buford, John, Jr., 175, 176, 177, 178, 179
Buford, Lucy, 155
Buford, Napoleon, 115, 122
Buford, Thomas Jefferson, 115, 188

Bulgaria, 408, 417
Bull Moose Party, 291, 365
Bull, Ole, 189
Bunker Hill, 398
Bureau County, Illinois, 147
Bureau of Investigation, 428, 449, 450
Bureau of Prohibition, 318, 371
burial mounds, 12, 32, 55
Burkhard, Pvt. Oscar, 35
Burlington, Vermont, 304
Burma, 192
Burnett, John, 96
Burns, George, 348
Burns, Ken, 276
Burns, Lucy, 312, 314
Burns, Tommy, 326
Burroughs, William S., 435
Busch, Adolphus, 276
Bush, George W., 192
bushwhackers, 174
Buster Brown, 451
Butterworth, William, 306
Byron, Illinois, 227
Byzantium, 16, 19, *See* Constantinople

C

C.C. Knell, 222
Cable, Philander, 154
Cadillac Automobile Company, 302
Caesar, Julius, 18, 24, 333
Cahokia, Illinois, 55
Cain, 140, 335
Cairo, Illinois, 41
Cajuns, 43
Caldwell, Idaho, 303
Calhoun, John C., 91
California Golden Bears, 225, 364
California Territory, 66
Calvary Catholic Cemetery, 151
Calvin, John, 28
Camden Mills, 130, 195
Camden Road, 125, 130, 194
Camden Road Bridge, 194
Camp Doniphan, 423
Camp Hauberg, 356
Campbell, John, 81
Campbell's Island, 82, 216, 217, 218
Camus, Albert, 435, 437
Canada, 34, 43, 44, 49, 76, 78, 80, 81, 99, 138, 160, 205, 211, 244, 311, 317, 355
Canarsee Indians, 30, 31, 68
Canon of Kings, Ptolemy, 15
Canton Bulldogs, 233, 234, 235
Cantor, Eddie, 348
Cape Cod, 32
Cape Horn, 112, 160
Capone, Al, 318, 328, 338, 371, 372, 373
Caribbean, 32, 45, 161, 162, 311
Caribbean Islands, 45
Carlisle Indian School, 234, 235
Carnegie Corporation, 244
Carnegie Institute, 244
Carnegie Mellon University, 244
Carnegie Museum, 244

Carnegie Steel, 243
Carnegie, Andrew, 238, 241–45, 289, 365
Carnegie, Louise Whitfield, 243
Carnegie, Margaret, 243
carpetbaggers, 191
Carse & Ohlweiler, 4
Carson, Kit, 143
Carthage, Illinois, 138
Case, Charles, 98
Case, Jonah, 98, 120, 147
Case, Louden, 88, 89
Casper, Wyoming, 159
Cass, Lewis, 106, 107, 145
Castle on the Mississippi, The, 359
Castro, Fidel, 448
Cathar, 22
Catholic Church, 19, 20, 28, 150, 257, 322, 336, 367
    Eastern Orthodox, 19, 22, 23, 24
Cavalry Corps, 178
Cayuga Indians, 58
CBS Television, 348, 350, 434, 445
Cedar Rapids, Iowa, 179, 392, 400
Centennial Bridge, 388, 450
Centerville, Iowa, 324
Central Asia, 16
Central Europe, 237
Central Pacific Railroad of California, 220
Central Trust & Savings, 387
Cervin, Olof, 257
Chama, New Mexico, 286
Chance, Frank, 305
Chaplin, Charlie, 430
Charles II, 31
Charleston Harbor, 64, 168
Charleston, South Carolina, 46, 64, 168, 342, 374, 379, 422
Charter of Liberties, 22
Chartist movement, 244
Chernow, Ron, 246
Cherokee Indians, 77, 95, 96, 97
Cherry Valley, New York, 129
Cheshire, England, 85
Cheyenne Indians, 213, 214, 303
Cheyenne, Wyoming, 303
Chicago, 1, 7, 40, 71, 86, 120, 127, 129, 130, 140, 152, 153, 156, 157, 203, 220, 221, 233, 234, 236, 248, 251, 252, 253, 257, 260, 263, 269, 270, 276, 279, 282, 294, 295, 297, 300, 316, 317, 318, 319, 321, 322, 325, 326, 327, 338, 342, 349, 353, 359, 371, 372, 373, 379, 383, 384, 396, 406, 421, 435, 439, 448
Chicago & Rock Island Railroad, 152, 153, 156, 220
Chicago Addition Rock Island, 260
Chicago Athletic Association, 203
Chicago Bears, 1, 233, 234, 235, 236, 271
Chicago Cardinals, 233
Chicago Cubs, 228, 229, 233, 235, 304, 305, 308, 342, 361, 383, 384, 455
Chicago Democratic Press, 130, 153
Chicago Examiner, 317
Chicago Outfit, 318, 322, 338, 371
Chicago Portage, 40
Chicago Tribune, 130, 317, 425

467

Chicago White Sox, 304, 326, 344
Chicago White Stockings, 227, 320
Chicago World's Fair, 270
Chicago Zephers, 455
Chicago, Rock Island & Pacific Railroad Company, 221
Chickahominy River, 211
Chickasaw Indians, 95
Chicken Delight, 453, 454
Chicken-In-The-Basket, 453
Chief Little Rock, 214
Chief Wapello, 85
Chilton, Sam, 179
China, 9, 13, 192, 398, 410, 414, 419, 431, 432
China Sea, 9
Chippewa Indians, 71, 87, 103
Chippewa River, 41
Chippiannock Cemetery, 129, 199, 200, 357
Chiropractic History Time Line, 279
Choctaw Indians, 77, 95, 168
Christiaensen, Hendrick, 30
Christianity, 19, 21, 29, 33, 60, 95, 273, 436
Chugwater, Wyoming, 353
Church of Christ. *See* Mormons
Church of England, 29, 36
Church of Jesus Christ of Latter-day Saints. *See* Mormons
Church Square. *See* Spencer Square
Churchill, Winston, 414, 416, 417
Cicero, 17
Cicero, Illinois, 193
Cigarmakers' International Union Local 144, 249
Cincinnati Bengal's, 254
Cincinnati College, 175
Cincinnati Conservatory of Music, 375
Cincinnati, Ohio, 85, 185, 293, 375, 385
City Brewery, 276
City College of New York, 432
City of Mills, the, 154, 253
Civil Rights Act, 193, 295, 366
Civil Rights Movement, 448
Civil War, 32, 56, 92, 101, 119, 129, 130, 157, 160, 162, 169, 171, 172, 175, 176, 177, 178, 179, 180, 181, 184, 187, 189, 194, 201, 204, 207, 210, 211, 212, 216, 217, 219, 224, 226, 239, 242, 243, 245, 250, 251, 254, 266, 267, 269, 273, 316, 413, 450
Civilian Conservation Corps, 379, 383, 399
Claim House, 116
Clay Cassius. *See* Ali, Mohammed
Clay, Henry, 91, 92, 146, 428
Clean Air Act, 261
Clemann & Salzmann, 222
Clemann, Hans, 222
Clemens, Samuel. *See* Mark Twain
Cleveland Bulldogs, 235
Cleveland Indians (NFL), 235
Cleveland, Grover, 219, 240, 241, 268, 288, 423
Cleveland, Harry H., 332
Cleveland, Ohio, 404, 444
Clinton, Iowa, 296, 307
Clock Tower Building, 187, 395
Clovis Culture, 11
Coal Valley House, 197
Coal Valley, Illinois, 197, 198, 384

Cockspur Island, Georgia, 122
Cody, Isaac, 136, 163, 166
Cody, Julia, 164
Cody, Mary Ann Laycock, 136
Cody, William "Buffalo Bill", 136, 163, 164, 180, 215, 216, 221, 270
Cold War, 365, 419, 426, 448
Cole, Nat King, 347
Colfax, Schuyler, 158
Colligan, John, 333
Colonel Sanders Kentucky Fried Chicken, 453
Colonial Period, 35, 38, 87, 161
Colorado Gold Rush, 212
Colorado River, 390
Colored Advisory Commission, 366
Columbia, 29
Columbia Broadcasting Company, 445
Columbia Park addition Rock Island, 256
Columbia River, 112
Columbia University, 312
Columbian World's Fair. *See* Chicago World's Fair
Columbus, Christopher, 5, 25, 26, 27, 28, 35, 41, 256, 269, 459
Comanche Indians, 172
Commander In Chief, 208, 434
Commerce, Illinois, 136
Communism, 321, 403, 419, 426, 427, 434, 435, 448
Communist Party, 419, 431, 434
Communists, 247, 257, 419, 427, 428, 429, 430, 431, 432, 433, 435, 440, 448, 449
Community of True Inspiration, 141
Compromise of 1850, 163
Compromise of 1877, 193
Compton, Arthur, 413, 414
Compton, Todd, 134
Comstock, Anthony, 428
Comstock, Medicine Bill", 215
Concord, Massachusetts, 51, 53, 165
Confederacy, 67, 76, 161, 168, 171, 172, 174, 180, 181, 182, 188
Confederate States, 168, 180, 187
Congress of Industrial Organizations, 402
Congressional Union, 313
Conner, Patrick, 212
Conquistadors, 29
Conrad, Joseph, 305
Considine, Bob, 433
Consolidated Foods, 454
Constantine, 19
Constantine the Great, 16
Constantinople, 16, 22, 24
Constitutional Convention, 58, 123
Container Corporation of America, 412
Continental Congress, 51, 53, 62, 80
Continental Oil (Conoco), 246
Coolidge, Calvin, 341, 361, 362, 363, 364, 367, 369, 370, 381, 390, 391
Cooperstown, New York, 379
Copenhagen, Denmark, 113
Cora Miskel, 349
Cornwallis, Lord, 56
Correll, Charles, 349, 350
Corrupt Bargain, 193, 239

Corydon, Indiana, 68
Costello, Frank, 317
Cosu, Alice, 314
Cotton Club, 326
Council Bluffs, Iowa, 220
Council of Economic Advisors, 369, 382
Council of Fifty, The, 138
County Cork, Ireland, 302
Courthouse Square, 259
Coventry Apartments, 156
Cowan, Dave, 456
Cox, Channing, 363
Cox, James M., 294
Cox, Thomas, 320, 327, 330, 337, 338
Cram Field, 338
Crawford, William H., 91
Crazy Horse, 214
Crazy Years, 322, 403
Cream of Wheat, 271
Credit Island, 41, 81, 112, 115, 387
Creek Indians, 75, 77, 79, 95
Creston, Iowa, 193
Crocker, Charles, 181
Crocker, Sewall, 303
Crockett, Davy, 77, 95, 97
crossroads of the nation, 112, 181, 204, 253, 281, 307, 385, 387
Crusades, 22, 23
Csatary, Laszlo, 417
Cuba, 27, 145, 163, 169, 272, 289, 448
Cuban Missile Crisis, 448
Cubs Park, 233, 234
Cullen-Harrison Act, 400
Cumberland River, 300
Cumberland Valley, 178
Curse of the Bambino, 345
Custer, Elizabeth "Lizzie" Bacon, 212, 214
Custer, George, 211, 212, 213, 214, 215
Custer's Last Stand, 214
Custis, Mary, 171
Cyrene, Libya, 20
Cyrus the Great, 15
Czechoslovakia, 403, 419
Czolgosz, Leon, 287

D

da Vinci, Leonardo, 28
Dairy Queen, 453, 454
Dakota Indians, 13
Dakota Territory, 212
Daley, Richard, 448
Dalitz, Moe, 316
Dallas Mavericks, 456
Dana, Charles, 177
dance marathon, 374, 375
Danforth, J.B., 282
Darius the Great, 16
Dark Ages, 66
Darrow, Clarence, 334, 335, 336
Dart Hall, 158, 188, 189, 216
Dart, Henry, 157, 158
Dartmouth, 129
Darwin, Charles, 335, 436
Dassler, Adi, 406

Daugherty, Harry, 339, 340
Daughters of the American Revolution, 402, 429
Davenport Bank & Trust Co., 386, 387
Davenport Civic Federation, 324
Davenport Commercial Club, 203
Davenport Daily Times, 232
Davenport Ferry, 115
Davenport Knickerbockers, 229
Davenport Ministerial Association, 323
Davenport River Rats, 229
Davenport Riversides, 229
Davenport, Bailey, 148, 151, 194, 227, 229, 250, 252, 254, 263, 279, 346
Davenport, Elizabeth, 85
Davenport, George, 85, 86, 89, 97, 105, 112, 113, 114, 117, 119, 120, 125, 126, 262
   Saganosh, 86
Davenport, L'oste, 85, 118
Davenport, Margret Lewis, 85
Davenport, Mary Grace, 148
David Hirsch & Company, 249
Davis, Emeal, 327, 328, 337
Davis, Jefferson, 106, 168, 170, 172, 184
Davis, Jim, 5
Davis, Jimmy, 4
Davis, John W., 362
Davis, Sarah, 169
Daynovsky, Benny, 298
Dayton, William, 146
Daytona Beach Raceway, 304
De Bow's Review, 168
de Champlain, Samuel, 33
de Coubertin, Pierre, 16
de facto segregation, 193
de jure segregation, 193
de la Mothe Cadillac, Antoine, 74
de La Salle, Robert, 41
de Quesada, Jimenez, 29
de Soto, Hernando, 40, 209
de Torquemada, Tomás, 25
Dearborn Independent, The, 345
Debs, Eugene, 291, 292
Decatur Commodores, 228
Decatur Staleys, 233
Declaration of Independence, 51, 53, 56, 59, 60, 62, 63, 67
DeClerk, Frank, 235
Deere & Company, 211, 256, 261, 278, 306, 327, 359, 384, 385, 389, 439
Deere Gentleman's Roadsters, 306
Deere, Charles, 129, 263, 306, 308
Deere, John, 129, 154, 204, 306, 308
Delaware Indians, 44
Democratic Party, 92, 117, 146, 190, 201, 269, 312, 334, 361, 366, 373, 378, 402, 419, 423, 434
Democratic Progressives, 265
Democratic-Republican Party, 92
Denkmann Paper Company, 356
Denkmann, Catherine Bloedel, 196, 199
Denkmann, Frederick (F.C.A.), 149, 200, 196–201, 204, 244, 353
Denmark, 113, 403
Denver, Colorado, 316, 340
Deo Vindice, 182
Des Moines Brewing Company, 203

469

Des Moines Rapids, 83, 84, 99, 122, 136, 296
Des Moines River, 41, 84, 87, 109
Des Moines, Iowa, 2, 83, 84, 88, 99, 109, 125, 136, 202, 203, 217, 322, 324
Des Plaines, Illinois, 453
Descartes, 60
Detroit, 38, 76, 109, 231, 241, 301, 302, 306, 309, 371, 385, 439
Detroit Automobile Company, 302
Detroit Tigers, 305
DeVaught's IGA, 1
Devil, the, 20, 262, 436
Dewar's Scotch, 447
Dewey, John, 267
Dewey, Thomas, 267, 425, 426
Diamond Lady Riverboat Casino, 297
Diana, 19
Dickinson, Charles, 93, 94
Didrikson, Babe, 403
Dillinger, John, 383, 384, 428
DiMaggio, Joe, 443
disco, 446
Disney, Walt, 270, 429
Distinguished Flying Cross, 427, 428
Dixiecrats, 366
Dock Street Theatre, 379
Doctrine of Plurality of Wives, The, 137, 138
Dodge, Horace, 304
Dodge, John, 304
Doheny, Edward, 340
Don Quixote, 354
Donner Party, 139, 220, 303
Donner Pass, California, 308
Doubleday Field, 379
Doubleday, Abner, 224
Douglas Park, 229, 230, 231, 232, 233, 234, 235, 236
Downtown Davenport Association, 235
Dr. Mick's Traveling Medicine Show, 349
Drake University, 232
Draught House, 395
Drew, John, 221
Driscoll, Jimmy, 349
driving on the right, 66
Drost, Dan, 333, 334
du Pont, Eleuthère Irénée, 401
du Pont, Pierre, 368
Dubuque, Iowa, 324
Duck Creek Chain of Rapids, 218
duck's butt, 444
Duke of York, 31
Duncan's Business College, 353
Dunfermline, Scotland, 241
Dunne, Finley Peter, 435
Dunsmuir, California, 341
dust bowl, 368
Dutch East India Company, 30
Dutch Inn, 453
Dutch Reform church, 31
Dutch West Indies Company, 30, 31

E

E Pluribus Unum, 134
Eads, James, 207, 208

Eagle, Edward L., 332
Eames, Charles, 255
East Coast, 33, 43, 46, 106, 107, 127, 131, 207, 248, 316, 317, 426
East Moline, 6, 114, 254, 359, 360, 413, 420
Eastern Europe, 23, 237, 298
Eastman Kodak, 304
Ebenezer, New York, 141
Economy Act, 381
Edina, Minnesota, 193
Edison General Electric Company, 270
Edison Illuminating Company, 302
Edison, Thomas, 270, 287, 300, 301, 302, 305
Edwardsville, Illinois, 121
Efficiency Movement, 365
Egan's Rats, 371
Eggnog Riot, 169
Egypt, 13, 14, 15, 192, 287
Eighteenth Amendment, 276, 292, 310, 311, 317, 320, 340, 361, 372, 400, 401
Einstein, Albert, 305, 413, 415, 437
Eisenhower, Dwight, 4, 234, 308, 374, 406, 432, 433, 434, 435, 440, 441, 442, 446, 447
Eisenhower, Edgar, 441
Elbe River, 202
Electoral College, 58, 91
Elks Lodge, 203
Ellington, Duke, 342
Elliot Bay, 341
Ellis Island, 237, 298, 328
Ellison, Ralph, 379
Elms Hotel, 425
Emancipation Proclamation, 162, 181, 187
Emerald City, 209
Emergency Banking Act, 380
Emerson, John, 116
Emerson, Ralph Waldo, 158, 165, 166, 189, 216
Emory University, 437
Empire State Building, 304, 368
Enemy Alien Registration, 293, 428
Energy Brick Company, 259
England, 5, 18, 21, 22, 26, 29, 30, 31, 32, 33, 34, 35, 37, 42, 45, 46, 47, 48, 49, 50, 51, 62, 74, 80, 85, 118, 126, 136, 137, 144, 165, 181, 237, 244, 272, 312, 314, 315, 354, 408, 459
Englewood High School, 231
Environmental Policy Act, 261
Era of Good Feelings, 80
Eretria, Greece, 16
Ericson, Charles, 253, 254
Erie County, New York, 241
Erie, Pennsylvania, 196
Erik the Red, 26
Eriksson, Leif, 26, 27, 41
Eriksson, Thorwald, 26
Europe, 10, 13, 14, 15, 16, 18, 20, 21, 22, 23, 24, 26, 28, 29, 30, 36, 42, 48, 74, 75, 80, 137, 192, 196, 241, 242, 287, 288, 293, 294, 298, 299, 315, 342, 344, 349, 354, 365, 403, 405, 407, 408, 413, 416, 422, 439, 440, 441
European Recovery Plan, 441
Evans, L., 197
Evanston, Illinois, 157, 401, 439
Evers, Johnny, 305
Excelsior Springs, Missouri, 425

existentialists, 166, 437

F

Faber College, 267
Fair Labor Standards Act, 380
Faith, Percy, 444
Falfurrias, Texas, 338
Fall, Albert, 340
Falls of the Ohio, 205
Far West, Missouri, 135
Farm Implement Capitl of the World, 361
Farm Security Administration, 380
Farnham, Charles Russel, 114
Farnham, Russel, 112, 113, 114, 120
Farnham, Susan Bosseron, 114
Farnhamsburg, 114, 115, 120, 131, 260
Farr, Gary, 279
Fascism, 419, 426
Fascists, 257, 345, 440
Fast Swimming Fish, 106
Faulkner, William, 343, 366
Federal Deposit Insurance Corporation, 380, 383
Federal Private Housing Initiative, 347
Federal Reserve, 368, 369, 382
Federal Reserve System, 368, 369
Federal Writers Project, 379
Federalist Papers, 58, 73
Federation of Organized Trades and Labor Unions, 249
Feigner, Eddie, 230
Feltex Corporation, 412
Ferdinand, Franz, 275
Fermi, Enrico, 413, 414
Ferris Wheel, 271
Ferris, George, 271
Fertile Crescent, 14, 15, 18, 19
Field, Marshall, 271
Fields, W.C., 348
Fifth Amendment, 433
Fifth Ward Democratic Club, 281
Fiji, 10
Fillmore, Millard, 145, 146, 175
Financial Times, 369
Finger Lakes, 38
Finkelstein, Henry, 453, 454
Finkelstein, Isador, 453
Fio-Rito, Ted, 375
First Amendment, 134, 286, 291, 355
First Continental Congress, 61
First National Bank of Rock Island, 154
Fisher, Eddie, 444
Fitzgerald, Ella, 347
Fitzgerald, F. Scott, 342, 343, 370
Fitzgerald, John "Honey Fitz", 446
Fitzgerald, Zelda Sayre, 344
Fitzpatrick, "Broken Hand", 143
Five Civilized Tribes, 95
Fixico, Donald, 213
Flagler, Henry, 238
Flanagan, Walter, 233
Florence, Italy, 28
Florida Keys, 379
Floyd, Pretty Boy, 382, 428
Flying Wallendas, The, 445

Fogg, Phileas, 313
Food and Drug Act, 290
Football Hall of Fame, 138, 254
Ford Flivver, 345
Ford Motor Company, 309, 345, 359, 418
Ford, Clara Ala Bryant, 302
Ford, Edsel, 302
Ford, Henry, 302, 304, 308, 309, 345, 367
Ford, Thomas, 98
Forest Park, Illinois, 429
Formosa, 410
Fort Amsterdam, 31
Fort Armstrong, 84, 85, 86, 87, 90, 98, 100, 105, 106, 109, 113, 114, 116, 117, 118, 127, 128, 130
Fort Bridger, 139, 164
Fort Crittenden, 163, 164, 176
Fort Detroit, 74, 75, 76
Fort Donelson, 171
Fort Harmar, Ohio, 68, 70
Fort Laramie, 139
Fort Leavenworth, Kansas, 163
Fort Lincoln, North Dakota, 214
Fort Madison, Iowa, 202
Fort Meigs, 76, 79
Fort Mims, 75, 77
Fort Monmouth, New Jersey, 432
Fort Monroe, 107, 108, 122
Fort Montrose, 132
Fort Oglethorpe Internment Camp, 293
Fort Pitt, 43
Fort Riley, Kansas, 212, 293
Fort Shelby, 82
Fort St. Louis, 70
Fort St. Paul, 122
Fort Stephenson, 76
Fort Sumter, 162, 168, 170, 172, 180, 224
Fort Wool, Virginia, 122
Forty-niners, 220
Foster, Abby Kelley, 311
Fourt, Cathrine, 85
Fox. *See* Meskwaki Indians
Fox River, 38, 395
Foxwoods Casino, 36
France, 21, 22, 23, 40, 41, 42, 43, 48, 50, 54, 65, 66, 80, 137, 142, 184, 191, 237, 275, 292, 293, 403, 408, 417, 423, 437
Franciscan Medical Center, 152, 385
Franciscan Sisters, 151, 203
Franco-Prussian War, 191, 238
Frank's Furniture, 1
Frankfurter, Felix, 291
Franklin, Benjamin, 46, 49, 46–51, 54, 56, 57, 58, 59, 60, 222, 305
Franklin, Deborah Read, 47
Franklin, Francis Folger, 47
Franklin, James, 46
Franklin, Josiah, 46
Franklin, Sarah, 47
Franklin, Sir John, 34
Frank's Foundry, 453
Franks, Bobby, 334
Frazee, Harry, 344
Frazier, E. Franklin, 300
Fred Mueller, 332
Frederick Avenue, Detroit, 295

Free Silver, 269
Free Soil Party, 145, 146, 163
Freed, Alan, 444
Freedom Riders, 5
Freemasons, 49, 195
Frémont, John C., 143, 146, 170
French fries, 29
French Intervention, the, 184
Freud, Sigmund, 341
Friedman, Milton, 364, 368
Frobisher, Sir Martin, 34
Fuller, Margaret, 165
Fulton, Illinois, 307

G

Gabel, Bill, 330, 331, 332, 333, 337, 338
Gable, Clark, 425
Gaines, Edmund, 98, 99, 104
Galbraith, Bonnie, 387
Galbraith, Robert, 387, 388, 412
Gale, Ellen, 189
Galena, Illinois, 86, 88, 89, 105, 119, 133, 170, 255, 261
Galesburg, Illinois, 175, 259, 322, 338
Galileo, 28
Galloway, James, 72
Galveston, Texas, 162, 180, 298, 299
Garbo, Greta, 375
Gardner, E.E., 286
Garfield, James, 239, 240, 295
Garland, John, 108
Gary, Indiana, 241
Gates, Susa Young, 138
Gaza, 15
Gehrig, Lou, 101
Geifman's Grocery Store, 385
Gellman Manufacturing, 412
General Electric Company, 270, 300
General Mills, 133
General Motors, 304, 402
General Survey Act of 1824, 122
Genghis Kahn, 23
Genovese crime family, 318
George III, 44, 45, 55, 56, 65, 66, 80, 85
George King. *See* Davenport, George
George, Elizabeth, 36
Georgetown (Washington D.C.), 339
Gerard, Joseph, 147
German Demokrat, 323
German Trust and Savings Bank, 203
German Turner Society, 174
Germany, 155, 191, 196, 197, 237, 238, 276, 315, 345, 354, 365, 402, 403, 407, 408, 410, 413, 416, 423, 426, 434
Gettysburg, Pennsylvania, 178, 179
GI Bill, 422, 439
Gibbon, John, 175, 176
Gilbert, Village of, 360
Gilded Age, 238, 239, 241, 250, 260, 268, 272
Ginsberg, Allen, 435
Glanvill, Joseph, 37
Glasgow, Scotland, 355
God, 9, 18, 20, 22, 23, 24, 29, 32, 34, 37, 48, 60, 63, 81, 88, 114, 134, 135, 138, 140, 141, 154, 165, 182, 211, 221, 244, 245, 246, 257, 274, 276, 310, 315, 325, 329, 335, 382, 409, 410, 420, 426, 436, 437, 448
God's Word, 20
Gold Standard, 269
Goldberg, Rube, 395
golden age of economic prosperity, 345
Golden Age of Exploration, 25
Golden Age of U.S. Army Corps of Engineers, 392
golden age of vaudeville, 374
Golden Era of Baseball, 344
Golden State Warriors, 456
Goldman, Emma, 274, 429
Goldman, Stanley, 348
Gompers, Samuel, 245, 249
Gompers, Sophia Julian, 249
Gordon, John, 182
Gordon, Waxey, 316
Gordon's Gin, 447
Gore, Al, 192
Gosden, Freeman, 349, 350
Government Bridge, 86, 115, 218, 220, 263, 279, 384, 387, 420
Government Island, 118, 154, 186
Gowen, Franklin, 247, 248
Grable, Betty, 375, 442, 443
Graham Cotton Factory, 194
Graham, Carl, 307
Grand Old Party, 192
Grand Union flag, 59
Grange, Red, 236
Granger, Gordon, 162
Grant High School, Cedar Rapids, 400
Grant, Ulysess S., 214
Grant, Ulysses S., 144, 170, 171, 174, 182, 183, 185, 189–92, 208, 219, 239
Grant's Meat Market, 197
Great Basin, 139, 159, 160, 175, 212, 213, 409
Great Britain, 36, 42, 43, 50, 57, 60, 66, 74, 79, 95, 137, 168, 275, 408, 417, 444, 447
Great Depression, 203, 222, 238, 239, 246, 247, 290, 296, 309, 336, 360, 364, 367, 368, 369, 370, 371, 374, 380, 382, 383, 384, 385, 387, 388, 389, 390, 391, 399, 403, 412, 420, 422, 423, 424, 439, 440, 442, 450
Great Famine, 23
Great Lakes, 40, 43, 50, 77, 87, 113, 157, 241, 250, 295, 299, 315
Great Outer Sea, 18
Great Plains, 10, 11, 130, 213, 368
Great War, 315, 373, 407, 409, 421
Greater Quad City Area, 361
Greece, 13, 16, 18
Greeley, Horace, 152, 190, 191
Greeley, Margaret Cheney, 190
Green Bay Packers, 233, 234, 235, 236
Green Bay, Wisconsin, 234, 236
Green Mountain Boys Band, 119, 120
Greene, Israel, 167
Greenglass, David, 432
Greenspan, Alan, 382
Greenwich Village, 435
Griffith Observatory, 379
Grimm, Charlie, 383
Grinnell College, 230, 232

Grinnell Pioneers, 232
Gris, Juan, 342
Guiteau, Charles, 240
Gulf of Alaska, 10
Gulf of Mexico, 41, 205, 210, 211, 393
Guyer, Edward, 254, 255, 258
Guyer, S.S., 197
Gypsies, 408

H

Haege, Thomas, 332, 333
Hagemeister Park, 234
Hagia Sophia cathedral, 24
Haight-Ashbury District, 435, 449
Hake, Otis, 400
Hakes, David, 197
Halas, George, 233
Haley, Bill, 444
Halpern's Department Store, 451
Hamburg, Germany, 202
Hamilton, Illinois, 126
Hamm, Theodore, 276
Hammatt, E.S., 226
Hammurabi, 14
Hannibal, Missouri, 209, 210
Hardin, Louis "Moondog", 444
Harding, Warren, 238, 294, 339, 340, 341, 361, 362, 364, 365, 381, 391
Harlem Globetrotters, 406
Harlem, New York, 31, 275, 295, 326, 349
Harmar Treaty, 68
Harper Opera House, 221, 222, 281, 348
Harper, Ben, 188, 189, 197, 221, 222, 257
Harper's Ferry of the West, 186
Harpers Ferry, Virginia, 166, 167, 172
Harper's New Monthly Magazine, 216
Harris Pizza, 352, 353
Harrison Land Act, 67, 68
Harrison Narcotics Tax Act, 329
Harrison, Anna Symmes, 67
Harrison, Benjamin, 288, 365
Harrison, William Henry, 66, 67, 68, 69, 70, 72, 75, 81, 127, 146, 268
Hart, Archie, 286
Harvard, 48, 129, 165, 287, 289, 369, 413, 446, 447
Harvey, Jerry, 451
Haskell County, Kansas, 293
Hastings Street, Detroit, 295
Hauberg Civic Center, 358
Hauberg Indian Museum, 3, 399
Hauberg, Catherine, 353
Hauberg, John, 252, 358, 353–59, 399
Hauberg, John, Jr., 358
Hauberg, Susanne Denkmann, 353, 356, 358, 450
Havana, Cuba, 289, 317
Haver, June, 375, 376, 442
Hawthorne, California,, 194
Hayes, Lucy Webb, 239
Hayes, Rutherford B., 192, 193, 239, 240
Hayworth, Rita, 442
Hearst, William Randolph, 292
Hebrew Bible, 15
Hebrew Temple, 451

Hefner, Hugh, 442, 443
Heidegger, Martin, 341
Hein's Billiard Saloon, 158
Heisman Trophy, 272
Helios, 19
Helsingfors, Finland, 356
Hemings, Sally, 63
Hemingway, Ernest, 342, 343, 344
Hennepin Canal, 219, 220, 259, 399
Hennepin Canal Parkway, 220
Hennepin, Illinois, 219
Henning, Arthur, 425
Henry Ford Company, 302
Henry VIII, 29
Hepburn, Katharine, 375, 430
heretics, 19, 22
Herky, 232
Herodotus, 17
Herrick's General Store, 197
Herrold, Charles, 350
Hershey Bar, 271
Hesse, Germany, 141
Hill, James, 200, 201
Himalayas, 18
Hines, Earl, 342
Hinze, Carl, 451
hip-hop, 446
hippies, 435
Hirohito, 415, 418
Hiroshima, Japan, 414, 418, 426
Hirsch, David, 249
Hitler, Adolph, 345, 402, 403, 404, 405, 408, 410, 423, 426, 434
Hoag, Steve, 235
Hobart, Garret, 287
Hoboken, New Jersey, 224
Holland, 30, 354
Holland's Rock Island Directory, 202
Hollywood High School, 375
Hollywood Ten, 430
Hollywood, California, 35, 284, 348, 375, 376, 427, 429, 430, 431, 443, 446
Holmgren, Dale, 354
Holocaust, 408, 437
Holsapple, George "Crimps", 333, 334, 336
Holy Land, 22, 192
Homewood, Iowa, 141
Homo sapiens, 13
Hood, Robin, 372
Hoover,, 366, 367, 370
Hoover, Herbert, 265, 321, 340, 341, 364–70, 377, 378, 381, 384, 390, 391, 402, 447
Hoover, J. Edgar, 293, 382, 383, 427, 428, 430, 435, 449, 450
Hopkins, Mark, 181
Hopkinson, Francis, 59
Hopper, Hedda, 430
Horse Lake Ranch, 286
Horseshoe Bend, 77, 79
House Un-American Activities Committee, 427, 429, 430, 431, 443
Houston, Sam, 77, 142, 143, 180
Howell, Varina, 169
Huber, Amelia, 202, 203
Huber, Cathariana Koehler, 202

Huber, Ignatz, 202, 276
Huber, Joseph, 277
Huber, Otto, 202, 203, 276
Huber's Beer Garden, 277
Hudetz, John, 235
Hudson Bay, 41, 58
Hudson River, 30, 38
Hudson, Henry, 30, 34
Hughes, Charles Evans, 273, 292
Hull House, 356
Humanism, 27
Humanist, 244
Humphreys, Andrew, 177, 178, 207, 208, 209, 216, 392, 394, 399
Hundred Years' War, 23
Hungary, 408, 417, 419
Hunkers, 190
Huns, 19, 21
Hunt Expedition, 112
Huntington, Collis, 181, 243
Hurricane Katrina, 209
Hutchinson, Thomas, 50
Hyde Park, 31
Hyde Park High School, 231
Hyde Park, Illinois, 270
Hyman's Furniture, 348

I

Ice Age, 10, 11, 13, 33
Iinternational Harvester Farmall, 388
Illiniwek, 12, 13, 39, 40, 393
Illinois River, 10, 40, 41, 56, 86, 219, 307
Illinois State Mental Hospital, 359
Illinois Territory, 88
Illinois Waterway Project, 396
Illinois Wesleyan College, 230
Illinois, Indiana, Iowa League, 228
Immigration Act, 238
Immigration Restriction League, 238
Imperial Cult, 18
In God We Trust, 7, 289
Independence High School, 423
Independence, Missouri, 423
India, 5, 9, 13, 14, 18, 23, 27, 30, 415
Indian Agency, 118
Indian Boundary, 71
Indian Confederation, 72, 74, 76
Indian Ocean, 9, 18
Indian Relocation Act, 1830, 94, 95, 97, 98
Indian Removal, 94, 97, 106, 107, 161
Indian Reorganization Act, 1934, 110
Indian Reserve, 44, 45, 54, 66
Indian Territory, 68, 71, 96, 97, 102, 213, 269
Indian wars, 137, 213
Indian Wars, 35, 187
Indiana Territory, 68, 71
Indianapolis Speedway, 307
Indonesia, 9
Industrial Revolution, 136
Inquisition, 23, 24, 28, 36
Intellectual Declaration of Independence, 165
International Council of Religious Education, 355
International Harvester Company, 261, 359, 360, 385, 412
International Harvester Farmall, 1, 2, 261, 264, 359, 412, 413, 439
International Olympic Committee, 403
International Softball Congress' World Fastpitch Softball Tournament, 230
International Workingmen's Association, 249
Interstate Commerce Act, 219
Interstate Highway System, 308
Iowa Alcoholic Beverage Division, 324
Iowa City, 142, 158, 159, 230, 231, 232, 384
Iowa Hawkeyes, 225, 230, 231, 232
Iowa- Illinois Memorial Bridge, 278, 421
Iowa River, 89, 109, 141
Iowa Soldier's Orphans Home, 320
Iowa State University, 232
Iowa Territory, 87, 89, 97, 105
Iowa's Gallant Seventh, 174
Ireland, 64, 237, 246
Irish Gang, 318
Iron Age, 15, 18, 21
Iron Curtain, 416
Ironwood, Michigan, 193
Iroquois Indians, 13, 38, 54, 58
Irving, Julius, 456
Israel, 15, 167, 299, 417, 424, 442
Istanbul, 16
Italian Broadway Mob, 317
Italy, 18, 21, 22, 408
Ivan the Terrible, 24

J

J.I. Case Company, 155, 261, 385, 412
Jabbar, Kareem Abdul, 456
Jackson County, Missouri, 135
Jackson, Andrew, 64, 66, 77, 79, 89, 91, 92, 93, 98, 107, 115, 124, 131, 146, 288
Jackson, Bertha, 302, 304
Jackson, Horatio, 302, 304, 308
Jackson, Hugh, 64
Jackson, Joseph "Shoeless Joe", 326, 344
Jackson, Rachel Donelson Robards, 64, 93, 94
Jackson, Robert, 64
Jacobson, Edward, 423, 424
Jamaica, 27
Jamaican Indians, 27
James "Dude" Bowen, 332
James Fort, 33
Jamestown, 33, 171
Japan, 10, 192, 407, 409, 410, 414, 415, 416, 417, 419, 440
Jay, John, 57, 58
jazz, 297, 342
Jazz Age, 342, 343, 344
Jefferson Barracks, Missouri, 98, 106, 168
Jefferson College, 169
Jefferson, Martha Wayles Skelton, 63
Jefferson, Thomas, 51, 57, 59, 62, 63, 65, 68, 69, 84, 91, 95, 377
Jeffries, James, 326
Jennings, Paul, 78
Jerusalem, 22, 135
Jesus Christ, 12, 13, 18, 19, 20, 27, 28, 40, 135, 138, 151, 437, 449
Jewish Center's Educational Center, 373

Jewish Free School, 249
Jim Crow laws, 193, 295, 459
John Barrell House, 114
John Deere's Town, 154
John Holt Boatyard, 200
John Looney, 280, 282, 286, 318, 327, 329, 330, 332, 333, 336, 337, 338, 351, 355, 373
John Petty, 197
Johns Hopkins Medical School, 343
Johns Hopkins University, 432
Johnson, Albert Sidney, 175
Johnson, Andrew, 187, 188, 193, 212, 268
Johnson, Dale, 234, 235, 236
Johnson, Jack, 326
Johnson, Joseph, 211
Johnson, Lyndon, 448
Johnson, Marques, 456, 457
Johnson, Samuel, 273
Joliet State Penitentiary, 336, 338
Joliet, Illinois, 453
Jolliet, Louis, 39, 40, 114, 393, 394
Jones, Geraldine, 437
Jones, Killer, 437
Jonesborough, Tennessee, 64
Joyce, James, 342
Juicy Fruit Gum, 271
Juneteenth Day, 162
Jung, Patrick, 106

K

Kahlke Boatyard, 115, 202
Kahlke, John, 202
Kahlke, Peter, 202
Kaiser Wilhelm, 276
Kai-shek, Chiang, 414, 432
Kansas City Massacre, 382
Kansas City, Missouri, 297, 316, 340, 423
Kansas Pacific Railroad, 215
Kansas Territory, 163, 166
Karlowa, Robert, 350, 351
Karmelkorn, 454
Karpis, Creepy, 428
KCBS, 350
Keelboats, 84
Keller, Helen, 171, 312
Kellogg House, 384
Kellogg, Frank, 286
Kellogg's Grove, 100
Kelly, M. R., 148
Kelly, Machine Gun, 428
Kemmerer, T.H., 323
Kendrick, Alexander, 434
Kennedy, Bobby, 6, 443, 449
Kennedy, Jacqueline, 93, 443, 447, 449
Kennedy, John, 6, 49, 93, 443, 446–49
Kennedy, Joseph, 446
Kennedy, Rose Fitzgerald, 446
Keokuk, 76, 81, 99, 109, 110, 114, 116, 141
Keokuk, Iowa, 132
Kerouac, Jack, 354, 435
Key, Francis Scott, 79, 344
Keynes, John Maynard, 381
Keynesian theory, 381
Keystone Bridge Works, 243

Kiao-Chow, Manchuria, 272
Kickapoo Indians, 86, 89
Kierkegaard, Soren, 436, 437
Kiev, Russia, 23, 298
Kimble, Spencer W., 140
King and His Court, The, 230
King Ferdinand, 24
King Gustav, 234
King Henry I, 21
King Philip II, 17
King, Martin Luther, Jr., 449
Kingdom of Judah, 15
Kinney, John, 90
Kiowa, Kansas, 274
Kirtland, Ohio, 135, 142, 147
Klingensmith, Norman, 176
Knights of Pythias, 257
Knox College, 175, 201, 230, 259
Knox County, Illinois, 259
Knox Manual Labor College, 175
Knox, Henry, 57, 95
Knox, John, 143
Knoxville Road, 56
Koch, Christopher, 329
Korea, 10, 410, 419, 433, 440
Korean War, 419, 431, 432, 440
Kowalsky, Lorene Jensen, 453
kranks, 229
Ku Klux Klan, 191, 237, 362, 367, 378, 423
Kursk, Russia, 416
KWQC, 454

L

La Follette, Robert, 265, 362, 428
La Follette, Robert, Jr., 428
Lady Astor, 419
LaGuardia Airport, 379
Lake Erie, 65, 75
Lake Itasca, 41
Lake Michigan, 40, 71, 86, 270
Lake Tahoe, 143
Lakota Sioux Indians, 214, 215
Land of Lincoln, 211
Land of Opportunity, 237
Landis, Kenesaw Mountain, 326
Landon, Alf, 402
Langtry Lily, 221
Lansky, Meyer, 316, 317, 328
Lardner, Jr., Ring, 430
Larkin, Charles, 120
Las Vegas, 317
LaSalle, Illinois, 338
Latin, 20
Latins, 18
Latter-day Saints. *See* Mormons
Lattimore, Owen, 431, 432
Latvia, 417
Law, William, 138
Lawrence, D.H., 342
Lawrence, Kansas, 166
Lawson, John Howard, 431
LDS. *See* Mormons
LDS Prophet, 138
League of Nations, 292, 345

LeClaire, Antoine, 83, 115, 116, 117, 118, 128, 136, 150, 153, 201, 279, 296
LeClaire, Iowa, 253
LeClaire, Marguerite, 116
Led Zeppelin, 366
Lee, Katherine Helena, 322
Lee, Lila, 374
Lee, Robert E., 122, 124, 125, 128, 144, 167, 171, 172, 174, 177, 178, 180, 182, 184, 185, 208, 212, 216, 217, 218
Leech Lake, Minnesota, 35
Leinenkugel, Jacob, 276
Lenin, Vladimir, 362
Leopold, Nathan, 334
Lewis and Clark, 84
Lewis and Clarke, 112
Lewis, Dora, 314
Lewis, Lillian, 222
Lewis, Ted, 348
Lewis, William, 85
Lexington, Massachusetts, 51, 53, 118
Lexington, Virginia, 184
Liberal Republican Party, 152, 190
Liberty Party, 146
Lifeline, 451
Lilienthal, David, 418
Lillard, Harvey, 280
Lillie Beer, 277
Lillienthal Tavern, 360
Lincoln Highway, 139, 307, 308
Lincoln Highway Association, 307
Lincoln Park, 2, 3, 71, 256, 258, 384, 456
Lincoln Tunnel, 379
Lincoln, Abraham, 92, 95, 100, 101, 104, 115, 117, 118, 144, 155, 156, 161, 166, 168, 170, 172, 181, 185, 192, 195, 258, 269, 282, 344, 361, 366
Lincoln, Mary Todd, 118, 185
Lind, John, 201
Lindbergh, Charles, 346
Lindley, Clarence, 12
Lion House, 140
Lithuania, 417
Little Bighorn River, 214
Little Bohemia Lodge, 383
Little Egypt, 270
Little Hell, 317
Little Hellions, 318
Little Rock Island, 307
Little Twig, Joe, 235
Livonia, 24
Lock and Dam No. 14, 395
Locks and Dam No. 15, 387, 394, 395
Locks and Dam No. 26, 396
Lodge, Jr., Henry Cabot, 447
Loeb, Albert, 334
London Blitz, 434
London School of Economics, 312
London, Jack, 305
Lone Ranger, 1
Lone Star State, 144, 180, 448
Long Depression, 238
Long Island, New York, 31, 344
Long, Aaron, 119, 120
Long, John, 119
Longview Park, 2, 456

Longworth, Alice, 339
Looney, Bill, 283
Looney, Conner, 331, 332, 333, 334, 335, 336, 338, 356, 373
Looney, Jerry, 283
Looney, John, 280–86, 318–22, 327–38, 347
Looney, John Connor, 281
Looney, Kathleen, 281, 331
Looney, Nora O'Connor, 281, 283
Looney, Ursula Mary, 281, 331, 338
Los Alamos National Laboratory, 432
Los Angeles, 157, 379, 403, 422
Los Angeles Lakers, 455, 456
Los Angeles Times, 411
Lost Colony of Roanoke, 34
Louisiana Purchase, 65, 74, 101, 162, 209
Louisville, Kentucky, 205, 206, 301
Louvain, Belgium, 450
Lowden State Park, 252
Lowell, Adelia, 148
Lowell, Massachusetts, 154
Lower Mississippi River, 10, 40, 54, 205, 206, 299, 306
Lower Mississippi Valley, 54
Luciano, Lucky, 317, 318, 328
Luke's Cottage Hospital, 151
Luther League, 355
Luther, Martin, 28, 29
Lyons, Iowa, 307

M

MacArthur, Douglas, 417, 418
Macbeth, 437
Macedon, 17
Mackin, Thomas, 151
MacMurray, Fred, 376
Madison D.C., 73
Madison Square Garden, 443
Madison, Dolley, 74, 78
Madison, Helene, 403
Madison, James, 57, 58, 73, 77, 91, 162
Mafioso, 317, 329
Magna Carta, 8, 22, 95
Magnavox, 1, 454
Major League Baseball, 229, 235, 304, 326
Malone, Moses, 456
Manchac, Louisiana, 55
Manhattan, 30, 31, 68, 317
Manhattan Project, 424, 432
Manifest Destiny, 68, 91, 143, 211
Manlius, New York, 373
Mann Act, 325, 326
Mann, James, 325
Manufacturer's Trust & Savings Bank, 387
Manufacturers Trust and Savings Bank of Rock Island, 356
Marajo, Brazil, 293
March on Washington, 449
March to the Sea, 182
Market Square, 286, 332, 333, 336
Market Street Gang, 317, 318
Marquette University, 405, 427
Marquette University School of Engineering, 427
Marquette, Jacques, 39, 114, 301, 393, 394

476

Marshall Plan, 416, 441
Marshall, George, 441
Marshall, John, 95, 96
Martin, Thomas, 197
Martinez, Marcel, 332
Marx Brothers, 348
Marxist Party, 430
Marycrest College, 279
Mashantucket Pequot Nation, 36
Mason, Stevens, 123, 124, 125
Mason-Dixon Line, 162, 181, 190
Massachusetts Bay, 35, 36
Massachusetts State Constitution, 61
Massasoit Indians, 34
Massey-Harris, 385
Matisse, Henri, 342
Matthews, J.B., 433
Matthews, Mark, 272
Maugham, Somerset, 342
Maumee River, 75
Mayflower, 32
Mayhew, Z., 148
Maysville, Kentucky, 258
Maytag, 142
McAdoo, William, 361
McCabe, Levi, 155
McCabe's Department Store, 155, 386
McCarthy, Joe, 163, 427, 428, 431, 432, 433, 434, 435, 436, 437, 442, 449
McCarthyism, 448
McClure, Alexander, 240
McConochie, William, 319
McCoy, Kansas Joe, 366
McDonald's, 453
McGrew, Henry C., 3, 100, 132, 134, 136
McKinley, William, 269, 286, 287, 289, 291
McLemore, Henry, 411
McParlan, James, 248
Mead, Smith and Marsh Lumber Company, 197, 198
Meade, George G., 178, 184
Meat Inspection Act, 290
Mecca, 22
Medal of Honor, 35, 459
Medici, 28
Medieval Period, 24, 25
Medill, Thomas, 263
Mediterranean Sea, 14, 15, 16, 18, 275
Meigs, Return J., 76
Mellon, Andrew, 238, 371
Memphis Minnie, 366
Memphis, Tennessee, 295, 300, 444
Menard, Father René, 39
Mencken, H.L., 372
Menjou, Adolphe, 429
Menominee Indians, 39, 55, 87, 241
Mesabi Range, Minnesota, 241
Meskwaki Indians, 39, 44, 45, 55, 68, 72, 82, 85, 87, 98, 102, 104, 109, 110, 112, 116, 141, 227, 358, 399
Mesopotamia, 14, 15
Metcalfe, Ralph, 405, 406
Methodist Mission, 299
Métis, 40, 54, 86, 114, 116, 234
Mexican Territory, 139, 143

Mexican-American War, 127, 129, 142, 169, 170, 180, 183
Mexico, 11, 29, 45, 80, 130, 139, 142, 143, 144, 160, 169, 184, 210, 212, 311, 329, 355
Meyers, William, 197
Michigan Law School, 334
Michigan Territorial Press, 124
Michigan Territory, 71, 101, 102, 123, 125
Michigan Wolverines, 231, 232
Michigan-Ohio War, 1835. *See* Toledo War
Middle Ages, 21, 22, 24
Middle East
   Ancient, 19
   modern, 14
Midtown Manhattan, 377
Midwest, 10, 11, 90, 110, 119, 137, 150, 152, 154, 199, 206, 207, 210, 211, 212, 248, 250, 252, 253, 265, 269, 298, 304, 307, 318, 322, 325, 328, 329, 338, 353, 361, 372, 386, 390, 392, 393, 399
Mieza, Greece, 18
Milan, 85, 89, 130, 194, 195, 197, 254, 277, 361, 413, 451
Milan Bridge, 194, 450
Military Academy. *See* West Point
Milky Way, 289
Miller, Arthur, 443
Miller, Kevin, 1
Mills Slot Machine Company, 319
Mills, Jenny, 6, 321, 322
Milwaukee Badgers, 234
Milwaukee Bucks, 456
Milwaukee Journal, 248
Milwaukee, Wisconsin, 157, 248, 271, 291, 439, 456
Minneapolis, Minnesota, 41, 133, 261, 316, 396
Minneapolis-Moline, 385
Minnesota River, 41
Mintonette, 225
Minuit, Peter, 30
Mirror Lounge, 283, 284
Mississippi Basin, 299
Mississippi Delta, 210, 293, 398
Mississippi Rifles, 169
Mississippi River Boom and Logging Company, 198
Mississippi Valley, 399
Mississippi Valley Conference, 1, 458
Mississippi Valley Flying School, 338
Mississippi-Rock River Canal, 126, 218
Missouri Compromise, 117, 162
Missouri River, 41, 69, 84, 87, 297
Missouri Territory, 86, 136
Missouri-Mississippi-Ohio River, 10, 205
Missouri-Mississippi-Ohio Valley, 393
Mitchell, Margaret, 179
Mitchell, Philemon, 154
Mobile, Alabama, 75
Model T, 305, 309, 345
Modern Manufacturing Era, 241
Modern Woodman Field, 229
Mohammad, 22
Mohammed, 6, 135
Mohawk Indians, 58, 66
Mohegan Indians, 35

Moline Plow Works, 261
Moline Workman, 154
Molly Maguires, 246, 247
Mongol empire, 23
Mongols, 22, 23
Monmouth, New Jersey, 54
Monroe, James, 74, 80, 171
Monroe, Marilyn, 443
Monroe, Michigan, 212
Monsters of the Midway, 225, 231, 271
Montana, Joe, 254
Montessori method, 301
Montgomery Ward catalog, 357
Montgomery, Alabama, 5, 379
Montgomery, John, 56
Montgomery, Lucy Maude, 305
Monticello, 63
Montreal, 38
Monument, Kansas, 216
Moore, Tim, 348, 350
Moran, George "Bugs", 371
Morgan County, Illinois, 88
Morgan, J.P., 238, 244, 268, 269, 367, 368
Morgan, William, 225
Mormon Battalion, 139
Mormon handcarts, 159, 160
Mormon Militia, 176
Mormon Rebellion, 175
Moroni, 134, 135
Morris, Robert, 54, 57, 59
Morton, Jelly Roll, 342
Mossad, 417
Mossell, Sadie, 300
Mother Nature, 10, 205, 209, 210, 218, 299, 392, 393, 398
Motion Picture Alliance, 429, 430
Moton, Robert Russa, 366
Motor City, USA, 306
Mount Blanc, Switzerland, 288
Mount Vernon, 52, 59, 62
Mountain Meadows Massacre, 176
Mr. Love, 3
Mt. Hood, 379
Mt. Toba, 9, 13
Mueller Brothers, 454
Mugwumps, 288
Muhammad, 22
Muir, John, 165, 394
Munich Institute of Technology, 202
Munich, Germany, 202
Municipal Stadium, 229
Murrow, Edward R., 434, 435
Muscatine, Iowa, 132
Museum of Science and Industry, 271
Museum of Wonders, 251
Muslims, 22, 23
Mystic Lake Casino, 36
Mystic, Connecticut, 35

N

Nagasaki, Japan, 414, 415, 418, 426, 432
Naismith, James, 224, 225, 226
Nantucket Island, 26
Napa, California, 264
Naperville, Illinois, 193
Naples, Italy, 13
Napoleonic Wars, 196
Narragansett Indians, 35
Nash, Frank "Jelly", 382
Nasheaskuk. *See* Whirling Thunder
Nashville, Tennessee, 64, 93, 300
Natalbany Lumber Company, 356
Natchez, Mississippi, 55, 169
Nater, Swen, 456
Nation, Carrie, 274
National American Women Suffrage Association, 312
National Association of Women's Suffrage Association, 312, 313
National Basketball Association, 186, 455, 456, 457, 458
National Broadcasting Company, 445
National Clay Manufacturing Company, 194
National Crime Syndicate, 317
National Football League, 233, 234, 235, 236, 254
National Hotel, 92
National Kindergarten College, 356
National Labor Relations Act (Wagner Act), 380
National League, 229, 304, 320
National Register of Historic Places, 253, 260, 395
National Republican Party, 92
National Research Council, 397
National Women's Party, 312, 313
National-Louis University, 356
Native Americans, 10, 11, 26, 32, 34, 35, 45, 56, 60, 65, 66, 73, 87, 137, 215, 459, 460
Nativists, 237
Nauvoo, Illinois, 84, 126, 132, 136, 137, 138, 139, 140, 141, 147, 159
Nazareth, 18
Nazis, 345, 403, 404, 408, 410, 412, 416, 417, 426, 434
Neal, C.W., 323
Neanderthals, 13
Near North Side, Chicago, 317
Negro Leagues, 229
Neidersaulheim, Germany, 196
Nellie Ball, 456
Nelson, Baby Face, 382, 383, 428
Nelson, Don, 454, 455, 456, 457, 458
Neo-Assyrian Empire, 15
Neo-Babylonia Empire, 15
Nero, 19
Ness, Eliot, 371
Netherlands, 66, 142, 377
Nevada Mountains, 139
New Amsterdam, 31
New Billburg, The, 325, 330
New Brunswick, New Jersey, 224
New Deal, 110, 378, 379, 380, 381, 384, 387, 391, 394, 402, 427, 440
New England, 32, 33, 84
New Guinea, 10
New Jerusalem, 137
New Netherland, 30, 31
New Orleans, 43, 55, 65, 74, 79, 122, 147, 153, 202, 209, 261, 296, 297, 298, 300, 393
New Plimouth, 33

New Testament, 20
New World, 26, 28, 30, 36, 41, 43, 68, 137, 196, 414
New York City, 13, 30, 31, 32, 46, 53, 54, 57, 78, 85, 107, 112, 113, 125, 131, 135, 141, 152, 158, 160, 190, 192, 197, 202, 212, 214, 220, 224, 233, 237, 240, 241, 243, 244, 245, 269, 274, 279, 282, 283, 287, 288, 289, 295, 298, 303, 304, 305, 311, 316, 317, 318, 320,326, 329, 340, 344, 348, 349, 350, 354, 361, 362, 365, 367, 378, 379, 382, 405, 422, 425, 430, 432, 434, 446, 452
New York Giants (NL), 304, 305, 344
New York Harbor, 237, 298
New York Knicks, 456
New York Philharmonic, 243
New York Sun, 288
New York Syndicate, 317
New York Times, 283, 329, 344, 365, 382, 446
New York Tribune, 152, 279
New York Yankees, 233, 344, 443
New Yorker, 444
Newberg, J.P., 251, 270
Newfoundland, 33, 34, 41
Newman, Paul, 338
Newman, Randy, 366
Ni'ihau, Hawaii, 411
Nicaragua, 163
Nietzsche, Friedrich, 420, 436, 437
Nimitz, Chester, 428
Nimrick, Gail Urie, 2, 8, 235
Nineteenth Amendment, 292, 311, 314
Nixon, Richard, 340, 447, 449
Nobel Prize, 290, 291, 292, 433, 442
Nobel Prize in Economics, 368, 369
Normandy, 21, 23, 178, 409, 416, 441
Norris University Center, 401
North America, 10, 11, 13, 26, 28, 29, 32, 42, 48, 55, 80, 95, 113, 122, 162, 256, 288, 414
North Atlantic Treaty Organization, 419
North Bridge, 307
North Korea, 440
North Mediterranean, 20
North Philadelphia, 295
North Pownal Academy, 240
North Side Gang, 317, 371
North Tarrytown, New York, 245
North, the, 26, 32, 45, 77, 117, 162, 163, 164, 167, 168, 169, 170, 172, 178, 179, 181, 182, 183, 184, 187, 188, 193, 244, 295, 419
Northeast, 26, 28, 127, 165, 211, 265, 269, 295, 315, 328, 366, 425
Northern Caucasus, 14
Northern Indiana Normal College, 353
Northern Lumber Company, 356
Northsiders, 318
Northwest Indian War, 67
Northwest Territory, 65, 66, 67, 72, 73, 74, 77, 123
Northwestern League, 228
Northwestern University, 157, 228, 230, 231, 232, 401
Notre Dame, 231
Nottinghamshire, England, 23
Nouveau France, 41

Nouveau Monde, 42
Nova Scotia, 26
November 18, 1905, 261
Novgorod, Russia, 23
Nuremberg, Bavaria, 417

O

O'Banion, Dean, 318
O'Connor, Bucky, 455
O'Leary, Catherine, 269
Oak Park High School, 225
Oak Park, Illinois, 342
Oakdale Cemetery, 174
Oakley, Annie, 270
Obama Administration, 397
Obama, Barak, 381
Oberlin College, 136
Objectivism, 381, 382
Occoquan Workhouse, 314
Odoacer, 19
Office of Scientific Research, 413
Ogilvie, P.H., 128, 129, 132, 148
Oglala Lakota Indians, 214
Ohio Gang, 339, 340, 361
Ohio League, 233
Ohio River, 12, 41, 54, 65, 152, 205, 206, 315
Ohio River Valley, 65
Ohio State University, the, 404, 406
Ohio Valley, 12, 106, 246
Oklahoma Territory, 213
Old Dominion State, 172
Old Spanish Trail, 176
Old St. Peter's Basilica, 19
Old Town Rock Island, 260
Oldfield, Barney, 304
Oliver Tractor Company, 385
Olsen, Ole, 348
Olympics, 6, 16, 226, 235, 264, 342, 403, 404, 405, 406, 426
Omaha Indians, 139
Omaha, Nebraska, 139, 303, 316
Oneida Indians, 58
Onoda, Hiroo, 415, 416
Onondaga Indians, 58
Operation Overlord, 441
Ordinance of Secession, 180
Oregon Territory, 66, 143
Oregon Trail, 139, 159, 303
Orion, Illinois, 56
Osage Indians, 13
Osbourne, Ozzy, 79
Oscans, 18
Oswald, Lee Harvey, 448
Oto Indians, 139
Ottawa Indians, 71
Ottawa, Illinois, 281
Ottoman Empire, 16
Outing Club, 357
Overland Campaign, 182
Owens, Jesse, 404, 405, 406
Oxford University, 50
Oyster Bay, New York, 288

P

Pabst Brewing Company, 271
Pabst, Frederick, 276
Pac-12 Conference, 458
Pacific & Atlantic Telegraph Company, 243
Pacific Affairs, 432
Pacific Northwest, 65, 112, 113, 213, 261
Pacific Railroad, 220
Page, Patti, 444
Paige, Satchel, 229
Paine, Thomas, 60
Paiute Indians, 176
Pakistan, 9, 16, 415
Palace Amusement Center, 374
Palace Hotel, 341
Palace of Fine Arts, 271
Palmer Infirmary and Chiropractic Institute, 280
Palmer School of Chiropractic, 279, 280
Palmer, Bartlett Joshua (B.J.), 280, 351
Palmer, David Daniel (D.D.), 279, 280, 351
Palmer, Elizabeth, 165
Palmer, Minnie, 348
Palmquist, Gustaf, 263
Palmyra, New York, 134
Palo Alto, California, 364, 429
Panama Canal, 290, 391
Panama City, 260
Pan-American Exposition, 287
Panic of 1837, 126, 128, 131, 219
Panic of 1857, 198
Panic of 1873, 191, 238
Pankhurst, Emmeline, 312
Parchman Penitentiary, 366
Paris Exposition, 271
Paris, France, 7, 23, 45, 66, 133, 240, 260, 342, 343, 349
Paris, Illinois, 322
Pasadena, California, 200
Patterson, Robert, 409
Patton, Charlie, 366
Patton, George, 409, 410
Patuxet, 33
Patuxet Indians, 33
Paul, Alice, 312
Paxton Boys, 50
Pearl Harbor, 407, 410, 411, 412, 428, 429, 441
Pedigo, Lawrence, 332, 336, 337, 338
Pennsylvania Abolition Society, 49
Pennsylvania Historical Society, 59
Pennsylvania Railroad Company, 242, 243
Pennsylvania State Pharmacy Board, 329
Pennzoil, 246
People's National Bank, 202, 203, 332
People's Party, 268
People's Savings Bank, 385
Peoria Enterprise, 228
Peoria, Illinois, 56, 116, 120, 228, 285
Pequot Indians, 35, 36
Persia, 15, 17, 23
Persian Empire, 16
Persian Gulf, 14
Peru, Illinois, 307
Petersburg, Virginia, 182, 183
Petersen's Department Store, 384
Pheidippides, 16
Phi Beta Kappa, 287, 290
Philadelphia, 46, 47, 48, 50, 54, 57, 58, 107, 185, 300, 316, 383, 446
Philadelphia 76ers, 456
Philadelphia and Reading Railroad, 268
Philadelphia Phillies, 383, 384
Philippine Islands, 272, 289, 415
Philippine Republic, 289
Philippine War, 289
Philistine States, 15
Phillips, Harry, 323, 324, 325
Phillips, Sam, 444
Phillips, Wendell, 158, 189
Phoenicia, 15
Picasso, Pablo, 305, 342, 343
Pierce, Franklin, 146, 170
Pike, Zebulon, 84, 86
Pilgrims, 29, 32, 33, 34, 36, 38
Pillsbury Company, 133
Pinckney, Charles C., 62
Pinkerton Detective Agency, 337
Pinkerton, Allan, 247
Pitt, William the Elder, 42
Pittsburg Pirates, 305, 383
Pittsburgh Gazette, 186
Pittsburgh, Pennsylvania, 42, 44, 241, 242, 243, 244, 304, 350, 351
Plains Indians, 212, 213, 214, 215
Plan Dog, 410
Planned Parenthood Federation, 275
Plato, 17
Playboy, 442, 443, 444
Plymouth Colony, 32, 33
Plymouth Harbor, 32, 33
Plymouth Notch, Vermont, 341
Plymouth, Massachusetts, 32, 33, 34, 37, 38
Poland, 14, 403, 404, 408, 412, 413, 419, 434
Polk, James, 143, 144, 146
Pollock, Louis, 430
Pontiac's Rebellion, 43
Pontiac's Rebellion, 50
Pony Express, 164, 176, 221
Poor Richard's Almanack, 47
Pope Boniface VIII, 66
Pope Clement VII, 29
Pope Innocent III, 22
Pope John XII, 36
Pope Lucius III, 22
Pope Pius XII, 433
Pope Urban III, 28
Populists, 268
pork-barrel legislation, 390
pork-barrel project, 219
pork-barrel promise, 392
Port Byron Academy, 357
Port Byron, Illinois, 86, 125, 218, 255
Portland Canal, 206
Portugal, 43
post-Civil War, 211
Potato Famine, 153
Potawatomi Indians, 55, 71, 72, 87, 98, 116
Potomac River, 77, 167
Potter, John, 282, 332, 333, 334
Potter, Minnie, 283, 332

Pound, Ezra, 342
Prairie du Chien, Wisconsin, 82, 83, 102, 103, 106, 109, 168
Prairie La Cross, 103
Prairie State, 211
pre-Civil War, 204
Preservation of American Ideals, 429
President Riverboat Casino, 297
Presley, Elvis, 442, 444, 445, 446
Pretzel Alley, 325
Princeton, 73, 224, 292, 344
Princeton, New Jersey, 54
Progressive Era, 265, 266, 268, 269, 275, 394
Progressive Movement, 267, 268, 273, 287, 292, 294, 310
Progressive Party, 291, 362
Progressive Republicans, 265
Prohibition, 265, 273, 275, 276, 277, 292, 294, 310, 311, 313, 315, 316, 317, 319, 320, 321, 324, 325, 330, 332, 336, 338, 339, 345, 351, 355, 359, 361, 371, 372, 373, 377, 400, 401, 402, 439, 446
Prophets, 22, 135, 141, 408, 437
Protestant Anglo-Saxons, 237
PT-109, 447
Public Works Administration, 273, 379, 390, 400
Pueblo, Colorado, 139
Puke State, 88
Pullman Palace Car Company, 291
Pullman, George M., 242
Pullman, Illinois, 237, 248
Purdue University, 231
Purington Paving Brick Company, 259, 260
Puritans, 33, 36, 37
Purple Gang, 371
Purvis, Melvin, 383, 384

Q

Quad Cities, 3, 85, 120, 236, 353, 360, 361, 420, 421, 439, 446, 454
Quad City Area, 421
Quad City Symphony Orchestra, 3
Quad-City Times, 8, 386
Quadricycle, 302
Quaker Oats, 271
Quashquema, 136
Quebec, 38, 40, 43, 49
Quebec City, 40, 75
Queen Isabella, 24
Quincy, Illinois, 132
Quinlan, William J., 115
Quint Cities, 361

R

Radarange, 142
Radcliffe College, 343
Radical Republicans, 188, 190, 191
Ramser, Jake, 285, 333, 334
Rand, Ayn, 91, 381, 382
Randle, Chasson, 457, 458, 459
Raskob, John, 368
Rauch Foundation, 385
Rauch, Albert, 384

Rauch, Lester, 384
Ray, Johnnie, 444
RCA Victor, 454
Reagan, Ronald, 128, 429
Reconstruction, 187, 188, 189, 190, 191, 192, 193, 204, 212, 215, 238, 239, 295
red baiters, 430
red baiting, 429
Red Banks, 38
Red Clay, Tennessee, 96
Red Sea, 15
Reed, Silas, 127, 131
Reformation, 29, 36
Relocation Camps, 409
Remington Arms, 252
Renkes, Jim, 278
Reno, Nevada, 308, 326
Republican Party, 92, 146, 152, 188, 192, 193, 290, 312, 366, 402, 440
Reynolds, John, 98, 100, 104, 132
Rial, Jay, 221
Rice, Thomas "Daddy", 193
Richard, Zachary, 366
Richmond, Virginia, 182, 183, 185
Richter, A., 323, 324
Riefenstahl, Leni, 404
RIHS Stadium, 230, 400, 412
RILCO Laminated Products Company, 356
Rio Grande River, 142, 143, 184
Riverdale, Iowa, 361
Riverside Cemetery, 6, 357
Riverside Park, 306
RKO Orpheum Theater, 374, 375
Roaring Twenties, 399, 420
Robards, Lewis, 93
Robber Barons, 181
Robbins, Welcome, 254
Roberts Commission Report, 411
Robin Hood, 23
Robinson, Jackie, 326
Robinson, Thomas, 263
Rocinante, 354
rock and roll, 444, 446
Rock Island & Peoria Railway, 197, 204
Rock Island Acrobats, 228
Rock Island Advertiser, 129, 188
Rock Island and Chicago Railroad, 130
Rock Island and Milan Steam and Horse Railway, 250
Rock Island Argus, 127, 148, 158, 187, 195, 217, 227, 228, 229, 260, 261, 281, 282, 283, 285, 286, 319, 327, 331, 332, 333, 351, 355, 358, 375
Rock Island Arsenal, 114, 119, 175, 179, 186, 187, 204, 217, 252, 277, 319, 325, 351, 385, 413, 421, 448
Rock Island Arsenal Golf Club, 203
Rock Island Band, 3
Rock Island Bank & Trust Company, 387
Rock Island Brewing Company, 202, 276, 277
Rock Island Central Trust and Savings Bank, 356
Rock Island Chamber of Commerce, 357, 388
Rock Island Churches
    B'nai Jacob Synagogue, 299
    Beth Israel Synagogue, 299
    Bethel Assembly of God, 2

481

Church Square, 147, 150, 263
Emanuel Lutheran Church. *See* German
  Lutheran Church
First Lutheran, 263
First Presbyterian, 151, 188
German Lutheran Church, 150
Grace Lutheran. *See* Zion Lutheran
Lighthouse Gospel Tabernacle, 374
Sacred Heart, 7, 257, 258
St. James, 150, 151
St. Joseph's, 150, 151, 155, 322, 336
St. Mary's, 151, 257, 322, 378
St. Paul's, 450
Swedish Baptist Church, 263
Tri-City Jewish Center, 155, 373
Trinity Episcopal, 151
Zion Swedish Evangelical Lutheran, 257
Rock Island City, 125, 126, 127, 129, 130, 131, 218, 337
Rock Island City Council, 138, 256, 263
Rock Island Club, 203
Rock Island Columbia Park addition, 256
Rock Island County, 90, 98, 100, 114, 115, 119, 120, 133, 157, 175, 195, 269, 337, 355, 357, 358, 413
Rock Island County Commissioners, 90, 114
Rock Island County Historical Society, 357
Rock Island County Pioneer and Old Settlers' Association, 357
Rock Island Districts
  Broadway, 151, 254, 257, 260, 263, 264, 282, 283, 346, 352, 450
  Downtown District, 150, 153, 221, 260, 319
  Greenbush, 257
  Highland Park, 347
  Hilltop, 347, 358
  KeyStone, 255, 256, 258, 259
  Longview, 264
  Old Town Chicago, 150, 260, 264
  The District, 6, 277, 319, 322, 327, 330, 331, 332, 333, 334, 336, 346, 347, 355, 373, 388
  Watch Hill (Hill Crest), 130, 346
  West End, 276, 299, 316, 346, 352, 412, 450, 451, 452, 453
Rock Island Fire Department, 262, 280
Rock Island Hotels
  Case's Tavern, 147
  Como, 331
  Farnham House, 156, 158
  Fort Armstrong, 347
  Harms, 351
  Harper House, 156, 221, 231
  Island City, 156, 158, 221, 228
  John Barrell's House, 147
  Rock Island House, 132, 147, 156
  Sherman, 332
Rock Island Independents, 233, 235, 236
Rock Island Islanders, 228, 229
Rock Island Junction, 254
Rock Island Law and Order League, 355
Rock Island Library, 1, 188, 244, 357
Rock Island Library and Reading Association, 188
Rock Island Line, 127, 141, 152, 154, 156, 158, 160, 200, 204, 220, 230, 254, 269, 281, 298, 299, 327, 385, 425
Rock Island Lumber and Manufacturing Company, 198
Rock Island Lumber Company, 356
Rock Island Mills, 128
Rock Island Millwork, 356
Rock Island News, 283, 284, 285, 286, 323, 330, 331, 333, 348, 355, 434
Rock Island Parent Teachers' Association, 273
Rock Island Parks & Recreation, 388
Rock Island Plow Company, 261, 356
Rock Island Plow Works, 261
Rock Island Police Department, 280, 286, 320
Rock Island Preservation Commission, 259
Rock Island Railroad Bridge, 207
Rock Island Rapids, 39, 82, 84, 86, 88, 89, 90, 99, 106, 110, 122, 125, 128, 155, 171, 200, 206, 216, 217, 218, 301, 307, 361, 395, 413, 421
Rock Island Rifle Company, 202
Rock Island Rocks, 400, 447, 454, 458
Rock Island Sash and Door Works, 356
Rock Island Savings Bank, 356, 387
Rock Island Schools
  Aiken Street, 273
  Alleman High School, 45, 151
  Audubon, 358
  Center for Math & Science, 258, 359
  Central Junior High, 4, 224, 452, 454
  Denkmann, 452
  Early Schools, 147, 148, 262
  Frances Willard, 273
  Franklin Junior High, 5, 452
  Hawthorne, 4, 148, 194, 451
  High School, 149, 179, 201, 230, 289, 373, 379, 400, 406, 451, 452, 457
  Irving, 148, 262, 263
  Jordan Catholic School, 258
  Lincoln, 155, 226, 260, 331, 400
  Longfellow, 1, 2, 4, 224, 253, 255, 256, 258, 259, 448, 460
  School Board, 149, 260, 262
  Sears School, 194
  St. Mary's, 151
  Union Square School, 148
  Villa de Chantal, 258, 331, 359
  Washington Junior High, 6, 452
Rock Island Theaters
  Airdrome, 352
  B&B, 352
  Best, 352
  Blackhawk, 352
  Colonial, 352
  Dreamland, 351, 352
  Fifth Avenue Theater, 352
  Fort Armstrong Theatre, 374, 375, 376
  Grand, 352
  New Lion, 352
  Princess, 352
  Rialto, 352
  Ritz, 352
  Rocket Cinema, 4, 376
  Spencer, 352
  The Elite, 352

482

West Side Hippodrome, 352
West Side Theater, 352
Rock Island Union, 203
Rock Island Village, 128, 194
Rock Island White Stockings, 228
Rock Island YMCA, 226, 227, 262, 354, 356, 374, 458
Rock Island Young Men's Literary Association, 188
Rock Island YWCA, 356
Rock Island, Missouri, 87
Rock Island-Davenport Ferry Company, The, 115
Rock River, 4, 12, 39, 41, 82, 84, 85, 89, 98, 99, 100, 101, 105, 112, 125, 127, 130, 132, 150, 194, 196, 198, 205, 219, 235, 250, 251, 284, 285, 359
Rock River Rangers, 98, 99
Rockefeller, "Devil Bill", 245
Rockefeller, John D., 238, 245, 246, 271, 321, 365, 401
Rockingham, 255
Rocky, 5, 6, 7, 45, 202, 375, 384, 446, 447, 450, 451, 452, 454, 455, 457, 458, 459
Rocky Mountains, 10, 11, 35, 41, 139, 152, 181, 205, 211
Rodman, Thomas, 186
Rodriguez, Jan, 30
Rogers, Elizabeth Selden, 314
Rogers, Henry, 238
Rogers, Roy, 4
Rogers, Will, 275, 339, 346, 362
roller dams, 394, 395
Roman Empire, 18, 19
Romania, 408
Rome, 18, 19, 28
Roosevelt Hotel, 425
Roosevelt, Edith Kermit Carow, 288
Roosevelt, Eleanor, 377, 378, 424
Roosevelt, Franklin, 110, 189, 269, 287, 288, 289, 290, 291, 292, 298, 353, 373, 390, 391, 400, 402, 403, 405, 407, 410, 411, 413, 415, 417, 422, 423, 424, 425, 426, 430, 432, 441, 449
Roosevelt, Jacobus, 377
Roosevelt, Johannes, 377
Roosevelt, Nicholas, 377
Roosevelt, Sara Delano, 377
Roosevelt, Theodore, 265, 287–92, 298, 321, 339, 353, 365, 377, 378
Rosen, Nig, 316
Rosenberg, Ethel, 432, 433
Rosenberg, Julius, 432, 433
Rosenfield, Morris, 155, 263, 373, 374
Rosenfield, Walter, 333
Ross, Betsy, 59
Ross, George, 59
Rotary International, 26, 357
Rothstein, Arnold, 316, 317, 328
Rough and Ready Club, 166
Rough Riders, 289
Rousseau, 60
Royal Proclamation of 1763, 44
Rubenstein, Richard, 437
Rumania, 417
Rus', 23
Russell, Bill, 455, 456
Russell, Charles Marion "Kid", 112
Russell, Jane, 442, 443
Russia, 24, 113, 192, 275, 294, 298, 341, 362, 365, 398, 408, 416, 417, 419, 426, 427, 429, 430, 433, 448, 451
Russian River Valley, 376
Rutgers University, 224
Ruth, Babe, 233, 344, 364

S

Sabin, Pauline, 401
Sac. *See* Sauk Indians
Sacramento, California, 152, 164, 303
Saginaw, Michigan, 38
Saint Ambrose College, 230, 279, 384
Saint Bernardine of Siena, 36
Saint George, 20, 21
Saint Peter, 19
Saints. *See* Mormon
Salem, Massachusetts, 37, 38, 118
Salinas Valley, 143
Salt Creek Valley, Kansas, 163
Salt Flats, 139
Salt Lake City, 140, 176, 308
Salt Lake Valley, 139, 158, 159, 160
Salzmann, Louis, 222
Salzwedel, Germany, 196
Samoset, 33
Sampson, Deborah, 311
San Antonio, Texas, 180
San Diego, California, 139, 422
San Francisco, 138, 152, 160, 220, 221, 302, 303, 304, 307, 308, 341, 365, 422, 435, 449
San Francisco 49ers, 254
San Francisco Chronicle, 225
San Juan Hill, 289
San Salvador, 27
Sandburg, Carl, 295
Sanders, Harlan, 453
Sangamon County Boys, 101
Sanger, Margaret, 274, 275, 315, 428
Santa Anna, 142
Santa Clause, 274
Santa Cruz, California, 143
Santa Monica, California, 304
Santo Domingo, 30
Saperstein, Abe, 406
Sartre, Jean-Paul, 433, 435, 437
Saturday Evening Post, 411
Sauk 1788 Treaty, 70
Sauk 1804 Treaty, 69, 70, 98
Sauk 1816 Treaty, 98
Sauk Indians, 3, 39, 44, 45, 55, 56, 68, 69, 70, 71, 72, 79, 81, 82, 84, 85, 86, 87, 88, 97, 98, 99, 100, 101, 102, 104, 106, 109, 110, 112, 116, 120, 125, 135, 136, 141, 179, 234, 235, 263, 399
Sauk Trail, 307
Saukenuk, 39, 44, 46, 56, 70, 76, 81, 88, 89, 98, 99, 102, 110, 113, 125, 136, 155, 205, 235, 250, 252, 263, 357, 361, 400, 460
Savanna, Georgia, 182, 255
scalawags, 191
Scandinavia, 21, 23, 26, 237
Schaab, J.M., 295

483

Scheuerman, Sharm, 455, 456
Schiff, Jacob, 298
Schlitz, Joseph, 276
Schnell, Matthias, 282
Schrank, John, 291
Schriver, Harry, 285, 286, 319
Schurz, Carl, 158, 189
Schuylkill County, 247
Scopes Monkey Trial, 7, 335, 341
Scopes, John, 335
Scotland, 249, 349
Scott County, Iowa, 116, 117, 174, 323
Scott, Dred, 116, 117
Scott, Thomas, 242
Scott, William, 337
Scott, Winfield, 97, 103, 139, 144, 145, 170, 172, 239
Screen Actors Guild, 429
Scripps, John Locke, 130
Sears Catalog, 439
Sears Post Office, 195
Sears, David, 128, 194, 195, 204
Sears, David, Jr., 195
Searstown, 194, 195, 250, 270
seasoned slaves, 162
Seattle, 202, 272, 276, 323, 341, 422
Seattle Brewing and Malting Company, 202
Second Battle of Bull Run, 178
Second Industrial Revolution, 241
Securities and Exchange Commission, 380, 447
seer stone, 134
Seminole Indians, 95
Seminole Wars, 180
Semitic Akkadian language, 15
Seneca Indians, 58
Sephardic Jews, 31
Servus Rubber Company, 356, 412, 413
Sevareid, Eric, 434
Seven Years War, 35, 42, 50
Seventeenth Amendment, 292
Severus, Alexander, 19
Sex Cities, 361
Seymour, Horatio, 190
Shakespeare, William, 28, 72, 437
Shaw, George Bernard, 342
Shawnee, 13, 67, 72
Shelly, Mary, 61
Shenandoah Valley, 51
Sheridan Plaza Hotel, 372
Sheridan, Phillip, 216
Sherman Antitrust Act, 246
Sherman, William Tecumseh, 182, 251
Shoot the Chutes, 251, 270
Shoshone Indians, 212
Show Me State, 88, 423
Shredded Wheat, 271
Shriver, Harry, 258, 319, 330, 333, 337, 373
Siberia, 10, 24, 410
Siegel, Bugsy, 316
Sierra Club, 355
Sierra Nevada, 152, 159, 160, 303
Silas, Paul, 456
Silene, 20, 21
Silent Sentinels, 313, 314
Silver Slipper, 317

Silvis, Illinois, 254, 359
Simmermaker, C.F., 386
Simonds, Ossian Cole, 263
Sinclair, Upton, 274
Sinnet, Alanson, 256
Sinnet, Frank, 256
Sioux Indians, 55, 103, 104, 163, 175, 176, 214, 215, 216
Sisters of Charity, 373
Sitting Bull, 214
Six Nations, 59
Sixteenth Amendment, 291, 311
Skinner, Otis, 348
Skowronski, Donna Dempsey, 452
Slade, Jack, 164
Slavs, 22
Sleepy Hollow Cemetery, 245
Smith College, 225
Smith, Al, 362, 366
Smith, Bessie, 366
Smith, Captain John, 33
Smith, Emma Hale, 134
Smith, Hyrum, 134, 138
Smith, John, 33
Smith, Joseph, 33, 134, 135, 136, 137, 138, 147, 225, 265, 279
Smith, Kate, 445
Smithsonian Museum, 304
Smoot-Hawley Tariff Act, 367, 368
Social Security Act, 380
Socialist Party, 292
Socialists, 250, 286, 426
Socrates, 17
Solid South, 269, 362
Solomon, Charles "King", 316
Sons of Israel, 299
Soo Line Railroad, 133
South America, 29, 45, 162
South China Sea, 9
South Korea, 419, 440
South Pacific, 410, 422
South, the, 9, 28, 32, 77, 95, 144, 161, 162, 163, 167, 168, 169, 172, 176, 178, 180, 181, 182, 183, 184, 187, 188, 189, 190, 191, 193, 195, 208, 211, 217, 237, 265, 266, 295, 300, 329, 361, 366, 371, 413, 414, 428, 439, 447, 452
  Deep South, 77, 187, 210, 211, 326, 366, 371, 425
Southeast Asia, 435
Southern Christian Leadership Conference, 449
Southern States, 168
Southern Strategy, 366
Soviet Union, 365, 416, 419, 427, 431, 432, 440
Space Race, 448
Spain, 24, 27, 29, 33, 42, 43, 54, 66, 237, 289, 293
Spalding Commercial College, 423
Spalding, Albert, 227, 228
Spanish Flu pandemic, 293
Sparta, Greece, 16
Speedwell, 32
Spencer Square, 3, 150, 325
Spencer, Edward, 157
Spencer, John, 88, 89, 98, 105, 115, 120, 128, 147, 155, 156, 157
Spiral Galaxy in Andromeda, 289

Springfield College, 224
Springfield rifle, 252
Springfield, Illinois, 118, 127
Springfield, Massachusetts, 225
Springfield, Massachusetts Armory, 252
Squanto, 33
St. Anthony's Hospital, 151, 203, 332, 385
St. Croix River, 41
St. Ignace, Michigan, 40
St. John's Military School, 373
St. Joseph, Missouri, 164, 299
St. Lawrence River, 38
St. Louis Bridge, 208
St. Louis Cardinals, 383
St. Louis Union Station, 425
St. Louis University, 230
St. Louis, Missouri, 33, 41, 55, 56, 69, 70, 79, 81, 82, 84, 106, 113, 114, 117, 119, 125, 130, 147, 152, 153, 156, 170, 198, 206, 207, 208, 216, 269, 295, 296, 297, 316, 318, 325, 331, 340, 371, 387, 396
St. Paul Ideals, 233
St. Paul, Minnesota, 41, 200, 208, 244, 296, 344, 390
St. Petersburg, Russia, 113
St. Thomas Catholic School, 169
St. Valentine's Day Massacre, 371, 372
Stageira, Greece, 17
Stagg, Amos Alonzo, 225, 271, 272
Staley, Augustus, 233
Stalin, Joseph, 413, 417, 419
Stalwarts, 288
Stampede Dam, 210
Standard of California (Chevron), 246
Standard of Indiana (Amoco), 246
Standard of New Jersey (Exxon), 246
Standard of New York (Mobil), 246
Standard of Ohio (Sohio), 246
Standard Oil Company, 245, 246
Standing Bear (Hauberg), 358
Stanford Cardinal, 225
Stanford University, 225, 364, 365, 429, 457, 458
Stanford, Leland, 181
Stanley Steamer, 304
Stanley, Francis, 304
Stanley, Freeland, 304
Stanton, William, 157, 314
Star of David, 59
States Rights, 425
steamboats, 86, 102, 103, 106, 107, 109, 148, 156, 201, 205, 206, 208, 209, 217, 218, 255, 270, 295, 296, 385
  Effie Afton, 156, 207, 218
  J.S., 296
  J.S. Deluxe, 296
  Kentucky No. 2, 200
  paddlewheel, 201
  Prairie State, 200, 201
  President, 296
  S.S. Admiral, 297
  Verne Swain, 296
  Virginia, 86
Stein, Gertrude, 342, 343, 354
Steinbeck, John, 370
Stephenson, Benjamin, 121

Stephenson, Village of, 121, 125, 127, 131, 132, 260
Stevenson, Adlai, 440
Stevenson, Mary "Polly", 50
Stitz, Lynne Urie, 2
Stock Market Crash, 367, 368, 385, 388
Stock Market Crash, 1929, 364, 367, 368, 371, 403
Stockholm Olympics, 234
Stone Age, 13, 14
Stone, Lucy, 311
Stork Club, 317
Stovenour, June, 375
Stozback, Germany, 202
Streckfus Steamers Company, 296
Streckfus, John, 295, 296
street numbers, 222
Street, Joseph, 118
Strode, James M., 105, 120, 121
Stuart, Gilbert, 78
Stuart, John, 118
Stuyvesant, Peter, 31
Sucker State, 88, 211
Sullivan, Ed, 348, 445, 446
Sullivan, John H., 255
Sumerian language, 14
Sumner, Charles, 166
Sun Records, 444
Sun Tzu, 330
Sunday, Billy, 320–22
Sunday, Nell, 321
Surratt, Mary, 344
Suzuki, Kantarō, 414
Svenska Kapell (Swedish Chapel), 257
Swanson, A.J., 154
Swarthmore College, 312
Sweeny, Donald, 397
Sweet, R.F., 151
Swingle, Ray, 286
Switzerland, 354, 355
Sylvan Island, 128
Sylvan Slough, 128, 256, 457
Sylvania, 454
Syracuse University, 437
Syria, 13

T

Tadaichi, Hara, 410
Taft, Lydia Chapin, 311
Taft, William Howard, 290, 291, 292, 311, 373
Tail-Gunner Joe, 427
Taino Indians, 27
Tainter gate dams, 395
Taiwan, 410
Talcott, Andrew, 123, 124
Tallahala Lumber Company, 356
Talmud, 23
Tama, Iowa, 110, 358
Tammany Hall, 240
Taylor, Zachary, 82, 106, 144, 146, 169, 170
Teague, Ron, 451, 458
Teapot Dome Scandal, 340
Tecumseh, 72, 73, 74, 75, 76, 77, 127
Tecumseh's War, 67

Temple of Nymphs, 18
Terre Haute Hottentots, 228
Terre Haute, Indiana, 147, 152
Territory of Virginia, 32
Texas Public Safety commissioners, 180
Texas Territory, 66
Thailand, 192
Thames Valley, 76
Thanksgiving, 34, 37, 230, 232, 256, 337
The Crash. *See* Stock Market Crash
The District. *See* Rock Island Districts
The Grand Trunk Herald, 301
The Great Change, 142
The Great War. *See* World War I
The Lost Generation, 342, 343
The Natural State, 259
The Outfit, 318, 371, 373
The Prophet, 99, 100, 106
The Q, 421
The Renaissance, 27
The Rock Island News, 130, 283
The Rock Islander, 130
The Strip, Michigan-Ohio, 123, 124, 125
The Untouchables, 371, 372
theodemocracy, 138
Theodosius I, 19
theory of evolution, 335
Third Reich, 403, 409, 417
Thomas, J. Parnell, 431
Thompson, Dow, 101
Thompson, J. Edgar, 242
Thoreau, Henry David, 165, 167
Thorn, Jonathan, 112
Thorpe, Grace, 234
Thorpe, Jim, 233, 234, 235, 441
Three-I League, 228, 229
Thunder Clan, 235
Thurmond, Strom, 425, 426
Tianjin, China, 432
Tiffany, Louis Comfort, 240
Tigris and Euphrates River valleys, 15
Tigris and Euphrates Rivers, 14
Tilden, Samuel J., 192
Timberline Lodge, 379
Time Magazine, 387, 393, 441
Tinker, Joe, 305
Tippecanoe River, 73
Tipton, Iowa, 386
Tiskilwa, Illinois, 147
Tisquantum. *See* Squanto
Tobin, James, 364, 369
Toklas, Alice B., 343
Tolbert, Tom, 456
Toledo War, 123, 256
Toledo, Ohio, 67, 123, 124, 125, 426
Tongue River, Wyoming, 213
Tonto, 1
Torah, 15
Toronto Star, 342
Torrio, Giovanni "Papa Johnny", 318, 322, 372
Tosches, Nick, 444
towboats, 201
Trail of Tears, 97
Transcendental Club, 165
transcendentalism, 165, 166

Transylvania University, 169
Treaty House, 116, 117
Treaty of Paris, 1763, 40, 42, 43, 44, 55
Treaty of Paris, 1783, 45, 56, 65, 66, 68, 81
Treaty of St. Louis, 70
Treaty of Versailles, 402
Trenton, New Jersey, 54
Tribal Confederation. *See* Indian Confederation
Tri-Cities, 129, 155, 202, 203, 221, 250, 258, 280, 282, 283, 296, 306, 318, 319, 321, 325, 328, 338, 346, 350, 352, 354, 358, 360, 373, 374, 385, 386, 412, 453, 454
Tri-City Auto Show, 308
Tri-City Jewish Center's Educational Center, 155
Tri-City Labor Review, 286
Tri-City Men's Rose Garden Club, 357
Tri-City Symphony, 357, 386
Trillin, Calvin, 298
Trinity Ladies Guild, 151
Triple Entente, 275
troglodyte, 14
Troy, 15
Troyes, France, 23
Truckee, California, 210
Trudeau, Garry, 165
Truman Special, 425
Truman, Bess Wallace, 423, 424, 425
Truman, Harry, 194, 405, 414, 417, 422, 423–26, 426, 432, 440, 441, 442, 446
Tse-tung, Mao, 431
Tucker, Sophie, 348
Tunick, A.L. "Al", 453, 454
Turkey, 13, 14, 15
Turner, Levi, 125
Tuscarora Indians, 58
Twain, Mark, 41, 122, 143, 192, 209, 210, 217, 221, 238, 240, 272, 289
Twelfth Amendment, 91
Twenty-First Amendment, 336, 400, 401
Twigs, David E., 180
Twin Cities, 261, 387
Tyler, John, 128

U

U.S. Army Corps of Engineers, 122, 171, 206–9, 210, 216–20, 252, 295, 387, 390–400
U.S. Army Corps of Engineers, Rock Island District, 216
U.S. Constitution, 48, 57, 58, 60, 61, 64, 65, 67, 73, 74, 117, 162, 266, 459
U.S. Housing Authority, 380
U.S. Military Academy. *See* West Point
Ulm, Germany, 415
Umbrians, 18
Uncle Tom's Cabin, 189, 221
Union County Division, 101
Union Ironworks, 243
Union Savings Bank, 386
Union Square. *See* Spencer Square
United Electrical, Radio, and Machine Workers, 428
United Nations, 345, 413
United States Steel Company, 244
United Sunday School Boys Band, 354

United Township High School, 360
University Athletic Association, 272
University of Birmingham, 312
University of California, 225, 362, 363, 364, 365
University of California Los Angeles, 456
University of Chicago, 225, 230, 231, 267, 271, 272, 371, 413, 437
University of Cincinnati, 175
University of Colorado, 457
University of Illinois, 13, 202, 230, 236, 325, 442
University of Iowa, 225, 230, 276, 384, 455, 456
University of Michigan, 441
University of Michigan Law School, 354
University of Minnesota, 231, 232
University of Mississippi, 179
University of Northern Iowa, 232
University of Pennsylvania, 48, 231, 300, 312
University of San Francisco, 455
University of Southern California, 406
University of Washington, 341, 379
University of Wisconsin, 231
University of Wisconsin-Green Bay, 38
Upper Iowa River, 87
Upper Midwest, 197, 252
Upper Mississippi Basin, 394
Upper Mississippi River, 39, 41, 44, 55, 84, 112, 119, 125, 126, 152, 198, 200, 201, 205, 206, 207, 216, 217, 269, 296, 337, 390, 391, 392, 393, 394, 396, 397, 398, 399
Upper Mississippi River System, 393
Upper Mississippi Valley, 269, 393, 394, 398
Uppsala University, 253
Urie, Hod, 235
Urie, Mike, 2
Utah Territorial Militia, 176
Utah Territory, 140, 141, 163, 175, 176
Utke, Gene, 452
Uxbridge, Massachusetts, 311, 312

V

Vale, Oregon, 303
Vallée, Rudy, 375
Valley Forge, 54, 59
Valparaiso University, 353
Valparaiso, Indiana, 307
Van Buren, Martin, 92, 96, 131, 142, 145
Van Dale, Helen, 321, 322, 325, 327, 337, 338
Van Dine, Nancy, 8
van Rosenvelt, Claes Maartenszen, 377
Van Sant Boatyard, 200
Van Sant, Samuel, 200, 201, 202, 204, 219
Vancouver, British Columbia, 341
Vanderbilt, Cornelius, 238
Vandruff Island, 126, 194, 195
Vandruff, Joshua, 89
Vargas, Alberto, 443
Variety, 429
Vassar College, 312
Vatican, 20, 21, 22
vaudeville, 251, 348, 349
Velie 40, 308
Velie Carriage Company, 308
Velie Motor Vehicle Company, 308
Velie, Stephen, 188

Velie, Willard, 308, 345
Verbiest, Ferdinand, 301
Vernes, Jules, 313
Vernon, J.L., 332
Vienna, Austria, 416, 434
Viet Nam War, 448
Vikings, 21, 26, 27, 75
Village of East Moline, 254
Village of Stephenson, 127, 131
Vincennes, Inidana, 68, 72, 73
Virginia Dynasty, 80
Visitation Sisters, 258
Vladimir, the Prince of Novgorod, 23, 24
Volkswagen, 345
Volstead Act, 310, 314, 315, 316, 320, 329, 330, 373
Voltaire, 60
von Bismarck, Otto, 191
von Hindenburg, Paul, 403
Voting Rights Act, 193

W

Wabash College, 437
Wabash River, 12, 73
Wabokieshiek. *See* The Prophet
Wade, Ginnie, 179
Wagner, Robert, 276
Walasiewicz, Stanislawa, 403
Walden Pond, 165
Waldorf-Astoria Hotel, 368
Walker, John Augustus, 379
Walker, Leonard "Fat", 337
Wall Street, 31, 268, 294, 370, 378, 379
Walsh, Bill, 254
Walsh, Stella, 404
Wampanoag Indians, 33, 34
Wapello Base Ball Club, 227, 228
War Hawks, 73
War of 1812, 75, 79, 80, 81, 84, 86, 106, 122, 127, 144, 145, 180, 288
Warner, Dudley, 238
Warsaw, Illinois, 84
Wasatch Front, 175
Washburn, Cadwallader Colden (C.C.), 132
Washburn, Israel Washington, Jr, 133
Washburn, William, 133
Washburne, Elihu, 133
Washington and Lee University, 184
Washington College, 184
Washington D.C, 308
Washington D.C., 73, 77, 78, 84, 87, 97, 106, 119, 127, 181, 269, 312, 313, 314, 339, 354, 422, 449
Washington Times, 428
Washington Wizards, 455
Washington, Booker T., 290
Washington, George, 4, 51, 53, 51–54, 56, 57, 58, 59, 60, 73, 78, 95, 122, 167, 171, 398
Washington, Lewis, 167
Washington, Martha Custis, 52, 171
WASP males, 459
Watch Tower Amusement Park, 250, 251, 252, 270, 346
Waterloo Gasoline Traction Engine Company, 306

Waterloo, Iowa, 306
Waterman, Ethel Baker, 386
Watertown Arsenal, 186
Watertown, Illinois, 359
Waupun, Wisconsin, 292
Wayles, John, 63
Wayne, Anthony, 67
Wayne, John, 429
Webb, W.E., 216
Weber, Christopher, 129
Webster, Daniel, 92, 126, 127, 129
Weizmann, Chaim, 424
Wellesley College, 270
Wells, George, 89
Wells, Rinnah, 89
Wentz, Augustus, 174
Wentz, Rebecka, 174
West Davenport, 255
West End Settlement House, 357, 450
West Point, 106, 115, 122, 125, 129, 144, 147, 169, 170, 171, 175, 176, 177, 179, 211, 234, 409, 441
Western Allies, 416, 432, 441
Western Asia, 23
Western Association, 228
Western Confederacy of Indians, 66
Western Conference, 231, 271
Western Europe, 24
Western European, 27
Western Interstate University Football Association, 230
Western League, 229
Western Plains, 211
Western Union, 243, 280, 301
Westinghouse Company, 270
Westinghouse, George, 270
Wexler, Irving, 316
Weyerhaeuser & Denkmann Company, 356
Weyerhaeuser Lumber, 197
Weyerhaeuser, Apollonia, 200
Weyerhaeuser, Frederick, 196–202, 204, 207, 238, 241, 244, 263, 278
Weyerhaeuser, Sarah Elizabeth, 200
WHBF, 1, 351, 375
Wheaton College, 455
Whig Party, 92, 144, 146
Whirling Thunder, 106, 107
Whirlpool Corporation, 142
White City, The, 270
White Cloud. *See* The Prophet
White, James, 136
White, Jo Jo, 456
White-Slave Traffic Act, 325
Whitman, Walt, 165
Whittaker, W.H., 314
Wickstom, George, 8
Wilcox, Jane, 358
Wild West, 153
Wild West Show, 270
Will, George, 73
Willard, Frances, 273, 274
Willard, John, 38
William & Mary College, 62
William Rufus, 21
William the Conqueror, 21, 42

Williams, Edward Huntington, 329
Willys Company, 309
Wilmerton, W. William, 284, 285
Wilson, Frank, 372
Wilson, John, 115
Wilson, Woodrow, 112, 132, 205, 265, 273, 278, 291, 292, 293, 294, 312, 313, 314, 321, 339, 340, 345, 361, 372
Winchell, Walter, 430
Winnebago, 13, 38, 55, 87, 89, 99, 100, 102, 103, 105, 106, 112
Winter Quarters, 139
Wisconsin Cavalry, 212
Wisconsin River, 39, 41, 69
witch cake, 38
witchcraft, 29, 36, 37, 38
Withers, Hannah, 93
WJ Quinlant, 115
WOC, 351, 361
Wolf, Martin, 369
Wollstonecraft, Mary, 61
Wolsey, Louis, 316
Women's Christian Temperance Union, 273
Women's Organization for National Prohibition Reform, 373, 401
Women's World Tournament of Softball, 230
Wonders, Eula H., 338
Woodbrooke Settlement for Social Work, 312
Woodruff, T.T., 242
Woodward, W.E., 161
Worcester v. Georgia, 95
Word of Life Christian Center, 155
Workingmen's Benevolent Association, 247
Works Projects Administration, 379, 400
World Series, 228, 304, 332, 344, 345, 445
World War I, 3, 194, 200, 241, 260, 275, 291, 292, 293, 294, 298, 310, 313, 315, 319, 321, 339, 340, 342, 343, 344, 345, 365, 373, 381, 402, 403, 411, 423, 424, 441
World War II, 161, 178, 194, 210, 227, 230, 264, 297, 309, 349, 352, 354, 359, 365, 368, 382, 386, 394, 406, 407, 408, 409, 413, 415, 416, 421, 422, 424, 426, 431, 432, 434, 435, 439, 441, 442, 447, 450, 459
World's Columbian Exposition, 269
Wright, Frank Lloyd, 341, 342
Wrigley Field, 234, 235, 383
Wundram, Bill, 8, 386
Wyandotte Indians, 38
Wynn, Ed, 348

X

Xavier University, Louisiana, 406

Y

Yakovlev, Anatoli, 432
Yale, 48, 155, 290, 312, 369
Yaropolk, 23
Year Without a Summer, 80
YMCA, 224, 225, 226, 354
Yorkshire, England, 259
Yorktown, Virginia, 56
Yorkville, Illinois, 395

Young Communist League, 432
Young Democrats, 449
Young Men's Christian Association Training School, 224
Young Men's Hebrew Association, 299
Young Men's Christian Association Training School, 225, 226
Young Republicans, 448, 449
Young, Brigham, 136, 138, 139, 141, 159, 175
Young, Steve, 138

Youth International Party, 449
Yugoslavia, 417
Yukon Territory, 10

Z

Zion, Missouri, 135
Zwicker, Ralph, 433, 434
Zwillman, Longy, 316

Acknowledgements

Early in the writing of Rock Island, on a quiet summer Sunday morning, I had the excellent opportunity to meet Beth Carvey, the Director of the Hauberg Indian Museum. The trip to the museum, which I remember to have been many times larger when I was a boy, is still a highly worthwhile visit, if only to chat up Ms. Carvey and draw on her deep knowledge of the Sauk and Meskwaki and their most famous warrior, Black Hawk. She graciously edited the Black Hawk and local Indian passages of this book and kindly explained the difference between Indian tribes and clans and gently pointed out that "Black Hawk was not a chief." That surprised me, but she is right. Her corrections are some of the hundreds that I made as I re-sifted Rock Island's glorious history, and very probably there are an equal number of errors and misstatements that have gone uncorrected. I constantly winced as I discovered authoritative data that contradicted what I had written earlier. Most of Rock Island's early history that was written after World War I relies on Argus articles and columns and old-timers' oral recollections — and, of course, to sell papers and books, some facts were enhanced, others deleted, and some were simply made up.

Refreshingly accurate and interesting historical accounts of Rock Island and its landmarks were written for the Rock Island Argus/Moline Dispatch by Diane Oestreich in her periodic Postcards From Home column. Oestreich's Postcards are reprinted on the Rock Island Preservation Society's excellent website and provide unique insights into the lives and times of Rock Island's pioneer families through old postcards and her narratives of Rock Island homes, businesses, churches, and public buildings. Oestreich not only charmingly writes about Rock Island's history, but she "walks the talk." Barbara and David Parker, the operators of the Victorian Inn Bed and Breakfast on 7th Avenue and 20th Street, tell of the evening in 1979 that a group of Broadway neighborhood women met, and at the end of the meeting, Oestreich had everyone join hands and pledge that they would reclaim their neighborhood. They have, and today with considerable public assistance driven by Mark Schwiebert, who served as Rock Island's mayor from 1989 to 2009, virtually every civic innovation, historical institution, and forward-thinking program emerged from Oestreich's pledge and was skillfully guided by Schwiebert. Rock Island's downtown is once again entertainment oriented, and the cornerstone of The District is Circa 21. Dennis Hitchcock's 35-year dedication to live dinner theater productions and his faithful reconstruction of the Fort Armstrong Theatre are inspirational examples of how a quality product can support an improbable business model. All Rock Islanders are indebted to the work of Oestreich, Schwiebert, Hitchcock, and the myriad of others who are helping to reclaim and restore Rock Island. Also, I would be remiss if I didn't acknowledge the 20 minutes Longfellow Principal David Knuckey spent on an August day four days before the school year started to show me around our school. With the exception of the auditorium/gym and the terrazzo-floored hallways, which are exactly as I left them in 1956, everything from the basketball hoops on the playground to the cheery, sun-lit classrooms has been improved.

I'm now an old-timer, but unlike those of prior generations, I had the Internet to quickly fact-check, and if a fact or statement or conclusion seemed questionable, it was usually an easy task to get a better take on the dubious matter by going beyond the first page of search hits, which gives more weight to recent popular history. Wikipedia is a fabulous resource and is generally quite accurate; however, on several occasions I found its articles to be contradictory or cited references that perpetuated inaccuracies. Writing Rock Island was like peeling the proverbial onion — the more I read and the more I talked to Rock Islanders, the more there was to write. I've missed a lot, and to better construct future copies of Rock Island, errors can be remedied and content suggestions made at: steveurie.org.

In 2007 a Central and Rocky classmate and friend, Nancy Neuhaus, created a very fine website for the RIHS Class of '62. The website brought together a group of classmates who daily share thoughts and activities. It was Nancy who provided the impetus and encouragement for this book. My classmates' memories and affection for Rock Island a half-century after most left surprised me, but growing suspicious of claims that Rock Island's grandeur peaked in 1962, I decided to find out if that were true. (I'm now convinced the peak occurred on November 18, 1905; pg. 261.) The journey was fantastically enjoyable, so my deepest thanks to my "audience" of classmates on the Rockpile who are as fine a group of real and virtual friends a guy can have, and for incenting me to learn about Rock Island's history and stimulating the memories of forgotten history lessons and events that sprang forth as I wrote. So, a grateful shout out to: Kent "The Prez" Arnold, Barbara "Bailey" Spence, Terry "Boltz" Baltzer, John "JB" Birkeland, Bob "O" Frink, Dick "Gas" Cummins, Donna "The Queen" Dempsey, Carl "DB" Hinze, Marty "Spider" Hoffeditz, David Kolovat, Lorene "The Editor" Jensen, Nancy Jo "It's a good Life" Powers, Alice Pronga, E. Gifford "Ed" Stack, Jerry Twitty, and Gene "The 6th Man" Utke. And I can't take a stroll down Rock Island's Memory Lane without bumping into Roger Adams, Becky Anderson, Sandy Anderson, Kathy Andrews, Pam Bartels, Betty Beauchamp, Barb Becky, Doug Benoit, Tarz Brandle, Judy Buckley, Phil Burke, Ginny Cale, Rocco Carbone, Carl Dahlen, Jimmy Davis, Jimmy Dixson, Peggy Dover, Bill Dunbar, Anita Eagle, Linda Echermann, Bill Edmund, Francie Eldred, Joan Foulke, Joe Fuller, Charlotte Frick, Julie Gard, Susie Geifman, Dick Goepple, Cassie German, Jeff, Kelly, Milt, and Anita Gersick, Gay Gray, Carla Hammerlund, Jerry Harvey, Jean Hilton, The Hungry 20, Ted Hinze, Bobby Holcomb, Bob Hotle, Sharon Inch, Kathy Johnson, Alice Junqueira, Ina Karish, Johnny Kish, Tom "Sleazy" Lee, Susie Letts, Judy Liljegren, Joane Linke, Marty Litvin, Teresa Lord, Bill Miller, Jan Moran, Merrill Morris, Judy Muhleman, Bart Newell, Jan O'Melia, Reese Orland, Pete Ortiz, Dennis Peterson, Mike Petersen, Neal Peterson, Jody Perkins, Rose Raithel, Susie Reed, Terry Rosenquist, Ann Salstrom, Bob Schauenberg, Carrol Scherer, "Rughead" Schroeder, Judy Sheridan, Gary Schuster, Jackie Staley, Sharon Stauffer, Steve Sullivan, Jan Summers, Ronnie Teague, Sally Temple, Sugar Thomas, Ron Utley, Nancy and Mike Van Dine (but Nancy more fondly), Dick VonDresky, Herb Wiener, Gail Wenos, Barb Wessel, Walt and Bill Wise, and Barb Zeffren. And, oh yeah, Mike Gersick who just won't let me forget.

I've been fortunate to have a wonderful Midwestern family overflowing with Zimmers, Prices, Stokers, Forgys, DeClerks, Stitzes, Nimricks, Wilcoxes, Coens, and Hales — all added a bit of insight to this history. My most heartfelt thanks go to the teachers who made me write, Michael Santos who showed me what it takes to write, and to my wife, Peggy "The Professor" Wilcox, who patiently and gently taught me how to write.

About the Author

Steve Urie is a 1962 graduate of Rock Island High School and is an undeserving but grateful 1967 recipient of a Civil Engineering degree from Marquette University. (His deep dislike for the work of the Army Corps of Engineers has festered since his grandfather and father told him about the Mississippi River when they were boys.) He has lived with his wife and editor, Peggy, in and around Truckee, California, for 40 years, where he worked as an IT systems engineer and small business owner. After many times bouncing from Ayn Rand Conservatism to Marxism to Libertarianism and landing on points in between, he has despaired of finding a political philosophy that matches his ever-changing ideology and is currently somewhere west northwest of center and is an unapologetic Independent. He is the proud father of Meg Raymore and grandfather of Ethan "Huck" Raymore. He is a lifelong Chicago Cubs fan and is currently planning a career in sports journalism.

www.ingramcontent.com/pod-product-compliance
Lightning Source LLC
Chambersburg PA
CBHW020727160426
43192CB00006B/142